POGROM
November 1938

Testimonies from 'Kristallnacht'

Editor RUTH LEVITT

Souvenir Press
Published in association with
The Wiener Library for the Study of
the Holocaust and Genocide

First published in Great Britain in 2015 by Souvenir Press Ltd
43 Great Russell Street, London WC1B 3PD

ISBN 978 0 2856 43079

Typeset by M Rules

Printed and bound in Great Britain by
CPI Group (UK) Ltd, Croydon, CR0 4YY

CONTENTS

LIST OF ILLUSTRATIONS

LIST OF ILLUSTRATIONS

ACKNOWLEDGEMENTS

The project has benefited from the work, skill, advice and interest of a number of individuals. They generously contributed many hours and much commitment and care to the translating, editing and research, for which the Wiener Library is profoundly grateful. The team also included two small groups of postgraduate university students: one group undertook guided research for the Glossary and the other undertook supervised text encoding. The arrangements were incorporated into their degree courses or internships, and provided mutual benefits: the students gained valuable learning and practical experience as well as knowledge about this aspect of history, which in most cases was unfamiliar to them; the Library obtained practical help with essential tasks. The Wiener Library thanks the university staff who facilitated these arrangements and provided specialist expertise and advice.

The Dulverton Trust provided a grant of £10,000 to support the publication of the book and communications about the project. Sir Malcolm Rifkind kindly introduced the Library to the Trust. Translating and editing was greatly assisted by Chris Bone, Martin Brady, Tim Gluckman, Richard McClelland, Beverley Simmons, Felicitas Starr-Egger, Michael Cavanagh and Peter Skrandies. Jenny Watson supported research for the Glossary. Erica Carter, Professor of German at King's College London, was very supportive of the project and enabled the following students to work with the project: Grace Etherington, Joshua Horwood, Maxwell Jones, Rishi Joshi, Charline Kopf, Agnese Pecorini, Alyson Richens and Sarah Standen. Charline Kopf and KCL students Kristin Bühnemann and Olivia Johnson did additional work. Professor Melissa Terras and Dr Julianne Nyhan of the Centre for Digital Humanities at University College London enabled students Stavrini Ioannidou and Olga Loboda to work with the project. The Library is very grateful indeed to all the students and staff for their work.

At the German Embassy in London the project has benefited from the interest and advice of Rosemarie Hille, Stefano Weinberger and Alexandra Wolfelsperger-Essig.

The Library is very grateful to the Mémorial de la Shoah (Jacques Fredj, Sophie Nagiscarde, Karen Taieb, Lior Smajda) for permission to include a selection of contemporary photographs as well as textual information about the political developments that preceded and followed the November Pogrom, taken from the book Mémorial prepared for its exhibition *La nuit de crystal* and published in Paris in 2008. The Stiftung Denkmal für die ermordeten Juden Europas (Ulrich Baumann) kindly gave permission to include two maps: Jewish communities in the German Reich, 1933; and 1283+ locations in the German Reich, November 1938, where synagogues and Jewish premises were destroyed or damaged. Research for the maps was done by students of the Stiftung and mapping was by MMCD New Media, Düsseldorf; the Stiftung commissioned these maps for its exhibition *Es brennt!* in Berlin in 2008. Michael Lenarz at the Jüdisches Museum Frankfurt am Main kindly provided the German edited texts and the Indexes to People and Places he prepared for the 2008 book of the German texts. The project also secured pro bono help from a web content management system provider, Imagiz (Pete Vox), which has been generous and invaluable and is very much appreciated.

Colleagues at the Wiener Library have contributed in numerous ways to the realisation of this project. In addition to Toby Simpson, Jessica Green, Marek Jaros, Kat Hubschmann, Neta Lavee and others on the permanent staff, Sharon Chiu (intern), Sue Boswell (volunteer) and Klara Podkowik (volunteer) provided valuable input.

The Library appreciates the very generous support of Ernest Hecht and Souvenir Press in enabling publication of this important material in English for the benefit of all those worldwide who seek to understand the relevance and significance of the November Pogrom.

Ben Barkow and Ruth Levitt
The Wiener Library
December 2014

DIRECTOR'S INTRODUCTION
Ben Barkow, Director, Wiener Library

The Wiener Library's mission is to serve scholars, professional researchers, the media and the public as a library of record; to engage people of all ages and backgrounds in understanding the Holocaust and its historical context through an active educational programme; to be a living memorial to the evils of the past by ensuring that the Library's collections are put at the service of the future; and to oppose antisemitism and other forms of prejudice and intolerance. The Library's reputation rests on its independence and the scholarly objectivity of its activities and publications. This book forms part of the Wiener Library's Pogrom: November 1938 project, which is providing information about the violent terror unleashed upon Jews in Germany and Austria on 9–10 November 1938. The book, together with an online web site (www.wiener-library.co.uk/novemberpogrom) and an e-book, is intended for teachers, students, historians, researchers, libraries, writers, journalists, politicians and others worldwide.

At the centre of these resources is the Wiener Library's unique collection of 356 eyewitness reports of the events of November 1938, which are available here in English for the first time. The vivid and compelling reports are accompanied by related material from the Wiener Library's own collections and elsewhere, and a detailed Glossary, setting the events in their historical and international contexts.

The project's testimonies are also of great interest because they are closely connected to the Wiener Library's own history. The Library today is the heir of the work that Dr Alfred Wiener (1885–1964), a German Jew, initiated in Berlin from the late 1920s to combat antisemitism, under the auspices of the Central Association of German Citizens of Jewish Faith (*Central-Verein deutscher Staatsbürger jüdischen Glaubens*). He perceived the rising threat from the Nazi Party and he was the driving force behind the setting up of an archive called *Büro Wilhelmstrasse* to collect intelligence about the Nazis that could inform campaigns to undermine their activities. The *Büro* became a small team collecting information about the rise of the Nazi regime and the details of antisemitic policies and regulations that Jews in Germany and the Third Reich were increasingly being subjected to. The *Büro* communicated this information internationally and Wiener wrote, lobbied and spoke in public.

The *Büro* and Wiener and his family were at greater risk once the Nazi Party had come to power in Germany in 1933. In order to be able to continue the work of collecting and disseminating information about the worsening situation for Jews under the Nazis, Wiener moved with his family to Amsterdam. There, he and Dr David Cohen, a prominent figure in the Dutch Jewish community, secured the interest and support of the Board of Deputies of British Jews and the Anglo-Jewish Association to establish a new organisation that could continue the efforts made by the *Büro Wilhelmstrasse* in monitoring, documenting and reporting internationally about Nazi policies and practices. Wiener again established a small team for this new Jewish Central Information Office (JCIO), and he found premises for it and an apartment for his family at Jan van Eyckstraat 14, Amsterdam-Zuid. For over five years between 1934 and 1939 the JCIO team gathered large amounts of documents and other evidence and issued numerous reports and bulletins recording events mainly in Germany and Austria, which it mailed internationally to governments, journalists, politicians, Jewish organisations and others.

Following the November terror in 1938 and mounting evidence of the Nazi regime's aggressive territorial ambitions, Amsterdam ceased to be a safe place for the JCIO to stay. Accordingly, the staff packed up much of the accumulated archive and shipped it to London in the summer of 1939. Throughout the war the JCIO served the British government by providing reports and intelligence from abroad. Increasingly the collection was referred to as 'Dr Wiener's Library' and eventually this led to its renaming.

At the heart of Holocaust education projects such as this (and the teaching and learning of history more generally) is the obligation to find ways to best describe and understand the past for the benefit of today's teachers and learners. It is not a simple matter to present the complex actions, perceptions and attitudes of people in possibly unfamiliar places and at moments in time that can now seem very distant and different. How we accommodate and comprehend our own ways of handling the passage of time shapes our ideas and the very narratives that we choose to consider. Alongside that responsibility we also have to understand the influences that customary commemorating of past events at their anniversary dates has in different places and for successive generations. Holocaust education and the study of such difficult history brings with it important responsibilities.

This project is helping to increase the Library's digital presence by removing barriers to accessing collections. In doing so, the project is furthering the Library's aim of attracting new audiences and better reaching existing audiences elsewhere. In addition to making the resources available digitally, by translating the testimonies the project is making this unique material available to a wider audience who use English rather than just those who can read German. This serves the Wiener Library's mission: 'To engage people of all ages and backgrounds in understanding the Holocaust and its historical context through an active educational programme.'

The Wiener Library is most grateful to Dr Ruth Levitt, Research Fellow, for designing, running and delivering this ambitious project for the Library – and for being willing to do so although the Library did not manage to secure the necessary funding for this work. She has identified and obtained the many texts and images that comprise the project's resources, she has commissioned, checked and edited the translations and other texts, and identified and obtained permissions to include many additional resources. She has also devised and created the Glossary and Index, which provide important additional ways to reach into the content. She has worked closely with the web system designer Imagiz to design and create the web site. She has established sound editorial principles and applied rigorous standards to support the educational and research aims throughout the project. She has initiated an international network of contacts. Upon all these firm foundations the project will continue to develop and grow.

EDITOR'S INTRODUCTION

Dr Ruth Levitt, Research Fellow, Wiener Library

On and around 9–10 November 1938 simultaneously in hundreds of towns and villages in Germany and Austria thousands of Jews were terrorised, persecuted and victimised. During these incidents over 1,200 synagogues and thousands of Jewish shops, businesses and homes were desecrated, looted and burned. Countless individuals were attacked, abused and beaten, over 90 people were killed, and over 25,000 men were arrested, deported and detained in the concentration camps at Buchenwald, Dachau and Sachsenhausen, many of them for several months, where they were brutally tortured and mistreated. Hundreds of these individuals died in the concentration camps as a result.

The sequence of events that preceded the November terror included increasing restrictions and disenfranchisement of Jews in Germany and Austria, a wave of arrests in May and June 1938, the expulsion of Polish-born Jews from Germany to the border with Poland in October 1938, and Herschel Grynszpan's mortal attack on German diplomat Ernst vom Rath in Paris on 7 November 1938. Nazi Minister of Propaganda Goebbels used this as the pretext for launching the terror, although there is evidence that it had apparently already been planned for some time.

Immediately afterwards, on 12 November 1938, Nazi leaders met to assess the outcomes of the operation and to discuss further expropriation, expulsion, deportation, and the extermination of the Jews. For those Jews able to emigrate, a swift departure was urgent but not easy, because of the intricate snares of bureaucratic procedures imposed on them along with punitive taxes and the seizure of a large proportion of their property and assets. For those who could not get out, ghettoisation, poverty and desperation intensified as more and more Jews were rounded up and sent to Poland as forced labourers, and random attacks and executions of Jews were common. Poland was invaded in September 1939, war was declared and the so-called 'Final Solution' that was the Holocaust gathered pace.

It is now (2015) 77 years since the so-called *Novemberpogrom*, also labelled *(Reichs)Kristallnacht* or *Novemberaktion*. These labels translate as 'November Pogrom', '(Reich) night of broken glass' and 'November operation'. Each term is problematic because:

(a) some people dispute that this was a 'pogrom', which they regard as 'exterminatory violence against a social group', rather than 'state-directed terror against the Jews'.*

The Oxford English Dictionary offers two definitions for 'pogrom':

(i) In Russia, Poland, and some other East European countries in the late 19th and early 20th centuries: an organized massacre aimed at the destruction or annihilation of a body or class of people, esp. one conducted against Jewish people;

(ii) an organized, officially tolerated, attack on any community or group.

(b) some wish to avoid the term '*Kristallnacht*' because they regard it as misrepresenting what happened by implying only windows were broken, thus diminishing the extent and severity of the murders and other harms caused to the Jews at the time;

(c) some wish to avoid Nazi vocabulary, such as the word '*Aktion*'.

Labels used for the November 1938 events carry significant associations, implications and interpretations, which may not necessarily be initially obvious. Nevertheless, these meanings can

---

*In discussion with historian Dr François Guesnet, University College London, a speaker at a workshop held at the Wiener Library in May 2014 on "Pogroms: Contemporary Reactions to Antisemitic Violence in Europe, 1815–1950."

infiltrate subsequent perceptions, commentaries and analyses about the events and consequences of November 1938. The same could be said for the term 'Holocaust', which is also a problematic label even though it is so widely accepted and used. As 'November Pogrom' and 'Kristallnacht' have become the most recognised terms for the 1938 terror, we have retained them for users' convenience even though they are not wholly accurate and we are not endorsing them. The project will enable users to develop for themselves a sound understanding of the events in their original and contemporary contexts.

The relationship between the events of November 1938 and the unfolding of the Holocaust is itself a further complex topic. Yet for most people alive today, particularly for young people in Europe and North America, the November events may be no more than a seemingly obscure incident occupying a few sentences in a history book. The Wiener Library project therefore attempts to present information in words and images that support much greater and deeper understanding of what happened in November 1938 and why.

The testimonies

The 356 documents comprising this special JCIO collection about November 1938 were created on 636 single-sided sheets of fairly thin white foolscap-size paper using a typewriter with a black ink ribbon. The texts were typed single-spaced and some have a few handwritten annotations, such as a question mark or brief comment; the name and sometimes the address of the person giving the report are also included in several cases. Each report has a unique number in the sequence from B.1 to B.353 (B. presumably is an abbreviation of Bericht [report]) with five additions (B.62a, B.175a, B.333a, plus B.1001 and B.1002 at the end), and two unused numbers (B.342 and B.343). There is no obvious logic to the numbering sequence: it is not arranged chronologically, geographically or by source. Several reports do carry a date, and an approximate date of some others can be worked out by context. Most of the dated reports were created in November and

December 1938; others were prepared in January and February 1939, and the remainder originated sporadically in the following weeks. The last few were typed in the early summer of 1939, just before the JCIO was packed up and moved to London in August 1939. Today the Library speculates that the reports were sourced using the JCIO's several usual modes of information gathering, including face to face interviews, telephone conversations, letters and written reports, selecting and cropping newspaper articles, and obtaining informal intelligence via conversations and correspondence with other organisations and contacts. The reports vary in length: the shortest is a mere 13 words, the longest is about 12,400 words, and the medium-length reports average around 800 words. Short reports (under 500 words) comprise 45% of the total, medium-length reports make up approximately 52% of the total, and the long reports make up the remaining 3%. The total word count of all the reports is approximately 195,000.

Almost all (333 or 93%) of the reports were written in German, although 18 reports are in Dutch, five in English and one in French. The whole set of documents is particularly significant because they were mostly collected in the days and weeks immediately following 9–10 November 1938 itself. These testimonies are different in nature from those based on memories recalled years later, which some other organisations have obtained. Testimonies collected later are inevitably modified and influenced by other intervening personal experiences as well as by versions and interpretations of the events by historians, politicians, journalists and others. The direct, unmediated nature of the Wiener Library's testimonies makes them all the more important and valuable. Until now they were only available in German, and thus restricted to a small proportion of the general readers, students, specialists and scholars worldwide who seek to understand the Holocaust and the events that heralded it.

Some time after the Library had been moved to London in 1939, the bundle of 356 documents was bound into a single volume between red leather boards, probably in the 1960s. Over time this binding became increasingly frail and started to disintegrate. In addition to the reports themselves, another bundle of pieces of white paper, these of much smaller dimensions (under A6 size) and in a small plain envelope, came to light at the Library; they are typed in black ink on one side with names and sometimes addresses or other information about the sources of reports B.130 to B.200, with perforations at the top suggesting they were detached from the same notepad in order to be typed. In 1998 the main reports were microfilmed for inclusion in *Testaments to the Holocaust,* a microfilm document collection published in that year, the 60th anniversary of the 1938 events. Around that time the damaged red leather binding holding the reports together was removed and the 636 sheets were rebound in two large-format folio volumes fitted into a slip case. A decade later, for the 70th anniversary in 2008, the microfilm reels were digitised and re-published by Cengage together with other content as an online database for subscribers. Also in 2008 the Wiener Library published the 356 reports in German as a small (20 × 13 cm), but thick (over 930 pages), hardback book entitled *Novemberpogrom 1938* (Suhrkamp Verlag; ISBN 978-3-633-54233-8), which included introductory essays by Ben Barkow (Wiener Library Director), Raphael Gross and Michael Lenarz (Frankfurt am Main Jüdisches Museum, Director and Deputy Director respectively).

Content and voices in the testimonies

Within the collection of testimonies several different styles of description, narrative and voice are apparent. Some are raw and personal, using language that conveys unconcealed distress, despair or anxiety, expressing great misery, fear or desperation. Some beg for help. Others are angry or defiant or scornful towards the perpetrators. Those that are written in a matter-of-fact, impersonal way, with little or no overt emotion or commentary, are equally chilling; a few try to present a scrupulous balance of positives and negatives. Some are minutely detailed, others are much less so; several are bravely stoical; a few manage an ironic tone of gallows humour; one or two present hair-raising escapes or describe attempts to hide as exciting adventures. Some of the reports record actual names and places, dates and times; whereas these details are omitted or anonymised in many others. Many of the reports present the plight and first-hand encounters that individuals had to go through, while a number of others give a broader overview or list details obtained from relatives or other people and places. Taken altogether the collection provides a highly specific set of word pictures from different personal perspectives, which corroborate many features of how the terror was perpetrated.

There is fulsome description of the way the arrests were planned and carried out in people's homes, who the intruders were, how they broke in, their disrespect in speaking to the occupants, physical violence, verbal attacks, the damage they did to furniture, fittings, windows and doors, the clothing they stole or ripped, the money and other possessions they looted, and how they forced the occupants out into the street and what transport they used to take them away. Then follow the details of arrival at assembly places, police stations, prisons and how they were spoken to and treated there, how long they were kept standing, whether they were put in cells, the deprivation of information, whether they had any food, water, sleeping accommodation or access to lavatories, what they could find out from other prisoners about what would happen to them, the personal information they had to give to their captors and guards, who was released (at what point and on what grounds), who was detained and when and where they were moved.

For those who were taken to concentration camps there are several very full accounts of the journey, lack of food, water or lavatory facilities, the treatment by their guards, impressions on arrival, their reception, the beatings and other mistreatment, the incessant routine of lengthy roll calls and the work or punitive drills they were forced to do under threat of punishments or death. There are full accounts of the food they were given, the washing and sanitation arrangements, the illnesses, wounds and medical treatment or lack thereof, sleep or lack therof, the cold, the heat and the uniforms they were issued. The psychological and emotional toll of torture emerges from these testimonies, even where the experiences are described in uncomplaining terms. Those who had completed the bureaucratic procedures for emigration before they were arrested as well as the financial and travel arrangements were usually released quite quickly. For all the imprisoned men, however, the physical and mental suffering that was inflicted on them is graphically conveyed, communicating the acute shock and bewilderment that many felt at first. This initial shock was soon followed for many by learning how to try to survive and what to do or avoid doing when coping with the brutality and the acute deprivation and distress they were under.

Testimonies about the November terror came to the JCIO from all over Germany, as well as from Austria, several of these provided by reporters in transit away from their homes or having already travelled abroad. Some recount the shocking information they gleaned from relatives and friends about attacks, beatings, lootings and deaths in other towns and villages or that they saw for themselves when visiting the homes or offices of family, colleagues and acquaintances. Several of the reports describe in detail how during the terror synagogues and houses of prayer were broken into, their contents desecrated, the buildings set on fire and allowed to burn down with the fire brigade looking on. In addition, there was deliberate humiliation of rabbis, synagogue staff and committee members.

A number of the reports shed light on the predicament of parents who were desperately seeking help to get their children to safe places away from Germany and Austria, including some by the same impoverished families and lone parents who were on the brink of breakdown or suicide. Among these is a compilation of short postcards to families at home written by children on a Kindertransport train carrying them through Holland to safety in England.

Translation and editing

At the outset, the editors of the project created some principles to guide the translating and editorial work. The objective was always to enable the reader to understand what the reporter had tried to convey and how they had conveyed it. It was important to always be aware that most of the accounts were expressed in German, over 75 years ago, very close in time to the shocking events and many of the individuals were in a state of bewilderment, shock or distress. The principles therefore sought to make English texts which retain the intention, style and voice of each source by maintaining the register and 'feel' of the language and preserving idiomatic colour and tone as much as possible. Furthermore, the English texts deliberately retain certain German words, followed immediately by their translation, where, for example, the reporter has specified particular concentration camp language, or the names of the many permits, regulations, taxes and processes, or the names of organisations. The German vocabulary, unfamiliar to many readers, is an important part of the history, but it must not be a barrier to understanding that history, and has been translated conscientiously. The work on the text was guided by a commitment to achieving clarity while not modernising, over-anglicising or 'sanitising' the texts. This was done even if a so-called 'better' translation might have been possible, in the sense of making it 'easier' for some of today's readers. Using anachronisms or turns of phrase that might fit when translating a modern source would have risked violating the significant historical origins of these testimonies.

To further assist readers who encounter unfamiliar words or facts, there is also a bespoke Glossary, which defines and explains all the specialised terminology and the main contextual factors associated with the November 1938 events. The Index identifies people and organisations, places and subjects in the eyewitness reports.

Other historically important documents that are included here contain some contemporary reports of the November pogrom, which the Jewish Central Information Office issued in 1938-39, and a number of photographs and maps.

November Pogrom Website

The November Pogrom website (www.wienerlibrary.co.uk/ novemberpogrom) has been created in conjunction with this book. The Wiener Library recognizes the growing expectations of users to access and engage with our collections in a digital environment, one that not only mirrors the physical collections, but enhances and enriches the user experience and understanding of the materials. With the simultaneous launch of the book's companion website: www.wienerlibrary.co.uk/novemberpogrom, users will be able to engage with the testimonies, contextual information, and search tools in a number of ways that are not possible in this book, including reading the English translations alongside PDF versions of the original testimonies. The political context and significance of the November Pogrom is set out on the website in texts first written for the Mémorial de la Shoah in 2008.

Ruth Levitt has teamed with London-based web designers, IMAGIZ and the Wiener Library's Digital Curator, Jessica Green, to design and create an educational digital resource that allows users to search and browse the testimonies using full-text search and a range of keywords, including the location, profession, and name of individuals and types of property damaged during the November Pogrom. In addition, the web resource includes a wealth of contextual historical information, archival images, and links to additional print and web resources about the November Pogrom and other Holocaust testimony collections. With the help of volunteers, the Library plans to continue to enhance and improve this resource over time by adding more contextual information, metadata, and new visual approaches to telling the stories of the individuals and events represented in the testimonies. The aim is to support a deeper understanding of what happened in the pogrom of November 1938 and its significance for us all.

PART I

B. 1 (For information only, not for distribution)

Delft, the 22nd November 1938

On 13.11. I arrived in Amsterdam from Berlin by aeroplane with my wife and in the following am trying to give an account from memory of circumstances which I have experienced myself in recent months or of which I have received authentic reports. As it was impossible to make notes about these events, despite everything they must be written down with certain reservations.

The desire to bring the Jewish problem to an ultimate liquidation in Germany has been evident since the beginning of 1938 and found its first decisive expression in the *Vermögenserklärung* [statement of assets] at the beginning of this year. The ways and means in which the information was demanded from Jews and in which the capitalisation of small and even smaller incomes formed an integral part, shows a determination to place as high a value on Jewish assets as possible. There followed the removal of taxation reliefs of every kind for Jews (allowances for children, taxation for Jewish welfare institutions etc.), the removal of public body status from Jewish *Gemeinden* [communities], and in connexion with this the compulsory collection of Jewish taxes, which became a voluntary payment, was no longer possible. The introduction of the so-called *"gelben Bänke"* [yellow benches; benches marked with yellow paint; Jews were not allowed to use other benches] was only a small pinprick. The radical movement received its own impetus through the invasion of Austria. The growth of the Jewish population, and the fact that all the measures which had been introduced into the *Altreich* [Old Reich] over the course of 5 years were brought in there in a few weeks in the "flush of victory", encroached on the *Altreich*. It came through the well-known revival of the boycott, the marking out of Jewish shops by inscribing the full name of the Jewish proprietor on the windowpanes, and publication of lists at the *Polizeirevieren* [police stations]. The next blow was the business of the arrests in the middle of June [*Juni-Aktion*; June operation], in which about

3,000 people were sent to the concentration camp, of whom 146 alone died before 30th September in Buchenwald camp near Weimar. Further measures led to the barring of Jewish doctors from the profession, of whom in total about 1,200 (400 of them from Berlin and Vienna) were, or are going to be, re-registered as Jewish *Krankenbehandler* [Jewish doctors licensed to treat Jewish patients] and of whom a large number have now been arrested again. The withdrawal of the so-called *Legitimationskarte* [identity card], *Stadthausierschein* [city hawker's licence] etc. wiped out the living of thousands more families. On 1st December followed the barring of the legal profession, on 1st January the ban on shops and commercial enterprises. At the same time measures of an administrative nature were in operation, such as the withdrawal of passports, the stamping of *Auswanderungspässe* [emigration passports] with a red capital J, the removal of weapons, the special registration numbers for cars in Jewish ownership, the compulsory introduction of the forenames Sara and Israel and the introduction of the *Kennkarte* [identity card] with fingerprints and clearly visible left ear.

In this statement a large number of less important measures have without doubt not been included. I will proceed at this point to outline the crucial development of recent weeks. The Czechoslovakian problem, which at the same time promised to bring in its wake a new "burden" of Jews through the existing Jewish *Gemeinden* in the Sudeten German region, has obviously led to deterrent measures in order to induce a voluntary evacuation by the Jewish population. From a reliable source comes news that in the event of a mobilisation the SA was to be granted a "Night of the long knives" on the day of mobilisation. The decisions about this are said to have been taken at the Party conference in September. That this news is well-founded is evident from the fact that on the planned mobilisation day, namely during the night of 28th-29th September, there were pogrom-like riots in smaller places where the news of the cancelled mobilisation had obviously not come through in time, which were particularly severe in Bavaria (Rothenburg ob der Tauber) and in the region of Hesse and Hesse-Nassau. In Rothenburg and other places in Bavaria and also in Hesse there were serious cases of mistreatment. The Jews were expelled within 24 hours from Rothenburg and other places and found refuge with friends and relatives in larger towns in the Reich. In a small town near the border the synagogues were completely destroyed and the whole *Gemeinde*, consisting of 21 families, was arrested and only released again 8 days later. It was thought that the measures sought to prevent news of this reaching the foreign press. In Langen near Frankfurt am Main the synagogue was broken into at night, the religious objects were stolen and the entrance was bricked up. The next morning a policeman went to the *Vorsteher* [chairman] of the *Gemeinde* and informed him that a master bricklayer had been given the task of opening up the door again, and the *Vorsteher* should hand over the key to the iron door. This is what happened. A short time later the *Staatspolizei* [*Stapo;* state police] appeared and arrested the *Vorsteher* because he had had the synagogue reopened without authority. There are no grounds to think that the police were working hand in hand with the *Stapo*. It appears much more likely that the police were well intentioned throughout. In another place near Frankfurt am Main, Seligenstadt am Main if I am not mistaken, on Friday evening a rope was stretched across the street the Jews used to go to the synagogue, so that they stumbled and fell over to the amusement of the adolescent spectators. At the same time, particularly in the Bavaria region, the more or less compulsory seizure of plots of land began for the most ridiculous prices. Some supposed purchaser or other was sent to the Jewish owner of the land in question, forcing him to sell his land at the given price, with the threat that otherwise he would be arrested. These methods were even used in a town like Würzburg. Numerous plots of land belonging to the Jewish *Gemeinde* were also expropriated in this way. Synagogues were seized and used as storehouses for grain etc. In Berlin during those days a special method was devised to keep the Jewish population in continual unrest and to wear them down. One day numerous raids took place on coffee houses, also a raid on the only open-air swimming pool near Berlin (Stölpchensee), which still allowed Jews entry. People who could prove their identity were generally not bothered, however what was considered valid identification varied completely. In many cases producing even out of date passports sufficed. In other cases this was seen as a serious offence which led to arrest, although an order to surrender expired passports had not yet been issued at that time; it only took effect on 15th October. Those people who were arrested were in general released again 2–3 days later. The head of the *Polizeirevier* in Grolmannstraße in Berlin-Charlottenburg, a *Polizeihauptmann* [police captain] Schneider, was particularly active in respect of such raids; it is said of him that he is a brother-in-law of the head of the German police, General [Kurt] Daluege. He was also the first to set up the so-called *Verkehrsfallen* [traffic traps] for pedestrians. They were situated in places where traffic was particularly heavy, such as the corner of Kurfürstendamm and Uhlandstraße, the corner of Kurfürstendamm and Leibnitzstraße, and the corner of Kurfürstendamm and Wilmersdorferstraße. Pedestrians who wrongly, or as was usually the case, were alleged to have wrongly crossed the road, were stopped and asked whether they were Jewish or non-Jewish. If they were non-Jewish, then they were allowed to go or the usual police fine of RM. 1.- was imposed on them. If on the other hand they were Jews, then they were taken to the police station, held for at least half a day and then fined between RM. 50.- and RM. 300.-, which counted as a previous conviction against them, and they lived in constant fear of arrest as a "*Verbrecher*" [criminal] during a raid. These were the same grounds for the arrests in June of this year, which were based on a law under which *Verbrecher* can be taken into *Schutzhaft* [protective custody] at any time. Those arrested then had to sign a form to this effect! The same scrutiny extended to Jewish cars, which had been given numbers over 350000 in order to make them immediately recognisable. As a result most Jewish car owners abandoned their cars, which meant considerable inconvenience given the distances in Berlin business traffic. These *Verkehrsfallen* became the accepted thing in the west and new ones were set up, typically on Antonplatz in Weißensee, where visitors to the Jewish cemetery had to cross the road, and in Iranische straße in front of the Jewish Hospital. It is easy to imagine how numerous the violations against the traffic regulations were here, when people overcome with sorrow and worry were going to or returning from the cemetery. Even the introduction of the *gelben Bänke* led to an escalation. Whereas on the squares where there were no such benches the Jews had still been able to use the public benches, that now changed and signs were put up with the following inscription, "For Jews in the administrative district… only those *gelben Bänke* designated with J are available for use." In this way they were therefore ordered to use the few *gelben Bänke*.

When it came to the incident in Antwerp [see press reports of an alleged attack upon some German passengers from the steamer Cordilleras on 26 October 1938 who were taking photographs in the Jewish district], it already seemed at that time that this occasion was to be used to set in motion the planned large operation. This was restricted at first however to the prohibition of all Jewish events. Included amongst these were the classes and language courses at the *Lehrhäuser* [houses of study], where the autumn term was just about to start and to which numerous students had already travelled from the provinces to the towns. These were principally so-called intensive courses, where work is done for 8 hours a day for 4 weeks. Only the *Kulturbundtheater* [Jewish Cultural Federation Theatre] was permitted to continue giving performances. The operation to issue *Kündigungen* [notices to quit] also started. They were given to thousands following the pattern in Vienna and caused the greatest confusion in Jewish circles, as substitute homes were hardly available with the current lack of accommodation. An operation was taking effect, which the *Arbeitsfront* [Labour Front; the Nazi trade union] introduced and which made matters particularly difficult, to place the owners of Jewish guest houses under more or less pressure to sell, so that numerous elderly people in particular became homeless, and so that temporary refuge in guest houses was made almost impossible for the numerous doctors who, as is well known, had been given notice to quit their homes within 6 weeks through a special law. All these measures had already led to complete despair amongst the Jewish population. The office hours of the Jewish aid organisations (*Hilfsverein* [Aid Association], *Central-Verein* [*Central-Verein deutscher Staatsbürger jüdischen Glaubens;*

Central Association for German Citizens of Jewish faith], *Palästina-Amt* [Palestine Office]) were overflowing with people to whom scarcely any advice could be given, as in the meantime the destination countries had withdrawn one after the other, because of the intensified pressure to emigrate and because of the forced illegal emigration. Advisers in the Jewish institutions increasingly became counsellors who had to prevent people from taking dubious measures. In this situation it proved not unfortunate that the three institutions named above, although aligned with each other in their work, were still able to continue working.

The last act of the Jewish tragedy was heralded by the *Polenaktion* [Poland operation]. On the night of 27th to 28th October between 4 and 7 o'clock in the morning all the male Polish-Jewish nationals of about the age of 16 upwards were arrested (in parts of the provinces also women and children) and moved to the border in *Sammeltransporten* [group transports]. The German Jews saw this merely as a prelude to their impending fate. It is even more astonishing that within a few hours this same society made it possible for thousands of Polish Jews to be fed before their transport left for the border, e.g. in Berlin and Hamburg at the railway stations, and that the same thing happened when some of these unfortunate people were transported back again in a state of complete exhaustion due to the measures introduced in the meantime by the Polish government. The Jewish *Gemeinde* of Berlin even undertook to raise part of the transport costs (if I am not mistaken RM. 60,000.-) and to allow these people to return to their homes. It must have been almost unprecedented in Jewish history that a willingness to help manifested itself in such a way, although it should also not be forgotten that the different standards between west and east European Jews and the tension that existed because of this had of course also not disappeared in Germany in any way.

The assassination in Paris fell into this troubled atmosphere. No Jew in Germany was in any doubt that henceforth the most serious events were to be expected. No Jew however could anticipate too that the consequences would be so brutally devastating. The first days after the assassination passed quietly as is well known. There were no riots of any kind. The speech that Hitler made on the evening of 8th November in the *Bürgerbräukeller* [*Bürgerbräu* beer hall] in Munich did not mention a word about the Jewish problem, so that it could be hoped that although the expected measures would indeed not fail to materialise, they would be dictated on reflection, not in the first excitement. On Thursday the 8th November followed the ban on the entire Jewish press in Germany, which on that day consisted of the three major newspapers, *CV Zeitung* [*Central Verein* newspaper] (circulation 40,000), *Jüdische Rundschau* [Jewish Review] (circulation 26,000), *Israelitisches Familienblatt* [Jewish Family Paper] (circulation 25,000), about 25 community periodicals, amongst them one from Berlin with a circulation of 40,000, 4 of the *Jüdische Kulturbund* [Jewish Cultural Federation] periodicals (Berlin, Hamburg, Frankfurt am Main, Cologne), the *Jüdischer Frauenbund* [Jewish Women's League] and the *Reichsbund Jüdischer Frontsoldaten* [Reich Association of Jewish Front-line Soldiers] periodicals, "*Morgen*", the historical "*Zeitschrift für die Geschichte der Juden in Deutschland*" [Journal of the History of Jews in Germany], *Makkabi* and some other small periodicals. Such banning of the Jewish press used to precede *antisemitic* excesses generally, because through this the Jews' means of communication between themselves was removed, every opportunity to acquire information prevented. On Wednesday the 9th November the editors-in-chief of the Jewish newspapers published in Berlin were ordered to the *Stapo* [*Staatspolizei*; State Police] on Alexanderplatz on the morning of Thursday 10th November. On Wednesday evening vom Rath died. On Wednesday evening and during the night of Wednesday to Thursday the organised mob in plain clothes moved from east Berlin into the centre and towards the west and systematically destroyed all the Jewish shops. As they were marked, this destructive vandalism was easily carried out without any danger to non-Jewish shops. The destruction was thorough. No item remained in place. The goods were flung into the streets, they were torn and most of them were stolen. At almost the same time the synagogues in Berlin and in the Reich went up in flames. The *Feuerwehr* [fire brigade] restricted itself to protecting the surrounding buildings and everywhere where the rampaging crowd appeared, the police vanished so as not to hinder the looters from going about their business. The public reacted completely silently in most cases, i.e. critically. There were occasional expressions of disapproval. These were stopped as such people were arrested. On Thursday the destructive rage continued in Berlin and in the Reich. It was replaced by the wave of arrests, in which in my estimation at least 10,000 Jewish men aged between 16 and 60 were affected.

On Thursday morning the Jewish organisations in Berlin had voluntarily closed their offices after forced entry during the night into the *Palästina-Amt* and the offices of the *Zionistische Vereinigung für Deutschland* [Zionist Union for Germany] and had partially destroyed them. Only the *Central-Verein* with about 15 people preserved an emergency service. Of its heads of department that morning Dr. Alfred Hirschberg, Dr. Ernst G. Loewenthal, Frau Dr. Eva Reichmann-Jungmann were ordered to the *Staatspolizei* as representatives of the press as described above. The reporter as well as the *Syndicus* [lawyer] of the *Verein*, Dr. Hans Reichmann, and his colleagues Dr. Werner Rosenstock, retired *Amtsgerichtsrat* [district court judge] Dr. Fritz Goldschmidt, retired *Regierungsdirektor* [senior government official] Friedländer took over their duties. Reports increased hourly of serious, even violent, riots in the provinces, sometimes with fatal consequences. Shortly after 13.00 hours 3 plain clothes officers from the *Staatspolizei* appeared, took over the telephone switchboard and called those present out of all the offices. They had to put on their hats and coats, were briefly searched and then released individually. The offices of the *CV* were sealed, the keys to the offices and the keys to the safe were handed over to the officers. None of those present was arrested. The tone in conducting the operation was forceful but proper. There were merely here and there words such as, "You'll see further details," "You'll soon be laughing on the other side of your face" (of course nobody had laughed) and similar. The reporter went to the home of Dr. Hirschberg and waited there for his return. It came at about 16.00 hours. All the other editors had also been released. They had been held from 8 o'clock in the morning until this point in time without any interrogation or anything else, then sent home and ordered to report on Friday morning at 10 o'clock.

In the meantime it turned out that numerous arrests had taken place of mainly affluent people, of lawyers, doctors and leading Jewish personalities. Thus the intention was evidently to remove all the people who would have advised or been able to reassure the Jewish people in these agitated days. The flight of Jewish men from their homes began. They slept mostly in households where there were no men, went away into the provinces, stayed hidden in the woods, travelled here and there through the night on the *Untergrund-* and *Stadtbahnen* [underground and suburban railways].

On Friday morning the editors were released at about 13.00 hours. They had had to sign a declaration that their newspaper was banned for 3 months. Whilst we were waiting in Dr. Hirschberg's home for his return, relieved because he had just telephoned, the *Kriminalpolizei* [criminal police] appeared, to arrest him. Whilst we were still dealing with them and were personally searched in turn, Dr. Hirschberg appeared in the home. He explained that he had just been released, and on his arrival the officers telephoned the chief of police. But in vain. Dr. Hirschberg was arrested. Already the previous day Dr. Hans Reichmann, who had been released that morning, had been taken from his home. In the course of Friday despite this the *Kriminalpolizei* still twice came to his home searching for him.

In Berlin not all men between the ages of 16 and 60 had been arrested. It also appears that this time as in June it had been made a requirement for the *Polizeirevieren* to arrest a certain number of men from their district, and this time to restrict them to intellectuals and the wealthy. This perception was confirmed by the following incident amongst other things: one of my colleagues was sought in his home on Friday and not found there. His Aryan wife was threatened with arrest if her husband did not report by the next morning. On my advice the man also went home and waited to be arrested. He was not taken however, and I have received a letter from him here dated 20th November. Probably they took another man in his place in order to fill the quota.

Blind Jews, even those blinded in war, lost their concessions on public transport soon afterwards. The *Jüdische Blindenanstalt* [Jewish Institute for the Blind] in Berlin had to dismiss its Jewish city representatives who sold basket and wickerwork to Jewish customers, as they no longer received a *Legitimationskarte.* The *Blindenanstalt* was required to engage Aryan representatives.

The surrender of weapons, which was only ordered across the board by law after 9th November, occurred in various forms from about the beginning of October. Generally a summons was served to appear at a set time at the *Polizeirevier.* Many *Polizeirevieren* however summoned several hundred people at once and made them wait for hours in sports halls or yards until the question was put to each about a weapon, driving licence for cars and other identity papers. One *Polizeirevier* in north east Berlin summoned the men to report several times daily at the time of the Jewish High Holidays in September, in the mornings at 7, midday at 12 and in the afternoon. Because of this, people with smaller businesses who naturally had to close their shops at this time, often were unable to carry on their businesses for days. With the surrender of weapons, which also covered fencing épées, sporting sabres and army revolvers, which must have been forcibly taken from the owners during the war, a declaration had to be signed that they were being surrendered voluntarily. Any compensation was obviously not paid. It goes without saying that every Jew who was still in possession of a weapon possessed the necessary licence for it.

It is essential to make clear that the laws of 12th November meant the complete material ruin of German Jewry. How this collapse itself took effect in detail can be shown through an example. Emigrating families as a rule used to sell their furniture. From the proceeds they would acquire either small pieces of new furniture especially for emigrating or they would use it to pay passage and freight to the new country. The breaking up of households in the hitherto traditional structure had alone in recent years pushed down prices considerably in the old furniture market. A renewed slump occurred because of the *Polenaktion.* In these days in Germany probably thousands of households must have suddenly broken up, unable to realise any price whatsoever for furniture, books, paintings, carpets etc, so that in numerous families the material basis for emigration was destroyed. Based on this example, it is easy to visualise parallel cases in other regions.

I am aware of the following details concerning the demolition of the Munich synagogue and of the Munich *Gemeindehaus* [community building] in Herzog-Maxstraße. *Oberstlandesgerichtsrat* [Judge] Neumeyer at the supreme district court was called to the *Innenministerium* [Ministry of the Interior], where it was disclosed to him that the demolition of the synagogue would begin on the following day. A declaration was required by the evening from him and from the *Gemeinde* respectively that the *Gemeinde* was in agreement with the demolition of the synagogue. This declaration was not provided in the desired form. There were barely 12 hours that night in which to remove the sacred objects from the synagogue. Then the *Gemeinde* was offered a selling price for the synagogue and the *Gemeindehaus* in the region of, as far as I remember, RM. 300,000.-, whereas the building costs of the synagogue alone without the land had at the time amounted to RM. 1 million. As these buildings are situated in a particularly desirable part of the city the value of the plot had risen from year to year. The demolition of the synagogue itself was completed in barely 14 days and a car park was built there for the opening of the German art exhibition.

Voice from the crowd: on one of the Holidays in September a young Jewish woman left the synagogue and stroked a little dog on the street. At this, the woman dog owner shouted, "Waldi, don't have anything to do with the Jews and be a good dog."

In recent months cases have increased in which the Aryan wives of Jewish men were summoned to the *Stapo* in order to put them under varying degrees of pressure there to get divorced from their husbands. Here is a little example of this too: At Rosenhain, the well-known shop on the Kurfürstendamm in Berlin, when it was Aryanised it had been arranged for the Aryan employee with a Jewish husband, who had converted to Judaism on marriage, to renounce Judaism again so that she could keep her job. A few days later she was dismissed nevertheless, because she had not dissolved her marriage and consequently the sign could not be put up at the business "We march united in the *Arbeitsfront*". Her admission into the *Arbeitsfront* therefore could not ensue because she was still married to a Jew. On the other hand the Jewish *Gemeinde* had declined to give the Jewish man a temporary job because his wife had renounced Judaism. With regard to the Jewish *Gemeinde* the matter could of course be resolved after a while.

Herr Oppenheim, now (1945) New York

B. 2   9th November 1938

The reporter is aware, as other reports also mention, that Herr Heidenheimer and Herr Metzger are not yet traceable. Whether Herr *Rechtsanwalt* [lawyer] Fritz Josefsthal is actually not traceable he is not able to say. It may be that he is in Berlin once again and has not returned to Nuremberg.

It is true that Dr. Fritz Lorch died in Fürth. He was in the Jewish hospital there to undergo a hernia operation before he emigrated. He suffered an embolism as a result of shock caused by the events and died.

Furthermore in Bamberg the restaurateur Herz with a heart condition also died through shock, about 60 years old.

The reporter has learned from good sources rather than his own knowledge that the owner of an export business in Nuremberg, Simon Loeb, about 60 years old, suffered a fractured skull in the pogroms. The reason is unknown. It should be possible to obtain confirmation of this rumour.

Leo Klein, a man of independent means aged over 70, former owner of Langer & Mainz, wholesale textiles, is reported to have suffered several fractures to his arms therefrom. Confirmation required.

Rechtsanwalt Justin Goldstein, Nuremberg, was mistreated such that he was so battered that he had to have stitches in hospital. His wife suffered a head injury and a nervous shock from it. It should be noted generally that the nerves of Jewish people whom the reporter knows are so agitated that even a falling plate or the smallest sound can seriously upset them.

Eyewitnesses have confirmed that the Essenweinstraße synagogue in Nuremberg was set on fire like the synagogue in Fürth. It should be noted that some days earlier all the *Thorarollen* [Torah scrolls] and ritual objects were stolen from the Essenweinstraße synagogue.

The Nuremberg rabbi Dr. Heilbronn was arrested. At the time of the pogrom Rabbi Dr. Klein was not in Nuremberg but in Riga with his children.

Kommerzienrat [commercial councillor] Rosenzweig, about 75 years old, *Vorsitzender* [chairman] of the Nuremberg *Gemeinde* [community], was arrested but later released.

Rechtsanwalt Dr. Walter Berlin was arrested as was *Rechtsanwalt* Landenberger, the *Vorsitzender* of the local *Reichsbunde jüdischer Frontsoldaten* [Reich Association of Jewish Front-line Soldiers]. The total number of those arrested may be about 200 people.

A Frau Löwy in Nuremberg, about 60 years old, was thrown down the stairs.

B. 3   18th November 1938

According to Herr X. from Düsseldorf, he has learned from reliable sources that the *Gemeinde* [community] and, as far as can be determined, a large part of the *Repräsentantenkollegium* [college of representatives], amongst them Herr Felsenthal senior, *Oberlandesgerichtsrat Franken* [senior lawyer at the Franconia regional high court and court of appeal], Herr Louis Elkan, as well as the two rabbis Dr. Eschelbacher and Dr. Klein had all been arrested. Frau Eschelbacher did not want to leave her husband's side and was in a cell at the prison with another Jewish woman who also did not want to be separated from her spouse. Then after some days the two women left the prison. On Tuesday Frau Elkan was allowed to take some clothes to her husband and visit him.

On the 18th November, in the morning edition of the *Algemeen Handelsblad* [General Trade Paper; Dutch daily newspaper], it is stated that *Justizrat* [state prosecutor] Löwisohn had been injured. Herr *Justizrat* Löwisohn has been dead for ten years.

But: opposite the house of Frau *Justizrat* Löwisohn lies the Karema restaurant, proprietor Herr Marcus. Frau Marcus has an injury to her forehead and was shot twice in the stomach. She was taken over to Dr. Löwenberg who lives diagonally opposite (next door to the house of Frau *Justizrat* Löwisohn) and who dressed her wounds. Herr Marcus, who had not been at home, heard of the wounding of his wife, rushed to Dr. Löwenberg and was shot and killed on the way. Herr Cohn, aged over 80, proprietor of the household goods firm Schickenberg in Düsseldorf, was driven out by the mob onto the street dressed only in his nightclothes. It is said that even his nightclothes were stripped from his body in the street. One of Herr Cohn's three sons is in hospital with seven knife wounds, a second son is also in hospital with a broken skull, the third son is an office worker in a steel business in Maastricht.

Fräulein ... from Düsseldorf, who is staying in Amsterdam on her way to America, stated that an SA man who was forced to take part in the operation declared afterwards that what he was forced to do was so appalling that if he did not have a wife and children he would have committed suicide.

Herr Moritz Klein, Amsterdam, Minervalaan 83, tel. 90648

B. 4   It has now been established beyond all doubt that Rabbi Dr. Jacob Horovitz [Horowitz] from Frankfurt am Main, one of the most valued and respected German rabbis due to his scholarly and rabbinical work and his humane readiness to help the widest sections of German and foreign Jewry, has died as a result of recent events. A short while ago he was arrested by the Gestapo after being falsely accused, and was released 14 days later when the falsehood of the denunciation became apparent. He suffered a nervous breakdown through the agitation of the custody and as a result was admitted to the Jewish Hospital in Frankfurt am Main. On the day of the pogrom he was made to leave the hospital and was forced to watch the burning of the synagogue in which both he and his father, Rabbi Dr. Marcus Horovitz [Horowitz] had taught for decades. He flew into a terrible fit of rage at this horrific sight which, together with his state of health, which had already been weakened by his arrest, led to his immediate death.

The youth rabbi, Dr. Lemmle [Lemle] of Frankfurt am Main, who was taken away by car, managed to escape from the car after petrol was poured over it and it was set alight whilst he was still inside. To date his fate is unknown.

It is certain that Herford will be added to the list of synagogues that have already been reported as destroyed by fire. All the male members of the *Gemeinde* [community] were also arrested.

In Dortmund credible eyewitnesses report that several Jews were stabbed to death, amongst them Frank, the lawyer.

In Düsseldorf men and women from the Jewish *Gemeinde* were dragged out of bed and led away wearing only pyjamas and nightdresses. They were forced to walk barefoot through all the broken glass.

Alfred Blank, a businessman from Dortmund, died in the concentration camp in Oranienburg [Sachsenhausen] "of a heart attack", according to a reliable report.

A Christian eyewitness reported from Herford that when he went past the ruins of the synagogue on Thursday afternoon, children were out on the streets ripping up *Thorarollen* [Torah scrolls] and altar cloths whilst shouting and cheering.

One of the largest office buildings in Herford was completely destroyed.

Gütersloh: during the night crowds forced their way into three Jewish houses in the town looking for weapons, smashed everything to pieces and set fire to the houses which burned down to the ground. The occupants had to get dressed in what they could find and go out barefoot onto the streets in the night, and were then taken in by Christians.

Bielefeld: most of the Jewish men were arrested and sent on transports away from the area.

Hans Goslar, *Ministerialdirektor* [senior government official]

B. 5 21st November 1938

The operations in Aachen and their consequences

The incidents in connection with the fires at the synagogue were described as follows:

All houses on the periphery of the synagogue were occupied by guards equipped with revolvers. No residents were allowed to leave the house on threat of death. The synagogue was completely burnt down. The rabbi Dr. Schönburger, who wanted to save the *Thorarollen* [Torah scrolls], was arrested and taken away but is out of prison now. The Jewish *Gemeinde* [community] was ordered to level the ground at the scene of the fire. If the *Gemeinde* failed to do this work it would be taken before the authorities.

The following personalities have been arrested:

Dr. Löwenstein is now in Buchenwald concentration camp. According to his secretary he has been arranging his departure for some time. Frau Dr. Löwenstein whom I contacted did not turn up at the agreed time; apparently they had taken away her *Grenzschein* [border permit].

Stern, a businessman: no precise information could be obtained. It was said he was shot; one of his employees however stated that Stern was alive but had been arrested, nobody knows where.

Hugo Kaufmann; former owner of the firm Herz & Heimann, textile factories, and also the factory owner Otto Meyer are in a concentration camp, in which is not known.

Königsberger, father and son, both arrested, son released on bail, father released, the son was later arrested again and transferred to a concentration camp.

Marx, a businessman, proprietor of the firm Marx & Auerbach also arrested.

Dr. Wallerstein departed for the USA on 5th October 1938.

The Jewish laboratory technician of a chemical factory was arrested but after his employer, a prominent National Socialist, intervened, was released since the latter had declared that without him the factory would have to close.

Dr. A., . . . , a 60-year-old man, was not arrested. I spoke with Frau A. myself; she was terribly upset and cried and insulted Jews abroad who were guilty of everything and explained as follows: "Please make sure that all campaigns abroad are stopped because Goebbels is stronger than foreign countries. We are all desperate." It should be noted that precisely this family have already had enough opportunity to depart and already have money in Belgium.

The businessman B., with whose wife I also spoke, reported: B. had been in his car on the return journey from Saarbrücken to Aachen and was arrested in a small village in the Eifel but released after some hours. Meanwhile he was already being sought by the Gestapo in Aachen. He lingered for several days, wandering around in the vicinity of Aachen. On Friday evening he came home completely broken, in a condition that prompted his wife to call a doctor, the doctor diagnosed myocardial inflammation. The doctor; an Aryan, grasped the situation immediately and prescribed complete bed rest and stated: If anybody comes to take your husband away, telephone me at once.

The mood of the population is passive, but abhors these operations. There is a tacit agreement amongst the Jews to ring the doorbell twice when visiting each other. There was no plundering in Aachen but windows and doors have been wrecked. Of those arrested about 30 have so far returned. Those who have been released do not dare go home and wander around in the Aachen vicinity.

Vicinity of Aachen

In Alsdorf all Jewish flats and houses were wrecked. A teacher Ruhland acted as ringleader. The perpetrators were all in plain clothes, equipped with blacksmiths' hammers and axes. The leader of the operation ensured that all items in the home that belonged to the Aryan owner were not destroyed, wash basins, toilets, etc. The same procedures were also reported from Höngen. In total about 20 people were arrested, some have since been released.

When some inhabitants went in person to the authorities to state this damage they refused to enter the Jewish homes.

In Borken after the wrecking all old and sick men and women were severely mistreated and imprisoned for some days.

The Holland family living in were to depart from Hamburg for Johannesburg on the coming Wednesday. On Friday a Gestapo official came and said: We have protected you until now but now you have to depart otherwise we will arrest you. The family preferred to drop everything and travel to Hamburg. – Some factory owners who are currently engaged in transferring their enterprises into Aryan hands have not been arrested because they have to introduce the new owners.

From small places in the Eifel there are reports that the Christian population is doing everything to look after the Jews who are wandering around in the forests, they take care of food and at night risk their own lives by bringing those unfortunate people into their own homes. Three mining families in Dülken were mentioned particularly.

As seen from Holland

Crossing the Dutch or Belgian borders is completely impossible. The checks are carried out very strictly by *Marechaussee* [police] escorted by soldiers with carbines. Both borders are hermetically sealed.

At the moment everything is quiet at the official border crossing at Aachen-Vaals. Taking photographs is forbidden by both sides. Jewish inhabitants of Aachen who possess a *Grenzschein* [border permit] are allowed through from the German side if they pluck up the courage to do so. The Dutch also let them through without problem.

The *Bürgermeister* [mayor] of Vaals, a Catholic, stated to a German-Jewish family in Vaals: "If you want to take in Jewish families from Aachen who are allowed through by the Germans and can prove that they will leave Holland in the foreseeable future, then they can stay in Vaals until that time."

On Saturday evening I went along the main street of Vaals, three men were walking in front of me. Suddenly one of them turned round, put his hand into the inside pocket of his overcoat and passed a newspaper to me with the word, "*Alstublieft!*" [please]. I immediately recognised that this was a copy of the paper "*De Nederlandsche Nationaal Socialist*" [The Dutch National Socialist], leader Majoor [Major] Kruyt. I spoke with one of the Hollanders about this matter. He explained to me that he found this operation very odd since this group had never before made any propaganda in Limburg. He thinks that this propaganda is connected with the operations in Germany. Attached is the copy of the newspaper.

Reporter: Herr Bettelheim, Amsterdam

B. 6 We have received the following report from a refugee who managed to cross the border to the Netherlands.

On the night from 9th to 10th November I was in a Jewish *Gemeindegebäude* [community building] so as to keep watch together with the *Verwalter* [caretaker]. We had already received the first reports about destruction of Jewish homes etc. on Wednesday. That had happened in the night from Tuesday to Wednesday in Dessau, Bebra and probably in other places as well. For example we heard from directly affected eyewitnesses that in Bebra the SA had entered their house during the night and completely destroyed everything. The residents had fled to the second floor. After the work was completed they heard: "Leave the lights on, everybody line up, march!" The destruction was so complete that, for example, a car which had stood in the garage did not have a single screw left that was usable.

A Polish citizen, owner of a small shop, was warned by Aryan acquaintances that "something" was going to happen on Wednesday (9 November) in the evening at around half past 10. Since the warning was very uncertain, and we knew neither where it came from nor what would take place, it was agreed during the evening in a conversation between the rabbis, members of the *Gemeindevorstand* [community board] and the C.V. [*Central-Verein deutscher Staatsbürger jüdischen Glaubens;* Central Association for German Citizens of Jewish faith] that we would first of all wait and see. It was impossible to pass the message on to others because there had often been such warnings and, given the over-nervous state of our people, in the worst case it would have created a total panic without anybody actually being helped by it.

I was then on guard together with the *Verwalter* until about 3 o'clock in the above-mentioned house. Also present were his wife and a Jewish girl, a business employee. Everything was quiet and the streets were empty. At about 2 o'clock a young man ran up to the house who, on seeing that it was dark, hesitated for a moment before going away again. I have since learned that by this time the synagogue had already been set on fire. People had gone there around half past 1, almost immediately after the conclusion of the SS *Vereidigung* [swearing-in-ceremony], which had begun at midnight. The occupants (rabbis and *Schammes* [sexton] with families), were driven out without being allowed the chance to take their possessions with them. At the same time fire was laid in the usual way with petrol or paraffin. The ringleaders must have been the same four to six SS men who afterwards came to us. There were no arrests.

At about 3 o'clock we decided to end the watch for that night since until then everything had been quiet and we could not imagine that at such a late or rather early hour "the *Volkswut* [people's rage] would boil over". We had just withdrawn and I was just about to have a rest when I heard a noise that I now cannot identify precisely. To be on the safe side I returned to our observation point from where we could keep an eye on the street. When I entered the room I immediately became aware of the noise of a motorbike engine. I ran to the window and saw an SA man on a motorbike whilst another emerged from the house on the other side of the road, sat himself on the pillion seat and gave the driver an address in the neighbourhood. Since both men were in uniform with chin straps lowered and a light had gone on in the house in question, it seemed very likely that the SA had been alerted. It was half past 3. After I had woken my friend we got dressed again and he positioned himself by the window so as to be able to observe what would happen. And indeed shortly afterwards an SA man emerged from the house. Meanwhile I had gone onto the street to see whether I could determine what had happened or was going to happen. I could actually see that SA men were hurrying towards an assembly point from all directions. As I walked along I saw a junior SA-*Führer* [SA leader]. He directed most of the men as they arrived either to get those not yet present to hurry up or to fetch them. With him stood a civilian who was complaining that it was taking too long. To which came the reply that they themselves had only been informed (apparently at the *Sturmbüro* [SA office]) at about 3 o'clock. I assume that the civilian was a member of the *Geheime Staatspolizei* [Gestapo] who had a hit list of Jewish homes and businesses.

I returned to my post and we resolved to wait further because we still really could not have known what was about to take place, and as a result could not decide on any counter-measures. Everything was quiet and the streets almost completely empty. The SA had literally been fetched from their beds for this special purpose. At about 20 minutes before 5 o'clock an older man in somewhat torn clothing showed up, looked at the house from all angles and appeared rather surprised that everything was so still and quiet here. He then went away. It occurs to me that in the town he had observed the destruction of the businesses and the fires at the synagogues, which at this juncture were already well underway, and now wanted to "take a look" at where we were.

At 5 minutes before 5 o'clock a small car drove up out of which four SS men in uniform jumped out. I recognised on one the insignia of an *Obersturmbannführer* [Lieutenant Colonel] (four stars, one stripe), and in what followed he gave the orders. We then ran into the home where the caretaker roused his wife and the girl.

The bell was rung briefly and there were knocks on the door. At the same time they started to smash the window panes from outside. Since I could no longer help, whilst the caretaker had to wait for his wife, I took my hat and coat and ran through the large hall to an emergency exit on the rear side of the house where I climbed over the wall. I then ran up the street and returned very slowly from a different direction as if I were going to or from my place of work. They were still busy knocking out window-panes. Some SS men had already climbed in and were smashing the crockery that had been piled up in the kitchen ready for the washing-up as well as chairs, a table and other fittings. I ran to a telephone callbox to inform the *Überfallkommando* [flying squad] but could not get through to them because I did not have any *Groschen* [pennies] on me. When I got back they were in the process of destroying everything on the upper floors. The window panes were knocked out along with the frames. I next informed the *Gemeindevorstand* and then phoned the *Überfallkommando* again from a different telephone box. It occurred to me that I did not get through to them directly but rather must have been connected via the central telephone exchange of the *Polizeiprä-sidium* [police headquarters]. That is unusual. I then ran to meet a

Jewish nurse. On the way I met an acquaintance in his car which I requisitioned for the subsequent course of events. In the meantime I had gathered from passers-by what had happened at the synagogue and the businesses. I returned with the uniformed nurse. The idea was that she would find out the fate of the *Verwalter*, his wife and the girl whom I had had to leave behind, and who could have been injured by the intruders. When we arrived, at first nothing could be seen of the fire. We assumed that the flames must stem from the blaze at the synagogue which lay in the same direction. However, the *Feuerwehr* [fire brigade] then drove up. At that time the flames began to flare up. The fire had been laid in such a professional manner that the ceilings had more or less all burned through by this time. The whole building was blazing away, although there was little flammable material in it due to its modern style of construction. Also, the fact that the flames blazed especially strongly out of a library housed there, in which about 12,000 books were piled up very close together, indicated the presence of a liquid fuel; books do not otherwise catch fire and certainly not so quickly. The nurse was refused entry to the building in a very rough and crude manner and was denied any information about the fate of its inhabitants. There were still only very few spectators on the street. The work of destruction itself was carried out by six to seven SS men at the very most. I then phoned the place where we had brought the child of my friend the previous evening, and was able to find out that everyone had been able to leave the house in good health. In this context it is worth stating that nobody was directly injured or murdered where I lived. That appeared to have been the result of orders. Those arrested were certainly badly mistreated, but not at the time of arrest. In general it seems that nothing was stolen. In other places during the operation not only were many people injured, but there were also serious cases of theft.

I stayed in close touch with the rabbis, *Gemeindevorstand* and *C.V.* the whole morning. We tried to establish what and where it had all happened and was still happening, and as far as possible to help people. They were still destroying homes and shops at this point. Windows and frames were being prised out, in some cases with crowbars, sledgehammers and pickaxes, and furniture, machines and other fittings were thrown out onto the streets. In the later hours of the morning there were many spectators of course. Half the city was on the move. Many Aryans were arrested too, those who dared to give expression to their disgust about the goings on.

Around 12 o'clock I came to the conclusion that the arrests which had begun in the morning at half past 6 were happening everywhere. They were carried out by blue-uniformed police. Since any further efforts were hereby rendered meaningless, I left by train using suburban stations and local lines. In the meantime the Gestapo have already called for me three times. I then travelled right across Germany to Hamburg. Only a few large shops had been destroyed (4–6?) there. For the rest people had restricted themselves to writing *Jude* [Jew] with red paint across glass panes in big letters. For the task of destruction they had alerted the pupils at a *Berufsschule* [vocational school] who had been told on the previous day where and when they should assemble and were then armed with crowbars. In close formation they then passed, amongst other places, the elevated railway station at Schlump. In the actual Jewish area on the Grindelallee things remained comparatively quiet. The businesses were closed, almost all were arrested. The *Israelitische Krankenhaus* [Jewish hospital] was still intact. It was overflowing with people who had suffered nervous breakdowns. I have heard nothing of any injuries. Some doctors were arrested. The synagogues were wrecked but apparently not burned to the ground. From a reliable Aryan acquaintance I heard that an older policeman from Eimsbüttel (a district in Hamburg) had told him that they had received orders not to leave their police station for the night from Wednesday to Thursday.

In Münster all the businesses were wrecked, although only some of the private homes were entered. However some shots were fired through windows into the homes. It appears that nobody was injured directly. Here even police officers had openly expressed their horror at the way in which people had behaved. The synagogue in Münster was burned to the ground and apparently also blown up.

Things must have been particularly bad in the smaller villages of the Münsterland on the Dutch border. In Drentsteinfurt the entire Jewish population is in hospital. Similar things must have happened in Burgsteinfurt, Gronau etc. When I arrived in Münster from the railway station, by chance I heard a young woman on the street explain to a soldier in a totally outraged manner how people in one place had played along as a Jewish couple was being driven through the streets.

Mönchen-Gladbach and Aachen appear to have got off comparatively lightly as apart from the businesses only a few homes were wrecked. It goes without saying that here too almost everybody was arrested.

First I attempted to cross the border at Aachen which, however, I did not succeed in doing. I then travelled back and was able to reach Dutch soil further north. On the way I received enormous help from many people I met, both Jews and Christians.

Through very reliable Christian eyewitnesses I have meanwhile also heard that my private home, which by the morning was already wrecked, was set on fire at 3 o'clock on Thursday afternoon. In addition it was then further wrecked in the night from Thursday to Friday. The final arson attack that I know of took place on Friday morning at 8 o'clock.

In all cases known to me the *Feuerwehr* restricted itself to ensuring that the fires did not spread. The fires themselves were not put out.

Heinz Nassau

B. 7   Aachen: Frau Spittel (Spittel und Franken textile factory) was beaten.

Düsseldorf: on the night of Wednesday to Thursday 20-year-old Oppenheim was knocked to the ground on the street by SA or SS men, and repeatedly mistreated. His mother and sister who tried to come to his aid were hit too. Medical help was refused.

Vreden (*Kreis* [district] Ahaus), Westphalia: three Jewish families live there. The men – Morgendorf, Heymann and a third – were fetched from their houses and totally covered in black (tar or soot?). Then one was clamped to the front of a two-wheeled cart, the second had to push it, and the third had to place himself on it. They had to trot through the town like this. If they did not go fast enough they were kicked, beaten and spat upon. The men were then forced to go barefoot across glass fragments.

Essen: Albert Bergerhausen and Walter Forst were fetched from their beds on the morning by an SS *Rollkommando* [raiding party]. They were only allowed to put on their trousers over the nightshirt, and then had to go to the synagogue where they had to watch as it was set on fire. During that there were cries such as "Throw them in too" – and similar.

Essen: Robert Blumenfeld (poulterers), Kasteienstraße, *Vorsitzender* [chairman] of the RJF [*Reichsbund Jüdischer Frontsoldaten*; Reich Association of Jewish Front-line Soldiers] was beaten and stabbed in the head during the looting of his shop.

Essen: the prisoners were first admitted to police prison. Then they were examined there for fitness for custody and work, and those aged over 55 were transported away in *wiern* whose windows were painted over, to an unknown destination. In prison they were comparatively decently treated.

Heinz Nassau

B. 8   16th November 1938

On 11th November I was arrested in my chambers and taken to what used to be the *Zuchthaus* [special prison] but has now been turned into a concentration camp. The old officials who made the arrest informed me that all the Jews had been arrested. There we were loaded onto trains at 8 o'clock in the evening and arrived near Oranienburg at about 3 o'clock in the morning. The station was about 2 kilometres away from the camp [Sachsenhausen] and we had to march there at the double. As there were many old people amongst us, several fell and were kicked and urged on with blows from rifle butts by the men accompanying us, all young SA lads.

On arrival at the camp, firstly names were called out and written down, and then from about 5 o'clock in the morning until 2 o'clock in the afternoon we had to muster and stand in the yard.

Anyone who moved was kicked and punched in the face. Our request to be allowed to leave was refused and answered with the crudest swearing by the guards. Finally in the afternoon a *Vorgesetzter* [superior officer] gave permission for us all be taken to the latrine. We were given food for the first time 24 hours after our arrest. The food was good.

We had to give up all our clothes and were given for them tattered concentration camp clothing made from worn out army uniforms, cotton drill clothing and suchlike. Similarly all our money was taken from us. In Oranienburg Jews are categorically forbidden to smoke and are not allowed to cater for themselves, nor are they permitted to buy anything in the canteen.

The next day there was *Exerzieren* [punitive drill]. For us younger people, many former front-line soldiers, this was bearable. Older people were left behind and were treated with kicks, with thrusts from rifle butts and with slaps and punches in the face, always accompanied by the crudest and foulest insults. In my section this happened to amongst others R., a businessman from H., over 70 years old, likewise J., the former *Anwalt* [lawyer], also over 70. Both were mistreated as has been described. During *Exerzieren* if prisoners went back into their lines after only a single exercise, the men were most cruelly kicked to the ground and then the guards mistreated them with hobnailed boots in the roughest manner without cause in their backs and buttocks.

At *Appell* [roll call] the Lagerkommandant [camp commandant] would walk to and fro at the front. Every now and then he would stop and swear in the crudest unrepeatable way at some of those who were lined up. He said for no reason to one of my neighbours, "I've got to take off my gloves now for you, dirty *Judensau* [Jewish pig]," and after he had done this very quietly, with all his strength he repeatedly punched the unfortunate one in the face and also under the chin.

One day all the inmates had to line up in order to watch the punishment to be carried out on a prisoner who had tried to escape. The man in question was strapped to a *Bock* [whipping block] and beaten with a heavy bull whip by two SA men who had volunteered specially for this until he lost consciousness. The victim had to loudly count every blow up to 25 himself until he fell silent because he lost consciousness, but even then the animals did not stop their mistreatment.

The *Stubenälteste* [room elder] reported that if the victim recovered even slightly, the second twenty-five would be administered.

There are attempted suicides every day. In my section an old man cut his wrists in an unobserved moment. During work the guards lure the workers to the barriers from time to time so that they can then knock them down. The current to the electrically charged wire fences is sometimes turned off because people run into these fences in their desperation to end their lives.

After six days I was released from the camp because my emigration was already arranged.

On release from the camp the usual parting speeches were made. "Atrocity propaganda" would also be punished abroad, because the foreign organisations were so supremely well organised that they would even lay hold of you abroad.

At this time 12,000 men are in Oranienburg, mainly Jews. 11 were released with me.

It has been arranged that on the day of vom Rath's funeral the assembled prisoners will stand to attention from early morning and will then be given no food all day.

B. 9 9th November 1938

Lessing, factory owner in Bamberg, founder of the "Traube" [Grapes], an inn for the *Jüdischer Kulturbund Bamberg* [Bamberg Jewish Cultural Federation]. Arson attack on the factory. He himself injured on the way to the factory. Last report about him from Monday the 14th November 1938. Card written by his wife and signed by him, sent to his brother in London.

Ingenieur [Engineer] Metzger, former director of the *Süddeutschen Eisenwerke* (South German Ironworks] in Nuremberg, travelled from Paris to Nuremberg on Wednesday night (9th November) to his family. He never arrived. Nobody knows whether and where he was taken out of the train.

Rechtsanwalt [lawyer] Heidenheimer, travelled from Nuremberg to St. Gallen on the night of Wednesday to Thursday. He never arrived.

The whereabouts of *Rechtsanwalt* Fritz Josephthal, Nuremberg (associate of Dr. W. Berlin), are unknown. *Rechtsanwälte* W. Berlin and Josephthal, Nuremberg, were released. The *Gemeindevorstand* [community chairman] Richard Jung is still in prison.

The former owner of the firm Lang & Mainz, Leopold Klein, and his wife, both aged 70, are now in hospital in Fürth after being injured during the house search.

B. 10 Shops and homes destroyed

Essen:

Confirmed, amongst others:

Shoe shop Edox (Willi Samson), Ad. Hitlerstraße

Shoe shop Schartenberg, Limbeckerstraße

Jeweller Futermann, Ad. Hitlerstraße

Jeweller Dublon, Ad. Hitlerstraße

Men's clothing Alexander, Limbeckerstraße

Women's fashion house Perl, Ad. Hitlerstraße (shortly before it was *arisiert* [Aryanised])

Furrier Ziegler, Theaterplatz

Furrier Verstaudig, Ad. Hitlerstraße

Carpet and pram shop Silber, Hindenburgstraße

Shoemaker Cohn, Hindenburgstraße

Wholesale haberdashery Jaeger (Frau Löwenthal), Hindenburgstraße (Aryan)

Wholesale haberdashery Gerson, Schlageterstraße

Wholesale perfumery Bloch, Rheinische Straße

Work clothes "Hosenmüller" (Hans Müller), Schlageterstraße

Women's fashion house Isselbächer, Rolandstraße

Ironing business "Bügelfalte", Rolandstraße

Children's clothing "Hamburger Kinderstube' (Frau Lilli Nassau), Limbeckerstraße

Perfumery Weinberg, Herm. Göringstraße

Dentist Steinberg, Thomaeplatz

Photographer Oppenheimer, Hindenburgstraße

Nassau and Samson flats, Haumannplatz (first destroyed
then set on fire)

Blum house, Max-Fiedler-Straße

Abel house, Max-Fiedler-Straße

Krombach house, Max-Fiedler-Straße

Herzfeld house, Max-Fiedler-Straße

Harf house, Friedrichstraße (set on fire)

Café-Restaurant Dreilindenstraße (formerly Loge) (S.
Samuel) (partly burned)

Hamburg:

Women's fashion house Robinsohn, Neuer Wall

Ladies' clothing, Gebrüder Hirschfeld, Neuer Wall

Photography shop Campbell, Neuer Wall

Women's fashion house Unger, Jungfernstieg

Aachen:

Shoe shop Speier, Am Elisenbrunnen

Heinz Nassau

B. 11 15 November 1938

Dear Madam,

You asked me for an overview of my journey, which I made
to Germany on 13 November. As I was in great disquiet about
my father and sister, last Saturday evening I travelled to W., where I
found my family well. W. used to have a thriving *Joodsche Gemeente*
[Jewish community] which under these circumstances now is
much reduced. I saw the synagogue there, which had gone up in
flames, a miserable picture. A fence in the vicinity bore the inscription "*Rache dem Judentum!*" [Revenge on Judaism]! The home of
the Jewish teacher next door had not one intact window pane, the
curtains were flapping out of the window. At a butcher's the large
shop windows were completely destroyed and much inside the
shop had also been destroyed. The windows were stuck with brown
paper from the outside. Two manufacturing businesses had been
completely emptied out, the goods there had been taken away by

lorry on Thursday. In my parental house everything was intact and
undamaged; in W. on the whole it still appeared human.

Thursday in the morning at 5 o'clock they had picked up
my father and sister from the house and shut them in a small
room with all the others from the *Gemeente*. 30 women and
children were in one room and 17 men. There were several old
people, one woman was already over 89 and quite deaf, they
had smashed all her windows as she had not woken up. Some of
them were interrogated, then the women were released at eleven
o'clock. There was an SA man on guard in front of every home
when they returned, he watched them the whole day. My sister
had the great fortune to have a decent person at her place, who
was so moved that he cried. The men, including my father of
77 years, were transported in a cattle truck to L. They had put
benches into them. All those arrested, including those from the
place itself, were brought to the abattoir, into the room where
the animals were slaughtered, where the axes and knives were
sharpened in their presence! There the elderly, over seventy,
were released after a caution, and my father was able to go home
again with three others. After his homecoming there was a
house search and all the cash was taken, also that of the *Joodsche
Gemeente*, and for the poor. The people there all have no money;
in fortunate cases they get a bit of welfare.

My sister's fiancé and his father were taken away to Oranienburg. They live at L.; some are appallingly housed there. There
are families there with no bed any more and no unbroken cup to
drink from. Six or seven deserted women were put together and
do not know where to turn. I spoke to one woman who had been
robbed of everything; her family consisted of 6 people, her only
daughter had been taken from her by death, one son in South
America, one 17-year-old boy in a youth prison and her husband
and son taken away. Everything in the house had been smashed.
The worst of it for these poor people is that they did not know
where their husbands could be. In L. meanwhile the lovely synagogue with official residence was burnt down, one supposes before
they had had time to take out all the valuables. When they came to
get the people in the morning they were surprised in their sleep,

they stood armed with clubs by the beds of the startled people. They could put on the most essential things by the light of a candle held by one of the brutes who completed their work of destruction if there was time. Wash basins were thrown at mirrors, nothing remained intact. My future brother-in-law came away in his nightshirt without socks or underwear, his distraught mother was taken to the train in pantaloons. Table silver as well as the ornaments were also seized from people who were going to emigrate. In W. the Jews also received a receipt for the goods that had been taken. I visited a pair of prominent families and I shall never forget the mute shock: it was as if the people had turned to stone.

H. de Groot-Cossen, Groningen

B. 12 Detailed report! CAUTION!

For appropriate use

At a burning Jewish youth centre in Essen a uniformed nursing sister who wanted to find out the fate of the *Verwalter* [administrator] and his family who could possibly be lying wounded in the burning building, was told by a fireman, "They can perish quietly! After all they did away with vom Rath. Make sure you leave this area or we'll smash you up too."

Frau Elli Samson in Essen, Haumannplatz 9, had already been perilously ill (nerves and heart) for some weeks. Doctor in charge: Dr. Fritz. When the SA intruded in the house to destroy it completely, the 60-year-old woman was taken from her bed and into the garden. When the maid, heavily criticised for being in service for Jews, requested a coat or a blanket for the sick woman she was told: "The old woman should perish quietly, she should be happy that we aren't smashing you up too." Frau Sansom has since been admitted to a hospital.

Fritz Nassau, owner of the firm *Rhein-Ruhr Maschinenvertrieb* [Rhine-Ruhr Machine Distribution] in Essen, private address Elsa-Brandström-Platz, was arrested at half past 6 in the morning on Thursday. He was later seriously mistreated and injured. I know nothing about his subsequent fate.

On Thursday morning around 10 o'clock a Dutch citizen

(Heyman?) appeared at the Dutch consulate in Dreilindenstraße in Essen. He had been seriously mistreated and injured.

In Münster a great deal was stolen during the destruction of homes. Above all almost all the silverware was taken. Savings bank books also disappeared.

The Jewish *Altersheim* [old people's home] Rosenau (*Daniel-Fleck-Stiftung* [Foundation]) was given instructions at midday that it had to be vacated by 5 o'clock. The home is situated beyond Essen-Werden.

Heinz Nassau

B. 13 My mother, a lady of nearly 80 years of age, lived in an old people's home in A. until the pogroms in Germany. The home was a private Jewish establishment. About 40 to 50 men and women were accommodated. The age of the residents must have been between roughly 70 and 85.

During the night of 11th to 12th November all the residents were awoken at 3 o'clock in the morning with instructions to pack their things and leave the house by 9 o'clock the next day. Those who had relatives in the locality, where few Jews lived, were lodged there or in the nearby vicinity. However, one must regard that accommodation as being very confined as a result of the pogroms. Where the old men and women who had no relatives nearby were accommodated eludes my knowledge.

Max Block, Amsterdam, Watteau-Straat

B. 14 21st November 1938

The *Fürsorgeheim* [Jewish girls' home in Neu-Isenburg] near Frankfurt am Main founded by Frau [Bertha] Pappenheim has been burned down.

Dr. Posen, The Hague

B. 15 18 November 1938

(For information only, not for circulation) *CAUTION!*

Herewith I kindly request assistance in order to rescue my mother from Germany.

I myself just fled from Germany and, by order of the *Luitenant-Kolonel, Administrateur der Grensbewaking en Rijksvreemdelingendienst* [Lieutenant-Colonel, Administrator of Border Control and State Aliens Office] at The Hague, was let through at the border office at A., because in my case I could prove that special risks to life and limb existed. I was librarian of the synagogue community and editor of a Jewish paper in B. and on the night of 9 and 10 November and also in the course of that day had the opportunity to observe what happened there and how the whole operation was coordinated. I have every reason to suppose that everything I saw is known in Germany.

I regard my mother as in particular, immediate danger because, as more happens, the German authorities will try to use her as a hostage now that they cannot catch me.

My mother has no more means to exist in Germany. The small business that she ran was totally ruined whilst our home was burnt and it was not possible to save anything.

To be sure, I myself cannot support my mother because I am not allowed to work here. So my uncle, with whom I am also staying at the moment, will take her in whilst some other acquaintances who live in fairly well-to-do circumstances have also said they are prepared to take her in. My brother in South Africa who has already been trying actively to fetch her, and shall soon succeed I hope, and my sister in Palestine, will be responsible for all the costs so there is in no case danger that she will be destitute.

For all further information it goes without saying that I am always at your service. German and Dutch references for my mother can also be supplied.

Letter from Julius Nassau, Bussum (Holl.), Groot Hertoginenlaan 26, Tel. 4325

B. 16 Rabbi Eschelbacher was taken from his home – which was completely wrecked – and imprisoned. Frau Dr. E. wanted to accompany her husband, but did not do so after she learned that she would not be allowed to remain in the same cell as him. Rabbi E. is said to have suffered a nervous breakdown in prison but his spouse does not know about it. Apparently he has recovered now.

What took place at Rabbi Klein's must have been terrible because his home has been totally wrecked. It has been established that he was mistreated but no details of that are known. His wife was also mistreated. Both were arrested as well as their son aged 13 and a paying guest of about the same age. However, on Friday Frau Klein and the two children were set free again.

The reporter himself buried six people – five men and a woman. These fatalities are strongly connected with the pogroms. Nothing would move the reporter to communicate the names of the fatal victims and the causes of death. He did say that a man suffocated in his room after the beds were set on fire.

The reporter also could not give an estimated indication about the number of wrecked homes. He did however state that hardly a home was spared including that of the cantor of *Gemeinde* [community] A., who was seriously wounded in the war, however. – Very many homes were robbed and plundered during and after the destruction; and not only valuables such as jewellery, gold etc. but also lingerie, linen etc.

Until Friday the 18th November Jews could still buy food in many shops, so that one cannot speak of an immediate food emergency. The *Wohlfahrtsamt* [welfare office] of the *Synagogengemeinde* [synagogue community] in which Frau Dr. Eschelbacher and Fräulein Levisohn are active, is also working.

In Dinslaken private houses were burned, not only the synagogue. At night there children were fetched from the orphanage and taken to a school room. After the orphanage was totally wrecked the children were taken back in again.

The reporter also could not make an indication of the number of people arrested in Düsseldorf but it is certainly a very large number. The younger of those arrested are said to have been taken to Dachau. The rest find themselves ten to a cell. Apparently they are allowed to cater for themselves, and can also play cards.

Herr Frank, Düsseldorf

B. 17 Zürich, 18th November 1938

Dear Sirs,

In response to your letter about destroyed synagogues in Germany, I am informing you of the following destruction of synagogues on the border, ascertained by eyewitnesses:

Tiengen [now Waldshut-Tiengen]: the synagogue there was completely burned out and became a slaughterhouse. The cemetery was also destroyed and all the gravestones were uprooted.

Gailingen: the Jews of the small town were ordered to be present at the destruction of the synagogue (which was rather a large building because of the former size of the Jewish settlement).

Konstanz: The synagogue here was also destroyed.

The business of a Swiss man in Nuremberg was completely wrecked. His home remained undamaged because of the *Hausverwalter* [caretaker]'s objections. According to a statement by the resident in question it is one of the few homes that was not destroyed.

Yours faithfully

Saly Braunschweig, Nüschelerstr. 36 II, Zürich

B. 18 21 November 1938

(Not for publication)

Children of 15 and 16 years are languishing in concentration camps and are only set free if there is proof that they will be admitted abroad.

Morendorff children. A girl of seven and a boy of eleven years were dragged through the streets with a noose that had been wound three times round the neck. Then they were thrown in the water. At the very last moment they were rescued, however. The children fled to the border three times. After telephoning the government they were admitted to Holland. They have now been brought safely to a Jewish orphanage. The children appeared indescribably poorly.

A child of eight years was found in a completely devastated house. Father away, mother, before she was taken prisoner, could only advise the child, "Go to Grandmother in Amsterdam". The child looked for his money box among the rubble, smashed it open and came to Amsterdam alone.

A child of 10 years was the only Jewish child at his school. A bigger boy said to him: "Your mother has been arrested." All other children were put in two rows and watched as the child who stood in the middle cried for his mother. The teacher said to him: "Your Mummy cannot see you any more, she has already been hanged." It was not true.

Eyewitnesses confirm that conditions are even worse than one is aware of here.

Many children flee entirely alone to the border from anxiety and uncertainty.

The Dutch people make an urgent appeal to the humanity and charity of people in other countries. The Netherlands has a strong financial *Comité* [committee]; homes to stay in are offered everywhere and requests by private individuals to take people. Protestant homes offer to cook according to ritual for the German children, unemployed ask to be able to help. Prominent Dutch people stand behind the Dutch operation for children which is completely neutral, consistent with the tradition of the Dutch people.

The government is very willing but cannot accept without limits. The Netherlands can make this a more contained campaign in the near future when other countries accept these children. (Thus Netherlands as transit country.)

Personal statement from Dr. [Hendrikus] Colijn to a friend. (Very reliable communications!) "If Roosevelt reports that a specific number of children can be accepted after a certain time, Holland can temporarily accept and feed them."

Various orphanages were totally destroyed. The children cannot stay there. (Including Frankfurt and Dinslaken.)

Frenle van Lennep

B. 19 21st November 1938

Herr Ullman from Elberfeld is in hospital in Düsseldorf with a head injury.

The old people's home in Werden near Essen, an establishment run by Frau Fleck – Düsseldorf, has been closed. Frau Fleck has now taken in a number of old ladies.

Wolfgang Neubuscher, 17 years old, in a concentration camp.

A 16-year-old child in a concentration camp.

A mentally handicapped child from Berlin driven out of a home. The brother, family breadwinner, in a concentration camp.

It had been reported from an absolutely safe source that the orphanage in Konigsberg, East Prussia, has been completely destroyed. Not a bed, not a chair remains whole. It is impossible for the Jewish children to be able to stay there.

B. 20 21st November 1938

In Dinslaken the orphanage was forcibly entered during the night, the children driven out of the building and into the yard and the orphanage wrecked. The children were then accommodated in various Jewish homes in Dinslaken and were looked after there by poor families. The children were then later taken to Cologne, where some were accommodated in the orphanage there and others in the *Chaluz* [Palestine pioneer organisation] house in Cologne.

In Dinslaken two houses under Jewish ownership were also burned down because they stood apart from the others and no other property was thereby endangered. The mother-in-law of the owner of one of the houses, a lady of nearly 70, had to be carried out whilst it was burning. The house of a widow with 2 children was completely wrecked and looted.

The reporter telephoned an Aryan *Anwalt* [lawyer] in D., who told him he could now vouch that nothing would happen to anybody else because the government had forbidden it. The properties are nevertheless "damaged".

Alfred Cohen

B. 21 If one entirely omits the political side of the events in Germany, then such an appalling quantity of human misery remains that each feeling person in the world is deeply struck by it. Whether guilty or innocent are now affected in Germany, in any case the most dreadful thing is the fate of the Jewish children. They most certainly have nothing to do with the so-called crimes that have been committed by "International Jewry" according to the Nazis; they are most certainly entirely innocent. But what will happen to them?

According to Berlin estimates, in the whole of Germany 35,000 men have been taken into custody. In most cases the women and children do not know where husbands and fathers are and how long they must remain in custody. Meanwhile the mothers are not in a condition to see to food for their children because in many cases they have been left behind without the means of existence. According to communications from various German places, shopkeepers refuse to sell food to Jewish customers. In smaller places, where each Jew is precisely known, it is impossible for Jewish families to obtain the basic necessities. In many towns milk for infants was not distributed once.

According to one report, in Frankfurt a. M. the risk of starvation exists for the thousands of Jewish children and women. In Vienna too the supply of food has become virtually impossible for the Jewish section of the population. Here and in Munich, in "Aryan" shops notices say that Jewish customers are not wanted. Jewish businesses are always entirely destroyed or find themselves in liquidation.

Almost more dreadful is the report of the destruction of a Jewish orphanage in West Germany. The children were driven out of the house and up to now no one knows where they are, probably they are roaming about in the country.

In families where the mother is no longer alive and the father is now incarcerated in a concentration camp the children are left behind without adult help. Acquaintances and family members, with whom they could perhaps have found shelter, are themselves helpless in destroyed homes. No one knows what should happen to the children. They have no chance of emigrating abroad in the normal manner unless foreign charitable institutions take up their case. A large field of activity is open before the Dutch population's wish to provide help. The future of Jewish children in Germany today is more disastrous than it ever was for German children in the war.

B. 22 A 13-year-old boy arrived here from Aachen at the *Zentral-bahnhof* [Central Station]. Mother dead, father imprisoned, child arrived alone. A policeman took the child in, took him home with him and now does not want to give him away.

The following announcement was made from the German-Dutch border at half past 10 on the morning of 18th November by a very credible party, whose guarantee can be wholly assumed:

For several days Jewish children have been roaming around in the woods along the German-Dutch border; they have walked there from various towns and villages, apparently with no father or mother, and are very frightened. When they arrive at the Dutch border they are brought to safety by the Dutch border guards.

B. 23 Report by an Aryan, recently in Munich, a well-educated man, Christian, who has left Munich as a result of the ghastly deeds:

He visited two families who had received the *Arisierungs-befehl* [Aryanisation order] and who were then forced to sign them immediately in the presence of *Beamten* [officials]. A man in the same building who refused sign this *Arisierungsbefehl* was battered to death with an iron truncheon in front of the eyes of other people and the reporter, who is prepared to testify to the truth of his report under oath.

Outside a Munich school a covered lorry appeared at 12 o'clock midday. When they came out of the school, 40 children – this concerns Jewish children – they were loaded onto the lorry and taken away. Nobody knows where.

The same reporter listened to the sermon of a National Socialist priest in a Munich church on the theme "Matthew: Lord, your will is done." He said it is stated that the blood of Christ would flow over the Jews; it was not stated when, but the moment had now come, it was God's will that this happened to the Jews.

In Minden in Westphalia all men aged under 60 were arrested and the synagogue burned.

In Hanover not only was the synagogue set alight but the cemetery was desecrated too because the cemetery chapel was set on fire.

B. 24 Not for dissemination, CAUTION.

11th November 1938

Your post has reached me, for which I would like to thank you particularly. How I came to get them is worth explaining in some detail. An *Armutszeugnis* [certificate of poverty] that would allow one to receive post duty-free does not exist for Jews. What to do? The RM. 100.– only arrived here on 1st November and before that I could not go to the post office (customs office). There my wife, as an Aryan, had to plead and beg and the official had a heart.

But who wants to talk about that when one sees what has become of Vienna. Yesterday Jews were hunted down in all of Vienna's *Bezirken* [districts]. I too was trapped and report: at 9 o'clock in the morning I went with some 80 prisoners to the *Polizeikommissariat* [police station] (Prater, Ausstellungsstraße), where some 1,000 poor victims had already been herded together in abandoned stables so that their bodies formed one solid mass. Everyone had to stand "hands raised" so as to make better use of the space. Every three to five minutes three or four people were ordered to go to the *Nationale* [to give their personal details]. The instruction was: three men from the far corner "over the heads!" Then the three or four men flew like rockets over the bowed heads to the opened door. I arrived at the *Nationale* c. 1 o'clock. Questions passed: "Are you homosexual, have you dealt with any scrapes, are you in a relationship with a person of German blood, etc.: which associations do you support?", and since there was a wait of around two more hours in a mezzanine room, I was able to see what was taking place in the yard below. The Jews were being handled by people acting like mad animals: they had to roll around on the ground without their shoes touching the ground – blow after blow, because it is not easy. Then hopping, jumping, squats – always accompanied by blows, then the people had to spit on each other, slap each other round the face, and if they did not punch with full force the partners were given extra blows. Others had to stand against the wall and were then threatened with execution, but even better – they were beaten accompanied by the words "*Du Saujud* [you Jewish pig]", "*Du Volksverräter* [you traitor against the people]" etc. Then people went into a hall where watches, rings, knives were taken from them – then on to a police doctor to decide if they were fit for prison or not. I went home because I was classed as not fit enough for prison. One question: how long can a human being – like a herring in a barrel – live without nutrition, must a person just "fade away"? I know that along with many, many hundreds of others I did not see a glass of water for ten hours, I am convinced that all of them had to endure a complete fast for 24 hours. That was still the police station. Homes were robbed and plundered. Homes were robbed of anything that was to hand. Money from RM. 1.– upwards, linen, radios, food were taken by people in uniform and without. Rings were taken off people's fingers, one saw all kinds of things. In the third *Bezirk* nothing was sold to Jews. For poor Jews there was no welfare support since the canteens had been completely destroyed. Until late at night everything possible was being dragged out of homes, a scandal for a *Volk* [people] who says of itself "*Über alles in der Welt*" [Above everything in the world]. True indeed in matters of cowardice and nastiness, hardness and barbarism, sadism, rapacity and beastliness – unparalleled in world history.

All *Tempel* [synagogues] totally destroyed, set on fire, blown up. Very sad to have to say that German is my mother tongue. The Jews do not take their children to school because every- thing is battered, large and small. What more can I say? That we were given notice to quit – insignificant when Jews are less than "animals". There is no law that protects Jews. Whether somebody has 100 medals or none, a Jew remains a Jew. Jews are without rights before the law. I visited families whose men were captured like me – deepest desperation everywhere since nobody can bring themselves to believe that the men are going to return home any time soon. It makes for surprises. Yesterday thousands of homes were "officially barred." The poor residents are supposed to go and sleep with families – but where? Instead of a firework the 9th November was officially declared not a day off school but rather as a day of robbery and plunder for the rapacious *Volk*. Starting at RM. 1.– everything possible was stolen. RM. 4.- – only RM. 4.- – was stolen from an 80-year-old woman. Those who had determined that the day should be a day of robbery – as if in mockery, the watchmen are going through the streets today, 24 hours later that is, whilst the gangsters put their booty to use. That people do such a thorough job is hardly surprising given that the Germans are noted for their thoroughness. Everything that is said about Vienna is untrue. It is underestimated a hundredfold. There is no compassion, no mercy, it is a brutish *Volk* enraptured by the most intense sadism. How the people were insulted, is of no interest now (since it does not cause physical pain). Those who did not prostrate themselves immediately when confronted by the police were punched or hit – it was awful to see and then have to hear the cries of pain. How many are dying or have perished already – there is no information. I was there and my report only covers part of what happened.

From today the *Kultusgemeinde* [Jewish community] has been occupied again – I mention that only in passing.

My child – despite being highly intelligent – is forced to wither away on account of not being able to go outside.

We have the home until the end of January and what may happen thereafter – nobody speaks of that. I have a definite feeling that we will never see each other again – never – and so I am happy that the longest journey . . .

Perhaps my wife will manage, as a more robust person, to move on in England where the child might also be able to get out.

It is really terrible to have to protect children before, during and after school. – Frightening, incomprehensible, for anyone.

B. 25 "Visits" to the homes of Jewish residents took place under the pretext of looking for weapons. In countless cases the residents were forced to leave home within a few minutes, their keys were taken from them and they wander in despair round the streets or in the vicinity of Vienna where they had fled to escape further persecution. Only later did they feel confident enough to go to relatives or friends.

One of my acquaintances wrote me a despairing letter from the streets on the night of 10th to 11th November in which she, a young life-loving person, announced her suicide if the efforts I had been making for a long time to obtain a position in a household here for her did not succeed very quickly. "She cannot stand it any longer it. It is ghastly." I received a letter from her dated the 13th November, by when she still had not had her key returned to her. "Whether we can survive this is a huge question."

During the "visits" young men *were* routinely taken away. Some had the "luck" to be released after some hours, their treatment during the time of their imprisonment was however barbaric. A former member of the *Union österreichischer Juden* [Union of Austrian Jews], Vienna *Kultusvorsteher* [Jewish community board member], head of a large branch of Merkurbank, Director Jacques Weiger, was so badly punched that his eardrum was damaged and he is lying in bed with severe pains in his body. Similarly a former member of the *Union österreichischer Juden,* Vienna *Kultusvorsteher, Prokurist* [company secretary] of the Wiener Giro- und Kassenverein Dr. Ernst Feldberg, who until recently had a position in the Vienna *Kultusgemeinde* [Jewish community] as director of the *Friedhofsamt* [cemetery office], was arrested in spite of his job in the *Kultusgemeinde* and badly battered.

The fate of thousands who were not released after their arrests but instead "properly" imprisoned remains totally unknown. That the authorities were not bothered by needing "reasons" for imprisonment is demonstrated by the fact that amongst those imprisoned and still held are doctors to whom *Bewilligung* [authorisation] had recently been granted as "*Krankenbehandler*", to treat Jewish patients. What is happening to those in prison is still not known, their location cannot be determined; it was stated merely that they have been sent to do *Zwangsarbeit* [forced labour] in *Altreich* [Germany].

"Less harmful" were those "visits" during which the uninvited guests satisfied themselves by taking valuables and money with them; one case is known to me in which the gentlemen were not content with watches and chains but also took a wedding ring. In some cases the "visits" were repeated a number of times.

The order concerning closure of all educational buildings and places of entertainment for Jews has not hit them particularly hard because already only small number of Jews visited such places. Most of them had not dared to go out onto the street for weeks for fear of jostling. It is also significant that – apart from at coffee houses and inns – the Jews are *"nicht erwünscht* [not wanted] even at confectioners.

Internal Jewish *Gemeindeleben* [community life] has been killed off completely; my prophesy concerning this at the end of my first long report has been proved correct in a shorter time than I had expected. It is known that the *"Zionistische Rundschau"* [Zionist Review] like all Jewish newspapers in Germany had to close. It may be less well known that rabbis have been forbidden to preach so that the unfortunate Jews in Vienna now also have to do without this spiritual support. As already reiterated in recent times, it can be assumed that from now on no evening services can take place and at best short morning prayers. Vienna is not affected by the banning of the [*Jüdische*] *Kulturbund* [Jewish Cultural Federation] because this institution had never been permitted to be set up there anyway. Recent endeavours on the part of *Dir[ektor]* Hellmer, working in Germany at one time and Director of the *Theater an der Wien* [Theatre on the Wien] before the turmoil, and which appeared almost to have borne fruit, have of course failed once and for all.

B. 26 The reporter was called on 15th November and told that Rabbi van der Zyl of Berlin was arrested and brought to Weimar [Buchenwald]. Apparently the rabbi will be released if it can be proved that he has an *Aufenthaltsbewilligung* [residence permit] for a different country.

Telephone call from Herr Heimann, Duivendrecht, at the instigation of Herr Oppenheimer

B. 27 14th November 1938

According to the reporter, on the night in question a mob intruded into his parents-in-law's house and wreaked havoc in such a way that the house is considered to be uninhabitable.

The couple B. were injured during it. The injuries of the wife are of a lighter nature whereas Herr B., the father-in-law, is now laid low in the Jewish refuge (hospital) in C, seriously injured.

The reporter added that numerous arrests have been carried out, as is known.

Rechtsanwalt [lawyer] Rudolf Haas, Noordzeebank

B. 28 15th November 1938

Nuremberg: few arrests but numerous homes destroyed.

Munich: many arrests but no homes ruined.

B. 29 Rumours: Rabbi Eschelbacher (Düsseldorf) missing. Rabbi Klein (Düsseldorf) in mental hospital.

The home of a relative aged over 70 of a gentleman resident here was smashed to pieces by the current head of large factory that used to belong to him, and by a mob of people.

B. 30 Krakow, 1st November 1938

My dears,

Hoping that you have received my telegram in the meantime. I would like to describe briefly to you what happened to me.

Early on Friday at half past 5 two officers came from my police station, I was to go with them at once and take RM. 10.- with me, it was a passport check. You can imagine the shock we had. At the police station I saw what the game was; since I lived in the house next door I asked the leader if I might fetch some things because I had nothing, it was flatly refused. I phoned Papa immediately so that he could inform Netti. They hastily brought me some clothes and food. We were assemled on lorries, transported to A.-Straße, from there we were taken to the railway station, there were c. 2,000 people.

There were scenes that one cannot describe in words. Women and children screamed, cried, collapsed unconscious.

They are like thieves, totally heartless, it was a veritable raid on poor, vulnerable people.

We left at half past 2 to 3 o'clock and were at the border at 12 o'clock at night. Nobody was allowed to go to the window or get out, everything was locked. We were threatened with cocked rifles and pistols in case we went to the window. The officers at the border post were very surprised because the transport had not been announced, suddenly all the German officers who had escorted us disappeared (200 men). During the journey we were all treated like criminals, it is a disgrace that this was allowed to happen at all.

Passports were checked and stamped until 3 o'clock in the night. Nobody had taken care of the accommodation. 2,000 people had to be accommodated in two small rooms, we were at the border station from Friday until Monday. No one can imagine the picture. The air made one choke, four people died in two days; it was a great pity that none of us had a camera to take pictures to send abroad.

All of us had no money and nothing to eat, we were forced to find a remedy in the quickest way because people became ill through debilitation.

Jewish getlemen and ladies came from the vicinity. They did everything that was possible. Very well-to-do people stood and queued at 2 o'clock at night until their turn came to receive a piece of dry bread and a glass of tea. There were tears in people's eyes, it was a situation that one can hardly describe in words. On Monday evening at 5 o'clock we arrived in K. We were all very cordially received, there was food that astonished us: sausage, eggs, bread and butter, tea, milk, coffee, cakes etc. Doctors and nurses were present. We were all fetched in cars and accommodation was taken care of. The people cost 100,000 zloty per day. I ate at midday and supper at A.'s, they are very fine people, and I obtained some money too.

I read your lovely letter at A.'s, and I was very pleased that you were so concerned about me. We did not end up in a *Sammellager* [transit camp], thank God, so you need not worry. I am very much in favour of the dear parents leaving Germany in the quickest way, since every day in B. there is something new.

There are negotiations about the expulsion of the Poles, it

is said that in c. eight days one can travel home so that we can organise matters in B.

Women and children were also deported from Stettin, Leipzig, Magdeburg, Cologne etc., sadly two of the small children died from the cold and poor nutrition (three and half months, and one year old). Fine conditions, it wants to be a "cultural nation", it is a crime what the government is doing.

Now I want to close because I am very tired, I have not seen a bed for three nights so you can imagine what I have been through.

B. 31 14th November 1938

Herr A. spent several weeks at a large chemical business in Berlin, where he was attending a medical course. He stayed with his wife in Charlottenburg with people one must describe as "Nazis". Nevertheless these people were horrified by the events of 10th November and emphatically declared their opposition to the way Jews were being treated.

On Thursday morning when Herr A. left the house he saw that a nearby shop selling fashion accessories was destroyed by a crowd of young lads. Going further, he passed the Neumann corsetry business, a large shop on the corner, and saw to his horror that the same thing was happening. The populace stood there in dumb terror. Nobody dared to try to oppose them. However eventually looting began. Women were fighting over lingerie etc. Herr A. observed exactly the same thing at a shoe shop.

At 2 o'clock Herr A. took the *Stadtbahn* [city railway] from Westend to Zoologische Garten station. When he passed Fasanenstraße he saw the synagogue still burning. A fire engine stood in front of it. But nothing much was being done to put out the fire. They only sought not to let it spread to the nearby houses. However the small administration building where the reading and lecture rooms used to be was completely burned down.

A Jew who drove past by car was suddenly attacked by a crowd of young men and in few moments beaten until he bled. Then a police motor cyclist arrived, the injured man was lifted into the sidecar and driven away. A passer-by who expressed his outrage was attacked in the same way and only just managed to save himself from the young fellows' rage. It is remarkable that amongst the perpetrators were not only the usual street riff raff but men with Party badges. (It happened at about ten past 2 in front of the burning synagogue in Fasanenstraße).

In the afternoon Herr A. travelled to Potsdam. There the same picture was displayed: every single Jewish business destroyed, the synagogues ravaged.

People rarely talked about this pogrom and only in secret. Amongst working people there was horror at this shamefulness and anyway fear that the workers would have to pay for the lost stock through taxes and compensate for hardship. It was said, even in so-called National Socialist circles, that it had not been as bad as this during the Spartacist uprising [general strike in Germany in January 1919] in Berlin. They regretted they had to be silent as almost everyone's employment depended in one way or another on the Party.

Representatives from the Party came to the chemical business looking for Herr A. three times and enquiries were made about him. This was probably in connection with the fact that he had repeatedly expressed his horror. But occasionally Germans also expressed themselves indignantly to him and said that they were ashamed to be German.

On leaving Germany Herr A. was questioned by SS men between Bentheim and Osnabrück and was also searched. There was evident fear that he had kept a record of what he had seen. It was argued that every Dutchman who said he was participating in scientific courses in Germany was certainly involved in politics. Was not the firm where he worked a Jewish one, etc.

The chemical firm in question, which incidentally is world famous, suddenly dismissed the last Jewish employees during these November days. They should really have stayed until the end of the year.

The medical course was led by an Aryan who said roughly the following however, "The names of the Jewish researchers Starkenstein and Neisser are admittedly no longer desirable in Germany. However the truth must be served and these researchers have done science a great service." Apart from many German doctors, a Dutch man (Herr A.), a Hungarian and a Turk were attending the course.

Herr A. heard from Austrians that in general there was discontent that the good jobs were in the hands of *Reichsdeutschen* [native Germans], whereby the Austrians had not come out of it well.

When Goebbels' decree was issued at 5 o'clock, the devastation had not yet stopped. At half past eight in the evening and even later the destruction in Friedrichstraße and in the arcade was still going on.

The Jews' anxiety was already great. Herr A., who used to go to a Jewish shop before this pogrom, was told by the female proprietor that as an Aryan he was not allowed to buy anything from her. First he had to prove that he was Dutch.

Herr A. had taken part in the meeting of Catholic youth organisations in the Camillus church on Karlplatz and spoke to the clergy. One of the priests pointed out that the Catholic Church still holds great power as long as it remains united. The churches are full and a good mood prevails amongst Catholics. This is also the case with the Protestants. However Catholic persecution is also expected!

A Dutchman who had expressed his indignation was arrested on Thursday evening. He would have been released if he had said no more; however he refused.

On the evening of the 10th November a policeman and an SS man stood guard at every business that had been destroyed.

B. 32 CAUTION

14th November 1938

The reporter seeks help for his wife's uncle, whose brother has lived here for several years. His wife's uncle, who is seriously ill, was arrested and in the opinion of the family doctor direct mortal danger exists if help does not arrive promptly. (The reporter is *Rein-Arier* [pure Aryan].)

The reporter, a language teacher, had held a beginners' course at half past seven on the morning of 10th November. Most of his pupils, exclusively SS men, were not present. He received the following reply to his question, "They have been ordered to smash window panes." As a result the course was postponed until the afternoon as the participants had to "do their duty" in plain clothes during the whole morning.

Then on his way through the town to the east where he had to give lessons, the reporter saw how the shops of Jewish business people had been wrecked and he recognised a number of his students, SS men in plain clothes, amongst those doing the wrecking. When the window panes of a Jewish shop in A.-Straße were broken, one old "onlooker" said to another, "Look at the mob, filthy rogues." The remark was relayed by another to a policeman and the man, obviously non-Jewish, was immediately arrested. In the east, even in the poorer quarter of B., all the Jewish homes were wrecked and the men arrested. No homes were damaged in the west, but the men were arrested. In cases where the men were not found after repeated searches, the arrest of the women and children was threatened if the men did not give themselves up. Two cases are known where this threat was carried out, and in another the wife fetched her husband from the coal cellar.

According to statements made to me from more reliable sources in Frankfurt am Main, patients at the Jewish Hospital in Gagernstraße were arrested from their beds. The rumour is going around that Rabbi Horovitz was burned in the synagogue; another rumour is that Horovitz must have been taken to a lunatic asylum.

Those who were arrested in Frankfurt am Main were assembled in the *Messegebäude* [trade fair building] and taken away in groups of 30. According to an eyewitness report they were mistreated in the most inhuman way in the open street.

A large number of homeless Jewish men from Frankfurt are roaming around in the Taunus without shelter because they are afraid of being arrested at home; a smaller number have been taken in secretly by Jewish and Christian friends in the vicinity.

Asked for his view of the purpose of the operation, the eyewitness stated that initially the intention was to occupy and destroy the street, but that it was widely accepted that there was a desire to exert pressure on "World Jewry", now or at a later stage, to pay a ransom in foreign currency. Even from more moderate circles it was said, "Let those abroad quietly bleed a bit."

Asked about the effect of the operation on the non-Jewish population, he reported that most watched completely disinterested. A smaller number were "glad" that at last things are being "tidied up" and an even smaller number were "ashamed". There does not appear to be any public protest.

B. 33 We learned through telephone reports from A. as well as information from somebody living there who came to Brussels that the house that has been in possession of the same family for 40 years was destroyed and its inhabitants, a married couple Dr. B. and his wife, were injured. Dr. B. is in the *Jüdischen Krankenhaus* [Jewish hospital] in C. Frau B. who was also admitted there, has in the meantime been discharged.

In Aachen 193 Jews were arrested; according to police information 60 of them were taken to Weimar. The members of the arrestees' families were referred to the *Rechtsanwalt* [lawyer] Karl Löwenstein. At his office they learned that he too was amongst those arrested. They were informed through daily newspapers about the wrecking of shops and burning of the synagogue.

B. 34 Berlin, 19th November 1938

I know that it is certainly unnecessary to write to you yet again about my misfortune. But I am writing nevertheless as I just have a special opportunity to do so. I am so grateful to think that you are doing everything that can be done. If only it was soon successful!

It is perhaps important for you to be aware of the following, so that you are able to intensify your efforts on behalf of A. and B.: one hears again and again that at the beginning of next week individual categories are to be released, disabled war veterans, war decorated, officers, old people. However the two belong to none of these categories! It is said that even business people who *arisieren* [Aryanise] are to be given priority – there is no question of that either. Therefore I am very afraid that the two will stay with the remainder who will be held for a very long time. Neither of them will be able to bear it! I am so desperate!

One also tries to achieve various things through the organisations, but to date the two have not even been released through the *Reichsvertretung* [*der Juden in Deutschland*; Reich Deputation of Jews in Germany] and the official from the *Hilfsverein* [*der Deutschen Juden*; Aid Association of German Jews], which is still working despite everything. Therefore I have little hope there. In fact what remains is only initiating an individual opportunity to emigrate. And that is what I am asking you for now, if it is at all in your power! Sadly, sadly there is still a long way to go, even if I can acquire the documents with your help which the consul has indicated to me would offer the prospect of an *Einreiseerlaubnis* [entry permit]. Then of course A. has no passport, and the *Unbedenklichkeitsbescheinigung* [clearance certificate] from the *Finanzämter* [tax offices], without which a passport will not be issued, is not currently being issued. It is said that it will remain thus until the billions have been collected. Oh God, oh God, one is banging one's head against a brick wall!

Nevertheless one must unceasingly consider everything imaginatively and tirelessly. I know you do that as do I. I am unceasingly grateful to you for this.

Frau Reifmann, Berlin

B. 35 12th November 1938

Below we report extracts from the events on 10th and 11th November in A., a German town with 30,000 inhabitants including 300 Jews, in B., a village with 700 inhabitants including 25 Jews, in C., a remote Jewish farm with agricultural students. – We still do not have a general overview today, 12th November. – Our report is based on facts which we have seen with our own eyes or which were told to us by those involved.

The operation began in A. on 10th November at half past 6 in the morning, when some prominent Jews, including women, were dragged out of bed. They were led in front of the synagogue, made to unlock it and witness the following. Uniformed SS men broke into the synagogue though quickly left again. Several bombs immediately exploded and the synagogue was in flames. The window panes of the neighbouring dwellings shattered. (The Christian residents of the surrounding houses had already been asked the previous evening to move their furniture away from the windows.) The *Feuerwehr* [fire brigade] stood by with their hands in their pockets and confined themselves to spraying the adjacent houses. Just four walls of the synagogue are still standing.

At the same time all male Jews between 20 and 70, about 60 in number, and also some women were arrested. The women were later released at about 9 o'clock and led home past the burning synagogue. The men were taken to the Gestapo hostel by use of the grossest means, even those who were seriously physically or mentally handicapped. Some, such as a 70-year-old man, were harshly mistreated, beaten until they lay there swollen and covered in blood. One was then thrown into water and "allowed" to go home. The others were partly locked in a cellar which they were not allowed to leave even to relieve themselves, others had to stand for hours facing the wall. Towards evening a few were released, mainly the elderly. Of the others, some were taken to the railway by lorries and loaded with kicks into goods wagons. We do not know where they were taken. Others were led away to the local prison.

Those released from custody can barely be induced to speak; though their wounds and the grey in their eyes speak for them. Those remaining in their homes, some of whom had been forbidden to leave, are close to despair. They are overwhelmed by their total ignorance about the fate of the men and fear of the immediate future. They receive telephone calls and telegrams from relatives in other places asking whether they can come and stay with them. The few Jewish businesses still in existence were closed by the police.

In B. the events took place as follows: at half past 6 all the men and a "*Judenknecht*" [servant of Jews; Nazi term for political enemies] were led in front of the synagogue by an

SS troop that had come in from elsewhere. After the Torah decorations had been removed by the SS the synagogue was blown up. – The men were then led away to the *Rathaus* [town hall]. There, once the local Gendarmerie had been dismissed, they were mistreated in the most appalling way without exception;everyone received about 80 blows with two clubs and was heavily kicked. One war veteran, a front-line soldier who had affixed his medal ribbons, was set upon particularly violently and his participation in the World War was doubted and derided by the young louts.

During this period houses were searched, confiscated and sums of money stolen. – Towards 6 o'clock in the evening the men were released again. They came home in a pitiable state. At 8 o'clock they were arrested anew. We do not know where they were then taken.

The Christian people in the village were completely uninvolved in everything that happened.

From C., the isolated farmstead, we are receiving a report that everything has been wrecked and the yard resembles a *Lazarett* [sick bay].

We have only reported the facts here. We are unable to depict the horror and the fear which has overcome the people involved. Sorrow at the destruction of holy places, the loss of so many valuables and of existence are accepted in silence. Only fearful worry for the lives of their relatives dominates these people.

B. 36 A Catholic Dutch gentleman resident in Amsterdam recounts and is prepared to swear to everything he recounts.

On Wednesday he had to travel to Berlin for a business trip, he arrived on Thursday 10th November at 7 o'clock, and saw that almost all the houses in Friedrichstraße had been wrecked. Shop goods were all thrown onto the street. The unrest lasted until Friday morning. The police stood there and watched without doing anything. When the staff of the various shops arrived for work, most people shook their heads. Only one individual laughed. Our reporter said he had to learn from this that the best supporters of Hitler comprise the 2% of panderers in the German people. Whilst he was with his business friend in the office, news came from Cologne that the home of his Jewish business friend's brother-in-law had been wrecked and all the furniture destroyed.

From a small town in Oderwald. The home of his business friend's brother was completely wrecked. Ten minutes later a third report from Frankfurt that a nephew was sought by the police. The man was able to flee in time. Our reporter had seen that typewriters were thown out of windows in Kronenstraße. Fur coats were dragged away by young people, account books were burned in the street whilst the police looked on laughing. During the evening meal the wife of the *Prokurist* [company secretary] was arrested. At lunchtime the private secretary received news by telephone that her father had been arrested, her brother half beaten to death and their shop completely wrecked. Meanwhile her father has been released again, the brother transported away to Oranienburg [Sachsenhausen].

In each police district people were arrested and taken away in cars in groups of 20 to 25 people. The disturbances occurred under the leadership of young people aged from 18 to 20 years. They always marched in groups of three with SA boots and red cravats. The people were not satisfied when the glass had been smashed and did not stop until the last fragment was knocked out. People stole appallingly. Our reporter saw in trams that stolen shoes were cut up. On Saturday at 4 o'clock he was visited by a Jewish woman who recounted that people were being tortured to death and very many had already lost their minds. People have been wandering around for four days and four nights. The situation in Oranienburg is dreadful. The prisoners have to rise at 3 o'clock in the morning and start work at half past 3. For breakfast they receive a piece of black bread and a cup of coffee. At 12 o'clock they receive a plate of soup. In the evening a piece of black bread again. If people have not done enough work they are brought to the quarry. One of the SA men who is the overseer threw his whip into the quarry and when a prisoner went down to fetch it, the supervisor simply blew up the stones with dynamite and the prisoner was killed beneath the stone rubble. Children from the age of twelve have also helped to loot shops, and it is generally known that drums of petrol were dragged into the synagogues. In Berlin not one single shop remains intact, even the smallest and poorest shops. The "[*Algemeen*] *Handelsblad*" [General Trade Paper] wrote that people are like rats in a trap; this example is misleading. One knows that a rat in trap will be finished off within an hour. Jews are tortured for longer. Our reporter has gained the impression that in smaller places the young people were paid a bonus for every smashing up. The more malicious they were, the more they were celebrated by the Party leadership.

One can estimate that ten thousand is the number who have been arrested. It is not at all possible to have an overall view of how many people have committed suicide.

When our reporter left Berlin he heard rumours that the local government there was hatching the plan for goods still to be provided to Jews. An Aryan gentleman who had been a front-line soldier told our reporter that the wartime foes had not faced each other so cruelly and cynically.

Second reporter. From East Friesland [in Lower Saxony]. In various villages and small towns Jews had been shot at with rifles and revolvers. Many Jews were murdered, others received terrible wounds. Our reporter saw how a boy of 19 who was his mother's breadwinner was thrown into water, but he could swim and when he crawled out onto the bank he was beaten unconscious, kicked into the water again until he drowned. Our reporter had seen many cases of mistreatment. When the synagogue burned the Jews had to march past in pyjamas whilst singing dirty songs. People were brought to the concentration camps in cattle trucks. A retired *schochet* [Jewish ritual slaughterer] aged 76 was robbed of his pension, he was trapped in a large henhouse and led through the small town. He was left with only RM. 1.-. All the homes were wrecked in these villages and small towns too. In some places the Jewish teachers themselves werer forced to set fire to the *Thorarollen* [Torah scrolls]. The Jews know exactly who the attackers were. But each one is afraid to name the perpetrators or even their wives.

B. 37 CAUTION

16th November 1938

A. in the Rhineland: a Belgian Catholic visited the relatives of an Antwerp Jewish family. – He encountered seven weeping and distraught women in a kitchen sitting on empty boxes that had been fetched from the cellar. – Furniture and crockery totally destroyed. No glasses, no plates. As the furniture was too large to go through the windows, the "spontaneous" *Volkswut* [people's rage] had first broken the window frames out of a number of windows to create an opening. So the women dwell in a home without windows. For clothing they possess only what they are wearing, everything else has disappeared. The men – including an elderly Jewish teacher – find themselves in *Schutzhaft* [protective custody], apparently in *Strafanstalt* [prison] Anrath, a *Zuchthaus* [special prison].

Krefeld: an 85-year-old woman had to flee to relatives. She is unable to eat because her false teeth could not be found under all the wreckage in the nocturnal operation – she cannot see because her spectacles shared the fate of all breakable everyday objects.

B apparently weapons were also searched for during the wrecking of the home of a Jewish widow living alone. During it, a large sum of cash disappeared as well as two savings bank books. Thus the woman is literally without a penny to buy essentials for herself.

Cologne: amongst the mass arrests is the physician Dr. Wallach, foremrly in Andernach, who was transported to the notorious camp at Weimar [Buchenwald] (stone quarry) despite a serious kidney complaint. Information about his fate has not been obtained until now despite urgent pleas.

Essen-Ruhr: the shoe shop Schartenberg (Limbecker Straße) was totally devastated and robbed. The proprietor Ludwig Schartenberg was shot by an SA man when he attempted to deal with the arson and put out the fire. The perpetrator was not arrested by the police and got away unrecognised. (Report not yet checked.)

Düsseldorf: various reports with contradictory details give accounts of the murder of the rabbi Dr. Eschelbacher, who it seems wanted to save objects from the burning synagogue.

A further report stated that rabbi Dr. Klein became mentally disturbed after mistreatment by the mob and was taken to an asylum. Various and differing reports are to hand concerning both incidents.

B. 38 28th November 1938

It has been reported that the *Rechtsanwalt* [lawyer] Dr. Heidenheimer who had disappeared on the journey to St. Gallen has turned up at Dachau concentration camp.

Of those arrested in Aachen who were transported to Buchenwald, Herr Gustav Struch has died.

Richard Haas

B. 39 Expulsion of the Polish Jews from Nuremberg

Polish Jews living in Nuremberg were taken from their homes without any warning on 28th and 29th October at 8 o'clock. They were allowed to take RM. 10.-. Those who had a woollen blanket could take it. They were taken from the *Polizeipräsidium* [police headquarters] to the railway station at half past 11 and at exactly midday went away on the train. The arrests were indiscriminate, from children to those aged 80.

Women with small children returned during the following days as a result of the Polish-German negotations. Later those who had still not yet been taken over the border returned too. In Nuremberg the number of those Polish Jews forcibly deported was about 200.

B. 40 22nd November 1938

Synagogues fires

In Cologne the synagogues on Roonstraße and Glockengasse burned out, also the synagogue in Deutz.

Furthermore the synagogue in Halberstadt was burned.

In Berlin these synagogues were burned:

1. Fasanenstraße,

2. Prinz Regentenstraße,

3. Franzensbaderstraße in Grunewald,

4. Lützowstraße,

5. Passauerstraße,

6. Kleine Auguststraße,

7. Lessingstraße.

The synagogue on Levetzowstraße has been damaged but apparently not burned.

A small fire occurred at the Reform Synagogue in Johannisstraße.

These synagogues were spared:

1. Oranienburgerstraße,

2. Artilleriestraße, as well as

3. Rosenstraße (Heidereuthergasse), in addition

4. the small synagogue in Sigmundshof.

The synagogues on Artilleriestraße and Heidereuthergasse are also thought to have been set on fire but because of the energetic intervention by the guard from the *Wach-* und *Schließgesellschaft* [security company] the arson attack could not be carried out because the intruders were fended off.

The fate of the synagogues in Lindenstraße and Rykestraße is not yet officially known.

B. 41 LIST OF SYNAGOGUES AND BETHAEUSER
[houses of prayer] SET ON FIRE

Aachen	*Temps, Nationalzeitung*	11.11.1938
Alt Breisach (Baden)	*Temps*	12.11.1938
Angermünde (Ukermark)	*Morgenpost*	11.11.1938
Arnsberg	*Westfälische Landeszeitung*	11.11.1938
Bamberg	*Paris Soir*	12.11.1938
Bayreuth	*Paris Soir*	12.11.1938
Berlin (9 of 12) (not Oranienburger and Münchener)	*Temps*	11.11.1938
Beuthen [now Pol. Bytom]	*Danziger Vorposten*	11.11.1938

▶

Bielefeld		
Bochum	*Privat*	
Brandenburg an der Havel	*Berliner Lokalanzeiger*	11.11.1938
Breslau [now Pol. Wrocław]	*Schlesische Tageszeitung,*	11.11.1938
	Danziger Vorposten	
Cassel [now Kassel]	*Populaire*	11.11.1938
Cleve [now Kleve] / Rheinland	*Luxemburger Wort*	14. 11.1938
Cologne -2-	*Westfälische Landeszeitung,*	11.11.1938
	Birmingham Post	
Cottbus (Provinz Brandenburg)	*Berliner Lokalanzeiger*	11.11.1938
Danzig [now Pol. Gdańsk]	*Basler Nachrichten*	15.11.1938
Dessau (Anhalt)	*Populaire*	11.11.1938
Dresden	*Danziger Vorposten*	11.11.1938
Düsseldorf	*Westfälische Landeszeitung*	11.11.1938
Eberswalde (Provinz Brandenburg)	*Morgenpost*	11.11.1938
Emmerich	*Algemeenes Handelsblad*	13.11.1938
Emmeringen	*Luxemburger Wort*	11.11.1938
Essen -2-	*Westfälische Landeszeitung*	11.11.1938
Frankfurt am Main -4-	*Morgenpost*	11.11.1938
Freienwalde	*Morgenpost*	11.11.1938
Freiburg / Breisgau	*Danziger Vorposten*	11.11.1938
Fürth / Bavaria	*Fränkische Tageszeitung*	11.11.1938
Gablonz [now Cz. Rep. Jablonec nad Nisou]	*Daily Telegraph*	12.11.1938
Gailingen / Baden	*Neue Zürcher Zeitung*	11.11.1938
Gleiwitz [now Pol. Gliwice]	*Danziger Vorposten*	11.11.1938
Goch / Rheinland	*Luxemburger Wort*	14.11.1938
Graz	*Salzburger Volksblatt*	12.11.1938
Halle	*Danziger Vorposten*	11.11.1938
Hamburg -2-	*Hamburger Tageblatt*	10.11.1938
Hanover	*Morgenpost*	11.11.1938
Hersfeld	*Times*	10.11.1938
Hildesheim near Hannover	*Luxemburger Wort*	11.11.1938
Hindenburg [now Pol. Zabrze]	*Danziger Vorposten*	11.11.1938
Ihringen (Baden)	*Temps*	12.11.1938
Innsbruck	*Salzburger Volksblatt*	12.11.1938

Klagenfurt	*Salzburger Volksblatt*	12.11.1938
Königsberg [now Rus. Kaliningrad	*Danziger Vorposten*	11.11.1938
Konstanz	*Birmingham Post*	11.11.1938
Krefeld	*Luxemburger Wort*	11.11.1938
Landsberg / Warthe [now Pol. Gorzow Wielkopolski]	*Morgenpost*	11.11.1938
Langfuhr-Danzig [now Pol. Wrzeszcz]	*Temps*	14.11.1938
Leipzig	*Morgenpost*	11.11.1938
Liebenau (Graz)	*Danziger Vorposten*	11.11.1938
Linz	*Birmingham Post*	11.11.1938
Lörrach	*Private*	
Lübeck	*National Zeitung*	11.11.1938
Magdeburg	*Danziger Vorposten*	11.11.1938
Mainz	*Bund*	12.11.1938
Mannheim – several –	*Hakenkreuzbanner*	11.11.1938
Marienwerder [now Pol. Kwidzyn]	*Danziger Vorposten*	11.11.1938
München	*Morgenpost*	11.11.1938
Neustadt (Schwarzwald)	*Bund*	12.11.1938
Nuremberg	*Fränkische Tageszeitung*	11.11.1938
Offenburg (Baden)	*Birmingham Post*	11.11.1938
Osnabrück	*Privat*	
Potsdam	*Temps*	11.11.1938
Randegg	*Neue Zürcher Zeitung*	12.11.1938
Reichenberg [now Cz. Rep. Liberec]	*Morgenpost*	11.11.1938
Salzburg	*Bund*	12.11.1938
Schmallenberg	*Westfälische Landeszeitung*	11.11.1938
Spandau	*Nieuwe Rotterd. Cour.*	11.11.1938
Stettin [now Pol. Szczecin]	*Morgenpost*	11.11.1938
Strausberg (Ob.-Barnim)	*Morgenpost*	11.11.1938
Stuttgart	*Morgenpost*	11.11.1938
Vienna, Schiffamtsgasse	*Völkischer Beobachter Wien*	11.11.1938
Neue Welt Gasse	*Völkischer Beobachter Wien*	
Tempelgasse	*Völkischer Beobachter Wien*	
Stumpergasse	*Völkischer Beobachter Wien*	
Unt. Viaductgasse	*Völkischer Beobachter Wien*	

▶

Schmalzhofgasse	*Völkischer Beobachter Wien*	
Hubergasse	*Völkischer Beobachter Wien*	
Siebenbrunnengasse	*Völkischer Beobachter Wien*	
Große Schiffgasse	*Völkischer Beobachter Wien*	
Kluckygasse	*Völkischer Beobachter Wien*	
Neudeggerstrasse	*Völkischer Beobachter Wien*	
Malzgasse	*Völkischer Beobachter Wien*	
Schopenhauergasse	*Völkischer Beobachter Wien*	
Zirkusgasse	*Völkischer Beobachter Wien*	
Steingasse	*Völkischer Beobachter Wien*	
Müllnergasse	*Völkischer Beobachter Wien*	
Pazmanitengasse	*Völkischer Beobachter Wien*	
Humboldtplatz	*Völkischer Beobachter Wien*	
Turnergasse	*Völkischer Beobachter Wien*	
Franz Hochedlingergasse	*Neue Freie Presse*	11.11.1938
71 Bethäuser	*Daily Telegraph, Reuter*	11.11.1938
Wangen	*Neue Zürcher Zeitung*	12.11.1938
Wattenscheid	*Private*	
Wriezen (Provinz Brandenburg)	*Morgenpost*	11.11.1938
Zoppot bei Danzig [now Pol. Sopot nr Gdansk]	*Temps*	14.11.1938

B. 42 22nd November 1938

In Potsdam, as in other towns, the synagogue on Wilhemsplatz has been badly damaged. Because the synagogue building, which stands on one of the most outstanding squares in Potsdam, is immediately surrounded on one side by the main post office and on the other by a residential house, they did not burn the synagogue down as has been done in other towns. Consequently the interior of the synagogue was heavily damaged using machinery. At the house adjacent to the synagogue, where the cantor lives with his family, stones were flung through the windows, so that those living in the house barely managed to reach safety.

The official opening of the now ruined synagogue was celebrated in 1903. It stands on the same spot where Frederick the

Great in his day had had a synagogue built for the Jewish people of Potsdam. In the new synagogue there was also a Prussian eagle with sword and sceptre as a symbol for that building.

Even the funeral chapel at the Jewish cemetery at Pfingstberg was destroyed and the cemetery itself closed. The graves themselves do not appear to have been damaged.

Originally all the male members of the Jewish *Gemeinde* [community] of Potsdam were arrested. Even the eldest, amongst them men of over 70 years of age, although they were later released. Still under arrest are, amongst others, Rabbi Dr. Hermann Schreiber, likewise his son Dr. Paul Schreiber who until his arrest was a teacher at a Jewish school in Berlin, in addition the first *Vorsitzende* [chairman] of the Jewish *Gemeinde*, *Rechtsanwalt* [lawyer] Dr. Marcuse. Also arrested was Dr. Fritz Hirschberg, the well-known Berlin physician and successor to Professor Dr. Boas, who has been living with his mother in Potsdam after giving up his practice.

Most of those arrested, amongst them Rabbi Dr. Schreiber, are in the concentration camp in Sachsenhausen.

A children's home in Caputh near Potsdam was also violently closed. It appears that the children accommodated in this home barely managed to save their lives as, according to a reliable report, a 15-year-old boy saved the life of the one-year-old child of a teacher.

B. 43 Preliminary remarks

The letter which is reprinted here appeared in "*Het Volk*" [The People], a Dutch daily newspaper with a wide circulation, on the evening of 17th November and may of course be used as you wish. The meeting referred to in the letter was attended by approximately 25,000 people.

Amsterdam, 15th November 1938

To the organisers of the mass meeting taking place on 15th November

Dear Sirs,

In the name of 26 people who have been forced to join the

German colony and definitely in keeping with the opinions of a much greater number of Germans in Holland, I ask you to be so kind as to read this letter to the meeting. The egregious events in Germany, which brought indelible shame to our fatherland, force us to unburden our conscience in this way in order to utter our deepest revulsion about what has happened. Unfortunately we are forced to give our views in this way. Admittedly today we are living here in a foreign country amongst you, who are able to express your opinion freely, but of course we have been spared from this very terror that reigns in Germany. If we were to appear openly under our own names we would certainly be labelled as traitors to our country and then our lives would be in danger here too. Furthermore, almost all of us still have relatives in Germany against whom the heroes of the pogrom would take revenge.

I can assure our indignant Dutch fellow citizens that millions in Germany also feel revulsion and shame at these barbarities.

To avoid any misunderstanding I further inform you that I and my friends are neither Jews nor emigrants. We have all been living in Holland for over 10 years.

B. 44 23rd November 1938

Today we received the news that a hospital nurse based here received news that her brother in Vienna has died in a concentration camp. The nurse received the news of the death directly.

Banker Einhorn, Amsterdam

B. 45 23rd November 1938

Dr. Marcus, the head of the *Palästina-Treuhandgesellschaft* [abbr. *Paltreu;* Palestine Trust Company] in Berlin, who had been arrested, was later released following a request by the *Reichswirtschaftsministerium* [Reich Ministry of Economic Affairs]. The *Paltreu* continues to operate as before. Consequently we are able to effect payments in *Haavaramark* [Haavara marks: payments under the Haavara Agreement] to Germany, also as before.

Dr. Max Jacusiel

B. 46 23rd November 1938

We have discovered from a completely reliable source that Herr Dr. Hirschberg, rabbi in Oppeln [now Pol. Opole], has been arrested.

Frau Dr. Hirschberg, Oppeln

B. 47 23rd November 1938

We are receiving a report that the following people have been arrested in Breslau [now Pol. Wrocław] and taken to the concentration camp.

Erich Julisburger [Juliusburger] and his brother-in-law from Breslau (businessmen).

Erich Boss and Karl Gronner from Breslau (businessmen).

Joseph Spanier, nurse from the Jewish Hospital in Breslau, who has worked there for two to three years, has been arrested.

Two Fuchs brothers were arrested in Breslau and are in concentration camp.

The third brother, Siegfried Fuchs, aged 16, was taken from the *Hachsharah* [agricultural training for Jews preparing to emigrate to Palestine] at Zobten [now Pol. Sobótka] (near Breslau) and arrested.

1–3   Letter from Herr Abraham from Berlin

4–5   Letter to Fräulein Fuchs from her mother in Breslau

B. 48 Amsterdam, 24th November 1938

Report from Frankfurt am Main

Independent doctors have been arrested, whereas in both hospitals the doctors were left. Only Dr. Meyer, ear specialist at the Gagernstraße hospital, was arrested. The director of the Gagernstraße hospital, Dr. Rosenthal, committed suicide by taking poison because he feared arrest.

The following are still active at the Rothschild Hospital: Dr. Schnerb, Dr. Löwenthal, Dr. Rosenbaum and Dr. Merzbach.

The synagogues were burned down at at Friedberger Anlage, Börneplatz, Börnestraße, Liebigstraße. As the fire at the Friedberger Anlage synagogue initially only caused limited damage, the fire was rekindled four times in total using drums of petrol and suchlike during the days that followed, which produced another spectacle for the crowds.

After the interior furnishings of the synagogue had been burned, the *Gemeinde* [community] was ordered by the police to demolish the buildings at its own expense because of the danger of collapse. This began immediately with the demolition of Friedberger Anlage on 17th November.

The police later cast suspicion on the Jews themselves for setting fire to the synagogue and issued a formal charge.

The *Tresor* [treasury] with the sacred silver objects in the synagogue at Friedberger Anlage was broken into with a welding torch the day after the first fire and the contents were stolen.

On Thursday 10th November many elderly men and women were also arrested in Frankfurt and taken to the large *Festhalle* [exhibition and trade fair hall]. They were left there until Friday afternoon without facilities to sleep and mostly nowhere to sit. Then the men over 60 years and the women were released.

Most of those arrested in Frankfurt are in the Buchenwald camp, from where they sent a pre-printed card to their relatives; the rest are in Dachau camp. The rabbi from the *Israelitische Religionsgemeinde* [Jewish religious community], Rabbi Horovitz, who has meanwhile been released through the intervention of the Czech consul, spent the entire 8 days in a police prison in Frankfurt am Main.

Rabbi Jos. Horowitz (previously Frankfurt), Scheveningen
Haagsche Str. 25 with Weissberger, and daughter (same address)

B. 49 Amsterdam, 24th November 1938

The following is known about the general tactics used in arrests taking place Germany:

The so-called *Arbeitseinsatzgesetz* [work deployment law] is formally applied as legal background for transfer to the concentration camps, under which male German nationals between the ages of 18 and 60 can be ordered to perform certain types of work according to the orders of the authorities.

Thus in all cases where a foreign consul has intervened on

behalf of a foreign national, the person in question, to whom the aforesaid law does not apply, has been successfully released. It is known that Czech as well as Polish nationals have been granted the protection of their consulate in this way. In individual cases where foreigners have been arrested, it was described as *Ausweisungshaft* [custody pending deportation], which can also be challenged by the consul, however, if adequate grounds to do this are lacking from the German authorities.

Cases are known where SS men have helped individuals who are sick to declare themselves to be aged 60 and to be released. Further, one case is known where a senior Party official has until now kept a Jew hidden in his private home, during which time his wife and children have been able to emigrate.

It is reported consistently from Nuremberg, Frankfurt am Main and Hamburg that from Thursday the 10th November it was made impossible for Jews to depart by railway, as a checkpoint was set up at the station and only Jews of foreign nationality were able to leave, whilst German nationals were arrested. In Hamburg such arrests were also carried out at travel agencies. In Hamburg on Monday the 14th November the obstacle to departure was removed again.

A report from Wednesday the 16th November from Frankfurt am Main states that strict street controls have been put into place there and people without Party insignia have to identify themselves. As a result a Christian Dutchman was stopped eight times during a single day.

see report B. 48

B. 50 For information only, not for circulation

Amsterdam, 24th November 1938

On Saturday the 12th November the Frankfurt Rabbi Horovitz from the *Israelitische Religionsgesellschaft* [Jewish religious community] was arrested at the hospital where he had taken himself the previous day on account of a stomach ailment, and was held for eight days in police custody in Frankfurt.

On the first day he was questioned repeatedly and received

repeated death threats as he was interrogated about the location of the silverware, etc., about which he could give no information as synagogue administration is not part of his duties. In connection with this he was taken to the synagogue building in person on the night of the 12th to 13th November in order to give information there. (The false report that a rabbi was pushed into the burning synagogue stems from this incident, as fire was smouldering in the building at the time).

Suspicion was also cast on him for having set fire to the synagogue, yet he could credibly maintain that because of illness he had not visited the synagogue on the day in question.

On entering prison his beard was shaved off and thereby seriously injured him with a razor, so the wound was stitched by the prison doctor. The injury then healed somewhat during his custody. It was subsequently stated in writing to him by the Czechoslovakian consul that he would be shaved during the internment and therefore his appearance was no longer consistent with his passport photograph.

Report received from Rabbi Horovitz (see report 48) by a man released from Buchenwald.

B. 51 Amsterdam, 24th November 1938

About Karlsruhe it is known that that the people who were arrested there, including Rabbi Michalski and the *Gemeindevorsteher* [chairman of the community], are in Dachau.

In Karlsruhe 19 *Thorarollen* [Torah scrolls] were successfully rescued from the synagogue.

Benjamin Wolff, Scheveningen, Gevers Deynootweg 50

B. 52 Amsterdam, 24th November 1938

The report by a man released from Buchenwald states that the people there have had to endure the most severe bullying. There were 500 men cooped up overnight in one dormitory. For two whole days they were given almost nothing to eat. Then they were secretly fed a laxative with the potatoes with appalling consequences.

B. 53 28th November 1938

It is not true that the *Kommerzienrat* [commercial councillor] Lessing from Bamberg has died. He lies seriously ill in hospital as a result of his mistreatment.

Rechtsanwalt [lawyer] Rudolf Haas, Noordzeebank, Rotterdam

B. 54 Synagogues

Cologne, Glockengasse completely destroyed.

Roonstraße seriously damaged.

Mortuary almost destroyed.

Potsdam, the mortuary as well as the synagogue has been burnt down.

B. 55 ATTENTION

Herr A., a Dutch businessman who owns a company in Berlin and who arrived here directly from B. on Thursday the 10th November, reported the following:

Members of the Gestapo forced their way into the home of factory owner Gustav Michaelis, proprietor of the carpet factory Michaelis & Berend in Nowawes, and asked him whether he owned any weapons. Because he remarked that many years ago he had given a pistol to his chauffeur, the chauffeur was brought in who confirmed what his boss had said.

When the Gestapo men nevertheless prepared to take Herr M. away, his wife explained that the chauffeur's statement had proved that her husband had told the truth too and there was no basis to arrest him. At which M. himself said to his wife, "You must know the reason I am being arrested is only because I am a Jew."

On the basis of his explanation he was led away amidst insults. Dr. Rawack, his son-in-law, was also arrested.

Herr A. also reports that in Potsdam not only the rabbi Dr. Schreiber but also all the male Jews registered with the *Gemeinde* [community] have been arrested.

On the operation itself Herr A. reports that he had already

ascertained early on Thursday when he entered Berlin that from Steglitz onwards all the window panes of Jewish-owned businesses had been smashed. This *Zertrümmerungsaktion* [destruction operation] is said already to have taken place during the night of Wednesday to Thursday at about half past two. However whilst one had been content with "merely" smashing window panes in the morning, in the afternoon a new operation began in which the businesses were wrecked and everything was looted.

SA men in plain clothes were involved in this operation who wore civilian jackets but SA trousers and used iron bars and crowbars to carry out their attacks on the businesses with the cry *"Juda verrecke!"* [Perish Juda]. They were usually accompanied by a representative with a list.

The press has already named a large number of the businesses that were destroyed.

In general the public expressed its horror at these events, and comments could be heard such as, "That's now our culture today", or "That's how our money is wasted."

The Christian employees of Herr A.'s firm went to the *Arbeitsfront* [Labour Front; the Nazi trade union] to point out that the business had already been sold to an Aryan. They were then told that they should do everything necessary to arrange for the Jewish employees to leave the business immediately. There was a desire on the part of the *Arbeitsfront* to do everything to "cross this business off the list", thus evidence of the fact that the *Zerstörungsaktion* [destruction operation] had been carried out according to precisely predetermined lists.

The fact that the Mikosch and Weiss-Czardas restaurants were attacked earlier, and also the well-known children's ready-to-wear clothing business of Arnold Müller, one owner of which, Metzger, is a Swiss national, shows that the property of foreign Jews was not spared.

Nothing happened to the well-known laundry company F. V. Grünfeld, although at first the crowd was said to have attempted to attack this business too. However as is well known the firm was recently *arisiert* [Aryanised].

Even cars owned by Jews were stopped and the windows smashed. The cars of Jews in the Berlin area are recognisable as they carry numbers starting with 350,000.

B. 56 11th November 1938

A lady from Düren in the Rhineland who has just come from there reported that during the night of Wednesday to Thursday all the Jewish businesses were destroyed in her home town. The synagogue was set on fire during the night. The fire spread so quickly that the *Küster* [synagogue sexton] and his family, who live right next to the synagogue, barely managed to escape with their lives.

Herr B. reports that the home of his mother, a lady of almost 70 years of age, in Glogau [now Pol. Głogów], was forcibly entered and all the furniture there was smashed too.

In Brunswick the former *Handelsgerichtsrat* [commercial court lawyer] Gustav Forstenzer, who until recently was the senior partner in the Frank department store, was arrested. In addition his two sons who are only 17 were also arrested.

B. 57 15th November 1938

A Dutchman who lived in Osnabrück for many years and fled during the recent disturbances reported to us:

At the end in O. there were still c. 150 Jewish inhabitants. All men were arrested apart from three under 60 and six over 60 years of age. All Jewish shops were destroyed. The property was confiscated. The synagogue was burned down. All the women are free.

B. 58 Amsterdam, 15th November 1938

Dear Sir,

Thank you for your endeavours; let us hope that today or tomorrow the gates will be opened here for thousands of miserable people, children, women and endangered men. Every hour matters greatly, the danger is indescribable.

There are several thousand men hidden in Germany and Austria, who are running the risk of being caught and put to death in camps every moment; so many are hidden in woodland etc. without food, so many are already caught and threatened with being struck down etc. It is no time for long meetings; when a ship is threatened with going under, a rescue proceeds without meetings, without *Schmussies* [nonsense]. When someone is drowning, many jump into the water to go to the rescue. When a house is burning, everyone rescues without empty talk. A much larger danger threatens the Jews in Germany and Austria which one cannot imagine if one has not seen it.

Now, Holland is really a model state, but initially several thousand should be allowed in who have relatives here who want to care for them, support them, have a large home and are in a position to feed them. Also when one visits the Jewish and possibly non-Jewish population, all should be obliged to take in or care for one person from the camps. A large crowd of people must be organised, must visit them personally at home with forms signed by several thousand people of affluent or average means to look after 1–2 persons, with which we will contact the Minister so that a certificate will be issued in the name of these and every other person whose stay is assured by the general public and who will be given temporary accommodation here for a few weeks. Each family can find room for 1–2 people, all human beings are obliged in this catastrophe; let us try to put ourselves in the position of those who find themselves there.

Tomorrow immediately mobilise a few hundred men and women who are respected; they will sign up for the obligation of receiving one or two people; the same thing must also be done in the other provinces. You will see that more than 50,000 people can easily be saved this week alone. Save thousands of Jews from starvation and murder as quickly as possible. Also organise a commission to get people out of German prisons, otherwise they are condemned to the worst without anything. Time is very costly in this danger, anything can happen any minute, organise everything necessary, a special train, with escort from the border, perhaps if possible, fetch it from Germany.

Jewish banks should tax themselves 10%, as should other prosperous people throughout the world; then we will not need to give money and even our lives to Hitler.

The misery is appalling!!!

Victims will die until all the powers make a decision. It is certainly possible to begin with a few thousand initially; there are even *Gem[einde]* [community] meeting places or empty homes here; then along the Stadionkade [in Amsterdam-Zuid] there are spaces for barracks which can be built in two days, while they can reside in schools, synagogues, clubhouses, private houses. Money is not lacking and they will not go hungry here. The world will provide, Holland need not be afraid, just open the doors before the fire. What Holland was first to achieve, that Holland was the first to help, will go down in history forever. We thank the Prime Minister and those who will help, their goodness will be rewarded.

With fraternal greetings

Friend of Humanity

B. 59 17th November 1938

Dr. Paul von Schwabach has now become another victim of the terrible rioting against the Jews who, as has been reliably reported, has taken his own life. Dr. von Schwabach was one of the leading personalities of the German banking world. Until the *Arisierung* [Aryanisation] of his firm he was joint proprietor of the banking house S. Bleichroeder, well known throughout Germany and founded as long ago as 1803 in Berlin by Samuel Bleichroeder. His uncle Gerson von Bleichroeder, the son of the founder, was not only Bismarck's banker but also financial advisor to the governments of Prussia and of the Reich. After the Franco-Prussian War Gerson von Bleichroeder was involved in leading the negotiations on the French war reparations in common with Graf Henckel von Donnersmark.

Regarding the development of the Bleichroeder banking house and its importance in the international loan business, after Gerson von Bleichroeder, his cousin and partner Julius Leopold Schwabach held the major share. Paul von Schwabach continued the great tradition of this house. He also held a leading position in Berlin society until the advent of the Hitler regime. His son-in-law is the former German ambassador in Lisbon and Brussels, Dr. Horstmann. His only son, Julius von Schwabach, also died some months ago from as yet unexplained causes. Paul von Schwabach was in the 72nd year of his life.

B. 60 Amsterdam, 24th November 1938

In Vienna the *"Volkswut"* [people's rage] broke out on 10th November. This rage was directed, as is everything nowadays of course, and in Vienna it was said that this *Volkswut* had forgotten to break out e.g. in Danzig [now Pol. Gdańsk], and so it first happened three days later under the same conditions as in the Reich. – Suddenly the synagogues began to blaze, suddenly all the shops were smashed up, people arrested, and the shops of Jewish proprietors closed.

I was able to observe the following myself: the SS, SA and police seem to have received instructions to arrest all Jewish men aged between 18 and 60 early on Thursday mornng.

The pretext for house seaches was a general search for weapons, in Vienna merely three revolvers were found, in distinction to the Reich. In contrast everything was confiscated, such as gold, silver, cash, valuable objects, in many cases even linen, clothes and otherwise anything that pleased the hordes. The procedure was nevertheless inconsistent.

When the men were arrested, the mob showed themselves as relatively decent in some houses, in other houses on the contrary they beat up the arrestees.

In Vienna it is said that the hospitals are overflowing. Many Jews released from *Schutzhaft* [protective custody] appear with bandaged faces and heads.

Another difference in the procedure is that some Jews are handed receipts for their confiscated objects but some were refused these because it did not suit the relevant SA men. Whether such a receipt actually means anything is anyone's guess.

In Hietzing (Vienna XIII.) for sure school youths between twelve and 14 years of age were allowed to leave the school at

10 o'clock in the morning with instructions to wreck Jewish homes and shops. Much vigorous use was made of that because many homes were smashed to pieces.

As long as those arrested were in the hands of the SA or the SS, things went very badly for them. Those who have been released from arrest naturally did not dare to recount anything about it. It certainly went better for those in the hands of the police, indeed the older policemen behaved extremely well. A struggle broke out everywhere, particularly in the Ostmark [Austria], but it appears that the Party units had the upper hand. In many cases those arrested were transported between different police prisons, and it was hardly possible to establish where they found themselves. Distributing information about it was abolutely born out of the feeling of sadism because wives were already given the information in the morning that their arrested husbands had been brought to Dachau, and it was possible these men would appear at home again in the afternoon.

Up to the present day the location of many of those imprisoned is not yet known. As already mentioned the hospitals are said to be overfull, especially the *Rothschild-Spital*, but of course there was no precise information to obtain about this.

For those arrested it was an advantage when preparations for *Ausreise* [departure] had already been made. In many cases these people were actually released again. But this is in no way routine, in many cases this had not helped at all, especially when the people could not be found.

It is noteworthy that in the view of the *Gildemeester-Aktion* [Nazi-run operation to evacuate Jews from Vienna] none of those arrested came to Dachau and also not to Buchenwald because these concentration camps were overfull, all the more so because *Ostmärker*s [Austrians] were sent to other camps in the Ostmark. But this is not certain, as I first learned of it on the day that I went away. In many cases people had to sign a declaration of a fixed date for their departure. But in any case everybody had to sign a declaration not to speak about the things they experienced, and actually it was possible to learn something from very few of those released again.

In Vienna's *Zentralfriedhof* [Central Cemetery] the *Neue Halle* [new hall], about which much had been said because it was a magnificent building in its day, has been totally destroyed. One cannot go through it any more because one fears being struck by masonry. Similarly the *Alte Halle* [old hall] has been destroyed, the roof is propped up with planks. All the synagogues in Vienna have been burned out. In many cases, e.g. at my father's, an auto-da-fé [bonfire] was organised in front of the home, in which prayer books and other objects were set alight.

The following also happened: one of my uncles was a guest at a doctor friend's. First all objects belonging to the doctor were confiscated, jewellery etc., then the doctor was arrested. Then to my uncle's home, took everything away there too, including the wedding rings, and everthing that could be found, arrested him, and a few days later it was not known where my uncle was, a man aged 50. He then returned since he already possessed a visa for Shanghai.

Residential provision is especially bad in Vienna. Business people had the keys to their businesses taken away by the Party. In many cases the homes of Jews had to be vacated within a few hours, the value of the home was assessed and bought from the occupants there and then. In one case a well-decorated three-room flat was valued at RM. 280.- and "purchased". Most recently the police have intervened against that. They instructed the care-taker in such cases to notify the police of such proceedings at once.

At the Emmerich border to the Netherlands (German side) they took a typewriter from me, a gold signet ring, a gold chain and a gold watch. This was my own fault, however, since I had neglected to register these objects in Vienna at the *Devisenstelle* [foreign currency office] and obtain an *Ausfuhrsteuer-Genehmigung* [export tax permit]. I was given a receipt for the retained objects in Emmerich and I was entitled to nominate a *Verfügungs-berechtiger* [person with power of disposal] in Vienna. Success is definitely doubtful.

Maximilian Loewy, brother-in-law of Oskar Hirschfeld, Vienna
Vienna Address: Biberstr. 4, Vienna I.
Now New York, Broadway 73 Str., Hotel Ansonja

B. 61 During a walk towards *Bahnhof* [station] Zoo-Kurfürstendamm on the morning of 10th November I convinced myself that in no Jewish shop was there even one window pane or glass display case still intact.

One saw crowds of young lads who had arrived later destroying furnishings and stock with hammers and other tools, e.g. in department stores, also in a cake shop, where the window panes had already been smashed. As a result of this destruction I saw e.g. a life-sized dummy fall onto the street from a department store. The crowd thronged the streets and silently watched these excesses with curiosity, without the often mentioned "*Volkswut*" [people's rage].

My brother and nephew were arrested and transported to the Sachsenhausen-Oranienburg concentration camp where it is claimed that they have not suffered until now.

Dr. Curt Meyer, Huize Clio, Cliostr. 6, Amsterdam

B. 62 The people were arrested at 5 o'clock in the morning on 10th November, some from their beds, some on the streets outside the consulates where they had already begun to line up that early. Arrests continued during the day through the efforts of whole Party units and security guards, in hotels, boarding houses, cafés, on the streets, in which it was always asked, "*Jude oder Nicht-jude?*" [Jew or non-Jew?] The number of arrests on this day amounted to c. 30,000. Committals followed until late in the night. The majority were first taken to police premises, where some were most severely mistreated and tortured, e.g. an eyewitness reported that a young chap was put in a cold shower in his clothes and then sent away in his wet clothes (Prater police station). Those arrested had to kneel down and those admitted later had to go to their places over the heads of those on their knees. After the last arrivals came the news that synagogues were being burst into and looted. This occurred at all *Tempel* [synagogues] in Vienna with the exception of the Seitenstet-tentempel in the *Kultusgemeinde* [Jewish community] although it has been completely emptied. Some people were taken from police stations to police headquarters or to the schools where e.g. at a small school in the VII *Bezirk* [district] 7,000 people had to spend the time standing all day long. It is noteworthy that as far as one could see mistreatment and sadistic torments were not carried out from bitterness or for revenge but rather were regarded as popular entertainment.

The classification was into three categories as follows:

1) "*Tauglich*" [fit], which the people immediately interpreted as "probably Dachau".

2) "*Zurück*" [return], which meant: back to prison. (Those were mostly people with emigration preparations or serious physical infirmities.)

3) "*Entlassung*" [release], were people over 60 years of age, partly also the very young, partly also women and foreign citizens who had been arrested individually.

The entire operation was mostly directed at Jewish citizens of the German Reich. For days nothing was heard about the fate of those arrested. Nothing precise is known even now of the destination and the whereabouts of those classed as "*Tauglich*" and transported away immediately; in response to inquiries one may obtain the answer "Dachau" from the authorities. Most of those catagorised as "*Zurück*" have actually been released in recent days.

(Not entirely authentic): some of those severely mistreated are said to have been held back so that the mistreatment would not be so clearly evident.

In some *Haftstellen* [detention centres] people committed suicide, e.g. three cases by jumping out of the window at a requisitioned school in Karajangasse: two cases were fatal, one case seriously injured.

On 10th November all Jewish shops were closed at once and for the most part emptied, food shops with the excuse that it concerned easily perishable goods, yet the other shops were looted too. The shops are still sealed up. House searches occured for c. 70% of the entire Jewish population, during which, especially in the *Bezirke* where many Jews live, all moveable items were taken away, some wrecked, people's jewellery, even wedding rings, cash amounts down to the last penny were removed, though not for the Party, but for private pockets.

Most of the homes were sealed up, the people were thrown out without being able to take anything with them, and later on too people did not succeeed in gaining possession of their homes or their property if it was still available. Without any guidelines those people were shoved arbitrarily into the homes of other Jews.

In two cases the relatives of two people under arrest who were calling on the *Kultusgemeinde* were affected by strokes from the agitation they felt.

At the moment the emergency has thus increased so dreadfully because the number of those without any form of subsistence has reached perhaps 60–70% of the entire Jewish population, and feeding them could no longer function in the first days on account of the wrecking of premises and materials. The depth of the emergency can be perceived in that they could not suppress complaints out loud, despite the presence of Party units in the *Kultusgemeinde* and in spite of people's fear.

Alfred Schechter, Vienna

B. 62 a (Related to B. 62, not for publication)

The *Sicherheitswache* [Austrian security police] behaved in an exemplary manner insofar as they could because they not only actively intervened but also comforted people and where possible also allowed them benefits in terms of food. Everything points to it not being an outbreak of popular displeasure but rather a well-organised operation by units of the Party. In the days following the operation, specially amongst the more insightful offices, there was an attempt to position the matter as a bit more harmless, and end it. But apparently the resistance was too great in Vienna, specially by the SA, so whilst arrests were indeed terminated, nothing else changed, which can certainly be ascribed to the reaction of the world's press; but with no cessation of statements from abroad the desire for moderation also appeared to have disappeared. That a desire for moderation existed can be clearly recognised from the remarks by Dr. Goebbels about "The cultural life of Jews in Germany" (*Völkischer Beobachter* [National Observer; Nazi newspaper]). It has never been the case that such an article has appeared on a peaceful theme concerning the Jews.

Question

What is more important for the Jews who still find themselves in the Reich: the publication of the truth in an irrefutable manner (what is reported falsely diminishes the truth, which is already sad enough), or a cessation by the news services, so as not to make the Jews' fate worse? In the opinion of the reporter, ultimately every response abroad may lead to new threats by Germany and worsening of the Jews' destiny without anything happening abroad that would benefit them. Unless the world is prepared to declare it will take in the German Jews, which is not yet certain, it is unclear whether one is inflicting further torment upon them before then.

Experiences concerning emigration

In the train the reporter travelled in were a number of people who wanted to go to Belgium illegally and already knew that the Belgian government would grant them facilities. This largely concerns people who do no credit to Jewry abroad because these are the sharpest ones who read too much into things and have their own news service. Would it not be possible to organise matters so that – when a country already declares it will allow 1,000 people over the border – one makes a choice and bring out those who constitute worthwhile material, who do credit to Jewry and create room for further emigration. Here one should note that such honest and decent people would not be that much of a burden on foreign Jewish welfare and thus not be that great a claim on the means.

Emigration to South America takes place for the most part in a type of backstairs politicking at the consulates, partly commercial, instead of official distribution of visas to the competent offices. There too one needs to have much more consideration for the emigration opportunities of those still remaining because it is not the best elements who are considered but rather those who happen to be in possession of suitable funds.

B. 63 16 November 1938

Dear Sir,

It was reported in the *Algemeen Handelsblad* [General Trade Paper; Dutch newspaper] of 13 November amongst other things that the Jewish orphanage at near Oberhausen had closed and that the orphans are wandering about aimlessly in the country. The Director of that orphanage is the father of the Director of our Jewish orphanage in Antwerp, Dr. Rothschild.

Two days before the murder in Paris, the Director of Dinslaken travelled to Palestine. According to communications from our Director here, it is indeed correct that the orphanage in Dinslaken closed. The children are not, however, walking about in Germany but were brought to the *Wirtschaft Rau* [Rau Inn] in Dinslaken, led by the sister of Dr. Rothschild, Mirjam Rothschild.

The children who had family members were returned to them, though the actual orphans are in the above-named inn.

I explain this to you as requested by the Director of our orphanage, so that your efforts to bring children from Germany to the Netherlands are informed and possibly you can do something for these children.

B. 64 16 November 1938

The person involved on the night of Wednesday 9 November was taken prisoner on Thursday 10 November and locked up with others in the cell at the police station in the place where he lived. On Saturday the prisoners were brought to another, larger, place where they were put in a prison. There were sixteen of them in a comparatively small cell.

Amongst other things they had to drill continuously: lie down, stand, lie down, stand, lie down, stand, etc. Meanwhile this one was beaten, then that one. In the meantime they had to open their mouths wide and then their mouths were spat in by their "guardians". They were commanded to go to the corner and on order had to do a small errand. Then they had to come in again. Then they had to "trousers down" and were forced to do their call of nature whether it was necessary or not, they had to! They were forced, amongst other things, the sixteen of them, to go and lie flat on the ground in two rows of 8 next to each other in such a way that the feet of one were opposite those of the other. Suddenly a rough guard came who cursed the *Judenlümmels* [Jewish slobs] here, and walked over them in his boots. The people then received beatings again.

Apparently the cell was watched from outside in case these people said anything. One of the unfortunate prisoners did seem to have said something out loud whilst he lay on the ground like "We've got it bad". Immediately one of the guards came inside (rough chap with large moustache) and in a rough voice ordered the man who had said something to stand up. The man lying next to him (who was the informant now released), who apparently did not understand that this command was meant for his neighbour, or through terror no longer knew if he were also included, also stood up. The man who had said something was beaten until he said what he had said; then he had exactly the same treatment again so that he fell in the corner. Then the guard focused on our informant with the words: "*Du Judenlümmel. Du lachst noch!*" [You Jewish slob. You're still laughing.] One can understand how the *Judenlümmel* who had seen exactly how his neighbour had had to suffer could still laugh least of all. An answer was naturally not expected but he also received many blows, which he will remember for the rest of his life.

Our informant, since released, has to report to the police station every day in the place where he lives. He lives amidst fear and dread that he will be arrested once more.

The fellow prisoners who have not yet been released have now been taken to an unknown destination, possibly to the concentration camp Oranienburg.

I can add here that I have been told, by parties who are trustworthy as far as I know, that in A. two people who would have lived exactly opposite each other were shot dead in bed. This also corroborates the continuing mortal danger that people face.

B. 65 22nd November 1938

Almost all homes were mercilessly wrecked in Nuremberg. Many Jews are said to have jumped from their homes many storeys high onto the street in order to find death that way. A great deal of mistreatment has taken place there, arrests not to such a great extent, in age not even up to 60 years. In one night in Nuremberg 170 houses were sold at fixed prices, documented in the presence of a notary. Thus e.g. a value of RM. 85,000.- was fixed at RM. 5,000.-. A case is known to me of an elderly gentleman to whom it was suggested that he sell his houses and he refused. He was then basically taken to a cellar and mistreated and beaten until he willingly consented to everything. When he emerged, it was said to him "Nothing has actually happened to you?" to which of course he replied, "No." – All synagogues were burned down.

In Fürth all Jews were taken from their homes between half past 2 and 3 at night, even very young children, sick people, pregnant women etc. and herded together on the large square. They had to stand there until 5 o'clock in the morning. Then they were led to the *Berolzheimerianum* [Jewish hospital] and brought to a large hall. They could sit down here. The women were sent home, as were the children. Then the men were called out singly and each individual dreadfully mistreated in front of the others. The people were then taken to Dachau.

In various places in the Baden region people were crammed into cattle trucks. They were taken to Dachau in two days without food, jammed against each other like cattle, which would certainly be better treated. They were not allowed to leave the trucks for a moment.

In Regensburg very many homes were wrecked and the synagogue burnt down. In addition younger sons (in one case aged 16) were arrested with their fathers and taken away.

In Lichtenfels (Oberfranken, Bavaria) the synagogue was burnt down. A Jewish woman wanted to save the ritual objects. Several children wanted to hinder her from doing so. When the woman fended them off, the children killed her and played football with the prayer books.

In Ingolstadt all the Jewish families were informed that they had to leave Ingolstadt within an hour after their homes were wrecked and the men were led away. They took themselves to Munich on foot.

Arthur Berg, Munich
Herr Wilhelm Neuburger, Courbetstr. 21, Amsterdam

B. 66 22nd November 1938

In Munich all the open shops have been wrecked and looted, particularly any existing jeweller's shops. The department store Uhlfelder was stormed, everything was smashed and set on fire. The fire was doused because of the risk that some 35 Aryan families in the adjacent houses might been been killed. In the large antiquities shop Bernheimer the most valuable antiquities were destroyed, carpets cut up, porcelain smashed etc. Both of the still existing synagogues were burned.

In all shops and restaurants and pubs large signs were erected, "*Juden zutritt verboten*" [Entry forbidden to Jews]. Nevertheless on Friday 18th November such signs were generally taken away again.

Radio sets were taken away from many homes, from where of course other things were also stolen. Telephone wires were cut through. After the men were arrested and taken to Dachau, two SS men appeared in nearly all the homes to demand that the women remaining behind departed from the city within 24 hours. But this demand was not complied with to the smallest degree. Only the occasional home was wrecked. The Villa Bach was set on fire. All the contents were robbed or wrecked. The people possess no more items of clothing. All accounts were confiscated from Jews, as were cars. At the end of the first week women were then allowed to be paid out RM. 100.- per week. Jews were arrested wherever they were encountered, on the street, in the tram, at railway stations. Well-meaning Christians advised them to report to the Gestapo for arrest because otherwise danger existed for the other members of the family.

The mood amongst the Christian population of Munich is thoroughly against the operation. I was shown the liveliest sympathy and compassion from all sides. It was generally assumed that the homes were going to be stormed on Friday evening (11th November). Aryans unknown to me from the vicinty invited my family to stay the night with them. The grocery shops asked if one needed anything, despite the prohibition on selling to Jews, bakers delivered bread despite the ban, etc. All Christians behaved irreproachably. A completely unknown Aryan lady from the best social class came to my wife with the comment, "Madam, I am ashamed to be a German". Another unknown lady sent a bottle of wine. People from the house gave advice to send warm clothes to me in Dachau. Aryan friends called by telephone to ask in what way they could help, of course not from their homes and only with their first names. Most people were also angry above all that Goebbels had claimed the *Volkswut* [people's rage] had vented itself, although they nevertheless had slept through the night. Time and again that was the first expression of an Aryan. One of the top Munich bankers (Aryan) explained to me in tears: "I am ashamed to be a German. Explain abroad that 90% of the German population are against these misdemeanours. It is only a small clique who have instigated this disaster."

Jewish refugees, who often had to walk hundreds of kilometres on foot, were looked after on the way in an exemplary manner by farmers, otherwise they would have frozen or starved.

Jews are not allowed to visit cemeteries in Munich. The *Chevra* [preparations for Jewish burial] are being done by Polish Jews there because apparently it is not wished to let it be known how many are dying.

See report 65

B. 67 22nd November 1938

The arrests in Munich began from 3 o'clock at night (from 9th to 10th November). The people were mostly arrested in a decent manner from the homes and taken to the *Politische Polizei* [political police]. Personal details were taken there, all in a decent way. Then the transport in autobuses to Dachau began. The sick were also arrested in Munich, they were even fetched out of their hospital beds. They too were taken to Dachau including aged men aged up to 75 years old.

During admission to the camp everyone was treated in the most humiliating way. We had to line up in rows. Everybody received terrible flogging and slaps round the face from various SS men. Countless people came away from that with blackened and swollen eyes. The rabbis were treated especially badly. One

Orthodox rabbi with a black beard had the hairs pulled out individually.

After the flogging, which had indeed been ordered from on high, we were led away to have quadruple photos taken. At this juncture one or two once again received some powerful slaps round the face. Then we were taken to another house again. There pockets were emptied. Everyone took his own things out of the pockets and handed them over to the cloakroom. One was allowed to retain handkerchiefs and silver coins only. An *Empfangsbescheinigung* [receipt] was issued for the remaining money. (I would like to stress at this juncture that I have received back all the things without exception that I handed in. Nothing was missing, no money either.) It continued, and one had to undress completely. The clothes were likewise handed in to the cloakroom.

Then we were driven through a hall where about ten people sat on stools, Aryan prisoners who had already been there for years, we had to sit in front of them. In no time individuals had their hair cut with a machine, the people with beards were also shaved. Then on to a further very hygienically equipped hall after the clothing had already been prepared. This consisted of trousers, jacket, a short-sleeved shirt, socks and shoes. As we later discovered, this clothing was already made in anticipation of war – blue-white (Zionist colours) striped *Drillichanzüge* [cotton drill clothing] –. A red triangle and a yellow one above it were sewn on the jackets we received, thus a *Mogen Dovid* [Star of David]. Later we ourselves even had to sew on our prisoner's number in ready printed characters.

In the hall we showered and washed and after that we went to a medical examination. At this point I would like to comment that whatever work there was in the camp was done by Aryan prisoners, some of whom had been in the camp for years and were being used in a type of trusted position regarding the newly arrived Jewish prisoners. These Aryan prisoners behaved in a quite worthy and highly decent way.

An Aryan prisoner takes down our personal details again, asks about childhood illnesses, and early infirmities or existing complaints, whilst at the same time in a whispered tone of voice draws attention to certain things that should not be reported. One then goes to stand in front of a doctor, once again some meanwhile receive floggings. When it is their turn with the doctor, those who do not report with "*Schutzhaftjude*" [Jew in protective custody] and name receive a terrible flogging. The doctor does not ask much, has the people turn round, and those who do not hurry away fast enough receive a kick. If someone has an operation wound on his body then he can certainly expect to get various slaps round the face.

Then we had to dress, were assembled and had to be counted off in cohorts of 200 people, who were then led to one of the camp barracks. These barracks are impeccably hygienic. The *Stuben* [rooms] are actually meant for 50–70 people and now have to accept 200. It was bearable in the *Stuben* themselves because they were well heated and the straw bed is not the worst.

After a brief arranging we were led to the large square and had to stand there from 10 in the morning to half past 12 o'clock at night. It was cold (those who arrived after us did not receive caps and so their shorn heads froze). The standing was dreadful. During this time SS men always went around the sections and beat one or the other person dreadfully. The manner of treatment was bestial. Anybody who assaulted creatures like that would be punished for cruelty to animals.

Whilst we were standing, more and more new Jews arrived in endless rows, and we had to notice that we who had arrived first were treated better than those who came later. Apparently the SS teams were ordered from above to behave thus. Because if an SS man did nothing for a while, one could observe a more senior SS man approach, whereupon he began to resume loud insults and became active again.

At night at half past 12 o'clock we were then led to the *Stube* where it was said to us that it was too late to receive food. However one could still have some warm tea. But sadly there was not sufficient, so it was not enough for all.

The next morning we had to rise at 5 o'clock. We received warm coffee and *Kommissbrot* [army bread], both tasted very good. Around half past 6 one had to go to *Appell* [roll call] so one already fell in at 6 o'clock. That lasted some hours, partly standing to attention, partly at ease. And again there were the corresponding floggings.

During the day names were read out in front of the camp barracks and lists put together, in the evenings at half past 6 it was Appell again which again lasted some hours with the corresponding floggings. And invariably still more trains with Jews arrived. In total there were about 15–18,000 Jews in the camp.

On about the third day the mistreatment came to an end. Our troop had developed into a structured mass that knew only iron discipline, iron standing to attention and looking frontwards were necessary in proximity to SS men so that they were not promted to hit.

Every group of 200 was answerable to a *Stubenälteste* [room elder], a so-called *Capo* (*Caporale*). He wore his name on an arm band. This *Capo* is an Aryan prisoner who in most cases has been imprisoned for four or five years already, that is since the beginning of the regime, mostly a former Communist. The man has of course to instill discipline amongst his people, and is sometimes somewhat rough in doing so, but in nearly all cases is a thoroughly well-intentioned and decent human being. Our Capo man once said to us: "Anyone who ever forgets what they have experienced here deserves to be spat in the face." He then went on that one had to muster willpower in order to survive. "And when the SS merely perceive that one has a will, then they also leave one alone in peace. But discipline must prevail."

The rations were not only ample but also tasted good in every respect. There was e.g. very good lentil soup, very good barley soup or yellow turnip soup, in the evenings potatoes with *Blutwurst* [blood sausage], liver sausage or herring e.g. mostly some warm tea as well. Also plenty of *Kommissbrot* which is also very good. However, Orthodox Jews are very badly off, and had to live on bread alone and butter and cheese that could be bought in the canteen and possibly also once biscuits. One often had to deceive these people in order to persuade them to eat something warm.

On the third or fourth day permission was given to purchase in the canteen. There one could obtain nearly everything that a human being needs, e.g. socks, *Fußlappen* [foot cloths], shaving equipment, toothbrushes, toothpaste, drinking glasses, cigarettes, things to eat, etc. Plenty of use was made of that of course. The atmosphere in the camp was comparatively good and comradely by now as a result of the fact that nobody, whether poor or rich, is excepted from their fate. We had to suffer from the cold above all, and especially those who were already suffering when they were admitted; most of them have already died meanwhile and more will die.

After various terrible cases became known, nobody in the camp has the confidence to report to the *Revier* [sick bay], i.e. the doctor. For example I could observe that two Aryan *Sanitäter* [orderlies] carried a man into the *Revier* who had been kicked and beaten unconscious by SA men and could no longer stand up. After barely a quarter of an hour the two orderlies returned with the sick man on the stretcher, without any consideration threw him off the stretcher onto the ground and went away. The doctor had stated there was nothing wrong with the man. Mostly those who make it to the *Revier* die. Of course nobody is present at the death.

Everybody has to attend the morning and evening *Appell*, even those who are ill. Naturally there were many people who could not take another step. They were then carried by two people and positioned, supported or propped up from behind. There were dozens who had to report in this manner. The *Capos* who felt human sympathy allowed these ill people to lie on the straw in the *Stuben* in the period between *Appells*. And of course their comrades attempted to make life for them as good as was possible. Also in the camp were those who had been seriously wounded in the war, even those with only one leg.

Between the two *Appells* morning and evening, the prisoners are to some extent left to themselves. They put themselves at the disposal of former *Chargen* [junior officers], [or] officers and exercise in the narrow streets of the camp. Whoever goes beyond the camp streets or e.g. leaves the barracks after the evening meal after lights out is ruthlessly shot. I have experienced several such cases. At night the SS also shoot ruthlessly into the washrooms in the barracks if someone spends time there with the light on.

On the towers at the two entrances to the camp machine guns are permanently pointed at the prisoners. Some have prayed: If only they would do away with us!

The Aryan prisoners were treated just as badly as the Jews. Amongst the Jewish prisoners who came later, we could tell that the SS became even more sadistic, hit yet harder at the *Appells*. All Jews are in agreement that each individual would be happy to give up everything, he only wants to get out of the camp, somewhere in a transit camp, and would gladly scrape a further living with his hands, only to get out of this hell.

See report 65

B. 68 22nd November 1938

The main priority and crucial is that the prisoners in Dachau concentration camp be helped. Above all what is missing here is woollen underclothing. Therefore it is essential that underclothing is supplied to the people in the camp through any *Hilfsorganisation* [aid organisation]. It would be possible for the camp authorities to provide the prisoners with underwear, equally to sell it in the canteen where everything else is to be had. It can be assumed that underclothing is thus only not sold in order that the people freeze and become ill. It would of course be a trifle for the prisoners to purchase underwear because they receive RM. 15.- per week paid out from their money, and can therefore puchase the essentials. If they do not receive warm underclothing, then one after the other will fall ill either through the cold or possibly rain. The consequences of that are ghastly, because nobody will report to the *Revier* [sick-bay] (*Krankenzimmer* [sickroom]) since the treatment there is terrifying. Thus the first and most important task, provided that the *Schutzhäftlinge* [protective custody prisoners] do not obtain their freedom, is at least to take care of warm underwear for them.

I am now one of the few of those favoured by God who have escaped from this hell, and know that the most important task of all is to help the camp people. The children and women will not suffer as long as there are Jews in Germany. But the misery for these children and women will first begin when the breadwinner returns ill from the camp or even dies. All camp people have learnt that they can survive through their manual labour. Moreover the 90% of Christians who are well disposed will certainly not let any Jewish child or Jewish woman starve.

See report 65

B. 69 Not for publication
    21st November 1938

Individual incidents in Dachau concentration camp
During the time I was in Dachau, four Jews died in my barracks in which 200 people were accommodated.

An old doctor aged over 70, who had various illnesses and reported at the *Revier* [sick bay], i.e. to the doctor, where the doctor said to him: "What's wrong with you, *alter Dreckjude* [dirty old Jew]?" The old man described what was wrong with him. The *Revier* doctor did not examine him, rather had him turn round, gave him a kick and said, "You're just lazy, *Du Schwein* [you pig]! Out!"

Geheimrat [privy councillor] Aufhäuser (banker), whose brother is a naturalised Englishman and Swedish *Generalkonsul* [consul general] in Munich, was beaten just like everybody else.

Baron Hirsch, whose parents or grandparents had endowed the HICEM [Jewish emigrants' assistance organisation] with 200 million, as is well known, was terribly battered. In order to force him to sell his property he was taken away for one day. He returned to the camp and let it be known that the property could not be sold at all because it belonged to his brother. But the latter could not be found. Baron Hirsch is a Catholic. (The story in Munich was that this absent Hirsch brother only wanted to donate to a museum a porcelain collection worth a million marks. However, this collection had been smashed to pieces in an attack on the Baron's Schloss Planegg. The castle was burned to the ground.)

The notary Walter, about 72 years old, was asked by an SS man: "*Was bist Du, Saujude?*" [What are you, Jewish pig?] Standing to attention, he replied "Notary." The SS man said to that, "So you cheated the people too." Walter: "I reject that." At once he was pulled out of line, an arm twisted (perhaps damaged), and he was taken away. Whether he has gone to an *Isolierlager* [isolation camp] or was perhaps shot immediately, we do not know. We all fear the worst for him.

The worst sadist appears to be the deputy of the *Lagerkommandant* [camp commandant]. He approached a troop of newly arrived Jews from behind. He gave one of them, who seemingly had not stood completely still, a horrible punch. The man fell down, was perhaps unconscious and could not get up. Thereupon the *Kommandant*'s deputy trampled around on the man, and when he still did not get up, had him laid on the *Bock* [whipping block] and whipped with the bullwhip. After that the man was certainly unconscious. (The worst punishment in and of itself is the frequent threat of whipping the naked body. And everyone has utter dread of that.)

A prisoner received such slaps around the face that he fell down. He could no longer get up again. An SS man had some pails of water brought and in the ice-cold night doused the man with it, apparently he had already undressed. (I was present at this incident but since it took place perhaps two rows behind me did not turn around otherwise the same would have happened to me. I stood to attention, rooted to the spot.) Through the dousing the man came to and stood up. Then he received yet more blows because he could not dress himself again quickly enough.

B. 70 22nd November 1938

In Berlin the three young rabbis, Dr. Jospe, Dr. van der Zyl and Swarsensky, have been arrested, according to reliable reports.

In Frankfurt am Main the rabbi of the *Israelitische Religionsgemeinschaft* [Jewish religious community], Horovitz, was dragged into the burning synagogue at Friedberger Anlage. He owes his life only to the fact that he is a Czech national and the Czech embassy championed his cause so actively at the last minute.

From Aschaffenburg it is reliably reported by family members that at least one 65-year-old man has been beaten to death. This case can in no way have been the only one in Aschaffenburg.

In Frankfurt am Main the appalling state of affairs still exists, that there is no milk and no food available even for nursing mothers, expectant mothers and small children. The families also would have had no means of procuring them, as on average in every family the male members have been taken away to the concentration camp and there is no money whatsoever available.

In the countryside in Bavaria, especially in Upper Franconia, everywhere, even in the smallest communities, the male Jews have been taken to the concentration camp.

To date unfortunately not a single case can be confirmed where prisoners have been released on grounds of the production of evidence that emigration could take place. Instead the most unbelievable complications and difficulties are made. In many towns, even in Frankfurt am Main, it is impossible to have passport photographs taken. In other towns the drawing up of the *Unbedenklichkeitserklärung* [clearance statement] as the basis for issuing a passport is being delayed. Everywhere the tendency appears to be not to allow people to leave but to hold them hostage, even where departure dates have been confirmed.

Cases from Vienna are known where the *Einreise-Zertifikat* [entry certificate] required by the *Palästina-Behörde* [Palestine Authority] was available four weeks ago without the release taking place. The grounds for the restraint of the people as hostages can only lie in the political area. The reason more often heard, that the billion must be paid first, is completely untrue, because all the bank balances of German Jews have been frozen for a long time and therefore it is entirely within the hands of the authorities to achieve this simply by making over the funds to the *Reichsbank* by bank transfer. No Jew still has the power to freely dispose of any such sums.

Herr *Ministerialdirektor* [head of government department] Hans Goslar, 22.11.38

B. 71 On admission to Dachau the rabbis were especially badly treated. The rabbis Dr. Baerwald and Dr. Finkelscherer from Munich received terrible beatings. Treated worst was the orthodox rabbi Dr. Ehrentreu (Munich) who had a black beard. The hairs were pulled out individually.

So far as our reporter knows the rabbi from Regensburg was released from Dachau after the second or third day.

Berg, Munich

B. 72 Amsterdam, 25th November 1938

According to a rumour circulating in Wiesbaden the Jewish footwear trader Sandel, who resisted the plundering of his shop, has been beaten to death.

Friedr. Wilhelm Schnitzler from Wiesbaden, Friedrichstr. 14, [now] New York City, 1 Sickle St. c/o Gutheim, Ap. E. 24

B. 73 Report from Cologne by a Dutchman

On the 19th and 20th of November I was in Cologne to seek out relatives and where possible to help them. I found a desperate atmosphere, especially amongst the women who burst into tears incessantly, since the fate of their men and their whereabouts were not known to them. The men went first to a labour camp in Brauweiler and from there to barracks in Dachau. Apparently they have not been treated inhumanely, but do have to do continual marching exercises, an unfamilier activity for the older ones above all, and thus stressful. All are shaven not only on their heads but also beards. C. 40 of the older ones returned to Cologne on Sunday the 20th November.

The housing shortage is extraordinarily great, homes are *gekündigt* [served with notice to quit], some to the 1st December, some to a later date. People are desperate because they do not know where they could be accommodated from that point in time. The homes currently in use are overfull with those who have fled from the province. As a result seven people are living at my aunt's in two rooms. What makes it even worse is that these people cannot pursue their emigration because they left all their documents behind in small localities as a consequence of their precipitate flight and cannot return there without endangering their lives.

The synagogues in Roonstraße and Glockengasse whilst still standing are nevertheless seriously damaged and inside are burnt out. The rabbi Dr. Caro has permission to visit prisoners in labour camps.

The following is known to me from a reliable source: Herr William Frankenstein in Solingen, 64 years old, seriously injured on his head from a sabre blow, and actually by a sacked employee. – A hairdresser Spiro in Cologne-Ehrenfeld died from the mistreatment he received. – I myself was convinced for myself that the entire furnishings at a family in Cologne-Braunsfeld were wrecked. – Apart from that I saw that planks have been nailed to the front of all Jewish shops, in particular at two Jewish pastry shops.

A man in his late seventies related to me that he was present when a relative's tailor's shop was totally destroyed. He warded off a blow from a weapon intended for the proprietor which would undoubtedly have killed him.

I myself have accommodated people in large flats so as to alleviate the most urgent housing shortage, and am trying to accommodate relatives here until their emigration has been completed.

G. Vigeveno, Amsterdam, Sarphatistraat 145, 25 years old

B. 74 Report from a provincial town

N. = Nuremberg, X. = Fürth

In the night from the 9th to 10th November at about half-past three o'clock I was warned by telephone about remaining in the home as my arrest was imminent. I then left the home immediately with my wife and son and wandered around in the streets. I met first of all the wife of a banker living in the neighbourhood, in the scantiest clothing, who was likewise trailing around, then as I went on a larger number of Jews, who were walking between *Kriminalbeamten* [criminal policemen] and apparently being taken away. One could tell where Jews lived by the illuminated windows and also from the crashing noises that came from the homes. A house in which only Jewish people lived was fully illuminated. Two guards stood in front of the house with their backs to the house wall and did not bother themselves about anything. One could see uniformed SA and SS people everywhere. A senior officer I know, woken by the hubbub, phoned the *Überfallkommando* [flying squad] and requested them to send people immediately, because apparently unlawful entry and other punishable actions had taken place at his house. The *Überfallkommando* replied that they could undertake nothing, everything had been ordered from above. In general squads of three to 25 men showed up armed with steel rods of which they made extensive use.

When we returned to our home, nothing had been taken but everything destroyed in the most vandalised way, paintings cut up, eiderdowns punctured and a valuable antique reclining chair smashed and the padding torn out. RM. 1,400.- was stolen from a relative. After wandering around for hours I was arrested at the railway station and together with c. 100 other Jewish citizens accommodated in the prison's gym. About six of them were injured including an 80-year-old gentleman wearing a bandage around his head, a bowl was smashed on his head. Amongst those arrested was the rabbi, aged c. 60, and a 77-year-old man. I myself was released after ten hours because I had a visa for America and am a front-line officer.

Moreover, it became known to me that older people were released from Dachau too. Mistreatment has apparently not taken place to a significant extent, only that in general the arrivals had their hair and beards shaved off of course.

Relatives, two ladies of 30 and 40 years, who own a house in X., were invited to sell this house for 10% of its value. When they refused and referred to a co-owner resident abroad, it was explained to them they would then have the opportunity to think it over for eight to ten hours in a cellar on bread and water. They then eventually submitted to this extortion. When the deal was notarised, a declaration was laid before them according to which they had sold "voluntarily", they requested that "voluntarily" be omitted; it was suggested to them by SS people that if they were still being so stupid they would both be taken away.

The large synagogue in N. was already demolished four weeks ago, the smaller some days before the night of arson. On the night in question it was also burned out inside. At the demolition of the large synagogue Hitler was in the city, the whole block was cordoned off by SS people.

I learned from reliable sources that 43 seriously injured people lay in hospital in X.

Essentially this is a matter of leg injuries to people who jumped out of windows or were thrown out. A jeweller in N., who had just been operated on, begged them to spare him because of that. He was dragged out of his bed in a brutal manner and died from the consequences of this treatment because the operation wounds opened.

The proprietor of the Café B. died of a heart attack resulting from the agitation, a Dr. S poisoned himself. A Herr A. S., who suffered from a nervous complaint and for whom his wife pleaded he be spared, was dragged from his bed, forced through the splintered pane of the door to the forecourt with the result that he suffered cuts all over his body. He then went to the police station barefoot and covered in blood, and from there was transported to the hospital by police officers. His Aryan wife who is a Swiss raised objections, at which the SS people explained to her, "It's all the same to us, *Du bist eine Judensau*" [you are a Jewish pig]. Women and children are injured too, a 70-year-old aunt of mine with her husband and son was beaten with steel rods. I had the impression that young SS people who were in uniform the previous day and celebrating the *Ereignis am Biertisch* [Beer Hall Putsch, 1923], had been made drunk and through that their inhibitions, if they had any at all, were completely removed.

In X. all men were arrested and driven into the market place. During this time all the homes everywhere were wrecked, likewise of course the shops and lawyers' chambers.

Rechtswanwalt [lawyer] Dr. Franz Bergmann, Nuremberg, at present Amsterdam, Linnaeusstraat 102

The 77-year-old arrestee: Rosenzweig

Jeweller Lorch

Kaffee Bamberger

Dr. S. = Süssheim

A. S. = Arnold Silbermann

B. 75 I have been here in Amsterdam since 20th November. When I wanted to fly to Amsterdam by aeroplane on Friday the 11th November with a visa for America, I was arrested at the airport and taken to the city prison. On the way there the *Kriminalbeampten* [police detectives] treated us properly, as befitted the circumstances. In prison we 220 Jews lay, in a room with space for 30 to 40 people. In total in F. at that time c. 600 Jews were being accommodated under arrest. Because of the narrowness of the room we could not lie on our backs but had to lie on our sides, pressing tightly against each other like sardines in a tin. We then went by train under police guard to Sachsenhausen concentration camp.

On arrival on Saturday morning we were received by SS, almost entirely very young men who behaved in an unbelievable way particularly towards the elderly male prisoners. We were continually sworn at and beaten the whole way from the railway station to the camp, which we had to cover at the double. In the camp there were only SS men, no police. We had to stand for 16 hours, were intermittently sworn at and beaten so that old men collapsed. Then, after we had to strip – our things were disinfected and as a result were completely unwearable – we arrived in barracks of which there are 60 in Sachsenhausen. The clothing supplied to us was new and had a red and yellow *Mogen Dovid* [Star of David]. Absolutely everything was quite new, especially even the towels. Obviously extensive preparations had been made for the reception of the Jewish prisoners. Even the barracks were newly built. Elderly *politische Häftlinge* [political prisoners] served as *Aufseher* [overseers] in the camp, who behaved relatively pleasantly towards us in agreeable contrast to the conduct of the SS men.

Here too in the barracks we lay quite tightly until on the following day some people were put in the *Tagesraum* [day room].

The day passed as follows: at 5 o'clock we had to get up, at 6 o'clock there was breakfast, at 7 o'clock was *Appell* [roll call] which was interrupted by swearing and kicks from the SS men. Meanwhile hair was cut and beards were shaved off.

I worked for the first time on Tuesday. Every activity had to be carried out at the double; we had to haul bags of sand and cement, sometimes also rocks. For food we were given coffee in a canteen [flask] to take with us and bread spread with something, but there was barely time to sit down and eat it because we had to continue to work at the double. Supper was then not bad.

A Rabbi Cohn was treated particularly badly and constantly sworn at and ridiculed. A large chimney stack that towered over the camp was pointed out to us by the SS men, who said that the following day we would be able to see smoke from ourselves coming out of the chimney.

On Thursday morning I was released on the intervention of my mother because I did have a visa for America.

In Hamburg I have seen how people have thrown stolen goods into the canal. In Jewish department stores the windows were smashed, everything that appeared Jewish was seized.

B. 76 For information only. CAUTION!

24th November 1938

Dr. David Taubes, 53 years old, former *Anwalt* [lawyer], widower, Vienna III., Weißgerberlände 50, was attacked on the street and seriously injured on the day of the pogrom (see B. 209).

The sales representative Jacob Samuel Taubes, 41 years old, married, one child, was taken by unknown persons in the street on 9th November and is missing since then.

Dr. I. Taubes, Amsterdam

B. 77 26th November 1938

My arrest took place during the night of Thursday to Friday, 10th November 1938 – in contrast to many of my acquaintances I was not notified of the imminent arrest. My home remained undamaged.

We first came to a dark room in Fuhlsbüttel prison in numbers that exceeded the capacity fivefold, stayed there without food the entire day and were then transported overnight in open goods wagons to Sachsenhausen, where we arrived at 2 o'clock in the morning. On the journey a young 17-year-old man from Bremen had a nervous breakdown because he had had to watch how SS men shot his mother, who cried out from the pain of seeing him led away and was then left lying there. On our arrival in Sachsenhausen a large number of SS men met us and immediately began such harsh mistreatment by kicking and beating us with rifle butts and truncheons that the *Schupo* [*Schutzpolizei;* police] escorting us stood there in bewilderment and quickly left and went back. We then had to march in lines of five, i.e. run – the physical exertion and the uninterrupted beating and battering by the SS was such that two of our group were left dead on the ground on the 15-minute march.

Then began the most terrible thing, the effect of which on me especially made all the physical mistreatment appear minor – in the camp we had to stand for 19 hours (for some individuals this time stretched to 25 hours) and were rewarded with kicks and blows from rifle butts during this time if one or two collapsed. The first to be called out was the rabbi, who had his beard pulled and was mistreated; he was given a sign to hold with the inscription, "I am a traitor to my country and an accessory in the death of vom Rath." He had to carry this sign around for 12 hours with arm outstretched. The SS men, of whom scarcely one was over 21 years of age, particularly had it in for all old, fat Jews of a higher social status and of Jewish appearance, e.g. rabbis, teachers, lawyers, whilst they treated sporty looking younger Jews more leniently. I cannot dispel the impression that a homosexual undertone influenced the actions of the SS men.

We were now shorn of beard and the hair on our head and had to stand for six hours again without food, drink and anything covering our heads outside in the rain – therefore we were without sleep and food for 2 days and nights and had to stand for the longest time. The first water that we could then take was so full of iron that we could barely keep it down as it was unhealthy.

In Sachsenhausen camp there were about 18,000 prisoners; of these 6,000 were from Hamburg. Most of them said that their homes had been completely wrecked, and they had had to spend the nights in all sorts of places until they were finally caught.

Thus a former senior legal official, who gave his name using his title, was treated particularly harshly, and with him the owner of a large catering business.

Every activity in the camp had to be carried out at the double, as well as en route to and from work, also as far as possible at work. If someone did not run, the SS men shouted, "Keep running, your highness, run, fat *Judenschwein* [Jewish pig]." Those exhausted and mistreated were not permitted to be helped, "The *Schwein* must stay where he's lying." Nobody went to our *Revier* [sick bay]; even if somebody did go, the doctor would not concern himself with them, only the *Sanitäter* [medical orderlies] who extremely skilfully and helpfully lent us their support. One could speak softly, although as a general rule anyone who spoke could be shot.

The work, to which we were driven at the double, was carried out in the *Klinker (Hermann-Göring)-Werke* [Hermann Göring Brick Works] and consisted of hauling bags of sand and cement. To carry the sand we prisoners had to take off our jackets and put them on again so that the back was at the front, then the jacket was held high and sand recklessly shovelled in, which we then had to carry with arms outstretched at the double for about 5 minutes [and] drop into the wagon. Then back again at the double. Bags of cement weighing a hundredweight were thrown indiscriminately onto the necks of 60- and 65-year-old men, they then had to haul this load in the same way at a brisk pace, throw it down and run back. Occasionally the sand was hauled on so-called stretchers; that was even more dreadful as this wood cut into the hands so that the flesh on my hands was cut through to the bone. After I had done five to six days' duty I finally then went to the *Revier* where my hands and feet were treated properly by the above mentioned .

I also want to stress that the SS men spoke to us indiscriminately as "*Du*" [familiar form of "you"] as a matter of course, and that we were particularly overcome with horror when it was known that the Vienna SS was on duty.

On the return march from work we ran in lines of five. Those who collapsed were beaten and then carried on a stretcher inside the lines of five, so that the people whom we had to pass on the streets did not notice several stretchers outside the lines. Anyone who was not standing to attention properly at drill had to '*rollen*' [roll], i.e. turn over and over in the sand until he lost consciousness. These unfortunate ones would often then run into the electric fence and were killed by the electric shock or by the guards who patrolled the boundary fence.

Finally on 21st November came the news of our release and indeed 70 of us were transported back. When we reported to the *Kommandant* [commandant] at the release, the senior SS officers were talking about whether it might not be advisable to slaughter or burn this or that particularly fat Jew. The effect of this conversation, considered to be a joke, on those with shattered nerves was terrible. However this was not the end of our journey through hell. On the morning after the announcement we had to stand from 6 o'clock in the morning until 6 o'clock in the evening in the pouring rain without head covering, then on the following day again from 11 until 3 without food and without being permitted to use the latrines. Eventually it was announced that the Jews would not receive any tickets to travel, and at the same time it was remarked, "You can walk on foot to Stargard [now Pol. Stargard Szczeciński] as far as I'm concerned." We then paid for those with no money amongst us, and then had to wait another twelve hours at the railway station before we could leave. Our clothes, which had had to be disinfected because all Jews were lice-ridden, were completely ruined.

Kurt Juster, Hamburg, 30 years old, Hoofddorp, Hotel "De Landbouw"

In the report:

Legal official = *Oberstaatsanwalt* Guggenheim

Owner of the large catering business = Herr Unger, Kempinski

B. 78 27th November 1938

A factual report

Preliminary remark: it must be assumed that as far as the mood in Germany is concerned, neither the overthrow of Austria nor the occupation of the Sudetenland has had a long-term effect. The mood in respect of satisfaction about Austria is lasting comparatively longer than with the Sudetenland. For the fear of war was very real and the joy in the so-called *Altreich* [Old Reich] is to do with having avoided the danger of war and nothing else. It is of course necessary to take an overall view of matters; for there is obviously still support for it to a large extent. However influential circles, particularly the Propaganda Minister [Joseph Goebbels], in no way failed to be aware of the real mood in the days when there was a danger of war. Anyone who was watching in person could not fail to be aware of the mood, both on that Tuesday as the troops marched out of Berlin bringing traffic to a halt for hours, and must have noticed that everywhere alike the people lining the streets stood there with stony faces not even waving, and also on the following Wednesday seeing the masses being led from the factories to the Lustgarten without making a sound. Under these circumstances is it any wonder that after the Munich conference on the one hand people looked for scapegoats because of the lack of enthusiasm and on the other hand contemplated how the mood could be improved. In fact food like butter, eggs etc. has become more and more scarce recently. Therefore even in October a growing tide of feeling against the Jews was discernible. Openly and in secret. Moderate thinkers shrugged their shoulders but declared that nothing could be done. However, the radicals demanded something more. In Berlin the places which put up, or were made to put up, the well-known sign "*Juden uner-wünscht*" [Jews not wanted] increased. In the autumn there was not a square, not even a small square, that did not have the signs with the Jewish benches. Sometimes only the sign was there but no so-called Jewish benches.

The facts: therefore after something had been in the air for a long time, after even a striking number of arrests had been made amongst Aryans (in commercial circles), there could be no further doubt that the shots at Herr vom Rath would constitute a signal. As early as the following morning attention was drawn to the fact that this would not remain without consequences for the Jews. On Wednesday 9th November in Berlin official messages had been published in the newspapers about attacks against the Jews in Kassel and in the Electorate of Hessen. That was obviously the official signal. And now to the night of 9th to 10th November.

At three o'clock in the morning precisely the building in which I lived and in which there was a small Jewish shop shook. Both the window panes were smashed in and the contents of the shop windows were also ruined. Whether that was the very first time there was an incident of course I cannot judge. I lived in the Kurfürstendamm quarter. Soon afterwards I heard the shattering of the window panes from this part of the city, as I used to sleep with the window open. One hour later the same thing happened again. There was a second attack on what remained intact of the shop windows even in the house in which I lived. Here from my window I saw a small car drive up, two men in plain clothes get out and smash the windows. Obviously everything had been arranged precisely; because the men got back in to do the same thing nearby. At about six o'clock in the morning a third group then came, who also wreaked destruction once again, as far as there was anything left to destroy. During these three hours again and again the rattle of guns could be heard periodically through the streets, and the smoke from the Fasanenstraße already hinted at what may have taken place. At any rate it was a well-planned operation which had been carried out by the SA, SS and *Hitlerjugend* [Hitler Youth] in plain clothes. In a barber's shop one man who had taken part said in my presence that they had been drinking until about three o'clock in the morning to prepare for the operation. During its execution many Jews had been "clobbered". The next morning a nightmarish picture presented itself and the smoking synagogue in the Fasanenstraße was like a beacon. The people examined the devastation silently, as far as I could tell, and probably to some extent also with inner turmoil. Yes, opinions about the outrage were also expressed quite openly. When I went over to the Kurfürstendamm in the morning, an old gentleman with snow-white hair addressed me on impulse as he spoke of an insult to decency for which the German people would still have to atone.

I left in the afternoon. Therefore I have no further experience of the events on the afternoon of Thursday 10th November in Berlin, which are said to have been particularly horrendous in the Hausvogtei quarter. However in Hamburg a similar picture presented itself as on the journey across Berlin. The large establishments like Robinsohn were completely destroyed and also looted. In Hamburg it was said to me that the *Tempel* [synagogues] were not set on fire but "only" destroyed. However after the Thursday in Hamburg nothing more is supposed to have happened publicly. Be that as it may, during a walk through the town I heard a very well-dressed lady say quite loudly that it was incomprehensible of the people of Hamburg. It is certain in any case that even on Friday evening there were difficulties getting Jews out on the large ships that were departing.

Concluding remark: thus these are some personal experiences, which do not even give an approximate picture of the reality, as I still had the unimaginable good fortune to escape from Berlin and also through favourable circumstances to get out of the country altogether.

On Saturday night Germany disappeared from our gaze. The big question, which in my opinion it is all about, is this, whether the world will now calm down, or not. The real police are completely neutralised and terror is the victor right down the line. As broadest sections of the German people are not antisemitic and also do business with Jews even now, it was envisaged that it would end in some form or another after the events of June. Yet nobody could foresee that it would turn out as it has. The tide of feeling may perhaps temporarily abate, but it will always make itself felt. Only if the big powers completely dissociate themselves from the regime will there be an end to it. That will indeed also be an end with fear, but that seems to me to be much better than a fear without end.

Statement made by Paul Dreyfus de Gunzburg, Basel

B. 79 According to a report from a reliable source the physician Dr. Hessberg (eye specialist) as well as *Justizrat* [state prosecutor] Heinemann have taken their own lives.

Ernst Nassau, at present in Bussum, at Julius N.

B. 80 23rd November 1938

It is reported to us that in Munich the Jewish shops were indeed destroyed but that nothing was stolen. In Munich the furniture was only smashed up in three villas yet in the remaining Jewish houses it was not.

The arrested men were transported away to Dachau in cars half an hour later, which is further proof that the operation was planned in advance.

Smager, President of the *Schweizer Isr[aelitischer] Gemeindebund* [Swiss Jewish Community Association], St. Gallen

B. 81 21st November 1938

Dr. Jacob Horwitz [Horovitz] is still ailing but not in danger. The rumours about his condition were caused by an accident that happened to another Dr. Horwitz (rabbi of the *Religionsgesellschaft* [Religious Society]), who was badly treated. The latter Dr. H., who is also an internee, is Czecho Slovak and has been claimed by his government.

As far as I could ascertain, Dr. Horwitz (rabbi of the Jewish *Gemeinde* [community] of Frankfurt) already has his permit to travel and will avail himself of it as soon as his doctors allow him to travel.

About the other two gentlemen I could not hear anything reliable.

Sammy Japhet
60, London Wall
London EC2

B. 82 Report from the concentration camp at Buchenwald near Weimar

On the notorious Thursday evening when the synagogues burned and the shops and homes were wrecked, I was arrested by the Gestapo with the explanation, "We must take you into *Schutzhaft* [protective custody] in connection with the events of this day." I was transferred to the *Untersuchungsgefängnis* [remand prison] and remained there one day. Treatment there quite correct, perhaps it could even be called friendly. Released towards evening, so that at first the thought occurred to us that we would be released to go home.

We learned better however through the fact that a row of buses suddenly drove up, into which we were loaded. Transported to Frankfurt-Süd [Frankfurt am Main South railway station], met there by a large crowd of *Schupos* [*Schutzpolizei*; police], who shouted loudly at us, but otherwise left us alone. Loaded onto a passenger train, order: "During the journey none of the windows may be opened; in the event of an attempt to escape those concerned will immediately be shot without warning." Journey to Weimar. The first acts of violence on arrival there. We had to go into the tunnel under the tracks, face against the wall, we were crammed closely together and mistreated with blows and punches. After the transport was counted off, we were herded on with crude shouts and cursing to run as quickly as possible up the steps to the buses that were standing there. The first kicks were planted on the steps. Here already it then became apparent that the boys and the agile came through comparatively well whilst the older or physically impaired were on the receiving end of the blows. Loaded into the buses already standing there, again with loud and crude shouts and many insults. Example: An SS man asks, "What are you all?" Of course no reply, as the question was not understood. Slap on the face. "We are all *Betrüger* [fraudsters], you must say! What must you say?" Slap on the face. At last comes the required answer. Slap on the face. "Speak up, you *Judenschwein* [Jewish pig]!" etc. In the bus the sudden command: "Spectacles off, heads down!" Punches immediately to all necks that were accessible until all heads held deeply bowed. We had to remain in this position for the whole journey; if anyone dared to raise the head, immediate punch to the neck.

Arrival in Buchenwald: order to get out. Even louder and cruder shouts and hail of insults. Order: "Hats off." Again herded at top speed and then a proper running of the gauntlet. We had to pass between two lines of SS men, one punched and kicked, the other beat us with knuckle-dusters and whips. One plump *Wachtmeister* [sergeant] had a short-handled whip in his hand like the

Russians' *nagaika* and it was doubtless also interlaced with wire or studded with pieces of lead. He struck the head with it and blood generally flowed after every lash. Again it was the case that agile younger men got away with a couple of blows whilst the older men, some of whom were suffering acutely, emerged from the alley bleeding and limping.

Report on the square in front of the *Kommandant* [Commandant]'s office, there allocation of prisoner numbers and allocation to the barracks. At the double to the barrack and there immediately ordered onto the *Pritsche* [plank beds]. Here an older prisoner consoled us, "Now you can all calm down, here you are safe." From my place I counted 22 men with bleeding heads. Mostly it was bleeding weals although on some individuals, however, the skin had split and the scalp lay bare. One of the older prisoners looked after the wounded insofar as he dipped a towel in water and laid it on the heads of the wounded to cool them. As he had neither many towels nor much water he had to remove the primitive bandage again after ten minutes in order to lay it on another man. Basically in Buchenwald there is no treatment of wounds for Jews. They have no claim to bandaging material, to medication or to any medical help whatsoever.

In the camp there were four barracks in which approximately 2,000 men had to be accommodated. *Pritsche* in four or five tiers above each other so that when everybody was lying flat and all the aisles and the central area were also occupied, most were able to lie down at least. All the same the room is not quite large enough, a number have to spend all night standing up. Two days later a fifth barrack was ready, so that in the end it can be envisaged that perhaps roughly 10,000 men have somewhere to sleep. There are no washing facilities. Already on the second day our hands are dark grey and sticky, so that we feel sick having to touch the bread with them. The camp must suffer from a shortage of water. At any rate it has to be saved even in the *Sanitätsbaracke* [medical barrack] to the extent that that the *Krankenwärter* [medical orderlies] complain that they can scarcely wash their patients. Another consequence of the water shortage: Jews are entitled to have coffee once a day. The daily coffee ration that was given to us amounted to at most only four or five mouthfuls, so that we all suffered from thirst and could often barely speak with the enormous amount of dust produced in the barracks, and for that reason it was very often necessary for us to clean our noses during the day by digging in with our fingers and so removing the crusts of filth. For the five barracks there was one latrine of perhaps ten metres in length. The usual field latrine: a tree trunk at sitting height with a corresponding pit behind it. It is self-evident that this latrine was not enough for so many people, and those who only wanted to urinate did not queue up for an hour to get to the latrine but urinated anywhere in the area, which naturally led very quickly to a contamination of the whole area. See below on the conditions during an occasional epidemic.

In the camp the prisoners are not allowed to wear a hat and are immediately ordered to take off collars and ties. On the first day we had to spend most of the day lying on the *Pritsche*, as there are only two alternatives. Either reporting on the square in front of the *Kommandant's* office or lying on the *Pritsche*. A day room does not exist, or even just space in which to move outside the barracks, even if only to a small extent. Once a day there is a hot meal; however, because of their thirst many only consume part of it.

On the evening of this first day came the first cases of mental disturbance. Next to me lay an old pharmacist, who suddenly began to talk incessantly. He said that he asked for coffee twice, had as a result deprived his fellow prisoners, realised his mistake and now had to report to the *Kommandant* in order to have himself shot. We tried for hours to dissuade him and in the end held him fast by the collar, however eventually tired and let him go. He reported to the *Unteroffizier* [junior officer] who was just doing his rounds, who nevertheless dealt with him really very kindly: "So now I'm going to tell you something, go now and turn in and shut your mouth, and if you do that, then that'll be the end of the matter, but if you don't keep quiet, then I'll come and shoot you!" The second case of mental disturbance went much more badly: an old gentleman from Frankfurt suddenly burst out with the cry, "Jews, help me, they want to kill me!" He could not be kept on his *Pritsche*, began to run around, again and again breaking into the frantic cry, "They want to kill me!" In the end one of the elderly prisoners confronted him: "Now finally shut your mouth, or I'll give you what for!" "Yes, but they want to kill me!" Another warning and when the old man again yelled out his characteristic cry, a punch landed on his head so that he flew back over several prisoners lying on the floor towards the stove, half pulled this over, however, then rapidly hid himself behind it, but immediately shouted, "They want to kill me." At this the elderly prisoner (who incidentally wore the green triangle of a common criminal) dragged him out from behind the stove and got three men as reinforcements and then seriously set to work. As a doctor I felt it was my duty to intervene and to make the people aware that one was dealing with an undoubted case of mental disturbance. I climbed down from my *Pritsche* and came forward below: "I am a doctor, the man is ill, would you perhaps allow me to see if I can cope with him?" Shove on the chest so that I lurched backwards. "We don't need any doctor here. We understand enough about these things and know what we've got to do with people like this." "If you make one more sound you'll be finished off!" When the old man still went on making his characteristic cry despite this, the four pounced, for perhaps one minute pelted him with punches to his head, which afterwards was a mass of blue-black; the place where his nose and his eyes should be could barely still be made out. The old man was half unconscious and of course kept quiet. As a result, great satisfaction on the part of this *Rollkommando* [raiding party]: "Yes, we already know how to deal with people like that, we've already shut up lots of people who didn't want to keep quiet. We've got all sorts of ways. If there's nothing else for it, then you've just got to believe in stopping it instead of one thousand or two thousand having to put up with it. If we don't cope with the fellow like that, then we take him outside for a bit. Then we'll make him keep quiet, we've learned how to do it nicely now, and we don't even need rope for it."

After about half an hour the old man had again recovered enough to burst out with his cry, "Let me live", at which a similar scene was played out as described above. The old man, of unbelievable tenacity, withstood it repeatedly, until in the morning at 6 o'clock we reported for duty, he lay on the floor of the hall in the dust and was still breathing noisily. However it cannot then have lasted much longer.

Another case from that night: one of the prisoners suddenly bursts out in fits of screaming, which ring out dreadfully through the entire hall and initially in fact were indistinguishable from hysterical screaming fits; later we often took these as a symptom of the start of a mental illness. One of the *Rollkommando* rushes up to him, "Shut up or I'll finish you off!" No effect on the prisoner and the first step is a kick up the backside, such that the man in question flies over two others. The screaming continues, at which the other man fetches a slat, with which he then wallops the screaming man so hard that the blows ring out loudly throughout the hall and everyone who should still have been asleep wakes up. The screaming continues, at which the other man ties a couple of rags to the point of the slat, sits down next to the screaming man, at the right moment pushes the gag deep into his throat. The screaming now stops of course, all that can be heard is the man still gasping. "See, we understand how to deal with people like you too, see, now you are all nice and quiet." The gag is now pulled out a little, or the pressure of it is increased again as necessary and ultimately pulled out when the prisoner had almost completely suffocated. After he had recovered, he started screaming again, and I believe, however it cannot be stated with complete certainty, that this time he was suffocated to stop the screaming. At any rate this man was dead by morning.

That night there were also two cases of heart spasms. The men affected were laid on a table which stood in the middle of the barrack, "You *Saujuden* [Jewish pigs] needn't come to us with such stories of heart spasms, we already know the ruse, since we also have our special methods to handle it." The treatment consisted of throwing water in the face of these prisoners. One of them, who was still lying on the table in the morning and was still alive, oddly enough had a wound in the region of his heart; where it came from, I do not know. This wound looked exactly the same as one on another man who had stabbed himself near his heart with a penknife. That night another man made an attempt to poison himself with Veronal. – Result of this night: three, perhaps even four dead in my barrack. As quite similar things are said to have happened in the other barracks, one can assume that at least 15 to 20 deaths per day could be recorded in the camp.

We were told, "Identification discs are the badge of honour of the soldier. You don't get that, but we advise you to stick a piece of paper in your pocket with the address of your wife on it, so that at least we know where to send the ashes."

On the second day, report for duty at 6 o'clock in the morning, attempt to create order in sections fails completely however, because no organised issue of commands and no communication of commands whatsoever were available. As a result of the unclear commands, frequent conflicts: if something is done wrong, there is beating with a slat or a wooden club. Where that involves a soldier, if he clicks his heels and shuts up, then it is fine. If he does not stand to attention or tries to explain his misunderstanding in an unsoldierly way, or to apologise, he gets fresh blows from the club, as it depends on the circumstance or on the mood of the man doing the beating whether the blow is made harder or weaker, or whether he hits the shoulders, the back or the head and the back of the neck. Heavier blows on the head and the neck make the person concerned slightly "groggy", then the situation becomes dangerous for him, for if he begins to teeter the command inevitably comes, "Heels together! Proper posture!", and as he cannot do that, fresh blows follow until he keels over. Those who have keeled over are either brought back to a standing position with kicks or left where they fall. Sometimes dozens of them could be seen lying around.

At last at about 10 o'clock we were led in a relatively disorganised way onto the square in front of the *Kommandant*'s office, and there they began to call out the prisoners by name according to town. A short pause to receive coffee, a somewhat longer pause to receive the hot meal. Otherwise this process went on without interruption until half past 6 in the evening, so that on this day we stood for roughly twelve hours. Of course the elderly and those who have not served in the military could not bear it but keeled over by the dozen.

That day new trains of prisoners came again, a new barrack was built remarkably quickly, but was not ready. I was one of those who were to be accommodated in this barrack. We were herded into the barrack until we were standing crammed rather closely together. Then the command for everyone to lie down, assisted by brandishings of the whip over our heads, and wherever we were standing we had to throw ourselves into the filth. Needless to say, people lay partly on top of each other and all over the place so that we could barely move. That night many started to suffer from diarrhoea. Those near the entrance tried to get out, asked the guard to be allowed to step outside, which was sometimes permitted with loud swearing and beating, also sometimes refused. At the latrine they stood in a long line. It frequently happened that somebody could not wait that long and he had to then more or less decide to drop his trousers just where he was standing and to pollute the area, reason enough for those on duty to swear and lash out at the *Schweinejuden* [pig Jews]. For hours that night almost without interruption one could hear the smack of blows and the cries of those being hit. At one point a shot rang out. It is clear that under these circumstances fewer and fewer people would have the courage to go outside and more and more would choose to stay in the barrack and let everything run into their trousers. Those who were lying distant from the entrance already more or less had to do this because they could not push their way through to the entrance. Also that night cases of acute confusion, as I have described those of the previous night, with the associated consequences.

The next day again report for duty at 6 o'clock. Again stand in front of the *Kommandant*'s office until 11 o'clock, again many people collapsed, especially those with gastro-enteritis. At 11 the command everyone turn left face and sit down so that one had the left-hand neighbour between one's legs. For four hours we had to stay in this position, which perhaps in the long run is far more strenuous than standing.

During the following night the taking of restless deranged men to the washhouse played a particular role. Of course I did not see for myself what happened there, that night also slept for four hours out cold from exhaustion. I heard that the events in the washhouse are said to have been roughly that somebody's head was pushed under water in a bucket with the usual threats and held down until they almost drowned.- One prisoner jumped into the electrically charged barbed wire fence, either in his confusion or even with the intention of committing suicide, another is said to have been found in the latrine.

Each *Vorgesetzte* [supervisor], or each elderly prisoner who occasionally or regularly acts as a *Vorgesetzte,* whips on principle.

Punishments: one punishment which is frequently used is whipping on the *Bock* [whipping block] which stands in front of the *Kommandant*'s office and from which the smacking sound is often heard. During this the skin of the buttocks often splits and bleeds. Another punishment which I have seen on a daily basis is leaving the prisoners standing in front of the punishment wall of the *Kommandant*'s office. They remain standing there for so long that they keel over. This punishment is compounded by the fact that a sandbag with different weights is hung around the person in question. Another punishment: tying the hand to one of the window bars and leaving the person standing there for hours. This punishment can be made harsher if both hands are tied to the bars at a height where the person in question still just touches the floor with the tips of their toes, which practically means that they are suspended by their hands. A further punishment: two prisoners have a fetter on both wrists and are locked together round a tree so that they can barely move. If they go limp, then the one hangs on the wrists of the other and through the weight causes him considerable pain.

B. 83 28th November 1938

The arrests of the Jewish men started on the Thursday morning after the night of 9th to 10th November in Breslau [now Pol. Wrocław] when the windows of the shops belonging to Jews were smashed everywhere. In Breslau approximately 3,000 Jews were arrested in total, amongst them originally even boys of 16 and old men of over 75 years of age.

Those under arrest were taken to the *Polizeirevier* [police station] initially and there locked in the air raid shelter that is situated in every police station. They were then taken by dispatch van to the *Polizeipräsidium* [police headquarters] where large air raid shelters are situated. Initially the Jewish prisoners were held in these shelters. Not until Friday afternoon were the youths and the old men over the age of 60 released separately. Most of the men under arrest were taken to Buchenwald and Sachsenhausen concentration camps. Some of the relatives still do not know where the arrested family members are. The Gestapo dismiss the unfortunate women with the greatest harshness.

The large synagogue at Ohlauer Stadtgraben was burned down like many other synagogues. The dome of the Great Synagogue has collapsed, the grounds around the synagogue are now fenced off. From the orthodox synagogue in Wallstraße the silver etc. kept there has been taken away in baskets by SA men.

The offices of the Jewish *Gemeinde* [community] were initially all locked and sealed, are now however back in operation. As most of the officials have been arrested, women are frequently working there. The same applies to the office of the *Hilfsverein* [*Hilfsverein der deutschen Juden;* Aid Association of German Jews].

Rabbi Dr. Vogelstein was not in Breslau on the day of the pogrom, neither was he arrested, unlike the second rabbi.

The large department store of Barrasch that was *arisiert* [Aryanised] a long time ago, as well as the well-known linen shop of Bielschowsky, were also damaged. The proprietors of the firms were expected to remove the names of the former Jewish owners in this way.

The synagogue located in the Jewish hospital has survived; of the Jewish doctors at this hospital all but three were arrested. It is hoped in Breslau that the doctors who have been licensed as *Krankenbehandler* [Jewish doctors licensed to treat Jewish patients] will be released again.

Most of the shops have been provided with wooden crates as the proprietors do not have the money to reopen the shops or refurbish them.

For the time being the Jewish cemetery lacks the appropriate resources to bury the dead. As a result of this during the first days after the pogrom the coffins were left there unburied.

Emigration is made exceptionally difficult, because until the fine is paid no *Unbedenklichkeitsbescheinigung* [clearance certificate] will be issued. The same applies to the emigration of juveniles where the parents have submitted a *Vermögenserklärung* [declaration of assets]. Extraordinarily high taxes are imposed on emigration assets, as usual.

B. 84 26th November 1938

Pogrom in the Rhineland

From a small Rhineland community in the Cologne district: on Thursday, the 10th November, a *Minyan*[gathering of at least ten adult Jewish men] (*Jahrzeit* [anniversary of a death]) took place in the morning at our synagogue. At the end, around 9 o'clock, the *Orts-Polizei-Kommissar* [local police inspector] entered the house of God, demanded to speak to the *Vorsteher* [chairman], and had the premises shown to him. He explained politely and quietly that according to instructions received he was obliged to order that: neither the synagogue nor the inner doors could be closed; all locks must remain open, also the *Betpult* [prayer stool] and *Thora-Schreine* [ark] which was shown and explained to him. The police officer then inspected the adjoining buildings, the Jewish school etc. in the upper floor of which the Aryan *Kalfaktor* [caretaker] lives; he is responsible for the cleaning and heating of the synagogue. The officer then commented: "Here next door nothing is to happen…"

Then, shortly after returning home I was arrested with almost all the other members of the *Gemeinde* [community]. Several hours later the "*spontane Volksmenge*" [spontaneous crowd] arrived from outside and only at around 12 o'clock midday did the prisoners in the police prison (which bordered on the *Feuerwehr* [fire brigade]) learn from the sounding of the fire siren that the synagogue was in flames.

It has been consistently reported from the villages and small towns in the Eifel that no local residents took part in the plundering and barbarity. All the perpetrators were people from outside. On 11th and 12th November in a number of places it was made known through town criers: everyone who took goods or objects out of Jewish houses and businesses had to hand these in at once to the *Ortsvorsteher* [local administrator] otherwise severe punishment was threatened. Most residents obeyed this demand and gave up the "ownerless goods" which had mostly been left on the streets during the wrecking.

From Aachen and Essen: "business" in stolen property was done quite openly on the street after the plundering. E.g. shoes and clothing were exchanged for suitable amounts, in both towns new footwear was traded for RM. 2.- to RM. 3.- per pair.

Mannheim: the synagogue was totally wrecked, arson seemed to be too dangerous because of the close proximity of neighbouring houses. – Consequently the explosions must have resulted from using dynamite detonators and high explosive bombs in the interior. – On Saturday the 12th and Sunday the 13th of November the synagogue was open for the public to visit. Collectors for the "W-H" [*Winterhilfswerk des deutschen Volkes*; Winter Relief for the German People] stood at the entrance and charged an entry fee of ten *Pfennigs* [pennies] from the great throng of curious onlookers.

Bonn: here too in a Gestapo duty room *Thorarollen* [Torah scrolls] and very many synagogue valuables were carefully laid out on tables. A uniformed SS man informed himself about the age and value of the objects, further about the purpose of their use, contents of books etc.through some older released *Schutzthäftlinge* [protective custody prisoners] (over 65 years old – only these have been released in Bonn).

Mittelstadt, near Aachen: a few minutes after returning home, Jews over 65 years old released from prison were ordered by telephone to report to the police at once for further imprisonment and to bring clothes etc. with them for 14 days – (between 18 and 19 o'clock in the evening, a Friday!, the 11th November.) It was explained to those who arrived by the officers on duty that nothing was known to them about this summons. The well-meaning *Bürgermeister* [mayor] received the anxious people, informed himself by telephone from various offices and sent these people home again because apparently an SA man had allowed himself a nasty hoax.

Westphalia: a German industrialist, Aryan, in a long private letter asks his Belgian business friends not to hold the German people responsible for the "atrocities of criminal elements". The letter concludes: "Quotation: That is the horror in the world, worse than death, that the scoundrel is master and remains master. Those are the words of a German, Wilhelm Raabe, in 'Schüdderrump' . . ."

B. 85 Report by a lady from Breslau [now Pol. Wrocław], whom I had questioned, who was *not* arrested (from the leaders of the *Gemeinde* [community]).

Synagogues all burned down. Where surrounding houses in danger of catching fire, completely destroyed.

All shops without exception completely vandalised and looted. Up to the third floor, even wholesalers. Homes and villas in Breslau here and there.

Upper Silesia many homes [destroyed]. Women also arrested one day there. Liegnitz [now Pol. Legnica] area treated more reasonably. However shops and synagogues likewise systematically destoyed.

All the men gone, in Breslau c. 90%, in the region 100%. War disabled and over 65s released. There is Less, Halpert, Markowitz, Spitz, Friedländer and otherwise only ladies. Myself unfortunately also endangered. Was in Militsch [now Pol. Milicz] on 10th November and made my getaway. Work senseless in the long term.

People: Better people are ashamed, little people indifferent, nobody's blood boils.

According to what I have heard, office manager Glaser was not arrested either.

B. 86 28th November 1938

In Hilden a businessman aged almost 60 was stabbed during the night of 9th to 10th November, likewise six other Jews, of whom four died and two survived. The stepdaughter was summoned and asked whether her stepfather had already often attempted suicide. Then she was asked if she had seen whom it was, to which she replied, "For the record I do not know whether it was an SS or an SA man or a civilian. For you personally: my neighbour, the hairdresser."

In a Dutch woman's home ten to twelve people were sheltered for one week. The only people not arrested were those who could go into hiding or wander around.

In Siegen in the night of 9th to 10th November, 76-year-old Herr Jacobi was taken away with ten other elderly Jewish men; since then there is no trace of them.

In Düsseldorf the Markus couple, owners of a Jewish café, were shot. The husband was dead immediately, the wife died after two days. [Later handwritten addition: Wife is living in Palestine – wounds healed. Rei[chmann], i.e member of JCIO staff.]

Older people have partly been released from the concentration camp, some because of frailty, illness, hernias. A larger number of the imprisoned were taken to the work camp at Brauweiler near Cologne. There an older officer said to them: "Things will turn round. The people who brought you here, will one day themselves end up here."

Cologne. In entire residential streets every single home has been wrecked; not one item, not one chair, not a cup remains intact. Grand pianos, upright pianos were thrown out of the windows onto the street. The mobs were partly led by "*Braune Schwestern*" [brown sisters; nurses; part of the Nazi welfare organisation] (who are now working in hospitals in place of the discharged nuns), who showed them which homes should be wrecked.

A 60-year-old man was seriously injured in the presence of his three small children (married late).

In the Urbach settlement near Bonn where youths from 14 to 19 years are trained for agricultural work, everything was wrecked. The youths, some of whom were mistreated, fled and were taken in by farmers.

B. 87 28th November 1938

My husband has satisfied himself personally that the synagogue in Oranienburgerstraße in Berlin was not unscathed. All the windows are smashed, chandeliers and beams brought down. 24 hours after the synagogue fires it was announced on the radio that the [*Jüdische*] *Kulturbund* [Jewish Cultural Federation] will perform again. The shows began on 22nd November (to houses one third full), on Sunday 26th November the cabaret had to perform again.

A 32-year-old man by the name of Hirschmann, seriously diabetic, was arrested on 10th November. The Gestapo officer who came for him told him that he should take some supplies with him. Three days later two SS men appeared at his home and asked his wife whether her husband should be cremated or buried as he had died. Herr A. was arrested immediately and following intervention five days later was released from Sachsenhausen. His nerves at breaking point, extremely upset, he denied reports, said only that the arrested men were taken to Sachsenhausen immediately and initially had to stand for twelve hours without anything to eat or being allowed to relieve themselves.

Those who could not endure it were beaten. The worst are the mental tortures. A major is in charge of the camp. He returned from a car journey to Berlin. 100 Jews (in this camp are also the rabbis from Berlin Dr. Swarsensky, Dr. van der Zyl, Dr. Jospe) were commandeered and had to stand by the gate, 50 on either side, and greet the returning major with the chorus, "Tonight did the Herr Major have a good..." (a most vulgar expression for being with a woman). Untrue! Reichmann [handwritten comment]

The people, except for a few exceptions who admit they are pleased about the events, are not only not in agreement, but I know from my own experience that Christians have said that they are ashamed to be German. It happened to me that when I was walking down the road with my little daughter who looks very Jewish, I was spoken to by a young lady: "The final chapter has not yet been written."

The worst camp is Buchenwald, in which young lads are in charge, the Vienna SS.

It has been announced that the *Kulturbund* in the Reich should perform again, without one knowing where, for what means and in front of whom.

B. 88 28th November 1938

In Frankfurt am Main Dr. Bernhard Rosenthal, head of the Gynae-cology Department of the Jewish Hospital in Gagernstraße, was taken away during the night of 9th to 10th November. He refused to abandon his patients who would be without any medical care. However, he had to go despite this. Under the pretence of having to get changed he poisoned himself in the neighbouring room.

According to rumours, which however have not been confirmed, his wife is also said to have taken her own life.

B. 89 29th November 1938

In the concentration camp ... on ... the manufacturer of cigar boxes, Hermann Hammerschlag from Gießen, has died. The death was notified to his family by a police officer who stated that H. had died of pneumonia.

B. 90 29th November 1938

On the Kleve-Cologne train I sat opposite an SS man in full uniform. He appeared to be a senior party functionary; on his uniform he wore three overlapping gold chevrons.

In the course of the conversation he stated that no one could claim there had been a romantic enthusiasm to go to war in September. Self-evidently one had to obey and had to do one's duty, not more.

B. 91 29th November 1938

In Solingen a Jewish gentleman owns a business premises with an assessed value of RM. 120,000.-. A tenant of this building who had first managed to have the rent reduced from RM. 12,000.- to RM. 9,000.-, declared that he wished to purchase the premises at the price of RM. 40,000.-.

If the owner were not to accept that, he would ensure that he went to a concentration camp since his subversive views were well known indeed.

B. 92 29th November 1938

The *Hilfsverein* [*der deutschen Juden;* Aid Association of German Jews] is working again under Herr Hans Jacoby [Jacobi]'s direction.

No longer are there food shortages. The signs in the shops "*An Juden werden keine Lebensmittel verkauft*" [No food will be sold to Jews] have mostly been removed.

The synagogues were closed by the police. The walls are still standing, the windows are charred.

It was reported to us from Cologne that on the night in question from 9th to 10th November the Deputy Rabbi of the *Orthodoxe Gemeinde* [community], Herr G., was phoned at c. half past 12 from *Polizeipräsidium* [police headquarters], Neumarkt, that he should be ready on the street with the keys to the synagogue, he would be collected in ten minutes by the *Überfallkommando* [flying squad]. The *Kommando* then drove him to the synagogue at St. Apern-straße. The *Thorarollen* [Torah scrolls] were collected and taken to the *Polizeipräsidium* under his escort. At half past 2 the devasta-tion of the synagogue happened. – The next morning the Deputy Rabbi was called from the *Polizeipräsidium* again with the request to collect the *Thorarollen* again and to store them in his home. The same measures did not take place at the other synagogues.

It seems that no new arrests occurred in Cologne during the week from 22nd to 29th November.

Unbedenklichkeitsbescheinigungen [clearance certificates] for emigrants have been issued in recent weeks. Passports have been issued to the relatives of people who were sent to concentra-tion camps. A technical difficulty and delay in issuing passports came about because *Anträge* [applications] for issuing passports have to be personally signed. That cannot apply to people who are in concentration camps. *Polizeipräsidium* refused to send such *Anträge* to Dachau for signature. Members of the family who travelled to Dachau with these *Anträge* returned again with the matter unresolved. Emigration can therefore only be continued to its full extent if the persons concerned are released from Dachau after the *Genehmigung* [permit] application from the *Hilfsverein*.

For some families who had notices to quit their homes by the end of November I succeeded in accommodating them with other Jewish families, partly with owner-occupiers living in their own houses, partly tenants renting from Jewish house owners. Nevertheless most homes have notices to quit by the end of March, some at the end of December. Accommodating these people will be very hard particularly as local families have to accommodate the influx of people from the countryside.

Up to now nothing is known about new buildings of urban barracks as ghetto quarters.

The mood of the Jews at this point can be characterised as a certain deadening in consequence of the insane commotion of the first days. Everyone is thinking of nothing but their own emigration without asking what kind of climate or what employment possibilities the land that is finally chosen might offer. The general motto is "Get out of Germany as quickly as possible." Even the oldest people want to leave as fast as possible.

The Jewish shops are boarded up, of course no shop business is happenng.

B. 93 It is reliably reported from Mergentheim that all the Jews from there were taken to Buchenwald.

According to a rumour the Rabbi Dr. Kahn is said to have been mistreated in the most dreadful way. He is said to have been pushed through a window pane and thrown onto the street. Then he was pushed back through the same window pane. A doctor who looked after the bleeding man is said to have been arrested.

In Hilden near Düsseldorf three people are said to have been shot. The Gestapo have impounded the bodies and ordered that the family members could only be informed after burial.

B. 94 29th November 1938

In Cologne by now a further 30 men were released, on average aged between 40 and 45 years. All these gentlemen have signed up to leaving Germany by 29th December 1938. They were released

through a *Gesuch* [petition]. I spoke personally to some of the
released men. The gentlemen came from Dachau.

According to Herr A. no mistreatment happened there.
People there were mostly occupied in marching and gymnastic
exercises. The food was ample and personal insults likewise did
not happen according to the statements of this gentleman. The
Vorgesetzte [supervisor] was the *Stubenälteste* [room elder], a
former Communist who was in charge of all Jewish gentlemen
in a so-called block consisting of four barracks. In the first days
people were walking around in clothing that was much too thin,
since many had been picked up at night when arrested from their
beds and admitted to Dachau in their pyjamas and nightclothes. –
The distance Cologne-Munich takes c. seven hours by fast train. It
cannot be assumed however that this journey took place in the fast
train, hence one can imagine the stresses of such a long journey
in completely inadequate clothing. The accounting of money was
done absolutely correctly according to Herr A.'s statement.

B. 95 29th November 1938

I was in Vienna until 24th November 1938 and thus in a position to provide an overview of the events from the outset of the
Aktion [operation], i.e. from March 1938.

From the following brief description it becomes clear that the
severity of the antisemitic operations ran in waves, and apparently temporarily waned when some other domestic or foreign
political difficulties apart from the Jewish question claimed the
attention of the government or the administration.

The operations were applied with great vehemence directly
after the *Anschluss* – one was continually asked on the street
whether one was Aryan, and on replying in the negative taken
away and involved in so-called *Reibekolonnen* [cleaning gangs]
for washing off slogans from the road embankments etc., which
stemmed from the [Kurt] Schuschnigg vote. No consideration
was given for women's clothing, they too had to kneel on the street
and wash with very caustic bleach – an acquaintance of my wife
sustained such a serious injury to her knee from it that the flesh

on the bones came off and after threee months the wound is still clearly visible. Even older ladies were taken and used in groups with others for every conceivable services to the SA e.g. as "ball boys" for tennis. A friend of my wife's was taken to a villa to clean it and was initially led to an apparently valuable vase that she had to dust. When she then used the dusting rag, the vase in question, which was seemingly broken, fell apart whereupon the SA people demanded a written admission that she had broken the vase and damage compensation, whereby she was threatened with rape. Some of my acquaintances who are absolutely reliable, amongst them a young man of 25, had their mouths smeared with shoe cream and ink poured in their mouths. Lorries are continually driven past cafés and take Jews away in large numbers, using them for *Reiben* [cleaning] or shoe-cleaning or some such work.

14 to 15-year-old *Hitler-jugend* [Hitler Youth] with weapons entered clothes shops and commandeered suits. Überfallkommandos [flying squads] incessantly trundled through the streets, rarely intervening to help Jews. The Vienna SA behaved worst of all whereas the German military were comparatively restrained and to some extent disapproved of the Vienna SA's approach.

The poster *"Arier, kauft nicht bei Juden"* [Aryans, do not buy from Jews] disappeared on March 25th for some time.

In April above all on Saturdays *Reibekolonne* of Jews were formed and marches organised on which signboards had to be worn by Jews with the inscription *"Nur ein Schwein kauft bei Juden ein"* [Only a pig buys from Jews] and by Catholics with the inscription *"Jesuitisches Schwein"* [Jesuit pig]. In this way so-called carnival processions were organised, which moved through the main avenue of the Prater and ended with the Jews having to amuse crowds by dancing, jumping and crawling in groups.

Rabbis and *Synagogenvorstände* [synagogue board members] had to sweep streets wearing *tallit* [prayer shawl] and top hat, the Horst Wessel song was played on the organ of the Jewish *Gemeinde* [community]'s synagogue. Jewish women with make up had their faces smeared with chlorine and were mistreated, dirndl dresses were stripped off them.

At shoeshop A., antisemitic caricatures were painted on the

shop window display – A. had to pay the "artist" for his work, and later also for its removal.

When Hitler visited, leaflets were apparently distributed by toadies with the wording, "Jews of Vienna, do not worry, Hitler will not leave Vienna alive." In Taborstraße where many Jews live, all windows were occupied by SS during the entry march, Jews had to remain in the rear rooms of homes. Then Hitler left suddenly during the night, and from the *Nordbahnhof* [north railway station] from where trains go to Czechoslovakia, and somewhere on the trip was diverted. Apparently this diversion took place so as to keep the location of his departure secret.

In May [Josef] Bürckel declared that he alone was taking charge of the resolution of the Jewish question. An alleviation was expected. Yet this did not come about, on the contrary in May and June such a large wave of arrests was applied that it was dangerous for Jews to be out on the streets.

At weddings the service was violated because on leaving the Lord's house, the young husband was arrested and taken to Dachau.

In July a quieter period set in, there were no "*Reiben*" and no arrests, only shops were harassed. In Baden bei Wien exceedingly many Jews were there on summer holiday, albeit they had to pay double the usual *Kurtaxe* [spa visitor's tax], above all very many young married couples, since everyone feared complications in marriages. One was able to go swimming unhindered.

The parks were gradually closed to Jews. Posters with skull and crossbones were fixed at the entrance by the municipal authorities.

During August in general people still went to cafés and cinemas, and in September it appeared as if the Jewish question had been forgotten, even swastikas disappeared. Only at the end of the month did the Sudeten Germans bring fresh unrest and continued the old harassments, supported by the press who at the beginning of October accused Jews of being warmongers. Now it became even worse, individuals were now threatened over the telephone with pogroms, villa owners thrashed and shot in *Laubhütten* [Succoth booths]. In synagogues the glass panes were smashed, rabbis mistreated, runner carpets made from *Thora-rollen* [Torah scrolls].

Inflammatory articles appeared in *Das Schwarze Korps* [The Black Corps; SS newspaper] on the back of the Antwerp incident [see press reports of an alleged attack upon some German passengers from the steamer Cordilleras on 26 October 1938 who were taking photographs in the Jewish district] and unleashed a new wave of arrests especially of Polish Jews. Tenants received 14-day notices to quit, Jews were accused of the attack on the Archbishop's Palace [on 8th October by the *Hitler-jugend* [Hitler Youth]], and baited in the press and also by Bürckel. Finally it became so bad that one no longer dared to go onto the streets.

In November more SA men showed up at our home and took away all money and jewellery and ordered me and my father to go to the *Ortsgruppe* [local group] at half past 1. When we came in there was a pile of silver and other pieces of jewellery although we could keep it until I had emigrated, i.e. some 14 days. I then went home and found out that a nearby *Tempel* [synagogue] had been blown up. My father never returned home, since then I have heard nothing more from him. Whilst waiting at the *Ortsgruppe* the arrivals, often 70-year-old people, were obliged to play childish games such as "Who of us wants to go to Dachau". At the school an acquaintance of ours hanged himself, many remained missing. Arrests took place randomly, in one family eight were arrested. The street was closed off by the SA whilst the synagogue was set on fire, and it raged in the interior of the synagogue. Women and children were also taken with the arrested on lorries that drove around all the time. Lawyers and doctors were seized in groups, had to work in these groups, were thrashed and had to sleep on coats since nothing else was available. Many were sent to the labour camp at Gänserndorf, very many to the quarry at Mauthausen.

On the morning of 24th November I myself travelled with my wife and succeeded in reaching the Netherlands after many commotions, supported above all by the Jewish *Comité* in Zevenaar. I also want to note that both my grandmothers had to leave their homes which were sealed.

B. 96 29th November 1938

I am head of the Jewish sporting, particularly swimming, organisation in A. At the beginning of June I was arrested one day and had to report every fourteen days. During this time many difficulties were made for me, because one of our athletes had kissed the hand of an Aryan lady, and as a result was prosecuted for attempted *Rassenschande* [racial defilement].

I was not arrested in November.

In A. only a few homes but all of the shops were destroyed. Every evening around 10th November large contingents of Jews, with 30 SA men at the head and 30 men from an SS division, were transported off in long trains. Until Sunday there were random arrests, according to my estimation 3 to 4,000 Jews. Whoever still dared to go out into the street at all walked with his eyes down in fear. From anxiety, many slept in other people's homes, but were even caught and arrested there. The villa of a spirit manufacturer B. was completely wrecked. Rabbis Hofmann and Lewin were arrested. Jews with visas were gradually released from the camp, but often so late that e.g. 63-year-old Herr C. could no longer reach his ship in time. During the first few days the *Gemeinde-verwaltung* [community administration] was not active; likewise for weeks practising any sport was impossible, although quite a lot of young people are still there.

It was credibly told to me that in Buchenwald it was not the work that was oppressive but the eternal bullying and the water shortage.

On release the prisoners had to undertake to disappear from Germany by 28th December.

There were numerous suicides during this time, as for example that of the proprietor of the large clothing business Xentaver.

B. 97 27th November 1938

Rabbi Frank in Worms has been arrested.

In addition it has been reported to the reporter by an eyewitness from Munich, that Rabbi Dr. Ehrentreu was subjected to life-threatening mistreatment before his imprisonment.

B. 98 30th November 1938

I spent five days from Thursday 10th November in the Sachsenhausen concentration camp, and can only say that the report given about Buchenwald in *Das Neue Tagebuch* [The New Journal] tallies exactly with my experiences except for the way the day was organised. We merely got up a bit later, but had to work in the same way, hauling rocks, shovelling sand and carrying bags of cement. We also had to drink cement water, which was particularly awful. The team of supervisors were all young men under 22 years of age, individual *Scharführer* [sergeants] under 25. We were left standing for hours, which was particularly hard for the elderly amongst us because we were also forbidden to relieve ourselves, often for six to ten hours. As a result I saw a 72-year-old lawyer from A. collapse next to me from these physical torments.

On the first day 60 lorries with c. 1,800 men arrived with us and were greeted at the camp by a crowd of grinning criminal faces, who immediately flung the crudest antisemitic swearwords and unrestrained mistreatment, particularly at the elderly. Then it was at the double to the barracks, which had been completely newly built; in our barrack were something over 150 men – the space was about 180 sq. m. large – so we lay crammed closely together.

We had to sew Mogen Dovids [Stars of David] onto our jackets ourselves. The food was not bad for someone who was used to soldiers' fare in the field. Old convicts were allocated to us as *Vorarbeiter* [foremen], who treated us much more fairly compared to the SA and SS men. Life was absolutely unbearable for older intellectual workers such as judges, lawyers and doctors, for whom the teams of guards particularly had it in.

B. 99 29th November 1938

My emigration is all prepared; when I returned to our home at 11 o'clock in the morning on Thursday 10th November from a trip into the town, we discovered an SS man at the door, formerly a representative of my firm, who said to us that we were not allowed to leave our home.

Shortly afterwards six men appeared, SS and SA in uniform, *Kriminalpolizei* [criminal investigation police] in plain clothes, who announced that we were under arrest, and then we were taken under escort by three men, SS, SA and a *Sturmhauptführer* [captain] on foot through the main roads of the town to the *Rathaus* [town hall]. There was nothing to be seen of "*Volkswut*" [people's rage], on the contrary people frequently greeted us. Already at the *Rathaus* were several people who had been arrested; in total c. 35 men had been arrested.

Statements were made, braces and ties were taken from us, and we were locked in a cell, twelve men together. After an hour eight men were called out. In front of the *Rathaus* stood a lorry on which were the *Thorarollen* [Torah scrolls], prayer books and valuables from the synagogue, which had to be unloaded by the eight men and taken into one of the *Kriminalpolizei's* rooms.

Then they were led back into their cell. The treatment was reasonable, if also rough, nothing happened, we received food, plank beds, blankets and straw mattresses. On the third day we also went outside for half an hour, physical exercise.

The car was impounded. On Thursday afternoon the building was searched by eight men, amongst them a former bookkeeper of the firm. Unimportant things were taken away, dishes were broken, the grand piano was chopped up with an axe. On Friday morning a *Polizeihauptmann* [police captain] inspected the home with an entourage of *Kriminalbeamten* [detectives].

The rabbi gave himself up.—The interior of the synagogue was destroyed but not set on fire, the equipment was thrown through the window. See article in "*A. Tageblatt*" [A. Daily Paper] from 10th to 13th November about these events.

No arrests were made during the night, no violence is known of, three to four homes were wrecked, amongst them that of Herr B. was completely destroyed, even the sockets were ripped from the walls.

We were released at noon on Sunday and departed immediately with our *Entlassungsschein* [certificate of release]. Before Monday all men under 20 and over 60 were released, the rest were transported away.

B. 100 Several Jews, reporter amongst them, were in the Pestalozzistraße synagogue in Berlin-Charlottenburg on Thursday
10th November when young lads in plain clothes, but clearly
recognisable as SS or SA, especially as they spoke about their
"*Formationen*" [units], forced their way in, grabbed hold of four
men and threw them with kicks into the cellar under the synagogue (reporter amongst them). They were beaten frenziedly
with sticks, one man was forced to beat another under the greatest threats, afterwards he was beaten with the stick until it broke.
Reporter was injured on the lip, one other had teeth knocked
out, what else happened in terms of injuries is not known. They
then had to stand for 2½ hours and after that clean the very dirty
cellar and were locked in. When reporter asked a question, a
loaded revolver was held to his forehead: "One more word and
I'll gun you down." Or they said, "Afterwards, we've still got time,
we'll all shoot together."

The leader of the band was undoubtedly an academic of 23 to
24 years of age. One of the men showed a stirring of humanity
when he was alone, "Stay calm, then nothing will happen to you,
you'll soon get out."

After 2½ hours they had to report for duty and were asked
individually what they earned. Then one of the men said, "If you
don't have enough here, it's all the same to me, you must pay RM.
10.-, then in an hour we'll set you free." Reporter offered RM.
15.- if they would soon be set free. Consultation on this, with
the result: "In quarter of an hour." In fact they were set free then
as well. Reporter then learned in a telephone call to his home
that *Kriminalbeamten* [detectives] had already been there to take
him away.

The Pestalozzistraße synagogue and the adjoining soup
kitchen for the impoverished middle classes were completely
destroyed. *Thorarollen* [Torah scrolls], altar cloths, prayer books,
top hats lay around on the street, everything destroyed and
dirtied. Christian children walked about with the hats.

In the town all the Jewish shops have been destroyed. N. Israel
[department store] completely wrecked. On Unter den Linden
the large jewellery shops of Marcus and of Posen, a fur business

in the Hotel Adlon and a gift shop completely destroyed. The crowd flooded through the streets, traffic was controlled by the police. Reporter repeatedly heard antisemitic remarks from the crowd, "What is there to get so excited about, the Jews have always made money, why shouldn't they hand it over to us?" and others, but one had the impression that there were SS men in plain clothes creating this atmosphere amongst the general public.

The synagogues in Heidereuthergasse and Münchenerstraße are said to be undamaged. According to a rumour Rabbi Dr. Swarsensky is said to have been set free again.

Reporter then left and stayed next at the border in Emmerich on 11th November. After a body search, during which small items of value disappeared, he was taken with others to a former school building, in which preparations had obviously been made to accept people under arrest, and held there from 6 o'clock in the morning until half past one in the afternoon. The treatment during this was reasonable on the whole.

B. 101 In Dortmund at night Jews were often forced to throw their furniture out of the window and then in nightclothes carry the broken items upstairs again themselves. The *Gemeindehaus* [community house] was totally ruined, all the files of the *Winterhilfe* destroyed, about RM. 1,000.- stolen. Jewish restaurants and cafés are nothing more than piles of rubble. Shops have all been destroyed, goods thrown onto the street.

In Lünen near Dortmund the mobs broke into the house of a 60-year-old Jew named Bruch and bellowing "Isaac" shot him down. His wife fled into the adjoining room, what happened to her is not known. The gas pipe to the oven was ripped out of the wall so that gas could flow out freely. In the house opposite an old man lay in bed. Before he could flee he was shot in the stomach through a blanket and died after four hours.

In Dortmund all men aged 16 to 60 were arrested, those not arrested had to turn themselves in. They were all taken to Sachsenhausen.

The reporter fled to Cologne and after spending two nights in a park fled to the Jewish *Asyl für Altersschwache* [Asylum for frail old people]. The asylum accepted 40 people every day who had been wandering around fearing house searches. Amongst the injured people were:

a 61-year-old man who received such a blow to the head that a splinter of bone penetrated his brain. After an operation on his skull he is laid hopelessly low.

Herr S. from Dortmund arrived in his pyjamas with a minor head injury.

Engineer F. from Dortmund, in whose home everything was smashed to pieces, was chased for 20 minutes while being mistreated. After he was able to flee in his pyjamas in a car to Cologne with a tooth knocked out and concussion sustained from blows to his head with a heavy object, he was accepted in the *Asyl*.

In addition a woman from Duisburg was admitted whose husband was stabbed to death.

B. 102 London, 6th December 1938

Report

Veteran *Prokurist* [company secretary] Winkler of the well-known ladies' wear shop Brill, [Vienna] II., Taborstraße was particularly cruelly treated during his imprisonment which lasted a number of hours. Both of his feet were broken and he is in hospital.

Weiger, former director of the Merkurbank, mentioned in Report no. 1 [B.25], is said to have lost the hearing in one ear due to a blow to his eardrum.

Amongst the countless Viennese Jewish personalities arrested and taken to Dachau on 10th November was the St. Pölten rabbi and former President of the *Verbandes der jüdischen Religions-lehrer an den Wiener Mittelschule* [Association Jewish Teachers of Religion at Secondary Schools in Vienna], Prof. Dr. Manfred Papo, who was "persona grata" in the *Wiener Stadtschulrat* [Vienna city school board] during the [Kurt] Schuschnigg era. He was arrested although he had an affidavit and could prove that he had a post with a New York Jewish *Gemeinde* [community].

On Friday the 11th November 200 Jewish funerals are said to have taken place at the *Wiener Zentralfriedhof* [Vienna Central Cemetery].

Reporter: Oskar Hirschfeld, London

B. 103 Dear Hans,

Only through Robert J. did I learn that you were at Walter's, because I did not set eyes on your visiting card in the whirlwind of my move. I also owe a letter to dear Annie who will certainly worry as long as she has no news. The relocation of my parents and Emil claimed all our time and nerves, and we are still by no means finished with that. All five of mother's relatives were ill, thank God they are well again. At present I am living at Irene's although that will probably not be for long since she may be leaving her home too. The parents have a courtyard flat, and a very nice lady with her son and another bachelor live with them. Our prospects have been very poor although we hope nevertheless to obtain a position in England. We do not know what we will start with Hugo since he has to remain here alone. If he had an affidavit then he could also travel to England until his departure. Unfortunately all of our imploring begging letters have been in vain. Nevertheless we cannot allow ourselves to abandon hope. Yesterday *Tante* [Aunt] Sophie sent RM. 25.- to us. Mother wept a great deal about this first pittance although it came as a divine inervention! I was just about to start an English waitress course but had to break off from it since my nerves have deserted me. I no longer live at home, in my flat.– I own my green sports dress with blouse and cardigan, a brown hat and shoes of the same colour and a winter coat. Dear Hans, do you think that is enough?

When you go to Walter's again, I implore you to visit André R. too and to sort out the disagreements. In case we are lucky and obtain a position we shall travel Vienna-Ostend, and I believe that we shall be able to make a stop somewhere where we can visit you, or you could come to Ostend where we can talk about everything else. It would be best if you could take André's worries off him. When we think of the parents, we could weep constantly. Papa is almost deaf and half senile and Mama cries all night when she thinks that Papa cannot hear it. She looks pitiable. My regards to Irene. In case your answer does arrive it will be forwarded to us by the post. Dr.[sic] comes today for the sale of their furniture. The packing will soon be over. God is with us. The letter is also for dear Mizzi of course.

I close, my nerves fail.

Write soon,

Your N.

B. 104 I wish to describe the following recent events in Germany which I myself experienced on the night of 9th to 10th November.

At around midnight my telephone rang, a gentleman from K. announced himself and begged me to take him in as something terrible had happened, and asked whether he could come at once. Of course I agreed to this, and this gentleman came to me dreadfully agitated, without hat, without coat, pale, and described to me the following occurrence:

He was sitting in a Jewish café when a gang of young uniformed SA men stormed into the café holding raised revolvers and cried, "*Rache für Paris!*" [Revenge for Paris] He heard a shot and at the same moment the entire café was smashed to pieces, during which this gentleman was able to escape. I add that in the meantime the owner of the café has died from his injuries. It was absolutely ghastly to observe this. He ran to the Königsallee (main street of Düsseldorf) where he saw that the window pane of a Jewish fashion house was being smashed in. He heard the people cry, "*Hängt die Juden an die Bäume!*" [Hang the Jews on the trees]

This gentleman stayed with me for a short time. Naturally I invited him to stay the night in my flat but he wanted to go home. I gave him money and a coat and did not believe that the homes would be affected too, yet hardly had this man gone when

I heard a dreadful rattling and racket in the neighbouring house. I ran to the window and heard a gang of young men already on the street there as well, saying, "So now in this house and to the families." I heard that they also wanted to come to me, quickly locked the door of my flat, my bedroom door, fetched my sleeping boy from his bed, since I was alone with him, and locked myself in the bathroom. Since two other Jewish familes live in my house, when I heard the same dreadful battering and screaming below, I assumed that the people too were being atta-cked, then the same thing happened on the same floor next to me, and a short time afterwards my flat door was also smashed in and c. 20 young people stormed in, immediately wrecked my whole flat with hatchets and pickaxes. The glass panes were smashed, the furniture squashed, everything broken to pieces, the pictures cut up, the backs and seats of the furniture chopped, the table top smashed to pieces, in short everything wrecked, and at the end all the furniture thrown in a pile. When these people had left the flat so as to continue their work of destruction in the neighbouring houses, I emerged from the bathroom with my boy and sought the other occupants of the house. A gentleman in the same house had been beaten about the head with a rubber truncheon when he had been sent upstairs. Nothing was left for these people either.

We were sent upstairs a short time later, and private indi-viduals arrived who began to plunder the flats and to steal. They dragged the genuine carpets out. They gathered the men's clothing, women's clothing, linen, silver, in brief whatever they could obtain was carried out of the flat. I assume that this did not take place everywhere, but report in this case only from us in this house. Whatever was still intact was destroyed by these people, and above all they looked for things which they could make use of. In the morning we were told we were not allowed into our flat, it was no longer our flat. I was not even allowed to get a suit for the child. The police, whom we had informed, came and said we must be allowed into the flat, yet the caretaker demanded vacating by 11 o'clock, i.e. we could only take with us baggage we had packed ourselves with our personal effects, which first of all had to be searched for from beneath the debris, of course. The caretaker was himself present with a rubber truncheon and did not permit the removal of my own spoons and forks, commenting that these were not personal, took them away from me, gave them to the caretaker's wife to take away. Nevertheless, later an order must have been issued according to which we did have to be allowed into the flat. (I would not have known where I ought to have gone since the same thing had happened to everyone, while the Jewish cafés had all been smashed up too and had suffered the same fate.) At midday the caretaker's wife came and said that we should go downstairs and showed us various things in the cellar, asking whether they belonged to us. We were allowed to take one or two things with us, whereas some had disappeared. There was not much to take. In this way one tried to save one's clothes and linen – so far as they were there. The coats that hung in our wardrobes, jackets and hats were so badly cut up that it was not worth taking them, while some female clothing had been completely smeared with men's pomade. Various items of value including jewellery had still disappeared although I got my wedding ring back. When I asked about my wedding ring and my watch, the caretaker's wife knew exactly where the ring had been in the cupboard, and I can only emphasise that I myself had seen the people in my flat when I had gone down in order to see what was happening in my flat, and was astonished to observe the landlord with the caretaker's people in my flat as well as people who who lived in adjoining buildings and whom I knew by sight, how they opened my handbag and also inspected everything in the flat. The landlord put back the sideboard which had been pushed over, had the carpets put in place and had my silver and other objects brought in, which I saw with my own eyes. I saw a pile of suits lying on the stairs as well as my suitcases all ready for my departure, which was to take place on the following day, with the woollen blankets for the beds and all possibly plundered items. I myself left the flat as soon as possible since I was able to save the furniture but nothing more. Moreover I had to deposit an amount for repairs in the flat, for smashed glass panes and doors as well as windows that had been broken, otherwise I would not have been allowed out. It was said that we had been treated very mercifully (in this residential district). In other districts furniture had been thrown out of the windows onto the street. When I went to my laundry to collect my things such as tablecloths, underwear and bed linen, this laundry, situated right at the back in a yard and hard to find even for me, had been destroyed. I was told that the laundry had been thrown into the yard and burnt, and this happened with linen items too, which can hardly be obtained in Germany. The business of these poor people was also completely ruined. At friends of mine who shared the same fate the entire house was likewise completely destroyed. The more expensive pictures had been ripped to pieces. To finish, all the taps were fully turned on so that everything was running with water, whilst the mains tap had been wrenched out before they left so that the water could not be turned off. A telephone connection with other people was difficult to obtain as most of the telephone equipment had been destroyed. Most men were arrested whereas the others wandered around outside so as to avoid being taken prisoner. The banks were blocked so in the first days one could not have access to one's money. Only the walls of the synagogues are standing whilst the Jewish school was also burned out. Whole pianos and furniture were thrown onto the street as well as the linen and clothes of the people who had been transported away. Men who were outside were grabbed on the streets, taken to the police prison where they were brought with 21 people to a small cell with six or eight beds while others were transported to a concentration camp.

People did not dare to go onto the street. Those who had to obtain something took a taxi – where possible. Occupancy of most flats was terminated with immediate effect. One conversed only in whispers, walked on tiptoes, flats were searched to see that nobody was being sheltered.

At present the priority is for people to escape with their lives and to get them out of hell as soon as possible. Everyone has the duty to help as quickly as they can and to bring people out.

B. 105 A Swiss report about a journey to Germany from November 1938

When somebody goes on a journey..., then it is generally expected that one only has something pleasant to relate. In my case it is sadly the opposite since I had to decide on going to Germany in response to an SOS call from my relatives there.

So with a heavy heart my father and I travelled into the unknown without suspecting what awaited us. My relatives, two women aged over 60, have lived in the Saar area since their childhood in a town of c. 10,000 inhabitants. It was already getting dark when we arrived at our destination and were astonished to discover such enormous bustle in this small town.

On reaching the house of my relatives, we first saw that everything was in darkness so that I already dreaded the worst. The shutters were closed although provisionally newly nailed with some planks, as was the door to the house, where the entire panel was missing. My aunt opened the door at our knocking, and on looking closely we could ascertain to our pleasure that nothing physical had been done to her. But what chaos awaited us in the interior of the house. The corridor with glass and wood splinters, shattered porcelain, slashed pictures and photographs, dirt, stones... exactly as if on a rubbish heap. The same picture in the kitchen, living- and bedroom.

At this point a short résumé, how this all played out: on said Thursday evening at about 8 o'clock somebody demanded entry to the home. One of my aunts opened the door and in front of her stood an almost two-metre tall SA man, who stated, "So, comrades, let's get on with it." Armed with picks, hammers, axes, logs and other heavy objects the horde, 50 to 60 people strong, pressed into the house, amongst them some girls and school children, threw cupboards, tables, chairs to the floor. They hit out with full force and anything the mob got hold of was smashed to pieces. As if by a miracle, two beds and a cupboard were spared, which in my opinion can be attributed to so many people in the house quite simply getting in each other's way. All food such as eggs, bottled fruit, jams was used for the purposes of thoroughly smearing the clothes. Both my aunts fled from the house completely broken by the spectacle, and with the help of the police reached police headquarters where they gave themselves up into *Schutzhaft* [protective custody] with other Jewish women. They spent the night there where they had the opportunity to sleep and the next morning were also given breakfast. At around 11 o'clock in the morning they were sent home with the information that nothing more would happen and that the house would be watched by the police overnight. In the meantime the windows and doors to the house had been temporarily patched up through the police, i.e. nailed up with planks. The few men who still live in the town were arrested and taken away to an unspecified destination. The synagogue was completely burned down, walls and roof still standing, the marvellous glass windows are smashed, the cemetery completely destroyed because the gravestones were ripped out of the earth and smashed up.

My father and I spent two full days working so as to recreate any sort of order at all, and one finds it hardly credible that such vandalism can exist in the so-called cultured Third Reich. My aunts were only able to stay in the kitchen during the first four days because they could have absolutely no heating as the pipes had been wrecked. They did not dare to go to bed for fear that the cruel game would start again from the beginning.

Now I must add that in this town at the moment c. 5,000 workers employed in building a fortification have to work two shifts of 12 hours. In addition there are another 300 policemen for so-called supervision. The comic aspect of the whole thing is indeed that on the said night the police were not allowed to intervene at all, rather were obliged to observe in silence. We were also assured that this wrecking was not carried out by the local residents but by those workers.

The German government had already begun to assess the value of the houses and land owned by German Jews, and such houses may only be sold to the state. The women were forced to sign a corresponding power of attorney and if they refused they were quite simply deprived of their property. The state pays 60% of the valuation but not in cash, rather the people were forced to sign *Anteilscheine* [share certificates], i.e. they will get to see nothing from that either.

B. 106 "... Whilst I am still waiting for a decision from Australia – as no rejection has arrived until now, a certain hope of a positive decision still persists – the situation here has intensified.

My children, a girl of not yet ten and a half years of age and a boy of not quite nine, constitute a matter of serious concern. One endures new fears daily.

Now I hear and read that in Holland *Hilfscomités* [aid committees] have been formed for Jewish refugees, or rather Jewish children from Germany, and a given number are allowed in and accommodated. Thus I allow myself to make the heartfelt plea, whether it would be possible to send my two children to Holland too, who are in the *Quinta* of an upper school, that is, the third preparatory class, until we are accepted, i.e. the fate of my wife and myself has been decided.

As you are involved so actively with this *comité* you will doubtless be able to judge best whether and under what circumstances it would be possible to agree to my request. I am thereby making the thoroughly self-evident assumption that from the standpoint there you also consider that such a sending away is advisable and advantageous for the children.

I ask you to forgive me for bothering you further on this, with the way things are developing and with our fear, and thank you most sincerely for your kindness in advance,

Respectfully yours

B. 107 "... With the polite request, to allow the two boys mentioned below to come here from Germany. They are both children of my niece. Their father does not earn a penny and the family must shortly vacate their home. It is important for them first and foremost to bring the two boys to safety and for them to learn a trade, perhaps here, for the purpose of emigrating onwards, as both have only just started apprenticeships.

In the hope that action can soon be taken as quickly as possible,

Respectfully yours

P.S.   Hans has started to learn carpentry

Peter has started to learn bricklaying

B. 108 "... I hereby ask you to be so good as to ensure that six-year-old Anna X., resident of Cologne, can come to Holland. I am also sending this request to you in the name of her parents. The parents have three children under the age of twelve and inform us that they must vacate their home and seek accommodation with relatives, and also that they do not have enough food, especially as they live strictly kosher. The child is one of our nieces. I declare myself to be emphatically and very willing to take her into my house without payment. It is only a question of temporary residence for the child, as the emigration of the family to the USA is arranged, in so far as it can be reckoned to take place in spring 1939.

I express my sincere thanks to you for your efforts in fighting for a good cause,

Respectfully yours

B. 109 "... As the mother of a ten-year-old boy and a six-year-old girl I find it difficult to ask you today to consider my children for residence in your country. My husband is ill and during the recent events in Germany my husband's sewing machine was thrown from the window on the second floor and all the clothes for fitting were cut up, so that we can no longer give our children the essentials. My acquaintance will gladly provide you with information about us.

I am most obliged to you,

Respectfully yours

B. 110 Metz, 20th November 1938

Dear Herr X.,

I am writing to you in the name of your cousin. She asks me to inform you that all her furniture has been destroyed. I myself travel there often and can only confirm it. Would it not be possible for you to obtain an *Aufenthaltsgenehmigung* [residence permit] in Holland for your relatives until the emigration to America? A stay in Germany is indeed impossible in the long term. One really does not know what is yet to come. I can only assure you that it was horrendous. All the synagogues in Trier have been destroyed, homes wrecked, people mistreated, it is not possible to put it into words...

Yours sincerely,

P.S. Clothes and jewellery have all been stolen.

B. 111 22 November 1938

In connection with what I wrote on the 18th of this month I hereby give you some subsequent information concerning the children for whom the request to stay in Holland was made through me.

7-year-old Ruth A. lives with her mother. Her father has already been abroad for a long time. On the night in question everything of Frau A. was smashed to pieces too. Her furniture, glass and earthenware. In short, nothing is left in the house. This child too, who attended a Jewish school, cannot go there any more; the teacher at the school is seriously ill as a result of the mistreatment that he experienced. Anyway, the school was set on fire. We request temporary residence in the Netherlands for this child. She can live with us at home.

Ursula and Gerd B., both born in A., now living in B., are children of a second cousin of ours. The father was arrested by the Gestapo long ago, and it is not known where he is. Most recently the mother was living with her children with her mother in Z. Her father was owner of the banking house R. there. Herr R. has also gone and everything in his wife's house has been destroyed.

Karl and Else E. are children of Max E. in Z. This man, wife and children were mistreated and their possessions destroyed. The mistreatment happened when they tried to put out the fire at the synagogue, which had been set alight.

B. 112 "The undersigned are asking us for help to save the children of our brother A. from B.

Our brother has been confined in prison in C. since 10th November. Today the wife writes that she was informed that he would only be released if he leaves Germany within three weeks. They are the only Jews living in a small place. Everything of theirs was completely destroyed and he has already spent years without work and in great need as a businessman in this position. We ask you nevertheless to help us to rescue the children.

We are taking the 11-year-old girl Anni A. permanently. The boy Karl A., 17 years old, has still not learned anything to date, however we ask for a place in an *Arbeitscamp* [work training camp], so that the boy is not completely useless. Our brother is blameless, was a front-line soldier during the World War.

Please help, the emergency here is great and only immediate help can save the children.

Respectfully yours…

B. 113 Copy of a card from Mannheim:

"Dear boy, we have finally received our visa for the USA. We can now save up for the costs of shipping our furniture, and even packing the glass and china no longer gives us any concern. Therefore everything is being resolved in an unforeseen way.

With best wishes…"
15th Nov. 1938

B. 114 23rd November 1938

Duisburg: From a report just arriving here can be inferred:
In this city (numbering c. 440,000 residents) there has been particularly brutal rioting. The "spontaneous" events took place

late at night. Noteworthy that the murderous rabble did not consist of locals. The perpetrators, mostly youths in their early 20s, may very well have come from Dortmund, in order to exercise "spontaneous vengeance" – in the city situated over 60 kms away. In north-west Germany this tactic of exchanging SA etc. appears to have been quite general: Dortmunders to Duisburg, Düsseldorfers to Wuppertal and Essen etc.; on the one hand to let no feelings of sympathy arise in case the operation should by chance be directed against personal acquaintances, on the other hand to avoid the identification of the perpetrators by the victims. According to consistent reports the mob was strongly under the influence of alcohol. Either the gangs became drunk beforehand, therefore – young lads famously react particularly quickly to the consumption of alcoholic drinks – in order to get them into pogrom mood (e.g. the "anniversary of the march on Munich [Beer Hall Putsch]" offered an external occasion for it) or during a break in the one-hour car journey to the area of operation free beer was donated. All the details of these measures must have been precisely arranged in advance of course, most probably well before the assassination of Herr vom Rath. Aryan eyewitnesses from Duisburg claim that the perpetrators pungently "stank of *Schnapps*". Only in this way can it be explained psychologically that no inhibitions emerged amongst hundreds of young lads about participating in this barbaric mess. To be particularly emphasised: if e.g. the Dortmunders "operated" in Duisburg and in so doing with "German thoroughness" did not forget a single Jewish household, then they must have been in possession of carefully prepared lists of addresses besides however, given the expansion of the urban area (almost 100 square kilometres!), having worked Groß-Duisburg in accordance with precisely divided districts for every pogrom gang.

The details can scarcely be repeated. Not only men but also women and screaming children were mistreated by bearers of Nazi culture and chased outside in their nightclothes. Whatever could be destroyed was ruined. Linen, clothes and suits shredded with the "*Blut und Ehre*" [blood and honour] dagger [of the Hitler Youth], fitted washstands, fitted majolica bathtubs were smashed with hammers, even wall panelling and linoleum flooring was wrecked. All male persons were seized without consideration for age limits (four exceptions are known, amongst them Rabbi N., a true minister, who has always given away his money for the needy down to the last *Pfennig* [penny], yet whose home was also completely destroyed). The "arrested" were first of all taken to the police prison where the treatment was normal. From there all the Jews were taken away on 12th November, destination unknown. Police officers claim that the transports were destined for Dachau. (For those abroad: Duisburg-Dachau distance c. 600 km.) On 22nd November, thus ten days later, the women had still no news where the men were.

Two especially well-furnished homes, one of them a centrally located villa, escaped on 9th/10th November – almost inconceivably; presumably because the absence of the men of the house was known. Home "A." was then subsequently smashed to pieces on 15th November, owner escaped abroad, villa "B." also wrecked on 15th November, owner had returned in the meantime and was seized.

A Jewish *Anwalt* [lawyer] was able to find refuge at the last moment with a Christian family. He "voluntarily" gave himself up for arrest on the following day because the Nazis had threatened his wife that she would be taken from her children and transported away if her husband did not report within 24 hours. A Jewish teacher also voluntarily gave himself up, his father, a frail man in his seventies, was said to have been taken hostage. A Jewish epileptic, 100% war-wounded, was released again.

The emotional state of the women, who were without news of the men for almost two weeks, cannot be described. Complete nervous breakdowns, incurable states of depression. After everything that the people have already suffered in recent years, robbed of income, businesses and all means of subsistence, now their last possession, the residence, the home, the children's legacy, clothing and linen etc. was utterly ruined. Many got into hopeless debt in order to raise the funds for the officially ordered repairs of the windows, heaters, water pipes etc. – For intellectuals (doctors, lawyers etc. too) the whole library was destroyed, including the only opportunity to prepare themselves for employment abroad. (Specialist linguistic works purchased with sacrifices!)

A Jewish scholar in the Aachen area was ordered to go to the Gestapo in Cologne, where artistic and antique artefacts were laid before him for his appraisal – everything coming from Rhineland synagogues, amongst them also *Thorarollen* [Torah scrolls] with the silver ritual objects etc. The objects had been carefully collected, obviously to special order in a certain district. Either the artistic value was recognised and it was desired to conserve them as museum pieces or, more probably, a far-sighted *Gauleiter* [Nazi Party regional leader] is convinced that rich communities outside Germany will purchase these sacred relics, some centuries old, in exchange for foreign currencies. If this case were to arise, only then would it become clear to the Nazis how stupidly they have behaved, and how much foreign currency value of the "*deutschen Volksvermögens*" [German people's wealth] they have destroyed through senseless barbarism, which could have brought in hundreds of thousands of dollars. One billion *Papiermark* [paper Marks; German currency 1914–1924] wrung out of the Jews from domestic assets are in technical financial terms of lesser value, but in accounting terms can only mean that the Reich's internal billion debt remains cut by one single Mark.

From the Hanau/Pforzheim area a reliable eyewitness report exists that the exchange of pogromists referred to above did not take place there, in almost all places the pillaging was done only by local murderous arsonists.

Occasionally reported that older Gestapo officers have even expressed to Jews their displeasure about the pogroms and the behaviour of the youth mobs. In one large mid-Rhineland city the senior Gestapo officer declared to a Jewish applicant who was waiting for an *Auswanderungspass* [emigration passport], "In your place I would not wait for these formalities at all, but rather cross the border illegally as quickly as possible . . .", this in confidence, after he had previously behaved harshly in the presence of other officers.

B. 115 23rd November 1938

If today I turn once again to the *Comité* it is because a very sad letter has been sent to me by my relatives. It concerns the X. family in Z. and two children, Erich aged 17 and Charlotte aged 14. They, who were caused much distress during the earlier excesses and had to leave their home, have now had everything destroyed of the little they had left. According to a note from very respectable Christian people clothes and jewellery have been robbed and stolen.

I am asked to support the two children so that they can come here. I am asking you to help me as quickly as possible. Steps have been taken from America for the family to be able to [go] there, so that the stay here would only be temporary and I will vouch for that.

Further, I am urgently begged by poor young parents in K. on behalf of their only child, two years old, to ask you that this child may come here, through you. Which I would like to do here most particularly.

With respect

B. 116 I cannot report anything of the events in Germany from my own experience, however know the following from a reliable reporter who has a so-called *Grenzschein* [border permit]:

The reporter was in Nuremberg in order to enquire about the fate of his relatives. In that regard in the night from 9th to 10th November 16 men appeared in these relatives' house – the husband is almost 70, the wife over 60 years old – and mistreated the two people and violently drove them out of the house. They were then bandaged by an Aryan doctor and brought by taxi to the Fürth hospital. On the way the car was repeatedly stopped by SS men so that finally policemen got onto the car's running boards in order to protect the patients' transport.

The old gentleman had injuries to his forehead and nose and had to stay in hospital for ten days, the old lady merely had a bruise and was soon able to be released. On their return their home was completely empty. Also at another of the reporter's relatives, Herr A., 30 men appeared and left nothing behind in the home. His house was then seized by the *Arbeitsfront* [Labour Front; Nazi trade union] – he himself fetched from the hospital in order to complete the legal formalities of the transfer of title.

The 50-year-old *Rechtsanwalt* [lawyer] Walter Berlin was considerably mistreated in prison, then however released with the explicit instruction to put Jewish emigration in Nuremberg into operation.

The rabbi Dr. Schönberger, who was released, took himself off to Luxembourg instead of caring for the *Gemeinde* [community].

In Aachen the *Rechtsanwalt* [lawyer] Loewenstein was arrested when he wanted to save the sacred objects from the burning synagogue. Gustav Struch from Aachen, whose health was delicate, died as a result of his imprisonment in Buchenwald. He was in Dachau in the Jewish section.

In Fürth Jews were driven into the theatre, the auditorium darkened and some of those present thrashed on the illuminated stage.

In Aachen only a few homes have been destroyed, essentially only a large and magnificent building which the large towel manufacturer B. had had built near the border.

Of suicides in Nuremberg I am aware of that of the proprietor of the Café Bamberger, secondly of a Herr Saalmann from Fürth, and of Herr Heidenheimer and Herr Otto Metzger, of whom the latter has died in Dachau.

B. 117 (Do not make use of this until the arrival of additions, c. 3–4 weeks.)

2nd December 1938

The 81-year-old Herr Bacharach from Nordhausen was arrested on 11th November and taken to Buchenwald. His relatives tried for over a week to find out more about his whereabouts and what was happening to him; however only on 20th November did they learn about his presence in Buchenwald through a gentleman coming to Holland.

Two *Gesuche* [petitions for release] were then submitted to which no response has been given to date.

The relatives then received the news on Thursday the 24th November that he was accommodated in Block 50 in Buchenwald, and on Friday the information from relatives in Berlin that he died in the camp, and it was from paralysis of the heart. He was then collected by car and buried in Weißensee. The old gentleman was up to three-quarters blind, had a double hernia and suffered from a serious heart condition.

In Nordhausen according to reliable reports all the male Jews over 15 years old have been arrested.

B. 118 30th November 1938

On the night of November 9th/10th at three o'clock in the morning the Jewish household where I was staying as a visitor with my wife was disturbed by a loud ring and when I came to the window I noticed several uniformed SA men jumping over the hedge close by the house. The door was opened by one of the maids and before I could get downstairs some of the glass doors were already beaten in. They did not reply to my question as to what they wanted but proceeded to follow me upstairs smashing whatever breakable objects they could find, starting with chairs whose legs they used for their destructive purposes. Practically all windows, especially to the front of the house (it is a very large and comfortable house) were smashed, electrical fittings, the panes of practically all book cases, the cupboards, etc. Sideboards were overturned face downwards with all their contents, book cases too and a very heavy oak dining table turned upside down on the remains of a sideboard. The whole destruction in the household took only about ten minutes. We and our friends could only repeat our questions as to what they wanted and stood in amazement wondering what would come next. No answer was given to us.

I was able to see clearly a typewritten list of all the names of the regular inhabitants of the house in the hands of the leader of the group, the lettering being the large type which is used for official purposes.

I told them that I was English but it made no impression and I was just told to go back to England. They left the house after the destruction without any explanation having been given.

For three hours afterwards we could hear the smashing and destruction going on in neighbouring houses.

B. 119 I saw a large number of people in Germany, who are actively trying to solve the problem, and so I received quite an insight into the situation.

The problem of the individual is of minor importance in comparison with the plight of the entire Jewish *Gemeinschaft* [community]. The problems of the immediate members of my own family are my own and will have to be solved by me personally at and beyond any financial sacrifice that I can afford. That, however, leaves the distress of the masses that can only be taken care of by those people who can afford to part with hundreds and thousands of dollars without effecting [sic] their mode of living, and fortunately there are quite a few such in the United States.

To inject a personal note and give you an example that you will no doubt believe and appreciate, I want to tell you the following. My own brother was sought by the Gestapo (Nazi police) at his own home. Fortunately, he was out and forewarned. He then went to my mother's into hiding and when they looked for him there he was moved on to some American friends of his. The police looked for him there as well, so he was hounded from place to place like a man who had committed a murder. He then told my mother that he could not stand it any longer and that he was going to give himself up. With the greatest amount of persuasion my mother insisted that he continue to avoid arrest, and after this kept up for another day he had the inevitable breakdown which affected his nerves and his kidneys. One tried to get a doctor but all the Jewish doctors had been arrested themselves and finally a gentile doctor was called in who seemed quite sympath[et]ic, and remarked that the condition my brother was in by then was quite understandable, and that he would have to be taken to a hospital whether he wanted or not. They tried to take him to the General Hospital in A. but after waiting for half an hour admission was refused as they do not treat Jews there. So he finally landed at the Jewish hospital where he is now.

Other men whom I know intimately are similarly hiding in the coal cellars and other places either in their own homes or in other people's, where nobody ever answers any doorbells and never turns on a light, thus pretending that they are not home. Of course these are only isolated cases as the vast majority is in concentration camps. A friend of mine whom I only saw a few weeks ago, a father of six children, was arrested out of bed at three o'clock in the morning, and consider that I only know the stories of those few whose names mean something to me, whereas there are thousands of others in the same misery.

A man in Berlin, not arrested only because he is over 65, was crying bitterly when he told me of the fate of some of the people in the concentration camps. Of course the Germans want the Jews to get out and they are all willing to leave every penny or piece of furniture they own behind, but the difficulty is that every country restricts immigration, that the process is so despairingly slow.

Herr B., being only about 50, has been arrested and is currently at the Oranienburg [Budenwald] concentration camp. Those few who have their emigration papers in order and are therefore able to leave are released by the German authorities. Before leaving the camps however they are made to sign under oath that they will not disclose any of the goings on at the camp. Nevertheless, such men are the source of information. When I told Herr C. that I was going to see Frau B. he told me that actually the life at the camp was dreadful and the sufferings not only comparable to the Middle Ages but as far back as Egypt when our people were made to work with a whip behind them. He asked me not to tell Frau B. as she was under the impression that it was not too bad.

The courage of the women is really incredible, and most admirable. This is demonstrated by Frau D., whose husband is in a concentration camp, and who has a baby two years old and is shortly expecting another one. The two daughters of Herr B., I would say about 16 and 14, were playing the piano and 'cello when we called there. Frau B. was out seeing a man who had just been allowed out of Oranienburg as he had his immigration papers. When she returned she was quite cheerful because her husband had sent her regards and because she was given the impression that her husband was quite well.

The rabbi of Frankfort [Frankfurt am Main] either died or was killed at the camp. A cousin of mine who is there told me that he had received word that his wife's uncle, a man of nearly 65, and a cousin of about 40 had both died at the camp. Fritz Warburg, Felix's brother, met a similar fate.

Children have arrived at the Dutch border and thanks to the efforts of the Dutch committee have found a home in Holland, and England. I was told by an eyewitness that those children were let out of Germany with a noose around their necks, and that you can still see the marks of same. There is a persecution mania in Germany and these people just have to be taken out unless one wants to stand aside while they are either being killed or dying as a consequence of their sufferings. Could you visualise, travelling in the *Queen Mary* or the *Normandie* and seeing a small boat in distress and standing aside idly and watching the spectacle whilst the passengers of the small boat are drowning? It is not sufficient to throw these people lifebelts. The boats have to be let down and everybody has to take a hand.

The burning of synagogues and ruining of shops and breaking of glass windows, quite a lot of which I saw with my own eyes, are coincidental. The latest concoction in Germany, the amendment of the *Abtreibungsparagraph* [abortion paragraph], namely that it is no longer illegal for Jewish women to have abortions because there is no interest in the procreation of the Jewish race, is also merely a joke by comparison with everything else that I have seen and heard.

B. 120 Reporter was in Z. until the beginning of December and can thus report from own observation about the events since the 9th November. On Wednesday evening, the 9th November 1938, as early as 11 o'clock c. 70 SA men forced their way into the

Gemeindehaus [community], struck *Vorsteher* [chairman] A., aged c. 70, and arrested him, destroyed everything that was in the building and chased the administrator, Frau B., aged over 60, with blows from a club into the cellar; all the others present were driven out of the building.

At c. quarter to 2 in the morning c. 30 men in uniform appeared in a one-family house, some of them with black coats. One amongst them was also noticed wearing the insignia of a political leader. As a result of the din from the forced opening of the front door the residents awoke from deep sleep although they had taken a sleeping powder, and saw six to seven people standing in the bedroom who were bellowing loudly, "Are you Jews?" When they answered in the affirmative, they forced them with clubs to get up and dress and chased them out of the house. During the residents' absence they smashed everything to pieces down to the last thing. Cut up pictures and mattresses and destroyed antique oak cupboards, chairs, chandeliers, absolutely everything that was there in the whole house. Frau C. was greeted outside by a jeering crowd of about 20 people, amongst whom were apparently pimps etc., with the constantly repeated shout, "This is what you did to the Sudeten Germans!" Herr and Frau D. then wandered around in the city for hours looking for each other and to ascertain the fate of the others. The man returned to the house first, which was a complete heap of rubble inside, and tried to telephone. Even that was not possible as the telephone had been cut in a professional manner [*nach Filmvorschrift*]. When the husband had rested about half an hour later in a dark corner of the house, SS men appeared and also smashed to pieces the single chandelier that was still undamaged in the house and then, making threats with the riding whip, left the house. The wife drove in a car which someone placed at her disposal, despite the general prohibition against Jews driving, zigzagging here and there until she had the feeling that the air was clear. She then went in and met her husband and stayed with him until the morning dawned, sitting on the ruins of their furniture in the dark. At every step there was a splintering and cracking in the house. It was such a bleak sight that the newspaper man who brought the newspaper in the early morning ran away. An SA man personally known to the husband has said that the order for this pogrom had already been given 14 days earlier, therefore long before the murder of vom Rath; on the Wednesday in question at 7 o'clock the orders were given out and the young people then led to alcohol. The wife states that when she left the house, such a strong smell of alcohol had filled the staircase that she was hardly able to bear it, she is also of the firm belief that ether had been mixed with the alcohol. For up to about three days the couple then stayed in hiding and eventually drove to Holland. We would also like to point out that police were not to be seen during the entire night.

From an absolutely reliable source the reporter also knows the following – in part he has satisfied himself of its accuracy with his own eyes.

In E. the 64-year-old very renowned *Anwalt* [lawyer] F. was arrested and the entire furnishings of his villa were smashed to pieces. Later hundreds of children were led through the house for days by adults, perhaps teachers, apparently to show them in what manner revenge is being taken on the "*Feinden des Volkes*" [enemies of the people]. The daughter of another Jewish *Rechtsanwalt* [lawyer] G. in the same place walked with her young husband through forests and small villages for three days in order to reach safety. A pastor H. of Jewish origin with an Aryan wife was taken to prison, and when another pastor wanted to come to her assistance in her distress, he himself was taken into *Schutzhaft* [protective custody]. A woman had to mop up the splinters of the broken glass and porcelain and sweep the house, was so insulted at the same time that a *Schutz-mann* [policeman] had to intervene for her protection.

Frau C. was able to experience the way this course of action dominated the thoughts of children, even of the smallest, when shortly before her departure she was travelling by tram and heard a child ask its mother, "Is this where the Jews are dying?" One also often heard the comment dropped, "They should have done that already in '33."

On the day of vom Rath's funeral, when Hitler was in Düssel-dorf, the picture of the murderer was hung on the *Gemeindehaus* by a woman. On 1st December numerous *Fachversammlungen* [professional meetings] took place; at all it was declared that all Jews would be lined up against the wall if something similar were to recur. A general ban on visiting restaurants was announced for Düsseldorf on the radio and in addition RM. 500.- offered for every Jew who is captured crossing the border.

In my home town, the wife declared, good-hearted Christians have placed food on the dung-heaps as the food shops were not allowed to sell anything.

In the synagogue all the seats were smashed, the copper roof had already been stripped before. A senior *Richter* [judge] J. was so mistreated that his jaw was broken in two places. An estate agent K. had 14 knife wounds inflicted on him with such expertise that in the view of the doctor in charge this could only have been done by a butcher or doctor. The curator of the *Archäologisches Institut* [Archaeolgical Institute] in Trier and a *Beamter* [official] of the *Orientalisches Seminar* [Oriental seminar] in Bonn collaborated in the pogroms as experts. Even members of the upper classes such as e.g. the *Generaldirektor* [managing director] of a transport business condoned the actions of the mobs, and merely regretted the events because they involved property, although in this case the end justified the means. The *Zerstörungswut* [destructive rage] in the houses went so far that silver spoons were broken, fur coats cut up and after the operation was over stones were still being thrown at the windows by adults and children.

B. 121 I was arrested with my father, aged almost 60, and taken to *Zuchthaus* [special prison] A. by prison van, which took on more and more Jews on the way so that it finally became unbearably crowded. There we first had to stand for one and a half hours after we were greeted by SS men with the words, "*Da ist das Judenpack!*" [There's the Jewish rabble]. Then our interrogation took place during which we were insulted in the most unheard-of way. A somewhat hard-of-hearing fellow prisoner who did not answer a question correctly was poked so hard in his stomach with the sharp edge of a table at which he was being questioned that he slumped down before my eyes; another young man came bleeding to us in the cell after his questioning, two of his teeth were knocked out. We were then forced to stand to attention in the corridor, face to the wall for hours until we were led away. Further new prisoners came on Monday and Tuesday, so that finally we were 82 in areas for 35. Some had to sleep on the ground. When we were first taken into the hall, the SS man commanded, "Under the beds!" No consideration was taken of age, even 60- to 70-year-olds had to crawl under the beds and try to clean the space under the beds however difficult it was for them. Of course we were all addressed with *Du* [familiar form of "you"].

At 6 o'clock we had to rise, at 7 o'clock was *Appell* [roll call]. Anyone who moved was slapped round the face. From Monday onwards marching exercises took place in the yard, alternating with *Appell*. At 6 o'clock we had to go to bed.

A Jewish fellow prisoner who made a comment unasked was given three days *Arrest* [detention] in a dark single cell in which there was merely a *Pritsche* [plank bed] and water and bread. During the entire period of our captivity it was impossible for us to wash ourselves or change our clothing.

I was freed after six days because my *Auswanderungsvisum* [emigration visa] had arrived, my father after eleven days because he had a serious renal colic. On release we had to stand at attention again for four hours, and make a declaration that we would leave Germany by 30.11. On release at the same time it was explained to us that *Halb-Arier* [half-Aryans] brought up as Christians, *Gemeinde* [community] officials, teachers, rabbis etc., war-wounded, fathers of more than three children, owners of businesses with more than eight Aryan employees, and of such businesses the *Arisierung* [Aryanisation] of which would be completed by 1st January, as well as front-line soldiers with decorations, were preferred for release.

My mother had not received any news at all about our whereabouts, so that she was in constant worry and agitation until my return.

B. 122 The number of arrests in Vienna is not assessable, according to reliable information it is said to be at least 25–30,000 people. Elderly people and some of those who can prove immediate departure have meanwhile been released with quite short deadlines for departure; however during the time of their imprisonment they were mostly treated in a very unpleasant way personally. The number of the injured and wounded is said to amount to 1,000 to 1,500 people.

For the purpose of accomplishing the mass arrests even private lorries have been requisitioned. The arrested men came to all the possible buildings, an acquaintance e.g. who was able to extricate himself as the result of an English permit and arrived here yesterday, told that with hundreds of others he came to a stable at the Vienna *Polizeikaserne* [police barracks], and that there they were indeed treated like animals. For six days no young Jewish man was to be seen on the street or in his home or in his shop. They were in hiding in cellars and in attics or in the vicinity of the city. Many a time Aryans who were outraged at the events gave them shelter.

In Graz the entire male Jewish population has been arrested. My last report about the numerous arrests of Jewish doctors [B.25], even those who only recently were accredited as '*jüdische Krankenbehandler*' [licensed to treat Jewish patients], is illustrated by the fact that the *Leiter* [chairman] of the *Kultusgemeinde* [Jewish community] hospital, *Prim[artzt*; chief physician] Borak, was arrested and has only been released after intervention by the *Kultusgemeinde.*

The "visitors" have repeatedly thrown the furnishings of homes and clothes onto the street or into the courtyard and held an "auction", insofar as they did not take them away themselves. – At least 250 suicides are to be recorded, the number of the starving goes into the thousands.

The former President of the *Kultusgemeinde*, Dr. Friedmann, is in Buchenwald, though not in the concentration camp but under *Polizeiarrest* [police detention]. The condition of *Oberbaurat* [senior architect] Stricker in Dachau is said to be very poor. The Vienna Rabbi Dr. Frankfurter, David Frankfurter's uncle, held for almost six months in prison and concentration camp because of this family relationship, has been released. The situation with *Reg. Rat* [*Regierungsrat*; civil servant] Dr. Oppenheim is unchanged.

My information about the ban on preaching by the Vienna rabbis rested on the ambiguous interpretation of a piece of news that the rabbis are not "functioning". This can be understood because they have all been robbed of their office, as apart from the *Seitenstettentempel* all the *Gemeinde-* and *Vereinstempel* [community and society synagogues] in Vienna have been completely destroyed in dynamite bomb attacks.

B. 123   As already mentioned c. 60 places of worship have been rendered unusable. Completely blown up are:

The Hietzinger *Tempel*, the newest and most modern *Tempel* [synagogue of Reform Judaism] in Vienna.

The *Tempel* in Siebenbrunnengasse, Vienna V.

The *Türkischer Tempel* in Zirkusgasse, Vienna II., one of the oldest, certainly however one of the most beautiful Sephardic *Tempel*s in the whole world.

Large fires were recorded at:

Großer Leopoldstädter Tempel, Vienna II., Tempelgasse, the largest *Tempel* of all anywhere in Vienna, where incidentally as reported, an attempt at arson was already made on the night of Yom Kippur.

Pazmaniten-Tempel, Vienna II., a conservative place of worship.

Schiff-Schul, the *Tempel* of the strictly Orthodox Jews of Vienna, which was also already stricken once in October.

The *Seitenstettentempel*, the oldest place of worship in Vienna, next to which the office of the Vienna *Kultusgemeinde* [Jewish community] is situated, was "only" totally wrecked and stripped out. On this occasion numerous Jews had the torn-up *Thorarollen* [Torah scrolls] tied to their backs, they had to put on *kittel*s [ceremonial robes] and *tallit* [Jewish prayer shawls] stolen from the *Tempel* and were chased through the streets of the inner city, the centre of Vienna! with the *lulav* [palm branch] in their hands. In individual *Bezirke* [districts] of Vienna, especially in Leopoldstadt, the "Jewish *Bezirk*", the prayer implements and prayer books were publicly burned and this medieval spectacle rapturously cheered by the crowd. The home of the senior rabbi of Vienna, which is in the house of the *Großer Leopoldstädter Tempel* mentioned above, has been completely wrecked. The ceremonial halls at gates I. and IV. of the Simmering cemetery, the latter only built a few years ago at considerable expense, are

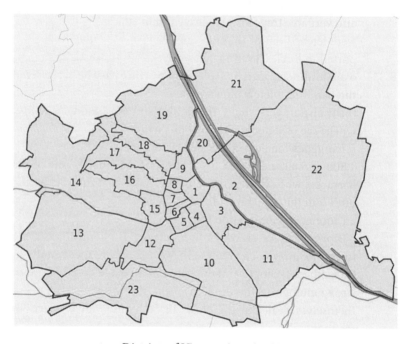

Districts of Vienna, Austria, 2011

KEY

1. *Innere Stadt*	9. *Alsergrund*	17. *Hernals*
2. *Leopoldstadt*	10. *Favoriten*	18. *Währing*
3. *Landstraße*	11. *Simmering*	19. *Döbling*
4. *Wieden*	12. *Meidling*	20. *Brigittenau*
5. *Margareten*	13. *Hietzing*	21. *Floridsdorf*
6. *Mariahilf*	14. *Penzing*	22. *Donaustadt*
7. *Neubau*	15. *Rudolfsheim-8Fünfhaus*	23. *Liesing*
8. *Josefstadt*	16. *Ottakring*	

no longer standing; visiting the cemeteries is only now permitted up to 1 o'clock in the afternoon. – The wife of a senior cantor, whose home was stormed, has gone mad from the horror – incidentally like many fellow sufferers.

Amongst the c. 30,000 arrested people are numerous women and children. As "substitute" for fathers perhaps not found at home, boys from 14–15 years of age were arrested, as were old people of 70 years of age for the sons not found. The arrested people were taken in the period from the night of 9.11 and during the whole day of 10.11 not only from their homes but also veritable traps for people were erected on the streets, people were fetched out of the tram, bus, station etc. They were transported in lorries, even in cattle-trucks, just as one takes pigs or oxen to the slaughterhouse. Already on climbing in, on holding the handrail, their bare fingers were hit with iron rods, during the transport with sticks and iron rods on their bare heads.

The arrested people were assembled *en masse* in the *Notarreste* [emergency detention units] and penned up, there were c. 4,000 to 5,000 people in the stable of the *Polizeikaserne* [police barracks] who spent more than 36 hours standing without food, until individuals who had the good fortune to be able to prove an immediate emigration were released. They were ordered to perform military exercises standing on the manure, they were forced to dirty each other's faces with muck, punch and slap each other's faces etc. If these blows given to each other were not strong enough in the opinion of the *Kommandant*, the guards themselves dealt out the blows in an appropriately intensified manner.

The results of this unheard-of bullying were suicides and mass transports to the hospitals which were overcrowded. Many "suicides" were also committed by those people where weapons were allegedly found during the official investigation.

Some homes were completely stripped out, some utterly wrecked, so that not one armchair remained whole. The Jewish shops, of which the majority were wrecked, have as yet not been reopened. Many homes were sealed and furnishings, clothes, linen etc. were forcibly "sold" or auctioned for a ridiculously cheap sum. In this way e.g. a superbly furnished, three-room home was sold for RM. 270.-.

The tendency was completely clear: take everything away and torture!

B. 124 The 10th November 1938 signifies the outbreak of the "*Volkswut*" [people's rage] in Vienna. This was ordered like everything in the Third Reich, and no evidence is needed that the Viennese would have been completely indifferent to Herr vom Rath. It is only interesting that this "*Volkswut*" e.g. in Danzig [now Pol. Gdańsk] completely forgot to break out punctually and had to break out first on Sunday instead of on Thursday with quite the same measures, only to be also called off 24 hours later.

The police, SS and SA appear to have had instructions to arrest all the Jewish men from 18 to 60 years of age in Floridsdorf, the XXI. *Gemeindebezirk* [district] in Vienna where the atrocities were already particularly severe after the turmoil, women were also arrested. As is well known, the general search for weapons constituted the pretext for the "visits"; it can be assumed with certainty that barely three old bayonets have been found amongst the Vienna Jews. During these house searches all gold, silver, cash were seized, in many cases linen, clothes etc. too. In some *Bezirke* there was looting. In Hietzing, a high-class Viennese *Bezirk* on the periphery of the city, the schoolchildren from 12 to 14 years of age were let out of school in order to wreck Jewish windowpanes and homes.

The "most harmless" punishment for Jews was eviction from home within a few hours. They had to pack clothes, linen, immediately insofar as they were allowed to keep them, and received the ridiculously small "*Schätzungswert*" [estimated value] for the furnishings left behind. (E.g. RM. 270.- was paid for a valuable three-roomed home.) The residents of seized homes, which were sealed, were accommodated with neighbouring Jews if they were not to wander around homeless on the street. (It was stated as follows in the language of the Nazis in the *Neues Wiener Tagblatt* [New Vienna Daily Paper] of 19.11.1938, in the leading article

Judenreine Wirtschaft [Jew-free economy]: "Where Jewish families move after separation from the housing association is up to the discretion of the Jews themselves.")

After the residents had already received many blows during the house searches, on their transport to the assembly points the arrested people were treated in the barbaric way described a number of times. After relatively few hours only those who could produce an immediate *Ausreise* [exit] permit or invalidity or sickness permit were released. If prisoners were not delivered to ordinary police stations they had much to endure, whereas the police are said to have behaved well in most cases, which would confirm that they have not changed in this respect since the experiences gained in the first months of the turmoil.

The inadequate information that the desperate relatives received concerning the whereabouts of their loved ones, now already held captive for 14 days, is a disgrace to civilisation and a sadists' delight. One day almost all received the information that the men were in Dachau – many of them returned home in the afternoon. Thus the family members were reliant on the attempt at personal verification, and one can imagine that in Vienna a regular service has now been set up between the members of individual friendly families, who position themselves at the individual *Arreste* [detention centres], police stations and hospitals, in order to perhaps see their loved ones at their admission. People have been seen with bandages on their heads, hands, arms and legs at such admissions, which enables conclusions to be drawn about their treatment. Family members mostly did not gain entry to the hospitals, which were overcrowded.

In recent days many have been released again, usually elderly people and people with an immediate opportunity to depart. One can deduce much from their silence and their faces.

One can place reports about the personal harassment of innocent people as a slogan at the head of the speech that Dr. Goebbels made on 13.11 (*Eintopfsonntag* ['stew Sunday'; a day when all citizens eat only simple, cheap foodstuffs]) in the *Germania-Festsäle* [Germania Festival Halls] in Berlin, "The German people were filled with an unprecedented outrage; one which incidentally did not turn against persons, only against objects."

Jews' shops have been closed down since the 10th November. On one of these days an attempt undertaken by individuals to reopen them was immediately thwarted by the police. Goods are removed to the extent that they are usable for *Winterhilfe* [*Winterhilfswerk des deutschen Volkes;* Winter Relief for the German People], what is to happen further is still uncertain. Only those shops which are suitable to be Aryanised are not allowed to be robbed.

The reports of various foreign newspapers (two London papers also carried the news) that Jews are forbidden to depart until the settlement of the financial penalties, have not proved to be well-founded. On the other hand German Jews have more than ever been subjected to the most severe bullying at the German borders. In Aachen on the Belgian border the early train is always allowed through without the Jews, who are held back there for four hours for "investigation", which for male emigrants is usually associated with terrible beatings. They are only permitted to travel further on the next train. – At the Dutch border one gentleman had his gold watch, chain, signet ring and typewriter taken away against a *Bestätigung* [receipt], he was even permitted to authorise a named relative to dispose of them [*Verfügungsberechtiger;* person with power of disposal]; whether the latter will ever regain possession of the items is of course a big question.

B. 125 26th November 1938

An NSDAP [Nazi Party] regulation of 13th November was posted in all the hallways according to which it is forbidden for Jews to sell their furniture. Through this order Jews have been robbed of the last opportunity to make the necessary new purchases for their journeys and to pay the costs of the journey. It can be assumed that this order will trigger a new rush on the emigration cash office of the *Kultusgemeinde* [Jewish community], even of those travelling who until recently still would have been in a position to bear the costs of their departure themselves.

The other day relatives of Jews who are being accommodated in the Dachau and Buchenwald concentration camps received a pre-printed form signed by the prisoner in question, the sense of which could be read as the following:

I am well. We have a one-month ban on writing and receiving letters because of the heinous murder by a Jewish criminal. I ask you not to bother the *Kommandantur* [headquarters] with superfluous inquiries as otherwise the ban could be extended.

It is probable that this ban is also valid for those arrested during the riots on 10th and 11th November; this would explain why their desperate relatives have no idea to date about the whereabouts of the prisoners, 14 days after the arrest.

B. 126 28th November 1938

The prayer objects, *tallit* [Jewish prayer shawl], phylacteries, were taken out of a drawer during the house search on 10th November at the home of Herr A., an orthodox Vienna Jew well over 80 years old, thrown through the window onto the street and there set on fire. During the house search itself jewellery, gold objects and cash in large quantities were taken from the lady of the house and the eldest son.

Fritz Roth, arrested on 10th November, was admitted after his imprisonment to an unoccupied monastery in Vienna, Kenyongasse.

The well-known head of a large Vienna bank, Dr. Bruno Siderer, made a suicide attempt from fear of molestation and despair about the events, as a result of which he lost his eyesight.

Another head of a large Vienna bank, formerly one of the leading personalities of the *Wiener Bankverein* [Vienna Bank Association], *Direktor* Ernst Goldschmidt, has been arrested although he is already in his late sixties and seriously ill.

Both bank heads enjoyed great popularity in Vienna and in particular were very intensively involved in Jewish welfare circles.

B. 127 30th November 1938

At the *Arbeitslosenamt* [unemployment office] Jewish young

men who until now have been in receipt of unemployment benefit received notification that they had been contracted for work service to Gänserndorf, a place on the northern train line two hours from Vienna where barracks are being built, which – according to rumours – are intended for Jews evacuated from Vienna. The creation of these barracks would also confirm a communication received by me that an evacuation plan for the Jews of Vienna exists at the Gestapo.

It is confirmed to me from several quarters that the *Feuerwehren* [fire brigades] sent out because of the *Tempel* [synagogue] fires were ordered to protect merely the neighbouring houses from the spread of the blaze, yet not to douse the *Tempel* themselves which were burning fiercely.

In the *Seitenstettentempel*, the oldest *Tempel* of Vienna, next to the office building of the Vienna *Kultusgemeinde* [Jewish community], even days after the 10th November the SA and SS were busy destroying the interior of the *Tempel* so that it is completely bare inside. This demolition could clearly be heard in the office building located next door which is constantly very much used by the public. – The places of worship that have not been burned down are supposedly to be used as warehouses, which would accord with [Josef] Bürckel's announcement in a major speech in Steyr directed "to all the workers in the *Ostmark* [Austria]" on the 16th November, where he declared the following: "That synagogues as the rallying point for all agitation against us had to disappear, goes without saying. Here and there they were – no doubt in memory of the Egyptian grain trader Joseph – converted into grain stores. I consider this to be the most practical solution."

A 70-year-old Vienna rabbi was driven out of his home with his wife. His son-in-law, who was first dismissed, then however reappointed to the management of the factory in which he had been the *Prokurist* [company secretary], was taken to Dachau on 10th November.

The Jewish head of an important Vienna company A. has been imprisoned for a day despite his war wounds – he possesses only one leg, and one arm is crippled –, and must have been particularly badly treated as he had to spend a week in hospital.

At the well-known, formerly Jewish, Vienna department store Gerngroß "*Eintritt Juden verboten*" [entry is forbidden to Jews].

B. 128 ATTENTION

1st December 1938

On Thursday 10th November I went down A. Straße in Z. to my home at midday with my husband. On the way I wanted to get something and went into a delicatessen whilst my husband waited outside. When I came out my husband had disappeared. In the street I heard that in the meantime Gestapo had stopped all passers by with the question, "*Jude oder Nichtjude?*" [Jew or non-Jew?] The Jews were taken away and immediately loaded onto lorries. I also saw that patrols were standing at the tram stops and were waiting for the people getting off. On enquiry I gathered the information from the police that they had nothing to do with the matter. Despite this I went back there and when I said that I was Aryan, obtained the so-called *Arierbeweis* [Aryan permit]. With this I went to the Gestapo where I was sent away by a young lad with the words, "*Wenn Du Schwein Dich mit einem Juden einlässt* [If you get involved with a Jew, you pig], then you have to take the consequences. You'll get a postcard and hear where your husband is." To the question, "Can't I send some clothes to my husband?" I received the reply, "I've said what's happening, if you keep on prattling you'll be put away yourself." After days of fruitless attempts to discover something, I then heard that there was only one way to force through inquiries with the Gestapo, by possessing *Ausreisepapiere* [exit papers] issued by consulates. For this purpose I actually obtained a letter from the Peruvian consul stating that there is nothing to prevent entry under certain circumstances.

Rechtsanwalt [lawyer] Friedländer from Breslau [now Pol. Wrocław] (wife Aryan) disappeared in the same way as the gentleman above; likewise *Rechtsanwalt* Eilenburg. *Justizrat* [state prosecutor] Eilenburg (brother of the *Rechtsanwalt*), wife also Aryan, was arrested too. After several days his wife received a message that on payment of a certain sum she could fetch the urn.

Frau B., whose husband also died in detention, made a scene at the Gestapo in her distress, "And if I am locked up or beaten to death 1,000 times, I have to say it: you are the wickedest monsters there ever were." They threatened her with arrest, but then just threw her out.

B. 129 30th November 1938

On 9th November at 2 o'clock in the morning the synagogue in the Fasanenstraße was on fire, half an hour later came the news that the synagogue in Prinzenstraße was burning. *Oberschammes* [synagogue attendant] A. suffered serious mistreatment, he had to walk barefoot through the shards of glass. The Kottbusser-damm synagogue was spared. A *Schupo* [police] officer forbade entry, people from the street gathered to support him, there was a real battle with beer glasses. – Contrary to another report the Oranienburgerstraße synagogue is said to have been spared, the Münchenerstraße synagogue heavily attacked.

In Sachsenhausen camp convicts are subordinate supervisors.

While the Jewish *Gemeindehaus* [community house] in Berlin was under guard, a dispute about authority emerged between *Arbeitsfront* [Labour Front; National Socialist trade union] and Gestapo; the latter proved to be a guardian angel.

The reports already existing of the destruction of Jewish shops have been confirmed. In *WilmersdorferStraße* all the wares were thrown into the roadway, doused in petrol and set alight. At N[athan] Israel [department store] the wares were thrown in the atrium. – The Jews now have to pay double rates for gas and electricity.

Rumours are doing the rounds that those who do not emigrate very quickly will be held back as hostages until the resolution of the colonial question.

Herr B. was taken from the train in Bentheim. During the body search his gold watch and chain was taken from him. He had to pay RM. 800.- in the *Unterwerfungsverfahren* [submission process] or he would be taken to court there. He provided the money by telegraphic transfer. – A lady who was wearing a not very valuable brooch was supposed to pay RM. 750.-; as she could not obtain the money, she was temporarily detained.

B. 130 Thursday, 10th November 1938

Report

Started at 7 o'clock in the morning, a continual bugle call from the *Feuerwehr* [fire brigade], a commotion amongst the people, what is going on, where is the fire. After an hour everybody knew, the Jewish *Tempel* are burning so that no conspiracies could take place there. The Schmalzhoftempel was diligently bombarded with stones by *HJ*-[*Hitler-Jugend*; Hitler Youth]-lads (white shirts), inside the *Tempel* it was already burning; the fire brigade was also present, who however merely had to protect the neighbouring houses, therefore (as at all *Tempel*) was not itself permitted to extinguish the *Tempel* fire.

Half an hour later:

XIII. Neidlinger Hauptstraße. 30–50 *HJ-Kinder* [Hitler Youth children] armed with iron bars went from Jewish shop to Jewish shop and first chopped up the company signs then tore off the scroll bars with much shouting, and it succeeded, one felt as if one were amongst savages, such shouting rang out, they wanted to say thereby that even children can do it. However, they had obtained long iron bars from their homes for this purpose, as already mentioned. These were already made available on Wednesday evening. In contrast the SS and SA obtained explosives for the *Tempel*. Many people who were watching made the following comments, "How can one let such 13- to 16-year-old lads do that, which will produce grown-up people by other means and dispossess Jewish shops, what will become then of such children when they become men?"

At the same time at Hufelandgasse XII., guardroom, a military vehicle, full of old Jews is being ordered by a only a very young SS man, field uniform, as follows, "Jump down from the vehicle, nothing more will happen than that you could break your feet, but that wouldn't do any harm at all." Then one saw very old men jump down, could hardly stand up again, yet were pushed rapidly into the guardroom by the SS men; the people who saw that shook their heads and one heard quietly say, "Awful!"

Corner of Arndtstraße–Meidlinger Hauptstraße the first shop broken into had already been plundered through the work of the *HJ*, a lorry drove by and men with SA armband stripes loaded up what they could and drove away with it. In the afternoon one already saw SA guards standing in front of the broken-into shop in order to request the people to move on. A few minutes away is the *Turnertempel*, it was burning fiercely until the evening, but the *Caféhaus* [coffee house] owner will not have been very pleased as very many windows of his premises, which is opposite the *Tempel*, are shattered due to the heat. The swastika flag was already flying over the ruins of the *Tempel* some days later, about to build homes or *Kaserne* [barracks], as the signs show. This is already so at the *Storchentempel* as well as at the *Turnertempel*. Today there are no more *Tempel*. Which has now happened in the homes.

Some evidence

Mother, c. 40 years old, with her 9-year-old son just at breakfast, all at once four Party men burst in, drag woman and child into the bathroom (the husband was already taken to Dachau some months earlier), lock them in there, wreck the furnishings of the home – not one object remained spared –, unlocked the bathroom again, took the 9-year-old lad, placed him in the bath, ran cold water onto him, they held the woman, smeared his face with soap and gave him then the soap to eat with the sentence, "*Judenbengel* [Jewish urchin], bite it off!"

He had to do it, earlier they gave the child no peace. The woman's face was smeared with dirt, chased her through the rooms so that she could see the men's rage, took the key to the home from her, sealed it and chased her onto the street with another Jewish party, just as they were, without coats, the child quite wet.

Reporter: Robert Steiner, 38 Rue Bisson, Paris XXe.

B. 131 Report about the pogrom in Frankfurt am Main from 10th–11th November 1938

Eyewitness account

The pogroms suddenly began promptly at 5 o'clock in the night to 10th November. First of all the synagogues were set on fire using petrol. The *Feuerwehren* [fire brigades] restricted themselves to merely protecting the neighbouring buildings. Young men (Jews) were forced to cut the *Thorarollen* [Torah scrolls] into little pieces and burn them. Around half past six in the morning small gangs of five to ten men broke into Jewish homes using force. At first the male members were dragged to the *Polizeirevier* [police station], the people were chased across the street even though they were only wearing a shirt as no time was allowed for them to dress themselves. As I did not look Jewish I managed to get to the city centre. It was about 9 o'clock when c. 50 SA in plain clothes suddenly appeared, some of whom were even known to me, and began to destroy all the Jewish shops according to a list, and where something was useful, they would take it. Then the wholesale shops were visited, destroyed, the fittings and wares were thrown into the street. In part wholesale shops were also destroyed by fire. The police were well represented in terms of numbers, yet in no case intervened. The following day the persecution continued further. Now even uniformed SS were deployed. Home was systematically visited by home according to the list of the NSDAP [Nazi Party] *Ortsgruppenführer* [local group leaders]. First the male members who were still there were taken with them in *Sammeltransporten* [group transports] by the city's buses to the *Festhalle* [large hall for trade fairs]. Then the women were asked about jewellery and gold and afterwards the home was searched. Everything that they found was forfeited in the so-called *Beschlagnahme* [confiscation]. Car owners had the keys and papers taken away and the car was confiscated. The furniture and fixtures and fittings were then destroyed at the discretion of the individual carrying out these measures.

Even the orphanage, where some hundred children were accommodated, was not spared. The children were put out on the street and the furnishings completely destroyed and burned. Even the *Gemeindehaus* [community building] in Fahrgasse was destroyed. The measures reached their climax on *Buß- und Bettag* [Day of Prayer and Repentance]. SS trekked from house to house and searched the homes. All the passers-by on the street had to identify themselves with their racial affiliation. Trams, cars were stopped and the passers-by arrested, in so far as they were Jewish. Consequently this actually succeeded in arresting all Jews of the male gender between 17–65 years of age. As I have stated, these very people were taken on the actual day of arrest to the concentration camps at Buchenwald and Dachau. Only those who could prove they had a real opportunity to emigrate were released, i.e. if their relatives had intervened to that effect with the Gestapo. I must point out that by far the largest proportion of the population did not take part in these violations. According to a statement by an SA man I befriended, SA from Munich were summoned to Frankfurt am Main specifically for this purpose. As the same additionally reported to me, all the pogroms took place by order.

In order to escape arrest and the abominations in the concentration camps, many prominent Jews of the city of Frankfurt am Main have committed suicide. Even Catholic houses and flats were searched for Jews. After the pogroms the Jewish houses and the streets where pogroms had taken place resembled a pile of ruins. Thus, because I was already in the concentration camp and had been granted leave for the purpose of emigrating and I had my emigration already arranged, I was released again after twice being arrested. This information that I give here is only a fraction of what happened in reality. This is in accordance with the true facts.

Reporter: Eugen Wolf, 9 Rue d'Ormesson, Paris

B. 132 STRICTLY CONFIDENTIAL

Herr A., a Frenchman, was employed in X. (Baden) as a teacher of religion.

Without previously having been harassed by the National Socialists in any way, he was himself also the object of persecution on 10th November 1938.

Early in the morning at 6 o'clock he was suddenly awoken by

the Gestapo and ordered to open the door. In his nightclothes he was obliged to open the door onto the corridor, in order not to allow the threat to break down the door to become reality, and already he was surrounded by about 12 to 15 men.

They asked him which nationality he was, at which he proved his identity with his French passport. With the words, "It's good that you are French," they then left his home. A few minutes later two men came back, the police minister [sic] and a plain clothes officer. At their request he showed them his French passport, at which they responded, "You're lucky that you're French. Disappear as fast as you can!" In the meantime a whole band of 25 to 35 men came and demanded entry. The wife, who opened the door, alerted them that the police were already in the room, whereupon the woman was brutally pushed to one side and hurled to the floor by the gangsters. One of the men attacked Herr A. so badly with punches that traces on his face, eyes and arms could still be seen in recent days by the police here.

Without being able to take the barest necessities with him, he then left the small town.

All his Jewish fellow brethren, like him, fled that very same morning.

Reporter: Henri Bloch, Schwetzingen (Baden), Bruchhäuserstr.

B. 133 27th November 1938

We have been informed by a gentleman who comes from Poland that the following synagogues have been completely burned down:

ROSENBERG [now Pol. Susz],

BEUTHEN [now Pol. Bytom],

GLEIWITZ [now Pol. Gliwice],

HINDENBURG [now Pol. Zabrze].

All the Jewish shops have been cleared out and looted. The men are in the concentration camp near Weimar [Buchenwald].

Reporter: unnamed

B. 134 The pogroms in Cologne began on 10th November at 4 o'clock in the morning. The participants were, according to the statements of the Jews living there, SA men in plain clothes. However young people in great numbers also in plain clothes, took part in the pogroms as well. They went through the streets in quite small gangs of c. 10 men. The population did not take part in them at all, only seldom out of curiosity, without approval but shocked expression. The gangs systematically smashed in all the Jewish shop windows and roll bars, fetched lorries onto which the contents of the shops were loaded and taken away, smashed up the furnishings, threw the smashed pieces onto the street and set fire to these frequently and went on.

Other gangs forced their way into the *Tempel* [synagogues], threw the furnishings onto the street and set fire to the *Tempel*.

In Aachen I saw how the Nazis ripped up a Torah in front of one *Tempel* and stuck scraps in their pockets, which they said might bring good luck. In addition they ruined all the pictures and ornaments in the buildings.

Others hauled the Jews out of the houses themselves, even sometimes out of the tram and various premises, mainly men whom they dragged to *Arrestlokale* [detention centres] and sundry *Sammellager* [transit camps], where they were beaten terribly. Dreadful scenes of beating also took place on the street in which even old men and women and children were not spared.

In Cologne for example, dreadful scenes occurred in the side streets off Bahnhofstraße. There and on Zülpicherplatz one saw small pools of blood everywhere. Only a small number of Jews were able to escape the *Aktion* [operation]. Many fled to the outskirts of the city. People with car spent the two nights in the car.

Horrible scenes of beating took place in Aachen in Harscampstraße and its side streets. They led away people with bleeding heads. At the end of Harscampstraße in Aachen is a *Tempel* that the Nazis had set on fire, and afterwards they pelted with burning pieces the Jews they had beaten up.

Reporter: Walter Singer, 8 Cité du Midi, Paris

B. 135 Transcripts of letters from children who travelled from Germany through Holland to England on 1st December 1938.

Frl. F. D., . My dear Fanny,

From this marvellous country, where everything with us is going wonderfully, I am sending you many, many happy birthday kisses. Give my best to all your other colleagues. Irma Lizzy Erna.

Hr. C. Z., .

My dear Peter,

From beautiful Holland your *Mutti* sends you a thousand good wishes. Are you better now? We are very well here. Much love and kisses to Granny and you from your *Mutti*.

Hr. S. L., .

My beloved Parents,

We are being received splendidly in Holland. We were given every kindness, everything that you could think of, as you can imagine. Like princes. So farewell! I am terribly glad. Love and kisses, Jan. Forgive the writing, I am writing on the train on the journey to Rotterdam. Your faithful son Jan.

Hr. D. I., Lübeck.

My dears,

We have safely crossed the border. My suitcase has not been opened. In Oldenzaal we were received splendidly, we were given hot food and soda. Even the press was there, we were photographed. I am writing against the wall, hence the scrawl. At 12 o'clock we travel from the Hook. Much love and kisses Werner. Harry sends much love.

Hr. H. A., Bremen.

My dears,

I am on the way to the Hook of Holland. We have left German soil and in Holland have been received most particularly well, with food and drink, photos etc. We are staying to start with in Harwich in a camp. We are here with children from all over Germany. At all the railway stations we were received enthusiastically. Love and a kiss Bernd.

Hr. B. I., Lübeck.

My dears,

The post is cheap, so I am writing already. The journey was splendid. We were cheerful and jolly. We have also already made acquaintances. The reception in Holland was excellent and the provisions first-rate. Greetings to everyone please, and particularly Helga, who I had almost forgotten. All the provisions are strictly kosher. I have hardly eaten any of my own rations. Now much love and kisses Kurt. Forgive the bad writing.

R. K., Bremen.

Dear *Tanten* [Aunts],

Tonight we are travelling to Harwich. How are you? I hope you are [well] my dears. The reception in Holland [is] indescribable. Chocolate, food. I don't know what the reception in England will be like. I have got from Herr K. a book, an alarm clock, a dictionary, a book about Bremen in four languages. Please forgive my writing, the train is jolting so much. So, much love and kisses to *Tante* Betti, *Tante* Fritze, Ilse, Hugo and Hans. Walter sends much love and kisses.

The R. brothers and sisters, Oldenburg.

My dear brothers and sisters,

We have safely crossed the border. The reception was simply first-rate. The ladies from the community handed out food, French beans and beef. We were given chocolate at another station. Everywhere we were received with hellos. We are all very jolly. Maxi too. What have the dear parents written? Send the card to our dear parents. Love and ten thousand kisses from your loving Giska. All my love Hans. Much love Jan.

Frau A. E., Hamburg.

Dear little Mu,

I am sitting here on the train to Rotterdam. It is really awfully nice so far. We are *only* nice people here, and it is so comradely and nice. The customs stories worked brilliantly. Now we are travelling through Holland at the moment. I cannot describe to you what the people are like. We are received at every station with cries of hurrah and joy and are always sent something else. Sodas, hot food, a bar of chocolate, an apple for each. One simply can't understand it any more. The newspaper sellers and porters and many, many people wave and welcome. We are always being photographed, we are having a good time, do not worry. Herr K. is here on the train. Liesel.

Frl. A. S., Hamburg.

Dear Anneli,

Now a large part is already behind us. We are all happy; the reception is really amazingly friendly. Hot and cold food is served continually. We talk a lot about you and Marga. (At any rate we are of very different opinions about Marga, but are you surprised after the last letter?) I have brought the picture for you today to be developed, it will be sent to you. Your little brother Hans. Dear Anneli, I send all my very best to you from this beautiful country.

Frau M. K., Berlin.

My dear *Mutti*,

I am now writing on the train. We will be there in 25 minutes. Oh, it is marvellous! At the first Dutch station we were awaited by Jewish and other people and were given wonderful food. Helga and I are happy. I could kiss the people here. Just be happy. Hopefully *Pappi* [Daddy] is coming, then my happiness will be complete. Please forgive the writing, it is swaying so badly. A long letter soon. Love and 100,000,000,000 kisses, your delighted Inge. Dear *Mutti*, love and a kiss, your Helga. Letter follows!

Frau A. S., Hamburg.

Dear *Mutti*,

We have done very well here. We are sitting here in a second-class carriage. I have been travelling well so far. Immediately after the border we were given hot food and also sodas as well. At every railway station we were given chocolate and cakes. At the Hook we are supposed to be photographed. I will write again soon. Much love to all. H.

Herr R. S., Berlin.

Dear Papa,

The first part of the journey is already over. In half an hour we will be at the Hook of Holland. At one station behind the border we were given hot food and fizzy lemonade. We were very nicely received at every station. From England I will write you a long letter about the journey. I have also written to the boys of the RWH on the train. Love from me to all our relatives, mainly Peter. Much love and kisses, your son Werner.

Frau E. P., Berlin.

Dear *Mutti* and all my dears,

In half an hour we will be at the final stop, the Hook of Holland, to board the ship. I will write to you straightaway in England. The journey will be wonderful, give everyone my love, follow soon. Much love and kisses, your loving Lielo. Pass on my best to all acquaintances.

Frau M. G., Berlin.

Dear *Mutti*,

I am in Holland. We were received in Bentheim with jubilation. I am very happy. Please forgive the writing because it is swaying so much. We are soon going onto the steamer. What are you all doing? Are you still crying? Please send best wishes to all acquaintances, particularly . . .

Frau G. R., Altona.

Dear *Mutti* and dear *Tante* Olly, *Onkel* [Uncle] Albert and Edgar,

We are now in Holland and I can scarcely describe the way we have been received. There was cabbage with mutton (in Bentheim), then soda. I am travelling with a very nice bunch in the compartment and we are very jolly. To us each Hollander is touching. Have you received the first card that I sent in the Weidenallee? We are almost at the Hook of Holland and travel on from there by ship. Is *Onkel* Fritz already there? In my compartment travelling with us is another very religious boy. We are all happy that everything is behind us. Hopefully it stays this good. I am sending the card to you, because I do not know whether *Mutti* will receive it in the Weidenallee. Much love and kisses to all, with love, your . . . Good *shabbos* [Sabbath].

A. M., Berlin.

My dears,

The journey is very beautiful. In Holland we have had a marvellous reception. We were very well fed, I will write particulars later. We are boarding the ship soon. All of us here have made friends beautifully. I am writing on the train and it is swaying a lot. We are getting off soon. Now it is 8.12 in the evening [and] I am writing to you. The region is incredible. In [a] couple of minutes we will be in Rotterdam. You will soon receive a long report from me to listen to. Now [we have] arrived in Rotterdam and are being snapped for the press. Everything is marvellous. Much love to all. Your . . .

Herr A. P., Berlin.

At this moment the train is stopping in Rotterdam. It is going on to the Hook of Holland now. Then by ship to London! I am happy. Hopefully you too will soon be happy. Love Edmund.

Frau M. St., Berlin.

Dear *Mutti*,

I am letting you know here that I have travelled to Holland

through Bentheim. We have been very well received in Holland and at midday were given vegetables with meat, we also were given something to drink. Card follows. Your son Harri.

A. R., Berlin.

I cannot write very well and clearly as the train is rocking dreadfully. We will soon be in Rotterdam. The reception in Holland was touching. We were taken in a... to the railway station. There were vegetables and then also a roast and lemonade. I write to you...

M. L., Perleberg.

Dear Parents,

Soon we will be in Rotterdam. Then comes Hook of Holland. I have put the watch back one hour. Have met Herr P. and the orphanage on the train. More from England. Much love...

J. L., Hamburg.

Dear Parents and Brothers and Sisters,

We have arrived in Holland, are now travelling on to England. With love and a kiss...

Frau R. M., Hamburg.

Dear little *Mutsch* [Mum]

We have now been over the border for a long time, next station "Rotterdam". In Bentheim we were fed wonderfully, vegetables, meat, soda, fruit, bread, cakes. It was so beautiful I could have cried. We shouted and organised a chant. Simply marvellous. One station after Bentheim we were fed chocolate by people, another din. It is too beautiful to describe. The train jolts damnably! Love and 1,000 kisses your...

E. J. Family, Bremen.

My dear J. family,

I did not have the chance to telephone you as we arrived in Hamburg very late. I spent the night in Hamburg in the hostel with three old ladies, and the ladies laughed and sang so much that I did not sleep all night. This morning we set off and met the people from Berlin in Osnabrück. We have [been] friendly received in Holland, and Frau M. and daughter greeted us. It is quite superb on the journey, we have a great deal of fun, in three hours we are going onto the ship. I would like to say a big thank you again to you, dear Frau J., for everything that I have learned from you. Please forgive me for writing so badly, but the train is swaying a lot. I will write to you again from England. Much love for...

Frau H. G., Lübeck.

Dear *Mutti*,

We are already on the way to Rotterdam. In Holland we have been very well received. At the border we were given a hot midday meal. Otherwise we are very merry and quite jolly, H. sends warm greeting and a kiss. Much love Werner.

Frau H. H., Wilhelmshaven.

Dear *Mutti* and *Opa* [Grandpa],

Now it is evening and many children are writing. We were *wonderfully* received in Holland. We received quite a lot. First there was meat with..., then lemonade, chocolate. In an hour we are going by ship to England. From E. I will write all about it in a letter to you. My writing is very bad. Much love and kisses your Inge.

Herr Dr. M. Z., Hamburg.

Dear Parents,

So far everything has gone very well. Whether I will meet D., I do not know, I do not know whether we are going via The Hague. We are very jolly. Much love Hansl. All my love Elisabeth. We are... fine!

Herr J. W., Berlin-Spandau.

Dear Parents,

Have been well received in Holland. The people are very good. We were given a midday meal and soda from the Dutch.

They are pleased with us. Soon be at the coast. It is 7.30 in the evening. I am writing very badly here. Will write more. It is just a note from me. We are all here. Love your son Horst.

Herr Dr. J., Hamburg – Othmarschen

My dear Parents,

We are already in Holland where we have been delightfully and marvellously looked after. The people behave *touchingly*. We were also photographed. If I receive the newspaper, you will receive a picture. Everything is too beautiful. We think of you a lot. This is just another sign of life which you see shows *how* magnificently things are going for us. Lots and lots of love, 100 kisses your Pitt. We are very jolly and have been singing. My very best Werner.

Frau R. E., Altona

Dear Recha,

We have been well received so far. Everything is in order. The children are happy and jolly. Your little Falck is sweet. Happy birthday and best wishes. All my love, your Toni, Lizzy. All my very best wishes, we are fine, your Erna. Happy birthday, all the best. It is beautiful here. Irma.

Herr K. S., Kloppenburg.

Before boarding the steamer for England. My dear unfortunate people. According to Dutch time it is quarter past 6. You will be astonished that we are writing again already, but we have not stopped being astonished either. Scarcely were we in Holland, the train stopped there and women brought vegetables, and can you imagine how it tasted. That was not all, there was sparkling water, chocolate, baskets full of bread rolls and apples. In every station there are sweets, and all the Dutch are coming with us to the ship. Forgive me for scribbling. At one o'clock tonight we are going onto the ship. Unfortunately you cannot see how well things are with us. In haste your Ruth. Soon going on the sea, so just much love and kisses your loving Hildegard.

Herr A. R., Bunde.

My dears,

We are here in Rotterdam and as we have been given more cards, just want to write to you. Today Thursday at 9.45 we left Hamburg. When we arrived in Oldenzaal we were given vegetables with meat and a drink. You will not believe how that tasted to us. At every station we were given something. We were very pleased. Soon will be going on the sea. Now will end. Much love and kisses, Hildegard.

Herren of the *Paulinenstift* [Pauline Foundation Girls' Orphanage].

My dear Sirs,

We are at the moment on the train right across Holland. At the first Dutch station we were heartily received. Women arrived with huge pots, plates and forks. We were given vegetables with kosher meat, tasted marvellous. At every later station we were given something else, everyone an apple, bread roll and a bar of chocolate. Our watches have already all been changed to Dutch time. Edith's brothers and sisters have already visited us. Your Gerda sends much love for everyone, especially for G. Love and a kiss Oavideljus. It is a good start. Everything is fine. Love Ilse. Much love from Wolff. Love Lilly and Margit, Love Clärchen and Eva.

Frl. E. R., Hamburg.

Dear Fräulein R,

The train is swaying a lot. The Dutch have looked after us so well that straightaway I have already gained a real desire once more to go to England, for I think that it will be like this there too. We have been photographed three times by the press. In Holland there was first-rate food, even meat. We are all first-rate. The journey goes forward very well with musical instruments. Everyone sends much love. Love to everyone. P.S. But all my very best love to you and Ger from your Davicde.

Frau M. Z., Oldenburg.

My dears,

It is 8 o'clock and we [have] just arrived in Rotterdam. It is marvellous. As soon as we were in Holland, we were given hot food and juice. Frau M. from Bremen was also there with her daughter, and she sends you much love. At every station we were given something. We already have lots of friends, girls and boys, who we all met by visiting. Greetings Love to everybody who asks after us. Hans is always going for walks with his friends and is very well-behaved. I already knew his friends from Wilhelminenhöhe. Much love . . .

Israelitisches Waisenhaus [Jewish Orphanage], Hanover.

My dears,

How are you? I am on the way to England. We are nearly at Rotterdam. At midnight we are going on the ship . . . That was an accident, the train went round a bend. I will send my address from England. So once again, sending you all my love from your Fritz.

Frau J. G., Berlin.

My dear *Mutti*,

I am writing to you from Rotterdam. Another half an hour and we are travelling in the ship. We were received *very* kindly in Holland and were given food there. I will shortly write you a detailed letter. I am well and cheerful. Love to everyone from me, *Tante* Erna, Fr., and others and everyone else I know. Kisses from Röschen.

S. B. Family, Frankfurt (Oder).

Dear Parents,

Safely arrived in Holland. G. is very jolly. We are about to go on the ship. In Holland we were given lunch, soda and chocolate. Now all my very very best love and kisses from your L.

M. M. Family, Leipzig.

Have just left Rotterdam, we were terribly nicely received everywhere in Holland, fed in Oldenzaal. Are about 22 children

Ben[t]heim, could not bring photo, because bought from beginning of November, cannot write well as on train, Much love and kisses Edgar. Travelling via Hook of Holland to Harwich (England). Must be quick as we are nearly there.

Herr N., Berlin.

Dear Herr and Frau N.,

Hopefully you are well. When you get this card, I will be in England. Love to everyone, much love, Ursula G.

Frl. M. F., Berlin.

Dear M. and Herr Fr.,

We are coming into Rotterdam at the moment. According to English time it is now 8 o'clock. Onkel Alexander was at the Schlesischer Bahnhof [railway station, now Berlin Ostbahnhof]. Tomorrow morning the ship will dock in England. More soon. Thank you very much for everything and much love from your Edmund. I feel as I have not felt for a long time. Love to Frau G.

Frau Else P., Hamburg.

My dear Else, dear children,

The journey was very beautiful, [we] were received everywhere very attentively. We are nearly in Rotterdam. Herr and Frau K. are very kind and are travelling with us. Much love and kisses your husband and father. Much love to comrades at home.

Frau K. W., Berlin.

Now we are about to change over to the ship, we are already looking forward to the cold sea journey, and when you receive the card, the voyage will already be over. So, dear Mama, no more regrets. In Holland we were received very well. Hot food, lemonade, sweet buns and chocolate, and the attention was excellent, simply superb. More details in the next letter. Things are really superb with me. I must end because I must get dressed for the voyage. I still have almost all of the food. Much love and kisses from Else.

Sent by Herr Flörsheim, Amsterdam

B. 136 The 48-year-old former editor of the *Neue Freie Presse* [New Free Press], [Kurt] Libesny, was arrested on 10th November, held for one day and so badly mistreated with blows that one of them smashed his spectacles and the splinter that penetrated his left eye led to the blinding of that eye. Released from prison, the unfortunate man returned home and – shot himself.

From a letter of a formerly very well-to-do Viennese Jewish house owner, "What is more I do not need to wrack my nervous brain about departure, as for some days the possibility of emigration has become 100% harder. In order to obtain the *Steuerunbedenklichkeit* [tax clearance certificate] and with that the passport, I would have to pay the following taxes:

25% *Reichsfluchtsteuer*		
[Reich departure tax]	c. RM.	58,000.-
20% *Kontribution*		
[tax for cost of *Novemberaktion* damage]	RM.	42,000.-
On sale of the house 9% Transfer	RM.	18,000.-
6% Appreciation in value	RM.	12,000.-
Income- and Pension tax	RM.	8,000.-
Expenses	RM.	4,000.-
Thus a total of RM.		142.000.-

which cannot be raised. As the first instalment of the *Kontribution* has to be paid on 15th December and I no longer possess RM. 1,000.- in assets, it will probably come to an executive sale of the house. The estimated value will be determined by the treasurer, the calling price is from experience 50% of the true value, so it will certainly be purchased, and the upshot will be I, who in his entire life owed nobody a single *Kreuzer* [coin], remain a debtor. In a word, if I can get out then my wife and I must obtain the travel tickets from the *Kultusgemeinde* [Jewish community].

We have had offers of lifts from various people, however I believe we shall forgo those, it is certainly cheaper and more comfortable to go on holiday with the rucksack."

Despite his well-known sense of charity in the city, the

letter-writer, in his seventies, received the *Ausweisungsbefehl* [deportation order] from the Gestapo by 1st February 1939. This decision was given to him in the following manner: he was asked how long he had already been living in Vienna, to which he answered that he had been in Vienna since the fifth year of his life. Thereupon he received the response, "Then you have misused the hospitality of this city for long enough, you have until 1.2.1939 to leave the German Reich."

Reporter: Oskar Hirschfeld, formerly Vienna, now London

B. 137 The destruction and looting took place by order of the Party and were carried out according to plan by the SA and the SS. There are no doubts about that in Germany, and inwardly all the people who still think normally are ashamed but do not say anything. In the streets the people – mainly workers – watched the destruction shaking their heads. Even Party members tell foreigners that they are absolutely not in agreement with this matter.

The Jews in Germany can only be helped by immediate evacuation. To help them financially is *senseless* as long as they are in Germany. If money to support them were still to come from abroad, that could therefore suit the . . . society. The money would be thrown away. To the extent that money is put at their disposal, it should only be used for travel to other countries and for financing their settlement.

The Jews are not suffering immediate physical emergency at the moment. They can still find the means to live. They will nevertheless be annihilated in some or other nasty way. They will be put in barrack camps. The Jew is even blamed that Germany is finished economically.

Herr L., who has otherwise still tried to understand Germany, is now in a very chastened mood too. He was in the Rhineland, and what he has heard there – from Party members – has opened his eyes. His representative in London is making no more visits on behalf of a German firm.

The situation in Germany is such that the people must be kept permanently in turmoil.

Reporter: an unknown Swiss Christian man, passed on through the *Schweizer Israel. Gemeindebund*, [Swiss Israelite [Jewish] Community Association] St. Gallen

B. 138 1. *Rechtsanwalt* [lawyer] A, a very distinguished lawyer in X., 70 years old, was taken away by the Nazis during the November days, allegedly in his capacity as *Vorsitzender* [chairman] of the Jewish *Gemeinde* [community] in X. (which office he held for years).

He was beaten until he bled and thrown into the lake. How he got out of the lake again he does not know as he was unconscious. Erich A., about 40 years old, has for several years owned a training farm in Y. near Z., where for years he has educated young Jewish people in horticulture and agriculture.

Herr A. was taken to the *Rathaus* [town hall] in Y. one morning and beaten with steel rods so badly that he got severe chest pains and lay there as if dead. The chest pains saved him from being deported to the concentration camp.

The pupils, aged from 14–18 years, likewise had to go to the *Rathaus* and were beaten there until they bled. One of the pupils has been seriously ill since then with a severe cerebral inflammation.

Reporter: *Notgemeinschaft deutscher Wissenschaftler im Ausland* [Emergency Association of German Scientists Abroad], London

Rechtsanwalt A = R. A. Bloch

Erich A = Erich Bloch

X = Konstanz on Lake Constance

Y = Horn

Z = Radolfzell am Untersee [Lower lake – part of Lake Constance]

B. 139 20th November 1938

"As stated, we have no idea where my father is at present,

whether in prison or concentration camp, but I regard every attempt to intervene from here as thoroughly wrong, even if it were possible, because it would only draw the attention of the Nazis to him and would harm rather than help."

Reporter: Hermann Eschelbacher, 12 Gladstone Terrace, Edinburgh 9, c/o Miss Elliot

B. 140 24th November 1938

"I can now inform you that my father was released from prison and is in Düsseldorf again, thank God! In Düsseldorf it appears to have been particlarly savage, hence the rumours. I myself heard e.g. by chance that my mother had been arrested, however there was no truth in that. In contrast unfortunately yesterday I heard that during the first days the mob broke into our home and literally destroyed everything, smashed the furniture into little pieces, cut up the cushions etc. Only one room was spared. That affects me very deeply, very much more than if our things had been confiscated. It seems to have happened the same way to a great many people, for I heard that many have joined the households of friends because their home had been destroyed."

Reporter: Hermann Eschelbacher, 12 Gladstone Terrace, Edinburgh 9, c.o. Miss Elliot

B. 141 Report

On 14th March 1938 two people in plain clothes appeared at my home, arrested me and brought me to the police in a car in which there were SS men. There a record was made of my personal details, in particular statements taken because of my membership of a Freemasons' Lodge. I was then taken to seven others in a cell where I met an eminent Vienna *Anwalt* [lawyer] known to me, and the *Justizminister* [Justice Minister]. The cell was normal in size, however extremely dirty and had only an open lavatory. The stay in the cell naturally mentally depressed us all terribly.

In the cell the light burned all night. During the second night I was suddenly called to the corridor where I found myself opposite an armed SS man who immediately bawled at me with the words, "Why are you lying down, *Jude* [Jew]? I've lived in Frankfurt and know you *Judengesindel* [Jewish rabble]." At these words, after he had removed his gloves he punched two powerful blows with such force against my jaw that he knocked out two of my teeth. I staggered back into the cell almost unconscious, and was comforted by the Minister with the words, "You must think to yourself it is like a rockfall in the mountains." On the following morning I was then taken for questioning at which now suddenly, instead of the accusation of membership of the Lodge, it was construed from some harmless letter or other that I was Socialist or Communist. My wife only learned where I am after a week, not even a school friend of mine who occupies a senior post in the Party and knew it precisely gave her information, he declared, "I am not even allowed to know his name otherwise tomorrow I shall be sitting in the cell next to him." The SS man who interrogated me was a particularly dapper, elegant tall person, he insulted me for three to three and a half hours with such words as "*Schwein*" [swine], "*Judenschwein*" [Jewish pig], "If you don't talk I'll hit you on the head with the chair." After my arrest at half past 9 in the evening several SS men appeared in front of my wife and our 20-year-old daughter, drove them out of bed and posed the most incredible questions to my wife who has been an employed doctor for 30 years. They began by asking, "How many German women have you deprived of their children, or don't you perform abortions?" To our daughter they said, "*Du Hure* [You whore], how many men have you already infected? Do you also sell cocaine?" Turning to his companions he then said – we live in a well-furnished villa, "*Judenhuren* [Jewish whores] now live in such palaces." He then asked about the purpose of the second bed in our shared bedroom and said, "You can easily have the second bed disposed of, your *Hurenkerl* [whore's chap] isn't coming back, at 5 o'clock he's already seeing already ten cold gun-barrels." The leader then looked at photographs in a carton and showed them round to his companions with comments like "*Negerfassade*" [Nigger face] and "*Zigeunerfratze*" [Gypsy mug]. After an hour they came back. The incident made such a frightful impression on my daughter that she said, "If they had shot all three of us that would have been better than this life." Then the men also took jewellery and a typewriter with them on their departure.

After we had been at the police station for five weeks – temporarily in individual cells where one had to sleep on the floor – we were brought to the *Landesgericht* [regional court] and received meat there for the first time, in the form of a piece of sausage. At the police station the air in the cell was dreadful, so we experienced the few minutes when we were led to the yard as a blessing. In order to kill time we made chess and other games from bread crumbs; I then stayed another nine weeks in the prison of the *Landesgericht* and had to withstand four or five interrogations during this time.

I first received permission to write after ten to 14 days. The treatment at the *Landesgericht* was better as it was carried out by old Austrian officials. As nothing could be found against me at the various interrogations, something different was alleged against me every time, at my penultimate questioning with the Gestapo it was stated to me that now I was known to be a pacifist. At the final interrogation, which was carried out by a *Reichsdeutsche* [native German] man in the presence of a senior Nazi official, I was asked how I imagined my future, when and where I wanted to go. I was given a two-month deadline, I should however be on my guard against spreading stories of atrocities, and sign a written declaration according to which I am permitted to make neither spoken nor written accounts of any kind about my experiences. The release formalities then lasted three or four more days. From my own experience I can also report the following:

A very rich manufacturer in Vienna was arrested in his villa and the negotiations – whether to shoot him through the mouth or how otherwise to dispose of him, possibly throw him into the water – were conducted in the presence of his wife and both their small children, because the men reopened the door to the children's bedroom which the wife had closed. The woman had to bring out all the jewellery present in the house which was taken away with the justification, "It is certainly not safe enough with the police." The manufacturer in question was a *Rittmeister* [cavalry captain] and had high military decorations. A sacked employee, from whom this entire operation apparently stemmed, had become the *Vizebürgermeister* [deputy mayor] of Vienna. On the occasion of the nocturnal visit to the wife, the officers left behind a notebook which contained a list of Jews living in our neighbourhood, and the following letter:

"Dear Parents, it is now very pleasant in Vienna, I am well. We can take the Jews' money away from them all day, when I visit, I shall also bring something beautiful with me."

Reporter: Prof. Dr. Theodor Bauer (53 years) and his wife from Vienna, now Wassenaar

B. 142 In the first days after the annexation of Austria, a complete array of Jewish editors of Vienna daily newspapers was arrested, namely those of *Der Telegraph*, *Der Wiener Tag* [The Vienna Day], *Die Stunde* [The Hour], the *Neues Wiener Tagblatt* [New Vienna Daily Paper] and the *Neue Freie Presse* [New Free Press]. Amongst the latter were also their long-standing colleagues Raoul Auernheimer and Ludwig Hirschfeld. The arrests took place in accordance with a certain system, as in the days after the turmoil, probably on the basis of lists prepared well in advance; one was not clear about the reason for these two arrests, particularly as information to family members was and is not communicated as a matter of principle. As for both writers the main reasons for the arrests did not come into question at that time. Neither were they economically particularly wealthy nor played a role in economic and financial life, nor had they been in some way more strongly active in political life in a sense that could not have been acceptable for the Nazis. (That both were Jews or at least of Jewish origin was, at the moment of their arrest, not the circumstance to be unconditionally concluded as the reason for the arrest, as this was indeed significant but at that time at least it did not play the only role in arrests; that only came later during the arbitrary arrests, when Jews were simply stopped in the street and imprisoned merely because they were Jews, indeed even taken to Dachau.)

Raoul Auernheimer was an aesthetic essayist and had written a series of belletristic books. He had never been a political exponent, not even as *Vorsitzender* [chairman] of the *Österreichisches P.E.N.-Club* [Austrian P.E.N. (Poets, Essayists, Novelists)]. On the contrary he had imposed intense restraint on himself in this position, so that he has even been the object of attack by various radical newspapers. He was taken to Dachau soon after his arrest.

The case of Ludwig Hirschfeld was particularly blatant. He was always only a humorous writer, not only for the *Neue Freie Presse* for which every Sunday he wrote undemanding, amusing observations, but also as author of droll stories entirely geared to the public taste. He was held in Vienna prisons.

From the 18th March also in custody in a Viennese police prison was the *Herausgeber* [publisher] and *Chefredakteur* [editor-in-chief] of *Die Wahrheit* [The Truth], Oskar Hirschfeld. At the same time in the same prison were former leading Austrian personalities such as the former *Heeresminister* [Minister for the Army] Carl Vaugoin (later Dachau), the former *Landeshauptmann von Niederösterreich* [Governor of Lower Austria] and *vaterländisch* [national] farmers' leader [Josef] Reither (later Dachau), an editor of the Catholic *Reichspost* [Reich Post] and author of a biography of [Engelbert] Dollfuss, [Hans] Maurer, (subsequent fate unknown), the comedian and playwright Paul Morgan (later Dachau), and the film actor Fritz Schulz (since released).

In the first four weeks the prisoners were not allowed to shave. The reason for this was as follows: fourteen days after the arrest the prisoners were taken in groups to a *Reichsdeutsche* [native German] photographer. Those led together into the photography room were called out for the picture one by one, a number was pinned on the left side of their chest, which apparently corresponded with the number on the list in the hands of the photographer, and then they were photographed from different angles with their unkempt beards. Afterwards they were questioned by the photographer, thus Oskar Hirschfeld was asked whether his paper often went abroad, which he denied, and whether it was printed in Hebrew script; the photographer did not understand the answer that the type face of the weekly paper was Antiqua.

The photographs were doubtless for newspaper purposes, like *Der Stürmer* [The Striker; Nazi tabloid newspaper] or *Das Schwarze Korps* [The Black Corps; SS newspaper]. That the photographer was so-to-speak a private individual can also be deduced from the fact that later when they were already allowed to shave again, the prisoners were once more photographed and fingerprinted in the same room, and indeed by *Wachebeamten* [guards] who stated that these pictures were intended for a separate album of criminals.

A short time later new prisoners came into Oskar Hirschfeld's cell, who stated that they had read the name "Hirschfeld" in "*Das Schwarze Korps*" and "*Die Wahrheit*" under a picture, it was however about a "Ludwig" Hirschfeld, and the picture did not bear the least resemblance to him, Oskar H. Already from that it follows that it was a case of mistaken identity. This was again confirmed by the account of another prisoner who returned to the prison from Dachau where he had been together with Raoul Auernheimer. Auernheimer was of the firm opinion that he had only been arrested because of his close friendship with Ludwig Hirschfeld, Ludwig Hirschfeld however had been the victim of confusion with Oskar Hirschfeld, the publisher of *Die Wahrheit*, and they now accused Auernheimer of collaboration on *Die Wahrheit* too.

The picture in *Das Schwarze Korps* did indeed show Ludwig and not Oskar Hirschfeld, with the caption that Ludwig H. now had the opportunity in prison to reflect on the lies he had circulated in *Die Wahrheit* about National Socialism.

Despite this it was possible for Ludwig Hirschfeld's wife to prove to the Gestapo that her husband had been arrested as the result of mistaken identity – she produced a confirmation from the *Neue Freie Presse* according to which her husband as a long-standing employee of this newspaper was obliged by contract to work for no other Viennese newspaper; it still took a full four weeks until Ludwig Hirschfeld was released. He had therefore had to stay for eight weeks for another, who in the meantime had also been arrested.

A similar thing happened to a Viennese neurologist, Dr. Bauer, who had been confused with a researcher into race with the same name, who was an opponent of the National Socialist theories about race. Although the neurologist was able to prove that he was not identical with the race researcher, he had to remain for weeks in prison.

Reporter: Oskar Hirschfeld, formerly of Vienna, now London

B. 143 After the reporter's house was searched, he was arrested on the morning of 10th November and taken to a smaller *Kommissariat* [police station]. Procedure was proper during the arrests, which – as in this case – were carried out by police officers, nothing was taken away from people either. It was different during arrests by the SA and SS, in the course of which acts of violence and thefts occurred. At the *Kommissariat* a crowd of Jews from 15 to 65 years of age was gathered. All were taken in open lorries to the *Bezirkskommissariat* [district police station] at Prater. Reporter was asked by an SA man to take off his spectacles, which opened up all kinds of perspectives. When they arrived at the *Bezirksamt* [district office] at Prater they heard shouting and saw Jews standing at the wall with their hands raised. They were immediately greeted with hoots and shouts by SA and SS *Verfügungstruppen* [support troops] and young lads in plain clothes, who had sticks and whips in their hands, "Down with the *Saujuden* [Jewish pigs]!" and dealt slaps round the face, blows and kicks. Then they also had to stand by the wall with their hands raised. Then gymnastic exercises were performed, lie down, stand up, always with blows and kicks. One stout Jew was rolled through the yard with constant kicks and blows. Others were forced to smear their faces with dirt. The reporter's brother was called out with some others and loaded with bales of cloth which came from the plundering and were to be dispatched. Anyone who collapsed under the load of the large bales was beaten. A senior police officer also took part in this whereas otherwise the police in general behaved very correctly. These people thus assigned did not take part in the gymnastics, had then to shout as ordered, "*Wir sind jüdische Verbrecher, Saujuden!*" [We are Jewish criminals, Jewish pigs]. One of them was beaten with a strap criss-cross over his face.

They were then all pushed into a large cellar and stood there tightly packed in intolerable air. After a report was made, the foreigners, people who had ship tickets, and people over 60 years old were released. At 12 o'clock at night the rest were taken in lorries to the *Kommissariat* in Karajangasse, a school. There they were met by the "*wütende Volksmenge*" [enraged crowd] and on the way from the vehicle to the entrance were pelted with stones and dealt punches and cudgel blows by SA and SS in steel helmets. One Jew shouted, "You've already beaten us enough, leave us alone!" His comrades shut him up so that nothing even worse would happen. About 2,500 men were crammed into the large gymnasium, some collapsed, had heart spasms. One could hear, "Let the dogs die," and other such expressions. Then a functionary appeared, *Gauleiter* [Nazi party regional leader] from the XX. *Bezirk*, a hairdresser by profession, who struck a pose and insistently shouted, "Gryns[z]pan, all Gryns[z]pan. This race deserves to be exterminated and that will happen!" The *Gefängnisleiter* [prison governor], an *Assessor* [assessor] from Berlin, had individual people called out, one had to beat up another, then it was said it was not enough, and then they were more soundly thrashed. The catering was good as the Jewish *Kultusgemeinde* [community] had paid.

In another prison (Kenyongasse) the people received only tea and bread for eight days. Sadistic jokes were the order of the day, "Who wants to volunteer for Dachau? You cowardly dogs are all going to have a turn." Or it was asked, "How old?" – "38 years old." "Good for the quarry." At night they were 109 people in what was usually a classroom. Three people lay on one sack of straw, there were no blankets, they had to cover themselves with their coats.

By Sunday two people had taken their own lives, reporter does not know what else happened. On Sunday the *Gefängnisleiter* came, "Today another of you Jews has committed suicide. Such a thing is not allowed to happen, loss of prestige. If something like that happens again, ten people will be shot out of each room." As punishment they were all placed against the wall for two hours, a machine-gun was positioned behind.

On Monday everyone had to have their hair cut and believed they were going to Dachau. Anyone who had departure papers in their hands or three war decorations was not shorn. Reporter fortunately had had a visa provided through his father, who was already in Switzerland, which was delivered to him by his mother through a guard. From midday on Tuesday interrogations began in the prison on Elisabethstraße. At 11 o'clock at night reporter was brought there with others. They already heard shouting from afar. In the prison yard SA and SS *Verfügungstruppen* formed a line and struck out with benches, bullwhips, steel helmets. They had to wait in the room, deaf-mutes and people with artificial limbs were also present. If it was noticed that someone had not been shorn, he had to kneel, somebody else had scissors pressed into his hand who had to shear him whilst they had to sing in different keys, "I am a *jüdische Verbrecher* [Jewish criminal]", and other senseless things.

Then they were interrogated by the Gestapo who took no notice of how people looked, but were quite correct, they allowed people to sit and lit cigarettes for them (which they had been allowed to buy for themselves in prison for RM. 2.50 – true purchase price RM. 0.80). During the interrogation it was asked what had already been done about departure. The people received letters "E" = "*entlassen* [release]", "Z" = "*zurück* [return]". [The] reporter received "Z", therefore return to Karajangasse. "D" meant "Dachau". Those who went to Dachau were greeted outside with slaps round the face and beaten until they were lying on the ground; then they were trampled on by feet. Once a policeman intervened when it became too bad. Older police officers wept but could do nothing. Reporter received the departure deadline of 15th December. He was very happy that he was going back to Karajangasse because it was even worse in other prisons. There the people were woken at night and buckets of water poured over their heads. When they came back to Karajangasse – there were 700 men, the others had gone to Dachau –, they fell onto the straw sacks exhausted to death. One of the supervising officers said, "You are here for your own protection, the people are rioting, we cannot restrain the SA."

Next day haircut again, which an apprentice of the *Gauleiter*-barber undertook. 104 people were in the room, RM. 1.- per man had to be raised, whether one had one's hair cut or not.

Thursday – the day of vom Rath's funeral – was the worst day. The people were divided according to age on the different floors: up to 30 years etc. At exactly half past 7 military vehicles appeared with SA and SS who arrived shouting and began to hit out. "*Advokaten* [lawyers] out here", "Dentists out here", ("Sex offenders out here"), "Workers out here". Then two were taken out who had to slap each other's faces and run at each other with their heads, and then were thrashed more. At 9 o'clock there was breakfast. One who had taken part in the thrashing said softly, "Endure [it]!" Then more beating, individuals taken out, kneebends had to be done and endured for 25 minutes in the most strenuous position, otherwise beating. Gymnastic exercises had to be done, the stairs crawled up. Brother of the reporter received 30 slaps round the face, according to a medical certificate a laceration of his eardrum resulted. A son of a *Wunderrabbi* [erudite rabbi who could work miracles] was beaten so badly that the cornea was torn. At exactly 11 o'clock there was peace, the SA and SS removed themselves. In spite of the appalling condition in which people found themselves, they volunteered for cleaning and washing down the areas: rooms, stairs, lavatories. Brother of the reporter worked together with a guard who told him he was an *illegale* [covert] SS man, "but such a thing can bring no happiness." He belonged to [Kurt] Schuschnigg's bodyguard, was head of the *Spionagedienst* [spy service]. Four *illegale* SS men were in it, even the chauffeur was an *illegale* SS man; furthermore Guido Schmidt, the former *Staatssekretär des Äußeren* [Secretary of State for Foreign Affairs], was now head of the Hirtenberger *Patronenfabrik* [Hirtenberger cartridge factory].

Release happened the next day. Then it emerged that the files on the reporter had disappeared. A new interrogation was arranged, the departure deadline set for 15th January 1939. After the interrogation they once again had to stand with noses pressed flat against the wall whilst the *Assessor* banged with the revolver. Then it had to be signed that nothing would be told, no propaganda about atrocities spread. "The arm of the Third Reich stretches around the whole world." We were thrown out with kicks, outside stood weeping women who were waiting for their husbands. All the watches were taken away, and at the end they were asked, "*Junge* [boy], how many spoons did you pinch here?" Marvellous demeanour of the Orthodox Jews was particularly accentuated.

Reporter: Carl Löwenstein from Vienna, at present in Amsterdam, van Woustraat 229, Jurist [lawyer], is emigrating to Bolivia.

B. 144 Reporter was arrested on 10th November by a *Kriminalbeamter* [police detective] and taken to Brigittenau police station. There he was put in a cell with 28 men after personal details had been recorded. The treatment was fair. In the afternoon the arrested men were taken to Karajangasse *Arrestlokal* [detention centre] (a former school). When the vehicles drove up, the square had to be cordoned off by SS *Schutztruppe* [SS troops], because the crowd, especially women, let loose with insults and violence towards those getting out. Reporter was put in a classroom with 78 men after an interrogation. Every two to three men could use one straw sack. Sleeping was inconceivable. After 12 o'clock at night an SS officer came into the room with a roar. "78 men" was reported. He roared, "78 Jews, that's called, repeat!" Then the academics had to step forward, who were addressed with "*Sie*" [formal "you"] and were asked about [their] profession. Then the businessmen. Individuals were asked, "What are you?" Answer: "Businessman". Roared to that: "You're a fraudster, repeat it!"

The next day the *Leiter* [governor] of the prison, an *Assessor* [assessor] from Berlin, ran riot with insults and brutality. On Monday or Tuesday the prisoners were taken in cars to Gestapo headquarters. In the yard they were met by the SS with wooden clubs and kicks and led to a hall with a stone floor. There those who had not yet been shorn were shorn in such a way that the man to be shorn had to kneel, another Jew received scissors and was ordered how to cut, if possible in such a way that the people looked disfigured. One Jew had a proper *Mogen Dovid* [Star of David] cut.

Anyone who apparently did not do something correctly was beaten, during which the others had to turn round. Then it was asked, "Who is hungry?" One could buy *Knackwurst* [saveloy] and bread. After the meal, which was observed, there were beatings with straps again. Then the people were interrogated and asked who had emigration papers. A division into three categories took place: "E'" i.e. "*Entlassen*" [release], that was people over 60 and the sick; "Z" = "*Zurück nach der* Karajangasse" [return to Karajangasse], "D" = "Dachau". Those who went to Dachau were immediately pushed into a lower room. C. 3,000 people went to Dachau or Weimar (did not know exactly).

The worst day was Thursday (day of vom Rath's funeral). They had to report early, then three or four SS men appeared in their room, who immediately shouted, "Now we're going to teach you, now there'll be a different tone." First had to eat again, sausage and bread, which had to be paid for. Then came gymnastic exercises standing face to the wall, hands reaching upwards. Fingers were beaten with straps. Lie on the ground, kiss the ground, lip smacking for ten minutes. Get up, stand at the wall again and reach up. A little rest, then academics step forward. Two *Rechtsanwälte* [lawyers] had to have a boxing match, intermittent shouting: "Look at the Jewish cowards!"; intermittent blows with the fist. Three or four pairs had to perform such fights. Even a *Kapellmeister* [choirmaster] was supposed to take part in a boxing match. Then a cup of coffee was thrown onto the floor and he had to lick up the coffee with his tongue. A *Rechtsanwalt* had to take off his shoes and socks, slide around on his knees and lick the floor with his tongue. The *Kapellmeister* had to sing a song. Then it was asked: "Who can recount something about Freemasons' lodges?" Those who came forward received blows. "Who will come forward voluntarily to be shot?" When one man came forward, he was asked, "Why?" And when he said that he spent four years in the war without one bullet having been being cast for him, and even now he had no fear, he was able to stand down.

An old rabbi had to kneel down, then one held a bayonet to his throat with the words, "*Du Schweinehund* [You swine], surrender your foreign currencies, do you want to see blood?" and gave him blows. Then it was standing at the wall again, academics and business people in particular were beaten with leather whips and steel helmets. Five people were unconscious, one *Rechtsanwalt* close to madness.

At exactly 11 o'clock the SS men disappeared and the guard came, the injured were bandaged. It was said that machine guns were put into position in the night from Thursday to Friday, and the SS were denied entry to the building. There are also said to have been arrests amongst the SS. According to rumours, in another prison people are said to have been jabbed with needles and forced to drink others' urine.

On release one had to sign that one would tell nothing. Beforehand watches and possible items of value were taken away. "Don't say that we have taken that, you donated them to us."

On release one said to the reporter, hearing that he was a Pole, "Why didn't you stay in Poland, *Du polnischer Schwein* [you Polish swine]?"

The last signature had to be provided by the *Assessor*, one was called for that, beforehand had to stand again with nose pressed flat against the wall. Reporter had to leave Vienna by 31st December, otherwise Dachau. Then a kick, "*Raus mit Dir, Du Schwein*" [Out with you, you swine].

The wife of the reporter told of the devastation of Jewish homes, everything was smashed to pieces and destroyed. At a relative's, who already had departure papers for Palestine, his large shop was robbed and then everything sealed up. He could only have his papers released by signing that he was voluntarily donating his firm to the Party. The next day a sign was on the shop, "*Arisiert*" [Aryanised].

After the reporter was turned back in Emmerich with his wife and two children of four and eight years of age, he was led across the border near Aachen by a German customs officer. "What crime have the two children committed then?" On the Dutch side they were helped by a Christian miner's family with eight children until they reached a *Comité*.

Reporter: Josef Schlesinger, upholsterer (35 years old), previously of Vienna XX., Universumstr. 34, at present in Amsterdam, Gelderschekade 79, c/o Baruch

B. 145 In Siegburg, a Rhenish town of some 20,000 inhabitants, so far as I know nothing was plundered. The synagogue, where the rabbi had delivered another sermon on Wednesday evening, was set on fire and burned out completely inside and photographed in this state. On Thursday the 10th November 1938 I was arrested at about 10 o'clock in the morning by a *Kriminalbeamte* [police detective] and then transported by the Gestapo to the work camp at Brauweiler with 40 people aged from 17 to 68. I want to point out that we had all been expecting something unusual, because in the newspaper on Wednesday it had said that the SS were to be sworn in at midnight.

After four days of fair treatment, we were then taken on foot on Tuesday morning at half past 3 to Groß-Königsdorf from where the elderly people were sent home on Saturday. Arrested with me was my father, who stayed in prison for only two days however.

We then came – we had in the meantime increased to about 1,500 men – to Dachau and were met there by about 100 SS men with steel helmets and bayonets. Myriad spotlights dazzled us and made us so dizzy that many fainted. We were reloaded onto a wagon which was about two metres above the ground and into which we had to clamber without help. That was naturally particularly difficult for the elderly, especially for an 87-year-old amongst us and for whom there was not the slightest consideration. In the wagon we were then escorted by Upper Bavarian SS men, who insulted and mistreated us so dreadfully that we said the customary mourning prayers led by the rabbi.

We then arrived at the camp and were squeezed so tightly into a room with 200 people that [the] unconscious were not even able to fall to the floor. We heard continuous shouting from the neighbouring rooms. We then had to step outside and were taken away at the double for examination, with the strict order, "Do not turn your eyes away from the neck of the man in front of you." We then had to stand in the hall right against the wall – some of us, who did not answer questions in the way the SS men wanted, were also mistreated here. We then went into another room with straw sacks – next to me lay my 57-year-old father-in-law, a Jewish teacher. I then remained in the camp for 12 days in total, the first registration lasted so long that we had to stand for a full eight hours without anything to eat, during which it was forbidden for us to look anywhere but straight ahead. We were then shorn and put under showers, first hot and then ice-cold. Whilst showering questions were directed at us and at the moment when the person concerned opened his mouth, the hose with the ice-cold water was directed into his mouth.

After we had been standing naked for a long time, we received garments, some of which bore the *Mogen Dovid* [Star of David] and some with numbers painted on them in colour – it gave the men a particular pleasure to give the overweight amongst us too tight garments. The daily routine always stayed always the same. At quarter to 5 we had to get up, then at 8, at 12 and 5 o'clock was *Appell* [roll call], in the meantime exercising and marching at the double practised, particularly squats. We had a locker and a knife for every four people. We slept two hundred people to the room, most had chills and fever because of the continual change of cold and heat. For all 200 people only eight lavatories were available. The surveillance consisted of SS men no older than 22, only the *Lagerkommandant* [camp commandant] was about 30 years old. If somebody moved at the order "Stand still", the SS man standing near him would unbuckle his waist-belt and lay into him.

I frequently saw lorries with dead and know too that a rabbi assisted at a funeral (A).

At half past 6 we had to go to bed, could however only sleep with difficulty because the air was intolerable, and in addition the spotlight was playing the entire night. We often heard shooting at night, perhaps this was connected to the warning constantly repeated at *Appell*, "At night do not go outside the door" – everyone who appeared outside the building was shot.

The treatment became harsher from day to day – on the *Appell-platz* [parade ground] orders were transmitted by loudspeaker.

Without exception we had swollen feet from marching in the clayey softened soil.

I was then eventually released due to a preliminary visa for China, with me about 150 who all wanted to emigrate or whose businesses had been *arisiert* [Aryanised]. On the day of release we still had to stand for hours until the formalities were completed. In particular the medical examination was very detailed as everyone whose bodies were marked with bruises or injuries had to remain behind.

Reporter: businessman Ernst Wallerstein (34 years), from Siegburg, at present in Amsterdam.

(A) Rabbi Köhler from Schweinfurt

B. 146 Report from Dachau

Report from a thoroughly reliable quarter:

The person concerned was transported to the town of Dachau from his homeland by railway carriage together with many hundred others accompanied by *Kriminalbeamten* [police detectives]. The journey lasted approximately ten hours. In some compartments the officers were humane and even provided water for the prisoners, in others not so, so that they suffered severely from thirst.

From Dachau railway station the prisoners were crammed into some cattle trucks – approximately 100 people in one cattle truck – so that only by standing pressed against one another could they complete the rest of the journey.

In the camp the people were first shorn as a matter of course. Some of the people received a uniform; the others could keep on their own clothes, as there were not enough *Drillichanzüge* [cotton drill suits]. The barracks in Dachau are built quite well and solidly and have stone floors. In principle such a barracks is equipped for 100 people. On one side is a dormitory in which straw is layered, on the other side there is a day room. In between are some latrines and a washroom. That would be sufficient for a hundred people, but in such a barracks 200 men are now accommodated so that the day room too is completely full.

Of course prisoners' watch, money, penknife etc. were taken away on their entry. But my informant got his things back on release. The shift begins at 5 o'clock with waking. Then there is coffee and bread – four men have to share one *Kommissbrot* [army loaf] per day. At 6 o'clock everybody goes out, at half past 6 report for duty; *Appell* [roll call] then lasts until 8 o'clock, for there were 12,000 Jews in this section of the camp alone. The counting itself lasts a long time, as counting such a large number of people leads to many mistakes.

After *Appell* drill exercises then take place until 11 o'clock, then lunch, at 1 o'clock report again, again drill until 6 o'clock, sometimes even longer. From 6 until 8 o'clock is free time, then the light is put out. Everyone who sets foot in the camp alley again after that is shot. Smoking is permitted in free time.

The worst thing is that people do not take their clothes off, have nothing to change into and the people who are wearing the so-called uniforms are almost always frozen and wet through. One can buy oneself woollen underwear in the camp for RM. 5.- but since most people have no money or do not get any sent to them or the money has not arrived, that is an impossible matter.

My informant was not in the camp for very long, only about three weeks, then he was called at *Appell* one morning to come for release. The release formalities lasted an entire day. The medical examination consisted of a doctor examining whether he also had any weals or bruises on his body from a kick or a blow. He asked about that with the word, "Accident?" Then he went on to the next formality.

At the end the *Lagerkommandant* [camp commandant] gave a speech, "You know that you should leave Germany as quickly as possible, do not stay there any longer than necessary, behave yourselves properly on the journey, do not tell any stories of atrocities, and above all, when you are once out of Germany, never again come back. Otherwise you and your relatives will be locked away for the rest of your lives."

After this speech the people were led under guard by police officers to Dachau station, some SS men saw to it that those who had more money bought tickets for those with none, and then still under guard they were shunted from Dachau to Munich. In Munich the imprisonment actually came to an end. It was however forbidden for them to remain standing, flocked together somewhat, in the station, which was difficult as the relevant trains only departed some hours later. The prisoners then went out of the station, there they discovered various Jews pressed together against a wall in a side street, some of whom they even took with them and then brought them back in time for the trains.

Beating was relatively infrequent in Dachau, as far as my informant established, i.e. official thrashings did not take place very much. It goes without saying that the SS men slapped faces and kicked to their hearts' content. The Aryan *politische Häftlinge* [political prisoners] are treated worse because they have to work extremely hard.

The camp is surrounded by electrically charged barbed wire and a trench, in addition flanked by some machine gun towers. In addition a large SS training centre lies directly by the entrance to the camp.

The worst thing is that when somebody becomes ill he is doomed unless his own robust nature helps him.

Reporter: Menko Max Hirsch, Antwerp

B. 147 A Scandinavian friend who was in Berlin in the days from 9th to 11th December 1938 informs me that he has the impression that the German people by and large condemns the regime and the recent pogroms. It is certainly difficult to achieve absolute clarity about this as nobody dares to speak out openly. In contrast he has indeed learned from comments by Christians with whom he has business dealings how dissatisfied they are and how they have said much against the existing regime in a concealed manner.

Report No. 147 was submitted on 12.12.38 by Herr Fred van Geldern, Deltastr. 12 b/ Walter, Amsterdam Z.

B. 148 Report

I was able to watch the incidents in X. with particular attention as I was not under arrest and as a senior official was able to move around unchallenged. I pursued my emigration and heard, when on the morning of 9th November I was at the Gestapo in connection with this, that a big operation was imminent. I thought that it concerned a search for weapons and that is why I took a weapon belonging to me and a friend to a wood at night where I threw it into a pond. On the morning of 10th November – I live right outside the town – my housekeeper told me that the synagogue had been set alight, all the Jews arrested, goods had been stolen and homes had been destroyed. I had been aware of so little of this that I only established it with certainty from telephone conversations.

In X. an infinite amount has been stolen and only small worthless items have been returned, the homes vandalised, I have seen for myself that typewriters and expensive adding machines with cartridges have been smashed to smithereens, crystalware has been crushed to splinters, most homes set on fire and everything has been trampeled on. The shops have also been looted; I was convinced that e.g. the whole precious warehouse of the *Rosenthaler Porzellanmanufaktur* [Rosenthal Porcelain Factory] had been completely destroyed. So much has been looted that an Aryan jeweller declared in my presence to a travelling salesman from Pforzheim, "This year there is no business to be done at Christmas, the SS has already got all the presents that it wants to give."

The population of X. is 92% Catholic – it was therefore to be expected that condemnatory remarks would be made. One of my Catholic acquaintances was rapidly dispatched to prison for this reason.

In X. as in Y. and Z. women and children were also arrested, although released again after six to eight hours. It was during their absence that the homes were destroyed.

Physical mistreatment, as far as I know, did not occur; instead the SS men satisfied themselves with hurling the nastiest insults. The SS men were, almost without exception, completely drunk; whether through alcohol which was given to them beforehand with this intention, or through schnapps and wine which they got hold of during their looting, I do not know of course. The most senior government officials from whom I have taken leave, and in fact officially in the offices, have almost unanimously and without exception declared to me, "We are sad and ashamed to be German. We envy you for getting out of here."

In total according to my estimate c. 300 people, all between the ages of 20 and 60, were arrested in X. Officers from the war and holders of the *E. K. 1* [Iron Cross First Class], as well as those severely disabled by war, have been released. The arrested Jews went to Buchenwald. As my brother-in-law, who is giving his impressions completely reliably and carefully, has told me, the newly built barracks in Buchenwald had already been built in June as barracks for Jews, as in the event of war it had been planned to put all the Jews into the concentration camp.

In Hirschberg the *Feuerwehr* [fire brigade] had driven up in front of the synagogue two hours before the interior was set on fire; the tombs were desecrated, children played in the street with *Thorarollen* [Torah scrolls] and organ pipes. Rabbi A., 63 years old, had to kneel for two hours in front of the synagogue while the synagogue burned down and while women and children had to line up round the synagogue to the shout of "*Alle Synagogen brennen!*" [Burn all synagogues], and was then transported to the camp, but has now been released again. A sum of RM. 30,000.- was demanded from the Jewish *Gemeinde* [community] for the demolition of the synagogue, the first instalment of which, RM. 15,000.-, a member of the *Gemeinde* has paid.

In the camp, as my brother-in-law has reliably reported to me, the food was adequate. The prisoners had to march for four hours each day, the rest of the day passed with *Appellen* [roll calls], at half past seven one went to bed; it was not possible to sleep because of the glaring spotlight. Prisoners were sadistically pursued in constant fear; as they marched in, coffins were carried out as if by chance, and at their first line up, when they had to stand facing the wall, the SS men discussed whether a shot in the neck or another cause of death would be more appropriate, according to the physical nature of individuals. To a Herr B., who is particularly stout, they said, "Well, tomorrow you'll sizzle beautifully."

Mistreatment was the order of the day, suicides also occurred more frequently – in their despair the prisoners ran into the live electric wire.

The seriously ill were doomed as there was a complete lack of medication. No consideration whatsoever was given to the sick, e.g. they also had to go out to *Appell*, even if they then ended by collapsing and had to be carried back on a stretcher. On release my brother-in-law had to stand for another seven and a half hours. The men marching off were then given sandwiches to take with them however, albeit with the accompanying words, "There are your sandwiches, you *Schweine* [pigs]."

Reporter: Kurt Krimmel, *Regierungs- und Baurat* [Head of the government planning department and building control office] (52 years of age). Beuthen, O.Schl. [Oberschlesien; Upper Silesia]

Key:

X = Beuthen [now Pol. Bytom]

Y = Gleiwitz [now Pol. Gliwice]

Z = Hindenburg [now Pol. Zabrze]

A = Prof. Dr. Kolintzki

B. = Wolf

B. 149 5th November 1938

From Vienna I have received news which proves that the situation has still not improved. The Jews still do not dare to go into the street in the evening for fear of being jostled. 14 days ago there were still notices near the *Tempel* [synagogues] with the following content, "It is requested to avoid every gathering on the street and to leave the *Tempel* buildings promptly after the conclusion of the service." Eight days ago evening prayers had been completely cancelled and one of my sources commented to me about this decision, "It was quite good, for the weather was bad, it has become winter this year in seasonal terms." Moreover I am expecting another detailed report from Vienna in the next few days which will probably also contain more details about the arbitrary arrests that have recently happened again in large numbers.

The Jews sent to Buchenwald are said to have to labour in a quarry.

It will interest you to hear that it is confirmed to me by thoroughly reliable acquaintances who have come here from Vienna in recent days that a distinctly anti-war mood prevailed in Vienna in the days before the Munich Agreement, which found expression on the street quite openly. Even well-known "*Illegale*" [illegals] have expressed their reluctance in a vehement manner to having to be drawn into a war because of the Sudeten Germans who never belonged to the Reich, which was already lost from the start because of the shortage of food. The atmosphere amongst Jews was understandably very depressed, for they feared all going into forced internment. But this danger did not depress them so very much as they saw the only possibility of an end to their suffering through a war. After the Munich Agreement great despair also seized the Jews because they now saw no way out at all to escape the yoke, then in addition came more new atrocities; in a word the spiritual mood of the Jews of Vienna is quite dreadful once again.

Reporter: Oskar Hirschfeld, London

B. 150 The Chief of Police
To the Jewish *Kultusverband* [Cultural Association] Ulm
Ref. Curfew.
The assassination of an official at the German embassy in

Paris by a Jew and the resulting frenzy in the foreign Jewish press has caused such outrage amongst the whole population, that in order to protect the Jewish population from danger I have no alternative but to impose a curfew in accordance with *Art. 32 Abs. 5, W. Pol. Str. G. B.* [Article 32 Paragraph 5, Württemberg Police Criminal Code], with effect from 9th November 1938 onwards, on all Jews from 20.00 hours in the evening until 06.00 hours in the morning. Violations of this ban result in punishment or immediate *Inschutzhaftnahme* [protective detention].

I request that this prohibition is made known to all members of the Jewish *Gemeinde* [community] immediately. The prohibition will be published tomorrow in the newspaper.

gez. [sgd.] Dreher

Reporter: S. I. G. [*Schweizerischer Israelitischer Gemeindebund;* Swiss Jewish Community Association] Zürich (Saly Braunschweig)

B. 151 The turmoil of recent times made it impossible to write to you earlier. Unfortunately I must inform you of the very sad news that my father has died in Buchenwald. All of us still cannot grasp it, for it is so hard and bitter, as my late father was a strong healthy man ... We sometimes see no way out, for opportunities to emigrate are becoming more and more difficult here. One must wait and see what the future brings ... You can be happy that you seized the very best time to emigrate ... We would so like to get away from here, but we are still not able to, because the approval of our house sale has so far not yet arrived ...

Letter from Frau Selma Kahn, Grebenau, *Kreis* [area] Alsfeld, *Bez.* [*Bezirk*; district] Kassel, to Rosenbusch Family, Amsterdam-Z[uid], Parnassusweg 32

B. 152 Report about the Buchenwald concentration camp

Sources of the report

The following report is based in the first instance on the detailed stories of three prisoners, whom the reporter himself has spoken to individually during the course of the month of July, each one only a few days after his release. Secondly information has been taken into account, which was given to the writer as being the substance of what two lawyers [*Juristen*] learned, who spent six weeks continually dealing with the processing of cases of internment from Buchenwald. Other sources, in particular the reports published in the British press, have not been used.

The precise names of the three prisoners mentioned above are known to the writer, however cannot be revealed here because the people concerned are still in Germany.

Camp population

According to a statement of the prisoners the composition of the camp population on about 20th June was as follows:

Number of prisoners in total:	c. 7,850
Jews included above	1,240–1,250
Ernste Bibelforscher [Jehovah's Witnesses]	300–400
Arbeitsscheue [work-shy]	c. 3,000
Politische Häftlinge [political prisoners]	800–1,000
'B.V.' (*Berufsverbrecher*) [professional criminals]	1,500–2,000

In addition to these prisoners there are only uniformed SS teams in the camp; civilians are never allowed to enter the camp – even the *Kriminalpolizei* [criminal police] have to wait at the entrance to the camp. The composition of the camp population is always posted on a blackboard in the area where the prisoners receive the money sent to them by their relatives.

The individual categories of prisoners

Of the individual categories of prisoners, the following can be observed: The so-called "*Arbeitsscheue*" [work shy] are made up in part of elements who really are reluctant to work, amongst them also a number of Gypsies, to a greater extent however of people whose crime was to leave their employment in order to take up better paid work elsewhere.

The "*Ernste Bibelforscher*" [Jehovah's Witnesses], members of the well-known sect, who amongst other things refuse to give the Nazi salute on religious grounds, are released from the concentration camp immediately if they undertake to "no longer believe in Jehovah". Without exception they refuse to do this however. In the concentration camp the *"Bibelforscher"* look after the Jews especially, often giving up some of their bread rations to them etc.

The number of Jews came to about 1,350 initially, i.e. after the large manhunt operation of 12th-18th June was carried out, as part of which the Jews first came to B. The departure of about 100 within five weeks is to a small extent the result of releases, to a larger extent of fatalities. In general Jews are released if it can be proved that they have an immediate opportunity to emigrate, i.e. if visa and ticket to travel are in place.

The different kinds of prisoners are already denoted by their clothing; therefore Jews wear a black stripe as *"Arbeitsscheue"* and a yellow one as Jews. Prisoners are accommodated in large barracks and in fact the Jews in special ones. Initially 462 men slept in one of the Jewish barracks, of these twelve were dead within the first week.

The course of the working day

As a rule the prisoners' day proceeds as follows: waking is at half past 3. At quarter past 4 is *Appell* [roll call]. This lasts until quarter past 5 – above all the frequency and long duration of the *Appell*s, having to stand to attention during them, is felt to be scarcely less agonising than the work, the mistreatment and the hunger. At quarter past 5 the *Arbeitskommandos* [work parties] report for duty, at quarter to 7 work starts. This then goes on without interruption until 12 o'clock. From 12 o'clock until shortly before half past 12 is lunch break, before half past 12 they move off again, and from 1–4 is work again. At 4 o'clock they are counted off again; this *Appell* lasts until at least ten past 5, that is if no one is missing; otherwise the so-called *Stufendienst* [patrols] search for the absentees (mostly in the forest), and the others have to continue to stand until he is found alive or dead; in some circumstances this can take from 4 o'clock until 8 o'clock. If no one is missing, then at twenty to 6 there is another work *Appell*, and from 6 o'clock until 8 o'clock they work again. At 8 o'clock there is then supper.

Rations

The prisoners receive coffee in the morning, but nothing to eat. At midday there is usually noodles, rice, pearl barley or suchlike or pulses. The food is said to be very good qualitatively, only much too little. In the evening Jews receive in total 300 g. of dry bread, which also has to last for the following morning. In the canteen prisoners can buy jam to put on it, which incidentally is said to be good. The result of this catering is weight loss, which as a rule seems to be between 20 and 40 pounds within six weeks. Aryans receive larger bread rations than Jews. But the precise detail is not known.

Types of work

The work of the prisoners consists predominantly of hauling rocks from the nearby quarry. Close attention is paid at least to the Jews, so that they are only allowed to perform this roughest work; one of the prisoners who had redeployed to the mason, asked for permission to work in the quarry itself, which was refused on the grounds that there was no question whatsoever of this for Jews. Besides hauling rocks prisoners are also occupied with felling trees and dragging them away. In each case they are forced to work with the most extreme exertion using all their strength, so oak planks say, which are normally carried by four workers, have to be carried by two prisoners here. In the same way in the quarry it is ensured that prisoners have to carry rocks of between one and two hundredweight – and even the old and sick.

Mistreatments

During the work itself mistreatment of all kinds, right up to straightforward murder, takes place daily. If someone collapses altogether under the workload or stumbles, then he is brought round again with kicks or blows from rifle butts or with a bucket of cold water. One of the prisoners told of the folllowing case: a Jew whilst hauling rock had picked up one rock which weighed roughly 40 pounds. At this he was shouted at to put the thing back and look for a larger rock. As the Jew went, the guard took the smaller rock and flung it with all his might at the Jew; he was hit in the neck and was dead. Prisoners are also continually dying in other ways as well as from the direct results of mistreatment. E.g. in July one of the Jewish prisoners died of a double renal pelvic fracture as a result of kickings. Mistreatments during work seem to happen for the most part through the *Vorarbeiter* [foremen], called "*Capos*". They are prisoners themselves (and indeed to an extent '*B.V.*' men, which means *Berufsverbrecher* [professional criminals], who are urged on by the SS teams to crack down as harshly as possible. The guards themselves stand near to the *Arbeitskommandos* [work squads] with weapons primed.

Outside work numerous mistreatments happen even during *Appell*s etc. Here especially punishments are also imposed and carried out for all possible offences, e.g. if somebody does not stand to attention or is not standing precisely in line etc. The regular punishments are 25 lashes, some of which are carried out in the presence of everybody in the camp in the evening during *Appell*. In most cases the result of these floggings is that the people concerned cannot then be released even if they can prove they have an immediate opportunity to emigrate – because it is not wanted that traces of mistreatment will be visible outside.

Medical care

Only those people who have either an open wound or a broken bone are allowed to report sick; hence all the serious internal illnesses that are caused through over-exertion during the work or through the inadequate diet, particularly heart disease, are not treated, and a large number die of exhaustion or a heart attack etc. This all the more as the rather large number of people over 50, at least amongst the Jews, in addition to those who were already suffering from heart disease on day one, the asthmatics etc., must take part in all kinds of work and also all the drills (endurance runs etc.) like the others.

There are doctors and *Sanitäter* [orderlies] present in the camp. These are prisoners themselves and have far too few beds, medicines etc., to be able to help effectively. For the most serious cramps they give a couple of drops of belladonna or the like in some circumstances. An SS doctor comes into the camp for a couple of hours each day, "but he will not touch a Jew", as one of the prisoners said.

Number of fatalities

When the *Arbeitskommandos* march out to work in the morning, they come past a place where always one or two, often even several, stretchers lie with the newly dead who are taken away. In total the number of fatalities in an average day is said to number six to eight. Of these fatalities one part is due to mistreatment, another to over-exertion, exhaustion, etc., a substantial part, however, to suicide. This is how it takes place as a rule – the despairing prisoners hurl [themselves] into the high voltage barbed wire surrounding the barracks. This was very common particularly in the early days.

Particular incidents

There is no ray of hope at all for the prisoners. Sunday seemed to us to be scarcely less terrible than the other weekdays; it consists for the most part of hours-long *Appells*. On a Sunday the prisoners even had to stand throughout the whole day, so that in the end from tiredness they could no longer stay upright. In between times they were drafted into groups to undress completely naked, after which the clothes are searched very thoroughly. It was said that a photograph has been published in an English newspaper of the gallows on which the recaptured murderer of the SS man was hanged in the presence of the entire camp population, and the whole camp is now being searched for the camera. Special punishments are imposed in other ways as well in some circumstances as a reprisal for foreign publications, for example complete deprivation of food for one day.

Conclusion

Those released from Buchenwald give the impression of being completely broken and frightened. As a rule the men weep as soon as they are asked something; often they only answer if their wife is nearby and encourages them. These people have doubtless become incapable of emigrating as a rule, because every bit of courage, every strength of nerve, has been taken away from them. Probably a larger part of them will perish abroad afterwards. Finally it should be noted that contrary to most of the press publications, the overwhelming majority of prisoners consists of non-Jews. Even amongst these the misery is horrendous; one of the released Jewish prisoners asserted that he had never before seen such dreadful misery in his life as in Buchenwald amongst the Christians.

Reporter unknown

B. 153 The numerous reports in respected London newspapers that traces of mistreatment were to be detected on the German Jewish children recently arrived here and welcomed with so much love, were confirmed to me by an Aryan Swiss woman whose English woman friend had taken in a child who recoiled anxiously from every approach. Soon the reason for the girl's fear became apparent. She had a swastika on her back – branded.

A young Jewish Viennese *Rechtsanwalt* [lawyer], Dr. Imbermann, after his arrest was taken to the Sievering (Vienna XIX.) SA barracks and there to a dark underground corridor at the end of which was a target. After one had asked him whether he knew what kind of "thing" that was, he had to stand with his face to the target, and the SA fellows shot off their revolvers behind him.

The *Seitenstettentempel* [synagogue] already mentioned a number of times by me, which has been completely wrecked inside, was able to be preserved for use for private purposes. On the ground floor of the place of worship officers of the *Kultusgemeinde* [Jewish community] have now been installed who receive clients.

Apart from the Gerngroß department store named in report no. 7 B.127], also at the renowned Vienna department stores Herzmansky and Falnbigl, which were likewise formerly under Jewish ownership, is "*Juden Eintritt verboten*" [Entry forbidden to Jews]

Reporter: Oskar Hirschfeld, London

B. 154 Dear Sirs,

I would further like to point out that, as I know from personal reports, the synagogue in Halberstadt is indeed still standing in its foundation walls, but the exceptionally valuable, because antique, furnishings have been utterly destroyed. To what extent the chandeliers, which date from the period 1660–1700, still survive, I do not know. In addition I do not know whether the curtains of the *Aron Hakodesch* [Torah ark], for the most part extremely valuable embroideries from about 1650, fell victim to the *süßen Pöbel* [sweet rabble]. The *kochende Volksseele* [seething populace] further amused itself by blowing up the mortuary at the Jewish cemetery, which was erected in 1895. This small excess did not really matter, however. For as I reliably hear, in Vienna not only was the mortuary dynamited but also the entire enclosing wall of the Jewish cemetery was dynamited there, so that the rabble could more easily vandalise the rest of the cemetery.

Excerpt from a letter by Herr Menko Max Hirsch, Antwerp, 26 Avenue Bosmans

[Handwritten:] B154, cf. BW 8/12

B. 155 A pronounced agitation of the masses was to be felt already for some weeks, I heard two women talking thus on the tram: One should slay the Jews at the next best opportunity. The sign "*Juden unerwünscht*" [Jews not wanted] appeared on various shops, cinemas etc. In Ansbach e.g., the seat of the district administration, already weeks ago this sign was on every shop without exception, whatever the trade; conditions were even worse in small places and in the countryside, people were forced by acts of terror or even by signing them away to sell their goods and chattels within a few hours at a knock-down price and to leave – to where? to the nearest big city of course. The same question, to where, before which all now stand. The murderous attack, some believe in a commissioned job, provided the desired trigger.

In the night from 9th to 10th [November] we awoke to the noise of furniture being thrown about and were able to establish that uniformed SA in small private cars, always seven to eight men in each, were breaking into Jewish homes and destroying everything like vandals. Cupboards of tableware were simply turned over, all the furniture smashed up, clothes in cupboards slashed to pieces, silver flung onto the floor and stamped upon, pictures cut up, grand pianos smashed up, no mirror, no window remained intact. One still cannot grasp today why everything was destroyed, and indeed destroyed in an organised manner, for the SA arrived with slips of paper so that virtually every home was destroyed, regardless whether it concerned a large villa of the rich or the smallest little attic room of the smallest.

Whilst only a very few of the homes were overlooked, even the shops of foreigners were utterly destroyed. In mine the six shop windows were smashed in, [they] broke in through them and not even a tiny piece remained in its place. Over one metre high the wares lay around completely destroyed, the machines hacked, important books stolen.

Items worth millions were destroyed, and indeed this was done solely upon orders from above and featured in the four-year plan, because in fact even the last toothpaste tube was squeezed-out so as to prevent anything being recovered. In some homes there were vile thefts, of RM. 4,000.- as at Anna's, whose husband is a retired official, at other people's, jewellery, whereas from others not the least thing was stolen but only destroyed. Now the poor people sit in their homes in the cold as the window panes have not as yet been permitted to be repaired by order.

Worse however than everything are the arrests, in N. everything was destroyed, few people were arrested, whilst in F. everyone [was] arrested, even the foreigners, no homes were destroyed, only the shops. In M. every man was arrested (in F. even the women temporarily), and almost without exception those arrested were deported to Dachau; there they were allowed to receive and send a letter of 15 lines every 14 days. Some money could be sent to them. Our brother-in-law Herbert is also there.

Nor did the matter go away so completely without bloodshed either. A friend of mine, jeweller F. L., had just undergone surgery in the Jewish Hospital in F., the sisters did not want to release him and he suffered a fatal stroke; Paul Lebrecht was thrown down the stairs, dead. Brother Langstadt suicide. Will not be the last. Other people lowered themselves on sheets at a window and remained in their nightclothes in the garden or garage. The funeral of an acquaintance, turnout three people, of whom one spoke a few words, had to take place in the open air as even the cemetery hall has been completely destroyed.

The synagogues were already plundered during the previous night, in N. of 40 *Sefer Torahs* [Torah scrolls] 27 were destroyed, the silver pendants stolen, and all that, even though this quarter was guarded and cordoned off by the police on this night because of the Führer's presence. Due to the draconian measures that now followed, for many people it is also no longer possible to buy food, even those who have money, even pharmacies refuse to dispense, and medical care is completely inadequate. All the homes must be vacated by 1st December, where to now, where to later, that is the question which dominates everyone, neither the material question nor the stomach question are in the foreground, this question and the people who have been arrested are the anxious questions which everyone asks themselves.

So help, help, help everyone, as one can, and those who believe they have done enough might do the same again, even that is too little. One must admit that through clandestine aid and comfort, which today many Christians provide for Jews, it has been proved that this vandalism is not coming to pass from the German people. Many groups must likewise endure the worst even if in another form,.

Many rabbis had their beards cut off, and [they were] arrested.

Reporter: unnamed, sent by [crossed out: S.I.G.] Juna, St. Gallen

B. 156 24 hour Jewish pogrom

Half past 6 in the morning: SA and civilians making a noise at the door, "*Juden aufmachen, Hausdurchsuchen*" [Jews open up, house search]. Everything is ransacked, the furniture is smashed to pieces, nothing is found, penknives are confiscated as weapons. On the street: these are completely dead. SA and SS as well as riff-raff rule the streets. Jewish shops are plundered, afterwards these have to be barricaded, they are sealed up, so that people will not steal from them. All the Jews who can be seized are arrested, whether on the streets or in their homes. Anyone who was amongst the lucky ones still to be free tried to find safety with Christians, of whom there were very many who had sympathy with the Jews. We go on further, we hear the detonations which stem from the fact that all the *Tempel* [synagogues] are being blown up, and what was left afterwards was nothing but rubble and ash. The mob is to be seen everywhere with joyful faces, they have after all accomplished a great deed. The families are robbed of their homes. 16 people squeezed into one room, in order to dwell like this for three days. What money and jewellery a Jew owns was taken away. Taking earrings out of the ears of small children was not shirked, or the last RM. from women's handbags. My acquaintances, who managed to have themselves released from prison, could not report enough about the suffering they had to bear although they were at the front in the World War and had experienced many such things and claimed unanimously never to have seen such inhumanity. The following events occurred in a cellar in which the Jews were accommodated: women aged 50–55 had to strip naked in order to perform a dance, demonstrated to them by the SA, for the men who had been locked up with them. Sick women had to relieve themselves '*coram publico*' [in public] in front of men and children on the W.C., of which there was only one for 200 people. Children aged from one month to two years received nothing to eat for two days as they were locked up with their parents.

I could continue this report for hours yet.

Reporter: Fritz Grünwald, 15 Rue Geoffroy Marie, Paris

B. 157 I am reporting to you in what follows about the events on 10th November in Mannheim.

Frau A. and her daughter in Mannheim had every single one of their belongings looted, down to the last shirt, the furniture was completely wrecked. Herr B. and his wife in Mannheim J [quadrate, district J] were taken to the lunatic asylum in Wiesloch; as ice-cold water was frequently poured over them there, the wife died of a heart attack. Herr C. in Mannheim D [quadrate D]. had every single thing stolen from him, likewise all his furnishings were completely ruined; the same thing happened to Frau D., who lived in the same building. Rabbi Dr. E. escaped during the night in the fog; everything in the main synagogue was stolen in a short time in the morning by the SA, the valuable articles loaded into a car that was standing ready, a number of children and women who were watching were chased away by the Nazis. The *Thoras* [*Thorarollen*; Torah scrolls] were set on fire, everything was stolen from the Wronker department store in the main street, the window panes were smashed, so were the furnishings.

The owner of the Café Schneider had his premises completely destroyed; he himself was half beaten to death in bed; the owner of the Café Schloss committed suicide as his premises had been destroyed; a synagogue located in the same building was looted and burned down. At the cemetery the most beautiful gravestones were torn out; the *Vorstand* [chairman] of the *Kultusgemeinde* [Jewish community], Simon, a man of 70 years of age, was beaten half to death and taken to the concentration camp. Likewise everything belonging to Frau F. was looted, everything belonging to businessman G. was stolen and destroyed and [he] was taken to Dachau, everything belonging to Dr. H. was also looted and he was beaten half to death and taken to Dachau.

The owner of the Ufa-Palast [a cinema], a 75-year-old man, threw himself from the third floor onto the road, where he remained on the ground. Everything belonging to the owner of the J. department store was stolen and burnt and [he] was taken to Dachau.

These examples show how people rampaged in Mannheim; there are more examples but to write them down would fill ten pages.

Reporter: Lewartowski, 19 Rue Fentier [du Sentier], Paris

Key to names

A = Frau Neumann
B = Herr and Frau Schwarzmann
C = Herr Röhrenheim
D = Frau Esslinger

E = Rabb. Dr. [Chaim] Lauer
F = Frau Hirsch
G = Businessman Weil
H = Dr. [Julius] Appel
J = Aronstern department store or similar

B. **158** 10th November 1938

Groß-Enzersdorf retraining camp, Vienna XXII., 5 o'clock in the morning

"Everyone get up, report immediately!" rang out the order of a Party man. In the camp are 16 men and seven girls aged 17 to 30. Had also two sick (Otto Brauch – hernia, Hans Albin – angina, high temperature). Report in the yard without food as well as without coats, taken to the *Kreisleitung* [district administration] where we already saw all the Jews from the small town. We had to surrender whatever money we had with us [!], we however threatened at the same time, anyone who is hiding something can prepare themselves for what is in store for them.

Then we were all, two-year-old children as well as 87- and 89-year-old men, crowded together in two lorries, and were driven to Winden (Burgenland), deposited us there with the words, "*Jetzt verschwindets, Juden!*" [Now get lost, Jews]. The two old men could go no further, also we did not know what we should do with the sick. The former *Kultusvorsteher* [Jewish community chairman] Z. was also with us, [we] came to the entrance to the town after enormous difficulties, could not and dared not go further, because a board placed there, "*Juden ist Eintritt verboten*" [Entry is forbidden to Jews]. At last a *Gendarm* [policeman] came, who asked us, we said how we had arrived there, thought we should wait. After two hours he came with a lorry and trailer. He told us to climb on, took us to Vienna I., Morzinplatz, to the Gestapo. It was already 7 o'clock, cold, nothing in our stomach, weeping from the women and children. Then immediately on to Elisabeth-Promenade. The whole yard full of "*Grüne Heinrichs*" [police vehicles], a noise, saw Jews climb out, were immediately welcomed with slaps round the face, punches. But we did not remain there either, they brought us back to Enzersdorf.

Stayed two hours locked in the *Tempel* [synagogue], were then taken to Floridsdorf to the *Polizeikommissariat* [police department]. Climbed out, yet could not even stand any longer for hunger, cold, everything was already overcrowded too, was already 11 o'clock at night. It went on to Karajangasse, XX. Order, "Men all get off", women drove on, to where we did not know. Taken to a hall, remained standing there until 2 o'clock in the morning, then our personal details were recorded, led to the yard and had to stand in the cold until 10 o'clock in the morning. Now foreigners as well as men over the age of 60 were allowed to leave.

We others were then crowded with Jews into rooms which at most take 40 people, were in total 206 people, understandable that one could not even turn round. The people who had fainted because of the poor air as well as from hunger were simply taken to the corridor and allowed to lie there quietly on the floor.

Now at last we received black coffee. One man in our hall jumped out of the window, we were on the third floor, he already could not bear the suffering any more, as at every opportunity people amongst us were hit. After that the *Kommissar* [inspector] came with drawn revolver, said should one more of us jump out, ten people would immediately be shot. As punishment we must stand to attention for two hours. If somebody wanted to relieve themselves, immediately received a punch because he had supposedly made a noise. Then we Jews except for a few had their hair cut or plucked in the shape of letters so that one could read "*Jud*'" [Jew] etc. on their head. Then after four days two people were taken to the Elisabeth-Promenade for the decision whether release or Dachau.

He who has been released had to go through a *Salzgasse* [salt alley], what that means is well known. But unfortunately only a few had the good fortune to go home, they were mostly 17-year-old lads.

Reporter: Robert Steiner, 38 Rue Bisson, Paris

Key

Z. = *Kultusvorsteher* [Jewish [community] chairman] Katz

B. 159 An incident in Z.: The fact that even during this sad time of the pogroms there was no lack of a certain humour and humane understanding, may be learned from the following true event.

In Z. Herr B., as the only Jew, was taken to the prison in the town. B. was seriously diabetic and when Frau B.'s husband's arrest was carried out, she immediately hurried, very concerned, to their family doctor. This doctor got in touch with the prison doctor and managed to arrange that B. could not only cater for himself but that the bottle of red wine, which he was in the habit of drinking, would be sent to him in the prison each day by his wife. The prison warder was also thoughtfully provided with a bottle of red wine each day. After only a few days B. was released and thanked the prison authorities for treating him well. He passed on various items of furniture to the prison warder at his request, as since then he has emigrated to America.

Reporter: Dr. K. Zielenziger.

Note:

Z. = Siegmaringen (Württemberg)

B. = brewery owner Franks

B. 160 Herr Paul Lissa, Frankfurt am Main, who was taken to the Dachau concentration camp, suddenly died there. The family has only received the notification [that] Herr L. suddenly died "of a heart attack".

In the Dachau concentration camp Herr *Rechtsanwalt* [lawyer] J. Riesser from Augsburg also died suddenly. He had also been taken to Dachau. A short time after his arrival his sister was invited to the Gestapo where they revealed to her [that] her brother had suddenly died of pneumonia. To Fräulein R.'s very energetic response [that] she did not believe this information because her brother was always in rude health and extremely strong and [that] one could not die in a few days from pneumonia, it was stated to her by a Gestapo official that he had to refuse her all information.

Reporter: Arthur Lehmann

B. 161 Report by an "Aryan" lady from Berlin:

On Thursday lunchtime at about 1 o'clock a gang of 13 or 14 men appeared in the *Konfektionsviertel* [clothing manufacturing district]. Three well-dressed men gave orders to the rest, who represented the "*kochende Volksseele*" [seething populace]. This group of ten or eleven men armed with long iron bars and axes forced their way into the wholesale shops in order to smash to pieces everything, but absolutely everything, that could be destroyed there. However that was not enough for this "*kochende Volksseele*". Clothes, furs, typewriters, coat racks, yes, even the flowerpots from the big showrooms were thrown onto the street. All the account books, work slips and card indexes flew onto the street. Everything about this that one reports is lame compared to the reality. From 1 o'clock until 6 o'clock came the sound of window panes shattering. Mountains of glass piled up on the streets and the paper from the account books lay over everything like snow. When the mob came back out of the individual buildings, the men had their pockets searched by the three ringleaders, for the *kochende Volksseele* was not allowed to steal anything. Below, the ringleaders and watchdogs ensured that the street was empty. Passers-by were held back with the words, "Street clear, window panes coming down here now!", whilst another redirected the traffic, and parked cars were pushed to the side in advance. I would like to point out particularly, that during the whole operation, the regular *Streifen-Verkehrs-Polizei* [traffic police patrol] was of course on the streets, without taking any notice at all of what was happening.

In one large wholesale shop the staff had temporarily left the premises and closed a heavy iron door, so that the gang could not force their way in despite their most strenuous efforts. At this the *kochende Volksseele* went and found a mason, who had to knock a hole through the wall from the neighbouring building, so that the mob could invade and then carry on with its work of destruction.

In the main streets it looked as if Berlin had been exposed to a bombing raid. Everything was dragged out of the shop windows onto the street. In the radio shops the large sets were smashed to pieces, in the wine merchants wines and spirits were ankle deep – everywhere, everywhere an indescribable chaos.

Reporter: an "Aryan" lady from Berlin

B. 162 Report

After my wife had first been told by the *Kriminalbeamten* [detectives] that there would be no question of my arrest, considering the completeness of my emigration papers, it nevertheless followed on Friday, 11th November 1938 in the morning. We, about 1,000 men, then went to Weimar in the custody of SS men, and there first of all had to stand for 12 hours, from 9 o'clock to 9 o'clock. After that we were ordered to remove spectacles and hats and were herded through the tunnnel at the double, pressed together in groups of 40–50 men; those standing on the outside were shoved and beaten with carbines, so that there were many bloody weals and elderly men unconscious. Then, to shouts of "*Verfluchter Jude*, [Damned Jew], run faster!" and similar, we were loaded onto lorries and taken to the camp [Buchenwald]. There we made our entry at the double, escorted by so-called *Kapo* men in blue uniforms, who carried out the supervisory duties in Buchenwald and behaved relatively well, as long as the SS were not standing behind them. We then had to stand for the entire day, lined up and without any head covering. For three days we received nothing to eat, then so little coffee that rain water tasted to us like champagne.

We were then taken to have our hair cut and had to collect and hand in the hair, because it was obviously intended to be used due to a shortage of material. Head wounds were simply cut around. We did not hear other terms of address, such as "*Sauhaufen* [herd of swine], *Judenhaufen* [herd of Jews], you'll be shot."

From my observation the youngest prisoner was 14 years of age, the eldest 73 years of age. The old men were treated particularly harshly. The most unbearable thing was the latrine situation, so dreadful that many simply did not eat anything for fear of having to use the latrine. We did not receive any bedlinen either and had to sleep on the bare wood without blankets. The barracks were intended for about 500 people and were occupied by 2,500; 5 beds were arranged on top of each other, the ground was clay on which those accommodated below had to sleep. The last barrack, 4a, was still being built. There was a constant shortage of water as the water was suspected of carrying typhus. Suicides happened frequently; during the night the prisoners would run into the live electric wire in their despair – I even experienced a case in which one Jew clearly driven to insanity bit through an artery with his teeth. Almost every night I heard shouting and gasping, obviously as a result of indescribable mistreatment by the SS men.

From 7 to 8 o'clock was reporting for duty. Then there was coffee which had gone cold and after that four hours of standing in a line, the midday meal, consisting of soup, potatoes and occasionally bread with cheese or herring. We had to buy dishes for RM. 3.- and pay again on release. I never received the travel money which my wife sent to me, also a card sent by me on 12th November was only posted on 26th November.

We were not provided with clothing and I did not get out of my things for the entire 14 days that I was in the camp, although they had become dirty and heavy through the eternally damp clay floor. The well-known punishments – being tied to trees with raised arms [*Baumhängen*] and 25 blows [25 *vorm Arsch*] – I have often seen carried out myself and observed that the Jews punished in this way almost always lost consciousness.

One day the order was given, "Millionaires step forward", and when eight to ten then came forward, amongst them the well-known Schnaps-Wolff from Breslau [now Pol. Wrocław], they were led away. Obviously to get money out of them.

An elderly prisoner fell into the latrine as a result of the unbelievable condition of the seat, and died. In every barrack a *Revier* [sick bay] was set up by Jewish doctors that worked well – diabetics and those with a heart condition however were sent to their doom helplessly. The result was that every day stretchers could be seen going past carrying the dead.

Most people's feet froze, because they could not decide to

take off their damp socks and shoes. Nothing happened to me healthwise, I just lost 12 pounds. We were not provided with clothing in our barracks and therefore also did not need to work. Those who were given clothing had a *Mogen Dovid* [Star of David] on their trousers and jacket, *Rassenschänder* [race defilers] a red stripe on their backs. Rabbi Hoffmann from Breslau, who is 65 years old, broke his leg in the damp clay and went into the *Lazarett* [sick bay]. A merchant from Breslau whom I know well called X. died as a result of beatings. I was summoned by the Gestapo in Breslau on 18th November, but first released on 26th November after we had spent a full day futilely reporting for duty and, after we had been shaved, all money was taken from the wallet. There were then 108 of us who all had visas who were released and taken to a village where we were left to fend for ourselves. Before release we still had to sign different disclaimers of demands etc. as well as the *Schweigepflicht* [pledge of confidentiality], not without having our travel money taken away from us again beforehand.

On discharge it was again explained to us that our brothers in faith would have to pay for it if we said anything about the events in the camp when we were outside.

In the camp was a large zoo with birds of prey, giant vultures and condors, as well as bear pits. Each day at *Appell* the animal keepers would come forward and clean the cages. Because of the many predators there was an unbearable stench in the camp.

Reporter: Hermann Schwarz, businessman, formerly Breslau, Strasse der SA 171, in transit to New York

Key:

X.= Neustadt

B. 163 Synagogue and mortuary in Erfurt were burned down on 9th/10th November 1938.

Reporter: Emil Fischer, Soerlaan 3, Amstelveen

B. 164 Report of 15th December 1938

As a result of the exertions or other causes in the concentration camp, Herr Dr. jur. Sussmann, Cologne, died one day after his release.

Special source *Direkt K.* (A. W.) [Alfred Wiener]

B. 165 The reporter has good contacts in Chemnitz as a result of a business connection over many years. He advises that the synagogue there has burned down and the *Vorsteher* [chairman] of the *Gemeinde* [community] arrested. His name is Alfred Kahn. Whether he has been released is uncertain. Further arrests have also been made. The rabbi was arrested and apparently mistreated. His name is Dr. Fuchs. He is said to have been in the police hospital until very recently. The reporter states that he knows from a reliable source that Herr Grünberg, former employee of the *Unita Strumpfwarenfabrik AG* [Unita Hosiery Factory] is dead, likewise Herr Fürstenberg of *Tietz AG.*

Reporter: A. Polak jun., Albrecht Dürerstraat 18, Amsterdam-Z[uid]

B. 166 WHAT IS NOT KNOWN ABOUT GERMANY

Foreign countries know much about the martyrdom of the Jews in Germany. It is therefore superfluous to repeat that which is well known. Those are the laws, regulations and prohibitions that appear officially. These are so hard, the German Jews are so intimidated, so afraid, so hounded, they have resigned themselves to it, in the way they resigned themselves to the Nuremberg Laws. These laws must really seem unenforceable to the foreigner. But they are being enforced, with this uncanny precision that never leaves the German, not even when it is to carry out the greatest atrocity. These well-known provisions, the "*legalen*" [legals] as one calls them in Germany, would be borne by the German Jews, simply, because – as paradoxical as it sounds – they love the country as hardly one of the select Aryan Germans does, because it is their home and they earn their living there, even if very quietly and secretly for years, because they know just how few places there still are for emigrants, and how hard it is to gain acceptance as such anywhere in the world – and because for thousands of years, with some respite, but still without an end, they have been wandering through the world ostracised and hounded. Even though there have always been Jews who brought advances and benefits to humanity through inventions, and scientific and artistic achievements.

As even today in Germany a standstill can be detected in respect of achievements and progress in every area.

The statutory laws now are not that which now make it impossible for a Jew to live in Germany. It is the unwritten ones, which are hidden from the members of its own population with nothing short of admirable skill. The people know incredibly little. Nothing may be told, anyone who disseminates facts will be locked up, harassed with the most astounding efficiency, and no privileges of the favoured Aryan will remain to him. So silence prevails, and only seldom does a grain of truth seep through to the masses. Only the worker is in the know. He is and was the only one who was educated politically, he is not anti-semitic, but anti-Nazi, but he is vulnerable and powerless and gagged by hordes of bestial men in uniforms and even more by camouflaged civilians, the henchmen of the *Geheime Staatspolizei* [Gestapo; Secret State Police].

The persecution of the Jews of recent weeks is a *PRIVAT-AKTION DES FÜHRER* [Personal operation by the Führer]. No intervention by Himmler, the leader of the SS, no plea by Magda Goebbels or Emmi Göring can bring about any mitigation. Since Munich the Führer feels himself safe, no war threatens him, so he employs all his uncanny intensity to the Jewish question. His hatred is applied to male Jews. Arising from his earlier time in Vienna and Munich when he turned to women without success, as he is gauche, inhibited and physically inept, but nevertheless desired women and longed to possess them. For the great ruler of the German Reich the sought-after women are naturally at his disposal. Yet the unknown man of earlier saw them slip inexorably from his grasp. Again and again the women he courted would turn away from him to young, fresh, lively Jewish men. From this stems one of his terrible rage complexes. "*Hitler*", the book by Rudolf Olden, deals with these incidents in a most objective way and is said to be completely true by Hitler's early fellow combatants and helpers, who today almost all stand against him. A new confirmation of the doctrine of the great Freud.

The impact of this rage complex is harrowing. And unstoppable. For the organisation is good like no other. Every official body says: *PRIVATAKTION DES FÜHRER*! He himself answered one of his first colleagues, who was championing the cause of two prominent Jews well known to him, "Anyone who undermines or thwarts my orders, will be shot." Anyone who speaks to the Führer of a mitigation of his policies for a single Jew, experiences one of Hitler's temper tantrums. The chairs destroyed with his fists during such moments each day amount to a considerable number. His doctor, who is treating him psychiatrically, only visits him in the company of an assistant. His adjutant and closest confidant, Brückner, was released from a sanatorium where he was said to taking a cure for alcoholism, because he simply could not be restrained and belonged in a high-security institution.

In the hands of these men now lies the fate of all, but also of all German Jews, who could only be captured. Officially today no one in Germany yet knows that all the Jewish men from 17 to 65 years of age were arrested. The hunt began on 10th November. Suddenly. Without reason or only a bogus reason. In the night of 9th to 10th November all the synagogues in Germany were on fire. Only a very few remain, where the fire would have endangered valuable neighbouring buildings. The *Feuerwehr* [fire brigade] arrived at some too early, in order to protect the surrounding buildings. The "*Volkswut*" [people's rage] erupted throughout the whole of Germany at precisely half past 2 in the morning. But the SA had mothers, brides, daughters, sisters, who passed on by word of mouth, "The SA carried the firebrands into the *Tempel* [synagogues]."

That same night the henchmen of the *Geheime Staatspolizei* forced their way into the Jewish houses, overran those who opened the doors to them and without more ado invaded the bedrooms. Afterwards during the house searches they ransacked everything for weapons. The law that a Jew is not allowed to bear arms had appeared the previous day. These dregs of humanity, who place themselves at the disposal of the *Geheime Staatspolizei,* conducted themselves in an unimaginable way. Swore at women and children in the most vile way and only rarely allowed the arrested Jews to get properly dressed. Many were driven onto the street in their nightclothes and loaded onto open lorries. All without the barest essentials, most without coat and hat. Often also troops of arrested Jews were driven through the towns, with provocateurs, who stirred up the people, that they were crooks and traitors to the Fatherland. Interrogations by the police and *Staatspolizei* [state police]. For hours and hours these distressed people had to stand erect, face to the wall. Anyone who slumped got blows from rifle butts. Some of them also stood in the courtyards of the prison institutions, inadequately dressed, in the icy wind, face to the wall, seven or eight hours. Motionless. Anyone who had a suitcase with them with essentials was allowed neither to put it down nor to change arms. Always blows with rifle butts. Age and illness played no part. At night without blankets on the prison floors, full of vermin. Completely inadequate food. During the interrogations only "*Judenschwein*" [Jewish pig] and "*Du*" [familiar "you"] was said. Holders of high military decorations were taunted about where they had wangled them from, and they were constantly shouted at, that they would be shot.

After two to three days most of these unfortunates were taken to the concentration camp. In cattle trucks, standing close together, for a journey of up to twelve hours, without a break. There was not the slightest embarrassment in connecting the ill-fated transports to official trains. But there were also trains of 30–40 coaches which ran separately across the country. Who should have said something?

Many times in Berlin, Munich, Düsseldorf, well-known Jews – doctors and others – were dragged out into the street and beaten to death. If an Aryan passer-by summoned the courage even just to say, "But that's too much", he was beaten so badly that he had to be carried away on a stretcher. Or his teeth were smashed in as an everlasting memory. So the Aryans heard the screaming of people being tortured to death and they had to stay silent, full of horror.

Synagogues and community buildings burned down. Some of the clergy were driven into the fires, some were not let out. In many places they had to give "performances" out in the open in full regalia: mumbling, knees bent, bowing in front of the howling mob. Always with blows from rifle butts from behind.

People were caught everywhere. Off the street, out of trains, in homes and hotels. Anyone who appeared Jewish was also taken away.

Most are now in camps. Nothing is known of them. Only that they have to do heavy work. Mostly an hour's march to the work place, ten hours' heavy work, an hour's march back and into the camp. Not once during these twelve hours permitted to rest or to sit down. They were not allowed to take anything with them into the camp, no articles of clothing, no soap, no comb. A very few individuals came back after two or three weeks. Fortunate people, whose cause was championed by an embassy of a foreign state. They said nothing, only about the great willingness to help and humanity of the current inmates of the camp, some of whom have already spent their life there for many years now.

A small section of the Jews now imprisoned is accommodated in prison institutions. They are better off as far as treatment is concerned, because the old staff of state prisons is fair. But they are not allowed to work, to write, to read, like the convicts. The *Pritschen* [plank beds] are strapped up at 5 o'clock in the morning, and they have to sit all day on their stool with nothing to do. No difference for the severely war wounded. They are not allowed out in the fresh air in the yard like the criminals. Presumably so that the inhabitants of the surrounding houses do not notice who is overpopulating the prisons.

No *Advokat* [lawyer] can help. Initially the relatives of those who had been taken away went to *Rechtsanwälte* [lawyers], who tried to help. After three days a ukase [decree] appeared: no *Advokat* is allowed to intercede for an imprisoned Jew. – If he does, he will become destitute if not locked up.

So these unfortunate men are abandoned to the crudest

arbitrariness. For how long? Who knows? Just as no one knows who is still alive. Germany is the land of tears. Everyone is under threat. Everyone is suffering – no one can help.

It is completely meaningless whether a Jew today volunteered to serve in the war, has the highest war decorations and a few weeks ago would still have been an officer in a regiment on active duty in the event of war. The severely war wounded suffer agonies, because no consideration is given to them at all, they are tormented and allowed to suffer like all the others. There are no doctors for detained persons. A 65-year-old had chest pains during the interrogations. He was locked up in a cell with a Jewish doctor who had also been arrested and was told, "There you have medical help." But there were no medicines or injections.

This factual report has been compiled by an Aryan Christian for Christians. Help your neighbours. In Germany no one can help. Get these unfortunates out. Anyone who has an entry permit for another country gets out of the camp. If it has been established, after endless research, in which one they are to be found. Usually even the authorities do not know where an individual is.

The regime cannot be compared with any other in terms of atrocities, now or in the past.

Some prominent men gifted Europe peace in Munich. This peace brought an unspeakable martyrdom to hundreds of thousands of people. No one could foresee that. But now only foreign countries can help.

HELP!

The letter writer is a German-American lady who lives in a Hanseatic city.

The letter was passed on before 15th December 1938 by Max Heimann, Brussels

B. 167 In Gablonz (Bohemia) [now Cz. Jablonec nad Nisou], on 9th-10th November 1938 the synagogue was set on fire. Whilst this was going on a sign was hung around a Jew – his name was

Robitschek – and he was pushed in the direction of the burning synagogue doors. Suddenly the organ began to play in the burning synagogue. The crowd was startled and found it eerie. After this nothing else happened to the Jew.

Reporter: Arnold Budlowsky, formerly of Gablonz, now of Hatton Garden 19/21, London EC1.

B. 168 In Duisburg-Hamborn, during the evening in the course of the operation on 10th November 1938, the SA mistreated a Jewish family – husband, wife and two children – in their home. Of the children the girl was twelve and the boy 15 years old. The furnishings in the home were destroyed. The family did not dare to set foot in their home for a considerable time. That was wise indeed for the SA arrived again the next day with hatchets. When an Aryan neighbour assured them that nobody was at home, they declared, "Then we are not allowed to break into the home," and withdrew once more. The father and son meanwhile have gone abroad.

An old gentleman aged 68 and a boy aged 16–17 from Essen are still in Dachau concentration camp amongst others. Two of those released from Dachau (emigration papers) are seriously ill. The people from Essen did not need to or were not allowed to work in Dachau. Yet they had to stand in the yard from 5 o'clock in the morning until 7 o'clock in the evening, dressed only in the thin *Drillichanzug* [cotton drill uniform] without underwear. Furthermore in the last week the temperature already fell to -8 degrees Celsius. Washing facilities scarcely available and then in a completely inadequate manner. The treatment of Jews from Vienna and the Palatinate is depicted as particularly bad.

In there is a former Dortmund resident who together with his brother-in-law has been "treated" with hydrochloric acid. The wounds are still visible. In this case the Dortmund police had rejected a request for *Schutzhaft* [protective custody].

The back of one of those released from the Buchenwald camp, who is at present staying in Amsterdam, forms a single scar.

Reporter: Heinz W. Nassau, Groot Hertoginnelaan 26, Bussum

B. 169 Currently in Amsterdam there is a Herr A., formerly of Essen and Bochum, recently of Berlin who, together with ten companions, succeeded in breaking out of the Oranienburg (Sachsenhausen) camp on 11th November where he had been for c. eleven months.

They knocked down an SS guard, were taken far away by a long distance transport and in this way after many other difficulties and dangers four men got as far as Antwerp in their *Drillichanzug* [cotton drill uniforms], from where they then were sent here. Three others were able to get through to Poland. He knew nothing about the fate of the remaining four men.

Reporter: Heinz W. Nassau, Groot Hertoginnelaan 26, Bussum
Herr A. = Seidemann

B. 170 Dr. med. Emil Hartogh, Hamburg, formerly of Wandsbeck, took his own life on 28th November 1938. Dr. H., who was a Christian non-Aryan and lived in Wandsbeck at Claudiusstraße 20, was one of the most eminent doctors in the area. He had so taken to heart the attacks that were repeatedly directed against him by the National Socialists – his name appeared amongst others on a handbill distributed in Wandsbeck that bore the headline, "Which Jewish enterprises are there in Wandsbeck?" – and the loss of his practice, that he has now taken his own life, after one suicide attempt had already failed. Dr. Hartogh was 63 years old.

Reporter: Albert Hartogh, formerly of Hamburg, now of Amsterdam.

B. 171 From a letter by an emigrant from San Francisco dated 23rd November 1938:

"... I am, as you will understand, very concerned about my parents, in addition to that is the depressing feeling that I myself am in a nothing less than enviable position and on the other hand barely able to help with the madness over there.

My mother wrote to me in a confused airmail letter of 11th November that our shop in K.-Straße has been completely destroyed and that her brother and a series of other relatives have been taken to the concentration camp. (The words concentration camp have been changed to hospital.) Another cousin, who was already taken to Sachsenhausen two months ago, suffered a "heart attack" there a couple of weeks ago from which he then died..."

From a letter from Herr Heinz Berggrün of San Francisco, passed on by Herr Ernst Wallach of New York.

Key

K.-Straße = Konstanzer Straße, apparently in Berlin

B. 172 The events of 9th to 11th November are, after the observations made in Germany, in no way to be considered merely as a consequence of the murder in Paris. Rather the act by Grynszpan was merely the welcome catalyst for the implementation of measures which had already been planned well in advance. Even hostile acts against Jewish *Gotteshäuser* [houses of worship] had increasingly become a reality in the autumn.

This is to an extent a case of "legal" acts. Some of the synagogues in Munich, Nuremberg, Dortmund etc. have been disposed of "voluntarily" by the synagogue *Gemeinden* [communities], some dispossessed in the *Enteignungsverfahren* [expropriation procedure]. In Dortmund a sum in the region of RM. 170,000.- was paid which was equivalent merely to the value of all the land whilst no account was taken of the substantial building. But even the purchase price of RM. 170,000.- was forfeited a short time later through the *Beschlagnahme* [confiscation], because during demolition of the synagogue building old leaflets had been discovered in a floor area which had accidentally been put there because the *Gemeindehaus* [community building] was being renovated.

In addition to these measures, which had at least some lawful basis however, damage to and burglaries of places of worship also took place repeatedly, even before 9th November e.g. in Westphalia.

Similarly even before Grynszpan's deed stones were being thrown at and vandalism was carried out on Jewish private houses. Such events were happening e.g. even in the summer in Hülchrath

(Rhineland) [now in North Rhine-Westphalia], in (Westphalia) [now a district in Selm, North Rhine-Westphalia] etc.

After the Paris murder the destruction of Jewish property and the burning of synagogues in the provinces of Hessen and Nassau already started before the death of the wounded man on 8th November.

It emerges from all this evidence, as also from the enlargement of the existing concentration camps, that the so-called reprisals would have been carried out in the same or similar form even without the welcome pretext.

The number of synagogues set on fire in November cannot be determined. In western Germany it can be established that no Jewish place of worship has escaped its fate. The degree of damage is very different though; in some of the great massive stone buildings in part merely the interior was burned out whilst the building itself remained intact, and precisely for this reason provides a ghostly sight with its empty window cavities.

The number of those arrested and those taken to concentration camps may amount to roughly 35,000. Of these 35% may have been released again in the middle of December. At present these are front-line soldiers and people whose imminent emigration can be proved.

The treatment of the prisoners was very variable; in Berlin it appears that no mistreatment was inflicted before transfer to concentration camp, or only very rarely, in Frankfurt highly unpleasant scenes (*Einzelexerzieren* [individual punitive drills], exercises by those lying on the floor and the like) occurred in the *Festhalle* [large hall for trade fairs].

The number of violent deaths is impossible to establish. The following have been killed: a Dr. Levy from Polzin [now Pol. Połczyn-Zdrój], the former proprietor of Tietz, Fürstenheim, in Chemnitz, four residents of Hilden (Rhineland) [now in North Rhine-Westphalia], coffee house owner Marcus in Düsseldorf, whose wife suffered a serious gunshot wound to the stomach. Jacoby, Küstrin, and Bamberger of Nuremberg are also said to have been killed.

The number of suicides is extraordinarily high; three such

cases are said to have taken place in Würzburg; in Munich a partner in the Aufhäuser banking house met his end by committing suicide, in Essen *Rechtsanwalt* [lawyer] Heinemann committed suicide with his wife, in Nassau an old man called Stern etc. A series of fatalities also occurred amongst elderly people due to the turmoil they had suffered.

The banker Wallich, Paul von Schwabach, both from Berlin, Dr. Hartog of Hamburg.

The mortality rate in concentration camps is very high; as things stand on 1st December the fatalities are said to amount to 180 in Buchenwald, 44 in Sachsenhausen-Oranienburg, relatively few in Dachau. The results of the cold snap in the second half of December cannot be predicted as yet.

Amongst those arrested the most by far were rabbis who were frequently treated particularly badly as they had relinquished their posts. Rabbi Klein, Düsseldorf, and his wife were thrown down the steps.

Because of the numerous arrests of Jewish teachers, education has sometimes been completely disrupted.

The economic consequences of the events are incalculable. The damage to property that has occurred also still cannot even be approximately determined. Nor can anything yet be stated about the impact of the so-called *Sühneleistung* [reparations].

In addition to these publicly known measures however, extortion took place about which nothing is known.

In Berlin wealthy Jews who want to emigrate have for some time not automatically been receiving their *Unbedenklichkeits-bescheinigung* [clearance certificate], which is the requirement for issuing passports. They are summoned by the *Stapo* [*Staatspolizei*; State Police] to an assessor, Müller-Scholtes, and compelled to make a special donation to the Graf-Helldorf-Fonds. This fund is supposed to be used to fund the emigration of less well-off Jews, however to date no case is known where funds have been provided from it. The sums extorted in this way already add up to RM. eight to ten million. Attempts by the *Reichsvertretung* [*der Juden in Deutschland*; Reich Deputation of Jews in Germany] to gain a certain degree of Jewish control have failed.

After the happenings of November the same Müller-Scholtes compiled a "millionaires list", which incidentally was predominantly made up of an array of non-Aryans involved in high finance who came from families baptised long ago (von Gewinner, Solmsen etc.). Five million had to be raised from the people thus selected. Although the Jewish *Gemeinde* [community] strove to achieve this aim, the attempt failed, not before Herr Müller-Scholtes had uttered to Herr Kozower, "If the millions are not collected, it will cost you your head."

All these events are completely unknown to the Aryans in their entirety. Individuals are merely aware of some details which are strongly denied.

The impoverishment of Jewry proceeds at a rapid tempo. After 1st January 1939 it will be barely possible for professional activity to continue, public welfare will basically cease from the same day, leased premises which until now have been debt-free can only continue to be retained against payment of rent. The educational burden of maintaining lessons to the same extent as to date amounts to RM. 25 million per year alone.

Signs of disorganisation and corruption are mounting within the entire population. Thefts within the *Reichspost* [Reich postal service] are increasing, the *Überwachungsbeamten der Zollstellen* [customs office supervisors] show a growing inclination to bribery – incidentally to the benefit of the Jews.

Fierce battles about areas of responsibility take place between the authorities; it is scarcely possible to find a properly authorised person to deal with. In Berlin meetings currently take place chiefly with the *Kriminalrat* [detective superintendant] Gans from the *Polizeipräsidium* [police headquarters] at Alexanderplatz. The *Judenaktion* [Jewish operation] seems to lie in the hands of *Obergruppenführer* [SS General] Wolf of the *Reichsführung SS* [SS High Command]. A Jewish source who has contacts in authoritative SS circles is frequently in a position to give advance warning of impending measures.

Reporter: Dr. Ernst Plaut, Essen

B. 173 Experiences of a young Vienna *Anwalt* [lawyer] in the period from 10th to 14th November.

Herr Dr. X. had, like many Viennese Jewish intellectuals, taken part in one of the re-training courses set up in Vienna by the *Kultusgemeinde* [Jewish community] with the approval of the Gestapo, to manufacture leather belts. At the beginning of September all the participants in this course were summoned to the police, amongst them also Dr. X.; an anonymous report had come in which accused the course participants of "*staatsfeindlicher kommunistischer Betätigung*" [Communist activity against the state]. After extensive, thorough questioning of the course leader and the course participants the police established that there was nothing to this report; it was another of those many unjustified accusations which immediately inferred "*kommunistische Betätigung*" from well-attended gatherings of Jews. The police even allowed the continuation of the course; its participants alone decided on its termination in order to avoid further unpleasantness. In spite of this clarified state of affairs, on 26th September Dr. X. received a summons to the Gestapo, where it was explained to him that as a participant in a course preparing for emigration he would have to leave the country within three months; moreover he had to promise to report twice weekly, and namely on Mondays and Thursdays, at the police station responsible for him in the *Gemeindebezirk* [municipal district] of Vienna I.

Dr. X. consistently complied with this instruction; at the same time he pursued his emigration to Australia with zeal. 10th November fell on one of the days stipulated for reporting, namely Thursday. Dr. X. knew that he would not return home again from this reporting, undertook it out of consideration for his relatives however, and was indeed arrested. From the police station he was first taken to the school in Karajangasse which had been converted into a police arrest centre. He had to spend the time there until Saturday in two small adjoining rooms with another 158 people; the space available to each person on average amounted to 25 cm², there was no possibility of sleep, they had to spend most of the time standing, the feet of the majority of the prisoners were swollen as a result.

From Karajangasse they were taken to the supplementary prison of the Vienna police prison in Hahngasse (Vienna IX). At first they stood there just as in Karajangasse, still under police surveillance, which – as was also confirmed from another quarter – was absolutely proper. On the other hand Dr. X.'s claim, that people on the street behaved aggressively towards the arrested men on arrival, differs from the descriptions of others, who declare that the people took no part in the ordered operation by molesting or insulting the arrested men.

On Sunday evening it was announced that *SS-Verfügungstruppen* [SS support troops] would take over duty in the prison building. "From this moment on," stated Dr. X., "my memory of the events is only of blood, blood and more blood." The police were withdrawn punctually at 12 o'clock midnight, and immediately afterwards one heard the tramp of the approaching soldiers. "The appearance of these men was that of an organised gang of murderers, I have no other term for it," reports Dr. X.

He heard that these men had taken part in a six-month training course in the *Altreich* [Germany], which only provides knowledge of the most barbaric torture of human beings; in fact before 10th November this *SS-Verfügungstruppe,* the appearance of which alone strikes one to the core, was not to be seen in Vienna.

From 2 o'clock at night until seven o'clock in the morning on Monday "exercising" was done under the command of this *Truppe*. The exercises consisted of:

1) Standing to attention facing the wall; at the slightest movement one received punches so that one immediately started to bleed;

2) Raising both arms and moving the fingers up and down; here too a lowering of the arms or slowing of finger movements was punished with punches;

3) "Gymnastics" which were carried out in such a way that every four men of the *Truppe* grabbed the arms and feet of one prisoner and wrenched the limbs in such a way that the unfortunate man had to do a cartwheel.

A "special pleasure" of the *Truppe* formed the hauling out of individual, especially prototypically Jewish-looking prisoners, who were pulled by their hair or had "emblems" cut into their hair.

At 7 o'clock the tormented men received a black coffee; many of them could not swallow at all due to pain and anxiety. Then it was: Report for questioning! The prisoners had to form a double row. The men in front of and to the sides of Dr. X., who himself has a strong constitution, were so weakened from the torture that he had to support them. The interrogation room lay at the end of a very long narrow corridor through which the prisoners had to pass individually. The *SS-Truppe* men positioned themselves so that the Jews had to run the gauntlet past them. They drove the prisoners forwards with punches, many of them stuck out a leg so that they fell over a man from the *Truppe* who, with the words, "*Saujude* [Jewish pig], can't you look out!" laid into the pitiable man. The prisoners were pushed through the door to the interrogation room in such a way that they banged their nose squarely on the desk positioned opposite the door, from there they were pushed back again and had to immediately "stand to attention".

Dr. X. noticed that on the desk of the – Austrian – interrogating officers were folders with the letters "D", "Z" and "E". "D" and "E" were clear to him at once, "Dachau" and "*Enthaften*" [release]. He learned what "Z" meant by chance, he heard from the neighbouring desk the words, "*Zur Überprüfung*" [to be examined], and deduced correctly from the context that it meant being held back in Vienna prisons to examine the assertions of the person being interrogated.

He was asked what he had undertaken to hasten his emigration, and stated truthfully that the approval of his entry to Australia had already arrived, and that every day he expected the permit so that he probably would even be able to emigrate before the appointed date. At that the officer drew a "Z" on his file. In view of his correct assumption Dr. X., with a stiff military bearing, which he believes may have made an impression, had the audacity to speak again, and said, "I can prove the claims I made at any time; I have the relevant documents at home, as I really was not at all prepared for my arrest. In addition I would like to allow myself to point out that I was enlisted from the year 1917, and was awarded the *Silbernes Verdienstkreuz* [silver cross of the order of merit]." At that the officer drew an "E" on the file and Dr. X. was led away by a policeman who stayed next to him, as Dr. X. believes, for his personal protection from further harassment by members of the *SS-Verfügungstruppe* until his release really did take place an hour later. E.g. a member of this *Truppe* really did approach Dr. X. and the policeman guarding him with the words, "What's happening then with the Jew?" to which the policeman explained, "He'll be deported!"

At the German border Dr. X. – as incidentally are most of those currently travelling abroad by this method – was taken from the train which travelled on, whilst the customs formalities took place only after the departure of the train, in the most unpleasant manner. The Jews had to spend the time until the departure of the next train – c. five hours – behind a type of cage bars, hungry, as in ignorance of this stop they had spent all the German money that they were allowed to take with them on the journey to the border.

Dr. X. told me too, as is indeed already well known, that the ceremonial hall at the Jewish cemetery has been completely burnt out, about which he was able to satisfy himself from personal experience; the ceremonial hall at the cemetery in Baden bei Wien, the spa town near Vienna on the southern railway route formerly greatly frequented especially by Jews, has been blown up, as he heard from a thoroughly reliable friend; the person concerned wanted to visit his mother's grave, which lay right next to the ceremonial hall, and could no longer find it for it existed as little as other graves that had been destroyed in the explosion.

Reporter: Dr. Reich from Vienna, now Australia, passed on through Oskar Hirschfeld, London

B. 174 I was arrested on 13th June 1938 at 6 o'clock in the morning in order, it was said, to be taken to a face-to-face meeting. In reality

I was to be transported to a camp because I had been fined RM. 1,000.- during the inflationary period. When we arrived at the Charlottenburg prison, I discovered some 100 Jews who were sharing my fate and with me had to sign a statement at the outset that began with the words, "I, a criminal Jew". We then went to Alexanderplatz and had to sleep there for two days, 70 men in one room with seven bunks. I must point out that I am very disabled by war, still now recognised as being 50%. However that did not delay my transport off to Buchenwald on Wednesday. My wife only learned where I was staying in a roundabout way. Through conversations in the camp I learned that the whole *Aktion* [operation] which then took place later in November had already been prepared in detail at that time, and that Dachau was going to be cleared out for the Jews in order to speed up their emigration. Amongst us were Jews up to the age of 75. We were met at the station by SS men, quite young men from 16 to 20 years of age, with blows from rifle butts and kicks, and then transported in lorries to the camp, where we had to report under the "gallows". With reference to this gallows we were told that not long before a Jew had swung there for a couple of days and that the same thing would happen to us if we showed any kind of lack of discipline. We then had to stand for all of the first day and whilst doing so received cap, trousers and coat, however neither underclothing nor anything to eat. The first meal we received the following noon. We had to sleep 500 men in one barn on the wet earth – we had merely gathered some pine twigs to lie on, which were also damp however. Our barrack was situated on the Ettersberg [a hill]. We had not received any linen either, so that we were very cold during the night. Our supervisor, the so-called *Blockältester* [block elder], was a brutish *Berufsverbrecher* [professional criminal] – in general our supervisors were *vorbestrafte* people [with previous convictions] who had already been in the camp for years. The *Blockführer* [block leader] was an SS man. We were then allocated to an *Arbeitskommando* [work squad] and had to work in the quarry, in particular carrying the broken rocks to the trucks under construction. Everything had to happen at the double, every normal step and any lingering elicited blows from the SS men. There was little to eat, 300 g. of bread, 1½ litres of soup, 15 g. of margarine, 15–20 g. of jam and in the evening a little tiny piece of inedible sausage. We had to get up at 3 o'clock. At 4 o'clock was *Appell* [roll call] which lasted for about an hour, then until 12 work in the quarry, then after a half hour break at midday work again until 4 o'clock, then *Appell* until quarter to 5 and then again work until 8 o'clock. At 10 o'clock we could then go to sleep in the barracks. New barracks had been built when we arrived where it was said the Jews are coming in. There were a lot of punishments. There were general punishments like standing still for eleven hours on the *Appellplatz* [parade ground] without being allowed to move or to relieve ourselves, and punishment drills like *Rollen* [rolling] and *Kniebeugen* [knee-bends].

In addition there were special punishments such as *Anhängen an Bäume* [tree-hanging] i.e. the people concerned were hung from a tree trunk with their wrists tied together, so that the arm joints dislocated and consciousness was lost after only a short time in terrible pain. Another punishment was tying people with their elbows bound together to a tree so that just the tips of their toes touched the ground. I was told reliably for sure, though did not see, that punishments were even carried out in which people were tied up so that their heads hung downwards.

There were 1,250 of us Jews and c. 6,500 Christian prisoners, so-called *B. V.*, i.e. *Berufsverbrecher* [professional criminals]. They had red stripes on their clothes, the *Bibelforscher* [Jehovah's Witnesses] blue and the *Asozialen* [anti-socials] black. There were then in addition the floggings, which were carried out by SS men almost daily during *Appell* in gradations of 20, 25 and 50 lashes for smoking whilst working and similar misdemeanours. The *Scharführer* [sergeants] were quite young SS men, the *Kommandant* [commandant], whose name we were told was Koch, was someone who had been convicted of murder who loved to go around in a white uniform and had a perverse brutish way of watching the punishment being carried out.

Then there were finally also the detentions, where the convicted man had to stand in a darkened cell for the whole time.

A clergyman, whose moaning and shouting I heard throughout the whole time, was in such a cell for two and a half months.

If one of the camp inmates disappeared, everyone had to stand still at *Appell* until he had been found again. One day – that was the most dreadful case I have experienced – a man who had obviously wanted to escape was brought back half dead; his clothes were hanging in shreds from his body. The dogs which were in the camp were then let loose on him and he was so badly bitten that he writhed in pain. He then received a flogging and was laid in a crate, both sides of which had been covered with barbed wire. Slats had been nailed across the top with gaps, then the crate was put out in the sun and he was left without food, so that in the end he must have starved in the crate, which we did not see again after two days. I have seen for myself how another man who had tried to escape was beaten to death with clubs. The SS men trampled on him with boots in order to be sure of his death.

The water supply was so poor that the men drank tar water. The old men no longer responded to food and refused to take any nourishment. In this way of course there were numerous deaths. I estimate that in the two and a half months that I was in the camp 150 to 180 died, in any case corpses were carried out of the camp and the barracks daily and probably burned. There were also numerous suicides of course. The despair was particularly great during the first days after admission, the men simply ran into the neutral zone, as they knew that they would then be shot. However acts of barbarism by the SS men were also frequently causes of death; thus I know that a young man called Lewisohn was intentionally run over by a lorry. The SS men carried out their constantly voiced threat of shooting to kill for the most harmless incidents.

At the start of a rainy period staying in the barracks was unbearable as it rained in. The rain brought many illnesses in its wake, as we had to stand for hours in the clothes that we had to put on when they were still wet. There were frequent cases of pneumonia, also many died from exhaustion and heart attacks. People with heart disease had it particularly hard, e.g. a Herr Kahn from Frankfurt am Main who was very popular and 73 years old. He was carried by us to the doctor, who refused all treatment however. We then carried him back and on the way met some SS men who knocked him off the stretcher and forced him to work. He was flogged so many times that he died two days later. The corpse that we carried back looked dreadful. Deaths from natural causes also became more frequent because the people who were not used to physical work were completely worn out by the 14-hour working day and poor diet. Our *Blockältester* beat a wine merchant from Trier, who was completely worn out, until he died. Seriously ill men also had to appear at *Appell* – they were then carried in on a stretcher and laid down by a tree. Often they died during *Appell*. A 73-year-old Herr Schnell from Berlin, who was seriously diabetic, received such a heavy blow to the head from an SS man that he was dead two days later. In general reporting sick was forbidden, probably because medication was not administered and e.g. gauze bandages were not available at all. The only contact we had with the doctor was on our release, who then examined us to see whether the mistreatment could be detected somewhere or other on our bodies.

Donations were constantly demanded from us for our superiors and Christian fellow internees without means; on average RM. 1.- of our money was made available to us each day. Nothing was stolen from the money to my knowledge, but it was virtually extorted from us. With me, 52 men were released because we had visas. We were brought back under heavy guard in lorries and prison vehicles to Berlin, where we were transported still in handcuffs to Alexanderplatz. My release took place on 29th August.

Reporter: Louis Gumpert, brickworks owner, Berlin W 35, Friedrich Wilhelmstraße 17, 51 years old

B. 175 From Dachau concentration camp an eyewitness who was imprisoned there for 21 days reports the following:

The notorious "Baumhängen" [tree-hanging] was imposed as "punishment" for such who were unable to join in the "sport", e.g. knee-bends twice slowly ten times; the offender had to climb onto a stool, then his hands were chained behind him to a tree and the stool was taken away. Then a little monkey was put on the tree, which played tricks on the defenceless shackled man, bit him in the face, searched him for lice etc., to the amusement of the SS men standing around. Duration: at least one hour as minimum punishment.

Old and sick Jews who complained of stomach problems etc. were taken to the *"Revier"* [sick bay] and there a quarter to a half a litre of castor oil was forcibly poured into them. Then ordered to "stand to attention" in the open air and this even extended to a full twelve hours during rain storms, every movement punished with blows from rifle butts and kicks, until the unfortunate men collapsed unconscious in the evening in their own filth. Subsequently then as punishment for "flagging" three to five days arrest in darkness or "bunker".

On the 30th November Dachau contained about 16,000 prisoners of whom 13,000 were Jews, 3,000 non-Jews – amongst the latter were 5–600 Sudeten German opponents of the Nazis.

The reporter was himself not beaten, firstly because as a proficient sportsman he had proved equal to all "sporting" harassments, secondly because, as one said to him, both his brothers were killed in action as war volunteers.

Exemplary Prussian order prevailed on arrival, release, in the files, depot for surrendered property etc. Comment of an SS officer on release, "Anyone who tells fairy stories in Germany about cruelty will be brought back immediately and then will never again get out for the rest of his life. Abroad, as far as I am concerned, you can say what you want because we sh ... on foreign opinion."

Corporal punishment in the usual form, tied to the *Bock* [whipping block], was seldom over with 25 [lashes], there were always "extras" because, "you needn't scrimp, with that we can be generous, only no false economy in relation to the foreign currency situation ..."

An elderly Jew, apparently a doctor, was turned away from the *"Revier"* as a malingerer, carried back into the barracks by his son on his back and then died three hours later in the presence of his son, who immediately afterwards was ordered away to stand to attention for five hours. Another inmate, an elderly *Justizrat* [state prosecutor], neighbour of the reporter, shouted during a fit of nerves when he saw the mistreatment of others, "They are indeed murderers!" and in the same second was shot dead by an SS man.

Reporter: Max Heimann, Antwerp, Helenalei 20s

B. 175a An Aryan bank director from Germany expressed his views about the position of the German stock exchanges as follows: He attributed the slump to Jewish sales which were made in order to provide liquid funds for the *Fluchtsteuer* [emigration tax]. Jewish security deposits in the region of about RM. 90 million are only supposed to be held at the DD-Bank [Deutsche Bank and Disconto-Gesellschaft] in Cologne.

He went on to report that condemnation and misgivings are being expressed about the pogroms in all sections of the population generally. In the place where he lives, a medium-sized town, a baker is being boycotted by the population and driven to sell his shop because his son took a particularly "outstanding" part in the operations of the 9th and 10th November.

A widow, Aryan, of a Jew who had died years earlier with a typically Jewish name suffered a raid as a result of the name plate on the front door during the night of 9th November. Nothing was stolen and nothing was destroyed because of the *Ariernachweis* [Aryan certificate] to hand. The *SS-Führer* [SS leader] in charge said to her after he had ordered his men to "step back", "Now then doll, you've had one *Schwein* [pig]. To thank me you'll meet me tomorrow night in private, I'll bring champagne and ... with me." The woman was so upset by this raid that she was still suffering from crying fits weeks later.

Reporter: Max Heimann, Antwerp, Helenalei 20

B. 176 The 65-year-old businessman Hamburg, co-owner of the firm *Gebrüder Hamburg* [Hamburg brothers] in Mainz, died in the Buchenwald concentration camp.

A letter from family members about this: "Ernst's eldest brother, 65 years old, will not be coming back from his journey to Weimar." Reporter: Dr. Kurt Zielenziger, Amsterdam

B. 177 ... my nephew Herr F. has forwarded to me your esteemed letter addressed to him. As I have still not received any reply from the *Comité* [committee] to date, I have aproached them directly and enclose a copy here.

Please accept, dear Herr X., my most sincere and heartfelt thanks for your efforts, but be assured that for us the matter is particularly pressing. Your efforts will fall on fertile ground and only bring you rewards. As you well know my good husband died on 10th November from a heart attack, I have also had an 81-year-old father, a 77-year-old mother and a 75-year-old aunt living with me for many years, and I no longer run my business. Everything will be done by the local *Gemeinde* [community] for my little daughter to get her away soon, however I am very worried about my boy. May I turn to you with a request or a suggestion, for I think day and night as to what can be done. As my boy is 18 years old and was already employed in the hotel profession as encl. witness statements testify, would it perhaps be possible for a shipping company in Holland or the Netherlands to in some way employ him as a steward or in the kitchen on a ship, even if it is a very small shipping company. He does not want any pay, just free board. Perhaps he could go to a Dutch colony? We are happy with anything. I look forward with the greatest interest to a very valued reply.

Respectfully yours and with deep gratitude

...

Reporter: R. A. Haas Amsterdam, Noordzeebank

Letter from Frau Olga Herz Bamberger, Nuremberg, Lindenaststraße [Lindenachtstraße] 21

B. 178 Dr. med. Klar in Munich, a former doctor, is said to have died in Dachau from a weak heart, as the reporter believes he knows from a reliable source.

In Weimar Dr. med. Germar (formerly Salomon), a baptised Jew, poisoned himself after he had been released from the Buchenwald concentration camp. The suicide occurred in the period from 5th to 12th December.

In Weimar the cemetery hall was also burned. In fear, the wife of the gardener at the Jewish cemetery, who had her home next to the hall, ran a distance of three kilometres dressed only in a shirt to the house of Rabbi Schifftan's widow. Other people living there who were Aryan protected and dressed the woman.

Information from Herr E. Fischer, Amstelveen, Soerlaan 3
15th December 1938

B. 179 Herr A. was taken from his home on 10th November early in the morning for an *"Auskunftserteilung"* [disclosure of information], and first brought to the Vienna police barracks, Vienna III., Juchgasse. There with 41 other fellow sufferers in a narrow room, which was only ventilated through two very small hatches, he had to spend all of Thursday and the night from Thursday to Friday, the latter standing because there was absolutely no possibility of lying down. On Friday morning the 42 men were squeezed into an extremely low and narrow police vehicle (called *"der Grüne Heinrich"* [Green Henry] in Vienna) and taken to the branch of the central Vienna police arrest centre, IX., Hahngasse, where they were put into the so-called *"Schubzellen"* [holding cells], otherwise [meant] for accommodating those to be expelled from the country. The treatment in this building was extremely cruel, the *Reichs-deutsche* [native German] *SS-Verfügungstruppen* [SS support troops] in field-grey uniforms were on duty, who could not do enough harassing and mistreating the prisoners. Some of them were brought into the yard for *"Exerzieren"* [punitive drill], like a young man with the words, "He looks like [Herschel] Grynszpan, I saw his picture in the newspaper yesterday." After a further dreadful night all 42 prisoners were called for "questioning" on Saturday morning. They had to stand in the anteroom of the interrogation chamber face to the wall whilst the SS men guarding them, who were heavily armed, brandished their guns. A bearded Jew was forced to sweep the floor with his beard. The "questioning" of Herr A. lasted one whole minute, he was able to prove to the interrogator, an Austrian officer, that he had an opportunity to emigrate to England immediately, and was released after ten minutes. The fate of his 41 fellow prisoners is completely unknown to him, he saw them again on his release in the anteroom of the building and assumes that they were all taken to Dachau.

Reporter: Oskar Hirschfeld, London

B. 180 25th December 1938

Information has been received from a trustworthy source that Frau Arnheim née Cohn, who is well known under her pen name of Eddy Beuth, and her sister Frau Marie Jersnitzer née Cohn have taken their own lives in Hamburg.

Reporter: Frau Julie Leipziger-Stettenheim, Berlin (daughter of Julius Stettenheim and widow of Leo Leipziger) and Professor Sinzheimer,

B. 181 My dears,

I will pull myself together so as to write you a few lines. We were very pleased to get your letter. Today we got up from shiva [*Schiwo*; Jewish customary period of seven days' mourning], and you can imagine how we are. Today at midday *Tante* [Aunt] Olga and *Onkel* [Uncle] Jacob came and they left again this evening. We have a lot to talk about and to settle. If you were here, dear *Tante* Käte, you could help us with lots of things, but alas there is nothing that can be done about it. Don't you have any friends at all in Switzerland or in Holland or in England who would take me as a domestic servant until my number (19113) comes up.

I would gladly work for my food. Try to help please, immediately. Perhaps I can thank you for it one day. As soon as dear Mama has settled her affairs she is moving with the A.s to X., so that dear Mama will not be so alone here. I can stay with the B.s, until they go away, they are very nice people. Herr B. was even here and visited us. The D.s live in X., often come with the B.s. My dear *Tante* is quite all right in the circumstances.

I don't have anything else to write except lots of love and kisses
From
Else
On Wednesday, G-d willing, am going back to X.
Reporter: unidentified
Original letter sent from Marköbel near Frankfurt a. M.[am Main]
Town X. = Frankfurt a. M.

B. 182 Visit to the Jewish hospital in X.

On Sunday I visited the hospital with our grandfather in which, amongst many other mistreated people was an old man whose two arms and legs were broken during the spontaneous operation like those of his wife by "throwing them down the stairs"! I asked the Jewish *Oberschwester* [ward sister] to give me a report about the sequence of events that night. I heard the following report:

Already in the days before 9th November we had to admit many of those fleeing, who, living in small places in the area, were attacked at night and mistreated. These people were always much more at risk because they were even more conspicuous living alone. They were brought in with serious injuries. Some, on noticing those breaking into the building, had jumped out of the window in their fear and despair, others came with symptoms of poisoning caused by suicide attempts.

On the night of 9th to 10th November at 4 o'clock in the morning there was a noise at the heavy iron gate of the front garden of the hospital. The sister asked from the window, in expectation of possible new cases, and noticed an SA *Kommando* [squad] which demanded entry. The gate was forced open before she even reached it. When she opened the door of the building the visitors stormed in and demanded that all the patients should leave their beds and go to the street. Under vigorous protest all the wards doors onto the corridor were opened, and each case individually examined "by particularly expert SA men". Only those freshly operated on were left in their beds, all the sick who were able to walk had to leave the building, clothed. All the Jewish sisters also had to go outside, and as a result the Catholic sisters on duty took over the watch. When the Jewish *Oberschwester* came back from her outing a seriously ill man had died as a result of the commotion.

All the people in the hospital were herded to a main square in X. where by now everyone who had been chased out of the houses had arrived or was arriving. The *Thorarollen* [Torah scrolls] were in the middle of the square, lying on the cobbles under the watch of the rabbi, who had meanwhile been beaten up. At the same time the synagogue was set on fire. Next to the *Thorarollen* lay the caskets and the documents from the destroyed *Gemeinde* [Jewish community] house. A flock of about 50 children, who came from the Jewish orphanage, were being urged along. Amongst the women who were standing isolated one noticed a woman who had two one-year-old twins with her. At seven o'clock in the morning the women were released, whereas the men were taken to prison and following that to the camp at Dachau.

When the Jewish sisters were back in the hospital, they discovered all the free beds, but also every other area, even corridors, occupied by sick and mistreated people who had meanwhile been brought in by the town's ambulance men. Christian doctors helped selflessly in the treatment of the unfortunate victims. They were in most cases head injuries and suicide attempts by grotesque methods. Those who had jumped out of the window had cut open their arteries with shards of glass before their deed or had taken some poison or other or large quantities of sleeping tablets. About a hundred people, mostly hopeless cases, were admitted there.

The Catholic Sisters were forcibly removed from the hospital and once and for all that very night on the orders of the SA.

Report about Z.

Released from Dachau report:

During the night we were driven out of the homes into the synagogue. There our rabbi was forced to read aloud from the pulpit some chapters from Hitler's *Mein Kampf*. Then rehearsals were held and finally the Horst Wessel song was sung by everyone present including the Jews. Whilst the synagogue was then set on fire, the men were transported to Dachau.

Characteristic of the situation and regarding the relationship between the brown shirts [SA] and the police, it is noteworthy that it was whispered by humane officers to the unfortunate men at police headquarters, "With us you can relax, nothing will happen to you here!" Personal details were recorded and about 350 thus admitted were transferred to the prison cells. Our father was finally bandaged at 2 o'clock in the afternoon, not without the doctor treating him giving vent to his anger. The seriously injured had already been admitted earlier to the X. hospital. Due to shortage of space our father was accommodated with three other criminals (fellow sufferers) in one cell, from which he was freed through connections on the third day of his imprisonment.

Our mother found the home systematically destroyed. What there had been in the way of glass and porcelain was shattered. The pictures on the wall were damaged in an especially humorous way, in that rectangular pieces of about 30 cms^2 were cut out of them with the bayonets. The wireless set was no longer recognisable, the sideboard tipped over onto its side, so that everything fell out and was conveniently trampled by the heavy boots of the SA. The bedroom was also seriously ravaged. The washstand had been turned into atoms, this, just like the bedside tables (marble tops) had crumbled. The occupants' watches, which were lying on the bedside tables, had been thrown onto the floor and later found again stamped completely flat. A briefcase with money was found later… but without the RM. 500.- which had been in there. All other large pieces of furniture can only be used for firewood.

It should also be noted that on the part of the police, it was made known so-to-speak officially that following this "spontaneous operation" considerable quantities of "*mitgenommene Gegenstände*" [removed objects] made of silver and gold, also sums of money were to be found at police headquarters, which could be collected! Wisely none of the people concerned reported having suffered losses.

Reporter: E. Fischer, Amstelveen, Soerlaan 3

B. 183 Factual report from Y.

On the basis of personal findings, visual inspections on the spot.

Persons concerned: the 81-year-old grandfather, a small little man weighing about 80 pounds; the 71-year-old grandmother, suffering from heart and spinal problems, who can barely move by herself without help; the son-in-law present in the house by chance, who wanted to say goodbye before his emigration from Europe.

Time of the events: the night of 9th to 10th November 1938, at 4 o'clock in the morning.

A personnel carrier with uniformed SA men drives up to the house of the above, they open the front door in a few minutes, and demand entry from the old people with shouts at the door of the flat situated on the first floor. Before the little old man, who had jumped out of his bed so as to open up [was at the door], the door was smashed in with axe blows, and eight men in SA and NSKK [*Nationalsozialistisches Kraftfahrkorps*; National Socialist Motor Corps] uniforms stormed into the flat shouting loudly and ordered the old people who were shocked to death to leave the flat immediately. Our mother fled into the stairwell in only her nightdress and a hastily donned coat. In the meantime the visitors wrecked interior furnishings of the flat, during which curiously enough those parts of the flat that belonged to the landlord were spared (window panes onto the street, bathroom, steam heating, gas meter and electricity). A horror-stricken Aryan living in the house who heard the cracking, splintering of wood, cupboards of porcelain overturned, telephoned the *Überfallkommando* [flying squad] because he believed it was a crime. It was indicated to him he should not concern himself about it, the matter was proceeding "*in Ordnung*" [correctly].

After an hour of hard work the visitors had or believed they had finished their work according to orders, and left the flat with mocking laughter. The despairing old people made their way back to their dwelling, wading through shards and, with the maid who by now had come running up (who had been threatened and locked in her bedroom in the rear building), tried to make some coffee, as they were naturally completely exhausted and frozen. Hardly had they sat down to drink (all the chairs had been destroyed), when after about 30 minutes a second "*Rollkommando*" [raiding party] appeared, which included civilians. All-out attack now proceeded, the old people were again chased out of the door, down the steps to the courtyard. Our grandmother was also dressed only in nightdress and coat on this trip, had only quickly put on a pair of low shoes. Father was in his underwear and had his slippers on. The uniformed thugs had taken up position on both sides of the first small steps and hit those passing with clubs. It goes without saying that the old man was bleeding heavily after a blow to the head, whereas my brother-in-law received several blows as a privilege. Meanwhile all the Jews living in the building had gathered in the courtyard. As the spontaneists still had [business] to do in the flats whilst all the entries and exits to the building were guarded, through an Aryan fellow resident our deeply suffering old mother managed to put on some knickers.

After a further half an hour the mob appeared with howls of joy and announced that now there would be "shooting". The unfortunate people anticipated the worst. The criminals ordered them to line up according to their instructions. The heavily bleeding people close to collapse were again and again corrected by blows and kicks as to their position and posture . . . until they were gradually made aware that only flash photographs would be shot.

At 7 o'clock in the morning all those concerned were moved to the front of the house and from there driven through the streets of the city on foot to police headquarters. Here the women were released at half-past seven.

Reporter: E. Fischer, Amstelveen, Soerlaan 3

B. 184 Our arrest was carried out by police or Gestapo officers, and actually did not involve any personal harassment. We were brought to the local police prisons. One day after our arrest we were informed that we were being held in provisional *Schutzhaft* [protective custody]. Further details could not be provided. The lists of those to be arrested must have been compiled at least nine months earlier because they included people who were already dead or who had emigrated. Even I was arrested under a profession which I have not practised for almost nine months.

After spending one or two nights in prison we were collected by a motor bus and brought to Dachau under police and SA guard, they behaved quite properly during the journey. This picture applied to the groups from places in southern Germany with the exception of the Palatinate and the city of Ulm on the Danube, where the people were dreadfully battered by SA and SS before their arrival. In part they were so badly beaten that this was their salvation, as they had to be transferred to hospital and thus temporarily spared before the concentration camp. People whose wives and mothers had sent packages to the prisons were unfortunate upon arriving at the camp. The SS had posted themselves by the camp entrance, i.e. just by the buses. These young SS men were handed the packages by the escort. The SS were armed with birch rods. Each name was now called. Individuals could only fetch their packages in return for a heavy lashing. So the lucky ones were those who arrived at the camp without any ballast.

We had to stand from the time of our arrival, at c. 4 o'clock in the afternoon, until around 10 o'clock at night. After that we were taken to the so-called *Schubraum* [shunt room or processing room], in which we, that is, c. 3,000 people, spent the night like cattle, lying on top of one another, in two large rooms. The next day we stood from morning until the afternoon in the walkways of the camp, without receiving any food of course, then came to the *Aufnahmeraum* [registration room], in which our personal information, possible previous convictions, previous membership of political parties etc. were recorded. Then we came to the washroom, were stripped completely naked, and our effects were set aside in a sack.

An ugly scene played out in front of the doctor. Individuals had to approach the doctor, line by line, to provide information about previous illnesses and the like. The clerk, who sat to one side of the doctor, a young SS man, was equipped with a birch rod and a pointed object, with which he either pressed into or struck the sides of the naked bodies. The wounds that resulted from this were such that they were still clearly visible after two and a half weeks. The worst of it was the mental anguish caused by knowing that in five or ten minutes' time you would be tortured in exactly the same way as your predecessor. However, the young SS man made the smallest nuances in carrying out this cruelty. E.g.people with slim, sporty bodies received the lightest strokes, whereas heavier people were mistreated more badly.

Otherwise, the day of arrival was only disrupted by slaps round the face, kicks, and lashings. We were informed by older prisoners that these occurred on arrival to enforce discipline in the camp. As soon as one was in uniform the worst was over.

People who had travelled in the famous *Wiener Sonderzug* [special train from Vienna] arrived with us. Several hundred Viennese men had been met by SS men at a pre-appointed time in Nuremberg. They had received no sustenance for four days in all, and travelled for 14 hours in the special train. During the night, they were forced to stare into the electric lights of the carriages without looking away or moving themselves in any way. Because of the pain that this caused for the eyes, nobody was able to do this for very long. However, as soon as anyone looked away or moved, they received terrible beatings from the SS guard. On top of that, they were forced to hit one another. The SS helped out if this was not done powerfully enough. These people arrived in Dachau with four dead, and in fact those who were beaten to death included the youngest person on the journey as well as three older men who had a very Jewish appearance.

Two more on the journey died during and shortly after arrival in Dachau. A number of people no longer had a human face, rather the face was a mass of raw flesh. In some faces one or both eyes could no longer be seen. Almost every single Viennese man had blue marks on the face. These people were so hungry that we gave them some of the black bread we had saved from the prison. Unfortunately this was spotted from afar by an *SS-Sturmführer* [SS lieutenant], who certainly did not know which group of prisoners was involved, nor the troubles these people had behind them, and so he sentenced the Vienna group to *Strafexerzieren* [punitive drill] for the whole afternoon, and which consisted mainly of countless knee-bends. One can imagine how many of them were completely done in, considering everything that they had experienced previously.

In the evenings we came to our barracks, and at this time the 15–16 blocks provided accommodation for 800–830 Jews each. There were therefore between 12–13,000 Jewish prisoners in Dachau. Alongside this, there were c. 4–5,000 Aryan prisoners there. It is calculated that Buchenwald, near Weimar, and Oranienburg [Sachsenhausen] had a much larger number of prisoners than Dachau. We estimate that the number of imprisoned Jews in all of Germany is at least 80,000.

Our prisoner uniforms had been made many months previously, primarily by the tailor's shop of the camp itself. The uniform consisted of a thin shirt and a thin, blue and white striped pair of trousers and a jacket of the same material, although the other prisoners had proper warm clothes. Our fellow sufferers informed us, however, that it had not been directly intended that we were to freeze in such a way, but rather our arrival had already been expected in spring or summer. I had the misfortune of being one of the roughly 8,000 prisoners for whom there were enough prisoner uniforms. The 4,000 Jews who arrived last were able to keep their civilian clothes, because the camp administration had seemingly not bargained on such a large influx. These companions in misfortune were naturally seen by us as being very lucky. They did not, at least, freeze to the same extent as we did, especially on the two days when the temperature dropped below zero, and on those days we stood in the teeming rain.

With the exception of Sundays, when we were awoken at 6 o'clock, we were awoken at 5 o'clock. We spent the night on *Pritschen* [plank beds] that had been lined with straw. However, the straw was so thin and became smaller day by day so that by the end of my imprisonment we were already lying down on bare wood. We lay so closely together that every single movement disturbed the neighbour.

Existing prisoners were made directly responsible for our supervision, and the majority of these had a red badge, i.e. they were former political opponents. One was able to make interesting observations of these people. Inwardly they were on our side, on the other hand it had been made clear to them that would bring forward their own release if they really "pestered" us. Because of this our treatment changed day by day, even hour by hour. So at one moment these supervisors were very nice to us, then again on account of a trifle we had to do 100 knee bends or crawl on fingertips or hop the knee bends, and there were more such pleasantries. We ourselves had, naturally, a yellow *Mogen Dovid* [Star of David] for a badge attached to the prisoner uniforms which were the same colours as the Jewish national colours. The other groups of prisoners, recognisable because of their varied coloured badges, comprised, alongside the *politische Häftlinge* [political prisoners], *Gewohnheitsverbrechern* [habitual criminals], *Arbeitsscheuen* [work shy] and so-called *Remigranten* [re-emigrants], i.e. people who had returned from abroad and were to be taught the ways of the new State in the camps. Amongst the political prisoners were the best of society, e.g. former representatives of the Social Democrats, as well as Austrian ministers; even the former mayor of Vienna, [Richard] Schmitz, who sometimes had to push a heavy road roller with other prisoners. At that time the political prisoners were building new SS barracks.

We did not have to work ourselves, only stand and *exerzieren*. Thanks to the thin clothes and harsh weather, standing was the most dangerous thing of all. This took place three times a day (only twice on Saturdays and Sundays) on the so-called *Appellplatz* [parade ground]. One had to line up here from about 6–8 in the morning, afternoons from 1–3, evenings again from 6–8, in files according to individual blocks. The worst was when the count did not tally. It once happened that one man too many had been counted, and so instead of two hours we had to stand for five. One time we had to listen to various trivial messages via the loudspeaker, which similarly lasted for around five hours. And one Saturday afternoon we were made to stand for six hours for some inane reason.

Every day new countermanding orders arrived, which cancelled out the others. In this way it was decreed one day that the sick and the elderly people were allowed to remain in the barracks, which one was usually only allowed to enter overnight and occasionally whilst eating. Yet on another day this instruction was repealed again, and the elderly and the sick had to march too. Amongst us were numerous people aged 65, 70 and 75.

After uniforms had been issued people were rarely touched by the SS, and then only when someone was not standing in line correctly, or otherwise acted in an undisciplined manner as the SS saw it. Otherwise we provided the selection of the ruined and dying from amongst us, i.e. nobody was beaten to death directly, but rather the weakest bodies were the first victims of this camp regime, then the next weakest etc. It is clear that the majority of deaths occurred amongst the eldest people. We counted c. 50–55 deaths in the first two and a half weeks. On one day, roughly two weeks after arrival, according to the doctor the highest death rate on a single day was eleven. Several prisoners had nervous breakdowns and left the barracks during the night. We had been informed early on that this fell under martial law, and in fact these people were "*auf der Flucht erschossen*" [shot whilst escaping], i.e. killed by the SS night patrol. Several individuals, whose names were announced, supposedly entered into an exchange of words with the SS as a result of their broken nerves, and self-evidently were shot. The vast majority of deaths resulted from stomach obstruction, pneumonia, heart attack, fever and other illnesses.

Reporting to the doctor took place at 4 o'clock, and examinations happened at 10 o'clock the following morning; and when there was a large crowd at 10 o'clock the day after. So long as people were not being spoken to by the doctor in the *Revier* [sick bay], which only took place in the most acute cases, they had to present themselves at *Appell* [roll call] just like all the rest. Because of this we were joined on the *Appellplatz* by the dying, evenings and mornings, and it happened that people fell down dead during roll call.

Releases occurred according to the following considerations:
People aged over 60, though not all of them, only some.
People who had finalised their emigration and who would be allowed to leave Germany within a short deadline.
People who had been recorded as essential for performing business sales.
(this was, however, only in the final days before my own release)
People of special merit and the wounded of the World War.

Upon release, emigrants were made aware of the fact that they and their families would be in a concentration camp for life if they were ever seen on German soil again. The emigration of Bavarian prisoners was 'eased' by the fact that the appropriate notary came to Dachau with a Party lawyer, and all of those who possessed property, businesses and suchlike had to give full authority to the lawyer to sell these at the best possible rate, so that any effort needed for the elimination of their property was removed from them.

Upon my release a number of my comrades came to me, threw themselves on to the floor, and pledged their eternal gratitude if I were able to arrange for their being transferred to a foreign prison. If my comrades still in Dachau were offered a walled-in territory, deep in the primeval forests by decree, then they would pray day and night for him who had brought them this fortune.

If a Jew living in Germany or abroad was ever to fire another shot or to give the regime there any other sort of leverage, then it is certain that hardly any of the Jews who are still resident in Germany would get away with their lives.

The report originates according to a letter of the 19th December 1938 from the *Landessekretariat* [local office] S. J. G. *Schweizerischer Israelitischer Gemeindebund* [Swiss Federation of Jewish Communities] in Zurich, Löwenstraße 1. It was recorded by the office of the *Lokalsekretariat* S. J. G. Zurich, because the member of the *Lokalcomité* [refugees aid committee of the local Zurich Gemeinde] who wanted to complete the report personally is currently ill.

B. 185 The following *Polizeiverfügung* [police order] was passed because the SA had refused to destroy the only Jewish shop in the town during the days of the pogrom.

Police order

By virtue of §32 ff. of the *Landesverwaltungsverordnung* [Regional Authority regulation] for . . . . . ., the shop of . . . . . . the Jew in . . . . . . is hereby closed with immediate effect by order of the police. In case of contravention, i.e. further business activity, I hereby declare a fine of RM. 500.-, in lieu of which in the event of non payment an alternative sentence of two weeks' imprisonment will be imposed.

An appeal against this order will be refused deferment effect, in accordance with §117 sec. II of the *LVO* [*Landesverwaltungsverordnung*].

Basis

The assassination by the Jewish race of *Legationssekretär* [Legation Secretary] vom Rath in Paris has stirred German people and general public to the greatest degree. It has also gripped the inhabitants of . . . . . . to the greatest extent. The *Wut* [rage] of the majority of the population is directed against the only official representative and activity of Jewry in . . . . . ., the shop of the Jew . . . . . . further activity by . . . . . . poses a danger for public peace and safety. It is to be expected that the population will vent their anger and take the law into their own hands. The police must then intervene.

The Jewish race breaches the public peace in general, ... [name to be confirmed] in particular.

His shop must therefore be closed in order to protect his person from attacks by the people and to restore peace in the population again.

On the grounds of the common good an appeal against the order must be refused deferment effect.

Stamp. . . . .

Herr. . . . .

Forwarded by Herr Eliel, Rokin 13, Amsterdam

B. 186 1. On 10 November they (SA) came to A. three times; the first time the interior furnishings were destroyed; glass and crockery broken, furniture smashed, books shredded, etc.; the second time the remaining decorations were taken too, in addition to the sum of RM. 2000.-, which he unwisely had kept in his own home. The third time A. was taken into custody, spent ten days in *Schutzhaft* [protective custody] with 13 others in one cell; nine of them are now in Dachau. For one and a half hours A. was made to do knee-bends until he fell over. Others had to climb ladders in a gym and were handled with bayonets. All were questioned: "*Was sind Sie?*" [formal "you"], or more likely: "*Was bist du?*" [informal "you"] – "I am a chauffeur", "*Nein, ein Schwein bist du, ein Saujud.*" [No, you're a pig, a Jewish pig]. Once more, "*Was bist du?*" If the man did not answer "*ein Schwein*" etc. he was flogged.

2. I was ten minutes from Vienna, with acquaintances, when the bell rang. A report from Dachau: *Ingenieur* [engineer] X. has died. It happened like this: on 10 November taken into custody and to Dachau, despite the fact that the journey to Australia was already sorted out for his wife and children as well as for himself, plus a bank guarantee at Sydney, travel tickets already purchased. A young man of about 35 years, and on 10 November 1938 in perfect health.

3. To the *Jüdische Blindenanstalt* [Jewish Institute for the Blind], and saw there the blind hit in the face with sticks and fists. Women relatives were brought there and asked: "Well then, do you still recognise the *Schwein*?"

4. A Jewish woman who had just given birth was taken from her home in the middle of the night; could take nothing with her, e.g. not even nappies for the child. In the street her handbag was searched and the money (30 Marks) taken from it.

5. A notable art critic in Vienna also taken on 10/11 [sic]. His hands were tied together and he was kicked around like a football for an hour; the man is now virtually mentally deranged.

I am now at No. 5. Is it necessary to go on to No. 20? I believe these examples are more than enough. Many abroad simply do not believe it. I was at the Dutch Legation in this town today, where we were also by chance in Vienna. It was said straight to my face: Yes, well, that's all Communist propaganda.

Reporter: Wim van der Kuylen, Pozsonyi út22, with Kàlmàn Imre, Budapest V

B. 187 Cologne: The premises of the large porcelain trader Marcan were also wrecked during the "*Juden-Unruhen*" [Jewish disturbance]. The major warehouse for the finest luxury porcelain was completely smashed to pieces. At the time of the "*Unglück*" [calamity] the warehouse was in the possession of a Swiss company and insured in Switzerland. It is reported that the Swiss insurance company has already filed a case against the Reich, the damages being estimated at RM. 750,000.

A party of *Auslandsdeutsche* [Germans abroad] had stopped off at a Cologne Hotel, amongst whom there happened also to be a man with a Jewish-sounding name. During the night he was sought out – after much knocking: "*Kriminalpolizei* [criminal police], open up immediately!" – he believed it was a practical joke by one of his fellow tourists and answered with a "German greeting". Upon which the official said: "I'm counting to three, and then we're going to knock the door in, you pay for the damage!"

Two SS men in uniform, two officials in plain clothes. Despite unsuspicious "Aryan" papers a disturbing interrogation nevertheless. Upon which a neighbour from the room next door appears and asks for peace at night. "Shut your mouth, or you'll get to know a concentration camp!" The man justifies himself as a subject of his Britannic Majesty..., a four-fold "Heil Hitler" and four Gestapo officials go forth to another hotel.

An Aryan industrialist from Düsseldorf applied for a new passport (November 1938). When it was issued at the passport office he had to sign a declaration on the back:

"I pledge that I will never enter into contact with any German émigrés when travelling abroad. It has been made clear to me that I face punishment if I act otherwise, similarly if I fail to remain silent about the existence of this declaration."

A more senior SS official had reported to friends: the lack of manpower does not justify us in feeding productively idle citizens. An employment law is being prepared that will provide for a Jewish workforce too. All Jews who do not emigrate immediately will be affected by this. It is anticipated that the new laws will come into force on 1st April 1939 at the latest.

An *arisiert* [Aryanised] company in Cologne was informed by the Oberbürgermeister [lord mayor] that the *Steuerverwaltung* [tax administration] had requested the appropriate excerpt from the commercial register, "so that you can be struck off the list of Jewish companies..."

Written No. Ju/Ka... "Ju/Ka" stands for *Juden-Kartothek* [Jewish card-file]

Reporter: Moritz Heimann, Antwerp

B. 188 20th December 1938

From Dachau:

A 42-year-old Herr Neumann from Nördlingen (Jewish) was officially reported as "died suddenly".

A Herr Wohlfahrt of Frankfurt am Main suffered "sustained injuries" from being shot in Dachau; a few days later a further inmate of the same name, brother of the first. A third brother and a brother-in-law of the two are also currently in Dachau.

The above-named three fatalities date from the time around 20th November 1938.

Herr Ferd. Levy, Neuwied am Rhein, was reported as deceased, death caused at the "*Aktionen*" [operations] of 9th/10th November.

Herr Alb. Jacob, Biskirchen an der Lahn, died in the "*KZ*" [concentration camp].

Kurt Singer, teacher from Nordhausen am Harz, born in Homberg-Niederrhein, died in the "concentration camp", presumably Buchenwald.

His father, Eduard Singer, who lived with him, also. The mother of the Jewish teacher, Frau Eduard Singer sr., has received delivery of both urns.

Reporter: M. Heimann, Antwerp

B. 189 I am an Austrian refugee just 16 years of age, who has luckily managed for several months to escape with my life from that hell – and by hell I mean Vienna, occupied by 15- to 25-year-old criminals.

I cannot describe here in a few short lines all the dreadful and horrible things that I experienced just five months ago. Even if I were to speak about it for years, it would be impossible to relate everything that I suffered personally.

I will try to report a little, however, of course only that which I personally felt physically or saw with my own eyes.

The days after the 13th March 1938:

At this time Nazis armed with revolvers and fixed bayonets often intruded into Jewish homes and businesses to loot them.

Jewish businesses were daubed with white or black paint and next to drawings which were supposed to show Jews one could read the following inscription on every Jewish business: "JUD oder SAUJUD" [Jew or Jewish Pig]", some time later: "BIN SCHON IN DACHAU" [Already in Dachau] etc. Jewish businesses were placed under the management of Aryan commissioners if they had not been "*arisiert*" [Aryanised] straight away, which means they were robbed by Nazis.

Jewish *Rechtsanwalten* [lawyers] were deprived of the right to practise their profession. 15,000 Jews were already out of work in April and being fed by the *Israelitischen Kultusgemeinde* [Jewish community].

Men and women were rounded up together at random on the streets or fetched from homes by the brown [-shirted] hordes for "*Reiben*" [washing]. They had to wash off the labels of the old regime, at which they were laughed at and mistreated by the Nazis.

Sometimes the SA occupied Jewish homes in order to listen to Hitler's speeches on the radio.

On the streets elderly Jews not infrequently were made to perform military exercises or gymnastics.

Imprisonments begin:

If a Jew attempted to leave for abroad he was arrested, because he was presumed to be a "*Fluchtgefahr*" [escape risk].

On the other hand, if a Jew had not attempted to leave, then he "wanted" to remain in Germany and was arrested anyway!

Prominent Vienna Jews mostly came into "*Schutzhaft*" [protective custody].

Life became insufferable and scores of Viennese made an end to their lives of their own free will at the moment of their arrest, though it often seemed that they had been shot by the Nazis who had forced their way into their homes.

Thousands of large lorries were driven by young Nazis through the streets of Vienna shouting "*Juda verrecke*" [perish Judah]. Nowhere was safe for life as a Jew any more, since even a five-year-old boy had a knife 20 cm long, with which he threatened "*Saujuden*" or was allowed to or should injure them.

I myself attended a *Realgymnasium* [secondary school] where the majority of pupils were Aryan. After Hitler invaded, the Aryan pupils beat the Jewish ones so severely that the Nazi director of our establishment felt obliged to issue the following instruction: "Aryan pupils in future will not be aggressive towards Jewish pupils in the school building, since the fate of these people is being determined outside the school".

I would like to point out that this directive naturally had not the slightest effect on the "German-Aryan" pupils equipped with revolvers, knives, boots, brown and white shirts: they continued to come to lessons in the same garb and clearly showed that the Nazis were there now.

After a while I had to attend a "Jewish school", at which young, National Socialist professors were said to deliver lessons on all subjects. They did not do this, and contented themselves with coming to school in SS uniform and threatening the poor Jewish pupils.

Outside school one did not have to "*Reiben*" [wash] any more. Homes were no longer occupied by Nazis who wanted to listen to the radio or loot valuables; now one was raided by the Gestapo in the home, and almost every Vienna Jew was arrested and dispatched to Dachau concentration camp. The period of mass arrests had begun ...

If someone rang at the door of a Jewish home, one did not

open it for fear that it would be the Gestapo. One dreaded going to the telephone, and one dared not speak in one's own home, because a microphone could have been installed somewhere and a rash word meant arrest.

If two Jews walked together in the street then they were exposed to the danger of being arrested by the SA, and if they did not give the identical answer to the Nazis' question on what they had been speaking about, then they would be arrested immediately.

During these months I spent more than one day unhappy, more than one night sleepless.

In Vienna every Jew aged over 18 years was threatened with unfounded arrest and the SPECTRE OF DACHAU!

On some days, orders came from Herr [Josef] Bürckel *Gauleiter* [provincial leader] of Vienna, and then, for example, 2,000 or another time again 800 Jews were arrested.

Neither my father nor my uncle avoided unfounded arrest.

In the same way as I stood in front of the prison for endless days and nights crying and confused, so did many children whose fathers, and many, many women, whose husbands or sons had been arrested without reason.

Mostly all attempts for release were in vain, and after two days the transport went to Dachau.

Jews were rounded up in the streets, from homes, from businesses and coffeehouses, no longer for "*Reiben*" but for "*Freifahrt nach Dachau*" [free travel to Dachau], as the "noble" Nazis described it.

There is no Jewish family in Vienna who is not affected by this insufferable misfortune; at least one man from every family is in *Schutzhaft* [protective custody] and whilst he is being tortured and martyred in Dachau or Buchenwald, his relatives in Vienna are close to despair.

People place such suffering upon people!

Whilst I am writing this and no longer suffer, things are even worse for the poor Jews in Vienna than at the time when I was still there. Evidence should be the lines written to me by a lady who has also escaped that hell for some time, and what was reported to me by a friend who is already in a foreign country.

The lady in question writes:

"I cannot describe to you what we have been part of, because a book would not suffice to record everything that we had to experience and suffer. I lived with my relative Dr. N. since 1st November. On the Thursday in question there were house searches for every Jew, and then we were all locked up, even the child. The 10 mark note that my cousin had lent me was taken from me though that was everything I possessed, and I had to sign that I had all my possessions.

In Aachen I was stripped bare, and then a train was going to Brussels, and I took this train, to be able at last to get out of the hell."

A friend reports:

"Firstly, I must apologise for my long silence. So much has happened since I last wrote to you that I could neither reply to any letters nor pay any visits, because the events left me not a minute free. We, i.e. my family, had to survive imprisonment and a house search . . .

After endless queuing and much running about we finally succeeded in obtaining a *Steuerbestätigung* [tax certificate] and thus we have fortunately arrived in X . . .

You can hardly imagine what has played out in Germany since the assassination of Ambassador vom Rath.

That we were not arrested or looted on that black Thursday is only attributable to the exemplary and honourable behaviour of our *Blockleiter* [block leader].

In total, roughly 2,500 male youths of our age (18 years!) were sent to Dachau . . .

It is so dreadful that one cannot write about what I alone have seen.

One cannot really celebrate one's freedom when one thinks of the lot of those who are left behind in that hell!"

Report of a 16-year-old male youth from Vienna, forwarded by Frau Dora Prywes, Antwerp, c/o Menko Max Hirsch.

B. 190 The reaction of the Christian population of Vienna to the *Aktion* [operation] of the 10th November varied. Intellectuals did not take part, but could only express their disgust at the events by ostentatiously turning away. There were numerous cases in which Jews found refuge from the persecution that – one can say with certainty – threatened all Jews from the ages of 20 to 60, with Aryans. The mob, in particular youths of 16 or 17, took part enthusiastically.

The following incident, which took place during the house search of the home of a Jewish businessman, a 55-year-old father of two children, Vienna II., Taborstraße, underlines the assertion above that all Jews in the age ranges mentioned were meant to be arrested. This house search took place there on the afternoon of the 10th November, and the occupier was asked where he had spent the morning. When he replied "In my shop", the search leaders exclaimed in surprise "And weren't you picked up there?" When the search – in which the family's silver was the main object – was over the businessman was taken away to an air raid shelter at the "Am Tabor" [inn] in his neighbourhood. The cellar was packed full of prisoners and a *Hitler-Jungen* [Hitler Youth] stationed at the door slammed it closed behind him with the words "*Derstickts, Saujuden!* " [Choke, Jewish pigs!].

As evidence of the callous behaviour which went on during the "house searches" I have heard meanwhile from a family member who has arrived here a further detail about what happened at the home of my father-in-law, whose prayer things were, as is well known, thrown out of the window into the street and burned. When my father-in-law, a strictly orthodox Jew of 83, horrified by what was happening, timidly asked "What shall I do?" he got the answer: "You? Die!"

When the desperate relatives of the people who had been arrested asked where they were being held they were almost always told that they were in Dachau. It seems that some relatives were told this in the morning, only for the people who had been arrested to come home in the afternoon without having been in Dachau. In Leopoldstadt a story went round, uncontradicted, that a certain Herr S. S., Vienna II., Heinestraße, who was detained only for a few hours because of a lung complaint, went afterwards to ask where he had been held and likewise got the answer "Dachau".

Of the way in which so-called *Aktionsjuden*, that is, those arrested during the *Aktion* of the 10th November, were treated in Dachau one hears that, in comparison with people arrested earlier, it was halfway acceptable. In the last few days numerous people who had been there have returned to Vienna, among others the Salzburg Rabbi Dr. S. Margulies. On the other hand, the following deaths in Dachau have been reported to me; I have not learned the causes of death: Beermann, fur dealer at Hohen Markt, Vienna I.; Richard Jacobi, owner of a well-known Viennese sewing machine and bicycle shop, Vienna IX., Liechtensteinstr., and Hans Mühlrad, owner of a men's fashion shop, Vienna II., Praterstr.. The last-named was a very active member of the [*Reichs*]*Bund jüdischer Frontsoldaten* [Reich Association of Jewish Front-line Soldiers] and was arrested in July this year.

In Kenyongasse, Vienna VII., the rear part of a convent was used as a *Notgefängnis* [temporary prison]. The cries of the arrested men could be heard around the neighbourhood all day. A prisoner released from there reported that they were not allowed to relieve themselves for three days, and when they could not stand it any more they were dragged to the "W. C." by the nose and had their faces shoved into the filth.

In the school at Karajangasse, Vienna XX., used as an emergency detention unit since the turmoil, two Jews threw themselves from the window, in one case at the moment when he heard his child calling his name from the yard of the building next door, which offered a view of the school and where relatives of those arrested had therefore been coming. One of these two Jews broke his hand in the fall, and the other was taken away by the *Rettungsgesellschaft* [rescue association], his injuries are not known. A doctor from Baden bei Wien went mad as a result of the suffering, had a laughing fit and was likewise taken away by the *Rettungsgesellschaft*. After the window incidents with the two Jews ten detainees were picked in each room and had to watch out that nothing similar happened again; if it were to, the ten "watchers" were threatened with the severest punishments, above all with "Dachau", though there was also talk of shooting.

The sick had to lie in a draughty corridor even with a 40-degree fever. So far as *Exerzierübung* [punitive drill practice] was concerned Herr X. has been able to report the following from the Karajangasse. The prisoners had to stand to attention in the yard all night. Here too the previously mentioned extremely painful exercise of moving the fingers up and down with arms outstretched was "popular". Herr X., who possessed a gold signet ring, had it taken away from him with the comment that it would only hinder him in the exercise. Prisoners were often ordered to box each other and even to tear out each other's hair and beards. Detainees were divided among the rooms according to their ages, in ten-year groups from 20 upwards.

At "dispatch" in the central prison, Elisabethpromenade, Vienna IX., Herr X. could also observe the bullying by the *SS-Verfügungstruppen* [SS support troops] stationed there. E.g. one of the prisoners brought in for "questioning" was ordered to "run", and when he obeyed this command was beaten for running too quickly. When another person who received this command went more slowly he was beaten as well because he had gone too slowly. When a prisoner, asked whether anyone had opportunities to travel abroad, replied with the information that he possessed boat tickets for January, he was yelled at for having named such a "late" date, taken away by the *SS-Verfügungstruppe* and not seen again.

A favourite frightener was to take a troop of prisoners off to the Westbahn, the connecting line to Bavaria, hold them there for an hour and a half and tell them that they were now going to be taken to Dachau; after this spell of torture they were put back in detention.

Reporter: Oskar Hirschfeld, London

The principal basis of this report is the account of Egon Trachtenberg, 31, of Vienna II., arrested on 10 November, to an acquaintance who has meanwhile arrived in London. Because

Herr Tr. is still in Vienna – he must leave the country by the end of January 1939 and will probably do so illegally – it is very important to be careful about the use of this report.The informant and his acquaintances are thoroughly reliable.

Father-in-law of Herr Hirschfeld: Leopold Loewy, Vienna II., Volkerstr.

Key:

S. S. = Siegfried Sommer

B. 191 The reporter states that on the morning of 10th November all window panes and shop windows were smashed in. During the course of the day the shops were completely wrecked and looted. Policemen stood there and did not interfere. Schoolboys, youths and SA wearing coats were involved in the work of destruction. In one Berlin newspaper it stated that not a thing had been taken away, the people had been disgusted to grab this Jewish trash. In two or three synagogues the *Synagogendiener* [synagogue sextons] saved the *Thorarollen* [Torah scrolls]. As they were already desecrated however they were buried in Weißensee. The *Thorarollen* from the Fasanenstraße and Prinzenstraße synagogues were burned in Wittenbergplatz.

It was worst of all in the provinces, particularly in Nuremberg, however. The reporter recounts what his parents in Nuremberg experienced. At half past 3 in the morning hordes broke down the street door with an axe, rushed up the stairs and broke down the door to the corridor with the axe. The parents – father 71 years old, seriously ill, mother 60 years old – in their nightclothes ran with other Jews living in the building up to the attic, but it was shut. In the flats everything was smashed to bits, carpets and pictures ripped up, nothing was left intact. Then the men ran up the stairs, beat the father till he bled, gave the mother a kick in the stomach so that she received internal injuries and then threw her down the stairs. Today, six weeks later, both parents who were supposed to leave the flat immediately but then could stay for eight more days, are still confused and have panic attacks as a direct result.

People were beaten to death, women in nightdresses and barefoot were chased to the police station, then sent home again. A blind man in his late fifties had acquired a 15 cm. long head wound.

[Julius] Streicher is supposed to have said that all the Jews, 3,000 people, would have to be out of Nuremberg by the Party Conference in 1939. Berlin, as the seat of government, Munich, as the city of the movement, and Nuremberg, city of the Reich Party Conference, must be purged of Jews first. In Berlin there are still said to be 140,000 Jews. Many Jewish homes in Berlin are being *gekündigt* [given notice].

Reporter: Kurt Wachtel, Berlin, Hohenzollerndamm, now New York

B. 192 On 20th May 1938 the reporter was picked up at his shop in Vienna. To his parents' question as to why the arrest was taking place came the reply, "He's a Jew, that's enough." He was first brought to the Karajangasse police station, abused with slaps on the face, punches in the ribs, blows from the butt of a revolver, robbed by the SS of all his money and valuables, shipped off with others by vehicle to the Westbahnhof, dumped in the carriage and set on the bench with a knock-out blow. Eating, smoking, talking, relieving oneself were forbidden during the journey. In every compartment stood an SS man brandishing a revolver. The journey lasted nine hours. There were 450 men in total on departure, on arrival nine were already dead; they had been shot.

In Dachau the work consisted of excavating and levelling a swamp. The hygiene facilities were good, the treatment relatively quite reasonable. In contrast to his subsequent stay in Buchenwald, Dachau could have passed for a sanatorium.

Transfer to Weimar happened in the middle of September. The Dachau camp was purged of Jews because of the imminent war. At Weimar station, where a large crowd of people was waiting, the *Kommandant* [commandant] welcomed them with the words, "The Jews are here." They were then lined up in rows

of ten facing the wall and then loaded onto buses. The Buchenwald camp is located on a mountain and the total length of the
perimeter is 3.6 km.; every 100 m. there is a watchtower topped
with a machine gun. At the outer entrance stands an inscription, *"Recht oder Unrecht einerlei – Deutschland dein Vaterland"*
[Germany your Fatherland – right or wrong; actually *Recht
oder Unrecht – mein Vaterland*; My country – right or wrong].
On the other door is *"Jedem das Seine"* [To each his own]. The
camp is surrounded by a 3 m. high barbed wire entanglement,
which at night is loaded with electrical current. Finally inside
is an 18 m. wide lawn, lastly past that a trench which it was not
permitted to set foot in. At night the camp is illuminated on
all sides by arc lights. Buchenwald contains 50 barracks with at
that time (September) 11,500 internees, of whom 40% are Jews,
60% others. The clothing consists of a shirt, long drawers, socks,
shoes, linen trousers, flimsy jacket and cap. On payment of RM.
12.- a pullover and gloves could be bought. All the internees
are identified by their clothing: Jews have a yellow triangle with
a red triangle on top. Jewish *Rassenschänder* [racial defilers] a
yellow patch with a black triangle, Jewish *"Kriminellen"* [crimi-
nals] a yellow patch with a green triangle, *"Asozialen"* [asocials]
a yellow patch with a solid black triangle. Aryans have the same
badges without a yellow patch, the Communists have a red patch
with the same symbols, the *Bibelforscher* [Jehovah's Witnesses],
of whom there are a significant number, have a purple patch, the
175-ers [homosexuals] have a pink patch.

The barracks were overcrowded and instead of 100 in one
area had to accommodate 180 men. The beds are mounted in
threes above each other. The washing bays work in the morning
and evenings each for half an hour as there is little or no water
available; often they do not work at all for four weeks. Lavatories
are built but cordoned off as there is no water, therefore there are
only latrines. Within the camp there is the 'sick bay', the hospital
barrack; admission there is almost impossible as only 100 people
can be admitted and there is always overcrowding.

The food consists of: in the mornings chicory coffee or soup,
15 g. margarine, 1 tablespoon of jam or syrup, ¾ lb. of bread

for the whole day; at midday more coffee with some cheese or herring or brawn, in the evening stew, tasty, but without a bit of fat. The eating bowls could be washed completely clean with cold water without soap, if there was water to be had, a sign that the food is completely fat free; if there was no water, the eating bowls were just wiped out with bread.

One of the most frequent illnesses was phlegmon, a festering inflammation which spreads internally caused by injuries at work which are not permitted to receive attention. After two to three days blood poisoning sets in and it becomes necessary to amputate limbs. Cases like these occur very frequently and these people are then never released.

The day's business begins with waking up an hour and a half hour before dawn, in summer at 20 past 3. Then we have to report for *Appell* [roll call] on the large compound set aside for this on the mountain. After this work is allotted. The route to the quarry where the work is done takes three quarters of an hour. The work is allocated by an Aryan prisoner called a *Kapo*, usually a criminal. The more he shouts and beats the men, the more he ingratiates himself with the SS. The workplace is marked out at a distance of 10 m. by *roten Fahnen* [red flags] (called the line of death as it is not permitted to cross it on pain of being shot), behind that surrounded by SS with revolvers. The kinds of jokes that are played are that an SS man suddenly rips the cap off a man's head and throws it away; the cap falls onto the line marked out in red. Anyone who does not have a cap is punished. If the man now runs after the cap and crosses the forbidden track, as happens repeatedly, he is immediately shot down. Work is done from 7 o'clock in the morning until 12 o'clock, then half an hour morning break. More work is done until 4 o'clock. At work it is not permitted to speak, smoke, or eat. The price of every infringement is a punishment. There are all kinds of punishments:

To be strapped by the SS to the *Bock* [whipping block] and *25 auf das Gesäß* [25 on the backside], either with the bullwhip, the dog lash or the cane;

Baumhängen [tree hanging]: to be hung backwards by the arms on the tree for an hour;

Sachsengruß [Saxon greeting]: to stand face to the wall for eight hours with arms crossed at the back of the neck, not permitted to eat or to relieve oneself;

Bunker [dungeon], which the SS are not so keen on as the men are then away from the work.

A favourite method is to watch the men from a watchtower through the telescope to see whether perhaps the number which is sewn on is no longer clean and then at *Appell* inflict one of the above punishments on the unsuspecting person.

Work is done in all weathers. If anyone collapses at work or at *Appell* he remains lying where he is, until at last he is then transported off. Bombastic phrases on such occasions, "*Verrecken soll das Judenschwein!*" [The Jewish pig should perish] or "A German is not ill, a German dies immediately!" Forms of address: "*Du Arschloch*" [You arsehole] or "*Jude no. . . .*" [Jew no. . . .]. At every opportunity they say, "Jews get nothing to eat on Sunday," which was very often the case too. Sunday work was done from 7 until half past 12.

Sunday food: whale ragout with jacket potatoes. Every 14 days one letter was allowed to be written and one letter to be received. Money was allowed to be sent; it was paid into his account, and the prisoner was permitted to receive up to RM. 10.- from his account each week. They said that everything could be bought in the canteen; usually it was closed, and the worst things were reserved for the Jews.

Separately, distinct *Strafkompanien* [punishment companies] were also operated. Here things were even stricter; one letter was allowed to be written and received every three months. At 4 o'clock Appell again, then collecting food, tidying our things, by half past 8 we had to be in the barracks. During the night no one was allowed out, they would immediately be shot. At night there were also sirens for air raid precautions, then in five minutes we had to be on the *Appellplatz* [parade ground].

Every day six or seven dead were transported off without being placed in a coffin; two crematoria especially were used for the incineration: Weimar and Jena.

In the month of July, when the camp was only occupied by 6,000 men, there were 165 fatalities.

Paul Morgan died there from pneumonia. The reporter was released on 29th October, as his emigration had been arranged. On release, like everyone else, he had to sign a non-disclosure statement to say that any kind of injuries he had inflicted himself, that he had not had to work, that anyone who spoke out disparagingly against the state would be immediately reported to the police, that he would keep completely quiet about the facilities and experiences in the camp; the most serious measures are threatened for failure to comply. One man, whose toes had been amputated, had to sign two blank forms in the hospital barrack.

In the camp the organisation is very poor.

The Aryans are frequently goaded by the SS, so that Jews were frequently attacked in the forest, robbed and hung from a tree.

"Anyone who leaves a concentration camp will not be granted their freedom, they will be given their life."

Reporter: Erwin Mann, businessman, 28 years old, formerly of Lerchenfelderstrasse 41, Vienna; last European address c/o Herr Jus Axelrad, 1 Gower Street, Bedford Square, London W.C.1, emigrated to Nicaragua.

B. 193 When the synagogue in my home town was set on fire we Jews who were under arrest were taken to a school opposite the synagogue and from there forced to watch the synagogue burning down and at the same time to be passive spectators as SS men played football with the Sefer Torah. Then an SS man came to us, had himself presented to the rabbi and cut off his beard. Then he attempted to start a religious conversation with him, which the latter however refused. He went away then with the words, "We are much stronger than your Jehovah."

We were then taken to Buchenwald, a camp that had in total about 22,000 inmates, 10,000 ordinary and 12,000 from the arrests of 9th November. There an *Alarmbereitschaft Hitler* [Hitler Alert] in grey met us, all vigorous young men from 18–23 years of age. The Alert consisted of about 2,500 men. We were driven with rifle butts into a tunnel, without any consideration that there were men over 70 years of age amongst us – the youngest was 14 years old. Many collapsed from fatigue as a result of the long journey, from the crush in the narrow tunnel and from the blows with rifle butts.

There were about 3,000 men from imprisoned with us. In the camp were 3,000 from Frankfurt am Main, 3,000 from Breslau [now Pol. Wrocław] and 1,000 from Kassel and Leipzig; in the camp in addition were the Viennese Jews from the so-called *Juni-Aktion* [June operation] – there were 5,000 of these who had been provided with clothing. We were accommodated separately from them, on the other side of a wire fence, and in fact in makeshift barracks. Those arrested in the *Juni-Aktion* were called *Aktionsjuden* [Operation Jews], whilst we were called the *Novemberjuden* [November Jews]. The *Aktionsjuden* were not employed at all; the *Kommandant* [commandant] declared, "We have no work and no feed for the *Aktionsjuden*."

I should just like to point out that in the tunnel, which was curved, we had to line up facing the short side amidst constant insults uttered by the SS men, and in the terrible crush throw our razors behind us and perform military exercises. Whilst doing this many sprained their joints and lost consciousness. We were adddressed alternately with the words: *Jude* [Jew], *Zuhälter* [pimp], *Betrüger* [fraudster], *Talmudgauner* [Talmud crook] etc. We were then asked what we had been until now, and every reply or silence was answered with a blow from a rifle butt, so that in the end almost everyone was bleeding. A Rabbi Ochs from Gleiwitz [now Pol. Gliwice] was particularly badly mistreated. As a result of the blows from rifle butts such a large number lost consciousness that a *Polizeihauptmann* [police captain] finally called a halt. The ordinary *Polizeibeamten* [police officers] in blue uniforms behaved properly, one even wept because he could not watch this unbelievable torture in the tunnel, which lasted for an hour and a half. We had to keep our heads bent the whole time and by this time could not keep upright because we had been travelling without food for c. 14 hours.

We were then led to the police lorries. Anyone who stumbled

during this or otherwise [fell] due to loss of blood just stayed where they lay, without anyone bothering about him. We were driven with whips onto the vehicle – it was c. one and a quarter metres above the ground, so that it was almost impossible to get on, particularly for the elderly, as there was no help whatsoever. The vehicle was closed with tarpaulins – we were ordered to look at the ground so that we could not observe what was happening outside. SS men stood on the running board and would look through peepholes into the inside of the lorry and for their amusement every now and then pull a head through these holes and beat it until the man fell back unconscious into the lorry.

When we arrived at the camp we were driven off with rifle butts and had to run over the gravel at the double, again driven by rifle butts, to the *Appellplatz* [parade ground]. At the gate which formed the entrance to the camp, at a height of about four metres, five or six machine guns, a loud speaker and the searchlight were installed – in addition there was the room used by the *Lagerführer* [camp leader], who held the rank of *Vizelagerkommandant* [Vice Camp Commandant]. Anyone who remained prostrate during the endurance run to the *Appellplatz* was struck with the whip. We were then put in order by location – during this it became apparent that many in our group were bleeding and had broken limbs. After we had then stood for three to four hours without having received anything to eat or drink and without being allowed to use the latrines we were taken to the camp barber and there our hair was cut, which we had to collect up. We had to then stand again for hours until eventually a log was recorded by older prisoners.

In contrast to the June prisoners we were not provided with clothing and – as already noted – also not given any work. The *Vizelagerkommandant*, who incidentally is the bearer of a *Blutorden* [Blood Order], announced that he had no employment for *diese Schweine* [these swine]. Frozen to the marrow and hungry we then went to the makeshift barracks, which were 250 x 8 metres large and four metres high. The floor was bare earth, turf. At the walls five planks like shelves in a bookcase were ranged 70 cm. above each other on which we had to sleep, so that the prisoners who slept on the uppermost fifth shelf had to perform something of a gymnastic routine every time. Our *Blockwart* [block warden]was a convict with many previous convictions by the name of Strauss from Frankfurt. In our barrack were 3,000 men.

Appell [roll call] took place daily. We had to stand for about five or six hours. The camp commandant called us his "*Vögel*" [birds] and began the *Appell* by asking whether all the "*Vögel*" were there. Later on the *Appell*s no longer took place regularly. A young chazzan Zeidler from Nordhausen was tormented to death by an *Unterscharführer* [sergeant] Zöllner. On the day of his burial his 69-year-old father was sought out, tied to a tree half a metre above the ground and, after he had been hanging there on a rope for half an hour and rigor mortis had already set in, laid on the ground, not before this inhuman *Unterscharführer* had kicked him in the stomach.

By the time I left the camp on 9th December 4% of our group had died. A comrade who was released on 12th, and whom I saw here – he is absolutely reliable – told me that out of 250, 17 froze to death during the cold snap. Before release we again had to stand for 12 hours, although we were not all in good health – e.g. I had a head cold. We were then shaved and shorn. The food was tolerable but insufficient. Water was completely inadequate. The situation with the latrines was particularly bad, they were simply dug out pits over which wide bars had been laid. More than once people drowned in the latrine. I also saw an SS man push a Jew in. A makeshift *Revier* [sick bay] was set up to which only the dying or the mad came however – cases of insanity were everyday occurrences. As there was no medication we collected RM. 400.- although in the end it was then not given to us on the grounds that Jewish doctors were so clever they could even cure people without medication. A doctor from Breslau went mad because he could no longer watch this neglect of seriously ill people. We had observed how hour by hour he became increasingly agitated about it.

Common colds due to rotten footwear were everyday occurrences. Most of us did not take our boots off at all, because due to the constant walking in the deep mud they were so sodden that we could scarcely get them off our feet.

At *Appell* thrashings were imposed and carried out. Subject to the whim of the *Kommandant*, 20–30 lashes were given, often only because a scrap of paper had lain on the spot where the prisoner stood.

Corpses were taken to the so-called washhouse designated for this purpose; I myself saw 25–30 being carried out. Of 97 prisoners from Hindenburg [now Pol. Zabrze] four died (among others Roth, Ehrlich and Berg), five out of 95 from Gleiwitz. The figures rose during frosty weather. That was the death rate in barely three weeks.

Our release was then announced over the loudspeaker. Once again, although there were numerous cases of influenza, we had to stand for ten hours, then our hair was cut and we had to stand for another ten to twelve hours, were then taken to the *Komman-dant*'s headquarters where we had to sign the well-known declarations that we had no claims, had been treated well and would say nothing about what we had experienced. Although we were all ill, the final medical examination merely checked for weals and other physical changes which could have led to a suspicion of mistreatment. If any such marks were present, then the release did not take place.

Sunlamps were used on the above-mentioned Rabbi Dr. Ochs to make his scars heal more quickly. On release it was announced to us by the *Oberscharführer* [SS staff sergeant] that we were not allowed to [travel] by express train and anyone who returned would stay in the camp for ever. One of the grounds for release was *Arisierung* [Aryanisation] of business. For this purpose the contract was sent to the *Lagerkommandant* for the prisoner to sign. When a Moritz Heimann from Beuthen [now Pol. Bytom] wanted to see the contract before signing it, the *Oberscharführer* said, "There is nothing for you to see, Jew, you must sign."

I should also like to point out that in the camp there was a small zoo with mastiffs, bears and eagles.

Report by Dr. Willy Schiller, *Syndikus* [Counsel], 39 years old, Hindenburg, Upper Silesia

B. 194 The precise conditions in the various camps is known to me from numerous reliable reports, although I was not arrested. I assume that the mistreatment and bullying, to which the arrested Jews in the concentration camps were exposed, are well known and only want to refer to the fact that SS men were commandeered from a camp located on the Dutch border in Esterwegen to Sachsenhausen, in order to teach the SS men there the punishment of so-called "Rollen" [rolling]. *The instruction was imparted to them* using the Jews located in the camp. The Oder canal was built near the camp and the imprisoned Jews were laid along the edge and in fact parallel to the edge. The SS men took a section of this line of Jews, marched forward and pushed them into the canal with their feet. The Jews then had to be back up on the bank within 20 seconds. If they arrived later the SS men trod on their feet and pushed them back into the canal again. No one remained uninjured, the injured and bleeding people were then laid in a heap which – as was reliably confirmed to me – was often one and a half metres high. The men then sat down quietly in their garden which was by the camp, ate bananas and openly delighted in the spectacle.

Consistent reports about these events have aroused in me the impression that it was a case of pathological-erotic release for the young SS men.

In total there were 3,000 SS men in Sachsenhausen.

Whenever the order was given that in the afternoon one was to go into the water, one knew immediately that it involved "*Rollen*"; a terrible panic would then spread. One Sunday afternoon the prisoners in Sachsenhausen were told that they had a free afternoon and should go and have a chat, play cards or do something else near the *Appellplatz* [parade ground]. As they complied delightedly with this concession and sat down casually in groups on the square, 50 journalists appeared who were presented with this scene of humane treatment in the concentration camp. At the same time the whole square was filmed from an adjacent tower.

One day all of the 18,000 prisoners were marshalled to sing in front of the *Lagerkommandant* [camp commandant]; the Jewish prisoners did not do it, despite being beaten.

When during the song *Das Wandern ist des Müllers Lust* [Hiking is the miller's delight] came the line *Die Steine selbst, so schwer sie sind* [The very rocks, they are so heavy], the Jewish prisoners wept so much that an SS man standing there turned around and wept himself.

During the early weeks prisoners in Sachsenhausen had to go on an endurance run each day for seven hours, later they had to work at the canal and in the forest.

A rabbi from Bremen was ordered by an SS man in Sachsenhausen to recite a Jewish saying in Hebrew and then translate it. To this when he said, "Behold, he that keepeth Israel shall neither slumber nor sleep", he was thrashed and forced to deliver a sermon about the Talmud.

Next to the *Appellplatz*, where prisoners were whipped, naked, almost daily, there was a garden for the SS men where they would sit comfortably at tables, drink and smoke. The *Lagerkommandant*, who was an animal lover, had laid out a small zoo and on a wooden wall mounted a row of cages of birds, which he particularly liked. Above was a large sign with the three words:

Bitte nicht quälen [Please do not torment]!

Right next to the daily site of the most brutal human torment!

The SS men were all trained in *Ordensburgen* [Castles of Order; Nazi training establishments for military leaders] and in my opinion were never suited to war, but only to cowardly mistreatment of the defenceless.

Reporter: Rabbi Dr. Nussbaum, Berlin

B. 195 On 28th October I was in Elberfeld, where I had business to do. I then went to the *Fremdenpolizei* [aliens police] in order to have my residency, which expired on 1st November, extended in order to be able to pursue my emigration to North America. The official came back to me after five minutes and sent me away with a second as an escort, apparently to the *Polizeipräsident* [Chief of Police]. But I was brought to the police prison. The prison official explained, "You are coming into *Abschiebungshaft* [custody pending deportation]." In the check for weapons and money I was allowed to keep RM. 45.-, also I was allowed to smoke. I was locked in a cell and begged the official to notify my parents. After an hour there were already ten Poles in the cell. Only then were personal details taken. Passports were retained.

Around 200 Poles were arrested in Elberfeld, men, women and children. After about two hours an official came to our cell with forms, in which it said roughly that that one declared oneself to be in agreement with being deported, and that there was a right to appeal within 14 days, whereby immediate deportation would not be cancelled, however. Everyone was in agreement to say no to this. I was the last to say no because I was summoned to the American consulate in Stuttgart on 15th November. After a quarter of an hour the chief official returned with three more men, to apply pressure. Our answer was again no. At this the officials went away with the words, "We'll show you how it'll be." The women were then separated from the men, received their passports and were released. They were told that the men would be deported at 7 o'clock. They could bring them clothes, etc.

The men were then taken away again one by one, and were told that they were going to Poland, but we did not learn where. Then taken to the railway station in heavily guarded buses. There I met my father and brother. 40 went into each third class carriage. We were treated fairly by the officials. Each carriage was given sausage sandwiches and a large pot of coffee. The carriages were then locked. No windows were allowed to be opened at the stations we travelled through. The train went via Hanover, Berlin and Frankfurt an der Oder to Neu-Bentschen [now Pol. Zbąszynek]. There we got off and were put on a Polish train. Before this we were checked for money, during which the officials were actually very generous. I was allowed e.g. to keep RM. 42.-, whereas another had to give up RM. 520.- from RM. 530.-. Then we travelled to *Alt-Bentschen* [Zbąszyń].

On the way from Neu- to Alt-Bentschen we saw about a thousand people on the country road, amongst them elderly, young children, prams etc. It was the transport from Hamburg, which had arrived at the Polish border at 5 o'clock in the morning and had been sent on by foot. These people had been met at the border by Polish guards with fixed bayonets, and when they wanted to retreat were pushed forward by the German *Schutzpolizei* [*Schupos*; police] and SS with pistols with the words, "You can proceed calmly, they're too cowardly to shoot." Then the Polish officials gave the order for everyone to lie down and everyone had to throw themselves on to the wet road. Three warning shots were fired and then everyone was allowed through.

We arrived in Alt-Bentschen at half past 7 on Saturday the 29th October. A customs check was announced, though this did not take place because of the large amount of chaos that was happening. A train was already in the station at Alt-Bentschen, which had arrived from Nuremberg an hour earlier but was still locked shut. These people were only allowed out at 6 o'clock on the Saturday evening.

In Alt-Bentschen there were said to be 11,000 people, in fact from Berlin, Düsseldorf, Wuppertal, Remscheid, Stuttgart, Dortmund, Essen, Duisburg, Hamburg, Hanover, Cologne, and a few from Vienna. A number who had enough money were allowed to travel on further into the country. About 6,000 remained behind. However, on Monday the 31st October a train travelling on from Alt-Bentschen was detained at Posen [now Pol. Poznan]. About 4,000 people were said to be in Posen.

No help was at hand because Poland apparently had not been informed of the German operation. We were all led into a large square. At 5 o'clock in the afternoon it transpired that one had to be registered and state where in Poland one had relatives, as one was probably going to be allowed to travel there the next day.

Then six Polish officials were present to take the details of all the people there. The stampede was so great, however, that the officials' table toppled over and no more was recorded. The population were very sympathetic. They brought straw and everyone attempted to get some so that they could sleep in the stables. The rest who did not go to the stables remained in the railway station waiting rooms or in the station hall. More registration on Sunday, Monday and Monday evening, but as there was still no help we attempted to make some order ourselves.

Monday morning it transpired that today people with children and old people would go on their way to their relatives. These were called by name again and had to leave the railway station at 2 o'clock to take possession of their tickets, because they should depart at 4 o'clock. At half past 3 a phone call from Warsaw said that everyone must stay in Alt-Bentschen.

The population was very helpful and also took in refugees, partly without payment and partly for a little reimbursement. The *Jüdische Hilfscomité* [*Hilfsverein der deutschen Juden*; Aid Association of German Jews] had also paid for this. I found a room from a lady with my father and my brother.

The population is very anti-German. German radio was only played continuously in a single inn. Nevertheless the Polish officials behaved themselves but were angry that no Polish was being spoken.

Up to Saturday the 13th November seven people had died, including a young girl of 19 years. Two children were born.

Reporter: Moritz Kupfermann from Wuppertal-Barmen, Werléstraße 18, currently Amsterdam, Plantage Badlaan 19, at Dillenberger. Polish national, 27 years old

B. 196 On 9th November 1923, the day of Hitler's first revolt [Beer Hall Putsch] in front of the *Feldherrndenkmal* [monument to the Generals, Odeonsplatz] in Munich, Göring amongst others was wounded by a shot in the leg. He was taken to the house of the Jewish furniture manufacturer Robert Ballin, and was cared for there and hidden from the authorities. The whole B. family, including members of the extended family, has since enjoyed the protection of Göring. This was also demonstrated in Dachau, since the two older Ballins were quickly released from the camp on the first or second day, and one or two days later Dr. Ballin, approximately forty years old, who admittedly is also a "*Jüdischer Krankenpfleger*" [Jewish nurse], was released.

In the books published by the party the assistance to Göring is not mentioned, but it was reported that Göring had been taken to the court pharmacy located in the Munich Residenz. The

Aryan doctor, who had administered first aid to Göring and who was an eyewitness of the incident, died a number of years ago.

Reporter: Wilhelm Neuburger, Amsterdam-Z[uid], Courbetstraat 21

The report may only be used with the consent of the reporter

B. 197 How does one obtain a *Steuer-Unbedenklichkeit* [tax clearance certificate] in Vienna? (from a letter from Vienna dated 20th December 1938)

"Trusting that one of the different emigration possibilities that I am currently working on will be successful in the foreseeable future, I embarked c. 14 days ago on the extremely frustrating journey to obtain a *Steuer-Unbedenklichkeit*. In order to achieve this one must first queue up at the *Kultusgemeinde* [Jewish community] to obtain a number. I did this three times from 4 o'clock in the morning and sacrificed RM. 10.- to gain a better place and finally obtained a number.

With the number thus obtained one must queue up again at the *Kultusgemeinde*, where the documents are now checked and the questionnaire is handed out, but only to those who can prove that they obtained an *Einreise* [entry certificate]. This second "queuing up" is also very onerous. For example, today I was waiting in line in the *Seitenstettentempel* [synagogue], which is now serving as a waiting hall, from a quarter past 7 in the morning to half past 1 in the afternoon without gaining admission. Those who had not been dealt with by 10 o'clock in the evening on the previous day were attended to first. The documents that were checked at the *Kultusgemeinde* are put into an envelope, which is then sealed, and one receives a pass for the former Rothschildpalais in Prinz-Eugen-Straße which is valid for a specific day.

One has to go there on the specified day, but at least one has the certainty that one will be admitted. The *Steuerunbedenklichkeit* is now only issued for a period of two months, and an extension – which had previously been an option – is impossible. A re-application is said to be forbidden as well. On the contrary, if you ask whether you can re-apply you are immediately threatened with imprisonment, even with Dachau, because they say you should only apply for *Unbedenklichkeit* if you really have obtained an *Einreise,* and if you burdened them with the work of issuing an *Unbedenklichkeit* for you without possessing it you would have deceived them."

Reporter: Oskar Hirschfeld, London

B. 198 At the corner of Sechshauserstraße and Ullmannstraße a certain P. is waiting for his wife, as he does every evening at 9 o'clock. By chance, a brother-in-law of P. came along and the two men started chatting. But suddenly both gentlemen (Herr P. is c. 55 years old, his brother-in-law, Herr E. c. 60 years) are manhandled by an SA man and are forced to accompany him into the inn opposite (Graf, formerly Seidelberger, corner of Sechshauserstraße and Kreuzgasse).

Pushed into the inn so that Herr E. fell flat on the floor, both men are forced to do the following on the orders of the SA man: "*Saujud*" [Jewish swine] (to Herr E.), "climb on the chair and start singing, loudly, or you'll be in for it." The guests present, who already had quite a lot of alcohol in them, not only slapped E. around the face, but also spat at him. Then E. was ordered to drink, the SA man grabbed him, punched him off the chair and he fell flat to the floor again (both Jews are small, fragile men, Mr. E. has a humpback), his face was rubbed with dirt as if it was fair game, ridiculed because of his humpback on top of that, he was really roughed up.

Now it was Herr P.'s turn, treated the same way as his brother-in-law despite him showing them his credentials as a front-line soldier. After the two Jews were no longer recognisable (clothes torn down, faces dirtied), the SA man said: "Now you can go." Yet neither had reached the exit before the SA man came up with the following good idea: "Come back you *Saukerlen* [swine fellows], now we are going to do a few exercises." However, then an SS man came along by chance, who had noticed the shouting coming from the inn, saw it and immediately started to talk to the

SA man. After that the two men were allowed to go home. Herr E. was so dazed that he could not find his way home although he lives less than a 10-minute walk away.

It was only after days that Herr E. was able to walk again, but he was still in pain.

Reporter: Robert Steiner, 38 Rue Bisson, Paris

B. 199 Germany, 9th, 10th and 11th November 1938

A couple of dozen SA men sit in a public house. They are whispering to each other. Some of them already feel the effects of the alcohol. At the stroke of 12 o'clock midnight everyone gets up. The guests cannot pay. As if by command the waiters stand next to the SA men. Well, they can pay in a moment. Everyone staggers out of the pub. Then they get into the lorries that have been waiting for them in front of the door. They now drive to a farmer known to them. Here they arm themselves with clubs and tons of petrol and dynamite. At 1, 2, 3 and 4 o'clock at night 15–18-year-old youths wander to the synagogues and Jewish houses.

Inside the holy places people are howling and bellowing like beasts. Curtains are being torn and cut. But that is not enough. The organs are being smashed to pieces with axes. Everything that is valuable is being looted. The holy *Thorarollen* [Torah scrolls] have been cut with butchers' knives. Benches are being knocked over, lamps knocked off the ceilings. The precious window panes have been smashed to pieces. Then petrol is being poured over everything. The people are appalled. But the drunken mob does not seem to notice its own evil deeds. They are acting on orders, and these must be carried out. Everything is well organised. This is not a public outrage. The *Vermögensangabe* [declaration of assets] was the introduction to this operation. Newer proof of economic hardship. An act of sabotage against the German people's assets. Jewish shops are destroyed, goods are thrown out onto the streets.

Jewish passers-by are arrested on the street. They drag the stricken people out of restaurants and pubs, and beat them bloody in front of their relatives. They mistreat fathers in the presence of their children. The Jews cannot expect help from any side. The people are intimidated. But the organised criminals have not yet cooled their heroic courage. Synagogues are set on fire after they have been devastated. Even private homes are burning. The Germans show again what barbarians they are. The government washes its hands in innocence. It will have no knowledge of these things.

People are queuing at the Jewish welfare offices. They are homeless. Everyone wants to leave the country as quickly as possible because they do not have anything left to live on. The poor people in the hospitals have to be pitied. People who are frail are dragged out of their beds into gymnasiums. Sons wanting to see their mothers are shot. Children in orphanages are locked into one room. Everything is wrecked. In the Hachshara kibbutzim [kibbutzim preparing Jews for emigration to Palestine] it is actually women who are tormenting the poor people.

When will the Jews find a bit of quiet? What will the future bring? How will mature young people live their lives? antisemitism is spreading in all countries. When will the diaspora come to an end? Will Palestine be the destination for all young people? Will a people of 16 million not find a secure home? Will we have to wait for the good nature of other countries? When will we be one people with one idea? When shall the caricature of the ever-wandering Jew change its face? And when will we be workers and no longer a people of cripples? People calls us vampires? Must we really live the lives of scroungers?

We will only become a people with a future if we have one idea and one will.

Ten Jews having nine different opinions will never find their way.

The report was posted anonymously with a Cologne postmark to the Comité voor bijzondere Joodsche Belangen [Committee for Special Jewish Affairs] in Amsterdam.

B. 200 Jacob Levy, cattle dealer from Oberbieber near Neuwied in the Rhineland, approximately 60 years old, died in Dachau.
Reporter: M. Heimann, Antwerp, Pelikaanstraat 86

B. 201 According to information from relatives in Amsterdam:

        1. the businessman Stern from Mühlhausen in Thuringia

        2. David Kaufmann from Kirchhain near Marburg

have died after their return home from Buchenwald concentration camp.

B. 202 The Pogrom in Frankfurt am Main

        Appalling conditions in concentration camp

The Jews in Frankfurt and the surrounding country have suffered just as severely from the pogrom of November 10th as the Jews in other parts of Germany, and the methods of the excesses show a common official instigation. All male Jews from the age of 17 were seized, whether in the streets or trams, in cafés or their homes, and taken to the *Festhalle* [large hall for trade fairs], where they were kept for two days and then transported in lorries on a seven-hour journey to the concentration camp at Buchenwald. Jews from Offenbach, Gmunden and other neighbouring towns were also taken to this camp. No consideration was shown to age or infirmity. There were several old men of 80 and even more, and there were many cases of people suffering from appendicitis and other diseases. There was even a boy of eleven.

The number of Jews from Frankfurt and its vicinity taken to the Buchenwald camp was 12,000 and another 3,000 were brought from other parts. There was no proper accommodation for more than 500, and the sufferings of the prisoners were therefore intolerable. They were divided up into groups of 50 and huddled into wooden barracks where the only sleeping accommodation consisted of wooden planks arranged in tiers of five, one above the other. No mattresses or blankets of any kind were provided and the men, who had not been allowed to take anything with them, were obliged to sleep in their clothes.

At first there were no sanitary arrangements of any sort, and the latrines had to be dug by the prisoners themselves. Nor was there any drinking water at first, and the men quenched their thirst with rain or drops of eau-de-cologne until they were able to buy mineral water (*Selter*[Selzer]-*Wasser*) at RM. 1½ per bottle. No water for washing was provided at any time, and mineral water with a handkerchief had to be used sparingly for the purpose. All food had to be bought at the camp canteen and those without money had to borrow from friends. Those who arrived with a considerable sum were deprived of the greater part of it by the camp officials. The bread was dark and clayey; there was no butter; there were few plates and no knives or forks.

Many men have died at Buchenwald: some of their previous maladies, some electrocuted by the heavily charged barbed wire fences against which they threw themselves in their frenzy. Others, who went raving mad and ran amok, were simply clubbed to death by their guards. In one night alone 40 dead bodies were counted as they were being removed. Many prisoners were brutally assaulted by the guards and had their faces or noses disfigured or their arms and legs fractured.

Everybody had to rise at five o'clock and retire at seven o'clock in the evening but there was no work to be done. Cigarettes of poor quality could be bought in a box of six for RM. 2.-.

The release of the prisoners began early in December. The first to be discharged were ex-servicemen and then followed the elderly people. They were liberated in batches of 40 and had to pay RM. 20.- per head for the motor-coach journey to Frankfurt. At present, so far as can be ascertained, only 4,000 Jews are still detained at Buchenwald. They include all those who have been injured or disfigured; these have to remain until their wounds have healed and they are once again presentable. All prisoners have their heads shaved and those released can easily be detected in the streets of Frankfurt, despite the manner in which they try to cover the baldness at the back with their hats.

The excesses in Frankfurt were begun in the early hours of November 10th, and were carried out systematically under obviously official instructions. All Jewish shops were attacked and looted and some were burned down; and all Jewish houses and flats were raided, wrecked and robbed. All the synagogues in Frankfurt, and neighbouring towns have been destroyed by fire.

The famous Rothschild-Haus [Rothschild House], birthplace of the "Five Frankfurters", which had been preserved for decades as a museum, has also been burned down.

In Offenbach a Jewish woman who recognised one of the Nazi band who invaded her home told him that she was surprised to see him committing such an outrage. He replied: "I'm sorry, but I have to obey orders." In Gmunden five Jewish houses forming a single block were completely burned down.

Although it is now over a month since the pogrom, all Jews in Frankfurt are still terror-stricken. They have a presentiment that some further disaster may soon befall them, and they are therefore anxious to get out of the country at the earliest possible moment. They besiege the British Consulate from early in the morning and are there all day and every day. The officials are doing their utmost to cope with the pressure, but those who obtain visas for this country are obviously only a fraction of the total number of applicants. Nobody is permitted to take anything but an insignificant sum of money out of the country and therefore money has lost its value for the involuntary exiles. They buy furniture with their savings as they are allowed to take that with them, but they must pay a tax of 100 per cent on all such purchases. As many as a dozen Jews were buying furniture at one shop the other day. So great now is the demand for this commodity that the manufacturers are complaining of a shortage of wood. Permission for these purchases has to be obtained from the local Nazi authorities, and payment is made direct by the bank at which the purchaser has been obliged to leave all his money.

B. 203 My experiences in Buchenwald concentration camp near Weimar until September 1938

I must first of all explain that this deals with facts that hundreds more have seen and experienced as well as me.

I was taken from my flat at half past 6 one morning by three *Stapo-Beamten* [*Staatspolizei-Beamten;* state police officers]; when asked they said it was for questioning. I was taken to the *Polizeipräsidium* [police headquarters] where to my astonishment I saw c. 200 people. I had to give my personal details to an officer and sign a *Schutzhaftbefehl* [protective custody order]. On the same evening I was transported to Weimar in a *Sammeltransport-Sonderzug* [group transport special train] under military guard with dogs.

It was 5 o'clock in the morning. To the left and right of the platform police officers were standing with weapons at the ready. We were met by SS. There was a hail of kicks and blows from rifle butts. We had to stand in the platform tunnel facing the wall and it was announced, "You are prisoners of the concentration camp and anyone who moves will be shot." Then we were loaded onto lorries that were standing ready, and again it was said that anyone who dared to even move their head would be shot by the armed guard standing at the back of the lorry. The journey lasted c. 30 minutes.

We could see nothing of the region we were driving through.

Here too at the entrance we were again met by SS guards with weapons under their arms. As old people could not keep up, the SS helped them along with rifle butts. We went through the camp gate, over which stood a slogan, *"Recht oder Unrecht – mein Vaterland"* [My country – right or wrong]. We had to strip naked, even though it was cold and wet. Then we dressed in prison uniform. Then our heads were shaved like the commonest criminal; after that we had to report for duty and do military drills, from which as early as this there were the first deaths, because many elderly men suffering from heart disease could not keep up this pace. It was like this for the first and second day, without a break and without any food.

We first received something to eat on the third day, namely half a litre of warm food and a two-kilo loaf of bread between five men. On the fourth day the prisoners were divided up for work. The Jews were used for the heaviest work. They went to the so-called quarry.

The day was divided up as follows: half past 3 wake up, then acorn coffee, at half past 4 *Appell* [roll call] and after that march to work, i.e. in gangs. Each gang had a *Vorarbeiter* [foreman], who was from the *Berufsverbrecher* [professional criminal] category. He had power over us, over life and death. These gentlemen drove us with a club, under the supervision of the SS guards of course, who witnessed every gang at 5 o'clock in the morning. The Herr *Vorarbeiter* and SS guards were responsible for the workload being maintained, which naturally was particularly difficult with the diet and unfamiliarity of the physical work. Thus every day various people were left lying dead. Shooting at so-called living targets was popular, in other words if a worker did not comply he was chased across the so-called cordon, then of course he was "auf der Flucht erschossen" [shot whilst escaping]; others were battered to death with a rock or were literally beaten to death.

The camp itself was surrounded by an electrified barbed wire fence, with a tower with machine gun posts every 50 metres. By day in addition to this there was another cordon round the area of the camp.

One day the *Lagerkommandant* [camp commandant] announced that the haulage gangs from the quarry, which had carried everything using four (men) with a litter on their shoulders until the beginning of June 1938, now had to carry the same and more using two. This of course was no longer carried on the shoulders but in both hands; however people now went down like flies as it was not permitted to take a break whilst working. The strength in the hands fails very quickly if c. two to three hundredweight have to be carried by two men a distance of two to three kilometres, and the result was that people did not comply and of course were considered to be *Arbeitsscheue* [work-shy] and refusers and were punished accordingly. I will come back later to the details of these punishments. In order not to fall foul of these measures, people tied their hands to the litters with rope in order not to attract attention, and preferred to let their hands be pulled out. When we had unloaded we had to return to the workplace or loading bay at the double. I myself sustained a hernia and torn lung through this inhuman work. As the food was only inadequate, strength very quickly ebbed away, and many died from exhaustion. There was no aid. People were so weary that at every *Appell* after work 30% of all the prisoners collapsed with exhaustion. These people were made to stand up again by means of cudgels, or they were dead.

Incidentally in the camp we had to sign to say that we are *Arbeitsscheue* Jews and that we have signed this voluntarily.

Now I come to a chapter, this is the so-called house punishments of the concentration camp. Anyone who has also seen and experienced these could believe that they had been transported back to the most gruesome dark ages, but it has to be accepted that back then it was not as bad.

First of all there was corporal punishment for the following misdemeanours:

for incomplete workload,

for talking at work,

for drinking water at work,

forgetting to salute a foreman or similar,

for collapsing at *Appell*, not standing to attention,

or one has not pleased a guard.

Then the number of the prisoner was written down and he was punished without interrogation. The *Bock* [whipping block] stood on the *Appellplatz*. The offender was pulled onto it by three SS men, one held his mouth shut, the second and third struck on the buttocks alternately from left and right using a leather club stuffed with lead pipe, c. 25–30–50 times [25 *vorm Arsch*] according to the severity of the punishment.

In many cases the people were dead or unconscious; if still alive, they had to pull their trousers down in order to show the *Kommandant* the holes in their flesh. Their lordships were so perverted. If a Jew died in this way, then the others were given notification that he had received a free ticket to Palestine.

A further punishment, which was also usually fatal, is "*Baumhängen*" [tree-hanging]. Every day 50–100 prisoners could be found tied to the trees. The hands were tied backwards round the tree and the body was hung 10 cm. off the ground, legs tied together. The cries of these prisoners could be heard for kilometres, until they lost consciousness and then slowly died.

During my imprisonment one prisoner was also publicly hanged in front of 15,000 prisoners. This man had tried to escape with another man and battered an SS guard to death. One of them escaped to the Č.S.R. [Czechoslovak Republic], but the other one was apprehended at his mother's home. In the yard, or on the *Appellplatz*, a gallows was erected that is still there today; the offender was executed by one of the prisoners who had been chosen for the task. The body was left hanging for 24 hours, and the whole camp, i.e. all the prisoners, had to stand on the *Appellplatz* for a long time in order to watch everything.

A further punishment was "*An-der-Mauer-Stehen*" [standing at the wall]: from 5 o'clock in the morning until 9 o'clock in the evening the person being punished had to stand on one spot and look at a white wall.

The worst was when someone had been asleep during work or had made an attempt to escape.

The offender was locked in a chest one square metre in size, which had barbed wire all round inside. The chest was placed in the sun and the prisoner fed with salted herrings for three to five days until he died.

There were no beds or similar; we were informed that we (Jews) had not earned any. We merely received two rough woollen blankets and slept on the ground. In one barrack (known as block) 4–500 people were crammed in, worse than sheep.

On Sundays the Jews got nothing to eat. People who were physically stout were specially picked on. They were hounded until they were dead or committed suicide.

The hygiene facilities were appalling. There were no lavatories or running water. Pits were arranged up to 20 metres deep, poles were placed across them, and there the call of nature was answered. It so happened that there was an outbreak of dysentery, people were so weak that they died as there was no aid.

If anyone had done it in their trousers, then he was reported by the block guard and then punished in the following way. A square box was filled with water, the prisoner got in and was scrubbed down with a besom, i.e. the skin was literally pulled from his body, and by the next day the patient had died. Over 50% of prisoners died during my imprisonment, i.e. from my block, in which there were 450 men. The camp was first built during my time. Elderly men died usually all as a result of exhaustion or the previously described conditions.

I am ready at all times to describe the conditions in more detail and to swear under oath in front of a commission.

A prisoner from the Buchenwald concentration camp.

The inmates call it *Totenwald* [Death Forest].

B. 204 20th December 1938

Note on the Situation of Jews in Germany

From reliable information it is evident that scarcely a fraction of what is really happening in Germany since the pogrom wave of November 10th has become known abroad, despite the accurate and detailed reports in the English and American press. This is due to the fact that any disclosures to the foreign press regarding the treatment meted out to many thousands of Jews in concentration camps would immediately place the prisoners in deadly peril; indeed, in some individual cases this has actually happened. The few facts about to be quoted must not be published.

In the small hours of 10th November (between one and three o'clock) no fewer than 500 synagogues throughout Greater Germany were set on fire at the express order of the Nazi Party authorities; in Berlin the order was given by Dr. Goebbels himself as Gauleiter Provincial Leader. The burning down of the synagogues was not only an act of revenge for the shooting of Herr vom Rath; it was done with the deliberate intention of depriving the Jews of their last stronghold and thereby accelerating their final "liquidation".

Since 1933, the service at all synagogues in German territory used to be attended by such large crowds of worshippers that the doors had to be closed immediately after, and sometimes even before the commencement of the service. The synagogue was the only place still left to the Jews where they might gather some spiritual comfort. This was realised by the leaders of the Nazi Party – hence the order to burn all synagogues simultaneously. Since that night not a single religious service has been held by Jews in Germany, whatever information to the contrary may have been given recently to foreign press correspondents.

It should be pointed out that numerous items of information which have been supplied to the press outside Germany have not appeared in the German papers and are completely untrue.

In the afternoon of 10th November the mass arrests of Jews began. 60,000 Jews aged from 16 to 80 were sent to the concentration camps of Sachsenhausen-Oranienburg, Buchenwald near Weimar and Dachau. It is almost impossible to convey an idea of the sufferings of these people, beaten, subjected to unspeakable tortures and in some cases murdered outright.

Those arrested on 10th, 11th and 12th November were, on arrival at the camps, forced to stand in rows for 17 hours without changing their position. Food was issued for the first time 24 hours after arrival. Many died, especially among the older men, as a result of this preliminary treatment. The new prisoners were placed in barracks, and 260 men had to sleep where there was room for only 50. They were compelled to lie on their side, closely pressed together, for want of space.

The inmates of the camps are made to rise at half past 5 when an *Appell* [roll call] is taken (the first of five or six) and the work distributed. At Sachsenhausen the prisoners are occupied with the preparation of iron and stones for bridges and the lining of canals; this work is done by all without regard to age or physical condition. It goes on without pause until 7 o'clock in the evening. Dinner consists of a hunk of dry bread distributed during the early morning *Appell,* and must be eaten while running, driven by SS men in skull-and-crossbones uniform, who lash the prisoners with whips.

In addition to the three concentration camps mentioned, there exists a so-called swamp camp near the Dutch border, known as Eschwege [Esterwegen]. To this camp only particularly hardened criminals used to be sent whom it was desired to dispatch quickly. Those criminals have been brought to Sachsenhausen, Buchenwald and Dachau to act as *Vorgesetzte* [foremen] of the imprisoned Jews.

People who spent months in the prisons of the Russian GPU [*Gosudarstvennoye politicheskoye upravlenie;* State Political Administration] swear that even there they had not come across such sadistic cruelty as is daily practised at the German concentration camps. One or two examples should suffice.

A particularly brutal torture, brought from Eschwege, has now been introduced at the camps. The Jewish prisoners are lined up in a recumbent position on the edge of a canal now being built near the Oder. SS men kick the prisoners into the canal, which is many metres deep, and they are made to scramble back to the bank and lie down again, only to be kicked into the canal once more; this process goes until the men lie prostrate, covered with blood. For a full week after 10th November the prisoners were forced daily to run round the canal for 7 hours at a stretch without any interruption; SS men were posted on both sides and threw sand into the jackets which the runners had to hold up; they were forced to throw this sand out on the opposite bank.

Most of the *Aufseher* [overseers] are lads from 17 to 19 years of age whose orders are always given at the point of the revolver. Since the slightest disobedience or inability to work is punished by immediate shooting, it is not surprising that there should be numerous deaths. It should be easy to understand, too, that unless the prisoners are saved quickly, they may lose all strength to live.

Nobody is dispensed from work. So long as a prisoner is still alive, however gravely ill he may be (the *Krankenstationen* [sick bays] at the camps were closed to Jews for the first three weeks), he is compelled to work and to answer every *Appell*. Both at Dachau and Sachsenhausen there have been cases of old men unable to stand up during *Appell*. They were deprived of food for three days, and those prisoners standing at either side who tried to help them by holding them up were publicly whipped.

A whipping is carried out in the presence of all the inmates of the prisoner's barrack. He is completely stripped and beaten by two SS men with leather whips. The screams heard from all ends of the camp at various times of the day and night are sometimes so harrowing that the prisoners try to stop their ears with any bit of stray paper they can find. The SS men organise daily hunts after rabbis, doctors, lawyers and members of the intellectual classes generally.

The camps are surrounded by an electrified fence, and when the SS men want to finish off a Jewish prisoner they order them to run towards the fence; the sentry there then shoots at him and the victim is reported to have been "*beim Fluchtversuch erschossen*" [shot whilst escaping], although it stands to reason that anyone trying to do so would be electrocuted by touching the fence.

Very soon after 10th November hundreds of Jewish women in Germany received urns containing the ashes of their husbands whose bodies had been cremated. Cremation is always resorted to in the case of Jews who die at concentration camps, to prevent the discovery of mutilations on the bodies.

Every Jew who is released for the purpose of emigration – and only those able to emigrate are set free – is made to sign a statement to the effect that he has not been mistreated, that he will keep silent about anything he might have seen at the camp, and that he will never, so long as he lives, engage in spoken or written propaganda to the detriment of the Third Reich.

The present account does not exhaust the facts by far. Some day a voluminous report will have to be written on the happenings of the last five weeks in Germany. The object of this note is merely to convey some idea of the tragic fate of German Jewry.

This fate threatens to become worse still. In January 1939, the "*Arisierung*" [Aryanisation] of the German economy will be completed and Jews will be thrown out of all branches of occupation. They will then be regarded as "*asoziale Elemente*" [asocial elements], and, in order to "prevent the demoralisation of Germany" it is intended to imprison them in labour camps where they will be forced to build roads and break stones.

It is important to mention that the German state, which hitherto had afforded some measure of relief to the poorest amongst its population, refuses such aid to the Jews. This means that the Jewish *Gemeinde* [communities] of Germany will have the care for thousands of people thrust upon them – a duty which, in view of their destitution, they cannot possibly discharge.

Thus we obtain the following picture of the situation: 60,000 Jews imprisoned in concentration camps, of whom only 25,000 have so far been released; a *Gemeinschaft* [community] about to be reduced to the state of proletarian paupers, bereft of the very means of sustenance, and threatened, literally, with death by starvation.

There is but one way to alleviate this terrible distress, and this is the opening of *Durchgangslagern* [transit camps] in various European countries, where the refugees could be re-trained for new occupations for a year or two in order that they may be enabled to settle overseas.

It is important, too, that the Jewish National Home in Palestine, which has long been German Jewry's only source of consolation and of hope, should contribute towards the solution of this difficult problem. 200 men who for many years have rendered signal services to Zionism are suffering in concentration camps. It is an intolerable thought that the Jewish *Gemeinde* in Palestine can do nothing to save some of the Jewish children in Germany (whose numbers are estimated at not less than 50,000).

Emigration alone can save Jews in Germany, doomed to a terrible fate; and this applies not only to those in the concentration camps, but also to the children. As new decrees, threatening another increase in Jewish misery, are due to appear very shortly, emigration, to be really effective, must be carried through immediately.

B. 205 13th January 1939
According to information from a completely reliable source

the following have died in Buchenwald and Sachsenhausen respectively:

Businessman Arnold Wollberg from Berlin, 72 years old, information provided by his wife, Ilonka Wollberg from Berlin;

Businessman Alfred   Schönberg, from Berlin, 58 years old.

B. 206 12th January 1939

According to the Basel *Nationalzeitung* [National Newspaper], no. 13 of 9th January, page 4, the well-known actor Paul Morgan has died in Buchenwald concentration camp, where he was taken in March 1938. Morgan was born on 1 October 1886 in Vienna.

The *Pariser Tageszeitung* [Paris Daily Newspaper] had already published a similar report a few days earlier.

The news is confirmed by report B. 192 from Buchenwald,

B. 207 In the second half of December 1938 or the beginning of January 1939 Ernst Feist from Berlin died after his release from the Buchenwald concentration camp as a result of frostbite to both forearms.

B. 208 The married couple S. are in a particularly bad and life-threatening situation, living in one of the smaller provincial towns. Herr S. is the joint owner of an ironmongery and coal firm.

Herr S. was in the concentration camp, however has been released. The couple has been evicted and must leave the flat within eight days. Expulsion is due to follow within 20 days. Frau S. has a young son of 15 months and is expecting a second child soon. Because of the coming child the young people have to date omitted to initiate any steps for emigration.

B. 209 I was not put into a camp either in the *März*-[March] or the *November-Aktion* [November operation] in Vienna. In November, when I became aware of the events, I went to clarify some of the questions related to my emigration and to speed matters up at the relevant office, and from there not home but to a friend's house. By chance as I was about to leave the house, it was searched and, following the question of whether I was a Jew, I was taken away by German SS men in full battledress. I will mention here that in my opinion I avoided imprisonment later because I lived with Turks and apparently the SS did not dare to enter their home.

I was thrust into a lorry in which there were a large number of heavily bleeding Jews. On getting out we were met by a double row of SS men standing ready for us on a flight of about 20–25 steps, equipped with all manner of implements, e.g. rubber truncheons etc. Whilst we went up the steps continuous curses were rained down upon us with such fury, cuts and blows that by the top of the steps we were all covered in blood. I was taken to a room with a tap and washed myself clean to some extent. My feet were in a pool of blood that showed me what had happened earlier in that room to my fellow believers.

I was then dragged into a second room, still half-unconscious and under loud insults, in which three obviously intellectual Jews were standing, passive and bleeding. For an introduction I received a slap round the face and had to stand against the wall to be interrogated. The SS man first asked me, "*Weißst Du Jud* [Jew do you know] why you are here?" When I did not answer, because I was simply not physically able to do so, and also did not know what answer he wanted to hear, he asked again, "*Jud*, what happened in Paris?" On my reply that a Jewish boy had shot a German official, he said: "and that is why you will now be shot: a thousand Jews for each Aryan." He then asked me what I was, and when I said "*Rechtsanwalt*" [lawyer] he asked: "How many have you cheated, more than ten thousand?" He repeated the question five or six times, until because of loss of blood and energy all strength finally left me and I became insensible. Obviously now the concept was ruined for him and he only cried, "*Raus* [out], *Jud*, go home!"

I dragged myself down the steps and then saw how two fellow believers, two from the three already mentioned, were beaten and dragged out of the room, what finally became of them and of the third I do not know. As I staggered down the steps, I was once again brutally beaten by SS men despite my awful condition, and kicked by two persons with heeled boots.

When I got back to my home, I hardly know how even now, I could not lie down because no place on my body was without wounds. My forehead was cut, I had large lumps at the back of my head, I could not move my legs, arms, shoulders and behind were swollen. Then, even though I was bleeding all over, I was put to bed and my landlords tried to obtain medical treatment for me. This was impossible because Jewish doctors were not there and Aryan ones did not come. At last on the following day a Jewish doctor who had been released came, and he established that my right side was completely paralysed and the left only partly mobile, the injuries came from rifle butts and blows from rubber truncheons and other implements.

I remained in bed for eight days and could only walk on crutches after 14 days. My brother was in Dachau, the replies that we were allowed to make to meagre letters from Dachau were so curtailed that we could only answer cards for cards and each letter with only one letter, whose scope could not stray outside that of the letter received.

In Dachau there were 12,000 prisoners, amongst them *Bürgermeister* [mayor] of Vienna [Richard] Schmitz, who was employed building roads, and the son of Archduke Franz Ferdinand.

The greatest difficulties were made in obtaining papers for emigration, and their completion often so long delayed that e.g. the *Unbedenklichkeitsbescheinigungen* [clearance certificates] became invalid and the process had to begin again. The *Finanzamt* [tax office], the police and the Gestapo impeded every correctly made application because in many cases they worked against each other.

B. 210   Addendum to the report about the circumstances of the *Wiener Israelitisch Kultusgemeinde* [Vienna Jewish community] at the end of December 1938

The figures given in the previous report about the extent of emigration were generally confirmed with minor variations by the reporter. According to his account, the ratio of those Jews who were themselves against leaving Vienna to those who were supported by the *Kultusgemeinde* [Jewish Community] in this respect was, until 10th November, 3:1; after this date it was 1:1.

With regard to the relationship between *SS-Obergruppenführer* [SS Senior Group Leaders] Eichmann and Kuchmann, who are responsible for the supervision of the *Kultusgemeinde*, and the senior men of the *Kultusgemeinde*, Dr. Josef Löwenherz, Emil Engel and Dr. Benjamin Murmelstein, the writer of the report explained that repeatedly a marked sadism characterises the tasks given by the former to the latter. Therefore they are very fond of setting extremely tight deadlines for extensive pieces of written work. In December alone, as well as the annual report, the submission was demanded of the following pieces of work within a very short period of time: "*Die wirtschaftliche und kulturelle Situation der Juden in Österreich vor und nach dem Umbruch*" [The economic and cultural position of the Jews in Austria before and after the turmoil], "*Jüdische Bevölkerungsbewegung in Österreich vor und nach dem Umbruch*" [Jewish population movement in Austria before and after the turmoil] and "*Das jüdische Organisationswesen vor dem Umbruch*" [Jewish organisations before the turmoil]. In addition to these large pieces of work supported by statistics and graphs, each week the so-called "*Wochenbericht*" [weekly report] has to be submitted. With regard to the content of these accounts it is essential to draw them up in a way that is acceptable to those who have ordered the work, but it is attempted by the authors occasionally, even without therefore having had as yet a sense of decency, to cite moments which actually prove the absurdity of the National Socialist Jewish policy. In general, as already communicated in the report, the emphasis must be placed on the extent of the emigration in all pieces of work that are to be submitted to the Gestapo.

The three leaders of the *Kultusgemeinde* had to undertake not to leave before the emigration of the Jews from the

"*Ostmark*" [Austria] is complete. All three must, in the event of foreign travel, which they may undertake only in the interests of emigration and the duration of which is precisely stipulated by the authorities, produce hostages in Vienna – amongst whom in particular there are family members. The 'privileged' position which Dr. M. enjoys has not prevented him from also being subjected to unpleasantness already on two occasions. On the one occasion he was arrested, in the summer on a Friday evening on the way home from his *Tempel* [synagogue] (Kluck-ygasse, XX.), together with a few *Vorsteher* [board members] of the *Tempelverein* [synagogue association]. The reason for this measure was as follows: A *Wachbeamter* [watch-officer], in a harsh tone of voice, had ordered the Jews who had come from the *Tempel* not to stop and to go home quickly. To spare themselves this kind of jostling, Dr. M. and his companions hurried away, at which however the *Wachbeamter* immediately took offence, all the more as Dr. M. had some Hungarian newspapers and the "*Jüdische Rundschau*" [Jewish Review] with him. He and the other gentlemen were detained until 11 o'clock in the evening at the nearest guard room, and it took numerous telephone calls, particularly to the Gestapo, to secure his release.

The second incident took place as follows: After 10th November the *Kultusgemeinde* was given the task of making lists of the "conscripts'" personal details and financial position as well as their chances of emigration. During the day the officials had to deal with the opening hours to the public, which as a result of the influx of the prisoners' family members assumed huge dimensions, at night most of the officials had to remain in the building in order to handle the correspondence, in particular however to complete the required lists referred to above within a short period of time. Therefore the senior officials of the *Kultusgemeinde* stayed in the building especially for eleven days, day and night; food was brought to them by young helpers of the *Kultusgemeinde* who, accompanied by one of the SS men stationed in the building, went to the local grocery shops (they had to be accompanied to ensure that the Jewish lads were not treated politely whilst shopping); in the *Kultus-gemeinde* meeting room folding beds were set up so that the officials could sleep in shifts for at least a few hours; if one of the officials had to do something urgently outside the building he received an *Entlassungsschein* [certificate of release] signed by the *Kommandant* [Commandant] of the SS squad assigned to the building that was on duty at this time, which specified exactly the time for which permission to leave the building had been given. The SS squad on duty at this time was no longer the same one that had each day assigned five men since the date of the re-opening of the *Kultusgemeinde*, with whom gradually an almost pleasant contact had been established on the part of the body of officials of the building. The new gentlemen differed in a very disagreeable way from those previously on duty both concerning their far greater number and also their demeanour; there were also repeatedly thefts of items of office equipment which were apparently attributable to the new SS men. At night time they very much enjoyed "inspections" in the individual departments of the *Gemeinde* [community] to check whether the completion of the lists was being worked on there in particular.

During such an inspection Dr. M. was ordered to make a "report" on the progress of the work, and as he did so, that very *SS-Kommandant* who had given the order to report back hit him in the face with all his might; however Dr. M. had to continue with his report. A female official of the *Kultusgemeinde*, Frl. Steuermann, who has strawberry blonde hair, was under suspicion that this hair was dyed – for the purpose of conforming to the Aryan hair colour; her hair was torn out so that in this way its authenticity was established.

Strictly confidential: In the past few days the leadership of the *Kultusgemeinde* has been asked to submit a plea to the Gestapo for the release of the former president of the *Kultusgemeinde*, Dr. Desider Friedmann, who is currently under police arrest in Buchenwald. This request, made by the Gestapo itself, seems to guarantee the possibility in the foreseeable future of the release of Dr. F., who has been held under various arrests since 18th

March, this all the more as already for many months a certificate for Palestine has been ready for him. In contrast one sees no possibility of *Oberbaurat Ing.* [Senior Government Engineer] Robert Stricker and the editor Bruno Heilig getting out of Buchenwald concentration camp, as any releases at all from this camp only take place in very rare cases. In response to interventions on behalf of the two aforementioned men, it was expressly declared that their detention would continue because of the so fiercely anti-National Socialist orientation of the Jewish newspapers that they were responsible for publishing, "*Die Neue Welt*" [The New World] and "*Die Stimme*" [The Voice]. (*Oberbaurat* Stricker is therefore not, as may have been assumed after the first hearings, being held because of his position in the Druckerei Steinmann [Steinmann Press], where "*Der Telegraph*" [The Telegraph] was produced.)

In Jewish Vienna there is general amazement that Oskar Hirschfeld, in spite of his position as editor-in-chief and managing editor of *Die Wahrheit* [The Truth], was only detained for three months in Vienna and then was released, without having seen Dachau, if one considers that the orientation of his newspaper was no less strong than the newspapers published by his two unfortunate colleagues. The fact is that Hirschfeld's *Referent Reg. Rat* [consultant civil servant], Dr. Weinmann from Cologne, was removed by the Vienna Gestapo shortly after the conclusion of Hirschfield's case; it can be assumed that he also showed himself to be as lenient in other cases and was therefore no longer acceptable in this house of brutality.

In addition to the manner of the release referred to in the previous report of the *Kultusgemeinde* officials detained by Dr. Blauer in the *Notarrest* [emergency arrest] XX. Karajangasse (*Volksschule* [elementary school]), nevertheless a second procedure was chosen to free the *Kultusgemeinde* officials who had been arbitrarily arrested on 10th November from the prisons. A *Kommandant* from the SS squad stationed at the building, together with a gentleman from the leadership staff of the voluntary youth helpers of the *Kultusgemeinde*, searched all the Vienna police inspectorates, and the gentleman had to identify the officials of the *Kultusgemeinde*, their researchers and assistants. Hoever, this activity only began rather late (that was in fact the reason why so many officials had already been sent from the police stations to the Karajangasse); before this the *Herr Kommandant* had no time, for he, together with Herr Eichmann, had to take part in leading the operation of destruction to which the *Seitenstettentempel* fell victim.

The number of Jews being held at the beginning of January in Dachau because of the '*Aktion*' [operation] of 10th November is estimated to be 3,000. Recently there have been continual releases, in the vast majority of cases however only when family members, who have to direct a plea to the Gestapo, are able to prove, in this and during the subsequent verbal summons, that they can leave immediately. In general, the behaviour of the officials hearing the cases towards the family member concerned is courteous. From the moment of the summons up to release usually takes eight to 14 days. On the other hand, in the past week a further increase in arrests has been seen; in addition, the Jews are also being subjected to further harassment; so in the past few days they have had to assist with the cleaning up of the excrement in Vienna that has accumulated due to the thaw – unpaid, of course.

Amongst the many atrocities of 10th November, the death of the well-known Viennese Jewish restaurateur Herr Schwarz, Vienna II, Rotesterngasse, caused in the most horrible way, has attracted considerable attention. The poor man, who came from a well-known Viennese Jewish restaurateurs' family, and whose business, taken over from his father, occupied the rank of the highly renowned Viennese Jewish restaurants à la Neugröschl and Tonelle, was severely distressed from the first day of turmoil. Immediately after the turmoil the restaurant was plundered by the SA, so that its refurbishment caused great financial sacrifice. Then it was announced that all Jewish restaurants in Vienna would have to close on 1st August, and Schwarz attempted suicide from sorrow at this news and was saved at the last minute. Now on 10th November he was trapped in his own refrigerator and died an agonising death.

Asked about the mood of the Aryan population, the reporter explained that they do indeed grumble a lot more or less openly, in particular about the sometimes noticeable lack of food, that however a release of this clearly existing dissatisfaction in some kind of revolutionary form cannot be counted on very soon; this is now to be expected not because of the severe methods of oppression, rather a certain resignation can be detected everywhere. (In Vienna a true saying is circulating in jest: "*Den Juden geschieht Unrecht, den Ariern Recht!*" [The Jews are being wronged, the Aryans are treated right!].) At that time, only two days after 10th November, the Viennese Jews were certainly sold nothing in very many grocery shops; the well-known Viennese coffee business Julius Meinl started it, the owner of which could not do enough during the Schuschnigg regime out of "sentiment for the Fatherland" and is also closely related to Jews by marriage.

The answer to my question, how one understands the particular severity of the National Socialist Jewish policy in Austria, which bears no relation even to the worst experience of the past five years in the '*Altreich*' [Old Reich], is very interesting; one believes that in all Gestapo directives the idea shines through that, in the opinion of the National Socialists, the slow pace of the emigration of the Jews from the *Altreich* during these five years has caused the ferocity of the measures directed against the Austrian Jews. Hitler has promised the German people a Germany free of Jews, and he still wants to witness this ideal. The slow pace of emigration from the *Altreich* allowed the fear to develop that he would not see this ideal state realised, and therefore in the *Ostmark* from the first day onwards draconian measures were introduced which were intended to bring about, and did indeed bring about, a mass emigration. Now that this experiment has succeeded, the intention is to get a similar grip on the *Altreich*, where measures of such ferocity were unknown until now; a leading functionary of the Vienna Gestapo, who visited a public authority there during a trip through the *Altreich* and talked conversationally about the expulsion of the Viennese Jews, encountered the liveliest astonishment from his German colleagues in the *Reich* over the applicability of such a directive; the functionary concerned related this episode himself. Only limited contact if absolutely necessary is permitted about official matters between the *Hilfsverein der deutschen Juden* [Aid Association of German Jews] and the *Wiener Israelitische Kultusgemeinde.*

There is still a significant detail to add to the destruction of the *Tempel*. At those places of worship where the Christian caretakers were PG [*Parteigenossen*; Party members], a plaque was mounted during the destruction operation, "*Achtung, Hausbesorger Parteigenosse!*" [Attention, caretaker Party member!]

B. 211 Observations in Berlin at the end of December 1938

Health services: The Jewish private clinics have all been *arisiert* [Aryanised]. There is only one Jewish hospital left, which cannot survive financially however and will close down in the foreseeable future. Jewish patients were also well cared for in Catholic hospitals until now. Aryan doctors can be consulted by Jews.

A Jewish old people's home is to close down in the near future.

There are said to be one or two Jewish *schools* left in Berlin, so that it has become impossible for most Jewish children still to go to school at all, as since 11th November 1938 they are no longer permitted in an Aryan school. Until now they were still able to attend Catholic schools.

Housing: There are Jews who still live in houses of Aryan owners today; however they constantly expect to be given notice. They may not enter certain streets and require a special *Erlaubnis* [permit] if they live in one of the banned streets.

Most restaurants bear the sign "*Juden unerwünscht*" [Jews not wanted].

Jewish cohesiveness: According to my observations the Jews are sticking very closely together and are helping each other out with funds.

Traffic: If a passer-by does not cross a road or a square in accordance with the rules, then he will be stopped by the

Verkehrspolizei [traffic police]. If he is an Aryan, then he pays a fine of RM. 1.-; if he is a Jew he has to pay RM. 20.- and this then counts as a *Vorbestraft* [previous conviction]. The following shows the way they do not baulk at any means of taking money off the Jews: before emigration every item that may be taken will be thoroughly examined by the *Devisenbeamten* [foreign currency officials], bed linen or underwear may not be exported in any quantities. In the case of typewriters or sewing machines the state requires 100% of the purchase price; for jewellery acquired after 1933, anyway for luxury goods, 200 to 300%.

As far as sustenance is concerned, the Jews get everything in Aryan shops and are treated well, as far as I can judge amongst the people that I know. In any case humanity seems to permeate amongst the Christians again. I have not heard a Jew curse the German people, only the authorities, although I believe that a tremendous hatred of humanity must have accumulated. During the worst November days Christians are said to have kept Jews hidden in their homes and brought them money and food. They felt ashamed in front of the Jews. Even *Kriminalbeamten* [police detectives] tried to save Jews from the concentration camp.

The most dreadful thing about the current state of affairs is the constant fear of the concentration camp, the terrors of which they now know. Very many came back suffering dreadfully, with frostbitten limbs etc.

The only thought that governs people is: Get away across the border as fast as possible, even if everything has to be left behind.

B. 212 As a repercussion of the Paris murder, the little village of Gailingen am Untersee also suffered from the National Socialist *Vergeltungsmaßregeln* [retribution measures]. A large number of Jewish families has been living in Gailingen for many years, who had to suffer greatly from this *Vergeltung*. The majority of the male Jewish population was taken to Dachau concentration camp and the synagogue was blown up. Information came to the people who had stayed behind 14 days ago that one of those who had been transported away had died in Dachau. And now the second death has already been announced; Rabbi Dr. Bohrer has also died in Dachau. Dr. Bohrer is the father of a large brood of children. A further member of the Jewish *Gemeinde* [community] in Gailingen was released from Dachau a few days ago and shortly afterwards suffered a fatal stroke in Munich.

These deaths, about which no more precise details are known, have seriously heightened the anxiety of the Jewish population about their family members.

From *National Zeitung* [National Newspaper] Basel, no. 114 of 10th January 1939

B. 213 The following report should convey calmly, clearly and precisely, free from all exaggeration and flights of fancy, that which the writer of these lines has actually seen and heard, so long as he can and also must answer before God and his conscience.

The events which took place during the burning down of the synagogues, the wrecking of homes etc. are indeed sufficiently well known that there is no need to go into more detail about them.

I

I was arrested on Saturday the 12th November on the street and first of all taken amidst verbal abuse to the appropriate *Polizei-revier* [police station], where personal details were established and recorded. Then c. 80 Jews were driven in a large bus to the large hall. On our arrival at about 12 noon c. 2,000 Jews were already there. One had to line up in rows of ten. In front of each row stood a table at which a senior police officer was seated who read the names out loud. One had to step forward as one's name was read out and say, "I am the *Saujud* [Jewish pig] so and so, born on, etc."

Woe betide anyone who forgot to say the word "*Saujud*". He was chased throughout the huge hall whilst being beaten. Money, everything one had with one was taken away. *Tefillin* [phylacteries] and *tallit* [prayer shawls] were cut to pieces amidst the most mocking remarks by the SS, "You'll get to heaven very soon, even without the Lord's prayer." One rabbi was forced to run throughout the huge hall attired in *tallit* and *tefillin*. An opera singer was forced, oh what irony, to sing Sarastro's aria from Mozart's *Magic Flute* "Within these sacred halls one does not know revenge." We had to shout in chorus, "We are *Saujuden*, murderers, *Rassenschänder* [race defilers]" etc. Then one was pitilessly made to do *Exerzieren* [punitive drill]. At the double, crawling on the stomach and with nose touching the dirty ground etc. They carried on with us like this until 10 o'clock in the evening. Of course there was nothing left to eat. At 10 o'clock the order rang out, "Prepare to march off." We were driven in buses to the railway under heavy SS guard, where the mob greeted us with shouts of "*Schlagt die Juden tot* [Beat the Jews to death], cut their throats!" Then one was herded into the wagons like cattle.

The journey itself passed relatively peacefully. However at 6 o'clock at the final destination a reception was awaiting us from the SS and the police, which cannot and must not be forgotten for the rest of one's life. We were pushed out of the wagons into a tunnel with blows from rifle butts. People who could not run fast enough were simply thrown down the steps by the SS, and they were simply trampled upon. There were very many injured whose blood just flowed from their faces. However they were not permitted to be bandaged. In the tunnel one had to stand again in rows of ten facing the wall, hat pressing into the face, and now the SS again began to beat us at random with rifle butts. Then we were herded into the prison vehicles. One had to raise the knees high and prop heads on them. Blows from rifle butts hailed down on our heads again. At 7 o'clock the vehicles stopped in front of the large gate at Buchenwald concentration camp. One was chased with blows again through the large gate and then had to report on the large *Appellplatz* [parade ground].

II

In the camp there were already c. 10,000 arrested Jews and c. 4,000 from Vienna, who have already been in the camp since

March. One now had to line up again in rows of ten, and each prisoner received a number, usually accompanied by a kick in the buttocks or a slap in the face. Then one's hair was cut. On this Sunday, it was the 13th November, we had to stand from 7 o'clock in the morning until 8 o'clock in the evening on one and the same spot. Of course there was nothing to eat. At 2 o'clock there was whale soup, to which [bicarbonate of] soda had been added. At 8.30 we were chased into the barracks. There were five large barracks in place, and c. 2,500 Jews were crowded in each one alike. Then followed a really insane night. One was not permitted to step outside, as then one would have been shot down by the guard. There was no drinking water. The result of the whale soup was that the majority of the barrack had diarrhoea. Thirst and the other events now caused mass hysteria. People began to shout and rave. Every so often the SS came, seized c. 20 to 30 Jews from each barrack and simply beat them to death in front of the barracks (will be contested!). Some of them were thrown onto the electric wire. The camp is surrounded by an electric wire in fact, which is charged with 360 volts. However in their despair some of the Jews ran into it of their own accord, and almost every day 8 to 10 Jews could be seen hanging life-lessly on the wire. Some in their despair simply let themselves be shot by the SS.

Dawn was breaking on the morning of the 14th November. On the horizon the sun was climbing, blood red. One had to report for *Appell* [roll call] again. At 9 o'clock there was some coffee and a small piece of mouldy bread; and then something else happened, which bears witness to the subhuman nature of the SS. From 9 o'clock in the morning until 7 o'clock in the evening they had us sit on the wet, soggy ground, legs crossed. Being excused to relieve ourselves was forbidden. One simply had to do it in one's trousers. No lavatories were in place and so-called latrines were only set up after a few days. There was no water for washing either. During imprisonment one was therefore forced not to wash and one had no other clothes either, so that one never got out of one's clothes for the whole period of one's imprisonment. The result of these appalling conditions can be vividly imagined. At 8 o'clock one was again chased into one's barrack, and the same sad scenes as during the night of Sunday to Monday were repeated.

Some people were dragged by the SS into the so-called washhouse, which in reality resembled a torture chamber where people were simply tortured and bullied to death. The writer of these lines was also dragged into the washhouse and had the opportunity to see and to hear what actually happened there. People asked themselves, "Is that reality or was it a fantasy brought on by overwrought nerves, what we saw there?" But unfortunately what was happening there was indeed clear from the dead who were carried out. For the cries of the tortured people were in fact no fantasy but harsh reality.

The author of these lines was fortunate to remain unmolested even in the washhouse. After four days, thus from 16th November, this kind of torture was stopped from above. After this time the SS was withdrawn from the Jewish barracks. The Vienna Jews were put in charge, who sacrificed themselves for us. In particular endless thanks are owed to the Viennese doctors who did everything to help the injured and also as far as was possible treated the sick. Medicines were not available at the beginning and Jews were simply not permitted to be treated and some of them had to die in the most dreadful pain, for Jews were not allowed to be admitted to the *Lagerlazarett* [camp sick bay]. The washhouse was afterwards turned into a sick bay for Jews, i.e. the sick were simply laid on the smooth wooden floor, without straw, without blankets etc. The barrack was open at the ceiling without windows so the wind whistled through. It goes without saying that there was no stove there.

Even when the atrocities by the SS stopped, several hundred people still died of illnesses such as symptoms of cold etc. Also anyone who had a temperature of 40 degrees had to report for *Appell* in the open air. Then it was merely said, "The *Judenschwein* [Jewish pig] can and should perish." Rations were more than inadequate. In the morning there was some brewed coffee and some mouldy *Kommissbrot* [army bread], one loaf a day between five Jews. Midday one litre of soup, peas or beans etc.·

In the evening a small piece of sausage or cheese and bread. One had to spend one day after another in this way. One was only permitted to write a card or a letter of ten lines once every 14 days. One was permitted to be sent RM. 10.-, however was not paid all of it and even if one was, it was after a deduction of 25% for administrative expenses.

Jews who are in the camp for political reasons wear camp clothing, as they have to do heavy work, most in the notorious quarries. Each Jew wears a *Mogen Dovid* [Star of David] in a different colour on his uniform. Red means *politischer Häftling* [political prisoner], green *Rassenschänder* [race defilers]etc. The quarry is located c. 25 minutes outside the camp.

The prisoners have to get the rocks to the camp at the double. SS guards are positioned every 20 minutes on the route, they throw large rocks at the poor prisoners and usually also injure them.

There are neither Sundays nor holidays in the camp. The working day is c. 16 hours long. There are so-called *Strafkompanien* [punishment companies]. They have to work in the quarry from noon on Saturday until Monday morning without receiving anything to eat. If a prisoner has done the least thing wrong then he is strapped to the so-called *Bock* [whipping block]. An Aryan receives 25 strokes of the cane on the buttocks and a non-Aryan 50 strokes. The author once saw the following scene amongst others:

"A heavy wooden wagon in boggy ground being pulled by c. 40 to 50 people in a yoke and alongside went the SS guards and relentlessly flogged their victims."

But in the camp nesting boxes are mounted for the birds and the SS also has a zoo where roe deer, three bears and stags are fed most attentively.

The author was summoned for release after fifteen days. One had to stand again for ten hours without anything to eat until all the formalities had been completed. One was thoroughly examined by the doctor. If anyone had any traces of abuse on his body then he had to stay in the camp until there was nothing left to be seen. When the *Entlassungsscheine* [release certificates] were given out one had to sign an undertaking not to talk outside about anything that one had seen in the camp. One was officially informed in the political section:

"You must leave Germany as soon as possible. If there is further harassment abroad then all the Jews living in Germany will be incarcerated with their families for life." And anyone who comes into the camp for a second time will also remain in the camp for life, regardless of whether he can emigrate or not.

The costs of the journey home had to be borne by ourselves.

With me 205 Jews were released on 28th November, amongst them 20 from Frankfurt. Many had not a penny on them, as everything had been taken away from them. So others (it was probably people from Upper Silesia who had money on them) had to pay for our journey home. Then when everybody had their tickets we were released. The *Lagerkommandant* [camp commandant] extorted more money for the *Winterhilfswerk* [Winter Relief] from our 205-strong transport. Finally at 7 o'clock one was chased out through the large gate under escort and was in so-called freedom. The result of the stay for the writer of these lines is briefly summarised as follows:

In the whole of someone's life it can never be any worse than in a concentration camp

One no longer need fear death

Hell is still a paradise compared to a concentration camp.

It must also be added that when one is released from the concentration camp the Gestapo orders one to leave Germany within a few days, under threat of being reincarcerated for life in the concentration camp if the person in question has not left the territory of the Reich by the appointed time.

B. 214   It is now reported by credible parties, although final confirmation is not to hand, that five persons have been killed in near Düsseldorf, namely

     Frau Willner,

     Frau Willner's son,

     Herr Heilighaus,

     Frau Heilighaus,

Herr Aron.

Herr Stiefel from the firm Adler jun. is said to have died in a concentration camp.

Alfred Blank, aged about 50, a sales representative from Dortmund, died in the Sachsenhausen concentration camp, probably on 14th or 15th December 1938. His ashes have been sent to the family.

B. 215 Report from Berlin, beginning of January 1939

Gloomy mood predominates. Anxiety about coming events, particularly war.

E.g. the recall of German servant girls from abroad is explained in public as not only that they are needed for domestic service and in the armament factories, but also that the savings which they bring with them are being targeted. The prevailing feeling is that the state is compelled to seize all money. It is literally feared that even the resident population will also be dispossessed, not only the Jews, the churches etc. For that reason a certain flight to tangible assets has gained ground, because fears about money are being harboured.

There is a scarcity of butter, eggs, and suchlike. It is necessary to queue up for them. Blame for that is being cast on the Jews, in particular those in America, who through their boycott of German goods prevent Germany from receiving foreign currency, which is needed for the supply of basic commodities and food. The public falls for these allegations and the mood towards the Jews is made worse as a result. But this distraction does not eliminate the fact of scarcity.

In part in any case it is suspected in public that food is indeed available, but it is being set aside as war reserves, which is possible. After all the hardships and deprivations of recent years, the prospect of war is regarded only with trepidation under such circumstances.

Indignation about the construction of huge buildings and new villages seems to prevail, whilst at the same time elsewhere house building has come to a complete standstill, although the

need exists. The somewhat dazzling facilities of the new buildings make a tasteless impression and mean a step backwards in
beautifully begun artistic development, particularly in interior
decoration.

Many Jews completely lack the means for the *Strafmilliarde*
[punishment billion; *Judenvermögensabgabe*; Jewish assets/
property tax]. They must often borrow the sums from other
Jews, who cannot count on being repaid.

When Jews emigrate, officials appear at their homes who label
the little clothing and linen that they are permitted to take with
them, and estimate the value of the items. A redemption sum
is to be paid to the state for the amount calculated. One must
also buy back one's personal property. The means for this are
obtained by selling the items not designated to be taken, first
and foremost the furniture. As one receives only c. a tenth of
the value, the proceeds barely extend beyond the redemption of
the things that one is allowed to take. In this way one leaves the
country without all the funds.

Engaged couples make use of the cheap availability of furnishings etc. from Jewish homes. In this way the state saves itself
the *Ehestandsdarlehen* [marriage loan], or with the help of the
aforementioned newly married couples can set up their homes
very extensively.

Weeks pass before all the formalities prior to departure
have been completed, especially before the *Unbedenklichkeitsbescheinigung* [tax clearance certificate] is available, signed
by all those whose signature is required (tax offices, *Devisenstellen* [foreign currency offices], police, customs etc., etc.). In
the meantime liquid funds are exhausted and levies, charges,
allowances etc. also have to be paid, until in fact people own
nothing more.

In a well-known case from another town the husband was
in the concentration camp from 11th November for four to five
weeks. Departure for America through Switzerland had been
arranged, but could not take place up to now however, because
fresh difficulties and formalities are always being placed in the
way and sums of money demanded. For redemption of the items

which husband, wife and mother may take with them, RM. 6,000.- was demanded, which sum was then reduced to RM. 4,000.-. The local relatives have made every effort to enable the departure. Enough money is available. But to date the people have not yet arrived here (in Switzerland), where they have been expected for weeks, in order to travel to America, where they aleady used to live.

B. 216 On 10th November at half past 9 in the morning, about half an hour after I had learned that in the city the synagogues were on fire and were taking place, a *Polizeibeamter* [police officer] appeared at my home in order to arrest me. When I asked what was happening and how long my questioning at the *Polizeirevier* [police station] would last, he replied that he was merely carrying out orders. His behaviour was not particularly friendly, although perfectly correct. I was taken by him to the *Polizeirevier*, where my personal details were written down and I was briefly searched for weapons. After that I was taken to the meeting room at the synagogue nearby, where there were already about 20 other arrested men. After barely half an hour we were transported by bus to the *Festhalle* [large hall for trade fairs], where several other batches of those arrested, I estimate 100, were gathered already, whose number grew over the course of the day to about 500.

We had to stand here until shortly before 7 o'clock in the evening; only for the elderly, roughly over 65 years of age, were there a few chairs available on which occasionally they could sit down. Going to the lavatory was permitted in groups of about 20 men. Here in general the regular police were on duty. Only occasionally a seemingly more senior SS officer appeared who distinguished himself by coarse, foul swearing.

In the *Festhalle* money, watches, wallets etc. were taken from us by police officers in exchange for a receipt. The treatment by the police officers was in general correct, only a few, among them the *Wachhabende* [guard commander], a still rather young *Polizeihauptmann* [police sergeant], occasionally allowed themselves cutting phrases, e.g. he said when some were talking, "You can do your scheming in your synagogue." I was particularly struck by this tone, as I would have expected quite a different tone from him as an officer. Without having received anything to drink or to eat (some had brought some food with them and could eat this, shared it also with such friends as had nothing), we were loaded back onto the buses shortly before 7 o'clock in the evening and taken to the Südbahnhof. First of all we had to stand for some time here in a draughty underpass, until we were loaded onto a third class carriage of a *Sonderzug* [special train] already standing there, the doors of which were locked. We were told that if a window was opened there would be live shooting.

I must further add that in the *Festhalle* was a batch of young detainees, apparently a school class or the residents of an apprentices' hostel. They had to march more frequently, at the double and similar, however without this degenerating into torment, and sing at the same time, e.g. *"Das Wandern ist des Müllers Lust"* [Hiking is the miller's delight]. Only this pressure to sing revealed to us, less perhaps to the children themselves, the crude nature of the guards. These children were in any case released in the evening, as were those who were over 65 years old and some who apparently were just about to emigrate. On the other hand however, B. for example, an old gentleman, a retired *Landgerichtsdirektor* [Regional Court Director] or *Landgerichtsrat* [District Court Councillor], who was at least 68 years old and was only dressed in underwear and a dressing gown, and was physically and mentally very senile, had been worn out by the already very noticeable cold. I met him again in Buchenwald, where only after several days did he get trousers and a coat, I do not know from where.

Moreover in our train compartment there was no guard. In Weimar, to where the train travelled without stopping, we were unloaded and here already another wind began to blow, as we passed from the hands of the police into those of the SS (so-called *Verfügungstruppen* [combat support troops]). Here we were also marshalled in an underpass, quite closely, the first row right up against the wall. If somebody was not standing properly or moved, there was also occasionally a shove. Then we were loaded onto transport vehicles, where, if we were not moving quickly enough, there were also more shoves. We were ordered to keep our head down. I did this too, was even falling asleep somewhat on the journey, when I suddenly got a blow on the head and the SS man was shouting at me in a rage that I had been looking out of the window.

After a roughly 10 km long journey we arrived at about 2 o'clock at the gate of Buchenwald concentration camp. Disembarking had to take place very quickly; if it was not going quickly enough, blows landed amongst us. Like most of the others, I had kept my hat on, not knowing that in the camp it was not permitted to wear a hat, which was struck off me with my spectacles by one of the row of SS men, which he himself picked up again for me however, as I could not find them. Then we had to go across the *Appellplatz* [parade ground] of the camp at the double, when those who were too slow were also again spurred on with blows from clubs. Here again we were marshalled into columns, where we were helped along more or less gently, and personal details taken down. Everyone got a number printed on a piece of canvas and we were informed that the loss of this number would be punished firstly with 25 blows, in addition to other penalties of death and torments of hell.

We then came to a barrack where we were met by prisoners from Vienna who had already been there for several months, who did the honours so to speak. At this point I would really like to add a word about the activities of our Viennese friends, who behaved magnificently in every respect. They calmed the new arrivals, initiated them somewhat in the conventions and customs of the camp. They occupied a particularly special position, as the camp administration gave them something of a free hand in organising matters. They told us straightaway that a certain discipline had to prevail, which is of course absolutely necessary in such a camp, and in respect of their arrangements too. We should not be surprised if they also sometimes shouted and swore dreadfully at us, sometimes even making as if to hit us, when the guards were nearby. That would all be theatre however, so that the SS men did not think they were not treating us properly.

The activity of one colleague from Vienna, Dr. Kries, who achieved extraordinary things, must be highlighted most particularly. The Aryan camp doctor was naturally too good to bother about the Jewish inmates of the camp. So all medical care lay in his hands, he involved the numerous colleagues there as necessary. Treatment was almost impossible during the first few days because no medicines and no bandages were available. That was the reason why, of the numerous diabetics who came into the camp, as far as I know, two died in a coma during the first few days, and for those with heart disease there was no remedy at our disposal either. Some fatalities during the first few days were due to this, quite apart from the fact that for those with heart disease or the unwell of all kinds such a stay is life-threatening in the highest degree. An elderly man was found one morning in the latrine pit. Apparently he had had a heart attack while he was sitting on the latrine. Many times each day the call rang through the barracks as to whether a colleague had a catheter on them, because urine had to be drained from elderly men with an enlarged prostate. It is well known how scrupulously cleanly such a catheterisation must be performed to avoid a serious bladder infection.

When I left the camp after eight days the colleague from Vienna, by talking to the camp administration, had managed to arrange for medication, above all insulin and bandages, to be placed at our disposal and with the help of other colleagues he could hold twice daily official surgeries. When I left, 75 insulin injections were being administered each day. The camp administration even made concessions to us to the extent that they placed the detention cells at our disposal for use as sick cells for the numerous acute psychotic illnesses; in addition seriously ill people were to be taken to the proper *Krankenrevier* [sick bay], which very soon was apparently completely full.

On the day after our arrrival, or rather on the same morning, we reported outside at about 6 o'clock. The principal occupation consisted of standing, in between which hair was cut and personal details taken down again. Only in the evening at about half past six was there something to eat for the first time, and admittedly actually a very good soup with fish, as all the food that we got was very good. I had therefore neither eaten nor drunk from half past seven in the morning of 10th November until the next evening at half past six. The thirst and the irregularity of food, also the irregular division of time, were what we had to suffer from most. In the morning there was no coffee, the first food on one occasion at 10, once at 12 o'clock, once the meals were quite close together, another time at quite long intervals. In my opinion this was because the organisation simply could not cope due to the sudden influx of about 10,000 people. I do not believe either that the very small amount of liquid (coffee) distributed represented a conscious torture, but there appeared to be a serious shortage of water in the camp. Thirst was so strong that we were completely parched and our lips and tongue became barky and cracked. The salty soups could not assuage the thirst. The diabetics suffered most here, and then were also favoured in the distribution of liquid, again under the leadership of our Viennese friends. There was sufficient bread, at least for those of us who did not need to work, occasionally some cheese with it, some sausage and a syrup spread. We were fortunate in the respect that, as the good weather changed after two days and rain set in, which admittedly turned the ground into a clay mush, it offered us the opportunity to collect and to drink the water that trickled down from the roof of the barrack.

At the same time on the third day however very serious diarrhoea affected almost everybody. Here I must include a report about the condition of the latrines. For the roughly 10,000 men, who came into the camp within four days, one single latrine with about seven seats was available. You can imagine the hygiene conditions that prevailed thereafter. Normally it already took at least half an hour to get to the latrine. In the night a bucket stood in every barrack. When the general diarrhoea set in now at the same time as the rain, the conditions were indescribable. People had no chance of waiting until they got to the latrine. On the way of course nothing could be done, at best they squatted down somewhere near the latrine. A new latrine was only just being built. Apart from this we had to sit behind each other for six hours that day on freshly tarred and gravelled ground, indeed in such a way that the person in front always sat between the splayed out legs of the man behind. Incidentally, in additon we also got quite good food that day, among other things a very good rice pudding, particularly appropriate on that day. Only a few were permitted to go to the latrine during this time. Therefore for most, everything went into their trousers. I was so glad just to still be barely able to make it. In any case due to a lack of paper I had to cut strips off my shirt and use them for this purpose. Also on the question of paper, one thing that sounds almost funny, however in such a situation is bitterly serious, the Viennese yet again proved themselves to be our salvation; I know not from where they conjured up newspapers, which were distributed sparsely, it is true, but fairly. Why there was no intestinal infection epidemic during this time is still not clear to me today. It seems that individual cases of serious intestinal infections did occur however. Thus I know that after my release one colleague with a weak heart died from an intestinal infection. Curiously enough, the diarrhoea died down very quickly despite us sitting for hours on the damp cold ground, so people had almost all recovered by the next day.

This sitting and standing for hours was naturally ingenious torture. With the large number of sudden new additions of about 10,000 men, of course the cooking pots were inadequate. Therefore one cooking pot with spoons passed from one to the other, without it being possible in any way to wash or wipe it beforehand.

We were accommodated in the camp in large wooden barracks. At first there were three such barracks. In the course of the following days two new barracks were added in lightning speed. These barracks were each for 2,000 men. They have four "storeys" of wooden floors above each other, on which people lie, without any straw and without blankets. We only had as a covering just what we had brought with us, I a thin coat. There was in our barrack a small iron stove for heating, but other barracks lacked this. We lay so closely together that we could barely move, in fact like sardines in a tin. Our clothes were never changed or taken off, we were covered to our knees in a thick layer of mud, and there was no washing. As an old soldier these things were easily overcome to some extent. Sometimes we did not wash or undress for weeks during the war either, and were also filthy. Then, however, it was an honourable filth, and we knew why were doing it. Also, we were not treated like cattle. But the accommodation was such that we constantly had the feeling that we were locked in like cattle in a dirty stall. Also the way we were driven into the barracks after *Apell,* for example, was exactly the same as the way cattle are driven into their stall; here too there was always the prospect of getting a lash with a riding whip from SS men who happened to be nearby if it was not going quickly enough, something that was natural given the large number of people.

Sometimes it was dreadful at night if some imbecile or other (people like that were also up there), or someone with an acute psychotic illness got into an acute state of anxiety and persistently and stridently cried for help. Occasionally such a person was taken out by the patrolling SS men and apparently beaten. Whether they were really seriously flogged or whether these sadistic people (for that is almost all of the SS there) only wanted to have a bit of "fun" with them, I could not find out for certain. In any case it was terrible to hear the cries for help and shouts of fear of these people. We could not help and did not know what was happening to the men. People must pack away what they possess of human dignity in the camp.

It goes without saying that "*Du*" [familiar form of "you"] was used, the official form of address was, "*Der Jude soundso*" [The Jew so and so]. If one of the SS men, usually the *Scharführer* [staff sergeant], asks what someone is, and he says to the relevant answer, "You've only gone and betrayed the Aryans, you *Saujud* [Jewish pig]" etc., then they have to keep their mouth shut. Words like *"Judenschwein"* [Jewish swine] are the order of the day. Woe betide anyone who forgets themselves enough to protest. I have repeatedly witnessed a punishment beating of 25 blows, once even about 40–50 blows. A *Bock* [whipping block] is always standing ready for this on which the person in question is laid and there gets the full force of his 25 blows with the bullwhip.

Another punishment I saw consisted of two men whose hands were tied together round a tree trunk so that their arms were at about shoulder height, and they had to stand for hours in this position. What their crime was, I do not know. A rabbi, I believe from Breslau [now Pol. Wrocław], who certainly taunted the men in a reckless fashion and asked them whether this was the famous National Socialism, was first thrashed and told that he would be put to death, but slowly. I am certain that they kept their word on this. At a white wall near which the floggings took place, splatters of blood could be seen up to the height of a man. Also people often had to stand for hours at this wall with their face close to the wall. One man who as I remember also collapsed after the flogging, and despite kicks and blows did not get up again, was dragged along the gravel ground. Whether he was dead or only unconscious I do not know.

We had to stand for hours at the large *Appell*s [roll calls], which took place particularly during the first few days (afterwards it was no longer possible because of the rain). The sick and even dying had to be carried out for *Appell* on a stretcher too. One or two of these people died during the *Appell*.

An elderly man was green and blue all over his body, apparently as a result of mistreatment. He was so weak that he could give me no further information. One man had an eye punched out. He went into the hospital some days later.

Above all some people came in a badly mistreated condition, particularly from the smaller places, e.g. from Thuringia and from the Kassel area. Scabbed over slashes on the head, black eyes etc., were frequently seen. I treated one fractured forearm myself. Our Viennese colleagues told us that they had seen many more seriously wounded during this period and a number of broken arms and legs. They had also been treated significantly worse in the early days than us, e.g. had had to do *Kniebeugen* [knee-bends] for hours.

One morning when we went out to relieve ourselves, two dead bodies lay on the ten metre wide strip of land which stretched out in front of the live electric fence. We had heard two shots during the night. Probably these men had wanted to go to the nearby latrine during the night, had gone a bit too far forward in the darkness and in their half asleep state and got into the forbidden strip of land and been shot from the watchtower. Or they had come to the wire and then been shot.

A young man whose father had become insane in the camp ran with suicidal intent into the wire which he grabbed with his hand; in the other hand he held his prayer book. The suicide attempt succeeded.

We had young people in the camp, among them a 14-year-old, however, probably because of his nice fresh nature, was treated well and was released after eight days, but also people of over 60, even over 70, were there. It was amazing how these people patiently bore everything. Even cripples were in the camp. Except for some people with artificial limbs, who were also released after eight days, there was, among others, also a completely crippled man, whose limbs were so crooked and stiff – for that matter he only had on a thin suit jacket without a coat – that he could only walk and stand with the help of two low sticks. His legs were bent completely backwards, a wholly poor, miserable cripple. He was, I believe, released on the same day as I was – thus after eight days. In any case he was standing in an adjacent compartment which it seems was also transported away.

As *Unteraufseher* [junior supervisors] over the camp inmates there were the so-called *Kapos*, some of whom had already been there for years. They were all Aryan. Their behaviour was very varied. While some were quite comradely and decent as long as there were no SS men nearby – if any were nearby of course there was continual shouting and foul language, pushing and beating, often however only for appearances – others were really downright rough and sadistic towards the working prisoners. Oddly enough, which often made me think, the so-called *Gewohnheits-verbrecher* [habitual offenders] (the various categories: *politischer Verbrecher* [political criminal], so-called *Arbeitsscheue* [work shy], i.e. also *Arbeitslose* [unemployed], *Rassenschänder* [race defilers], *Bibelforscher* [Jehovah's Witnesses], *175-ers* [homosex-uals] were designated by a triangle in a certain colour) were on average much more good-natured than the *politische Verbrecher*. Whether they particularly wanted to get into our good books I do not know. However it is not possible to make generalisa-tions about it. There were also decent people among the political criminals and scoundrels among the criminals.

I could only observe the workers at work to the extent that they were busy in the camp itself, mostly with woodwork, building barracks. They have to work for about 14 hours each day with half an hour break at midday. They have to drag and slog continu-ally, are occasionally treated with kicks and blows by the *Aufseher* [overseer] if it is not going quickly enough or mistakes are made, above all if an overseer has it in for one man in particular.

I only saw the quarry workers when they came back from work, a sight that I will never forget. Gaunt figures, each one carrying a heavy rock of about 40 cm³ on one shoulder, for this method of rock transport is cheaper than using a vehicle. This is how they came back into the camp in the evening.

During "vom Rath-week" the Jewish workers – Buchen-wald has almost only Jewish prisoners – received only half food rations. They suffered bitter hunger and we often secretly slipped them some of our bread. When we did this it was touching that these people still sometimes whispered to us, "Don't lose heart, it is not so bad when you get used to it."

What the treatment during the work in the quarry was like and particularly in the *Strafkompanie* [punishment company] I do not know from my own observation. In any case it is certain that the slightest mistake was strictly punished.

Incidentally, in the camp I never saw anything myself of blows from rifle butts. (It was mentioned in various reports that I read). I do not believe it either, for in the camp itself only the guards on the watch tower carried carbines; otherwise the SS men usually only had revolvers and riding whips.

It happened quite unxpectedly that on the morning of the eighth day the loudspeaker suddenly heralded, "The Jew Dr. X. from Y. with all his "effects" (thus with my summer coat) to the gate." After a short wait, during which several others, altogether about 20 people, also turned up there, we were taken to be shaved by a "*Kapo*", who also whispered to me that we were to be released. The quick release after only eight days was in my case because I was already in the middle of my emigration preparations and a letter from a senior foreign diplomat had arrived, saying that he would give me a visa for his country at any time.

And this last day was a day that I will never forget and which made a deeply shocking impression on me. The clerk, who once more recorded our personal details, the young Viennese boys who shaved us, the workers who we met, the attendants at the *Revier* [sick bay] where we were fleetingly examined once more to see whether there were perhaps signs of corporal punishment, all of them whispered to us, "You fortunate people!" There we thrust unnoticed to one a few cigarettes which we happened to have in our pocket, there a piece of army bread to a starving worker. But the feeling, now to get out of here and not to be able to take out the others who had already been in there for weeks, months and years with us, was dreadful.

Afterwards when we were led back to the entrance, we came past the *Appellplatz* on which our other colleagues were having a meal. They waved to us and called in a low voice, "Goodbye!" No one begrudged us it, but it was as difficult for us who were leaving as for them. However before we were released we still had to stand again for about four to five hours in two ranks near the gate in the piercing wind and damp, right under the watchtower. And as an SS man was standing guard right here who really wanted to make himself look big, we were not allowed to move during this time or he would call down a foul remark and a threat. In the case of a second section, also about 20 men strong, who it seemed were also being released, among others also stood the aforementioned completely crippled man, who was shivering in the frost as he had no coat.

Finally we were taken back to the *"politische Abteilung"* [political section], where we had to sign an undertaking that we had not seen or suffered any kind of ill-treatment etc., etc. "And if you tell any horror stories, you'll be arrested again immediately and then you'll never get out of the camp. And if you say anything abroad, be aware that we have our scouts everywhere and then you will be 'eliminated'. You know very well what that means." Only the final official in plain clothes was decent, who finally released us and who could be believed to feel a trace of sympathy for us.

Then we were taken by an SS *Scharführer* through the forest to the edge of the camp, where he left us with the wish, "Don't get drunk!" We walked to the nearest village which was about 2.5 km away, where at the inn we were served first of all real coffee, mineral water and bread and cheese by the landlord and his wife. The people seemed to know what was needed if someone came down from up there. I was sober after the previous evening. They were friendly and decent, no questions about the camp. Even the three old villagers who were drinking their beer in the inn were silent, but not unfriendly. In cars which were ordered after this, we then drove down to Weimar, and as filthy as we were, covered with a coating of mud reaching to our knees, we travelled on the scheduled express train to Frankfurt. Not one person on the train made a remark about the dirty company who came onto the train. They knew what the dirt meant on travellers who got on in Weimar and looked like that.

One gentleman who came back some days later told me that on the train, when he got on, an Aryan lady stood up and offered him her seat. When he demurred that he could not accept, she said, "But that is the least I can do for you!" With such remarks, the sincere joy of many Aryans, particularly of ordinary people, when they saw us again, cannot be passed off.

Two things have been learned from the stay in the concentration camp: to do everything that can be done to arrange for those who are still in Germany, or more precisely in the camp, to get out, and secondly constantly to tell oneself in every life situation: anything is better than the concentration camp!

For a man who is on the whole healthy, the stay in the camp was bearable for eight days, particularly if he was an old soldier and kept his mouth shut. However, what does eight days mean against the weeks and months that other people have had to endure and are still having to? Therefore also probably because of the increasing cold in particular, the rates of sickness and death later spiralled very steeply upwards. First and foremost pneumonia (pulmonary inflammation) was cited to me by colleagues as cause of death. One colleague died from an intestinal infection and a weak heart, one man from phlegmon of the base of the mouth (as a result of the mouth drying out from not drinking enough). One teacher from the *Philanthropin* [High School for the Jewish community in Frankfurt am Main] had to have both legs amputated as a result of frostbite, as cases of frostbite were generally common. A gentleman I knew, who was incidentally extremely short-sighted, came back while I was still in X., with a high temperature and with a serious intestinal infection. Another elderly teacher had a broken ankle.

A colleague who has now (January 1939) arrived here estimated the number of deaths recently to be at least about 10% of the headcount!

B. 217 Deaths in Buchenwald and Dachau concentration camps

1) The banker Jacobius of Mendelssohnstraße, Frankfurt am Main, died in Buchenwald concentration camp in January 1939 at the age of 30 to 35.

2) The bookseller Joseph Kende of Am Opernring, Vienna, died in Dachau concentration camp in November 1938 at the age of 70.

B. 218 At the end of May, that is at that time in Vienna when arbitrary mass arrests were carried out [*Juni-Aktion*], the reporter's business, which he ran with his father, was rung by the *Polizei-direktion* [police authorities] and initially his father was asked for. As he rightly suspected the purpose of the call he explained that his father was not available, whereupon he was asked who was speaking. He said the son, thereupon was asked whether he was able to supply information on the commercial aspects of the company, which he confirmed. Thereupon he was instructed to report to the *Polizeidirektion*. There he was arrested and initially brought to the *Notgefängnis* [temporary prison], Vienna XX., Karajangasse, *Volksschule* [primary school], where he remained for several days.

From there he was taken to Dachau by one of the many mass transports of those days. Even on the transport the prisoners were granted a dreadful foretaste of that which awaited them in Dachau. The words of the *Kommandant* [commander] of the SS troops who had taken over from the quite friendly police detention, explaining that "another wind was blowing", would come true during transportation. They were horribly beaten, as these transports generally offered the SS troops guarding Dachau prisoners the first opportunity to vent their sadistic urge. The reporter recounted rumours circulating in Dachau that the railway staff had not only sometimes refused to clean the wagons after the transports, which had been covered all over in blood, but that once they had even refused to move the train any further because the screams of the martyred had almost driven the train driver mad. The fact is that each transport produced deaths and very badly battered people who would have to live with their injuries for the rest of their lives.

In Dachau the prisoners had to rise at about half past 3 each morning, in order to report at 5 o'clock. They had to work hard daily for ten hours, the work consisted mainly of making the vicinity viable (laying cables, making roads, breaking stones, felling trees etc.). Moreover there was assiduous "*exerzieren*" [punitive drills]. The prisoners included all age groups, thus amongst them a Vienna *Rechtsanwalt* [lawyer] of 72 but also very young Vienna newspaper sellers who had been accused of circulating the (strongly anti-National Socialist) Vienna daily and evening newspaper *Der Telegraph*, which they had naturally only done for economic reasons, not based on an attitude of support. Treatment was very harsh, though accommodation and food were half way tolerable. In the accommodation strict separation of Jews from was applied although the work was often accomplished collectively, so that the reporter had the opportunity of meeting, amongst others, many prominent leaders of the [Kurt] Schuschnigg regime, who were handled particularly toughly. The very old and the seriously ill were not picked for heavy work, they had to prepare all nails and wires.

Once the work to be done in Dachau was half complete, all the Jews there went to Buchenwald, the Aryans remained behind. The first to return to Dachau were "*Aktionsjuden*" [operation Jews] arrested on 10th November, their treatment is said to have been quite tolerable, according to information obtained by the reporter in Vienna after his release from Buchenwald. Their principal activity consisted of "*exerzieren*".

The transportation to Buchenwald repeated the atrocities on the transportation to Dachau to a considerably intensified degree. The new SS men who took over the prisoners wanted to show that they exceeded the previous guards in severity, evidence of which they succeeded in providing at this first opportunity. The reporter explained verbatim that the conditions in Dachau could be described as "paradise" in direct comparison to those in Buchenwald. It was impossible for him to depict all the sadistic atrocities of this dreadful concentration camp, because merely the memory of it is too upsetting.

The work and daily arrangements were similar to Dachau, although there was less "*exerzieren*", instead very hard work. The work was also similar to Dachau, it is interesting that, amongst other things, a number of prisoners were occupied in laying out a plantation of medicinal herbs. Here too individual prisoners were excused from work of a heavier nature and were occupied "undercover", as the expression has it. Thus the well-known Vienna comedian Fritz Grünbaum was made to darn stockings, whereas a colleague of his, Ferdinand Leopoldi, who was accused of particular devotion to the Schuschnigg regime, had to do heavy outdoor work.

The reporter himself, in the last stage of his imprisonment, when his *Entlassungsgesuch* [petition for release] was already in motion and had prospects of fortunate settlement, was occupied in the workshop as a skilled precision engineer.

The living and sanitary conditions in Buchenwald were appalling, hundreds of people were crammed into one camp block. The food was meagre and bad. In the canteen there was little to buy so the prisoners found it difficult to use the RM. 30.- they were allowed to have transferred monthly for extras to eat; it happened repeatedly that the money that had been sent to them did not reach their hands. The camp doctors were unbelievably brutal, if they made the effort to treat the sick at all. After the death of Herr vom Rath the following decree was implemented: half rations, writing and receiving letters forbidden, treating the sick forbidden.

Most of the many fatalities in Buchenwald cannot be attributed to external causes, though it did happen that those mistreated with blows died as a consequence of that mistreatment; it was no wonder, when the blows were struck with very thick sticks and unheard-of force in great frequency and rapid succession, whereby the tormentors did not make the effort to remove their victims out of sight of their fellow prisoners, who many times had to watch repeatedly the martyrdom of their colleagues; the beatings were repeatedly done during *Appell* [roll call], which was a brutality in itself; thus *Schutzhäftlinge* [prisoners in protective custody] once had to stand to attention for five hours in snow and ice. It often happened that the thick stick was broken in use on the prisoner.

Another external cause of death was the electrified wires that thickly surrounded the entire concentration camp. Although their danger was known, it happened now and then that prisoners, driven crazy by pain or fear of the perpetual torture, ran into the wires and thereby caused either very severe burns or collapsed at the place where they made contact with the current.

However, the majority of fatalities were caused by pneumonia, which was badly treated in unheated or very inadequately heated barracks by malicious doctors; or total exhaustion. The fact is that, particularly in the most recent period of cold, there were very very many fatalities. (This information was also given to me by another informant, who told me that very large numbers of urns continuously come to Vienna from Dachau and Buchenwald.) With regard to important personalities, the reporter confirmed to me the decease of Paul Morgan, and he told me furthermore that two particularly noted *Advokaten* [lawyers] of the Vienna chambers, Dr. Oswald Richter and Dr. Sperber, both died recently; they had been taken into *Schutzhaft* [protective custody] because of their situation as Social Democrats who were chiefly able to be involved with defending Socialists. In Buchenwald the prevailing view was that anyone who tolerated imprisonment badly and evidently bore marks of imprisonment (bad appearance, enduring traces of mistreatment), had absolutely no prospect of being released.

Relatives received urns of the deceased for RM. 8–10.-, soldered coffins for RM. 800.- to RM. 1,000.-. Whilst the reporter was present in Vienna, a family with whom he was friends received an urn containing the remains of their strong 24-year-old son sent from Dachau.

As a particular brutality the reporter depicted the treatment of a Vienna engineer Popper, who, because he had apparently been working too slowly, was strung up by the hands and had to dangle thus for one and a half hours; in spite of his loud cries of pain he was not let down. Most of all the prisoners suffered from the cold; frozen feet and open, festering wounds were very common.

The reporter was released with orders to leave Vienna, where he was authorised to give himself up, within five days. But at this point he received another *Aufenthaltserlaubnis* [residence permit] for one month. Amongst those who were released recently is the head of the cemetery office of the *Wiener Kultusgemeinde* [Vienna Jewish community], Felix Willmann, who served nine months in the concentration camps at Dachau and Buchenwald.

B. 219 Herr B. was arrested on 10th November and in the first instance brought to Hahngasse (Vienna IX., auxiliary prison to the central Vienna police prison), where he was accommodated with 200 other Jews in a room ten metres long and five metres wide. Whilst the treatment by the police during the day was very friendly, this changed when at half past nine in the evening the SS-*Verfügungstruppen* [SS combat support troops] took over command. Herr B. literally declared that he did not believe he could survive the night. The prisoners had to do "gymnastics" in the manner described in a previous report; in addition to the "gymnastic exercises" referred to there, Herr B. also listed as particular harassments kissing ground and boots, indeed even licking up sputum, and mentioned that the following "exercise" was particularly gruelling: the Jews were ordered to mass in the corner of the room at a given signal, and anyone who did not reach the corner quickly and was considerate towards the next man in the dense mass forming there, was beaten until they bled. Frightened of these beatings, everyone ran into the corner and had to push and shove the next man, which was extremely painful.

On 11th November the prisoners were brought to the Vienna Westbahnhof in order to be transported to Dachau, where they were met by the escorts with rifle butts. Every twelve men were accommodated in a very cramped train compartment, so that one man had to sit on another. During the whole journey for 14 hours they were forced to stare into the compartment light, and they were not allowed to move. According to B.'s statements one man was shot and two were beaten to death during the journey.

In Dachau, where at the time of their arrival there were only Aryans – the Jews who had been imprisoned there previously had been taken to Buchenwald – they were given thin, blue and white striped, *Zwilchanzüge* [cotton drill suits]. One man had gone to relieve himself on arrival and had then stood back in line, which was noticed without the man himself being identifiable. As he did not come forward when ordered, and his companions did not point him out, everyone had to do "Strafexerzieren" [punitive drill] from Saturday morning until Monday evening without food whilst the SS men consumed their food in a particularly provocative manner in front of the Jews.

In terms of general living conditions, B. reported that the living quarters were halfway fit for human habitation, the prisoners liked the food especially as they were always very hungry from all the *Exerzieren* [punitive drill], that waking was at 5 o' clock, that they were allowed to smoke in their free time. Treatment by doctors was extremely inadequate; even with a high temperature they had no objection to the patient reporting for *Exerzieren,* so that one prisoner, a Herr Wellisch from Graz, with a temperature of 40 degrees did actually collapse and die during *Exerzieren.* The prisoners suffered from the cold mainly due to their thin clothing, even in the lowest temperatures they had to do *Exerzieren*, which because of the movement was still halfway acceptable; worse was standing to attention for hours in snow and ice. Each day there were roughly twelve deaths.

Herr B. claims that his release was brought about as a result of his status as a front-line soldier, on the basis of which his wife submitted a hastily agreed plea to the Vienna Gestapo; in fact he spent only four weeks in Dachau. He was released together with 240 other Jews, nine of them from Vienna. On release they still endlessly had to go through numerous formalities which went on for a long time, e.g. they were weighed, whereby it was established that he had lost six kilos during his imprisonment. A *Reichsdeutsche* [native German] prisoner, on whose imprisonment RM. 500.- had been found, had to use this money to pay the fare to Munich of all those released. They still remained under supervision until the arrival of the train, then they were free. In Munich they were met by representatives of the local Jewish *Gemeinde* [community] who organised their onward journey to their respective destinations very well. Those released had to declare how much cash they had on them and according to what each had, pay towards their onward travel expenses, however in such a way that everyone still had RM. 2.- for the rest of the journey.

The Jews placed in Dachau were, according to Herr B., referred to as *"Aktions- oder Schutzhaftjuden"* [operation or protective custody Jews], whilst those placed in Buchenwald were spoken of as *"Hochverräter"* [guilty of high treason], although vast numbers were amongst them who were all indiscriminately captured on the street, in particular during the *Aktion* at the end of May. Only recently has the release of the latter category begun.

B. 220 … During the mobilisation before the Munich conference my father had to place his Opel delivery van at the disposal of the army, and indeed, as I am informed, he received a substantial payment for it from the government and the vehicle back in an impeccable condition in addition, which he sold shortly afterwards. (How can that be explained?).

Shortly afterwards however he received a summons from the *Geheime Staatspolizei* [Gestapo; Secret State Police], in which he was ordered to sell his shop immediately, which until then still seemed to be doing relatively well. The murder in Paris and the new riots, decrees etc. followed. During these days in which the Jewish men by the dozen were fetched from their beds in the morning and taken off to the concentration camp, our former maid Marie, a Catholic from Pomerania, took my father in, and he spent several nights in her home. SA men appeared several times at our flat to take my father away.

During the days of the pogrom no fewer than six male members of my family including my cousin lived at a maiden aunt's, who had a two-room flat in Moabit. Others spent the night in Grunewald despite the November cold. My cousin's father, *Gemeindevorsteher* [Jewish community board member] in Schwerin, was put in the city's police prison on the grounds that he had set the synagogue on fire. Two other cousins "died" in the concentration camp …

B. 221 According to consistent reports by two foreign colleagues, a German professor at the University of Bonn has been removed from his post because his wife was found by the Gestapo helping two Jewish women, who had to escape from Germany, to pack their things. His son, who was studying at the university, had to leave the university.

A 78-year-old woman from Karlsbad was dragged out of her house in her dressing gown on the day of the pogrom, transported for four hours by lorry to Plauen with other prisoners and held in prison there for four days. Then, almost dying, she was taken back to Karlsbad, from there to Saatz [now Cz. Žatec] and deported across the border to Czechoslovakia.

B. 222 Herr Dr. X. reports on four cases of suicide, which happened within a rather short space of time in his circle of relatives or friends:

1) Frau Selma Goldschmidt, Berlin, aunt of the reporter, poisoned herself with Veronal in the middle of January 1939;

2) Frau Goldschmidt, friend of 1) also took her own life;

3) Frau Hedwig Michaelis, Berlin, native of Potsdam, ditto;

4) Frau Clara Arnold, c. 75 years old, cousin of the mother of the reporter, ditto.

In no cases was economic hardship the motive for the act, but only a weariness of life when faced with persecution.

B. 223 From a letter from Berlin in the middle of February 1939:

"Our old friend, Dr. Willy Sobernheim, could not bear it any longer, which I am very sorry about..." It emerges from this correspondence that the well-known Berlin ear, nose and throat specialist, Dr. Willy Sobernheim, a man of c. 60 years of age, has taken his own life. Dr. S. belonged to the well-known Sobernheim family.

B. 224 There can be no doubt that the destruction of shops had been prepared for a long time; at the time of the destruction on 10th November lists that had been made were already out of date. My firm in the *Konfektionsviertel* [clothing manufacturing district] of Berlin had already been *arisiert* [Aryanised] to such an extent that the new owner was present with his skilled workers when the *Zerstörungskolonne* [destruction squad] appeared. It was on the afternoon of 10th November; the intruders were only convinced with difficulty that the business really [was] no longer in Jewish hands, such that they finally gave up their plan.

They wreaked havoc all the more fiercely on the premises of the ready-to-wear firm located beneath us. Everything was ruined and thrown onto the street, typewriters, tables, dummies etc. The goods also landed on the street, as did the bills and letters torn from the files.

Documents were found right up Charlottenstraße as far as the Friedrichstraße station the next day from the well-known children's ready-to-wear firm Arnold Müller on the corner of Leipzigerstraße and Charlottenstraße.

Contrary to official claims, a significantly large amount must have been stolen, as not one thing of all of the goods thrown onto the street was still there the following day.

B. 225 On 10th November at 8 o'clock in the evening I was taken away by two *Kriminalbeamten* [police detectives] in plain clothes to "an interrogation with the *Kommissar vom Dienst* [duty police inspector]." Whilst I was waiting there, gradually yet more arrested men came. We were taken by taxi to the Alex [Berlin police headquarters at Alexanderplatz]. There it was said that the *Kommissar* had already left. We were accommodated for the night in the *Polizeigefängnis* [police prison] in a large room, with about 250 men, where there were plank beds for sleeping. The next morning we received coffee and a piece of bread. We were then led to the yard, made to stand in rows and asked whether there was anyone over the age of 60 amongst us. Anyone who had a passport or valid ship's papers was also released.

Those remaining behind were taken in three large lorries with covered benches to Oranienburg-Sachsenhausen by two *Schupos* [*Schutzpolizei;* policemen]. When we drove out of the gate of the *Präsidium* [headquarters], c. 100 adolescent lads were standing there, loudly shouting, *"Juda verrecke"* [Perish Judah].

On arrival in the camp SS men were standing ready to receive us; we had to jump off the lorry, in doing this several fell over and were kicked by the SS men. They also bellowed, "Can't you run, you *Judenschweine!* [Jewish pigs]" Hats had to be removed. We then had to report on the *Appellplatz* [parade ground] and stand without moving from 2 o'clock in the afternoon until 8 o'clock in the evening, and without receiving anything to eat.

During this the *Lagerführer* [camp leader] made a speech, "You probably know why you are here. You are political vermin of the Third Reich and enemies of the National Socialist government. You do not know how to behave in accordance with the new Third Reich, you will be taught that here. You will stay here for five years, and if you do not behave properly in that time, the time can be extended to 20 years." One of the *Lagerältesten* [camp elders] came afterwards and whispered to us, "Don't believe what the thug says, you won't be here for five years, you'll all be back home again by Christmas."

We were then led to a barrack where we had to get undressed, bathe, our hair was cut and old military clothing was given to us. The fat people amongst us got convicts' uniforms. Then we were allocated to barracks. In each barrack 350 men were accommodated, i.e. 175 men in each wing, everyone got straw and a blanket, on the whole everything was quite clean and tidy. There were also washrooms and lavatories. Despite this it was unbelievably narrow, and the dust from the straw bothered us greatly.

For the first three days we did not have to work. We were permitted to walk around in the camp and talk. On Monday we were divided up for work. People over 45 years of age had to work three quarters of an hour away in a so-called brickworks. C. 1,500–2,000 Jews worked there. Up to Monday new arrests were still constantly taking place, then the influx stopped.

The younger men were occupied thus; they had to hold up a corner of their jacket and sand was shovelled in, with this they had to run round in a circle in order to empty it out again somewhere else. With the sand they could go at walking pace, they had to run back. This was performed from half past 7 in the morning until 3 o'clock in the afternoon with half an hour break in which one was not permitted to sit down.

In the morning *Milchsuppe mit Haferflocken* [porridge] was provided, at work we received a third of a loaf with either a piece of brawn, fish paste or Harz cheese. As one had no paper to wrap the things in, one had to put them in the pocket as they were. During work eating was forbidden, it was only permitted to eat during the break. The SS *Verfügungstruppe* [support troop] was in charge.

On return at half past 4 there was *Appell* [roll call] in the *Kasernenhof* [barracks yard], then we could go into the barracks to eat. The hot food consisted of soup with potatoes and sauerkraut or white cabbage. There was also frequently fish soup containing whale meat in microscopic quantities. On Sunday there was a pulse soup. There was as good as no meat at all in the food, so that one was always hungry, because whilst working in the open air [neither] the quantity, and even less the quality, of the food was adequate. Sunday was also worked. It was well organised, the food always came on time.

The worst thing during the first eight days was the march back from the work, as people were beaten dreadfully by the 17- and 18-year-old SS men who were in charge. The fat men and the plodders in particular were picked on. In my barrack there was a man who had to lie down for eight days, his back had been so badly beaten with a rifle butt.

A Herr Levy from the Jewish *Winterhilfe* [*Hilfsverein der deutschen Juden*; Aid Association of German Jews] who weighed c. two and a half *Zentner* [hundredweight; c. 125 kilos] was bullied dreadfully. One evening the *Blockführer* [block leader; SS guard] came and bellowed in the barracks, "Where is the fat *Rechtsanwalt* [lawyer]?" He had to come out and do c. 25 *Kniebeugen* [knee bends]. He came back half conscious. Then he was told to crawl on the ceiling beams in the barrack.

One who was due to be released was asked whether something of his was missing. He replied, "A gold ring." He had to roll around on the ground in the dust. If he gave the same answer to the repeated question he had to roll around again, and do this until he gave the answer that nothing of his was missing.

On release all civilian suit pockets had to be turned inside out, which were searched by the SS men. One man had forgotten to turn his trouser pocket inside out, because of this he was violently slapped in the face. The civilian suits had been taken away from us for cleanng, i.e. they had been boiled and rolled up wet and brought back to us like this. It goes without saying that because of this the things had become completely unwearable. Dry-cleaning establishments subsequently would no longer accept the things as they could do nothing with them and one simply had to throw them away. It was my bad luck that I had been wearing a very new suit and new winter coat which I had bought for my emigration. I had to throw both away.

There was as good as no medical care at all. There were two doctors for 3,500 people. If one had been injured whilst working then one of the *Sanitätern* [medical orderlies] in the barrack did the treatment, and very well indeed. They were usually former Communists who had already been in the camp for years. People with internal illnesses however were doomed, they had no treatment. There were many case of abdominal bleeding.

By means of small bribes it was possible to obtain easier work e.g. on the cement mixer or barrack building, roof tiling etc. Here elderly prisoners, usually Communists, were in charge, who looked after us very well. For only 25 *Pfg.* [*Pfennig;* pennies] or a couple of cigarettes, which could be bought in the canteen, they were very accommodating.

Everything one wanted could be bought in the canteen, though we mostly had no money to do so as that which had been sent to us was only paid out to us at long intervals and in small amounts. On release however we got everything back that had been taken from us or received for us.

Punishments were decreed for alleged neglect whilst working or unauthorised talking to Aryan professional workers who were employed there. The person in question was called upon in the evening at *Appell* and then had to stand bareheaded without moving for three hours by the guardhouse at the entrance gate [*stehen am Tor*], and it goes without saying got no supper.

A dentist, Albu, who was busy tiling the roof, had infringed the prohibition to speak and had probably slipped a couple of cigarettes to a worker, although it was only permitted to talk about work matters. He had to *stehen* [*am Tor*] for three evenings one after the other and was half dead on the last day.

Two fatalities occurred in my barrack. One old man of over 70 years from Schönlanke [now Pol. Trzcianka] died presumably of exhaustion or a chronic illness. A Herr Born from Brandenburgische Straße, Berlin, died from mistreatment, and in fact in the following circumstances. Everyone was asked what their occupation was. The simpler the occupation one gave, the better. Every academic was dubbed "*intellektuelles Schwein*" [intellectual pig]. For that reason instead of pharmacist I too gave my occupation as chemist. Herr Born replied "millionaire" to the question, why I still do not know to this day. Consequently he was beaten dreadfully and kicked in the stomach. He was a rather fat man of about 40 years of age. He was also badly bullied at work. He was ill because of all this and went to the *Lazarett* [sick bay], however he was thrown out again. Water was poured over him and as wet as he was he had to *stehen am Tor* in front of the guard. In doing this he literally froze.

There was also a group of 50 children, apparently a *Hachshara* [agricultural training for Jews preparing to emigrate to Palestine] group from Westphalia, in the camp. They were treated quite well however, they had their own barrack, and they let them play and occupied them with writing.

On release the *Lagerführer* gave the usual speech. We were not allowed to say anything. "Our arm reaches as far as North America. And the way back into the camp is very short."

What was worse for us was the position of our wives and mothers, who for eight days did not know where we were, and did not give credence to any news that we were quite all right.

The activity of the *jüdische Gemeinde* [Jewish community] on behalf of the released men must be emphasised quite particularly. There were already two of their men in Oranienburg who looked after us and made sure that we were provided with travel tickets. Similarly we were met at the Stettiner Bahnhof [Berlin Nordbahnhof; Berlin North Station] and everyone was asked where he had to get to and whether he needed help. The men from Hamburg were taken to Rosenstraße, fed and then taken to the Lehrter Bahnhof [now Berlin Hauptbahnhof; Berlin Central Station] to get the train, when again those who had no money were provided with tickets.

The destruction in the Berlin shops had been carried out thoroughly and totally for the most part. Not once did the lowered shutters hinder the wreckers. That is why they had entered the well-known clock and jewellery shop of Brandmann by tractor.

In a cigar shop ten baskets full of trampled cigars were swept up. In addition the iron stove and the till were smashed.

In a large grocery and food shop not one bottle, not one jar remained intact. Nothing was still usable, the food had been shaken out and trampled upon.

The Jews had to remove the fragments themselves, no Aryan was permitted to help with this. The police checked that. The police also asked whether any goods were missing. One replied of course that nothing had been taken away. Even so in round terms 60 looters were sent to Sachsenhausen, who had been involved in stealing the goods.

The Jews had to pay for the repair of the shop windows themselves. The insurance companies were not permitted to pay anything out to them, the insurance money was confiscated by the state. However, the Jewish *Gemeinde* made it possible through a collection from some rich members of the *Gemeinde* to refund their damages to all the shopowners in full.

B. 226 Amsterdam, 7 January 1939

Saturday morning 31 December 1938 was sent to Vienna as courier of the *Nederl. Kinder Comité* [Dutch Children's Committee].

In accordance with my instructions I went to The Society of Friends, Singerstr. 16, for a meeting with Heer Lipopsky, in charge of the department for *Kindertransport* to England and the Netherlands, who was not available, however.

Then I visited Herr Gildemeester, for whom I had been given a message. He was not, however, inclined to discuss anything as he presumed the Gestapo would hear everything and that could have unpleasant consequences for him.

Herr G. brought me to the [*Aktion-*]*Gildemeester* [Nazi-run operation to evacuate Jews from Vienna] office, where I spent some hours and was told the following:

It is as difficult for the emigration offices to get Jews over the German border as it is to get admission for them to another country. Each Jew means money for the German government, how they get it and by what means is immaterial to them. Even when all papers are in order, ticket paid, etc. the emigrants are sent back from the station and [they] try to get more money out of them.

Furthermore the head of the *Gildemeester* office, Herr Fasal, had many complaints against the director of the *Kultusgemeinde* [Jewish community], Herr Löwenherz, who according to him not only paid [no] attention to the urgency of cases (in this case pure Jewish children) but was very partial in his choice for the transports e.g. Polish Jews enjoyed his favour. According to Herr Fasal, that is also the reason for much disagreement between the *Kultusgemeinde* and the *Gildemeester* office, and cooperation is particularly bad. It is evident that children who are in entirely bad circumstances and who have obtained permission from the Netherl. government to reside in Holland still do not come with the transport although others are arbitrarily chosen in their place. This is laid down by the *Kultusgemeinde*. The *Nederl. Comité* is under the impression that these children have already been sent away and will do no more about them. Not cases in the greatest need, therefore, but favouritism.

One of the difficulties at the moment concerns the emigration of boys of 16 and 17 years, as they are in continual danger of being sent to concentration camps, mainly if they are of large stature. One can guess what this indicates for these children when one thinks that they undergo the same treatment as adult men.

On Sunday afternoon I went to the Swedish Mission and there heard about the possibilities of emigration to Sweden. These are also not great. There are already many children from Czechoslovakia there. 7 January a transport of 100 Evangelical children left and during January the *Kultusgemeinde* organised a further transport of Jewish children to Sweden.

One hundred families have gone to Ecuador, who can find a life there [sic]. Thereafter I was at the *Gildemeester* office for some time again, where I was told about a great plan for emigration to Abyssinia. The costs of it are 100,000 pounds and would be carried out by England. Given Mussolini's attitude to the Jews and the climate there, many think this is an impractical plan, anyway unsuited to providing emigrants with a permanent place to stay.

Monday morning I found Herr Lipopsky and he told me the following about the *Gildemeester* office:

This office has asked the committees of all countries to become officially recognised as an emigration office. None of these committees has complied with this and therefore the G. office is trying to achieve independence as far as possible. Favouritism plays a large part here too. On the first transport to Holland e.g. all 20 children were allocated by the G. office, children of its own staff. Furthermore, they arbitrarily take everyone who turns up, whilst it is emphatically stated that the K. G. [Kultusgemeinde] looks after Jews, The Society of Friends after Evangelicals. Because of this the work is very thwarted, the children have to report to different offices, and these meanwhile do not know from each other if the children have gone with a transport or not.

The only thing that the G. office looks after for the *K.G.* and for the Soc. of Friends are the group permits with which the children travel. The cooperation between the G. office and Herr L. is thus limited too, and there is no talk of mutual working. In case of the greatest need they get in touch with each other.

From Herr L. I had the impression that Herr G. himself is an entirely trustworthy person, but he is used as a tool by the staff of his office. Three weeks ago Herr G. also went away as he had nothing more to say at the office and he was recalled again because his name and possible contacts were of great importance to the office. Some things were confiscated from the till, though it is hoped to get these back again on 15 January; according to Herr L. this is not likely.

The Gestapo had also been at the house of The Society of Friends and looked through all the books, which seemed not to indicate much, however, and they were left alone.

It sometimes appears that the children who have transport opportunities and are on Herr L.'s list cannot be found any more. This happens because the families are often suddenly displaced from their house and then no longer have another fixed address. This explains sending other children than those who are given to Herr L. by the *Nederl. Comité.*

Then Herr L. went with me to the Swedish Mission to take lists of Evang. children who could possibly emigrate. In the waiting room there I saw various cases of frozen limbs as a result of spells in a concentration camp, incl. one young man whose hands remained thick and blue. He had already been in Dachau twice and was in danger of being arrested all the time. Further variously crippled men (frozen feet) and one man with a totally bandaged head (frozen ears). Many cases occur particularly as the men are sometimes made to exercise day and night scantily clothed in a cotton jacket and trousers with a pair of shoes and bald shaven uncovered head. Whoever puts his hands in his pockets from the cold is struck with a club.

Herr L. told me afterwards that in a transport to the camp 200 men were loaded into a cattle truck and stood for 5 days and nights without food and water. Strong lights were brought onto the roof of this truck and the men had to look into the light without a break. Whoever bent his head was beaten to attention again. The truck was shot at if there was the slightest sound. The number reaching the camp no longer alive is not small. On arrival there they have to exercise for hours. If they complain of thirst, coffee is thrown on the stone floor which they can lick up.

In the race crimes section each man gets 5 kicks in the belly with a spiked shoe for each crime committed, many die here too. Another torture is to tie round the men's legs with a rope and in the room hoist them up to the ceiling with heads down, then the guards undo the rope. Many are smashed to pieces on the stone floor. This is a bloodbath each time. Men are laid on the floor in rows, they have to open their mouths wide and they urinate into their mouths. There are many indescribable variants of this policy.

As regards small things there is punishment of 20 lashes with a spiked stick, not administered by a single guard but by 20 different ones, so that each stroke is administered by a tireless arm. Each prisoner must sign a paper where only one small square is left blank for the signature; the rest is covered up so that no one knows what he is signing. They must also sign a piece of paper which says that they were never mistreated, had always eaten and drunk well, and they were forbidden to speak about their treatment in the concentration camp, on pain of death.

Machine guns are mounted at the four corners of the camp; anyone who goes outside after sunset is shot down without further ado. Prisoners may talk to each other for an hour a day; whoever says a word outside that time receives a number of blows. There is nothing to eat, drinking water is inadequate and polluted. There is also no heating, while the shelter is totally inadequate. There are men returned from Dachau who lost 30 pounds in one week.

Fatalities are reported to the family so they can come and fetch the urn; the body itself is never returned.

There is also a concentration camp for women guarded by men. One can imagine what this indicates. It seems not to be rare for Jewish girls of 12–14 years to be assaulted by SS or SA men. The emigration chances of these children are naturally extremely small, because one must wait for the results of this outrage. A few cases have nevertheless been transported to England.

All these stories were told to me by Herr Lipopsky, himself a full-blooded "Aryan".

The general misery in Vienna is unbelievable. There are people who have not had a roof over their heads for weeks, walking from doorway to doorway, who dare not report for emigration from fear of being arrested. Others, who no longer possess a cent, can get food at the *K.G.* to the value of 15 *Pf.* [*Pfennig*; pennies] per day.

From a statistic of one of the Jewish cemeteries in Vienna it appears that in the first weeks after 10 November 130 dead per day had to be buried. Many cemeteries were set on fire and the bodies lay open above the ground until the Jews themselves covered them with straw. The number of Jews killed on 10 November and later cannot be counted; they talk of hundreds.

The *Nederl.* [Dutch] government has provided for adult Jews, with which they are permitted to cross over the Dutch border with a valid passport. These cards are valid only three weeks. For those coming from Vienna, sometimes 4 to 5 days go by. As application for a pass without the possibility of emigration is pointless, and the minimum time required is three weeks, the cards expire before a pass is obtained. Nor can these cards be extended. In these ways emigration is made harder because a new application does not succeed. The cards should be valid for at least six weeks, as there is sometimes a delay through unpaid tax or fine.

In relation to the various offices in Vienna one has the strong feeling that Austria is treated harshly by the Netherlands, as the number of Austrian children in relation to the total number of emigrated children is particularly small, while the need in Austria is certainly no less.

The motto of the Gestapo in Vienna is: "*Die Juden sollen nicht verreisen, sondern verrecken.*" [The Jews will not travel but perish.]

B. 227 I was in Dachau for ten weeks in all, that is from 10th November 1938 to 18th January 1939, when I was released on the basis of a *Vorvisum* [preliminary visa] to Panama.

On the morning of 10th November I was taken from home, with my brother, by four people from the Gestapo. We arrived in prison and stayed there from Thursday until Tuesday. During this time our particulars were taken, but the reason for our detention was not explained to us in any way. There were five people to a cell. On the Tuesday we were taken into the yard where around 400 Jews had assembled to be taken away, of whom a great many were in their 50s or 60s. Then we were driven by bus to the railway station – the station and the streets were strictly cordoned off. We then travelled in a *Sondergefangenenzug* [special prisoners' train] to Dachau. There the escorting Gestapo officers told us that we should not get too upset about the reception which was awaiting us, it was the worst thing that was going to happen. There then followed straight away the command *"Juden raus!"* [Jews out!]. SS men with steel helmets and carbines appeared, searchlights shone, the carbines were drawn. We had to fall in and move at the double to the goods train that was waiting for us, while ceaseless blows with rubber truncheons and rifle butts rained down, even on those who had fallen. We were then loaded into cattle trucks – there is no other way of describing the way in which we were flung into the wagons – and the journey began with 250 people in each truck. We were threatened at the outset that we could be shot even if we looked out of the truck. Many people fainted because we were standing so tightly pressed up against each other.

On arrival at the camp itself the searchlights shone so brightly that we were almost blinded. We had to move at the double to a particular assembly point. Many people just lay on the ground, what happened to them I do not know. We now had to remain standing for two hours in the fog, wet through with sweat. We then went in a group of 800 into a room, and then one by one into an adjoining room where we were to spend the night on damp sacks of straw. We received a little tea and bread. But sleep was out of the question because we were lying so closely packed together that our heads were between the feet of the man in front. At 5 o'clock we had to get up and fall in. By this point two of our people were already exhausted.

We were then photographed and taken to be washed. SS men were in charge, they questioned us there and squirted water into our open mouths with a hosepipe when we tried to reply. At 7 o'clock there was some food, insubstantial and not very much of it. In the dormitory there were 200 of us lying on straw, not straw sacks, and of course there were no bedclothes of any kind. We each received one blanket, which of course was not enough against the extreme cold that soon set in. There was *Exerzieren* [punitive drill] every day. *Appell* [roll call] was at 6 o'clock, then *Exerzieren* [punitive drill] from 8 to half past 11, then a meal, then we had to stand for an hour, with *Exerzieren* again from 2–5 and then from 5–6 there was a *Zählappell* (roll call count). On Sundays we often had to stand to attention for 6 hours without any exercise at all while the SS just "pestered" us.

We received only a quarter of a loaf a day. That went on till Christmas! Then there was no work because of the frost, and we just had to stand all the time, on one occasion, because one of us was missing, for two and a half hours in 18 degrees of frost in cotton drill suits. The *Appell*s went on unchanged after Christmas – all the sick had to be there, including those with lung ailments. It regularly happened that sick people died during *Appell*s. I remember one incident in which a Jew with a fever of 40 degrees had to appear at an *Appell* in these circumstances with pieces of wood that he had tied under his feet. There were 13,000 Jews and 4,500 Aryans in the camp. The oldest were 84 and 87 years old. 40 people died on one day.

At first you could buy all sorts of things in the canteen, then after Christmas there was nothing worth having, for Jews there was absolutely no bread and no butter any more. On the days when money had come for us we could only get 6-*Pfennig* [penny] cigarettes.

We did no more work after Christmas, it was just constant cleaning. The slightest untidiness or spot of dirt was strictly punished, e.g. with eight days of scrubbing the latrines or carrying food. One day, because a towel was not completely clean, 150 people had to hold their towels motionlessly out in front of them with outstretched arms for hours on end. On another day we had to stand upright from 8–6 without food beside the so-called *Jourhaus* [camp entrance building at Dachau]. Then there was the *Strafe des Baumhängens* [tree-hanging punishment], in which our chained hands were fastened to a tree so that we swung in the air. The punishment consisting of 25 strokes was carried out in the "Bunker" [prison] by a sex killer who had been released from jail.

One day when one of the walls of our barrack cracked because of the cold we had to pay for the repair. We also had to provide materials such as soap, scrubbing brushes, cloths etc. that we needed to keep the barrack clean, but we were never allowed to go to the counter. In the washroom we were only allowed to appear when stripped to the waist. One day a Viennese journalist, A. (55 years old), stayed on in the washroom and put his shirt on, when an SS man went up to him, punched him in the face and threw [him] onto the stone floor so that two of his teeth were missing afterwards. He then had to make a written statement that his injury resulted from an accident. The doctor in the *Revier* [sick bay] hardly ever bothered to check.

There were frequent foot inspections, as well as towel inspections and checks of razors, toothbrushes, soap and so on. Every day at the foot inspection it happened that the SS men stamped on feet with their nailed boots when they did not like something.

Everything that was bought had to stay in the camp. Because it was bitterly cold in the wooden barracks we were never able to undress and had to sleep in the same clothes and on increasingly rotting and damp straw for the ten weeks. One day two Aryans escaped and one was discovered after a short while, tied by the feet and dragged into the camp behind a motorbike, where he obviously arrived dead. Until these two people were found we had to stand outside in the cold of the camp.

During my time in the camp my hair was cut four times. On my release I was told that we were not allowed to say anything about our experiences and the organisation of the camp. We could do so abroad, but nobody would believe any of it.

B. 228 From a report by Herr X., who was arrested on 10th November and spent eight weeks in Dachau.

Herr X. was able to report on his arrest, transport to Dachau, detention there and release, similar to all those so-called "*Aktionsjuden*" [operation Jews] arrested on 10th November. Therefore in what follows only the particularly noteworthy has been picked out from his report.

After his arrest, Herr X. was taken with hundreds of other Jews to the former monastery building in Kenyongasse, Vienna VII. As well as the gymnastic exercises which were also maintained at other *Sammelstationen* [assembly points], the SS team also managed the following perversities: at around midnight the detainees were taken from their "dormitories" to a large hall. Once there, they were asked whether there was a rabbi amongst them, whereupon a rabbi from a small synagogue in Vienna II., Untere Augartenstraße responded. He was placed in the middle of the room, hairs were pulled out one at a time and emblems were cut into his beard and the hair on his head. Then he was required to recite the Prayer for the Dead for himself, which he was then made to repeat multiple times, in an increasingly loud voice, so that he had to almost scream by the end. Finally it was explained to him that he was to recite the Prayer for the Dead (Kaddish) for the entire group because they were all to be shot at 4 o'clock. The rest of the Jews joined in the prayer, the scene was shocking. Then they were left alone and were almost convinced that the SS would carry out their threat. The hours passed in agonised nervousness. At ten minutes past four the doors were torn open and all were required to return to their dormitories.

One of the best-liked tortures was standing at the wall, whereby the tortured had to press their noses firmly against the wall, they themselves were forced to count and awaited the *coup de grâce*, yet after a short while the martyrdom was suddenly ceased.

Herr X. was taken to Dachau in one of the last of the transports that then took place several times a day. As normal passenger carriages were no longer available, he was placed in a cattle truck with 87 others, in which it was impossible to stir owing to the overcrowding. The doors of the truck were opened for very brief moments only twice during the almost 14-hour journey, when the escort team "enquired" how the group was feeling in a mocking manner accompanied by foul language. Each individual was mauled so badly with a knuckle-duster on boarding that they entered the car covered in blood. They had to provisionally bind their wounds with their dirty undergarments. During transport seven Jews lost their minds.

Since, as stated, Herr X. came to Dachau with one of the last transports, he and his fellow sufferers, who were accommodated in Block 30, received no *Zwilchanzug* [cotton drill uniform], unlike the other prisoners, because these had all been handed out. This had the advantage that they retained their warm civilian clothes, although they had to remain in their completely dirty undergarments seven weeks long.

Herr X. is 54 years old.

B. 229 It is reported from Vienna that *Oberbaurat Ing.* [senior architect and engineer] Robert Stricker has been released from Buchenwald and returned home. The four owners of the well-known Schiffmann department store in Vienna were also released at the same time. They were similarly arrested in the first days of turmoil and also taken first to Dachau and then to Buchenwald. The Schiffmanns, in particular *Kom. Rat.* [*Kommerzialrat*; commercial councillor] Max Schiffmann, played a major role in the Zionist and Jewish sports movement in Vienna. Max Schiffmann was also a *Kultusvorsteher* [community board member] of Stricker's *Judenstaatspartei* [Jewish State Party].

There is still no news available as to the fate of Dr. Friedmann.

In connection with the above report it is announced that *Oberbaurat* Stricker – like *Reg. Rat.* [*Regierunsrat*; civil servant] Dr. Oppenheim – had to agree not to leave the country, although a *Zertifikat* [certificate] that has been available to him in Vienna for a long time would give him the opportunity of immediate emigration to Palestine.

Dr. Oppenheim could also travel to England but is not allowed to do so, the only "concession" which has been granted to him so far is that he "only" has to report to the police twice a week instead of twice a day as before.

President Friedmann is also expected soon.

Since the 21st March people travelling out of the country are allowed to take only RM. 30.- in foreign currency with them, and only RM. 10.- in German currency are allowed.

B. 230 You want to know how and what occurred in X. on our Black Thursday, 10th November 1938. On 8th November the mobs were already running riot in Erfurt, Kassel, on that day they broke into the local synagogue as well and only tipped the pulpit over; we all thought that was the end of the matter. On 9th November everything was quiet. On 10 November, just as we had eaten our evening meal, there were three or four massive blows on the front door, which burst it open, and four fellows armed with axes and heavy hammers came in shouting "*Raus, raus, raus!*" [Out, out, out].

They pushed into our room and then: smashed all the windows together with the frames, knocked over the furniture and piled it up, then left again. Whilst this was going on we fled to our neighbours who are Aryan. Barely ten minutes later came a band of about 15 men, nothing but locals, town officials, shop people etc., all from the SA but all in plain clothes. They smashed up most of the things, they went away and a quarter of an hour later a third gang came, four tall strong louts who threw everything out of the windows, the washstand with a heavy marble top, our good beds, mirrors and pictures, nothing was spared, and we had to flee and sat at the back of our barn from 9 o'clock until quarter to 3 until we could come out again.

The women had to go to the so-called night refuge, where tradesmen usually spent the night, and the men to the prison until everyone could return home the next day. Now we could see our chaos, it was impossible to get into a room, everything lay ruined all over the place, no electric light worked, we boarded up the windows with cardboard until permission came after several days that workmen were allowed to work for Jews.

There were Jewish families, though, who had it even worse than us. The former rich banking house K. suffered most, over RM. 100,000.- worth of art treasures were said to have been destroyed and today it is said to be poor. The Jewish old people's home is completely destroyed inside. The synagogue interior has been smashed to pieces, thank God the *Thorarollen* [Torah scrolls] had already been made safe.

I almost forgot to write that the ruffians had sat our rabbi, who is very pious, in a chair and had cut off his beard. They threw all his clothes into the cellar, tipped jars of jam over them and strewed them with bed feathers; the gangs did the latter in nearly all Jewish homes.

The whole thing was planned in advance: in May all Jews had to hand in their weapons, in July came the *Vermögenserklärung* [statement of assets], then the Paris murder, that was the signal and after everything had been smashed in two came the 20% *Vermögensabgabe* [assets levy], from which we were not spared either; no Aryan shop sold anything to Jews any more, even my hairdresser who had served me for over 30 years was not allowed to any more though he had a very decent attitude, but most business people were frightened.

B. 231 From the *Gemeindeblatt* [Community newspaper] *Montevideo*, December 1938

A member of our community, Herr Max Seliger, has had

the news that his mother Frau Rosa Seliger, née Ehrmann, has passed away at the age of 91. A few days before her death the dying woman had to leave Bad Orb, where she had lived since her marriage and was universally well-liked, along with the few other Jews who still lived in the town. She died in Frankfurt am Main.

The parents-in-law of our *Gemeindemitglied* [community member] Herr Hans Friedheim, *Sanitätsrat* [medical consultant] Dr. Goldberg and his wife lived in Burgdamm near Bremen, and had not sent any news to their children since the recent disorder in Germany. The answer that the latter received to a telegram sent there was that both are dead. Dr. Goldberg and his wife were the only Jews resident in Burgdamm near Bremen. They were respectively 78 and 65 years old.

The Kahn brothers, Maldonado 897, have received news that their father Louis Kahn, most recently resident at Königstein in the Taunus, was arrested on 16th November 1938. Four days later Herr Kahn was dead. He was 58 years old and in full health.

From the "*Gemeindeblatt Montevideo*", January 1939

Herr Bernhard Weiss, here, has received news that his 33-year-old brother Max Weiss was arrested in Germany on 9th November 1938 and died on 14th November 1938.

B. 232 From *L'Univers Israélite* [Jewish Universe; weekly journal] 20, 3 February 1939

Suicide of two Austrian refugees

M. Leopold Lipschutz, aged 69, had been obliged to leave Vienna the day after the *Anschluss* [Nazi German occupation and annexation of Austria on 12 March 1938], where he edited the *Kronenzeitung* [Crown Newspaper], a newspaper supporting the policy of Chancellor [Kurt] Schuschnigg whose friend he also was. He had come and settled in Nice with his wife, Frau Thérèse Lipschutz, aged 58, and his son Franz, aged 24. In October, after spending some months in a hotel, he moved to a home in the

Boulevard Victor Hugo with his wife, the young man living separately in a family *pension*.

The journalist had great difficulty in adapting to this life of exile. He had often said to political exiles like himself that he had had enough of living like this, that is to say, with the thought that his country was under the Nazi yoke. He got his wife to share his despair and both were found dead in their bedroom, poisoned by barbiturates. Before carrying out his tragic design M. Leopold Lipschutz had written several letters, one of which, addressed to the police commissioner, stated his fatal decision, caused by the situation of his country after the *Anschluss*, and also by the fact that he was frequently the target of threats. The man now reduced to desperation was well known in Viennese society. He was the president of "Concordia", an association that brought together the best writers and journalists of Vienna.

B. 233 From the *Pariser Tageszeitung* [Paris Daily Newspaper], no. 914, 8 February 1939

RICHARD WILDE DEAD IN BUCHENWALD

The writer and journalist Richard Wilde, who ran the review section of the Berlin *Acht-Uhr-Abendblatt* [Eight o'clock Evening Paper] until 1933, died a few days ago in Buchenwald concentration camp.

Richard Wilde, who wrote several genuinely successful comedies for the stage, once even wrote a play with Hjalmar Schacht, the recently deposed *Reichsbank* [German central bank] President. When Hitler seized power and Wilde lost his job – he lived modestly from the proceeds of a Berlin lunch café run by his resolute wife – he approached his one-time colleague Schacht. He often recounted how Schacht received him on that occasion. The *Reichsbank* President was charming as always and explained to him "in confidence" how little he agreed with the new course of events, but "there is nothing one can do."

B. 234 From the *Basler Nachrichten* [Basel News], no. 32, 2 February 1939

EMIGRANT TRAGEDY
Lugano, 1 February 1939

As reported by the *Gazetta Ticinese* [Ticino Gazette], on Tuesday afternoon a Rivapiana [now Minusio] fisherman noticed a boat around 300 metres away from the bank in which lay a young woman who was injured. The doctor who was called ascertained that the woman had been injured by two revolver shots.

Immediate enquiries established that the woman is an Austrian who has been living with her husband Dr. Valentin, the well-known Jewish surgeon from Vienna, at a guest house near Rivapiana for some time.

Both had left the guest house at about half past 12 in order to go out in the boat as they often did. Since Dr. Valentin has disappeared, it is suspected that he turned the weapon on himself after having attempted to kill his wife. The woman's condition is hopeless.

B. 235 According to a Berlin report from early February 1939, Frau Selma Goldschmidt, née Abramcyk, the widow of the bank director Julian Goldschmidt, has taken her own life with Veronal. Frau Goldschmidt was 78 years old.

B. 236 An eyewitness reports as follows about the operation of 10th and 11th November 1938 in Berlin:

Immediately after the assassination of Legation Secretary vom Rath considerable fear was expressed in Berlin Jewish circles about the consequences of the assassination, so that from that day forward numerous Jews did not spend the night in their own home any more.

Like all other eyewitnesses, this gentleman reports that the destruction operation started on the night of Wednesday to Thursday and that synagogues were set on fire that night. Amongst others, the synagogues at Lessing-, Klopstock-, Ryke-

and Lützowstraße, which have not previously been mentioned in the newspapers, were completely destroyed in this way. In the Lützowstraße synagogue the *Thorarollen* [Torah scrolls] were torn to shreds.

He also reports, in agreement with others, that a fresh tumult began right after Goebbels' incitement in the afternoon, it was not until the afternoon of Thursday 10th November that the looting and complete destruction of businesses began.

The reporter went through a number of Berlin districts that afternoon and was thus able to confirm the appalling way in which the looting was carried out, completely destroying the Jews' property. Through this operation many Jewish businessmen have been robbed of all they owned.

In the well-known Brandmann watch and clock dealer on Alexanderplatz everything was smashed into tiny pieces, even the large grandfather clocks. School children filled their pockets with gold watches and rings.

In bookshops in that area, for instance Lewin's bookshop, at Wolf Sales, all the books were burnt and torn up. At Gonzer in Orianenburgerstraße the *Thorarollen* were torn up too, the *tallits* [Jewish prayer shawls] were cut up and befouled. The robbers also forced their way into the home there, smashed up the furniture and stole money.

There was just as much damage at Saalberg's so-called "*Haus der Geschenke*" [gift house] in the Konigstraße.

The following scene illustrates the way in which the attack was carried out in one of the numerous antique dealers' in the Lützowstraße. There are many antique shops in that area.

A man with a thick briefcase appeared in the shop. The lady owner greeted him with the words "How can I help you?" The man: "Is this a Jewish shop?" The owner: "I am Jewish myself, how can I help you?" The man (shouting) "Get the hell out of here!"

Intimidated, the woman took a few steps back to retreat to the home that connects with the shop. At the same moment the man slung some heavy object into one of the display cabinets standing in the shop, which was full of valuable cups. That was probably the signal for the copycat attack. The shop was immediately full of hooligans, who smashed up not only the shop's entire inventory but also everything else, in senseless fury, including numerous precious objects. As a result of this destruction it was not only the display windows, the shop furniture and the goods that were completely destroyed, but the precious shop fittings were also violently smashed up.

Even empty shops had their windows smashed if they were identified as former Jewish businesses.

In the Grenadierstraße, the area where the poorest Jews live, there were indescribable scenes.

Remarkably, one small street near the *Rathaus* [town hall] had remained entirely undamaged. It was probably simply forgotten. Early on Friday the police appeared in the Jewish shops there and noted that the shop windows and the shops were not destroyed.

The *Palästinaamt* [Palestine Office] in Meineckestraße is also said to have been completely destroyed. The files were ripped up and typewriters thrown out of the window.

The doors of the Jewish *Gemeindehaus* [community building] on the Rosenstraße were kicked in. The Jewish *Gemeindehaus* on Oranienburgerstraße was occupied by the Gestapo.

Numerous arrests took place as early as Thursday 10th November, many men aged between 18 and 60 were arrested. The *Polizeireviere* [police stations] explained that the arrests were nothing to do with them. They also claimed that people with an *Auswanderungspass* [emigration passport] had nothing to fear. There was naturally no way of finding out whether this information was true.

As a result of the arrests most Jews did not spend the night at home any more, but hid with people they knew, in many cases with Christian friends. In the *Hansaviertel* many Jews spent the night on the floor of a Jewish school.

One of those arrested was Dr. Horowitz, surgeon at the Jewish hospital in the Elsasser Straße.

Despite the fact that a large part of the public refused to have anything to do with the terrible scenes, it became public that Party circles had complained that no blood had yet flowed.

Telephone connections with Jewish families in provincial towns was mostly impossible, either because the people were not at home or because the exchange was not putting through calls to Jewish subscribers.

On the issue of the estimate of people's financial resources, Herr X. rightly notes that these are greatly overestimated. E.g. all pensions and annuities have been capitalised. For a civil servant who receives a pension of perhaps around RM. 4,000.- this income is calculated as if he had capital of RM. 100,000.- This naturally produces completely unjustifiable capital estimates and enormous amounts have been calculated that either never existed at all or do not exist any more.

B. 237 [Julius] Streicher's personal adjutant, [Hanns] König, died suddenly in Nuremberg a short while ago; cause of death: suicide. He received a splendid funeral and was buried in a grave of honour. Streicher himself gave a great funeral oration for him and published an obituary in which he commemorated the dead man in noble terms, who had "voluntarily departed from life".

A little while later strange rumours were making the rounds. König was said to be mixed up in some very nasty business, he had procured women and girls and sent them to the doctor himself. According to the stories the suicide could be traced back to these affairs, which had caused a great deal of trouble and bitterness.

Numerous arrests took place at the same time as these rumours. There was even an attempt to force a doctor who had carried out abortions on König's orders to commit suicide, which however he categorically refused to do. There was a great scandal in which Hitler himself intervened.

The suicide König, just recently heaped with honours, was removed from his honoured grave in the cemetery of honour and buried somewhere else. The first grave was levelled, the wreaths and ribbons were taken away. There was a pilgrimage of Nurembergers to see the place for themselves.

As an epilogue, decrees by the *Polizeipräsident* [police chief] and the *Bürgermeister* [mayor] are being published in the newspapers rebutting the malicious and false rumours and threatening those who invent and spread them with the most serious prison sentences. All persons arrested on these grounds will be identified in the paper.

Names of several people who have been arrested are published in the *Fränkische Kurier* [Franconian Courier] of 1 March and in the *Nürnberg-Fürther Neuesten Nachrichten* [Nuremberg-Fürth Latest News].

B. 238 In Nuremberg, Fürth and Bamberg the following persons died as a result of ill-treatment during the days of the pogrom in November 1938:

1) Paul Lebrecht, Mittlere Pirkheimer Straße 20, aged about 50, was taken to the Jewish hospital in Fürth with a broken skull and died two days later, without having regained consciousness.

2) Simon Loeb, Mittlere Pirkheimer Straße 22, was thrown down the stairs of his house with his wife, after which they both remained lying helpless in the garden for two hours, seriously injured. Eventually they were collected by an ambulance, which took the husband to the city hospital in Nuremberg, where he died after half an hour. His wife was separated from him and brought to the Jewish hospital in Fürth, where she remained in ignorance of the fate of her husband for days. Due to the mistreatment she had suffered she had a deep wound on one side of her face, twisting her lip so that her face looked completely distorted. She was in total despair about the death of her husband. The burial, like all funerals of pogrom victims, had to take place in absolute silence and with no relatives present.

3) Herr Schumann, also of Mittlere Pirkheimer Straße, had a serious eye condition because of which he was almost blind.

Sometime previously he had been to a famous eye surgeon in Utrecht for an operation, and was due to return soon for a second operation. He was hit in the affected eye in such a way that there is now absolutely no chance of an operation or a cure. Both he and his wife were taken to Fürth hospital with head wounds.

4) Fritz Lorch, Emilienstraße 3, was in Fürth hospital following an operation for a fracture. As a result of mistreatment and the commotion he had an embolism, from which he died. His emigration to America had been as good as arranged.

5) Bamberger, owner of the Bamberger Café in the Lindenaststraße, was one of the first people killed.

The following persons took their own lives:

1) Hedwig Süssheim, Adlerstraße, had already lost her husband, who was a Social Democrat Member of the Bavarian *Landtag* [State Parliament] in 1933. Since then she had constantly had to suffer searches of her home and harassment. She had not emigrated so as not to leave her mother. She poisoned herself with gas. She owned a famous collection of antiques, which was taken away from her and made over to the *Germanisches Museum* [Germanic Museum].

2) Frieda Bloch, Wodanstrasse 78, poisoned herself with gas.

3) Leonhard Frankenburger, *Justizrat* [state prosecutor], about 70 years old, poisoned himself with gas. He had been secretary of the A*nwaltskammer* [legal chambers] in Nuremberg for ten years.

4) Alexander Frankenburger, *Geheimer Hofrat* [Privy Councillor], brother of the above, the same age, was taken, dying, to Fürth hospital. He founded and resourced the tuberculosis charity in Nuremberg and set up the tuberculosis sanatorium in Nuremberg on his own.

Their sister, also very elderly, had slit her wrists, but was rescued and later taken to Holland by a distant relation.

5) A married couple called Behrend also committed suicide, the husband died in Fürth hospital, the wife was rescued. She had two daughters abroad, one in Holland and the other in Switzerland. She has probably taken refuge with one or other of them.

6) Karl Sahlmann, of Friedrichstrasse 11, Fürth, shot himself.

7) Anna Engelmann, of Bamberg, widow of a doctor, poisoned herself. A note was found beside her in which she had given instructions that in no case should any attempts be made to revive her in the event that she was found alive.

8) Grete Bing, Bamberg, similarly committed suicide.

9) An unknown man was discovered hanged.

10) Dr. Weinstock, medical practitioner, took his own life in March 1939 in Nuremberg.

11) Willy Lessing, *Kommerzienrat* [commercial councillor], board member of the *Kultusgemeinde* [Jewish community], went to the synagogues in the night when he heard they were burning. He was badly beaten up and later attacked once again on the way home and mistreated so badly that his cries could be heard for streets around. Then he was taken to his home. He suffered terribly for eight weeks, and abcesses formed on his injuries which had to be drained. Finally septicemia set in, from which he died.

B. 239 In the night of 9th to 10th November the front door bell of a large detached family house rings at exactly three in the morning. The lady of the house opens the door dressed only in her nightdress and a housecoat and sees the whole forecourt is full of SA. They demand access and tell her to return to her bedroom. Following her protestations they allow her husband to remain in bed.

The intruders enter the living room and begin their work of destruction. For twenty minutes all that can be heard is the crashing of axes, the splitting of wood and the shattering of porcelain and glass. They were extremely thorough. They smashed the panes of the glass-fronted book cabinet with a heavy lead crystal carafe, a flower pot was left hanging in a glass cabinet, nothing was spared, neither pictures nor curtains nor the piano, which was tackled with an axe. Then the destroyers left.

The occupants of the house dressed themselves provisionally, aware of the danger of a further attack, which was indeed not long in coming. Half an hour later the group returned and this time the people themselves were mistreated. The husband, who was still lying in bed, received a number of powerful blows to the head, his wife, who raised her arm to protect his head, also received a strike to the arm of such violence that it was black and blue for a week afterwards. The husband was driven from his bed to screams of "*Aus dem Haus raus, aus dem Haus raus*" [Get out of the house, get out of the house] and forced down the stairs accompanied by repeated blows to his head and back. The couple, both of advanced years, run for their lives down the stairs and out onto the street; the man is barely conscious due to the loss of blood and blows he has sustained. Fortunately an Aryan doctor lives on the next street corner. The wife rings the bell and he takes them both in, treating the husband who is completely exhausted and on the verge of collapse.

The doctor then rang the police who sent an ambulance escorted by a police officer, which then took both people to the Jewish hospital in Fürth. When they arrived the entire building was in turmoil, there were SA, doctors, nurses everywhere, and patients had been chased into the garden and it had even been attempted to force seriously ill patients out of bed. When the car with the two people arrived the driver was bawled at: "Who sent you here?", to which he replied concisely, "*Polizeipräsidium* [police headquarters] Nuremberg", after which the wounded were allowed to get out of the car and be brought into the building.

All doctors and nurses had to make their way to the Marktplatz in Fürth where all the city's Jews had been rounded up. Patients who could walk also had to go along. It was attempted to force the woman who had just arrived to go with them but she was left in peace when she protested vociferously that she too had been wounded.

In the course of the night innumerable people who had been injured and mistreated and those who had attempted suicide were admitted. Every room was occupied by more patients than it was supposed to take and others had to be put up in corridors.

Once they had been sent back to the hospital, doctors and nursing staff wore unchanged clothing for days. All the women who came to see their relatives stayed on and helped.

The injuries were almost all of the same kind. Blows to the head, dealt with enormous force, even to women.

One married couple was admitted, each with double fractures to their arms; as she had attempted to protect her husband the wife had been dealt a blow to the arm with such force that it broke in two places.

Two disabled women had been dragged from their beds and left lying on the floor.

One man was admitted who had been paralysed down the right side following a blow and had lost his ability to speak as if he had suffered a serious stroke.

A four-year-old child from Neustadt an der Aisch was admitted with a broken chin.

No one doubted for a moment that the entire operation had been prepared down to the last detail and that it was not in any sense the product of a general *Volkswut* [people's rage]. It has been proved that the instruments used to smash and destroy things had been produced to order weeks before in the *Maschinenfabrik* Augsburg (MAN). At two o'clock on the agreed night there was once again an *Appell* [roll call] on the *Marktplatz*, weapons distributed and *Oberführer* [SS Brigadier General] [Hanns] Obernitz again gave precise orders.

One SA man responded as follows to the question as to whether [Julius] Streicher would have had the authority to order such action: "This order comes from none other than the Führer himself." And to the forlorn question, "Is it all really necessary?" he merely replied "An order is an order."

The vast majority of the Aryan population responded to the events with apathy; some of those who had heard about it in advance warned their Jewish acquaintances.

Despite claims to the contrary, a great deal was stolen and looted.

Amongst the wreckers there were also special *Zerstörungstrupps* [destruction squads] who did not simply content themselves with smashing everything to pieces. They literally cut carpets, curtains, and clothes into strips so that they could never be repaired. One lady who had her clothes and those of her maid rendered unusable in this way was forced to pay the maid a set price of RM. 480.- as compensation.

Works of art were certainly not spared, even those by the great masters. One gentleman pleaded desperately that a small authentic Rembrandt should not be destroyed but rather handed to the *Germanisches [*National*] Museum*; he would gladly donate it. He was not listened to and the picture was ripped to shreds. During the night a number of great German art works were victims of the frenzy of destruction, including works by such names as Gabriel Max, [Moritz von] Schwind, [Andreas] Achenbach, etc. Furthermore, a large quantity of very beautiful old family portraits, often fine examples of Biedermeier art, were senselessly destroyed. Similarly, finely crafted and inlaid mirrors, faïence and valuable collections of porcelain were smashed to pieces. Later many Aryans came to see what had happened, it is absolutely unimaginable for anyone who did not hear and see it. One waded around in shards and no one who experienced it will rid their imagination of the shattering, smashing and splintering. Strangely, numerous Aryans later turned up offering to buy damaged goods, perhaps because they thought they might acquire some valuable objects cheaply.

The case of two children is tragic, a boy and a girl, who were both highly musical. Their most valuable possessions, the violin and the piano, were smashed to pieces so completely that a repair was unthinkable.

In one home the Aryan maid protected most of the possessions from destruction with great courage. The family was on the verge of emigrating and had sold the vast majority of the things to the person moving into the home. The sale was not quite complete, but this way she saved the things. She explained that many things had been given to her as gifts.

The brutality against women in particular was unbelievable. One lady was threatened and prevented from entering the room of her mother who was seriously ill. One old lady who asked whether it was all really necessary was told "Shut your mouth or you'll get a beating." Another asked them to spare a picture on the writing desk of her son who had fallen in the war, as it was her last memento of him. She was told: "Who cares? That was in the Second Reich."

It was often the case that residents were chased out onto the street in their shirts and barefoot in order to be photographed. One man who lived near to Streicher's home had to clear his home in three hours in the middle of the night. He managed, with difficulty, to find a place to stay with friends.

In Fürth the entire Jewish population was herded together on the Marktplatz and forced to stand there from half past three until 8 o'clock in the morning. Amongst them were a number of 83- and 88-year olds and very young children, some of whom were brought along in perambulators. In the morning they were herded into a hall building that had once been donated to the city by a Jew. From there the women and children were released whilst the men were transported to Dachau. Notices immediately appeared on all shops, "*Juden Eintritt verboten*" [Entry prohibited for Jews]. Jews could not buy anything whatsoever and were secretly taken care of by Aryan friends who shopped for them.

The particularly beautiful old synagogue was burned down and along with it innumerable valuable artefacts were lost. Groups of Jewish children were brought there to watch the spectacle. One fireman reported, "In the 37 years I've been with the *Feuerwehr* [fire brigade] I have helped to put out many a fire, but starting one is something completely new."

Every squad who carried out the destruction or started fires had a leader who directed the operation.

In Schweinfurt a school class was sent to a c. 80-year-old woman to destroy her home.

In Würzburg the leader of the attack on the synagogue was the university Vice-Chancellor [Ernst] Seyffert. Nor did he shy away from getting involved in the detail of its execution and cut up the carpets of a respected Jewish citizen with his own hands.

In general so-called *gebildete Leute* [educated people] also participated in the vandalism. Thus one lady recognised her attacker to be the landscape gardener who had once designed the garden for her at considerable expense.

In many Franconian *Gemeinden* communities the people had literally not a scrap to eat and nothing to drink.

As late as February a man from a Franconian *Gemeinde* was admitted to the hospital in Fürth who had to be fed because his hands had been smashed.

The dispossession of Jewish real estate was handed over to an organisation known as "*Heim und Haus*" [House and Home], which was set up specifically to this end. It acted summarily by presenting the people summoned to its office with a contract of sale in which the plot of land was to be sold for a fraction of its real value. The seller did not receive any money but he was forced to pay rent if he was allowed to continue using the house. Anyone who refused or wanted time to consider the offer was threatened with being put up in a cellar of the building; anyone who emerged from there was prepared to sign anything.

People waiting in the lobby to be called had to stand to attention with their hands raised whenever one of the officials appeared. As bullying, one of them was always passing through the room so the people did not get a moment's rest. Anyone who agreed from the outset to accept anything and everything laid before them came off best, although that was not the end of it; e.g. houses in which former occupants were allowed to remain often had to be cleared at very short notice. This often had catastrophic consequences because those who formerly owned the villas now found their houses full of people who had been hounded out of their rented homes.

The Jewish *Gemeinde* in Nuremberg had to hand over its old people's home, nurses' home and cemetery. It did not receive any money but was forced to pay RM. 350.- rent for the old people's home. A new cemetery site was taken from it for RM. 100.– and it was then forced to pay RM. 80.- a month for it. During the night after the "sale" closed 57 graves were knocked over and on the day [Hanns] König was buried a further 27.

Two years previously the *Gemeinde* had sold at a loss a piece of land that had originally been bought as a site for a second synagogue, but which had become superfluous following the gradual dissolution of the community. It had received RM. 60,000.- and a mortgage was set up for a further RM. 60,000.-. The *Gemeindevorsitzende* [community chairman] was summoned and forced to relinquish the mortgage, without the slightest compensation of course.

Following the example of the authorities, private individuals naturally also did not shy away from extortion: one lady had sold all her goods and chattels for RM. 400.- and drawn up a written contract of sale. The following day the buyer turned up claiming that he had agreed to far too high a price and was only prepared to pay RM. 200.– and threatened to call the SA if his demands were not acceded to. The seller gave in. The next day the man appeared once again, this time extorting a further RM. 100.– from the lady, supposedly for transport of the things.

One day the "*Heim and Haus*" [home and house] office, which had installed itself comfortably in one of the most beautiful Nuremberg villas, formerly in Jewish hands, was suddenly closed down, the majority of its officials were arrested and a number of them sent to Berlin. Apparently they had been earning excessive commissions from the dispossessions.

A particularly terrible measure is the decree on surrendering jewellery and silver because it particularly affects old people who have saved these things as final possessions to protect them from starvation. There were indescribable scenes at the places where the surrender happened, and the people were treated in the most despicable manner.

In the case of Jewish dentists, equipment and instruments, some very valuable and in many cases acquired over a long period in preparation for emigration, were confiscated and expropriated. For the three remaining authorised dentists in Nuremberg, who were forced to practise from common premises, the *Kultusgemeinde* [Jewish community] was compelled to buy back one of the sets of equipment, the most worthless of the three. The others were auctioned off. As with dental items, so too other medical equipment, instruments and appliances could not be taken away for emigration.

All sales of things after the 10th November were subject to *Arisierungsabgabe* [Aryanisation duty]. The things were valued by an expert and then e.g. the following calculation was made: A grand piano valued at RM. 500.- allegedly had to be repaired at a cost of RM. 250.- because it had suffered damage during the destruction operation. Of the remaining RM. 250.- one quarter, RM. 60.- , was deducted. The seller received RM. 186.- of the RM. 190.- .

The *Arisierungsabgabe* flows into the coffers of the *Winterhilfswerk des deutschen Volkes* [Winter Relief for the German People] rather than the Jewish *Hilfswerk* [*Hilfsverein der deutschen Juden;* Aid Association of German Jews].

The duties demanded for things that the owners want to take with them are even worse. E.g. a gentleman's gold watch was valued at RM. 300- ; the duty to be paid if the owner wanted to take it with him was set at RM. 900.- . He did without the watch and asked for permission to sell it instead. 25% was again deducted from the sale price, which was far below the actual value, so that the sum he finally received for it was ludicrously small.

A young pianist had received as a present the wonderful Steinway grand piano of a rich lady. It was the only item he wanted to take with him when he emigrated. A duty of RM. 8,000.- was demanded from him. He could not pay it and had to leave the piano behind.

A rich couple who had been seriously injured on the night of the pogrom (double fractures to their arms) was required to pay RM. 93,000.- duty. They had to leave all their valuable carpets and jewellery behind.

The bullying that people were exposed to extended cunningly to all possible areas. The aim was to wear people down. Files were allowed to disappear just as people were due to emigrate and then suddenly turned up again after they had made desperate attempts to get their affairs in order.

One was forbidden to send parcels and packets abroad. Only

one international *Antwortschein* [reply coupon] could be sent each month and only to one individual. One had the sense that the longer the representative to the conference in Évian negotiated in Berlin, the more severe the measures became.

In Berlin the *Helldorf-Fonds* [fund] was set up for which Berlin Jews were expected to pay enormous sums, supposedly to pay compensation for destroyed foreign property.

As an indication of the deranged thinking of those in power it is reported that Streicher received a *Thorarolle* [Torah scroll] found on the site of a burned synagogue as a birthday present.

The *Gauleiter* [provincial leader] of Würzburg Dr. Hellmuth named his newborn daughter Gailana. The explanation follows: around the year 750 Würzburg was ruled by a *Herzogin* [Duchess] Gailana, renowned for her immoral and blasphemous lifestyle and as a consequence vehemently opposed by three pious bishops. She had all three beheaded. The three martyrs were canonised and one of them named Kilian became the patron saint of Würzburg. The *Gauleiter* thus named his daughter after the ungodly Gailana, but christened his dog Kilian.

B. 240 EXPOSÉ

Regarding the *Israelitisches Altersheim für die Pfalz e.V.* [Jewish Old People's Home for the Palatinate] at Neustadt an der Weinstraße, Rhineland-Palatinate.

The *Israelitisches Altersheim* in Neustadt, perhaps the most beautiful such home in Germany, was set on fire on 10th November 1938 and completely destroyed with its valuable furnishings. It is the only old people's home in the Reich that was destroyed in this way.

The home accommodated 72 residents (excluding the staff). They were all chased out of bed very early in the morning and driven out into the street, barely dressed. Two of them could no longer be found and are still missing to this day. Several others died in the following days and weeks.

Most of the residents were first taken to the *Israelitisches*

Altersheim in Mannheim, which was already overcrowded and could therefore offer no accommodation suitable for the old people. They were kept corridors, hallways, sculleries, cellars and stairways in the most miserable fashion. This state of affairs was intolerable, and it was possible after some days to obtain a floor in another building in Mannheim, in which 50 people in all had to be accommodated in five rooms. No further explanation is needed as to how they had to live there. Three people had to sleep on every two mattresses.

This dreadful state of affairs cannot be justified any longer; moreover the Jewish *Gemeinde* [community] of Mannheim and the Mannheim police are demanding in the strongest way that the premises be vacated.

Our efforts to obtain other premises – in the Palatinate – with the help of the authorities have been unsuccessful up to now. For these reasons we can see no other option than to turn to our foreign brothers and request their help in this exceptional emergency. We have so far had some success in France, in that the Jewish authorities agreed to the reception of ten old men into two old people's homes. Efforts to move a further number to France will be continued.

We now request most sincerely that Holland might also accept an appropriate number of our old people, so that they may see out the evening of their lives in peace.

For the management of the *Israelitisches Altersheim für die Pfalz e.V.*

(signature)

B. 241 On 10th November 1938 the residents of the *Altersheim* [old people's home] in Emden in Ostfriesland, all people between the ages of 70 and 80, were driven out of the home to the open space in front of the school, where the other Jewish residents of the town were also required to assemble. They were led past the burning synagogue and forced to sing as they went. They were made to do gymnastic exercises and knee-bends in the school yard. The next morning they were taken back to the home.

As a result of the pogroms a number of fatalities are to be recorded:

Daniel de Beer, butcher in Emden, was shot and left for dead. He was taken to hospital, where he died of his injuries after c. 14 days.

His wife Frau Rosi de Beer, mother of two small children, also had to go to the school yard with the children in the night. She was taken in by relatives in Holland. However, she was only allowed to leave after she had had all damage to her shop and home repaired at her own expense. She also had to pay the hospital fees for her husband herself. As it happens, his corpse was released in an orderly fashion for the funeral.

A young girl, Lina de Beer, was locked in her home where she lived with her brothers. She escaped by climbing over the roof and was then taken in and looked after by Christian neighbours. The same Christian friends had, during the deportation of the Polish Jews, donated a large number of blankets to the unfortunates.

Sally Löwenstein, Emden, died on the transport to the camp, apparently of heart failure: it turned out later that blows from a rifle butt had killed him.

Leopold Cohn, Emden, aged 39, was pushed into the water by some of the mob, whenever he reached the bank they threw him back in again, until finally he emerged half dead. Then he was taken to the concentration camp. But despite this he came home again alive in the end.

Louis Pels, an ailing man, was beaten to a pulp and his whole cheek cut up. Smashed china lay around in piles in his home, as in almost all Jewish homes in the town. He later came to Holland (Groningen) but was completely distraught as a result of what he had experienced.

Emden's rabbi happened to be away on a trip when they came looking for him. Locked in her home, his wife was forced to witness the synagogue fire. The rabbi was identified with the aid of a photograph, which they took from his home, and arrested whilst he was still travelling. The couple later came to Palestine, where the wife died shortly after disembarking as a result of all the distress she had suffered.

In Norden in Friesland people were dragged out of their beds at night in their shirts, tied to one another in pairs like cattle and put in stables where they were beaten up. Then they were taken away to the concentration camp.

B. 242 Dear F.

I have been in London since yesterday. My thoughts are even more confused than they were after my release. I came here by plane after violent arguments with the Gestapo, which ended with me having 24 hours to leave the country. H. collected me, I am living at her place now, and I would be quite lost without her. I am barely capable of speaking the language and this enormous city has made a powerful impression on me. I really don't know whether I like it, it is so big. But that will wear off in the end and is beside the point. It's much more important to be really free and to be able at last to talk for once without fear and trepidation. You see, the transition to humanity took place rather quickly, and my head feels as dull as it did in the camp.

It is getting better slowly now, since I have been able to talk to H. She is a marvellous person and helps me in all sorts of ways. I really don't know how I got like this, but I have become a frightful egotist and accept all her help as a matter of course.

Yes, I really wanted to write to you about my experiences in the camp, but it is difficult. however I want to try to describe some of it for you. I will write to you more often, and so you will hear the most important things in small doses.

So, listen: I was picked up on... (at the end of May [*Juni-Aktion*]), was kept in a school with many other Jews and waited for what was to happen. Two days later, on Monday, we were suddenly loaded into cars and began the guessing game about where we were going. First along the Elisabethprom-enade, then by the *Landesgericht* [regional court], then up the Mariahilferstraße. Well, as soon as I saw that I felt much better: then suddenly we were off to Dachau. The journey (to) Dachau was endless torture. Those beasts beat, stabbed and killed. I can't tell you any more about the journey and don't want to, because constantly talking about death and murder is now for me – just boring. Enough, I survived.

In Dachau yet another short, delightful and raucous reception. Then it was changing, haircutting and after a 14-hour journey and 12 hours of changing the reception formalities were concluded. Then to work. Ten hours a day of shovelling and pushing wheelbarrows, without looking up, a hellish tempo, and then standing for the *Zählappellen* [roll call head counts], standing, standing and more standing. With this *Frondienst* [slave labour] it is no surprise that morale in Dachau is poor. Most of the Aryan *politische Häftlinge* [political prisoners], who were our *Vorarbeiter* [foremen] or the *Stubenältesten* [room elders] in our barracks, had got into the habit of adopting the SS's methods of torture. So I was very happy when after three weeks I found a decent *Vorarbeiter* who took me into his *Arbeitskommando* [work squad] and protected me. He was a young student and former member of the SS, who had become convinced that his views were wrong soon after the *Machtergreifung* [seizure of power]. You need a lot of strength or strong friends to see people dying beside you every day.

But F., I can't be writing to you constantly about the camp, with every word I write another thousand things occur to me. I won't write any more about the camp for now. Only one thing more, so that you don't think we had lost all our sense of humour. These verses were thought up in Buchenwald:

In Buchenwald, in Buchenwald
Da sitz' ich viele Wochen bald
Es walten guten milden Geister
Unter den Namen Gildemeister [Gildemeester]
Sind es Menschen oder weiße Schatten
Die hier durch die Sch... Waten?

[In Buchenwald, in Buchenwald / I've been sitting here for weeks now / Kindly spirits are at work /Under the name of

Gildermeister [Gildemeester]. / Are they men or white shadows / Who are wading through the sh... here?]

But now I want to know from you how you got out, what you are doing, etc. Please, dear F., write soon and in detail, I'm very curious. Finally, thank you so much for your telegram.

Greetings to you

Your old friend

B. 243 15th December 1938

I would like to describe our situation very briefly to you: due to the events of the last weeks we are utterly destitute. Neither my parents nor one of us siblings has even the smallest possibility of earning – and we are a family of seven. Can you imagine what our future now looks like? In all this there might be one hope that could make our desperate situation bearable, hope of emigration – but that too is not in the least available. We are given notice to be out of our home as of 31st January 1939. All our efforts to find a new home have been in vain – and it is scarcely seven weeks until the 31st. But that is not the worst.

My father was taken into *Schutzhaft* [protective custody] five weeks ago... Yet this still did not seem to satisfy cruel fate. Another crushing blow hit us: the upsetting events of late caused my mother to have a serious nervous breakdown... If you wish I can send a medical certificate regarding that.

Can you now understand that, despite what you have written, we desperately clutch at you to obtain your help? From this can you conceive what emotions these crude facts must awaken in the souls of small, innocent children? Do you understand now that in this case it is really a duty to help? In the name of my parents and of my siblings and in my name, I imploringly ask only one thing: help!

(Followed by personal details of four brothers 17, 13, ten and eight years of age).

From a letter by the same boy to his mother's brother: I have just spoken to the doctor about dear *Mutti* [Mum]. He told me it would be a downright crime if *Mutti* stayed in S. any longer. She has to get out of here under any circustamces. It would be best if she could find a place somewhere abroad. It would be downright suicide if she had to stay here any longer.

B. 244 ... As you know, Hermann Gutmann had been away (!), he returned last week Thursday, he caught an infection in one arm, the same arm that had suffered severe damage due to the cold and a few hours after he was back had to resort to hospital. Dr. X. was there immediately when he arrived. The matter looked bad. Dr. Z., who is now surgeon in L., immediately talked about the danger of amputation, which, to preserve the arm, was postponed, but nevertheless had to be carried out today.

In all this unfortunately it still cannot be foreseen whether the infection has passed into the body, the doctor immediately administered injections to counteract this, but in the last few days had to recognise that the body is utterly weakened and does not possess strong resistance. We hope that even as a cripple he will at least survive as a human being and father.

If I am writing to you now, it is with the plea that despite all difficulties you try to get the children Walter and Alfred from there to Holland. There is real urgency here, they are half-orphans for whom the possibility of being full orphans shortly is unfortunately rather close...

Letter from the *Reichsvertretung der Juden in Deutschland* [Reich Deputation of Jews in Germany] of 3rd February 1939

... We learn that the circumstances in the case of the two children Walter and Alfred G. are particularly sad and recommend urgently the children are allowed to enter Holland as soon as possible.

The children's mother died about two years ago, the father was engaged six months after his wife's death to Fraulein A. and intended to marry her soon. He had to go away in November and on 30th December died in the hospital to which he had been admitted on 24th December as a result of a wound infection.

During his absence his fiancée has been running the household and still does, since the 82-year-old grandmother is the only person in the house. The household is to be dispersed very shortly...

B. 245 Ref. Hanover
17th November 1938
Herewith I recount to you the particularly sad fate of my cousin Dr. H.'s family. He has been a sufferer from a severe nervous disorder for years, is now located in a concentration camp with his 18-year-old son.

His wife is located in hospital in X. with a serious illness and the second son, 12 years old, is at home alone. If it were possible at least to find accommodation in Holland for the child, that would take one worry from the family, of course the same would be equally urgent for the detainees...

B. 246 Ref.
16th November 1938
Deeply impressed by reports of desperate parents who have already been suffering the bitterest need from a small place in Germany, I turn to you to ask whether you have the possibility of bringing their child here, a girl of 14 years.

The parents, who have been very poor for some time, have been supported by a brother of the wife. This brother, who himself has a wife and several children, was arrested on Friday after his business was destroyed, and both families find themselves in great need because the population of the small place is unwilling or does not dare to help them, and they certainly have no provisions...

B. 247 Ref. Wesermünde [now in Bremerhaven]
15th November 1938
I have just heard that my cousin's husband has been arrested.

My cousin herself has gone mad from despair after this horrendous experience and had to be taken into an institution. The
children are left helpless and for me it is a terrible thought
that the children had to witness such a disaster so explicitly. I
received a cry for help with the urgent request to take the children in until it is possible to make definite decisions about their
future calmly ...

(The children are seven and two and a half years old.)

B. 248 Breslau [now Pol. Wrocław]
3rd February 1939
Since we have been without any livelihood and therefore
without any income since 10th November, had to give up our
home and were only able to find accommodation with relatives for a limited period of time, since my husband had been
interned until Christmas and we do not have any connections
which enable us to find accommodation anywhere abroad
for ourselves and our children, you and the English *Hilfscomité* [aid committee] were our only hope. We are in complete
despair and have nothing left to lose but our bare lives. If it
is now really not possible for you to grant our plea and you
are unable to intercede at least for our children, we really
have only one very last resort left, which we have so far shied
away from for understandable reasons. But another negative
reply will certainly abandon us to despair. Indeed I can not
think of a single more desperate and therefore more urgent
case than ours. So much has been said and written about our
foreign fellow believers' willingness to help. We have not had
any proof of this so far, because when we use even our last
Groschen [pennies] to plead for help through begging letters
sent abroad, so far only refusal has come from all sides. We
have to fend for ourselves and have nobody who will act on
our behalf. Every person living abroad should be happy that
he is not the one for whom someone is having to intercede.
It is so bitter to have to give one's children away, but it is a
thousand times more bitter if one has to beg to get rid of them,

we do not wish on any of our fellow believers living in peace and comfort that they should ever get into the position of feeling this bitterness.

The chairman of the Jewish *Gemeinde* [community] in X. can confirm the truth of my statement. We belonged to that *Gemeinde* until the end of 1938. As there is really no needier case than ours, I ask again for consideration and friendly goodwill. Otherwise we really have no other way out.

B. 249 Vienna, the 14th January 1939

... My brother in New York is trying to get us to America. Since our quota, as you know, will only have its turn in two years' time, my brother wanted to get us to Cuba in the meantime. For this purpose he had already deposited the *Landungsgeld* [landing charge] there. Since, apart from the financial part, there were also other conditions to be fulfilled to obtain the *Einreise* [entry permit], such as the medical examination, which had to be carried out only by a doctor assigned by the consulate, all three of us had to go to the consulate in Bremen for this purpose.

Since Bremen is not far from the border post Kleve [Cleves], we decided to go to Kleve on our way back for the purpose of orientation. We arrived there on 6th December at 8 o'clock in the morning. Herr X. advised Lenchen to go to a certain inn called *Zur Goldenen Rose* [At the Golden Rose], where we would get the necessary information. Not familiar with the place, we looked for the inn and it transpired that it was located on the Dutch border. Not even the driver with whom we drove to the inn could provide any information about it. Lenchen booked a room with the intention of resting for a few hours and then travelling back. When Lenchen came out of the inn, customs officials came towards us and accused us of wanting to flee across the border. We were stopped and arrested.

The next day, the 7th December, Lenchen was found dead in bed, the right hand wrapped around the body of the child, pressing it hard to her chest. When the child woke up cheerily it found its *Mutti* no longer with it. This is in plain words the report about the terrible tragedy, which a poet's imagination could hardly have accomplished.

Now here I lie, wholly buried under the wreckage of this dreadful catastrophe, and still cannot pull myself together to save the child.

B. 250 Ref. Gießen

21st December 1938

... Have registered the boy (b. 9th November 1923) here for entry into Holland a few weeks ago with you. Given that my nephew has already been arrested twice, the boy's father is still in custody and the mother is working for food in Gießen. The boy is currently in hiding in F. Has no accommodation and no food, but can be arrested again any day.

Please help in this matter. It is very important to free the boy promptly from his misery.

26th January 1939

... On 23rd December you wrote to me that the above child would be treated as an urgent case. Now that another four weeks have gone by and I have not heard anything from you in the meantime, I would like to ask you again to speed up departure for the boy. I would not burden you so often with my letters, but in this case help is urgently required. Given that the boy has already been arrested twice and has experienced horrendous things and has no home any more ...

B. 251 Extracts from letters to the *Kindercomité* [Children's committee] in Amsterdam

Ref. Emden (Ostfriesland [East Fiesland])

17th November 1938

... It concerns the children of my brother-in-law and sister-in-law in Emden. According to certain trustworthy information, my brother-in-law was taken away to an unknown destination in the recent events. We fear greatly for his fate because he is a seriously diabetic patient who can only remain healthy on a strictly controlled diet.

The contents of his house – according to these reports – were doused in petrol and totally destroyed by fire.

It is clear that under these circumstances the position of his two children gives us great cause for concern, chiefly in connection with reports concerning the prohibition on selling food (to Jews) and blocking of their bank accounts.

It is on these grounds that I turn to you with this request, to apply your influence so that both these children are given temporary leave to settle here until they have obtained the necessary papers to emigrate to Palestine...

B. 252 Ref. Dortmund

22nd November 1938

... It concerns my sister-in-law's children, a girl of ten and a boy of eleven. The following facts have only just been brought to my attention:

The Dortmund *Anwalt* [lawyer] Frank was murdered in my sister-in-law's house;

as far as I am aware, most of the furniture has been destroyed;

the children have suffered a lot psychologically through the "nightly house visits". They cannot calm down.

it appears that the rental agreement has been cancelled, as I gathered from the note;

the children's single mother has completely lost her equilibrium and there is no relative left in Germany;

I emphasise again that the children's father maliciously abandoned his wife in 1933 and has never supported her, so the financial circumstances are bad...

B. 253 Letter from a concentration camp

"I don't know if this letter will reach you, I have sacrificed my last belongings for the transport, I don't know where we are. My name is A., lived in M., still have a wife and six children aged three to 14 there, am Jewish and stateless.

Save us. Very urgent!"

B. 254 Ref. Lahr or rather Offenburg in Baden

17th November 1938

... As my relatives informed me, both of my brothers-in-law were carried off to concentration camps during the *Volkswut* [people's rage]. I would now like to ask most respectfully that you might intercede so that at least the children can be brought here, since they are in the most serious danger and their mother is close to despair. She cannot provide food for the children and has almost reached a point where she will commit suicide with the children, since they are on the point of starvation. Apart from the two children there is another boy aged eleven at home ...

B. 255 21st December 1938

... The undersigned has received approval for his nephew to come to Holland for training as a *Palästina-Pionier* [Palestine Pioneer]. Confirmation of the authorisation is already in the hands of the boy (15 years old).

However it is impossible for the boy to come here, as the German police are refusing to give him a passport and are demanding an *Unbedenklichkeitsbescheinigung* [clearance certificate] because of the tax.

In this respect I must point out that the boy's father was shot dead during the recent pogrom in Germany and that his mother is in hospital with serious gunshot wounds to the lungs and abdomen. The boy is in B. in an area where he can no longer remain and it is therefore desperately urgent for him to leave ...

B. 256 Ref: Gerderhahn near Erkelenz

14th December 1938

Since 18th November 1938 I have had one of my sister's boys

here; her husband suffered serious mistreatment in June 1935 from a National Socialist and died two months later as a result of the mistreatment.

The boy is the eldest of four children and came here by train via Roermond on 18th November, having been provided with a valid *Kinderausweis* [child's identity card]. He asked me if he could stay here as his mother can no longer buy food and he can no longer go to school.

My sister's is the only Jewish family living in G.

I ask now most sincerely as I want to ensure that the boy is legalised and is permitted to stay here ...

B. 257 9th November 1938

... I have two sons aged 14 and 15½ years of age; the elder is learning joinery, the younger is still in his last year at school. Both boys must leave the country as quickly as possible as the danger exists that they are particularly at risk, like I myself, due to the close link to my brother, X., the former Independent Socialist *Reichstagsabgeordneter* [Reichstag deputy] now in the USA.

It is well known that even today from time to time the German press publish articles filled with hatred against my brother. His exact address in the USA is known to the German authorities and even today he is spied on by Germans, as the themes of his speeches are well known by the Gestapo. Consequently within Germany I dare not use the affidavit received from my brother. For this reason I must use my short stay here to ask the *Comité* to do everything to help me, so that first and foremost my children get across the German border very soon. I cannot describe these things from inside Germany.

I would like to mention that my dear wife took her own life six weeks ago in despair over the whole situation.

If it were possible to enable my children to stay for the time being and undertake further training abroad, perhaps in Holland, a worry, a very great worry, would be taken from me ...

I would be most indebted to you, if you would at least open a possibility of life for my children, so that I can look into the future with courage again.

I ask you, if you write to me or to the *Hilfsverein* [*der deutschen Juden;* Aid Association of German Jews] in Berlin, not to mention my brother's name, as otherwise we would all be placed in the gravest danger.

B. 258 Ref. Limburg an der Lahn
          15th November 1938

In Limburg an der Lahn last week all the adult Jews were arrested, men and women. People aged over 60 were released on Saturday evening. The fate of the children, there will be roughly seven children in the *Gemeinde* [community], is still not known.

It has just become known in the circle of Jews living here who come from Limburg, that the Jewish men and women of the *Gemeinde* are thought to have been taken to Dachau.

It is imperative to save the children. Considering the situation in Limburg I am asking for notification as to whether it would be possible to send here all seven Jewish children from L. They could all be accommodated here in the houses of the people who come from L. without the need for outside help.

Unfortunately we do not know all the personal details of the children. I myself have a nephew and a niece in L. The parents are away, I assume that the children are with their grandmother.

B. 259 Ref. Goch in the Rhineland [now North Rhine-Westphalia]
          28th January 1939

... May I ask you to do your utmost to ensure that our *Antrage* [application] is granted and the children, who as a result of the *Aufenthaltsverbot* [exclusion order] issued against them are facing a life threatening situation, are saved.

B. 260 26th November 1938

The undersigned request you kindly to assist them as regards admitting Judith R. of D. into the Netherlands. The child is the little daughter of the former organist of the liberal synagogue H. and assistant organist at D. On account of the destruction of the D. synagogue and devastation of the synagogue at H., the same is destitute.

During the night of the pogrom the same stayed mainly with non-Jewish citizens, in the cellar. Because the man is entirely destitute, parents and child must suffer hunger. It is not possible to send them food, as the man is not on the dole, has to pay import duties, whilst he has command of nothing.

Hoping that you will be favourably disposed towards the fate of the abovementioned little one, I sign thanking you in advance and with greatest respect.

Below on the application form: Father seriously ill in hospital, his condition is very bad, the mother is with him all day, the child is alone at home unsupervised.

B. 261 November 1938

The undersigned urgently asks for help for his son. He has been attending the Samson Rafael Hirsch *Real Schule* [secondary school] in Frankfurt am Main and has been staying in a *Beth Neorim* hostel that was set up by the *Aguda*. This has been closed, as I have just discovered, since Friday 25th November, lessons at the school abandoned. And now I do not know where the boy is.

We had to leave Z., which is near Kassel, and were taken in by a charitable family in Kassel. We, one daughter, my wife and I, occupy one room in turns and do not know what to do about the poor boy. Heinz is a capable and hard-working person with an agreeable nature, aged 15. He would have finished school at Easter and after the *Aguda* we intended him to attend a Belgian state *Baugewerbeschule* [building trade school] in Antwerp. What will come of this is now completely uncertain, so that we are very worried.

As you can imagine, our means are at an end, a small manufacturing business which was established in 1873 by my late father, that until recently had a good reputation, is no more.

Please help me and do concern yourself with the progress of our boy. We are very, very grateful people.

B. 262 23rd January 1939

Your Royal Highness

Standing before a seemingly insoluble problem, with the courage, which the desire to keep my children lends me, I dare to direct this letter to Your Royal Highness.

In brief, the facts of the matter are as follows:

My husband was in *Schutzhaft* [protective custody] for seven months, has now been released and expelled, so that we have to leave the country within the next few days. As there is no other possibility of leaving available to us, we have signed up to a *Sammeltransport* [group transport], on which children under the age of ten years old are not permitted to be taken too. All our relatives here are, like us, on the point of emigrating, some of the initiatives for children, which take children of emigrants abroad, have been discontinued, some of them do not take children under the age of ten. My lad is however not quite eight years old.

And therefore I see myself facing the burning question of what I should do with him.

In this dilemma the thought came to me of you, Your Royal Highness, for you already have here amongst us the reputation, which surely every woman in the world envies you, the reputation of being a mother, not only to your own child, but mother in the absolute sense of the word.

For precisely this reason it is to Your Royal Highness that I now turn.

I enclose two pictures of my lad. For a long time his little face today has not been as round as in these pictures, but I am confident that it will once again be full and smiling like it was in those days, for I firmly believe that Your Royal Highness will want to help him.

It is surely unnecessary to describe to Your Royal Highness what I feel at the thought of having to leave the country with my husband without the possibility of returning, and to leave the child, who is our only one, here with strangers, without knowing how and when I can have him back. Your Royal Highness will be able to understand my feelings so well, that I feel that there is no need to draw out this already interminable letter even more.

At the same time neither do I want to dwell on the scale of the gratitude which my husband and I would show to Your Royal Highness, if you were to help our child to leave, and later, when we have settled somewhere, to return to us. The prospect of our gratitude is surely the last thing that will determine the actions of Your Royal Highness.

I am in no doubt at all about what Your Royal Highness will do.

The only concern which I have is that this letter reaches the hands of Your Royal Highness.

P. S. I am sending this letter through a friend who is travelling through the Netherlands, because this way of dispatch seems to me the most reliable.

B. 263 26th December 1938

The *Haagsche Comité voor hulp aan buitenlandsche kinderen* [Hague Committee for Aid to Foreign Children] informs me that it has written to you, as you may be good enough to find accommodation for my daughter, and I beg you to find somewhere for my daughter Eleonora to stay where she will do well, as we have to be away from here in the middle of January at the latest.

My husband committed suicide last month and we must leave although we were born in Vienna and brought up here, because I am Czech through marriage.

The local *Kultusgemeinde* [Jewish community] only helps German children and I would not know where to go if no help came by then, as we do not speak Czech, have no friends and no means in the Czechoslovak Republic.

My daughter attends three *Mittelschule* [grammar school] classes and is a well-behaved and good natured child, well-accomplished, speaks English and French, plays the piano and has nimble fingers.

Please help the girl most urgently, and I hope for favourable news soon.

B. 264 Ref.

6th January 1939

... I have returned after six weeks in *Schutzhaft* [protective custody] in Dachau and must shortly leave the country. In the past you have kindly promised me your support in finding accommodation for my children in Holland. Now many Viennese children have recently already had the luck to reach Holland on such transports; as I am dreadfully worried about leaving here without knowing that the children are provided for, I allow myself once more to avail myself of your kindness and to ask you to help me find accommodation for my children.

I myself cannot take the children with me as little choice remains to me about the destination in the short time available to me, and I am even having to settle for unpleasant overseas countries. I must unfortunately also separate from my wife, as on the one hand she cannot come to decisions for herself whilst the children are not provided for, and on the other hand the costs themselves in such undesirable overseas countries are so great, that there is not enough for me and my wife...

B. 265 Ref.

21st November 1938

... In the meantime I have again received terrible appeals for help from the X. family. They write to me that the father of the two children who have already been requested by me was seriously mistreated during the pogrom despite his serious illness (heart disease). The home has been completely vandalised and the people have nothing more to eat, so that it is a matter of very great urgency to get the children away from there.

The mother was for roughly 20 years the *Vorsitzende* [chairwoman] of a Jewish welfare association and has done endless good for the poor and the sick, so that this family really deserves that now it too will be helped for once...

B. 266 Ref.

November 1938

Would ask hereby and enquire whether a possibility exists to accommodate my son in Holland. Have been a widow for eleven years, have only the one child who I have brought up with difficulty. Have now suffered a nervous breakdown a few days ago due to anxiety, have absolutely no relatives here who would look after me. Am now homeless and in great distress, I cannot watch the way my child must starve, and am close to despair with the child. He is, thank God, a healthy and strong boy, if you wish I can send a picture and a testimonial from the Jewish school...

B. 267 Ref.

16th November 1938

I would very much like to have my niece, Ellen S., 15 years old, in Holland, whose father and mother are living in hiding in Cologne as their own home has been completely destroyed as well as that of the mother-in-law in D. It goes without saying that I will be responsible for everything...

B. 268 Ref. (Hanover)

20th November 1938

The child, a girl of ten years, has had a nervous breakdown. She is living with strangers. It was at school, when the looting began. The school children were all taken to the schoolyard in groups, and the biggest had to help. Whilst doing this the child began to scream and to shout, "I want to go to my *Mutti* [Mummy]", to which the answer was given, "You won't see your mother again, she has already been hanged." That was not true, she had only been arrested. The child was then put on a train to Hamburg where she wandered around until she was found the following morning...

B. 269 Ref. Frankfurt am Main

16th November 1938

I hereby beseech you to procure as quickly as possible the *Einreiseerlaubnis* [entry permit] for the following two children of four and five years of age. The father of both children, who was a doctor in F., has been under arrest since 10th November. The mother is seriously ill with pneumonia so that the children are not being looked after at all...

B. 270 Ref.

21st November 1938

May I urgently request your intervention for admission of the minor J. L., born 30 April 1923 and thus not yet 16 years old. He has already been taken prisoner and then set free again because he was not yet 16 years old. As soon as he is older, however, he will be taken prisoner again, because they cannot imprison his father, who was 100% invalided in the war...

B. 271 Ref.

November 1938

Moreover, my attention was requested in the case of A. G., which is being handled through you. This boy is 16 years old but he appears so big and strongly built that he was taken to be an adult and was transferred to a concentration camp. His family, who are naturally in great distress, have told the family in Amsterdam dreadful tales about this. Would it be possible, through channels known to you, to promote the claim that this child receives priority in connection with the moral and physical ordeal to which he is exposed?

B. 272 Ref.

14th November 1938

The undersigned requests permission for the children of members of her family living in Germany to be allowed to come to Holland, a girl of 13 and a boy of 10 years.

Both children find themselves in direct mortal danger, their parents' home was completely destroyed so they no longer have a place to stay.

B. 273 Ref. in Rhineland [now North Rhine-Westphalia]

14th November 1938

I herewith request your co-operation in accommodating two children, a boy of 14 and a girl of 11 years.

The father is an 80% war invalid and now arrested, and the mother is a mental case after caring for her husband all these years. The three people are now entirely without income ...

B. 274 Ref. in Westphalia

22nd November 1938

I am turning to you with the following case, as tragic as it is urgent, with the plea for help. It concerns my two nephews aged 16 and 12, who lived in A. until the days of the pogrom. The children's father was arrested some weeks ago. During the most recent events the elder boy was also taken away – no one knows where – the younger suffered mistreatment. The mother has been in hospital since the pogrom and Hans is staying with strangers. The home has been completely destroyed. The family with whom the boy is staying are going to emigrate in the near future.

B. 275 Ref. Neuwied

7th January 1939

In response to your letter of 4th inst. I inform you that I am willing to take in the two C. children ... May I ask you to handle the case as quickly as possible, as the 15-year-old boy has already been arrested twice and taken to prison ...

B. 276 Ref. Brilon

5th January 1939

... The boy is from my husband's first marriage; his mother was Catholic, but is now dead. The boy, who was also previously Catholic, has been living for two and a half years in the *Israelitisches Kinderheim* [Jewish children's home] in K., where my husband had him become a Jew. Since there is no Jewish school in my home town, the boy remained in the home, particularly as he was continually threatened in the street when he spent the holidays here. After my husband became unemployed we could no longer pay for the boy, and so the *Direktor* [Director] sent the boy to me with no regard for my impoverished situation; I do not even have anywhere for the boy to sleep, as I have already sold furniture in order to be able to live. The means of the small Jewish *Gemeinde* [community] have been completely exhausted and the relevant welfare offices provide in the first instance for old and sick people and are overstretched ...

For our boy unfortunately there now exists the danger of intimidation on the street, as everyone here knows that he was previously Catholic ...

B. 277 From Moers

29th December 1938

Dear Paul,

After I described my desperate situation so often to you now already, I am waiting with the greatest impatience for a conclusive answer. You know that in the very near future I shall no longer have a roof over my head. What will happen then? I know no other way apart from that. It is extremely urgent that the children and myself are provided for. Why do other children get away? I have been alone now for a year and a half with the three children and see no help from any quarter. You are there and there will probably be a way that for our children departure becomes possible too. The position is certainly urgent, and there is nobody here who can help me. Go immediately to the *Comité* once again and report my plight there. What otherwise will happen, I no longer know.

In great despair

B. 278 Ref. in Westphalia

18th November 1938

It concerns a nephew and two nieces of 13, 11 and 7 years...
The parents of the three children named here are living in Menden in Westph. (Iserlohn district); these two households are the only Jewish families in Menden, where it appears that dreadful things have happened in Germany, from notices and reports of the recent events gathered in the daily newspapers.

The shops with associated homes of both families have been completely destroyed. The fathers of the named children have disappeared and probably ended up in concentration camps or indeed were subjected to an even worse fate.

The surviving members of both the families referred to are at present together in one room, where the grandfather, who was seriously mistreated, is in bed. Both families have no food at all and the lack causes them the greatest distress. The source of income of both families has ceased to exist...

B. 279 Ref.

17th November 1938

With reference to my conversation with you, I am passing on to you in the attached the necessary details about the mother of the three children from M. I have learned that the father, who was a *Rechtsanwalt* [lawyer], is in the Dachau concentration camp, and that the mother is in hiding since she too is being sought by the Gestapo. At present the children are with neighbours, where however they can also no longer stay. My relatives want to try to cross the Dutch border tomorrow with the children. The children have been provided with *Kinderausweisen* [children's identity cards].

In M. there is no one else who is able to take care of the children. The grandparents have taken their own lives, at our relatives in Frankfurt all the men have also been arrested, the women themselves are helpless. The children are unprovided for, and there remains only the street for them, whereas here in Holland people are ready to take the children in and to look after them ... (twins of eleven years, girls and a boy of 13 years).

B. 280 Ref. Dresden

17th November 1938

... The name of the child is ... born May 1924. Their father was arrested during the night of Wednesday to Thursday, the 9th/10th November, with no explanation – whereabouts unknown. He ran a knitwear factory which he had sold and the proceeds of which have been confiscated. The mother to whom I have spoken myself was, as it appeared to me, mentally so upset by what has happened, that she is not in a position to look after her child. As I hear it, she is without any financial means ...

B. 281 Ref. Hamburg

14th November 1938

My brother, 16 years old, was also taken into custody during the *Verhaftungsaktion* [arrests operation], set free again because of his age, however, and was then supposed to be taken again despite this. Consequently a terrible danger exists, especially as my elderly father has a nervous disorder and suffers from convulsions (St Vitus' Dance). A re-arrest could cause my father's death ...

B. 282 Ref. Hamburg

... Father has been arrested. His large cattle trading business is closed. Mother is working as a maid in Hamburg. The child is alone with its 86-year-old grandfather who does not have enough to eat himself. The parents were rich people with a good name and a good business...

B. 283 Ref.

19th November 1938

... Father is in captivity, mother incurably ill, child without means ...

B. 284 Ref.

5th January 1939

... The lady who accepted my application confirmed to me that the application for a permit will be forwarded to The Hague immediately, especially as the boy's father was very ill in hospital for 16 weeks and the Gestapo checked up on him daily after he came home from hospital, exactly during the stormy days of the German events of November, to establish whether his condition allowed detention. The 10-year-old boy had to witness this...

B. 285 Ref.

17th November 1938

I urgently request herewith an *Einreiseerlaubnis* [entry permit] for Rita M., 13 years old. According to a letter from the rabbi the father has been picked up, the mother [is] without means and the child herself at serious risk on health grounds.

B. 286 Ref. Vienna

24th November 1938

... Parents of the girl have been put out on the street and are homeless, in addition mistreated...

B. 287 Re.

1st December 1938

Concerned about the fate of German children, we the undersigned request Your Excellency to permit Lotte and Ursel H., 12 and 10 years old respectively, to reside in the Netherlands, as these children find themselves in the most extremely difficult circumstances on account of their faith. Their father has already been on remand for more than a year and a half, whilst their mother does not want to leave him alone in Germany...

B. 288 Ref. Munich

17th November 1938

... Father arrested, presumed in Dachau. Mother had to flee from Munich, current whereabouts unknown. The child is living at home without any means, left to his own devices. His former Jewish *Lehrlingsausbildungsstätte* [apprentice training centre] has been destroyed.

B. 289 Ref. Hamburg

16th November 1938

With reference to the telephone conversation of yesterday evening I am requesting that you take urgent steps to obtain an *Aufenthaltserlaubnis* [residence permit] for Ruth N. (11 years old), whose father has been dead for years and whose mother has been arrested, whilst all the furniture in the home has been destroyed.

B. 290 Ref. Düsseldorf

22nd November 1938

... In Düsseldorf two children are completely unsupervised since the father is in the concentration camp and the mother is seriously ill in hospital. The girl is ten years old, the boy seven years old.

Hitler speaking at the Nazi party rally in Nuremberg, 1935

Jewish communities in the German Reich, 1933

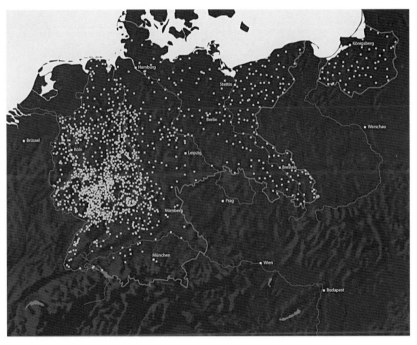

Towns in Greater German Reich and the Free City of Danzig where synagogues and Jewish prayer rooms were destroyed in November 1938

B.48.   Amsterdam, den 24. November 1938.

Bericht aus Frankfurt am Main.

Die freien Aerzte sind verhaftet worden, dagegen wurden in den beiden Krankenhäusern alle Aerzte belassen. Nur der Ohrenspezialist Dr. Meyer im Krankenhaus Gagernstrasse wurde verhaftet. Der Direktor des Krankenhauses Gagernstrasse, Dr. Rosenthal, hat aus Furcht vor Verhaftung Selbstmord durch Vergiftung begangen.

Im Rothschild-Hospital sind weiterhin tätig: Dr. Schnerb, Dr. Löwenthal, Dr. Rosenbaum und Dr. Merxbach.

Verbrannt wurden die Synagogen Friedberger Anlage, Börneplatz, Börnestrasse, Liebigstrasse. Da das Feuer in der Synagoge Friedberger Anlage zunächst nur begrenzten Schaden anrichtete, wurde auch an den folgenden Tagen, insgesamt viermal, erneut der Brand unter Benutzung von Benzinfässern und dergleichen entfacht, wodurch der Volksmenge wiederholt ein Schaustück bereitet wurde.

Nachdem die Inneneinrichtung der Synagoge ausgebrannt war, wurde die Gemeinde von der Polizei aufgefordert, wegen Einsturzgefahr die Gebäude auf eigene Kosten abzubrechen. Mit dem Abbruch Friedberger Anlage wurde sofort am 17. November begonnen.

Die Polizei hat nachträglich die Juden selbst der Brandstiftung an den Synagogen verdächtigt und eine dementsprechende formale Strafanzeige erlassen.

Der Tresor mit den silbernen Kultgegenständen in der Synagoge Friedberger Anlage ist am Tage nach dem ersten Brand aufgeschweisst und seines Inhaltes beraubt worden.

Am Donnerstag, den 10. November, wurden in Frankfurt auch viele alte Leute und Frauen verhaftet und nach der grossen Festhalle verbracht. Dort wurden sie bis Freitag Nachmittag ohne Schlafgelegenheit und meistens ohne Sitzgelegenheit belassen. Dann wurden die Leute über 60 Jahre, sowie die Frauen entlassen.

Die in Frankfurt Verhafteten befinden sich zu einem grossen Teil im Lager Buchenwald, von wo sie eine vorgedruckte Karte an ihre Angehörigen gesandt haben, zum andern Teil im Lager Dachau. Der inzwischen durch Intervention des czechoslovakischen Konsuls wieder entlassene Rabbiner der Israelitischen Religionsgemeinde, Rabbiner Horovitz, war die 8 Tage über nur im Polizeigefängnis Frankfurt am Main.

Rabbiner Jos. Horovitz (früher
Frankfurt.
Scheveningen. Haagsche Str. 25
Eu Weinberger
und Tochter (same address)

©2005 Wiener Library, London.
Private reports on Jews in Germany
Document Reference: 046-EA-0450

November Pogrom
Eyewitness report B.48

The CV Zeitung, newspaper
organ of the Association of
German Citizens of Jewish
Faith, 2 February 1933

German Jews waiting to obtain an emigration visa. Berlin, 1933–1939

The Zbąszyń displaced persons waiting at a soup kitchen, Poland, November 1938

Jews made to clean pavements in Vienna on 13 March 1938

Czechoslovak-Jewish refugees expelled by the Germans from the Sudeten territories of Porlitz and Koslitz, 26 October 1938

A Jew with a non-Jewish wife humiliated by SA troops who consider that this marriage has tarnished German honour

Shopfront of a cafe and beerhall defaced with antisemitic slogans in Vienna in 1938

Demolished shoe shop in a street in Vienna after the November Pogrom on 10 November 1938

Herschel Grynszpan surrounded by policemen after his first interrogation at police headquarters. Paris, 7 November 1938

A crowd watches the burning synagogue in Graz, set on fire by Nazis in March 1938

A wrecked shop belonging to Jews living in the Rhineland, 10 November 1938

Devastated interior of a Munich synagogue after 'Kristallnacht'
in November 1938

Jews arrested during the November Pogrom line up for roll call at Buchenwald concentration camp, November 1938

Slave labourers from Sachsenhausen concentration camp at work in the 'Klinkerwerk Oranienburg' in 1940

*Destination zones of Jewish emigration from Germany and Austria
through Jewish agencies, April 1933 to June 1939*

*Mrs Krampflecek, a
91-year-old refugee
from Vienna arrives
at Croydon airport,
31 March 1939*

Jewish refugee children travelling from Berlin shortly after they crossed the German/Dutch border, 1st or 2nd December 1938

Jewish refugees from Germany boarding a boat for England, 2 December 1938

JEWISH

AFFAIRS

Published by
THE INSTITUTE OF JEWISH AFFAIRS
330 West Forty-second Street
New York, N. Y.

| VOL. I, NO. 4 | NOVEMEER, 1941 | TEN CENTS |

Projects for Jewish Mass Colonization

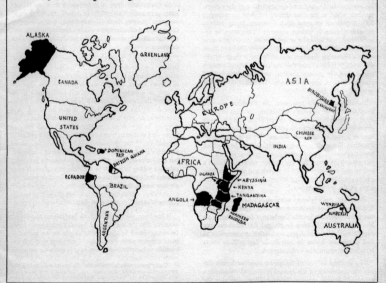

THE INSTITUTE OF JEWISH AFFAIRS, sponsored by the American Jewish Congress and the World Jewish Congress, is a research body engaged in investigating Jewish life during the past 25 years with a view to establishing the facts of the present situation, determining its direct and indirect causes, and suggesting lines on which Jewish rights may be claimed at the end of the present war.

Director: Jacob Robinson; Research Fellows: Jacob Lestchinsky, Arieh Tartakower, Max Laserson.

JEWISH AFFAIRS is published monthly. Each number is devoted to the Jewish aspects of a current issue.

Excerpts may be reproduced in any form, provided that the source is acknowledged.

Jewish Affairs, Vol. 1, No 4, November 1941

*Members of the Jewish Central Information Office staff in
Amsterdam, c. 1938; Margarethe and Alfred Wiener on far left*

B. 291 Ref. Floss, Upper Palatinate

14th November 1938

Herewith I request most respectfully to make it possible for my little niece, 13 years old, to come here as soon as possible. Since her mother was divorced without blame, the child has been living with her grandparents in a small village in the Upper Palatinate. Until May 1938 she was in W. at the *Lyceum* [secondary school], however was not allowed to remain there any longer. She then went to the Jewish school in F. and lived in the *Israelitisches Mädchenstift* [home for Jewish girls] in N. On 10th November the *Mädchenstift* was utterly destroyed and the children driven away. Today I have finally learned that the child is with her grandparents once again. But the child cannot remain in this small village either, in which only three Jewish families live, and probably has to suffer poverty like her grandparents and her mother...

B. 292 From a questionnaire

29th November 1938

The child, a girl of seven years, lost both parents in Barcelona in August 1936 in a tragic manner so is a complete orphan.

She lives with her grandmother who fled with the child at that time. A placement abroad is urgently required, especially as the economic circumstances are also very poor. The grandmother draws welfare support in Germany...

B. 293 Ref. Erlangen

19th November 1938

... It concerns Max F., b. 6th January 1924. The father is dead. The mother, whose home was completely wrecked, and was herself arrested with the boy for several days, is living in hiding with the child with some old friends in Nuremberg. I pay for everything for the boy who is my wife's brother and whose nerves have suffered greatly.

More details about Arthur H., b. 1922. The father, 65 years

old, is in a concentration camp. The whereabouts of the mother are unknown. The flat or rather the building has been completely wrecked. As the boy is a wanted person he is living in hiding in S. with two single 70-year-old ladies, his father's sisters. His mental state has also suffered to such an extent that if help is not granted soon to the two children the worst is to be feared...

B. 294 Ref. Bochum
          17th January 1939
          ... I have a favour to ask, to accommodate my cousin's son, since I unfortunately cannot put him up, in Amsterdam if possible, and namely for the following reasons:
          The boy's father was released from the concentration camp on 17th December, had to go straight into hospital and on 23rd December died as a result of blood poisoning from frostbitten hands. He was in business with my father for 20 years and lived with my parents during this time so that he was more a brother than a cousin to me. It is therefore quite natural that the well-being of this boy, whose mother has to wait for emigration in Germany, is close to my heart. If he were now to be accommodated in Amsterdam I could do one or two things for him, above all continually report to the mother about her son...

B. 295 Ref. Kempen in Rhineland [now North Rhine-Westphalia]
          18th November 1938
          Would like to ask you most politely to take the following children into your protection, the father finds himself in a concentration camp, not known where, the home has been destroyed, the grandfather, 76 years, in prison, left behind mother and children and mentally ill grandmother...

B. 296 Report on the events in Graz on 10th November 1938
          In Graz the formerly esteemed and generally popular senior

rabbi, university professor and historian was taken from his bed at an early hour, dragged by his beard to the cemetery, was ordered to dig his own grave there; he was left there in the most appalling state.

The well-known Graz furniture dealer *Kommerzialrat* [commercial councillor] X., earlier president of the Graz *Kultusgemeinde* [Jewish community], was taken from his home in underwear during the night, beaten beyond recognition, was left lying in a pool of blood; he was so disfigured that his own wife was unable to recognise him.

Girls from the better Jewish households were driven in *Schubwagen* [bogies] to the river Mur where they were all ordered to jump into the water. The girls were driven half mad by the torture.

B. 297 Report by X. on his three-month detention in Oranienburg [Sachsenhausen] concentration camp.

X., who had sought to cross the Belgian-German border illegally on foot, was stopped by the customs authorities on 13th November and was taken to Oranienburg, together with five other Jews who had undertaken the same attempt, where he was held for three months and only released on the grounds of an *Einreisemöglichkeit* [entry permit] to England. X., previously a very dashing young man, looks wretched, is suffering from nervous tics and has a frostbitten right hand as a visual reminder of the treatment in the camp.

In the camp, in which 6,000 Jews and 8,000 Aryans, of whom 3,000 were so-called "*Asozialen*" [Asocials], activities consisted of work from 7 o'clock in the morning until 6 o'clock in the evening with a single lunch break of only twenty minutes, at which the meagre food had to be consumed standing up. Particular prisoners also had to stay outside the barracks at night, they were required for *Stehrapport*, [reporting to inspection rounds], therefore had no opportunity to have the evening meal, which was handed out inside the barracks and was not allowed to be put aside, and were therefore reliant on the charity of their fellow sufferers, who saved the rest of their evening meals for them.

Work, which consisted of carrying rocks and cement, always had to be done at the double. Disregard of the running speed resulted in severe mistreatment. Many times it happened that Jews were first severely beaten and then pushed into cement pits and "packed" in cement. The victims of this mistreatment were usually always the same prisoners who were treated aggressively by their brutal guards, whereas others often remained unmolested for months. E.g. X. was only once hit on the head.

The accommodation was quite good, in free time prisoners were permitted to smoke. Food was very scarce, prisoners sometimes only received the money that had been sent to them once a month.

The exercise of speaking in unison was very popular, such as one, the meaning of which sounded like: "We are criminals, we have the murder of the German diplomat vom Rath on our consciences!" Those who did not shout this phrase loud enough had to repeat it outside the line.

Medical treatment was very deficient, most deaths occurred from pneumonia and frailty, each day one could observe the removal of one to two black coffins. It also happened that a prisoner who had fallen into bed exhausted in the evening was no longer alive in the morning. The case of one Jew was extremely tragic, who died of a heart attack at the exact moment that he should have left the camp.

Amongst those still located in the camp is the Vienna writer Hans K. who was arrested immediately after the turmoil because of his Jewish-monarchist activities, and who has already been in Dachau and Buchenwald. The disposition amongst the Aryans is decidedly Communist.

B. 298 20th March 1939

Once again the Germans have thought up new atrocities against the Jews. I can cite the following factual report as one who was affected by the events.

On 10th November 1938 my family and I were startled from our sleep at half past 5 by continuous ringing and banging on the door, and it was demanded that we opened it. I was arrested and had to go along immediately. This operation was carried out by an SA *Obersturmbannführer* [Lieutenant Colonel] and a *Hitler-Junge* [Hitler Youth] who was perhaps 15 years old. I was not given any time to dress and so I could only go along scantily clothed. At least I still had something to cover my body. One Jew appeared in nightshirt, another in dressing gown and a third came barefoot.

I was taken to the gymnasium of a school were Jews had already been brought since c. 2 o'clock in the morning. I was received there by police, SA and SS men, all of whom excelled at striking and mistreating us with all possible beating devices such as bullwhips, whips and sticks. I myself got nothing, thank God, apart from some kicks so that I could hardly walk. But the picture that presented itself to me was terrible. Only the blood of poor, wounded people sprays in such a way, and the terrible screams of pain of those who had been struck were nerve-wracking. After the beasts had staunched their sadistic lust we were ordered to knee-bend with arms raised, face to the wall so that they could shoot us. Moreover, what was about to happen was all the same to me. Now a new hail of beatings was deployed and blood sprayed about in such a way that my coat was completely spattered with the blood of other Jews. I was lucky again in this situation too, I received nothing, perhaps because someone amongst them wished me well.

After this *Aktion* [operation] we had to line up in rows and shout "*Juda verrecke!*" [perish Judah] aloud three times.

Subsequently we were loaded into cars and brought to Buchenwald concentration camp near Weimar, where we were also received with mistreatment. It was quarter to 7.

Two Jews were beaten so badly in the gymnasium that they could not be transported: they had to be taken to the hospital. One of them is still unable to walk today, on 20th March 1939.

On the *Appellplatz* [parade ground] of the camp, at the command "*Stillgestanden!*" [Attention!] we had to stand for twelve hours, albeit people aged up to 79 were there. These beasts of hangman's assistants do not have a human heart whatsoever. In front of me stood a man of 69 years who had been hit on the top of the skull and had blood flowing down him. Although he lost consciousness he was not removed but still kicked and further roared at, whether the *Schwein* [pig] did not want to *verrecken* [perish]. As if by a miracle this man has now become healthy again.

We Jews had a particular place in the camp and did not come into contact with the other miserable prisoners, who at that point had already been robbed of six years of their freedom. We were almost 11,000 people and were accommodated in five barracks without straw and without blankets. The sparsely clothed were naturally very cold but we were given extra stuff by the others who were there.

For 48 hours those beasts had given us no food or drink and the treatment was terrible. The worst night was the night from the first Sunday to Monday, when some were battered to death.

I observed the following case: I lay by the window whilst the guards thrashed a man until he fell lifeless: next they dragged him by the legs across the *Appellplatz* and kept beating him until he disappeared from my view. What became of him and who it was, I do not know.

The strangest thing however, is that from that night onwards, no SS man or guard was allowed to enter our camp and we finally had peace. Discipline was maintained by us Jews ourselves.

The sanitary facilities were indescribable, at first we only had one latrine for the many people, eventually one more was built later. There was absolutely no water for washing or drinking. I was there for four weeks, and one can imagine what condition one found oneself in. Because of the muddy ground the soles of the shoes of many rotted, mine included, and each day was a further agony.

At our release these brutes took their anger out on us once more, in that they insulted us with foul language, and we first breathed a sigh of relief when we reached the other side of the camp boundary. We thought wistfully of the others who had remained behind, whose suffering first began when the terrible cold set in a few days later.

Unfortunately many Jews died there because they did not receive proper medical treatment, medication was lacking, and the smallest cold could bring death. Thus did one of my best friends die, who had caught a bladder infection and went down from it.

B. 299 In Germany when one wants to emigrate one must make an exact inventory of the things in order to bring one's belongings. Each handkerchief, each pair of stockings, every single item has to be stated and classified as specified, 1) before 1933, 2) 1933–1939 and 3) required for the purposes of emigration. This list has to be submitted to the *Zollfahndungsstelle* [customs investigation office]. It passes the list on to the *Devisenstelle* [foreign currency office] and it gives the *Zollfahndungsstelle* the *Genehmigung* [permit] to be checked.

We were investigated by a very mean official. Amongst other things he remarked, "It's not our fault that you have to pay money for this, but the Jews are renown for getting away with it." Then he told us that all these measures only existed because our pressure from outside is so strong. At the end he advised us to leave Germany as quickly as possible, as this was not the final operation.

Of my wife's jewellery, a diamond ring and a pearl necklace were confiscated, which had to be taxed immediately and then deposited in the safe of the Dresdner Bank. The tax turned out to be very low and was actually only RM. 850.-; their actual worth was about two and a half thousand. Later, the same jewellery had to be offered for sale to a pawnbroker and he only paid us RM. 315.-. An unprecedented robbery. We were still in luck, we could still keep our silver as well as a few gold trinkets. However, if our luggage had been dispatched 24 hours later then we would have been forced to open our cases once again.

Naturally there is a lot of complaining everywhere that all our valuables are being stolen, as silver fetches hardly anything and inherited things are not allowed to be kept.

Some of the Aryans are not in agreement with it, but they cannot help us. Fear of punishment, which is not insignificant, leaves even the most decent characters silent. Several of my good Aryan friends cried and begged us not to think so badly of all Germans.

The newest harassment is that in Germany one is not allowed into either the restaurant carriage or the sleeper carriage. However, this is not permitted to be communicated in the Jewish press but has to be passed on by word of mouth.

At the beginning of March this year the Jewry in our town was once again put in fear and harassment by the Gestapo. At half past 9 in the evening a larger fraction of the Jews was ordered by the police to go to the Gestapo immediately. One can imagine the people's fear, and what was the outcome? A mass deportation to Shanghai would take place and people were already selected for this. The rich Jews were forced to sign, and in fact these were not inconsiderable amounts; if these were insufficient, the official threatened that other means would be invoked. In the meantime, however, nothing has come of it. Yet once again the people are without their money.

B. 300 Fatalities in concentration camps

In the following report reference will be made solely to the victims of the *Juni-Aktion* [June operation] and the *November-pogrom*.

1. The operation of 13th June seized so-called previously convicted Jews. The order of the *Reichskriminalamt* [Reich Criminal Investigation Office], which carried out the operation at the instigation of the *Reichsführer SS* [National Leader of the SS, i.e. Heinrich Himmler], states "All Jews who were punished with a prison sentence of longer than one month or a fine, for the non-payment of which a prison sentence of longer than one month was imposed, arrested and brought to a concentration camp without questioning." More than 2,000 Jews were arrested

simultaneously across the whole of Germany. Of these around 900 came to Sachsenhausen, the rest to Buchenwald. At the same time thousands of *asoziale* [asocial] elements of Aryan descent and gypsies were arrested across the whole of Germany and brought to the same camps. The purpose of the operation was to place pressure on the Jews to emigrate, but at the same time these many thousands were necessary for the construction of both concentration camps, and hence also these arrests doubtless occurred.

The treatment of the more than 2,000 Jews arrested in June is not comparable to the treatment of at least 30,000 *Aktionsjuden* [operation Jews] arrested in November. The victims of the June operation were treated incomparably awfully, and the percentage of dead was far higher than in November.

During June Jews in both camps were worked to death with agonising, pointless labour. They collapsed and died in the heat, during work performed at the double, under the ban on drinking water – in Buchenwald a water shortage prevailed, in Sachsenhausen it was risk of dysentry A smaller proportion was "auf der Flucht erschossen" [shot whilst escaping]. The SS guards of both camps had not experienced Jews in such numbers before. Now they believed they were permitted to indulge their shooting fury. Those shot in June were shot down without reason. People were sought out as victims who were "noticeable". Thus e.g. in Buchenwald the somewhat mentally backward young businessman Wystiniecki was shot down in a quarry by two SS guards; when he still showed signs of life whilst lying on the ground, he was shot again. In Sachsenhausen the sport "Rollen" [rolling] was practised; during their work, prisoners were not allowed to cross a line marked by small flags. Prospective victims were made to walk to the top of a hill and were commanded to "lie down and roll". Those made to roll had to brake their bodies before the flag boundary. Vigorous individuals succeeded as long as they had not become dizzy. To induce dizziness, the procedure of walking up and rolling down the hill was repeated x-times, until the rolling body rolled over the flag boundary; then they were shot.

In Sachsenhausen, 90 of the 900 victims of the *Juni-Aktion* died from illness, over-exertion and shooting.

The killings ceased at the end of August 1938. Instructions may have been issued to discontinue arbitrary shootings. The source of these instructions is not apparent. Possibly from publications in the foreign press, which carried truthful reports.

At the 1938 Party conference, Dr. [Joseph] Goebbels inveighed against English newspapers, in particular the *News Chronicle*, which had painted a truthful picture of events in the camps. He said, almost word for word: "The unfortunates had to work from 4 in the morning until 8 at night – and this is why they died." (Derisive cheering.) The working hours of both camps were not given correctly, however.

2. In relation to the *Novemberaktion* [November operation] no prisoners were shot in Sachsenhausen camp, aside from the 25-year-old prisoner Dammann, who shot himself through fear of punishment for deliberately bribing a *Vorarbeiter* [foreman].

The number of fatalities in Sachsenhausen itself could be 80 or 90 (total number of inmates 6,000). Causes of death are: 1. over-exertion, 2. ending of usual medical treatment and medicines, and stoppage of diet, 3. septic illnesses, 4. consequences of frost and pneumonia.

Died in Sachsenhausen, amongst others:

1. Businessman Schmierer from Berlin
2. Businessman Reich from Schneidemühl [now Pol. Piła], aged over 60, from pneumonia
3. Dr. Robert Meyer from Berlin
4. Businessman Rosenthal from Gevelsberg (Westphalia), perforated stomach ulcer
5. Abattoir owner Marx from Westphalia, heart attack
6. Dammann, Berlin, 25 years old, suicide by shooting.

Died in Buchenwald, amongst others:

1. Warschauer from Berlin, 25 years old, pneumonia

The number who died in Buchenwald camp is so monstrously large that it must almost be cast in doubt: it was given as 550 by a very reliable source. This is the number allegedly given by those employed in the office.

Numerous prisoners died immediately after release or during the course of an agonising and lingering illness:

1. Businessman Herzberg from Schönlanke [now Pol. Trzcianka], (consequences of frost), around 60 years old, prisoner in Sachsenhausen

2. Hotel owner Ohrenstein from Harzburg (pneumonia), severe mistreatment in Harzburg before deportation to the camp, about 60 years old, prisoner in Buchenwald.

3. *Rechtsanwalt* [lawyer] Martin Ehrlich from Gleiwitz [now Pol. Gliwice], about 50 years old, prisoner in Buchenwald.

B. 301 As a result of the arrests in connection with the pogrom on 10 November 1938 and detention in concentration camps the Jewish *Gemeinde* [community] in Hamburg has lost the lives of about ten people. Known, with names, are:

1. Otto Sussmann, bank employee, previously with the Warburg firm, about 40 years old, married, father of two children, died in Sachsenhausen concentration camp of pneumonia

2. Le[e]ser, bank employee, formerly with the Warburg firm, age about 50 years

3. Rosenthal, businessman, age about 50 years

4. Fränkel, businessman, age about 40 years.

B. 302 21st March 1939

Louis ten Brink, born 25 April 1874 in Emlichheim, arrived illegally in Holland on 20 December 1938 in order to stay here. Despite the *Comité*'s advice he went back to Germany the next day because he did not want to leave his sister alone. From that time on he had to report to the police every day. After about three days he was arrested in Neuenhaus and did not return. Nothing was heard of his whereabouts. On 19th March 1939 the family heard from the police that he had died.

B. 303 Deaths in Sachsenhausen and Buchenwald concentration camps and after returning from the camps.

1. Dr. Ernst Feist-Wollheim, from the family of Caesar Wollheim, prisoner in Sachsenhausen, died in hospital after his return from the camp of sepsis and erysipelas [skin infection] as a result of frostbite. He had lost his sanity and any will to live. He left a wife behind.

2. Max Aronheim, formerly of Reetz [now Pol. Recz] in the Neumark [New March or East Brandenburg, now Pol. Nowa Marchia], grain merchant, married, died during his first days in Sachsenhausen allegedly of heart attack. His wife Lotte, née Adler, born in Stargard [now Pol. Szczeciński] in Pomerania, lost her sanity, was admitted to a sanatorium and committed suicide there. No children.

3. Karl Katz, cantor of Jastrow [now Pol. Jastrowie] *Gemeinde* [community] in the Grenzmark [Frontier March of Posen-West Prussia, now Pol. Marchia Graniczna Poznańsko-Zachodniopruska], c. 35 years old, died in the *Revier* [sick bay] in Sachsenhausen, allegedly of heart attack. He left behind his wife, two small children and his elderly father.

4. Jonas, Berlin, died of heart attack in Sachsenhausen.

5. Hermann Bacharach, b. 14th April 1859 in Rhina (Hesse), resident in Nordhausen, pensioner, died of heart attack 24th November in Buchenwald.

6. Kurt Seidemann, c. 40 years old (*Juni-Aktion* [June operation]) died in December 1938 of sepsis in Buchenwald. He was unmarried, from Berlin.

7. Pharmacist Michaelis, Berlin, died c. 50 years of age in Buchenwald (*Juni-Aktion*).

8. *Rechtsanwalt* [lawyer] Robert Meyer, *Syndikus* [legal adviser] of the Hertie department store A. G. (formerly Hermann Tietz), died in Sachsenhausen (*November-Aktion* [November operation]).

9. Horst Loewenberg, Berlin NO 55, Lippehnerstraße 24 (*Juni-Aktion*), unmarried, 22 years old, died on 2nd October 1938 in Buchenwald.

10. Heinz Blumenheim, Berlin-Wilmersdorf, Landhausstraße,

unmarried, c. 30 years of age (*Juni-Aktion*), died January 1939 in Buchenwald.

The individuals named here are buried in Berlin.

B. 304 On Thursday the 10th November I was arrested in the street early in the day by a *Wache* [civil guard] and taken to the nearest *Wachstube* [guard station] "to provide some information". It was quite clear to me what that meant, not only because the May/June arrests [*Juni-Aktion*], which had begun in exactly the same way, were still a terrible memory fresh in our minds, but also because the days shortly before the 10th November had been tense with fear and expectation as we waited to see how the government would react to the incident in Paris. Moreover, the artificially whipped-up and incited "*Volksstimme*" [voice of the people] did not bode well. I had to wait for a long time at the *Wachstube*, sitting alongside others who had also been taken, and we were taken under escort to the appropriate *Kommissariat* [police station].

A few hundred people were already gathered there in the courtyard of the building – it was around 11 o'clock in the morning – and here we were allowed to see our relatives for the last time, because I must stress that the Vienna police turned out to be exceptionally accommodating to the point, even, of disapproving of the whole *Aktion* [operation], something that would have a significant impact later on. So we received the odd affectionate gift from our relatives and were able to pass on important information to them.

For we had shared all our different experiences amongst one another: how one person had been taken from his place of work, another from his home, and a third from his office, or even from a train waiting to leave for a journey abroad, and how in the house-to-house searches, supposedly meant to uncover hidden weapons, everything of value that could be found, including jewellery, money, silver cutlery, cameras, typewriters etc. had been confiscated. So in this regard we were able to warn the women, if it was not already too late. It was to be the last conversation for a long time.

New prisoners kept arriving at the *Kommissariat* all the time. The stream was continuous until around 4 o'clock in the afternoon and only then came to an end, which led us to assume, rightly as it later transpired, that the *Aktion* had come to an end. In fact anyone who had not been admitted by this point or was captured later was freed shortly afterwards. We on the other hand stood around in the courtyard of the *Kommissariat* waiting to see what would happen. It was already 11 o'clock in the evening, by which time we had been standing there for 12 hours, before a group of us was taken in for questioning, then all of a sudden at midnight *SS-Verfügungstruppen* [SS combat support troops] (in grey military uniform with steel helmets) entered the building. We heard a series of brief commands and they prepared us to be taken away.

We were formed into separate units facing the wall, not without some blows and screaming, and driven away in buses. Climbing aboard the buses gave these fellows their first opportunity for a bit of fun – if they thought things were going too slowly they lashed out with crops and belts. Unfortunately it was the old and the sick who came off worst, just as they were also to become the main object of the sadistic excesses that were to follow.

Our journey took us to the IX. *Wiener Gemeindebezirk* [Vienna District IX], we thought our destination would be the central Vienna police prison on the Elisabethpromenade but instead we continued to the Pramergasse, also in district IX, to the *Polizeireitschule* [police riding school]. On leaving the bus we became victims once again of the same sweet little game that was played when we boarded; we entered an enormous complex of buildings and became aware of large groups of Jews from other districts of Vienna already lined up in formations. We had never seen such a large number of Jews in one place. We reckoned there must have been around 4,000 men, and then there were as many again on the aforementioned Elisabethpromenade, in the *Sofiensälen* (a huge Viennese entertainment establishment), even more in the Karajangasse (a *Notarrest* [emergency detention unit] set up in a school in the *Wiener Gemeindebezirk*), along with those from neighbouring provinces (Baden, Mödling etc.) sent to Vienna and held in the former *Bezirksgericht* [district court] in district VII. All in all a gigantic number.

We were also lined up in military file and stood there under guard for half the night to Friday 11th November and then all of Friday without being allowed to move a single step out of line, let alone being given a bite to eat. Towards evening the severe formations were relaxed, we were allowed to go to the toilet, could each buy a single *Semmel* [bread roll] from a baker who appeared, and were allowed to sleep on the ground. When you bear in mind that the *Semmel* was made of ground bark mixed with horse muck and similar ingredients, and that we still threw ourselves to the ground in unison as if following a command, just to get a bit of rest, then you can judge for yourself how exhausted everyone was, having already been on their feet for 36 hours.

Of course there was rumour upon rumour. Whilst someone claimed to have got "authentic information" from one guard, someone else had it from another – the first claimed we would be home within two days, the other already mentioned Dachau for the first time, but we could not believe that, we were innocent after all, we took him to be a pessimist. But how right they were, those who prophesied the worst.

As far as food was concerned nothing appeared – apart from that single *Semmel* – until the morning of Saturday the 12th November; this encouraged the optimists to be hopeful, since 48 hours had, of course, elapsed since our committal. Finally there was some movement in the crowd, we saw bread being distributed, but far too little for the mass of people there, which led to a crush of the kind you see at the feeding of a beast of prey's cage. Subsequently it transpired that the Vienna *Wache* had decided on its own that it could not face watching this inhumanity any longer and had handed over some of its own rations. Later, at the instigation of the *Wiener Israelitische Kultusgemeinde* [Vienna Jewish community], more bread was distributed, this time also to those who had not received any the first time.

One can hardly imagine the mood of the crowd, exhausted,

hungry, fearing the very worst, it is a miracle that people for the most part remained calm, although outbursts of hysteria and epileptic fits were the order of the day, leading one to believe that an outbreak of mass hysteria was imminent. This situation finally came to an end on Saturday towards the evening when they began to take us away.

We were piled into open military vehicles, each with two SS men sitting at one end with fixed bayonets, and it was made abundantly clear to us that an attempt to escape would be punished by being shot. The route went along the Ringstraße and Burgstraße into the Kenyongasse in district VII where we were delivered to a former convent school.

On getting down, screams, blows, lined up in the corridor facing the wall, then ordered to the fourth floor, a small room, undoubtedly former sleeping quarters of a holy sister, now completely bare. Aside from a single hysterical outburst by one colleague the night passed peacefully, on the hard floor of course.

Next day, Sunday the 13th November, there were a number of inspections and it looked as though the gentlemen concerned still had no idea what to commence with us. We had a premonition when we caught sight of people who had been dealt with by the SA at the *Kommissariat* Vienna district II, in the Ausstellungsstraße (which according to information from different sources was the worst place people were sent to in Vienna on the 10th November, O.H.); terrible evidence of how they had been "dealt with" included bleeding heads, emergency bandages, black eyes etc.

Sudden visit in the night to Monday the 14th November, everyone jumps up half asleep, the *Zimmerkommandant* [room commander] announces "43 men", receives a blow to the face of such force that he reels, he should have announced "43 Jews!" And now the order "*Wippen!*" [squats] begins. That went on for an hour. Anyone who did not do it exactly right was ordered out into the corridor and returned bleeding and covered with weals from the whip. Always accompanied by terrible screaming, we heard everything from the neighbouring rooms and it was much worse to have to listen to the screams of those being tortured than experiencing it oneself.

We were fortunate that in our narrow room there was not much opportunity for things to get out of hand, but next door there were larger classrooms and there sparks really flew. In one room in particular there was a rabbi in a caftan who seemed to attract the attention of these beasts more than anyone else. They beat him up completely, broke his teeth and both cheek bones, and fractured the base of his skull, the latter with their steel helmets and nothing was worse than having to listen to the noise they made and the wailing that accompanied it followed by a groaning. When we later caught sight of him in a spare moment his face was so swollen that we could barely identify any human features at all in the physical wreck that remained.

Insofar as an escalation was possible, then this disastrous room was also home to an even more unfortunate resident, a young man, something of a dreamer, who suddenly had the idea of going over to the teacher's desk and writing a poem of supplication on the blackboard, in which he proposed a reconciliation between the Jews and the NSDAP [Nazi Party]. This madman was caught in the act during an inspection and had his idea literally knocked on its head with such force he ended up dead on the floor.

Other deaths followed his, and from talking to others it was later possible to say with certainty that 20 dead would be no exaggeration, not least given that a number of people who committed suicide to put an end to their suffering had to be added to the list.

And *Wippen* over and over again. Anyone who could not keep going had a bucket of water poured over them and then it started again. In the short breaks we were allowed, during which we lay on the floor covered in sweat and with hearts thumping, the windows were thrown open in order to finish us off as quickly as possible.

Suddenly in the night the guard appeared and told the *Zimmerkommandant* that the guards wanted to have a good day and that all money should be handed over. If anyone was found to have any money left they would be shot. After what had happened we were in no doubt that they would be true to their word and handed over all our money, there were RM. 540.- in the room, so that we did not have a penny in Dachau.

Just like the night to Monday the 14th, the Monday proceeded with *Wippen* and torture. All the time terrible screams in the building, brutal blows, blood flowing, was this still human beings?

Finally, on Tuesday the 15th November it all seemed to come to an end and we were prepared for departure and had to pass through a hall with about 50 young officials seated at tables who interrogated us and had us sign a piece of paper that stated we were in effect willing to hand over all our possessions. Starving, 48 hours without a moment's quiet, the racket in the hall with the clattering of 50 typewriters, I had no idea what I was being asked and what I signed, it was a cunningly devised system to extort "confessions" and concessions.

We were then immediately put into police vehicles (known in Vienna as "*Grüne Heinrich*" [Green Henry]) and were taken to the Elisabethpromenade. Once again the optimists thought this was the end of our misery – how wrong.

We certainly received our first warm meal – soup and then beans and bread – sleeping standing up in the corridors because even in a building as substantial as this one there was no space to accommodate so many people in the cells, and then all of a sudden the SS beasts, whom we thought we had seen the last of, arrived on the scene and we knew that our ordeal would continue. We were again brought before a *Kommissar* [inspector] who had the details of our interrogation in the Kenyongasse in front of him and decided as he saw fit who should go to Dachau and who should go home.

In the meantime the inhuman treatment by the SS continued there too, you could hear the terrible sound of belt blows and the wailing of the victims coming from a special room.

I was selected for Dachau and arrived with my comrades at the Westbahnhof in a "*Grüne Heinrich*" on the 16th November at around 2 o'clock in the morning, where we had to run the SS gauntlet and were beaten again before being herded into cattle trucks. Here we spent the 16-hour journey, 70 men with nothing to eat or drink, not able to relieve ourselves, and arrived half suffocated in Dachau, and were luckier than those who had travelled under escort in passenger trains and who had been forced to stare into the light for the whole journey and subjected to inhuman beatings throughout. Many of them lost their sanity, jumped out of the windows and were "auf der Flucht erschossen" [shot whilst escaping].

Although it sounds absurd, for us inmates from Kenyongasse, Dachau (see attached sketch [missing]) was almost a relief after so many inhuman and unpredictable outrages. Because there were drills all the time and everything was organised according to a strict, pre-ordained set of rules. We were woken at 5 o'clock in the morning, by half past 5 everyone had to have washed, gone to the toilet and be lined up in formation ready for breakfast, and during this half hour a group, which changed weekly, also had to be responsible for tidying and washing the rooms, the bathrooms, the toilets and the passages.

After breakfast, consisting of a black drink which had nothing to do with coffee but at least was warm, we lined up in formations once again and the whole camp, Jews and Aryans, marched to the *Appellplatz* [parade ground] for the so-called *Zählappell* [roll call head count] which happened twice a day, morning and evening, and during which possible disappearances could be ascertained instantly. We arrived at the *Appellplatz* by a quarter to 8 in the morning and had to stand to attention for an hour until the *Rapportführer* [reporting officer] had informed the *Lagerkommandant* [camp commandant] of the current state of the camp and then, following the command "*Abrücken!*" [move out], we marched back in formation to our workplaces.

For us *Aktionsjuden* [operation Jews] work consisted of "*Exerzieren*" [punitive drill] and exercises until 12 o'clock, followed by lunch, consisting of vegetables with microscopic quantities of tinned meat, or rice with milk, or sago with milk, and a bread ration of a quarter of a loaf of *Kommissbrot* [army bread] per man per day which one had to divide up for oneself accordingly.

At 1 o'clock the lunch break was over and we marched, again in formation, to the *Appellplatz* to be allocated into work groups, whereby the Aryans were selected for work outside the camp under special guard. Following the allocation we Jews marched back to our barracks and carried out our "work", namely marching and exercises.

That continued until around 5 o'clock in the afternoon, at which time we had to present ourselves for the evening *Appell* [roll call] on the *Appellplatz*. By their very nature these *Appell* were the most unpleasant institution in the concentration camp. On arrival in Dachau we mostly had to hand over our clothes and shoes and in return were allocated army shoes, socks and a uniform made of cotton drill that was basically nothing more than a pair of pyjamas. We were also shorn, so when the rain and snow ran down our heads and shoulders during a roll call that had already lasted an hour and showed no sign of ending, and in bad weather we were obviously kept standing longer than when it was good, most of us reckoned we would not be able to survive this treatment for very long. Later, when the big frost set in before Christmas and the icy winds on the open *Appellplatz* blew right through you until you felt numbed to the bone, and then crawled away bent double with agonising pains all over, it looked like something out of Dante's *Inferno*.

One was happy to get back to one's bed – we slept on open straw covered with a flannel blanket – quickly ate supper, soup or sausage or cheese and lime blossom tea, washed out the bowl and lay down.

During this frost period the first consequences of the pitiless standing around in the open for hours began to be visible: everyone had hands and feet swollen from the frost; in many cases these blisters had burst and were the beginning of the end because they always got infected. In Dachau there were in fact two barracks for hospital treatment. But they were only for those with infectious diseases or a temperature of over 40 degrees;

with frostbite you only received out-patient treatment, by Aryan prisoners with nursing skills, and only between 3 and half past 4 o'clock in the afternoon.

When one considers that as the cold got worse 200 to 300 people sought treatment every day, and could only be treated during this short period by four *Sanitätsgehilfen* [medical orderlies], then one understands why no more than one in ten went there and the frostbite steadily got worse. In the end the *Sanitäter* [orderlies] had no choice but to risk serious punishment by stealing the bandages and ointments and selling them to the Jews for a few Marks so that the doctors who were imprisoned with the others in the barracks could continue the treatment. Unfortunately they were frequently caught in the act during inspections and received severe blows.

When this treatment was no longer sufficient and people began to die from the cold it apparently even became too much for the camp authorities, and in the final days before Christmas our work, i.e. spending time in the open air, was restricted to the morning and evening *Zählappell,* and the rest of the day was spent inside, where at least there was some heating.

By Christmas we had already been there for five weeks, we had had one bath on arrival, the straw had never been replaced and it comes as no surprise that lice started to appear in some of the blocks. As a punishment the occupants of these blocks had to undress completely on the *Appellplatz* and finally got to have a shower, fresh underwear and clothes, and their straw bedding was replaced. One block (barrack) had a bit of good luck amidst all the misfortune because it suffered a case of typhus, which put the entire block into quarantine for three weeks at a time of the bitterest cold (-15°) and meant we could not go out at all.

I can honestly say that it was a bitter period, there was not a single day when one did not feel one's life was in danger, and I was happy beyond measure when early in the morning on the day before Christmas my name was called out in the list of those to be released. It did not matter that we got nothing to eat that day from 6 o'clock in the morning until 7 o'clock at night, we were going to be free at last, and the heavy gates shut behind us once and for all after 60 terrible, painful days.

B. 305 I was arrested out of my bed at 7 o'clock on the morning of 10th November 1938 and taken first to the *Polizeirevier* [police station] and then to Fuhlsbüttel *Zuchthaus* [special prison]. There we were loaded into wagons without knowing where we were going. The transport was going to Sachsenhausen.

In the train we were supervised by *Schupobeamte* [*Schutzpolizei*; police], who behaved properly and only forbade us to speak to each other. There were several people amongst us who had already been taken to Sachsenhausen following the *Juli-Aktion* [July operation]. They told us that we had to be brave, the worst thing was the arrival and the route from Orianenburg station to the camp. We were supposed to walk this route, which normally takes 40 to 50 minutes, in a quarter of an hour. The waiting SS men received us with blows from their rifle butts and pushed us onto the path. Because I am very unwell and find walking particularly difficult (I am well over 60 years old) it was impossible for me to keep up the pace and after three minutes I fell down in a faint. I was picked up and flung head first into a lorry; it was only because I instinctively put my hands in front of my head that I was able to stop myself crashing with full force against the side of the vehicle. Because I could not stand, within the first minute I was pulled upwards so brutally that my coat and jacket were torn off.

We arrived at the camp at half past two in the morning. After that I was standing on the *Appellplatz* [parade ground] in shirtsleeves with nothing to eat until 5 o'clock that afternoon. Older prisoners who were coming back from work gave us pieces of their bread, insofar as it was possible for them to do so unnoticed.

The taking of personal details then took place at 5 o'clock in the afternoon; during this, after the person whose turn it was had given his details he had to run back to join the left side of the group as fast as possible past the line of SS officers who were flanking us. As I was doing this I stumbled and as I was apologising I was obscenely insulted and beaten violently on the backside. When I eventually reached my comrades they received me with tears in their eyes, having seen that one of the young SS men, all of them youths of 18 to 20, had tripped me up with his leg.

When we were finally allocated to the barracks the worst part of our sufferings had come to an end. The *Barackenältesten* [barrack elders], all of them older and mainly *politische Häftlinge* [political prisoners] who were in charge behaved very properly towards us and did what they could to give us every possible relief. As a result I was ordered to work in the office after a few days and generally did not need to appear at *Appell* [roll call]. The office was run by a prisoner priest of the *Bekenntniskirche* [Lutheran Church] and as well as me a Jewish teacher worked there. The SS came to check our work but because they did not understand what we were doing they had a certain respect for it, as uneducated people do generally have for every so-called intellectual activity.

We experienced enough terrible things nonetheless. On one occasion a man near me in line fell down dead; he had been beaten too much.

Our *Barackenältester* was strict, but as he said himself you could talk to him. Certainly he could not do anything to change the fact that we had to lie packed together like herrings at night. You could not turn over so you had spend the night in the position in which you had lain down in the evening or crush your neighbour. For me this was a particular torture since I have to get up several times during the night, yet my comrades kindly helped me.

Medical treatment was very bad, hardly anyone dared to go to the so-called *Revier* [sick bay]. I avoided it as well, although I badly needed medical attention.

I was released after 14 days. Obviously one was advised to leave the country as quickly as possible. All the officials whom I had to do with whilst arranging my emigration were not only correct but notably cooperative. Because I had been working on behalf of the Jewish *Gemeinde* [community] of my home town for many years I was well known to everybody. Although I had no more right to this title I was still always greeted everywhere as '*Herr Rechtsanwalt*' [Mr Lawyer]. One had the feeling that some people were glad to grasp the opportunity to make someone understand that they were in no way in agreement with the methods of the regime.

B. 306 In Germany since the autumn of 1938 every Jew has had to possess a *Kennkarte* [identity card] with photo, fingerprint and an exact personal description. In general the issue of these cards is carried out smoothly. But in the II. *Bezirk* [district] of Vienna a special procedure was brought in.

Here, after the *Karte* had been issued the recipients were asked to wait a moment in the antechamber. They were then taken one by one into a room where there was a photographer with his apparatus and several young men and women helping him. The person was then repeatedly photographed, initially just the head from all sides, then with a number fixed to the chest like a prisoner. Then it was "Take off your clothes." Despite their utmost reluctance people had to undress completely before all these men and women in order to be taken again from all sides. Further, fingerprints were taken again, and all body measurements taken, during which the men obviously measured the women, hair strength was measured, blood samples taken and everything written down and enumerated. One can imagine what this procedure meant for the tormented victims. As a result many people who had learned of this instantly ran immediately they had received their *Karte*. When this became apparent the procedure was brought forward to the beginning and the *Kennkarte* were not given out until the after the naked photography had been done.

Things have probably not been so inhuman anywhere for the Jews as in Vienna and the rest of Austria. Especially bad things have taken place in Burgenland. In small villages here people have been driven out of the house literally naked. They have been beaten and battered. They have been made to sweep the streets and burdened in every imaginable way. Burgenland has been literally cleansed of Jews.

Transports to the concentration camps of the people arrested in July was frightful. Particularly terrible was one transport in a passenger train with windows and doors tightly shut and heating fully on despite the summer heat. The prisoners sat crammed against each other and had to stare at the ceiling lights all the time. Now and then one of the SS men came in and ordered them to get onto their knees. Anyone who did not get down because of the lack of room was hit over the head. Eventually the air was so stale that people could hardly breathe any more and desperately gasped for air. The brief moments when the door was torn open so that someone who had not been staring upwards could be beaten came as a relief. Everybody who has been in one of these transports is clear that it was the worst of all their sufferings, even though most have spent over three quarters of a year in Dachau or Buchenwald. The journey lasted from 8 o'clock in the evening until 2 o'clock the next day, when they reached Dachau. There the prisoners were loaded into cattle trucks and driven into the camp.

Reception with blows. Then orders to form rank and file immediately. Thereafter the SS men took any opportunity to shoot. Anyone who got a little bit out of line was in danger of being shot. That is how an SS man was once shot by his own comrades. People were so beaten and mistreated that scars were still visible 10 months afterwards.

Collections were often organised among the prisoners in Dachau so that penniless colleagues could buy necessities from the canteen. The SS usually kept a large part of the money. On one occasion, the *Kommandant* [commandant]'s large dog died, and the Jews were blamed and obliged to provide a replacement. There had to be another collection, but one of the prisoners offered his own similar dog as a substitute and had it brought.

When it became cold in December the prisoners received permission to buy gloves in the canteen. After three days they had to hand them in again.

The misery amongst the Vienna Jews has increased constantly. They have almost all been turned out of their homes and live three families together. The majority of them are already eating the mass meals from the *Kultusgemeinde* [Jewish community], since they can no longer cater for themselves and for example are beaten at Zettel Market, where Jews are not allowed to buy because of food shortage.

B. 307 New York City, 29th December 1938

My Dears

By now you will have received the airmail letters we sent from here, from which you will have gathered that we have now arrived safely. As mentioned in the letter I had wanted to write to you from the ship, but had not been able to on account of a rather stormy crossing. I will now finally do what I had intended and describe to you what happened to us following the crisis in Czechoslovakia. Of course I can only do this in the most general terms otherwise I would have to write a whole novel.

As you know we moved to X. on 10th October. The reason for this was that I did not want to stay in Z. any longer under any circumstances. As soon as the mobilisation was announced the rumour spread in Z. that if war broke out the Jews would all have their throats slit because they were responsible for it in the first place. This was passed on to a number of acquaintances by trustworthy people, and some acquaintances had already left Z. in the last few days. We did not do so, however, although we did listen to the radio day and night to see what would happen. Initially I took the whole thing to be nothing more than gossip and assumed that everything had turned out for the best because war did not actually break out. However I decided from that point to live only in furnished accommodation, because you are more mobile if something happens. So we put our furniture into storage with a removal company and rented two furnished rooms. I spent a lot of time in X. chasing up the authorities to make sure that our preparations for emigration were progressing. However this sort of thing is now much more difficult and protracted than it used to be because you have to sort things out with many more offices than before. We had reserved a place on a ship for the 28th December and wanted to travel together with A. However we changed this in the light of what had happened.

Before describing the events of 10th November (exactly four weeks after our move to X.) I want to mention that there was a simple but particularly moving celebration of Chanukah on board the ship. A gentleman who had already been living in Jerusalem for five years, and had apparently once been a newspaper editor, gave a speech, the motto of which I would like to adopt as the title for my descriptions, in particular because you, my dear . . . and you too, my dear . . . have written to say that we should forget what happened. Certainly one has to look to the future, but I would like to leave it up to your discretion to decide, once you have read what follows, whether it is perhaps right not to forget the things that have occurred, but instead make sure that our children know about them one day too.

The motto of the gentleman's speech was as follows: "Children of Israel, do not forget what Amalek did to you."

Previously we had only known from school what it was like to experience a pogrom in which the *Tempel* [synagogues] are destroyed, now we know for ourselves. On the morning of 10th November I drove into town to visit the removal company in order to sort out various things relating to the containers. I passed a Jewish jewellers and its blinds were down and there was broken glass on the street. I thought to myself that there must have been a burglary because we had not heard anything at home about what had happened. En route to the removal company I then saw that the windows of the Jewish shops had been smashed in and that some of the merchandise had been thrown out onto the street. In short, I encountered gangs of around 15 to 25 men armed with axes and pickaxes who were in the process of smashing everything to pieces. When I arrived at the removal company the glass rained down from the windows of the *Klauβ* [orthodox synagogue] right next door to the office. Inside much had already been destroyed and lots of curious people were looking through the door, which had been smashed with an axe.

So these were the first things I experienced that morning on my journey into town. Initially everyone thought that the synagogues and shops would be destroyed and that that would then be the end of the matter. However, as a result I wanted to pay the removal company and buy our tickets for the ship as soon as possible so that we could leave suddenly if necessary. I telephoned... in Amsterdam because we had heard that it was not easy to get permission to gain entry there. For this reason I changed the booking to the Holland Line, because that would mean going to Rotterdam to board the ship. If we used the American Line it was possible that the Dutch would tell us that we had to board in Hamburg.

Jewish bank accounts were being kept under particularly strict surveillance by this point. Gaining access to our money in Z. was only possible after a number of telephone calls and after I had also got the removal company to make a call. Despite this, the payment for the container had to be approved by the Gestapo and the *Kreisleitung* [Nazi municipal authorities]. At the banks you also could not have unlimited access to your money and often had to collect a series of small amounts. A decree was also issued by the *Bankenvereinigung* [banking association] in Berlin to the effect that to prevent a sharp fall in prices Jews could not sell their stocks and bonds. One could only sell stocks and bonds up to a maximum of RM. 1,000.- if the account was not in credit. For this reason I spent the credit in my account so that I could sell RM. 1,000.- worth of securities. One had to make an effort to wade through all these things because it was often the case that by midday instructions that had been in place in the morning had suddenly changed.

From the removal company I went home and reported what had happened in the city. I then went to get food for the people in our house because we could no longer eat at the Jewish restaurant following its wrecking. En route I visited a good friend as he had telephoned *Mutter* [Mother] to say that I should not go into the city. Whilst I was there a man joined us and reported that the gangs were now going around private homes smashing everything to pieces and that the men were going to be arrested. Immediately I then returned home to *Mutter* and prepared her and the other people in the house for a possible visit from these people. As I stood guard behind the curtains one of these gangs did indeed come down our street, however passed us by and turned round the corner. We then saw books, cushions, clothes, household goods etc. flying out of the windows onto the street three houses down from our home. It was essential to act in these minutes. *Mutter* kept saying I should not stay at home. I therefore spent some time driving here and there around X. and saw that the destruction was fully underway in the homes. I parked the car next to others on the roadside because I did not feel safe in the car any longer.

Now walking around on foot with my briefcase containing the passports and the visas for the USA, I had to show utmost self-control and not run away if I came across one of these gangs. There was nothing for it however but to keep up with the onlookers and then disappear into thin air. Although I stayed close to home I did not feel comfortable knowing that *Mama* was alone there with the old people. I telephoned *Mama* and we met in town as it had all pretty much come to an end there and the gangs were all now in the residential areas. *Mama* came over immediately with a sausage and a piece of bread for everyone for lunch. We drove past the furniture store and saw that nothing had happened there. (I later heard that that they had wanted to destroy everything there too, but the Aryan removal man had been able to prevent them from doing so.) We then decided to travel to Z. because we could not tell whether what had happened in X. was merely the result of local decision making. In any case *Mutter* had a doctor's appointment in Z. that day because he wanted to change the bandage on her injured hand. We telephoned Z. and discovered that B. had been arrested. We did not know, however, that they were intending to arrest all the men, because his deputy was on the phone. We ate the food that *Mama* had brought along in the car en route. In Z. I rang acquaintances and was told that the

men had been taken away there as well, and that the same thing
had happened to the homes. We decided to travel to Y. next
and then possibly from there visit the doctor in X. In Y. we
were told by... that all of the Jews had to be out of the city
by evening... had not been taken and while we were there a
Schupo [uniformed policeman] turned up to demand a signature confirming that he would leave the city by the evening.
We then drove to *Onkel* [uncle] C. who was packing, and in
the evening went over to... (In the meantime he has made it
to Detroit with *Tante* [aunt].) We took C. and D. with us to X.
to join their acquaintances. In the evening when we arrived in
X. we telephoned our landlord and were told that nothing had
happened in the flat there. So the day was finally over and we
returned home. One heard that everything had died down in
the afternoon, yet one was not confident that someone would
not still turn up and collect those who had been forgotten.
Occasionally one could not sleep, one could not eat on account
of the agitation, or one slept soundly and could also eat due to
the agitation.

Now one really could see misery everywhere. People kept
arriving in X. from... and other towns because the Jews had
been expelled from the... GAU. The old people's home in... was
burned out so the old people moved to the Jewish old people's
home and to the hospital in... Mattresses, bed linen etc. were
quickly collected and the home, which had not been affected,
was nothing less than a refugee camp, and so overcrowded that
the mattresses had to be laid out on the floor for the refugees.
Anyone who had acquaintances elsewhere tried to reach them
in order to have somewhere to sleep and food to eat. People
kept turning up at our place too until they could finally get to
their acquaintances. The people arrived with a small suitcase
or a bundle – just as in the pictures one has seen of refugees
in wartime. It will doubtless interest you to know about what
happened in... and we got to hear quite a bit because people
were arriving all the time. It was bad because many people did
not know where their relatives or acquaintances had ended up.
Everything happened in such a rush that initially everyone had

to see to their own affairs and then one would meet someone by chance who would be able to say where the others were. We heard the following about... from acquaintances who came from...

In the morning the synagogue was already in flames, petrol had been poured during the night for this purpose. Once it had burned out the synagogue was blown up and is now nothing more than a pile of stones surrounded by a wooden fence. Nothing happened to the cemetery, and we visited *Papa*'s grave and that of our grandparents on the Sunday before we left. *Papa* died six years ago on 6th December and this time I could not go to a synagogue to say Kaddish because they had all been destroyed. On 7th December we set off at 2 o'clock in the morning for Amsterdam in... because I had a meeting at midday with... and did not want to stay in Germany any longer thereafter. In... everyone was expelled and had to leave... at midday. But before they were allowed to go to the train there was an inspection at the platform barrier of the men by the SS and of the women by the [*Nationalsozialistische*] *Frauenschaft* [National Socialist Women's League]. The Jews had their jewellery and money confiscated, apart from some small change, so that they were virtually penniless when they arrived. The people were happy to have got away with their lives, the pictures were terrible. The men were arrested and the women arrived in this state with their children. And initially no one knew where the men had been taken and what they would do to them. In... some of the men were put in prison and others taken to the Jewish café. Initially they lay on straw in the café and apparently they were not treated very nicely there either. From there the men were sent to... and then transported to Dachau. Three men, including..., had their visas for the USA and were therefore released in...

Initially no one dared go back to... However one day the refugees in... were suddenly expelled again by the Gestapo and were supposed to return to where they had been living previously. People therefore really did not know what they should do because every town had its own arrangements – there were no longer any real laws to speak of. In . . . it was particularly good because the *Kreisleiter* [Nazi municipal leader] there was something of a hero when it came to these things. Almost all of the homes were more or less wrecked and more than a little had been stolen. First the women were allowed back into the wrecked homes and had no idea where to begin clearing up. The homes had been sealed by the police and one first had to go there to get the key to gain access. *Mama* was with . . . who often used to visit us and who lived with . . . at her mother in law's in . . . She also had to go to the Gestapo in . . . in order to get into the flat. They had forgotten to wreck this flat, which was also a stroke of luck for us because we had left our clock etc. there as I had not yet taken them to . . . because when *Mama* was in hospital, initially I stayed with . . . in . . . In . . . I ended up running a law office pure and simple as soon as the women discovered that I had not been taken away. Alongside my own affairs I had endless petitions to write to the Gestapo on behalf of acquaintances concerning the release of the men who had been arrested. From time to time the men were released once they had received an appointment at the consulate. This is where I also heard that . . . had been released, I do not know if it is true but it may be the case because he had pushed ahead with his plan to emigrate to the USA. During the wrecking old Herr X., who suffered from a heart condition, had a heart attack. No one knows who buried him because there were no men left in . . . A certain Herr Z. in . . . also died of a heart attack. It is said that Y. died in a concentration camp. P. was apparently *auf der Flucht erschossen* [shot whilst escaping].

It was impossible to get a clear picture of everything that had happened, and of course in all the excitement all kinds of rumours did the rounds which later turned out to be false. I myself could not return to . . . until the Sunday before our departure. Acquaintances and someone from the *Kreisleitung* with whom I had a telephone conversation advised me not to go to . . . In our house the whole of the first floor has been let to an army officer. On the second floor the large pane of glass in the corridor was smashed and the fine gentlemen moved on when they saw that our flat was empty. Apparently they had also wrecked the furniture on the third floor. Frau ... had gone to her relatives. The flat is let to a *Feldwebel* [sergeant] and Frau ... intended to give up the flat once we had moved to ...

On the Sunday after going to the cemetery we went to visit ... who was there that day.... is also in Dachau and ... is with ... staying with her [their] parents. Her father was also picked up but released again, and the brother picked up. It is barely possible to describe how ...'s flat looked. The heavy furniture had been hacked up into firewood, the pictures slashed, all the crockery and mirrors smashed into a thousand pieces. This chaos was strewn around all the rooms. Only old and dirty linen remained, and the same with the suits. Silver and new things were all missing. It is impossible to imagine how it looked, and even with my descriptions you cannot imagine how the wrecked homes looked. There is no point trying to describe it in any more detail because one would not know where to end. We ate at ...'s and there too much was wrecked.

... went with his family to ... to stay with his brother-in-law and also lodged with us. By now he will be on his way here and initially intended to go to Luxembourg until the steamer was due to depart, where ... has emigrated to. *Onkel* ... also stayed with us and his place had also been completely wrecked. He also wants to come here but is a long way down the registration list at the consulate. Elsbeth and her acquaintances have stood surety for him.

We were in ... for one night because I did not have any time during the day, and was out and about sorting out our emigration every day. They had not wrecked any of the homes there and Kurt was not picked up. *Tante* Frieda is due to go to Sweden soon to stay with ... has stood surety for ... and ... have not had any luck getting surety yet, but we hope to sort this out as well because they have a low number at the consulate. We hope to be able to get them out soon.

On the street in ... I met ... from Amsterdam and he came round to me at midday. I explained to him that we have a visa for the USA and want to go to Holland. He immediately wrote me an invitation from home, and following my telephone conversation also had one from … He had left Mannheim to stay with relatives and was imprisoned there until he received a summons from the consulate. However he was not badly off there and was happy not to have ended up in a concentration camp.

Now I want to stop describing all these wonderful things because I could go on for page after page and there is no point. From these lines you can get an impression of what these fine people we have been living with are like. I am sure there are also perfectly decent people there, yet it is a fact that something of this kind has happened in Germany in the 20th century.

You will now doubtless understand why I began by quoting the motto of the speaker at the Chanukah celebration, and just want to mention once again that these occurrences should remain in the memory not only of this generation but also the next, and that no Jew should ever forget something of this kind.

"Children of Israel, do not forget what Amalek did to you."

However now I just want to mention briefly all the things that at the time had to be sorted out for emigration. I am not doing this just so that I can tell you all the things I had to do, but rather so that you will understand if and when you ask yourselves whether this or that could not have been sorted out first.

As you know we were summoned to the consulate on 9th August thanks to the surety stood for us by … Because a formality had to be sorted out with the surety we only received our visas on 12th September. It goes without saying that at the time I immediately delivered the letter to the Brazilian consulate in Frankfurt. At the time the secretary in the consulate told me it could take three months and *Mama* should be grateful if she got a visa at all as there was only one letter of recommendation. As I have already told you, *Mama* did get her visa so it is not necessary to write about that all over again.

I also applied to emigrate to Uruguay. To this end I handed over RM. 1,000.- for both of us. The visa was to be issued in Hamburg and the consul in Frankfurt told me I should pack everything and then travel to Hamburg. There I would receive the visa once the formalities had been taken care of. Yet during this period there was the business with Argentina where people prepared everything and were then banned from going, so they did not get their visa in Hamburg, they had given up their homes and had no visas.

For this reason the whole thing with Uruguay seemed to me to be too risky because I could not get the visa in Frankfurt before everything was packed. This is all sorted now and I have taken the paperwork with me in case it comes in useful at some point.

So at this critical point *Mama* had her visa for the USA and so did I. We had to go to Frankfurt a number of times until *Mama* got the Brazilian visa. E.g. we were in Frankfurt one day when they were still arresting people there, although the *Aktion* [operation], as they called the whole thing, was supposed to have died down. The Uruguayan consul advised me to go to Hamburg immediately and leave on the next ship because they were still going to round up more people in Frankfurt. Not surprisingly it was a major struggle to keep one's head during this period. There were long queues of Jews at the consulates and the offices of the shipping lines and the faces of these beleaguered people were a terrible sight to behold.

You now know all about the visa question. Then the containers had to be sorted out, because we were fortunate in that our furniture had not been smashed to pieces. Because we had moved to... on 10th October the relevant *Devisen-stelle* [foreign currency office] for us was in..., and they were much more conciliatory there than at the office in... Once we had been registered in... for four weeks I intended to submit the application for permission to pack to the office in... The cutlery and the linen had already been packed into containers ready for the move to... So immediately after 10th November I submitted the list of what we were taking in..., because you had to have lived in... for some time before it could be dealt with. We had bought some electrical equipment from a Jewish family, but in the meantime these people had been arrested on 10th November. So once we had collected the things we had bought from the wives of the business owners we had to submit a supplementary list. I wanted to buy some photo equipment for myself but the *Devisenstelle* would not allow me to take it. We only had to make a small duty payment to the Golddiskontbank [gold discount bank] for the new things, and in this respect got off very lightly.

As you know, I had an *Unbedenklichkeitsschein* [clearance certificate] for both of us from the *Finanzamt* [tax office] in... and the city of...We now heard that no more of these *Unbedenklichkeitsscheine* were being distributed, and that before one could be drawn up people would have to make the 20% *Kontribution* [tax on Jews for the cost of *Novemberaktion* damage]. Yet as I have already explained to you, no one was allowed to sell securities, so how was I supposed to pay this 20% and on top of that the *Reichsfluchtsteuer* [Reich departure tax] for *Mama*, which I had not yet paid. The time limit offered protection, and I had the *Unbedenklichkeitsscheine* extended again and again. But during that period one only went to the authorities with some trepidation, because one did not know if one would be arrested after all if someone caught sight of one there. In the... they recently also instigated an accounts check. And then there was usually the *Zollfahndung* [customs investigation], which checked every last detail with a fine toothcomb.

So I made photocopies of all the *Unbedenklichkeitsscheine* that I had, then had them witnessed by a notary and used these documents instead. I frequently had to go to the *Devisenstelle* in... and then received permission for *Mama* to pack, though in my case there were still some questions to be answered. Following various visits to the *Devisenstelle* the official told me they did not recognise me. On the basis of the *Unbedenklichkeitsschein* I was able to ensure that I could pack as well. However when he then informed me that the outstanding question had not been answered I thought again that I might be arrested.

Two days after receiving the *Packgenehmigung* [packing permit] we filled both of the containers and the suitcases and had everything sent to Rotterdam. Through a notary I had already made sure that... had been sent power of attorney over everything and arranged that I would write to him from Holland. He would then sort out the *Reichsfluchtsteuer* and the 20% *Kontribution* with the *Finanzamt*. I am now waiting for a reply to find out whether he has done so. I wrote to him from Holland once the containers had arrived in Rotterdam so that they did not get held up for any reason. We could not transfer anything under these circumstances and I was told that for the time being no *Sperrmark* [blocked Marks] were being sold. However in Holland I heard that it is possible after all, and will see what remains after the taxes have been paid and how it can be transferred.

We spent a week in Holland and boarded ship in Rotterdam on the 13th of this month.

B. 308 London 4th May 1939

... Consistent reports have been conveyed to me by several Jews from Dachau I have met here who were arrested as a result of the *Novemberaktion* [November operation] that in January this year the prisoners there were kept on so-called "*Stehappell*" [standing parade] for 36 hours at a stretch, because a Sudeten German prisoner had escaped. This man had managed to slip into the stores and get hold of a uniform, in which disguise he came through and out of the camp unimpeded. He was picked up near Munich however and brought back to Dachau. The prisoners there were fetched out of their beds and had to be present when the escapee returned. As reported, he allegedly received only 25 strokes and 14 days in isolation. However, he was not seen any more, and even prisoners who were in isolation themselves told their comrades that they had not caught sight of him.

B. 309 9th January 1939

In Herne those who were released from *Schutzhaft* [protective custody] were obliged to emigrate in the shortest possible time. And it is reported that owing to non-compliance with this obligation there have been various arrests and transfers to prison in Münster i. W. Specifically, up to now we have been able to establish the following gentlemen:

Baumgarten, Harry	Herne
Franke, Salo	Herne
Franke, Heinz	Herne
Franke, Walter	Herne
Baer, Fritz	Herne

Further, in the district we actually have case after case of people, even over 60 years old, without foreign languages, with unsuitable occupations, who have received the stipulation of immediate emigration from the authorities. So e.g. in Herne, Witten, Hattingen, Bochum, Wanne-Eickel, etc. We have the greatest doubt about advising passage to Shanghai in these cases and ask you urgently for immediate information about other possibilities at your disposal.

B. 310 The experiences of a twelve-year-old Jewish child in Vienna in the winter of 1938/39 emerge from the following extracts of a series of letters.

February 1939

Dear Sister,

I have another big favour to ask you. I have received the following sad, deeply sad letters from Vienna. C. ten days ago I got one from a little girl who is almost twelve. I have told you about her already, she had come to England with her sister and was called back by a relative because the children of Martha (a cousin of her father) were very seriously ill. The little boy recovered, but the little girl of four, whose picture I once showed you, died. Leni has now written to tell me that the child has died and that Martha is refusing to eat and doesn't want to see anyone, not even her little boy.

I wrote her a consoling letter and then yesterday received an even sadder one, also written by the girl. Martha is in hospital and has had a nervous breakdown, but not just as a result of the death of her little girl. She wrote the following: "It has been very hot here in the last few days and in order to cool down we had to spend a day and a night in the cellar. When we came back up again burglars had been there and stolen everything – money, linen, clothes, jewellery, even things belonging to the little boy – and that's when *Tante* Martha had her nervous breakdown."

They only have what they were wearing at the time. So to my request. If you have anything your daughter really can't wear any longer and anything you yourself don't use then I can send it to Martha. It would be a big *mitzvah* [good deed] and I am sure your husband will agree.

The girl now has to look after the little boy. She spends the day with friends and at night sleeps alone with the boy in the flat. Isn't this a terrible tragedy? . . .

Vienna, February 1939

Dear Frau Z.,

I take the liberty of thanking you very sincerely in the name of my *Tante* Martha for the parcel. My *Tante* is very ill and is in hospital. But first I would like to introduce myself to you so you know who I am. My late father and *Tante* Martha were cousins. I am eleven and a half and my name is Leni and am now always going to stay with my *Tante* because my Mama also died a few weeks ago. I will keep the parcel safely until *Tante* Martha comes home. Then she will write to you herself. She got sick because she was very agitated. In October my *Papi* died, six weeks later my *Mami*. *Onkel* Jacob disappeared last May and I can't tell you where he is because I don't know. In January Sonja died, Martha's little girl. She was four years old. But *Tante* Martha has another child. He's called Hans and is one and a half years old. Now something else has happened, I can't tell you everything, it was all too much for my *Tante*. She has often told me about you and is very fond of you.

She always spoke so warmly about you. And she showed me pictures of you and your little daughter. So once again many thanks and warmest greetings from

Leni and Hansi

I am going to the hospital tomorrow, I hope my *Tante* will be able to write to you herself.

Vienna, 10th March 1939

My dear good *Tante*

I received your kind letter. And thank you very much for letting me call you *Tante*. I am very fond of you and *Tante* Anna because *Tante* Martha likes you so much. Unfortunately she is still very ill and can't write to you herself. Hansi and I are staying with a woman in the same building. I don't want to look after Hansi any more. He's very naughty. He won't let me wash and dress him. He bites me and scratches me all the time and cries for his Mama. I go to school. The teacher likes me a lot. The things you sent will fit *Tante* Martha because she has got very thin. They are too big for me, but *Tante* Martha will sort everything out for me when she's well again…

Vienna, March 1939

Dear good *Tanterle* [little aunt]

Your card arrived yesterday. I can't give you the address of the hospital. Dear *Tante*, I will tell you the truth, although *Tante* Martha has told me not to. She was in the District Court in January. What *Tante* Berta wrote is true, that burglars were here and stole everything. In the heat of the moment my *Tante* said some unfortunate things, which is why she has had this misfortune.

I can't describe everything to you as it happened, you would have to see it with your own eyes to understand it. I wouldn't have written to you about all this if you hadn't asked me for the address of the hospital. *Tante* Martha mustn't know that I have told you the truth and *Tante* Berta also. I visit her every Wednesday. I am sending you a note which she slipped me. Once more, please don't tell anyone that you know everything.

Lots of kisses Leni.

Please don't send me any more cards because the lady I live with reads everything.

"Thank you very much for the beautiful things. Best wishes and kisses Martha.

I am in hospital and can't write anything else."

Vienna, March 1939

Dear *Tante*

I am sending you a letter from my *Tante*. Hansi is now spending his time with Frau F. until my *Tante* comes home again.

Lots of kisses from Leni.

From prison, March 1939

My dear good *Täntchen* [little aunt]

Yesterday my little Leni was here with me and admitted to me that she has told you the whole truth. Dear *Tante*, will you now think ill of me? I don't know if Leni told you everything in detail, I can't talk much to her here. They took everything away from us and we just stood there with nothing more than clothes we were wearing. In the heat of the moment I said some words I shouldn't have and that's why I've been here for the last three months. Please don't think ill of me as a result. After all, dear *Tante*, your brother was also here for 13 weeks last year, as you know, and that didn't make him a bad person. Thank you thousands of times for the lovely things. If I didn't have them I would have to wear the same dress all the time. They fit very well, although the shoes are rather large, but I can still wear them. You can't imagine how happy I was about everything you sent and above all because they came from you.

I am always thinking of you. Please don't be angry that Leni told you I was in hospital, I was too embarrassed to tell you the truth. Please don't tell *Tante* Berta anything about this. Even though I'm here I'm not despondent and I hope that I will soon be able to be with my little boy again. Leni is a good child and if I didn't have her I would be completely alone. For this reason I will always keep her close to me. I would be very happy if Leni could bring a letter from you on Wednesday. She comes and visits me every Wednesday. A thousand greetings and kisses

Your Martha.

Very best wishes to your husband, daughter and to *Tante* Anna.

I am sending you a picture of me. It was taken here and isn't very good. I'll give the letter to Leni. I hope it arrives safely. Once again, please don't tell Berta anything about this.

Vienna, April 1939

Dear good *Tanterle*

I received your letter. I haven't got the parcel yet, but they always take longer. I will write to you as soon as it arrives. This time it wasn't possible to include a letter from *Tante* Martha. "*Onkel*" was watching too carefully. She isn't allowed to write or receive letters. Dear *Tante*, you say we should put our faith in God. I don't believe in God. Why has he punished us so harshly? I can't begin to describe what we've been through. God has taken my beloved parents. My brother was in the same rest home as your brother last year and died there. It's the same home that our *Tante* is in now. The most terrible thing was that the burglars were here and took everything away from us. At the time we [were] hidden in the cellar for three days and didn't dare come out. Can one still believe in God in these circumstances?

Just look, dear *Tante*, at how badly "*Onkel*" treats us – I'm not allowed to go to the cinema, to the theatre, I'm not allowed to go to the park, some days I'm not allowed to show my face on the street. Isn't that enough? I'm not quite twelve years old but sometimes I feel as if I'm 100 years old.

But I'll stop now or you'll get angry. Hansi now spends all his time with Frau F., she gets 15 Marks a month for him from the *Gemeinde* [community] and I eat in the girl's refuge. Hansi is very naughty but a cute little scallywag. I'm sending you a picture of him. He didn't want to stand still so we tied his hands to the railing. I photographed him. In the next letter I'll send you a photograph of me. My *Tante* has a lawyer. I don't know what else I can write to you.

Your Leni.

Vienna, May 1939

Dear, dear *Tanterle*

I received your kind letter and read it with great pleasure. I am always so happy when you write to me. As far as the subject of God is concerned I want to ask you some time what you imagine him to be like. I know you'll tell me that God is an invisible force, but you have to believe in him all the same. Let me now give you a little example. If I wrote to you telling you that I have sent you 1,000 Marks, but you'd never receive it because the money remains invisible, would you still believe me? You'd tell me that you'd believe it when you see it. That's what I say too. I only believe what I see. And you also say that you could tell me about many things you have seen. Dear *Tante*, you certainly haven't seen the kind of things I've seen. But I'm going to change the subject or you'll get angry.

I think a lot about everything and say what I think. I'm sorry you've got such a weak heart. If I was there I could have taken the workload off you. I can already cook a bit. I can make coffee and I've also made *Powidlknödel* [plum jam dumplings]. I am sending you a picture of me. I'm wearing everything you sent me. You'll laugh because I was photographed with the doll. I still like to play sometimes. Please don't laugh at me or get angry with me. I'm pleased you're going to the *Comité*. Perhaps you can sort something out. I'd be very grateful if you could . . . Please write to me again soon. Your letters are a real comfort to me. For today best wishes and a million kisses

Your Leni and Hansi.

Vienna, 15 June 1939

My dear good *Tanti* [auntie]

Today a man came to visit and said you had written to the *Kultusgemeinde* [Jewish community] that you hadn't had any post from us since January. He also gave me a note for *Tante* Martha which I am sending you. I don't understand why you haven't received any post. I have written to you and I also sent you a picture of me. The man was very angry and said I was a stupid creature and that the *Kultusgemeinde* had better things to do than be pestered about things like this. Why haven't you written to me? Don't you believe what I told you about *Tante* Martha? I will try to get a confirmation from them and then send it to you. But please don't write to the *Kultusgemeinde* again. Please reply immediately so I know that you've got my letter and please also tell me whether you got my picture in the last letter. The one in which I am wearing the dress, pullover and cap which you sent me. Have you been able to make any enquiries in the emigration office about *Tante* Martha? Do émigrés get an *Arbeitsbewilligung* [work permit]? *Tante* Martha is a qualified book binder. I will travel to New York and *Tante* Martha would leave Hansi here for the time being so she can work there. Please, please reply. I send a hundred thousand kisses

Your Leni.

Please reply.

(The inquiry directed to the Vienna *Kultusgemeinde* by relatives in Holland was intended to ascertain whether the *Kultusgemeinde* knew about the fate of the family. Clearly they were not informed about it as demonstrated by the behaviour of the investigator and the note he handed over.)

"To Martha X.

Your *Tante*, Frau Z. in A., requests that you write to her as she hasn't heard from you since January of this year.

She has turned to us, the Vienna *Kultusgemeinde*.

15 June 1939"

From prison, June 1939

My dear good *Tante*

Thank you very much for trying so hard to sort things out for me. I hope I will be able to leave here soon. Leni and Hansi are travelling to America. At the moment I can't join them because I wasn't registered with the American Consulate. However Leni has now registered me. But I have to wait for at least a year before I can travel. Please don't turn for help to the Vienna *Kultus-gemeinde*, we don't want anything from people like that. They only support children under their own patronage. Leni has asked for help three times, she wanted to give me the money so that I could improve my situation, and they didn't answer. I hope that I'll be able to go back home even without their help. I hope to receive an answer from you soon. Thank you very much for you kindness and I hope that one day I will be able to repay you for everything.

A thousand good wishes and kisses

Martha.

Vienna, June 1939

My dear *Tante*

I received your letter today. The man from the *Kultusgemeinde* asked me whether I knew you so I told him yes, I do know you. I didn't know I wasn't supposed to do it. But I didn't say that my *Tante* is in prison. That's none of the *Kultusgemeinde*'s business. I get food for myself and Hansi from the Jewish canteen and the woman with whom Hansi is living has only received 10 Marks for him on two occasions. Three times now I have submitted an application for support to the *jüdische Fürsorge* [Jewish Welfare] on behalf of my *Tante* and haven't had a reply. They always say there's no money. Do you really believe that the *Kultusgemeinde* cares about its own people? You could perish like a dog and they wouldn't care. When I'm 14 I'm going to drop religion entirely.

Please don't turn to the *Kultusgemeinde* any more, we don't want to have anything to do with them. I'm going to New York, perhaps in two weeks even, and if *Tante* Martha agrees Hansi can come along as well. I'm travelling with a party. And *Tante* Grete is in New York. She invited us. Thank you for being so good to us. But you don't need to worry about me and Hansi any more. If you could send *Tante* Martha an entry permit for Holland we would be very grateful to you. But first you will need to ask if she would be allowed to work there. *Tante* Grete has handed the matter over to a solicitor in New York and we hope that *Tante* Martha will soon be able to come home. So in the name of *Tante* Martha please understand that we don't want to have anything to do with the *Kultusgemeinde*. Please don't show the lady from the *Comité* this letter. Otherwise she'll write to the *Kultusgemeinde* and then we won't even get any food. Perhaps the *Comité* could help *Tante* Martha by sending her something so that she can improve the quality of her food.

Now I'll answer your questions. My sister is seven years old and has been in London since December. My brother Julius was 18 years old and died in Buchenwald. I was twelve on 2 June and am still alive at the moment. My good *Papi* was 53 years old and died in October. *Tante* Martha won't tell me what he died of. He was a police inspector until March 1938. My dear *Muttilein* [little Mummy] had been ill for seven years and the death of my *Papi* was the end of her. She was 53 years old as well. My *Papi* was the cousin of *Tante* Martha. *Papi*'s mother and *Tante* Martha's father were brother and sister. Now I've told you everything. When I have got away from here I will send you a nice card from America, and when I'm grown up I'll send you lots and lots of dollars. All best wishes and a million kisses

Your Leni and Hans.

The food from the canteen is very bad. Not even pigs would eat it. That's how much the *Kultusgemeinde* cares for its people.

B. 311 It is reported that a businessman Schnell from Berlin-Steglitz died in Buchenwald in June 1938.

Similarly, the sudden death of a Dr. Marbach is reliably reported. More precise information is unobtainable.

B. 312 6th June 1939

It is reported by a reliable source in Paris that in May 1939 Frau Grete Eppstein, née Hoffmann, took her own life in Berlin. Frau Grete Eppstein is the daughter of the well-known couturier Hermann Hofmann, Berlin Friedrichstraße, and the wife of the well-known Berlin theatre lawyer Dr. Eppstein who is at present seriously ill.

Frau Eppstein was accused of allegedly smuggling foreign currency and she poisoned herself in the bathroom with Veronal tablets whilst the Gestapo was in her home. It has been established that the accusations raised against her were entirely unjust.

B. 313 Corruption

One of the most noticeable phenomena in Germany is the corruption amongst civil servants and other officials, which can be said to increase daily.

To start with a few examples:

I myself visited the *Polizeirevier* [police station] 156, Schaperstraße in December to apply for *Auswanderungspässe* [emigration passports]. There the civil servant asked questions about our financial circumstances in order to fill in a form. "You see, now you will have to bring all that money to the bank, but nobody ever thinks about us civil servants." I was baffled somewhat and asked: "Excuse me, what do you mean?" In response he repeated his earlier statement, and I replied by saying: "What do you mean by this – as far as it is possible, I am very happy to do what I can." In response, he said that "he had not entirely meant what he said." Then he left the room and I did the same. Outside he told me his name (Kusch) and said: "Well, when you emigrate, you will think of me, won't you?" I told him to let me know his wishes, and that I would be very happy to see what I could do. A few hours later, when I was sitting at the table in my home, the bell rang and the official appeared (in uniform with a coat over it). As I opened the door to him with some amazement he said that "he only wanted to tell me that he would like a round table and a rug measuring 2 by 3 metres." Incidentally, the *Auswanderungspässe* were issued surprisingly quickly.

One of my friends, *Rechtsanwalt* [lawyer] W., to whom I told this story, rang me up a couple of days later to tell me that what had been "the round table" in my case had been "the typewriter" in his.

With regard to another case, I know of the following.

An elderly Polish Jewish woman visited the *Fremdenamt* [foreigners' registration office] in Karlstraße to deal with a passport matter. One of the officials told her: "Isn't it good that we are all honest here. We don't take any money." The old lady, Frau Th., replied: "That is because you still belong to the old school", whereupon the official declared: "You put that very well."

Apart from these telling anecdotes, the following has to be said: corruption is particularly thriving when it comes to the dispatch of removal goods and luggage belonging to Jewish emigrants. The different hauliers dealing with the shipping of the emigrants' property are known for either having good connections with the authorities or not. This question is much more important than the estimates of removal costs for Jewish emigrants. A company like Franzkowiak, for example, enjoys an excellent – and for itself very lucrative – reputation because of its influence amongst officials. Since there are no binding rules at all with regard to what can be taxed and how much can be charged, arbitrary behaviour is left completely unchecked (as is corruption). The following is typical in this regard.

The conditions vary from place to place. In Berlin, emigrants generally manage to take all their belongings with them, although for newly bought goods (from the year 1938) a fee of 100% must usually be paid. On very rare occasions people are not allowed to take with them particularly expensive or valuable items. In contrast, authorities elsewhere act much more strictly. In some cities, for example in Nuremberg or Magdeburg, their practice is extremely harsh and very valuable newly bought goods are almost never allowed to be taken, whilst for other valuable goods fees of up to 500% may be charged. Moreover, it is known that a lot of people use large banknotes to pay the small clearance fees due at the foreign currency office and that they usually leave the change behind.

Possibilities for cultural life in Germany

At the moment there are neither Jewish bookshops nor publishers. Everything has been transferred to the *Abt[eilung] Buchverlag* [book publishing dept.] of the *Jüdischer Kulturbund* [Jewish Cultural Federation]. From what I have heard, this leads to an enormous body of Jewish antiquarian books having to be pulped, since the *Kulturbund* has nowhere near enough space to store things. Moreover, the new law has had the following consequences:

Until now Jewish companies had been allowed to print Jewish publications; this has stopped.

Now everything has to be printed at a particular company, whose name I cannot remember right now, but whose owner is a *PG* [*Parteigenosse*: Party member] with a golden Party badge.

This goes so far that, for example, the new South America journal of the *Hilfsverein der deutschen Juden* [Aid Association of German Jews] (the new edition of the 1936 journal), which had already been fully set at the Lichtwitz company, can no longer be printed there but must now be printed at the new company. All future editions will have to be printed at the new company.

"*Joci causa*" [for the sake of a joke] the following detail:

The old publisher of the *Hilfsverein*, Herr Schmoller, who used to be in charge of advertisements, appears at the *Hilfsverein* with a completely unknown second gentleman who had been made head of the *Abteilung Buchverlag* at the *Kulturbund*. He introduces this gentleman to the editor of the journal *Jüdische Auswanderung* [Jewish Emigration] as his successor: "You did not want this, Herr X. did not want this, and I had also not wanted to give up the business, but now you will have to work together."

Moreover, the sale and even the free distribution of *Jüdische Auswanderung* was prohibited for at least six weeks, despite the fact that the correspondence review is needed at every *Auswanderungs-Beratungsstelle* [emigration advice centre] and very obviously serves to promote emigration which is wanted by the government.

The *Jüdisches Nachrichtenblatt* [Jewish Newspaper], the one remnant of the Jewish press still in existence, is published under a system of double censorship. One censorship, that of the office of [Hans] Hinkel, is considered to be harmless. On the other hand the second censorship, carried out by the *Reichsführung SS* [SS High Command], in fact the editor [Leo] Kreindler, is subject to so much pressure that a whole range of articles give the impression that they had been written directly by the Gestapo. In particular it is being said e.g. that a letter that was published in the second or third issue of the paper, which complained bitterly that the foreign Jews were doing nothing for the German Jews, and that the emigrating intellectuals etc. only pursued their own interests etc., had come into the paper as a result of the following circumstances:

A copy of the letter had been sent to the Gestapo at the same time, which had insisted on it being published. I cannot vouch for the accuracy of this claim, since Herr Kreindler has for a long time avoided entering into discussion with me.

Concerning the migration situation

The situation is currently characterised by the fact that of the 30 to 35,000 people who had been arrested at the end of November, all have been released – with the exception of approximately 2,000. I cannot guarantee these numbers. However, these tens of thousands of people were only released under the strict condition that they must emigrate as soon as possible. The time limit set for emigration varies. In very many cases it is three weeks. A limit that normally does not give enough time to organise any kind of orderly emigration even technically, given the complicated nature of passport and customs rules etc., the difficulties of obtaining an *Unbedenklichkeitsbescheinigung* [clearance certificate] etc. In reality, the contradictory nature of this situation is evident. However, the conclusions which are drawn from this are entirely contradictory:

The Gestapo tries to simplify all formalities related to emigration in accordance with the "Vienna model", i.e. the Gestapo itself centralises the *Devisenabfertigung* [foreign currency clearance], the issuing of passports etc. in one process. Of special importance in this regard is the famous article published in the *Essener Nationalzeitung* [Essen National Newspaper]. The adoption of this procedure would indeed make it technically possible to carry out emigration more quickly. It is also very clear that currently the pressures to emigrate are not matched by immigration opportunities and that therefore mass emigration enforced by whatever means must, under some circumstances, quickly lead to the further decrease of existing opportunities. In any case, the Gestapo does not seem to be interested in this. On the other hand, the *Reichsstelle für Wanderungswesen* [Reich Office for Emigration Affairs] is very familiar with these issues, and therefore it basically supported and forwarded a petition of the *Hilfsverein* [Aid Association], which requested the extension of the period granted for emigration after release from concentration camps. The office even took the stand that (in accordance with the request of the *Hilfsverein*) basically a period of three months should be granted for emigration. Moreover, should emigration not have taken place within this period, a further extension should be granted, if the local *Auswanderungs-Beratungsstelle* confirms that the departure has so far been impossible. Thus the *Reichsstelle* demands the opposite of what the Gestapo wants, not a simplification of the formalities, but an extension of deadlines. Politically, this means of course that the *Reichsstelle* wants to ensure that its offices are in a position to intervene. The *Reichsstelle* is very much afraid of the reorganisation with which it is threatened, and has even asked Jewish organisations about what is supposed to happen. "We are completely in the dark." – "We don't know anything other than what was published in the article in the *Essener Nationalzeitung* and naturally this is not applicable to the situation in Germany. The circumstances here are, of course, completely unlike in Austria." (Remark made by a member of staff of the *Reichsstelle* on the telephone to the *Hilfsverein*).

The above only highlights a part-extract of the fight of the Gestapo against all other authorities.

The situation with migration policies is that the Gestapo creates such a strong pressure to emigrate through the concentration camps and the releases at short notice, and through the expulsion of stateless persons, and even nowadays of Germans, that any meaningful orderly activity of the *Reichsstelle* is no longer possible. Other issues, e.g. the arrest of advisers working for the *Hilfsverein*, which is not uncommon (during the *Novemberaktion* [November operation] at least half a dozen advisers were put into concentration camps), show that the Gestapo is no longer interested in any regulated form of emigration. One consequence of this amongst others is that taking action against private companies, especially travel agencies and the numerous secret agents, etc. which exploit the misery of emigrants, becomes almost impossible. One of the travel offices, who contributes most shamelessly to taking advantage of emigrants and to the destruction of immigration opportunities by sending migrants out with completely insufficient visas, declared with a smile, after it was pointed out that it would be possible to bring legal actions against it for the misuse of *Auswanderungspässe*, that the relevant authority was the one that is now sending the clients in the first place. Because of the immense pressure to emigrate and the very limited visa possibilities, people queue for hours in front of travel agencies to buy the most dubious of visas. No description of the misery of refugees in Shanghai or Bolivia will stop them from booking. They become abusive towards the *Hilfsverein* when the organisation tries to resist this urge to emigrate *à tout prix* [at any price].

Where the current developments will lead to, no one can imagine. Even if one only counts the 30,000 men who were in concentration camps and add their relatives to this number, i.e. ignoring all other urgent categories of emigrants, i.e.:

those stateless persons or Poles, Romanians and Hungarians etc. who have received their deportation orders,

those who with the *Genehmigung* [permit] from the *Stadtpräsident* [mayor] who took part in *Umsichtungskurse* [re-orientation courses] and now press for emigration, and

finally the great mass of those who just want to leave because they have lost all opportunities to earn a living and also frequently have been evicted from their homes;

even then, one will arrive at a figure of 100,000 people who really have to emigrate urgently and leave Germany within six months. Compared to this, as is well known, the possibilities to settle in other countries are very limited: around 2,000 people can go to the USA (in total), further 300 to 400 per month to Australia, further perhaps 500 people in total to Argentina, Brazil and Chile (in all monthly) – this exhausts the number of existing concrete possibilities to emigrate in a more or less orderly fashion and just leaves certain areas where people could only be deported to *en masse*, places like Shanghai or Bolivia, which do not allow for large-scale migration. Moreover, there are limited possibilities of being granted *Transitaufenthalt* [transit residence] to European countries, with all the associated financial and other consequences. Without doubt the situation would be different if generous resettlement plans had been prepared in a timely manner. For the moment it will be necessary to improvise without any preparation, if at least some of the people are to be rescued in one way or another.

B. 314 Julius Katzenstein from Eschwege died in Buchenwald on 29 November 1938 in his mid-50s as a result of complete exhaustion caused by psychological depression. His younger brother, who was also in Buchenwald, returned home at the end of December with severe frostbite in the arms. He has suffered so seriously physically and mentally that he will never completely recover.

A third brother of the[se] two was in Dachau for c. three weeks after having previously been in the *Polizeigefängnis* [police prison] in his home town for a week. His wife did not know where her husband was for two weeks or whether he was still alive at all. On 10th November the couple's home was completely smashed up. The effect on the children aged 15 and twelve was such that the younger boy suffered from facial twitching for weeks. The family has since emigrated after having been robbed of all their possessions, their silver and their valuables.

B. 315 Events during house expropriations in Fürth.

One of the first to be called about handing over their house was Herr T. with his wife. They were taken to the *Rathaus* [town hall] at 11 o'clock at night and there told the reason why they had been made to come. There were a few other Jews there in the same situation.

Herr T. is 72, his wife 62 years old. They were taken into the cellar of the *Rathaus* and initially had to dig over heaps of sand for a while, during which they were tormented with such remarks as *"Da siehst Du, Du Jud, was arbeiten ist, du hast doch Dein ganzes Leben nichts getan,"* [Now you see, you Jew, what it is to work, you've done nothing all your life], to which Herr T. replied "I've probably done more than you." Reply: "Yes, probably buried some old Jew in the cemetery."

After the digging the couple were placed on the sand piles and beaten with steel rods on the behind so badly that they were suffering from the injuries for five weeks. The husband was held down by his ear so firmly that it tore; he had to leave behind the completely bloodied handkerchief with which he wiped the blood away. The wife fainted after the severe mistreatment. They gave her Hofmann drops [spirit of ether].

The couple were allowed to go back to their home at 4 o'clock in the morning, obviously after they had previously agreed to the sale. The husband, having asked once again whether he could think things over a little received in reply "Yes, five minutes," and when he then asked "And what then?" the answer was "Then you go back into the cellar." Obviously he then consented straight away. On their release they were both threatened with death if they told anyone their experience that night.

Afterwards the wife had a nervous breakdown which kept her in bed for weeks and required the attendance of a nerve specialist.

B. 316 At Tiengen in Südbaden [now Waldshut-Tiengen in southern Baden-Württemberg] all the gravestones in the Jewish cemetery were wrecked and the cemetery, several hundred years old, turned into a sports field.

The 70-year-old *Vorbeter* [prayer leader] was taken to Dachau and killed there on the second day after his arrival.

B. 317 *Rechtsanwalt* [lawyer] Dr. Ortweiler writes from Sao Paolo:
"My brother was killed in December in Buchenwald."
The dead man came from Meiningen.

B. 318 May 1939
Professor Lust of Karlsruhe, an extraordinarily well-known and esteemed man there, recently committed suicide because he could not bear it any more.

B. 319 From German schools
In one school an Aryan schoolboy is said to have been punished for bad behaviour. Instead of the usual punishments

the teacher decided that to make the punishment worse he had to sit next to a Jewish pupil for an hour.

A Jewish father was advised to take his child out of school voluntarily, otherwise the teacher would see to it that he came home crying and bawling every day.

One of the worst Nazis is the head of a Nuremberg girls' school, who had the only two Jewish girls in one class of his school come up to the front and told them that it was scandalous that they were still there because they belonged to the inferior race of *Rassenschänder* [racial defilers]. He bullied the two children in this way so severely that they went home overcome with tears.

A four-year-old Christian child comes home from the kindergarten and says "We've been told we mustn't speak to the *Judenstinkern* [stinking Jews] any more."

B. 320 A married couple, Dr. and Frau Jonas, committed suicide in Altona. There were no financial reasons.

B. 321 A Herr Kahn from Duisburg died in Dachau in March 1939 at the age of about 34 years.

B. 322 Otto Sussman of Hamburg died of pneumonia in Sachsenhausen in December 1938 at the age of 43. So as not to stand out he had gone to work despite a high fever and returned half dead to the barracks in the evening. He left a wife and two children. His profession was bank official.

A Herr Kallmann from Hamburg returned from Sachsenhausen with severe pneumonia and died two days afterwards. He had married very recently and had made preparation for his emigration before his arrest.

B. 323 On the afternoon of 11 November 1938 I was visited in my home by two policemen under orders from the *Polizeirevier* [police station] in the district where I lived, and requested to follow them to the *Polizeipräsidium* [police headquarters]; I arrived there as evening approached, with another older man. In the courtyard were already about 150 men standing around who had been arrested during the afternoon. After waiting for about an hour we were loaded onto lorries and driven to Oranienburg, straight to the camp next to the village of Sachsenhausen.

Whilst the treatment by the policemen who arrested us and also by those who accompanied us during transportation had been reasonably decent, in some cases even courteous, the reception by the teams of guards at the camp from the outset was characterised by a brutality and roughness that I would not have believed possible. We were chased from the vehicles with vile insults. A large proportion of those arrested, most of whom were over 50, some over 70 even, fell to the ground on jumping from the vehicles: those who wanted to help them were prevented from doing so, our hats were torn from our heads and we were chased into the camp past a line of guards with a tremendous amount of swearing, pushing and shoving with rifle butts and blows.

If people fell over as a result of being pushed and shoved with the rifle butts, or for any other reason, the others were forced to walk over them. As I was later told, an older man on the previous transport who had fallen unconscious on the way from the station to the camp had been beaten and trampled so badly in this manner that in fact he had died on the spot.

It must have been around 10 o'clock in the evening when we arrived inside the camp. Around 2–3,000 men were standing there in the darkness occasionally illuminated by searchlights, in groups and lined up in rows of ten; I was later told that they had arrived during the day or even the previous night. With only short interruptions we had to stand on the *Appellplatz* [parade ground] until around half past 2 or half past 3 the following day. Then we went to get dressed, washed, followed by an *Appell* [roll call] at half past 5, so that all in all we had been standing for 18 or 19 hours on end. There was no food. When the SS men who were guarding us moved away for a moment, the *politische Häftlinge* [political prisoners] in charge of us gave us some water to drink.

In the main we were forced to stand bolt upright and in line. The *SS-Scharführer* [company leaders] or *SS-Blockführer* [block leaders] on guard duty entertained themselves and passed away the time with the most vulgar insults, threats, mistreatment. The mistreatment consisted above all of kicks in the backside with their heavy boots and being hit in the face. The insults mainly consisted of asking individuals about their profession and position and then using vile words about them.

From the outset one had the feeling that the main intention was to wear us down with the most degrading and humiliating behaviour possible. So for example they forced some people to pick up and chew crumbs which had fallen to the ground from the bread they had brought with them. Then others had signs pushed into their hand which had to be held with the hand raised and on which were insulting inscriptions such as "We Jews are the wreckers of German culture."

Now and then, also under threat of mistreatment, choruses were formed which had to repeat sentences in unison like those mentioned above. The SS men were especially fond of making it clear to us that we were now finally done for and destroyed, making sarcastic remarks to the effect that the Jews would be held here for life and that they now had the law and the power on their side. One of the SS men was proud of being nicknamed "the Satan of Oranienburg" and said he would treat us accordingly.

The following incident seems to be symptomatic of the extent to which the guard teams were determined to keep us under pressure: in the group in front of me there was a particularly large number of academics – doctors, judges, rabbis, including an *Oberstaatsanwalt* [senior prosecutor]. When the latter gave his name and former profession he was asked like everyone else about his income, the size of his home, the extent of his pension etc. Once the SS interrogator had made it clear that he was a destroyer and that for him everything was now lost, it suddenly occurred to him that the *Oberstaatsanwalt* must recognise him from former times; he said something along the following lines: "Tell me, do not we know each other? You were the one who sent me down for six months in 1931 together with five of my comrades." When the one being spoken to said he could not remember, the SS man continued: "We've always said to ourselves here, so where is X. hiding these days? We've been waiting for you for a long time. Now you can congratulate yourself because we're going to get our own back on you."

Although it was clear to me, as it was to other comrades of mine, that threats of this kind were largely theatrical, this theatre was still very unpleasant because it was accompanied by mistreatment and compulsory knee-bends etc.

Early in the morning, around 8 o'clock, the *Lagerkomman-dant* [camp commandant] himself appeared with the *Lagerführer* [camp leader], walked along the ranks, made an insulting remark about these rogues who, in his opinion, had to be taught the meaning of orderliness, asked how long we had been standing here, but without doing anything whatsoever to make sure we were accommodated quickly. In the night at about 1 o'clock our personal details were collected, again accompanied by blows and mistreatment. In the afternoon at around half past 2 we went to change and bathe in the washroom. An incident in the washroom which serves as a particularly striking example of what happened has stayed clearly in my memory. Needing to use both hands to get undressed, and feeling himself to be temporarily unobserved, the man next to me had attempted for a brief moment to put his hat on. An SS man who happened to be close by after all swiped the hat from his head, punched him in the head a couple of times and screamed: "*Du Scheißjude, gibst Du zu, dass Du ein Scheiß-jude bist!*" [You f***ing Jew, admit you're a f***ing Jew!]. Despite what had just happened my neighbour maintained his composure and said firmly and deliberately "*Ich bin Jude*" [I am a Jew]. This was followed by further blows and the same threatening order. Despite three or four repetitions of this scene the man in question continued to maintain his composure and just kept repeating "*Ich bin Jude.*" The SS man then demanded that he report to him during the washing session.

Washing and changing consisted of darting from one table to another where personal details were taken, valuables, money and clothes had to be handed over, and then the head shorn in a few seconds, something that had already been sarcastically promised to those with a fine mane. Then there were cold and hot showers and, in place of the relinquished outer garments and underclothes, prisoner's clothing distributed which consisted of thin underwear along with trousers and jacket of thin striped material or old soldiers' coats from the war. Whether the clothes fitted or not was not taken into account at this point. In the case of more corpulent people the trousers and jacket simply could not be buttoned up. Initially they had to sort this out for themselves by tying the suit together with string and covering the open patch with newspaper.

From the outset everything was accompanied by the threat of a disciplinary punishment that was apparently common in the camp, "*24 auf den Nackten*" [24 on the backside]. This punishment consisted of the delinquent being strapped to a *Bock* [whipping block] and thrashed by a number of SS men with a whip with pieces of lead on the end.

The behaviour of the prisoners who were in charge alongside the SS was in total contrast to the brutal and vicious behaviour of these SS guards themselves. Wherever humanly possible they tried to make the situation more bearable, constantly reminding us that the first days in the camp were particularly hard and that, although it did not seem very likely to us, we would get used to it. Also worthy of particular mention is the fact that an older man who was clearly sick and could not cope with standing ended up writhing on the floor early in the morning. When the prisoners guarding us repeatedly tried to have him carried away the SS men said that he should stay there until the *Zählung* [count] was over. When the orderlies arrived with the stretcher and carried him off he died on the way to the *Krankenrevier* [sick bay], we were later told.

It is revealing that no questions were asked, it would seem quite intentionally, about service at the front or any individual's military history, either when personal details were collected or at any other time. It was made clear from the outset that all orders and medals were to be removed. When a friend of mine handed over an *Eisernes Kreuz 1. und 2. Klasse* [Iron Cross First and Second Class] and a *Verwundetenabzeichen* [war wounded decoration] as we relinquished our valuables, the SS officer collecting them said "We'll make sure you get another *Verwundetenabzeichen.*"

Before moving on to a description of life in the camp it would seem to me that a short description of the camp organisation would be useful. As far as I could tell the entire camp consisted of three separate parts separated by guards, barbed wire, and fences. The outer camp, in which living quarters and industrial buildings had been erected, was the *Mannschaftslager* [staff camp] and included the barracks for the SS responsible for guarding the camp, an officers' mess and canteen as well as offices and the industrial and wood yards containing workshops as well as supplies of wood and metal; then there was the inner camp in which the prisoners spent most of their time unless they were occupied with work outside the camp.

This inner camp consists of around 70 to 80 barracks arranged in a semi-circle of three rows around a square designated the *Appellplatz* [parade ground]. Within the barrack grounds is another area separated by a special wall and courtyard known as the Bunker, which is there to house individual prisoners. It is here that the renowned Pastor [Martin] Niemöller amongst others is apparently accommodated. In prisoner circles the *Bunker* was always referred to with particular disgust; this was where prisoners were temporarily held who had broken the rules. It is said that real cages, not cells, are there. We only knew about these things from hearsay because there was obviously no access.

Two or three other barracks were also separated from the rest by a special wall, the so-called isolation barracks, which housed the punishment sections. These punishment sections dealt with groups of prisoners who for one reason or another were treated especially harshly. During the period of my internment there were around three hundred Jehovah's Witnesses in the isolation barracks, amongst others; I was told that these Jehovah's Witnesses had been told to sign a declaration in March

1938 which stated that they revoked their beliefs as Jehovah's Witnesses and which would lead to their release. Not a single one of the three hundred signed the declaration. Since then they have been imprisoned in the isolation barracks under particularly harsh conditions.

On my arrival it struck me that these people, with whom verbal or any other kind of contact was impossible, were distinctly in an even worse condition than the others, even though everyone was undernourished. One had the impression that some of these people were completely debilitated. Yet the spiritual strength that they had maintained despite everything was evident from a chance discussion between the *Lagerkommandant* and one of them. Whilst working in the industrial yard the *Kommandant* addressed the man asking, when he would abandon his faith in Sabaoth [the Lord]. When the Jehovah's Witness answered that he would never abandon his faith in Sabaoth, who was eternal, the *Lagerkommandant* replied, "Then you'll never get out of the camp."

The individual accommodation barracks usually contained four large rooms, two day rooms and two night rooms, intended for the intake of around 75 men. Between the rooms there was a washroom and a toilet room. In the sleeping rooms the beds were stacked three high. Under normal occupation of 150 people per barracks the accommodation rooms and the washing and toilet rooms would not, in terms of the standards that can be applied to mass accommodation of this kind, have given any cause for complaint as far as hygiene was concerned. But things were very different in the case of the accommodation for 6,000–7,000 Jews squeezed together in the so-called "new" camp, i.e. in the accommodation blocks built a few months previously, at an occupation rate of 350 to 400 persons per barracks rather than the normal 150. And when the number of prisoners decreased as a result of releases, sickness, and fatalities, people were simply moved together, which meant that the density within individual barracks remained at around 350–400 men.

Of course there were no beds, there would not have been enough room for them. There was just straw. As time went by, however, sacks of straw were delivered and an average of two blankets per person were provided for the night. There were no pillows or anything like that.

Two of the barracks in the inner camp constituted the so-called "*Krankenrevier*", and in the middle there was also the kitchen, the shop and the washing block. The washing block contained about 100 showers so that one hundred men could always be dealt with in one go. It has to be admitted that at a normal rate of occupation the hygiene facilities of this washing block, like the toilets and washing facilities, would have been able to meet demands. It also has to be said that the cleanliness of the inner camp could not be faulted, and indeed that the whole place did not give an unsightly impression.

The inner camp was reached through a special gate set in the surrounding stone wall. Along this stone wall there is a path which on the inward side is bordered by a defensive wall of barbed wire which is apparently electrified. Machine guns are placed on special towers along the perimeter wall which are able to target the entire area within the inner camp.

It is within this environment that the totally regulated life of the camp, both monotonous and terrible, is played out. After rising in the morning darkness first the crush in the wash-rooms to rinse face and upper body at the available taps. Further personal hygiene including tooth brushing was impossible given the crowd of people. Then breakfast, consisting of sago soup and dry bread, which was available in sufficient quantities. On Sunday there was some jam. Breakfast had to be consumed at great speed so that we would be on time for the *Appell* in front of the barracks. Then we proceeded in tight formation and rows of ten to the *Morgenappell* [morning roll call]. Then we fell in for the distribution of work. During the first weeks that was still bearable because only the youngest and fittest were assigned to the labour which everyone most feared in the brick works, road building and in the settlements. However, the demand for numbers, especially in the brick works, then rose to such an extent that even people aged up to 59 were called up for this work.

Following the departure of those ordered to work outside the camp, the remainder had to start *Exerzieren* [punitive drill], at least during the first weeks; these were only interrupted by the *Mittagsappell* [midday roll call] which lasted about an hour. From then until the *Abendappell* [evening roll call], i.e. about 5 o'clock or half past 5, there was uninterrupted marching of the most strenuous kind, a torture, almost more so for those prisoners forced to give the orders than for those who received them due to the monotony of the proceedings. In general there were around 8–900 men marching on the *Appellplatz* and sometimes wheeling to the right or left at short intervals had to be performed. Now and then passing SS men added to the bullying by ordering marching at the double and knee-bends. Stepping out, even to go to the toilet, was strictly forbidden. After five or six hours at the earliest there was a short pause to this end, unless a particularly harsh SS officer was nearby.

After about two or three weeks it was decided that the marching should stop. From now on it had to be standing. It almost goes without saying what that was like with completely inadequate clothing in November and December weather (apart from thin underpants and an equally thin vest we had not received any further underclothes, and most people did not have any head covering). It was very fortunate that it hardly rained and that there was unusually mild weather before it got bitterly cold in mid-December.

That was the life for those who due to their age or frailty were so "fortunate" that they did not have to go to work, and in particular work outside the camp.

The ones hit hardest of all were those who had to toil in the brick works, building roads, and in the settlements. The march there and back, often of up to a thousand prisoners, shoved along with rifle butts by their escorts, was a torture itself. Much of what took place at the brick works was so atrocious that it almost defied description. Particularly in the early days they really had it in for people who, on account of their education, seemed ill-suited to this physical work. Rabbis, academics and other brain workers were unbelievably mistreated by the *Vorarbeiter* [foremen] and the guards. Yet this was not always the case. The behaviour of the guards varied. Amongst their ranks there were also groups who tried to be humane and go gently on people.

The majority of the *Vorarbeiter* were also decent, as long as they were not being observed and checked by companies of sadistic SS. Most of them even tried, as best they could, to make life easier for the other prisoners. The *politische Häftlinge* in particular, but also those who were designated "*Berufsverbrecher*" [professional criminals] could be trusted to show consideration and solidarity. However, the advice that these people gave me at the beginning, based on their own experience, sometimes turned out to be excessive. So, for example, on the first day before we marched off I was advised not to approach a guard too close or step behind him when he called out, because this call was just an excuse on the part of the guard to have an opportunity to shoot. In fact, as I discovered, the guards were forbidden to shoot. The idea apparently was to avoid a repeat of what happened in the case of the *Juni-Aktion* [June operation], namely that a number of prisoners were shot daily during the first weeks.

Despite this ban on shooting a relatively large number of people died in any case without special intervention; as a result of overexertion or for other reasons many keeled over and died at their workplace. I know of a 50-year-old man who was selected for work at the brick works despite the fact that he suffered from a heart condition; he had a heart attack and died on the spot.

Very many fatalities occurred during the very cold December days. The following incident is typical: one day a man collapsed and died as he marched out of the inner camp. On the orders of the guard team the corpse had to be carried to the workplace and then brought back in the evening. This happened because it was feared that otherwise there would be discrepancies at the count.

With a break for half an hour at midday, following the *Mittagsappell* which also lasted half an hour, worked continued until the return march to *Abendappell*. Sitting down was not allowed during the midday break. The breakfast that was carried had to eaten standing. For about a quarter of an hour smoking was also allowed.

When shovelling one was not allowed to stand up straight even for a moment without running the risk of being reported for a disciplinary punishment.

The work in the wood yard as a rule was less strenuous. The supervision was also not as rigorous there. Nevertheless the monotony and tedium were both tiring and irritating, along with the cold.

It was seen as a special privilege to be assigned to *Stubendienst* [room duty]. However, as the number of people doing *Stubendienst* was reduced again and again this privilege only benefitted a few older and weaker people. Even here too there were a number of very unpleasant tasks, such as carrying the enormously heavy food pans, so heavy that older people and those with hernias could not carry them. Collecting food and bread was also not an unadulterated pleasure for other reasons. Aside from having to stand for hours in the freezing cold outside the kitchen, one of the three *Scharführer* [sergeants] was exceptionally brutal. He would often brandish a broom or stick when food was being distributed and took every available opportunity, without any excuse, to hit people in the face who had to come near him and to cause commotion and anxiety in those queuing up for food at the kitchen by making them move at the double.

To be fair to the other SS people working there, it has to be said that one of the others was evidently particularly humane, and that under his supervision the distribution was calm and trouble free, the third was somewhere in the middle insofar as he was sometimes very quiet and then would occasionally try to fit in with the conventions of the camp by punching and kicking people.

Bread distribution was not so bad because one of the SS men there was very quiet, whilst the other was often strict, not with blows but by forcing people to stand stock still for little or no reason and also by bullying those collecting bread in other ways. Occasionally an SS man known to be a particular *Schweinehund* [bastard] turned up at the kitchen who would take the opportunity of choosing particularly weak people when there were unusually heavy sacks or loads that they were not able to carry. The following incident has stayed with me: he asked one of the prisoners in a group adjacent to me what his profession was. He had been a senior civil servant. Having received answers to a number of questions about the man's position and future plans he posed the following question: "You have to admit that you were unworthy of the post you formerly held." The prisoner, who had answered all the previous questions, stayed demonstratively silent. This earned him some blows to the chest: "Answer me, you know I have ways of making you talk." The prisoner continued to remain silent. The punches continued with the result that the prisoner fell backwards without providing the desired answer. This continued for a time until the prisoner finally spoke, but made it quite clear that he did not have an answer to the last question. This marked the end of the incident, which had demonstrated that the SS man did appear to have some scruples after all.

The maintenance of order was largely achieved by the threat of disciplinary action and by the deployment of something that is generally typical of National Socialism, collective punishment. If a prisoner did something that could possibly be construed as incorrect the whole block was punished. It was often the case that such occasions were artificially created by those SS men renowned for their harshness. The Damoclean sword of punishment in the form of *Strafexerzieren* [punitive drills], *stehen am Tor* [standing by the gate], barrack arrest was always hanging over everyone.

If it was observed during the morning wash that someone had not bared their upper body properly, that he kept hands in his trouser pockets, that he had not stepped up quickly enough etc., then the whole block would be punished. Another excuse for punishment was when the block lined up for an *Appell* and the people at the front and sides were not aligned correctly. One imagines that it was partly impossible to keep an absolutely straight line at the sides because some particularly rotund people were not in a position to get in line properly and moreover that everyone had to fall in at the *Appell*, including those who for reasons of illness or whatever could not walk.

On the first night it seemed to be impossible to accommodate everyone in the sleeping room; although most people lay on their sides to save space it turned out that four or five people definitely could not be accommodated. It was forbidden to put these few people in the *Tagesraum* [day room], which was completely empty. Instead, places were found for these four under the threat that the whole block would have to stand outside with no clothes above the waist if space was not made for everyone. In another block that very punishment had been carried out the previous night.

In respect of work duties some measures affording relief were introduced over the coming weeks for older and weaker people. After being examined by the *Lagerälteste* [camp elder] these people were allocated sock darning and potato peeling duties where they could at least sit under cover.

The entire camp was under the supervision of a *Lagerkommandant* who on account of his appearance was known as *"Vierkant"* [foursquare], a stocky man whose speeches were characterised by a large dose of cynicism. The substance of the speech he delivered on the third day after the arrival of the Jewish prisoners, following the *Abendappell*, was roughly as follows: "You have been interned here on account of your hostile attitude towards *Volk und Staat* [people and state]. A concentration camp is not a prison, not a penitentiary yet also not a sanatorium or convalescent home, but rather an educational institution run on National Socialist lines. The principal aim is to educate people in strict discipline. Disciplinary punishment involves 24 *auf den Nackten* until you can hear the angels singing in heaven, being hung out to dry, accommodation in solitary confinement or in the punishment section, *stehen am Tor* etc. etc. If you should get the idea of trying to escape I would point out that no mercy will be shown, bang, a shot will ring out and that's the end of the story, and my SS lads are definitely good shots."

When giving the same speech to some newly arrived Aryan prisoners, which I heard by chance, he added "The aim, insofar as you are Aryans, is to turn you into good *Volkesgenossen* [national comrades]. In the case of Jews the purpose of the education is to teach them how to behave when they encounter a *Wirtsvolk* [host people]."

The tone this *Kommandant* was able to strike becomes apparent from the following utterances. When on occasion a section of prisoners was commanded by its leader to face left as a sign of respect, he shouted "Keep your noses straight, I do not want to see your *Stinkrüben* [ugly mugs]!"

I experienced his first greeting on the morning after our arrival, thus after standing for about 12 hours. He inspected the line of prisoners and, on seeing some scraps of paper on the ground, turned to his adjutant with the words: "Cleanliness does not seem to be something these rogues know about, oh well, they'll get to know it here." The *Lagerkommandant* supervised the entire camp together with the guard teams. The so-called *Lagerführer* [camp leader], who clearly had the rank of *Hauptmann* [captain], was responsible for the inner camp and the treatment of the prisoners.

The systematic torturing and bullying that were routine within the inner camp: standing around for hours, the long, uninterrupted work duties even on Sundays, restriction of free time, being locked in barracks, heating ban, the herding together of people in barracks, all this was clearly on the orders of the *Lagerführer*. I draw this conclusion from the fact that when the usual *Lagerführer* went on leave for a few days we experienced considerable relief, manifested above all in the fact that the lower ranked guards were much more lenient, that we were given the opportunity to write, that Sunday work was suspended and that at midday sitting down was permitted in the barracks.

Below the *Lagerführer* the supervision was led by SS men designated as *Scharführer* or *Blockführer*. Their behaviour towards us varied. There were doubtless those amongst them who, except on days when they were supposed to wear us down, behaved decently and, when not being observed by those above them, went about their duties peacefully. But some of the SS men had manifest sadistic tendencies. Whenever they could find an opportunity to mistreat people they would beat them, kick them and hit them in the face. They particularly had it in for physically clumsy, very obese and mentally inferior people.

Luckily for the prisoners the number of SS men was not so large that they could be everywhere. The delegated supervision in the barracks was largely in the hands of Aryan prisoners who were also our *Vorgesetzte* [superiors] as *Vorarbeiter*. There were also the so-called *Blockältester* [block elder] and *Stubenältester* [room elder] and around eight or nine other Aryan prisoners who supervised each block. Out of a sense of human solidarity they made an effort to make life easier for the Jewish prisoners wherever possible, although they thereby put themselves in danger of serious punishment. A number of them, former SA men who did not behave in this way, only constituted a small minority. On occasion, e.g. one *Stubenältester* would be punished for allowing a few people who entered the barracks freezing and soaked to warm up by the stove for a few minutes. Given the large and diverse mass of people living in the barracks, it was not easy for the *Stubenältester* to keep and maintain order, distribute the food equally, ensure that working hours and other camp rules were observed, and on occasion it was miraculous that they carried out their duties with such consummate composure and self control. One has to bear in mind that most of these people had been under lock and key or behind barbed wire since 1933 and that their nerves had often enough been put to the test. For the most part they were *politische Häftlinge*, Marxists or Communists, who did the supervising.

In the camp the different categories of prisoner were marked by different triangular badges which had to be sewn visibly onto jackets and trousers. The political prisoners had red triangles, the *Berufsverbrecher* blue, the so-called *Arbeitsscheue* [work shy] brown, violet, and pink. *Rückwanderer* [en; returned emigrants] in particular had special markings. One-time Party members in so-called "*Ehrenhaft*" [honourable custody] constituted a special category. They were often deployed to supervise the other prisoners. The highest-ranking group of prisoners, who had also doubtless agreed certain rules of honourable conduct amongst themselves, were the political ones. It was characteristic that amongst them it was completely forbidden to use physical force against other prisoners, although depending on the circumstances the temptation was there often enough. Amongst those labelled "*Arbeitsscheue*" there were mainly prisoners from the *Juni-Aktion,* a mixture of Aryans and Jews. In most cases there was no question of them being work shy, but they were well known as opponents of the Nazis and were to be made harmless or intimidated in this way. Amongst the *Berufsverbrecher* there were also many people who were anything but. Moreover the real career criminals demonstrated considerable solidarity with the Jewish prisoners.

The Jews were designated with a yellow triangle which was sewn across either a brown triangle, for the *Juni-Aktion* or a red triangle for the *Novemberaktion* [November operation], thereby forming a *Mogen Dovid* [Star of David].

Three *Appell*s took place every day. The entire population, with the exception of those in the *Krankenrevier*, thus c. 12–14,000 men, appeared for the early morning and *Abendappell* on the *Appellplatz*. Everybody was counted and reported and it was particularly bad if any discrepancies came to light during the *Abendappell*, e.g. if someone was missing. The *Appell* was then not over until the discrepancy had been resolved. Thus an *Appell* of this kind, which normally lasted more than an hour, could drag on into the late evening, which was terrible on cold December days. Everyone who was not in the *Revier* or *Lazarett* [hospital] had to appear, and if they could not walk they had to be carried. I can still remember a man with serious bladder problems who groaned and screamed continuously. Everyone stood there on the square from 12-year-old boys to 84-year-old men. However, after a few days people over 81 were put up in the *Revier*. But I know the case of an 80-year-old who had to turn up for the *Appell* for three weeks.

On some days the *Abendappell* were followed by a singing class. Three or four songs written and composed by prisoners were sung in chorus. Anyone who did not sing along or had not learnt the text properly was in danger of being beaten. Generally a number of prisoners were also called out by number during the

Abendappell. These were people who had attracted attention or whose names had been noted down and who had to spend the rest of the evening after the *Appell* '*stehen am Tor*' [stand by the gate]. Sometimes right through to the following morning.

During the first weeks prisoners due to be released were also called out at the *Abendappell*. Later those for release were only announced the following morning. Special events repeatedly took place during the *Mittagsappell*. People were selected to be photographed by journalists and appear in the pages of *Der Stürmer* [The Striker; Nazi newspaper] or "*Das Schwarze Korps*" [The Black Corps; SS newspaper]. Rabbis and "millionaires" were generally chosen; amongst the latter, however, various people were also selected who owned considerably less than a million.

One day a prisoner was returned to the camp who had escaped and was led around to a drumbeat and accompanied by a rabbi and a Protestant pastor wearing placards bearing a sarcastic inscription which I can no longer remember. Afterwards the pastor and the rabbi had to *stehen am Tor* for three or four hours.

The punishment "24 *auf den Nackten*" was carried out publically during the *Appell*. I did not experience this myself, however, because during the weeks of my stay there it became known that this whipping had been forbidden by the ministry responsible for overseeing the camp. During this period whipping was also not mentioned in official announcements.

Amongst the prisoners it was well known, however, that whipping still took place in the "*Bunker*". From hearsay I also know that whipping was carried out on one occasion during *Appell* in the first few days after I arrived. I did not even notice it myself on account of the huge crowd of people on the *Appellplatz* and my own extreme exhaustion from standing for so long. I also heard that during the big freeze in December two prisoners received this punishment. The prisoners had fallen asleep at work in a sheltered room due to the cold, did not appear for the *Appell*, and were only found after a search lasting several hours.

It was particularly bad if you became ill. Before being able to see a doctor in the *Revier* you had to expect to stand for at least five hours on the *Appellplatz* with the *Revier* patients. One of the doctors would not treat Jews on principle and also decreed that patients would have to stand through to the next *Appell* after being seen. I know of a case in which a man suffering from tuberculosis of the kidneys had to *stehen am Tor* for a whole day. The result was that even those who were seriously ill no longer reported themselves sick or at most went for outpatient treatment, which was provided by Aryan prisoners in a much more humane way. People suffering from fever were sometimes put up in the *Revier* through the special intervention of the *Stuben-* or *Blockältester;* once they were there their treatment and care was acceptable and they were not exposed to the danger that, in order to identify malingerers, the supervising doctor would demand that one or other of them should *stehen am Tor*. I heard of two cases where patients treated in this way died either during the night or the following day. The average death rate must have been around seven or eight people per day, although it is important to bear in mind that severely ill people were quite often released early.

During the first days some prisoners attempted to commit suicide by trying to get within the range of the *Sicherungs-maschinengewehr* [security machine gun]. They could only be restrained by their comrades with difficulty. I know of one instance in which a prisoner did manage to realise his intention. Of a halo of bullets fired at him only four hit their target, but they were fatal.

Food consisted of a warm meal handed out after the *Abend-appell* as well as a soup at breakfast and the so-called "*Portion*" [portion] which was supplemented on Sunday by some jam. Besides there was also a sufficient quantity of bread. The *Portion* consisted variously of brawn, known in camp language as "*Lagerspeck*" [camp ham], margarine, some cheese, occasionally also smoked or salted herring. The so-called "*Lagerspeck*" was bad, comprising cheap gelatine and offal scraps; the cheese however was edible. The warm meal often contained whale meat which was well-processed, and sometimes peas or beans. The fish soup was not popular. In terms of the kind of expectations one might reasonably have regarding mass catering of this kind, the quality of food preparation could not generally be deemed bad. Generally some coffee or tea was also provided, although it was very weak. One day there was even goulash with potatoes, which was very appetising. On this particular day the kitchen was being presented to the *Reichswehrkommission* [Reich Army Commission] which consisted of various senior officers and which, I heard, had been invited to the inauguration of the new mess. Like other commissions, this one was accompanied by foreign journalists who were very wisely not brought into the camp where the Jews were, however.

The food was adequate for those who had only been in the camp for a short time and therefore still had certain energy reserves, but not for those who had already been there for a long time and were dependent on the camp catering. This alone explains why a large proportion of the detainees piteously begged for bread or other leftovers regardless of the severe punishments that threatened them. There was provision in the camp rules for every prisoner to be handed out RM. 15.- sent to him by relatives. However this payment only began after three weeks. From then it was possible, however, to get all kinds of food cheaply in the canteen. The complete emaciation suffered by the majority of inmates after a few weeks was less a result of the lack of sustenance than the continuous cold they had to endure outside with entirely inadequate clothing. They tried to improve the situation by wrapping a towel, which everyone received, or newspaper around their chest. But as soon as word got out the SS instigated checks during *Appell* and the threat of serious punishment was applied to such misdemeanours. People who were vulnerable to internal illnesses suffered especially. Incidentally, almost everyone had bronchitis to some degree.

On the day of release ordinarily one had to stand out in the open again, from 7 o'clock in the morning until 4 o'clock in the afternoon, until one's freedom was restored under the usual formalities.

B. 324 Herr Bohne from Berlin died at Sachsenhausen in November 1938. He was c. 47 years old and suffered from a serious heart condition so that he collapsed and died one day as a result of the heavy work. His profession was salesman in the confectionery industry.

Amtsgerichtrat [local court judge] Pasch, formerly at Wedding District Court, was in Sachsenhausen for four to five weeks. He was diabetic and very sickly. After his release in December 1938 he had to have a foot amputated due to frostbite and died as a consequence.

B. 325 Only one Jewish family lives in Kemel near Wiesbaden. During the night of the 9th to 10th November the elderly married couple were driven out onto the street in their nightclothes where they had to see and hear in the dark how their home was destroyed. Eventually a baker took pity on them and brought them into the bakehouse of his shop so that they did not have to freeze. One of the couple's sons fled into the woods in the night. The next morning he was found and taken to Buchenwald together with his three brothers and brother-in-law. The parents were allowed to return to their ruined home in the morning.

B. 326 I report only facts which are known to me personally or which I have learned from reliable people, and I am speaking above all from the standpoint of a Leipziger.

On Wednesday 9th November it became known around two o'clock in the afternoon that there were plans to attack the two Jewish cafés. The Jews who were there were able to save themselves in time, so that in the cafés there was only the destruction of the fittings to complain about.

Towards evening it became known to the Gemeinde- und Synagogendiener [community and synagogue sexton] that there were plans to set the community synagogue on fire. He communicated that it seemed superfluous and anyway pointless to try to take any protective measures. In the early part of the night the community synagogue (Gottschedstraße corner with Zentralstraße) and the Ez-Chajim synagogue were set on fire and were quickly in flames. The home of the *Synagogeninspektor* [synagogue administrator] was in a neighbouring part of the community synagogue. He did not return home until after 11 o'clock, had gone to sleep when he was awoken by the noise and the light and, terrified, tried to escape. However the staircase was completely choked with smoke, no exit was free for him any more, only with difficulty could he make himself understood by the people who had gathered round. Thereafter the *Feuerwehr* [fire brigade] was called and his wife rescued by ladder. All his goods and chattels were still in the home. It is noteworthy that this part of the building was not burnt down too. Later it was established however that its furnishings were no longer to be found at the premises. These included a grand piano, the *Thoravorhänge* [Torah curtains] and the robes of the community rabbi and the cantor and the administrator's furniture. On the administrator's writing desk lay a briefcase in which a sum of around RM. 325.- had been counted out, intended to pay a bill the next day. There was also jewellery on the writing desk. When enquiries about the briefcase were made later, it was discovered in police custody. The administrator was asked to retrieve it from there. During several visits to the police station he was repeatedly put off and finally roughly told that he should not dare ask about it any more. An attempt to clarify the matter with the *Geheime Staatspolizei* [Gestapo; secret state police] officials supervising the community office also failed; the community was resigned to finding the amount to pay this bill again.

At the news of the fire, the orthodox community rabbi and a *Synagogenvorsteher* [synagogue board member] arrived at night at the Ez-Chajim Synagogue (at Apels Garten and Otto Schill Straße) with the aim of rescuing *Thorarollen* [Torah scrolls]. They did not reach the synagogue but instead were seized and suffered serious injuries; in particular the *Synagogenvorsteher* suffered wounds that took two weeks to heal. The rabbi's injuries were near his eye, but were not dangerous.

The buildings on the land of the new Jewish cemetery in Delitzscher Landstraße were also set on fire in the night. The large cemetery hall, the small cemetery hall burnt out completely, but also the living quarters by the new hall were completely destroyed. The people living there only got away with their lives. It should be added here that the community was later made responsible for ensuring that the remains of the buildings were completely demolished. The synagogues and the cemetery buildings have been levelled to the ground.

At the same time as the arson at these community buildings the site belonging to Bamberger & Hertz gentlemen's outfitters at Augustusplatz corner with Grimmaische Straße was also set on fire. This fire was already reported in the morning edition of 10th November and was presented there to seem as if the firm's owner had set the site on fire himself in order to commit insurance fraud, since the firm's opportunities for making sales have (recently) become very poor and its financial circumstances have been seriously affected. In a part of the building on the Augustusplatz side the site contained a café that occupied the ground floor and the inside part of the first floor there. Yet the fire burnt in such a way that the business premises of the firm Bamberger & Hertz were completely burnt out, although the space occupied by the café and the office space above it remained completely untouched. The obvious suspect reported to the *Staatsanwaltschaft* [public prosecutor's office] straight away, which however declared that there was no evidence against him. Consequently he went home, was arrested and taken to the concentration camp, and after being held there for seven weeks, taken to the police prison again. There it was attempted to force him to put on record that he acknowledged that he was in some way responsible for causing the fire. He refused, even when they only demanded that he explain that he was not able fully to clear up the suspicions against him. He was finally set free.

The large shop premises of the Uri Gebrüder [Uri Brothers] company were relatively little damaged. Only the numerous shop windows were destroyed and the window displays vanished. The stock was later valued by a trustee and after liquidation the site renovated and used for the textile trade fair.

Smaller and larger mobs appeared in numerous homes and senselessly destroyed their fixtures and fittings. Furniture was smashed up, and they took particular pleasure in shattering mirrors, crystal and similar objects.

Arrests started in the early morning. Partly these were carried out in an orderly way by officers of the *Kriminalpolizei* [criminal police] or the Gestapo, mostly with the collaboration of SA and SS men, but partly mobs of obviously unauthorised people came and dragged Jewish men out of their houses to take them to the police. In the Eutritzsch area of town women were also taken away at first, they were all, men and women, some with children too, put in a public square, then all the women and a few of the men were released again and the rest led away without being allowed to take anything with them. In the Zoo district they chased the prisoners to the Parthe that flows there, made them go down a set of steps that leads down to it, drove them into the water densely packed together, but then let some of them go back home later. Police took the rest away to transfer them to the concentration camp. Some of the people who were arrested were first taken to the court prison and the others to the homeless shelter.

People who had been arrested were treated properly in both sections of the court prison. On the other hand the people who were taken to the homeless shelter were mistreated there in the most shameful way. An overseer, he was designated *Werkleutnant* [work lieutenant], who was in charge of these arrestees quite plainly took it on himself systematically to make sure that the people had no peace during the night. This official appeared at short intervals, yelled at them, made them stand and set up a long-distance run in the hall during which even men over 60 years of age had to jump over obstacles. Others, who could not take part in this due to visible ailments had to form a circle and sing *Weißt Du, wieviel Sternlein stehen?* [lullaby "Do you know how many stars there are?"]

In the course of the morning men over 60 were picked out

one by one and mostly released after a few days. The rest were taken to the Buchenwald camp, that is, provided they were not over 60 years old, the rabbis and cantors of the community, members of the community boards, chief doctors of the Jewish hospitals, also the great majority of authorised Jewish doctors and lawyers, owners of the large firms, but also a considerable number of unemployed and German citizens as well as stateless people. The transport to the railway station left around midday on Friday.

B. 327 The general *Judengesetze* [laws relating to the Jews] in the Third Reich are known. Before I go in detail into the events of 10th November 1938, I would like briefly to list the reasons which led to the ruin of our business. Customers started the boycott immediately after the seizure of power, it intensified continuously, not so much voluntarily as through coercive means on the part of the state and the Party. (Withdrawal of the *Winterhilfe* [*Winterhilfswerk des deutschen Volkes*; Winter Relief for the German People], welfare support, support for families with lots of children, exclusion of children from individual schools, threats of non-promotion of near relatives, exclusion [from] Party organisations etc.).

However, since this did not lead to the destruction of Jewish businesses fast enough for the Party, a boycott by suppliers was later instigated. First the *Reichsnährstand* [Reich Food Corporation] blocked the delivery of flour and semolina, then consignments of foreign goods were also blocked (oil, citrus fruit, later partly cocoa, chocolate, rice). At the end of 1937 the *Staatliche Salinen München* [National Salt Mines Munich] informed us that they would no longer supply salt; in the middle of 1938 the *Süddeutsche Zuckerfabrik* [South German Sugar Works], with whom we had done a lot of business for decades, made the same announcement. At the same time, the manufacturers of branded goods partly started to block deliveries, first Oetker, Bielefeld.

Early on a number of customers cited the Party in cases of non-payment. Since all our demands were justified, we mostly took no notice of that, although we sometimes received directly threatening letters from the Party telling us not to take any action against debtors.

Initially, contact with the authorities was still polite. At the end of December 1937, the *Bezirksamt* [district office] Weißenburg refused to issue *Reiselegitimationskarten* [travel permits; *Durchlaßscheine*], which was actually nine months before the corresponding Reich law was passed. This made any travel impossible, which would inevitably lead to the demise of most wholesale businesses. In 1938, the *Finanzamt* [tax office] belatedly collected the sum of RM. 35,000.- for *Umsatzsteuer* [turnover tax], since allegedly the conditions for a reduction based on wholesale did not apply, even though there was a written permit from the *Finanzamt*.

During a meeting at the *Finanzamt* to apply for a refund the clerk said that if an appeal was lodged the *Landesfinanzamt* [regional tax office] would carry out a further audit of *Umsatzsteuer* for the period up to 1935. This was indeed scheduled for November 1938 and was only not carried out because of the events in November.

In ... the situation was such that for years it had been almost impossible to let children out on the streets on their own. Adults were also not safe from being accosted by school children; until the start of 1938 complaints to the *Gendarmerie* [constabulary] resulted in some peace, later even complaints were pointless. Window smashing was in part prevented by the glass insurance companies. Any purchases made in Jewish shops and talking to or greeting of a Jew by a non-Jew were immediately reported to the *Bürgermeister* [mayor] who called the "culprits" in. They were excluded from city deliveries, support etc. In May 1938, hairdressers agreed *en bloc* not to serve Jews any more. Individual craftsmen had already done this earlier.

At the beginning of autumn 1938 during the Czech war crisis animosities visibly increased. Being jostled by people large and small, stone throwing, window smashing, removal of shutters during the day were not uncommon. The unrest and nervousness increased even further when it was learnt from various Jewish *Gemeinden* [communities] (Leutershausen, Ellingen etc.)

that Jews had been forced to leave their houses on the high holidays, leaving their goods and chattels wherever they were, and sell the synagogues at ludicrously low prices (in some cases for a few marks).

I want to add that my 17-year-old daughter witnessed a mob attack during the *Juni-Aktion* [June operation] in Berlin. The Jewish girls boarding school was attacked; a telephone call to the Berlin *Überfallkommando* [flying squad] prompted the question as to whether non-Aryans were involved, in which case it would not be a matter for the *Überfallkommando*.

On 10th November 1938 between 4 and 5 o'clock in the morning I heard steps in the garden. When I looked out of the window eight to ten men (SA) were standing, heavily armed with axes, hatchets, daggers and revolvers. By the time I woke my wife and my 11-year-old son a man was already in the bedroom who ordered us to go to the basement and immediately started to smash everything to pieces: the washing jug and bowl, mirrors, windows, furniture, doors etc. After we (which included my sister-in-law and daughter) had been in the basement for a short time I was called up. When my daughter wanted to come with me she was pushed back. Somebody yelled at me: "*Du Lump* [you wretch], you know that since 12 o'clock midnight you have been declared fair game for us, give us your documents." By the time I had unlocked the desk I had received such a blow to the face that my glasses fell off and broke, my right eye swelled up heavily and my pupil was paralysed. The doctor explained later that I could have lost my sight from this blow. Then I was shoved into a corner and indiscriminately pelted with items of furniture. That I only sustained three flesh wounds and no serious injury has to be described as extremely lucky. In the meantime, the entire house was wrecked in the way described above. In the kitchen every last piece of crockery was smashed; in the basement my wife was hit on the head with a full tin of food; the women had to smash wine bottles and preserving jars themselves.

The mob came after the SA, then the school children; each party destroyed and stole yet more. It can be stated without any doubt that the SA took away the contents of the writing desk: a gentleman's gold wristwatch, a new gentleman's wristwatch, RM. 120.- in cash, a wedding ring, a necklace. A lady's gold wristwatch and a girl's ring were also stolen on the same Thursday. It should be added that a part of the large tiled stoves and the grand piano were also destroyed.

By the time my wife got round to packing a few days later, all the wardrobes and drawers were almost completely empty, so that almost all the clothes and most of the underwear had been stolen. All Jewish homes in ... were treated in this or a similar way. In the meantime, the synagogue with all the *Thorarollen* [Torah scrolls], all the prayer books, *tefillin* [phylacteries], *tallit*s [prayer shawls], the over 100-year-old *Memorbuch* [memory book] etc. were also set on fire and burnt. The unusable *Thorarollen,* which had been stored in the outbuilding, were not burnt. The city did not pay anything for the large plot where the *Bezirksamt* [district office] Weißenburg synagogue, the bath house, the teacher's home had stood, nor for the outbuilding and the garden, since the cost for clearing up equalled its value. The Jewish cemetery was also repeatedly desecrated before and after the 10th November.

On the 10th November, after the various destruction operations, we were allowed to pack some underwear and clothes and had to go to the railway station through rows of the rabble and accompanied by their jeers. Other members of the *Gemeinde* were already there, others already left on earlier trains. Some who remained were badly mistreated the same evening; partly by the SA, in the *Rathaus* [town hall] the over 70-year-old doctor ... in particular, who was so upset by it that he took his own life. The remaining Jews had to leave town the following day, which brought the century-old Jewish *Gemeinde* to an end.

We went to Munich, where I met my brother who had travelled a few hours earlier. After a short stay my brother and I were arrested. After various personal details had been taken down we were taken to Dachau. There, various personal details were recorded again, we were photographed and had to wait for hours until we got to the bath house. There we were brought before the doctor after the bath and had to announce: "*Schutzhaftjude* [protective custody Jew] X. respectfully reporting." Because we had not announced ourselves loud enough, with most of the other prisoners I was slapped round the face in front of the *Stabsarzt* [medical officer]. Examinations were not carried out; we were simply asked: "Ill or had an accident?"

However, the sick, the old, cripples, diabetics and the mentally subnormal all remained in custody; in our barrack e.g. an elderly gentleman who had polio, could hardly walk and speak and was incontinent.

After the "examination" we came out into the open from the warm bath house dressed only in short shirts, socks, trousers and *Drillichjacke* [cotton drill jacket]. We all had to stand until midnight whether we had been imprisoned early that morning, like individual gentlemen from Munich, or later. SS men watched us and if anybody was seen not standing to attention properly there were slaps around the face and shoves. After 12 o'clock we were led to the barracks. There we received the only food of the day, tea and *Kommissbrot* [army bread]. The barracks themselves were split into four dormitories; each dormitory consisted of two rooms, intended for 50 men. However, they were occupied by 200. The washroom and toilet were accordingly insufficient. Initially four men had to make do with one towel, which was also used for drying the crockery. Later towels and underpants could be bought in the canteen.

The daily routine was roughly as follows: wake-up at 5 o'clock, wash, coffee. We were allowed to eat in the barracks, but there were blocks where almost always one had to eat and drink outside, i.e. standing. This depended on the *Stubenältestenr* [room elders], who, of course, were never taken to task by the SS in charge for bad treatment of the Jews. Since the rooms had to be cleaned before the *Appell* [roll call], it was necessary to leave them at half past 5. We then had to wait for some time on the camp road before we were led to the *Appellplatz* [parade ground]. After the *Appell*, the *Zimmerdienst* [room cleaning group] (which included me most of the time) was allowed to stand down, whereas most people had to march and do *Exerzieren* [punitive drills] in all weathers until after 11 o'clock.

Initially Jewish former officers were allowed to be in charge, later only Aryans. After lunch, we usually had 30–60 minutes' free time, then it was *Appell* again, marching and *Exerzieren* again and after a short break, evening *Appell*. After the evening meal we were free until bed time (8 o'clock).

On the *Appellplatz* as in the whole camp and even in the barracks, one was [never] safe from SS checks. These almost never passed without beatings and shoving. On one occasion I was helping a sick person along when an SS man came and ordered me to let him walk by himself and gave me a push from behind for no other reason. Similarly I had a broom thrown at my head when I did not carry out an order fast enough in the barracks, but, luckily, without being hit. Everybody had to go to the *Appell*, whether sick or old. So it happened that the sick and weak often had to be carried by 2–4 men. People who reported to the *Revier* [sick bay] or the doctor were often sent away 2–3 times before they were seen; then they were often discharged without any or insufficient examination and without decent treatment.

Special events

On one occasion all the Jewish blocks (c. 10,000 men) had to stand on the *Appellplatz* from lunchtime till 6 o'clock in the evening. Standing still for 30–60 minutes on the *Appellplatz* was not uncommon, especially during the evening *Appell* we were often bullied by having to stand still for longer than usual instead of being allowed to move.

An SS man asked an acquaintance (aged over 70) his name. When he gave it without the prerequisite addition *Schutzhaft-jude* he was twice slapped round the face so hard that he fell over. Shortly afterwards the man was released and died two days [after] his release, another man 2 hours after his return to Munich.

An approximately 60-year-old man with a bladder complaint asked to be allowed to relieve himself. When this was refused and he replied something, he was hit so hard that he fell over. His comrades were forbidden to help him up. In the presence of the SS he was so badly beaten by the *Stubenälteste* (an Aryan prisoner) that he was dead when he was carried off the square.

One evening a Munich *Sanitätsrat* [medical consultant] reported to the doctor with appendix pains. He was refused treatment and had to return to the barracks. The following morning the *Sanitätsrat* called for help. A few minutes later a colleague had to confirm that he was dead. It could not be ascertained whether a ruptured appendix or heart attack had been the cause.

One gentleman died of a heart attack on the *Appellplatz*. He was simply left there and it took 20–30 minutes before the *Sanitätspersonal* [medical orderlies] came to pick him up with the words "Another one's croaked."

On release day after having coffee we had to stand from 5 o'clock in the morning until the train left Dachau at 4 o'clock in the afternoon without any other food.

According to Aryan prisoners, the whole "*Juden-Aktion* [Jews operation] of November 1938", as the matter was called in the files, had no connection with the vom Rath affair, since preparations in Dachau had been completed considerably earlier.

Even whilst I was still in Dachau, my wife was threatened that I would not be released from the concentration camp until my siblings abroad had their mortgages on my property cancelled. In fact, although I was released earlier I had to sell my house for RM. 14,000- which had a value of at least RM. 23,000.- taking all the warehouses into account. A further RM. 2,500.- was deducted from that for damages caused by the SA on 10th November during their wild frenzy of destruction.

In the above report I have, almost without exception, mentioned only facts that I have seen with my own eyes; anything else, especially from other blocks, I have left out, even if it had been reported by an absolutely trustworthy source.

B. 328 There are people whose look speaks of the fear of death when they open their lips. Dread resonates in their words when they are able to free their hearts from experiences that are almost impossible to render in human language. They are prisoners released from German concentration camps. A few of them were able to return to the light of life after weeks or months, because they or their relatives managed to emigrate to some distant country. Verifiable emigration is the only key which enables the gates of the concentration camps to unlock outwards. Few are able to get hold of this key because almost every gate in the world is being bolted against emigration. Even the small South American countries today demand proof of larger or smaller payments from the emigrants. Namely the foreign currencies that are so scarce in Germany. Despite this, one or another prisoner can still be freed through acquisition of the necessary emigration papers and money.

On leave – not released!

Upon release from the concentration camp the prisoner is first handed over immediately outside the camp gates to *Kriminalbeamten* [detectives] who receive him. None of those is allowed to enter a concentration camp. Protected from any gaze, the *Totenkopfverbände* [Death's-Head units] of the SS reign alone. If the prisoner returns to his home town he is issued with a fixed deadline by when he must have emigrated. Up to that day he must register daily with the police. Thus as long as he continues to breathe German air he is further placed under the heaviest psychological pressure. When the day of release arrives he is told: "You are not released, you are only on leave. The arm of the Gestapo is long! You are forbidden to recount in the slightest to anyone what you have experienced or seen. You are forbidden to show your body to anyone! Otherwise you will lose your life! Our international organisation is sufficiently large and powerful to carry out your punishment anywhere in the world."

Those released prisoners find themselves under this dreadful pressure; the following picture can be compiled from their harrowing reports. Consideration for them makes it a human obligation to use these with greater prudence and blurring all traces. The information that our individual informants provided has been carefully checked and compared for accuracy and reliability. There can be no doubt about the truth. If someone asks himself whether such a situation is possible in the centre of Europe, inside a country with an ancient culture, then one must unfortunately answer that these reports and words are anyway only able to render an inadequate picture of the horrifying truth. In fact things happen day after day that even a satanic vision could not imagine. However, in order to remain faithful to the truth at least to some degree, terminology must be presented in what follows that the half-civilised person does allow past his lips, but which is the language of the concentration camps and their personnel. *Le style c'est l'homme* [the manner reflects the person]– applies here too, although the term "person" seems to be missing.

June 1938

Several things were published about the German concentration camps in the first two or three years after the formation of the Third Reich which aroused the world's horror. Then it gradually went silent about these. One believed they dealt with incidents, outrages from the first revolutionary phase of National Socialism. One thought that with the consolidation of National Socialist power this worst form of terror had been slowly liquidated, one accepted that with the successes of the Hitler government internally and externally and with its stabilisation, those elements would be gradually eradicated on whose account the inhumane incidents of the years 1933–35 had been made. This belief is erroneous! This is alarmingly proven by the summer of 1938. From 13th to 20th June 1938 a wave of arrests gushed spontaneously and unexpectedly over the whole Reich, bringing fear and horror in countless homes. During that week Jews and non-Jews day after day were dragged from their beds at the crack of dawn by *Kriminalpolizeibeamte* [detectives]. Nobody knew why or wherefore. Everyone felt themselves to be in jeopardy. Many no longer dared to sleep in their homes, some went away. For the first three or four days of the operation the standpoints from which the arrests were undertaken were completely opaque. The picture gradually emerged that those with previous convictions could be taken into *Vorbeugungshaft* [protective custody] in accordance with a decree from the end of 1937 of the *Reichsminister des Inneren* [Minister of the Interior]. The precondition for arrest was a sentence of a very minor level, often some sort of police punishment for violating closing time, a traffic offence or something similar. The wave of arrests hit randomly in one form or another, but anyway people who if they were to blame for something had atoned for it long ago. The "*Sonderaktion Juden*" [special operation Jews] were processed with particular sharpness; however almost no one knew why his arrest happened, let alone which dreadful consequences it would have for him. One learnt next to nothing about the fate of those arrested. The anxious worry of uncertainty weighed on their families. Then it gradually seeped out that those arrested were taken first to local police officers, for whom they had to write down a curriculum vitae, and then on from there to the gloomy, red, imposing building of the *Polizeipräsidium* [police headquarters] on the Alexanderplatz in Berlin, the casemates, halls and "bunkers" of which were filled ever tighter with living prey. The same is true of the *Polizeipräsidien* of other big cities. A few – very few – of the arrested were released again very soon, be it because they could produce papers concerning their impending emigration or because of particular conspicuous physical disabilities, e.g. one-armed or one-legged war wounded; but also by no means invariably so for such disabled. Eerie activities, comings and goings dominated in those nights and days in the red building on Alexanderplatz. In the yard the rumbling of lorries overloaded with their prey did not cease. Rooms designated and equipped with "*Schlafpritschen*" [plank beds] for 20 to 30 prisoners were tightly jammed with a hundred or more men who awaited their fate in highest nervous tension. It was not long before they would learn of it. They were allocated to replenishment of the concentration camps.

In the week beginning Monday 13th June, transport after transport departed there. No kind of escape existed any more. In one of the transports on 17th June was a man who during imprisonment at Alexanderplatz had prayed incessantly by himself as a devout Jew. Now, at the moment of departure, he lost his strength. He fell to the ground jerkily with severe heart spasms. Fellow prisoners turned to the *Polizeiaufseher* [police overseer] and showed him the man, who was completely unfit to be transported, begging him for a doctor. The *Aufseher* still possessed sufficient humanity to enquire of his superior. His decision was negative, however. Even this man had to be transported, lifted and propped up by his comrades in fate, in the transport vehicle which could barely contain the number of inmates ... This one example should serve in the place of many and illustrate the style and form of this operation.

The world has already heard something of the concentration camp in Dachau and its horrors. It is known that since the coup in Austria it serves primarily for prisoners from Vienna and Austria. But now two new names of concentration camps emerge, about which the public has heard little until now. It seeps out that the transports of those whose freedom has been stolen without a judge's decision mostly trundle in the direction of Weimar, once the city of the highest German culture, and to the vicinity of Berlin, to Oranienburg. The two names, responsible for unutterable sorrows and many, many, tears, are: Buchenwald near Weimar and Sachsenhausen near Oranienburg.

If the number of deaths resulting from the disturbances in the Sudetenland from 12th to 17th September 1938 totalled 30, then the number of fatalities during the first weeks in these two concentration camps was not less but higher! Meanwhile these have steadily increased from week to week, though not at the same tempo, and by the end of August 1938 accounted for about 150 known cases. But by no means each fatality is known anyway. The full extent of the June *Verhaftungsaktion* [arrests operation], which the *Kriminalpolizei* abruptly stopped through two secret orders on 19th and 20th June, is genuinely not known. In any case, according to the statement of population estimated in the camp, Sachsenhausen was filled with about 10,000 men, and this figure can also be a yardstick for Buchenwald. The number of Jews amongst the prisoners there was assessed at 1,500, around 1,000 in Sachsenhausen. In the latter the decrease through fatalities was not so rapid as in Buchenwald where the number of Jewish prisoners declined, mainly through death and partly through release, to around 1,200.

RM. 3.- charge for cremation ashes

Notification of deaths to the unlucky wives or other individuals left behind by the victims probably occurred in the unique form of a police announcement, those involved were only then able to report to police stations to take receipt of the ashes of their husbands in exchange for a fee of three marks. The cause of death was given briefly as "*Gehirnschlag*" [stroke] or "auf der Flucht erschossen" [shot whilst escaping]. What these words meant is detailed below. This unbelievable valuation of human feelings corresponds exactly to the valuation of a human life by the men in the concentration camps, the executors of the Third Reich. The concentration camp means sentence of death without prosecutor and without judge, slow, agonising, mental and physical destruction full of horrible orderliness, compared to which the implementation of the death penalty of a murderer by gallows, axe or the electric chair is humane.

"We are not humane..."

The transports trundled into the concentration camps in long processions from day to day, packed full of their unfortunate human prey. The executioners were already standing ready to receive them. The first punches, kicks and curses happened randomly and indiscriminately as soon as they jumped off the wagons. Hell had taken delivery of its victims. The spirit of this place was left in no doubt from the speech of the *Lagerkommandant* [camp commandant], which followed soon afterwards: "You are not in a prison here, nor a gaol – prisons and gaols are humane. We are not humane!" And the motto already fell from the lips of the *Kommandant* – named von Jananovsky according to his signature – that was to become the red thread running through the days and weeks that would now begin to pull the prisoners, the expression:

"*Peng – und Scheißdreck wird weggeräumt!*" [Bang – and filth is removed!] Bang: that was the unerring shot of the SS sentry from his carbine, filth – that means a human life; a lifeless body that is "removed" – and whose alleged ashes a widow can take delivery of in exchange for a RM. 3.- fee. Anyway a shot in the heart from the carbine is the mildest of deaths, sought voluntarily by some, in order to be released from the agony that they are unable to bear any more. That is then "auf der Flucht erschossen".

"Zur roten Fahne" *[to the red flag]*

Amongst the prisoners it is known as going "*zur roten Fahne*". The methods by which they are brought to it are as refined as they are hideous, and it often requires true strength of character to escape this temptation. Examples will follow. However, one case of this strength of character is cited here. It is that of the former doctor in Vienna Dr. Niedermeier, who was the only Austrian prisoner interned in Sachsenhausen, and the subject of exceptional tortures. His "crime" consisted of writing a pamphlet against sterilisation during the Schuschnigg government. Scarcely were these grounds for his arrest known when the *SS-Führer* [SS leader] of Sachsenhausen built a Laube [arch] as it is known in camp language, around him, i.e. standing in a ring around him, insulting him most dreadfully, threatened him with cutting off his genitals, and levelled him with kicks. Everywhere he showed himself in the camp or at work, his *Quälgeister* [torturers] drew each other's attention to him. During work on a firing range for the SS he was summoned to a high mound of sand and was made to stand with his face towards the assembled *SS-Führern* and his back towards the slope. Under crude insults and to the amusement of his *Quälgeister*, the doctor staggered from a dreadful punch to the larynx, so that he fell head over heels, backwards down the slope of the hill. Then he was summoned back up again. He hurried back to the top of the hill, half dazed, and had to stand in the same position. A new punch. Again he toppled down. Again he had to go up. And thus the same spectacle was repeated anew. In camp language this is called "*fertigmachen*" [preparing] the prisoner. Preparation for the "*rote Fahne*". These small red flags surrounded the working area of the prisoners, they bordered the so-called "neutral zone"', which no prisoner was allowed to cross. The *SS-Posten* [SS guards] stood ready to shoot him with loaded carbine "*auf der Flucht*". Despite the exceptional tortures to which he had be exposed day in, day out, Dr Niedermeier did not cross the line of red flags, which they wanted to force him to do. Because he had thought of his five children. How is he today? Is he still alive . . . ?-

A fellow sufferer, one architect Neubauer from Munich, a man aged about 50, was unable to muster the same steadfastness against the tortures. Eventually he chose to go to the red flags, and to receive the *coup de grâce*. He was subjected to the following process, amongst others, which was occasionally carried out on prisoners: the prisoner in question had to dig a deep hole close to the workshops and get into it. Other prisoners had to fill the hole until only his head was showing, like a cabbage in a field. In this indescribable situation, the SS men threatened him with their revolvers, laid into his head as though it were a target, and carried on their joke with his helplessness and fear of death until he was dug up again.

Clothing

The life, more correctly vegetating, of the detainee begins with the surrender of civilian things and his being clothed in prisoner uniform. The outfit that now forms his clothes is thrown to the prisoner without regard to whether or not it fits him. Small, slender people receive things intended for those of a larger size. Broad and fat receive those for the small and slender. People with a belly – and the majority of prisoners are in riper years, even including some over 70 – are particularly ignored. Each belly particularly evokes the instinct to torture, as do each disability and each weakness. An example: one fat man received a pair of trousers that was much too tight for him and which he was unable to button over his belly with his best efforts. Now he was shouted at: We'll show you, *Du Schwein* [you pig], that the trousers fit you. He had to stand with the trousers in front of an SS man seated on a stool and who pushed violently on his belly with a boot whilst other SS men held him from behind.

A music director from Breslau [now Pol. Wrocław] named Rosendorf sank to the ground in misery because of kicks to the belly. The bloody traces left behind by the steel-capped boots could still be seen by other prisoners shortly before his death.

Kicks to the belly with heavy, steel-capped boots, kicks to the backside, so common that the victims were no longer able to sit down from pain, kicks to the calves, red scars which can still be seen weeks after release, kicks from the front and, above all, from behind, are the daily lot of the prisoners. Kicks, kicks, kicks. People die of "*Gehirnschlag*" [stroke] from kicks. People are literally trampled. It happened thus in Sachsenhausen, e.g. that one man lay on the ground, just a lump of flesh, whilst the *SS-Blockführer* [block leader] roared and kicked at him to stand up, until one of his inferiors informed him, "*Die Judensau ist schon tot*" [the Jewish pig is already dead].

Like the fat people, all those with a disability who have the misfortune of being arrested, and the elderly, less mobile, are also targeted with a particular ferocity. More is demanded from the older people, who have mostly achieved something in life as traders, leading staff, academics and intellectuals in advanced years, than by the strictest army in the world from a young, eighteen-year-old recruit. To be regarded as an "intellectual" is a particular stigma. Those with glasses were especially targeted. The glasses are anyway mostly shattered by the first blows and thumps. There is no replacement for them. The short-sighted one who has now been robbed of his glasses has to suffer particularly, on account of his clumsiness. For every human suffering prompts the SS men's urge for hate all the more strongly. A man with one eye already lost his artificial eye during the first mistreatment after his arrival. All attempts to find a replacement were in vain. Can one imagine this excruciating situation? Can one imagine the excruciating situation of those people whose trusses, which they have to wear for an inguinal or scrotal hernia, were taken away with their civilian clothes and who now have to carry out the unbelievably heavy physical labour regardless of being without their truss? In Sachsenhausen there was a man – he should also be a specific illustration for the totality – with a hand mutilated during the war, somebody who had lost a part of his health and creativity in the war. Here he was given no special consideration, on the contrary! In the concentration camp "*Dank des Vaterlandes*" [gratitude of the fatherland] consists of an intensified martyrdom. Things went so badly for the man whose right hand had been shot to pieces that he had to report sick after a few weeks.

Doctor or Unmensch [monster]?

To report sick is certainly the greatest risk an inmate in a concentration camp can take. If he does so, it only happens in final despair and with the fear of death in his heart. This was so even for that war-wounded man. Prisoners who wanted to report sick had to report to the camp doctor. They were not examined by him in order to determine their illness, they simply had to state their name and illness themselves. The "doctor" at Sachsenhausen stood there motionless and for each one he only made a sign with his thumb, to the left or to the right. To the right meant that the patient would receive treatment, to the left meant: heaviest work! The thumb almost always went to the left. In Sachsenhausen this meant working on the *Schießplatz* [shooting range], which was built by the prisoners for the SS troops; anyway the heaviest work, during which the "malingerer'" who had wanted to report sick was treated especially severely, was often enough in his state of health to dispatch him to the next world. The doctor's thumb went to the left even for that war-wounded man with the hand shot to pieces. He could scarcely drag himself on the half-hour forced march to the workplace. Finally there, the veteran was forced to carry out the heaviest work of all: digging up the stumps and roots of felled trees. Goaded again and again by curses, blows and kicks he worked, semi-conscious, the long and tortuous hours of a day, which seemed almost without end. The heavy tree stumps, cleared from deep in the ground, were then loaded onto a trailer. The whole work gang made the return march to the camp, the trailer with its heavy load at the head. It had to be dragged by prisoners harnessed at the front like horses. And this at the fastest speed, always ahead of the advancing forced march. Amongst the human draught animals, who wheezed and groaned in their harnesses, was the sick man with the hand shot to pieces. He was literally dragged along, his legs did not carry him, all strength had left him. Thus did the procession enter the camp. At the end of the work day all prisoners had to stand in file in front of the barracks. They had to report at attention for *Appell* [roll call]. The man with the maimed hand stood in his row. The last of his strength gave way from his body, he could no longer stand upright and collapsed. Harsh orders, kicks. He had to stand up. One last attempt to stand upright. In vain. He lay helpless on the ground. Senseless rage amongst the *Vorgesetzte* [superiors]. Only a faint whimper could be heard from the small heap on the ground. Wilder kicking, regardless of where they landed. Then the whimpering stopped too. A war-wounded man was literally trampled into the ground at *Appell* in a concentration camp. He was not alone...

"*Der Dank des Vaterlandes*" [the gratitude of the fatherland]

Particular targets of hate were the former front-line soldiers and veterans amongst the Jewish prisoners. It was even denied that Jews had fulfilled their duty with honour during Germany's most difficult time, in the world war. One persecuted them in particular out of the instinctive feeling that one had to justify the relentless antisemitism for oneself, because one refuted such men in comparison with oneself in one's wrongfulness and senselessness. One hated particularly those Jews who had been distinguished by their bravery in the face of the enemy, their *Eiserne Kreuz* [Iron Cross] or *Verwundetenabzeichen* [decoration for the war-wounded] was already ripped from the jacket upon arrival in the camp, trodden upon, they were ridiculed, cursed and mistreated. The primitive torturers in their black SS uniforms were unaware that they were simultaneously besmirching German *Soldatenehre* [military honour]. They lacked any understanding of it. Only the smallest number of these young fellows had learnt about the war. They had only been drilled in the annihilation of an apparent enemy who could not defend itself. But often in the evenings the old front-line soldiers amongst the prisoners stated that they would rather have spent four more years in the hell of Verdun or the barrage at the Somme in the face of the enemy than four weeks in a concentration camp, where the most horrible enemy of all could strike the defenceless in the back at any moment.

The quarry at Buchenwald

In Buchenwald near Weimar the day begins with being woken at three in the morning. The barrack buildings here are still so insufficient that, according to the reports of freed prisoners, they had use sheep pens for sleeping accommodation, where they spent the nights crammed together on the ground. Fatigue from the superhuman work was so great that they were able to sleep, despite the pain caused by their mistreatment during the day. Employment happened here from 3 o'clock in the morning onwards, 13 hours daily of heavy physical work! The worst work that one could be allocated to was work in the quarry, its approach route alone lasted an hour. Quarry work, hewing, dragging, loading and transporting the stone, is the heaviest work probably anywhere. For people from intellectual professions it is intolerable, quickly leads to loss of strength and in the long term to certain death. From this one can easily explain the particularly numerous fatalities at Buchenwald. Apparently the forced labour of the Jews building the pyramids in Egypt is taken as the model here. What went on there in the quarry at Weimar can only be suggested in the following reliably reported incident: a middle-aged prisoner, not strong, had just attempted to heave up a lump of stone with enormous effort. The *SS-Führer* [SS leader] who was supervising called him and the man dragged himself and the stone over to the guard. He shouted: "*Du Judensau*, are you trying to slack off work? Lifting such a small stone? Give it here and take a larger one" – The man gave the stone to the *SS-Führer*, who took it in both hands, and walked back to the quarry to use every bit of strength to lift a larger stone. As he bent down the *SS-Führer* walked up behind him and struck him in the neck with the lump of stone in his hands with such force that the prisoner collapsed forwards silently.

Those who collapse in the quarry and cannot stand up again are grabbed by the ankles by two men and face down dragged back to the camp over sticks and stones, over jagged rocks and tough tree roots. When the body has reached the camp there is definitely no life in it. Dragged to death ...

No water . . .

In July 1938 and into August an extraordinary summer heat wave sweltered over all Germany. The tortures of the prisoners were further increased through it. Buchenwald is in an elevated position. As already stated, this camp was still very provisionally established and unsuited for the mass billeting that it had to accept during the notorious week of 13th to 18th June. Water had to be pumped from below. The water supply was extremely deficient. The prisoners, who had to perform the heaviest work for 13 hours a day in the blistering heat, were denied the simplest thing required by any living being, drinking water. A torture beyond compare! A full ten days long these unfortunates were without any water whatsoever! The greatest number of fatalities was in those days.

"Life" in the camp

Whilst the day begins in Buchenwald at 3 in the morning and daily work lasts for thirteen hours, in Sachsenhausen waking is "only" at half past 5 in the morning and the work lasts "only" eleven hours. The camp consists of 60 blocks, most of these wooden barracks serve as quarters for the prisoners. A concentration camp is guarded day and night in three concentric circles by a threefold cordon. The outermost barrier externally consists of the electrified barbed wire all around. In between can be found the towers occupied by machine guns ready to fire, as well as searchlights for night which tirelessly spy all over in the dark and miss nothing. Wherever the slightest thing moves at night, the searchlights concentrate their beam and firing begins at the next moment. Daily existence for the inmates in the camp and at the workplaces beyond the camp takes place with the incessant threat of death from the machine guns and carbines. It is hard to imagine the discipline in the camp without experiencing it. Incessant checking of prisoner numbers assembled from blocks happens day after day. Numbers checks in the morning at reporting for duty, counting off for the march to work. Strict check on the march to the camp, new check in the evenings at *Appell* when the entire personnel is mustered by blocks. Woe if one is missing, if something does not tally! In Buchenwald when something did not tally at the count and the result of the counting compared to the camp population showed that one man was missing, the prisoners had to line up in blazing heat in rank and file and remain standing to attention for twelve hours, according to multiple consistent reports. The unfortunates had to remain standing thus in the position as described, beneath the muzzles of the machine guns without daring to move a muscle. Woe to him whose knees gave in! Even the most natural of human needs was no reason to move from your position throughout the whole time. Sweat dripped from bodies. Muscles failed. It was an outrageous type of torture. The inmates of Sachsenhausen were in the same situation for an hour and a half once when the difference between the count and the official figures differed by five men. Then it transpired after repeated recounting that a gang of five men had not been included inadvertently. This was a terrible warning sign permanently in front of their eyes for the inmates in Buchenwald: one remembers that a long time ago, months before the last *Verhaftungsaktion* in June, two Buchenwald concentration camp prisoners had killed the *SS-Posten* [guard] who were supervising them and had fled: one of them managed to reach safety abroad, the other was caught and executed. In the centre of Buchenwald concentration camp, a gallows projected towards heaven, on which hung the corpse of the executed man, preserved through embalming. Day in, day out the inmates of Buchenwald had him before their eyes.

Number checks

Vordermann [person in front] and *Seitenrichtung* [side alignment]: the alpha and the omega of camp organisation. *Vordermann* and *Seitenrichtung*, the exact positioning of prisoners beside one another and behind one another in rank and file, which always gives an overview of their complete presence. One was mustered thus in the camp and marched thus to and from work. The speed of the march is extremely fast. It is more running than walking. A continuous run. The perpetual movement without a pause, which does not recognise any fatigue, must choke the people, most of whom were no longer young. The march back to the camp was at this speed after 13 or eleven hours of hard work. No notice was taken of exhaustion. Mistreatment, kicks do for them. Whoever wanted to remain behind was exposed to the heaviest punishments one can speak of, as *Arbeitsscheu* [work shy]. The prisoners in different categories have badges on their jackets in the shape of triangles of various colours. There are the *politische Häftlinge* [political prisoners], the *Gewohnheitsverbrecher* [habitual criminals] and the *Arbeitsscheuen* [work shy]. "*Gewohnheitsverbrecher*", with a green triangle are the inmates who actually committed a punishable deed, but had served the sentence, so were not now actually in the concentration camp for an offence. "*Arbeitsscheue*" is the official designation for the Jewish prisoners here. Yet this designation for people who were suddenly wrenched out of their profession, their home, their family by the Gestapo in June 1938, shows the arbitrariness of this measure. Perhaps the following incident is representative of this: in Sachsenhausen a prisoner was called out to appear before the *SS-Führer* shortly after his internment. He announced himself correctly, as is demanded of all Jews there: "*Arbeitsscheue* X. (surname) Y. (forename)." He was asked what his occupation was and reported: "For 20 years in a leading, regularly employed position at the Z. firm in H." – a major mercantile undertaking. These are the "*Arbeitsscheue*"! They wear a brown triangle and for labelling as Jews a yellow triangle too. Both triangles together form the Star of David.

Hygiene

The state of health amongst the prisoners in the concentration camp is a terrible chapter. The food, cooked with a large amount of [bicarbonate of] soda, which has at least improved in quantity recently in Buchenwald, the soup-like consistency of the warm food and the *Kommissbrot* [army bread] cause diarrhoea and gastro-enteritis. The number of toilets in the camp is completely insufficient. In Sachsenhausen there were only three latrines for a thousand Jews, who were initially penned up separately from the others. (There is more to say on isolation in Sachsenhausen.) The uniforms that they received subsequently had to be worn by prisoners day in, day out. In the height of summer they were soaked in sweat down to the last thread, in rain soaked through. There is no changing of clothes. At night jackets also serve as pillows. The boots that are also provided often do not fit. In Buchenwald there were initially no boots at all, so the prisoners were forced to wear their ordinary light footwear for marches and work. They fell apart quickly. The prisoners dragged themselves through their miserable existence – always at top speed and pushed forwards by mistreatment and fear – on emaciated feet, with bloody soles and, often, deep sores. Much devastation was caused by the terrible heat in July. Caps were not available for the thousands of newly arrived prisoners. Their heads were shorn bald as though they were in prison. The sun was as relentless as their tormentors. They toiled in its blaze for entire days. For many, terrible sunburn on the head, on the face, and on the hands and arms was the consequence. Their skin fell from them in rags. The pain of sunburn is terrible, and often accompanied by fever and shivering. The appearance of ulcers and boils is widespread. On top of this can be counted the results of their mistreatment, blows and kicks. One sees a lot of infections, above all on the hands, which could have been prevented through a normal level of hygiene. In the sleeping quarters the prisoners were merely given blankets for the night. But in Sachsenhausen e.g. in the blocks for Jews the individual by no means always received the same blanket for sleeping. On top of this it was expressly forbidden to wear trousers and underwear during the night. Thus infectious diseases, boils and ulcers were spread from individual to individual through this exchange of blankets. It has already been explained what it means to present yourself to the doctor and register as sick. Once again one example will serve here in the place of many. A prisoner running a high fever, and who felt himself completely unfit for work, registered himself as sick. The thumb of the doctor in Sachsenhausen went to the left, and so the sick man had to march out with the others to build the *Schießstand*, which in Sachsenhausen replaced the quarry at Weimar. Here his "cure" took the following form according to eyewitness reports: he had to drag a heavy tree trunk, which a strong man alone could hardly heave, up the high, sandy hill to the SS guards standing close to the notorious red flags. Then the trunk was kicked down the hill, and once again he had to drag it up the hill, again and again, roughly 50 times! Accompanied by the ever-weakening strength of a man suffering from a fever. In this case, the goal of "*fertigmachen*" the man for the red flags, i.e. deliverance by being shot by the SS, was not achieved. Indeed, the SS had their own methods of curing the ill in their terrifying empire, the concentration camps! Naturally, this form of existence often results in patients suffering from so-called lumbago, which has similar symptoms to rheumatism in the shoulders, the back and the neck, as a result of which the prisoners buckled, and are no longer able to stand upright or walk in a straight line. These wretches are not taken to a sick bay and do not receive any medication whatsoever. Even in their terrible state they have to drag themselves to work and do everything required of them. Their black-clad torturers come from behind and force them upright violently. It is no wonder, then, that the few allowed to leave the concentration camp come out as people broken in body and soul, who require months of care and recovery, which the pressures of imminent emigration hardly allow. A Jewish butcher from Berlin who, as his job suggests, had been the incarnation of prosperous and powerful life, was allowed to leave Buchenwald after just a few weeks, with emigration as his main priority. Yet he was now a creature with a heavily bent spine who was unable to walk, but had to crawl on two sticks. A most pathetically miserable sight. Apparently he had sustained a serious back injury from his mistreatment. He went to South America.

Isolation

The isolation of the *Juni-Aktion* [June operation] Jewish prisoners during their imprisonment in Sachsenhausen was peculiar to this camp, and the description of this is vital for a full understanding of what happened there. Whilst a concentration camp itself is hermetically sealed from the outside world, the Jewish prisoners of Sachsenhausen found themselves subject to an extra level of isolation, by which they were strictly excluded from the other life in the camp. This isolation and all the increased terrors lasted for six weeks. Whilst the Jewish inmates of Buchenwald were allowed to mix with the other prisoners without special separation when they received their money, which they could use to buy small items, as well as the other items they had during their imprisonment, none of this took place in Sachsenhausen. It was only after the first six weeks that the Jewish prisoners were able to receive their own money or have money sent to them, with which they could buy extra items in the canteen to supplement their diet. It should be noted here that a certain percentage was deducted from each sum they received by the camp authorities, which was retained for the costs of their return journey. So the involuntary guests even had to cover their own travel expenses. The first signs of life from Buchenwald prisoners were received 14 days after their arrest; there they were at least allowed to write to their families in the strictly prescribed framework – naturally that they were well and that swift emigration should be secured – as well as receive post. In this way the name Buchenwald became common knowledge whilst that of Sachsenhausen remained shrouded in impenetrable darkness. Because there, the Jewish prisoners did not even have the least bit of contact with the outside world throughout the entire six-week period of isolation. The roughly one thousand people had to sleep in wooden barracks, which had not been built to cope with such numbers. They had to sleep on the floor, pressed up against each other tightly, with their prisoners' jackets as pillows. The space between their barracks, where they had to report was very narrow and surrounded by barbed wire, where they were made to line up and wait. Smoking, the only solace for many, was impossible, because they had no money with which to buy something. On Sunday, in their few free hours when they gathered closely packed in the tight space between their barracks, they were occasionally able to see beyond the boundary the camp's most famous inmate: Pastor [Martin] Niemöller. He was the only person to be kept in solitary confinement, and walked slowly in circles, smoking a cigar. During the period of isolation, these prisoners were not even able to buy one of the few newspapers which were allowed in the concentration camps. They did not possess even the smallest piece of paper to use when relieving themselves. Everything had been taken from them, even their handkerchiefs. They were unable to wipe the away the sweat that streamed from them during work. They received no field flasks in which to take water with them for work in the searing heat. In this way they were exposed to the same merciless, agonising thirst as their companions in suffering in Buchenwald.

The Vorgesetzte [superiors]

Yet, who are the executors of this inhumane system in the Third Reich? In the case of the unconditional discipline of the SS it is the *Lagerkommandant* who sets the tone, and whose will everyone beneath him strives to fulfil. The tone that he gives is characterised by the slogan that has already been quoted: *"Peng – Scheißdreck wird weggeräumt."* Here, each crude act, each moment of brutality counts as credit, and each man attempts to prove that inhumanity is his strength. The direct superiors of the prisoners are actually the *Blockführer,* SS men who comprise a lower rung in the organisational structure of the camp. The *Blockführer* stands at the head at the block. Terrible friends! Yet there are also nuances here. There are *Blockführer* who are relentlessly strict though nevertheless fair, and there are others who exercise their darkest instincts on the prisoners. No human imagination could easily conceive of the kind of things that were possible with them, even after what has been described so far. An example taken from the solitary confinement in Sachsenhausen speaks for the entire system. One night, the inmates of one of the blocks were suddenly awakened. They were ordered to dress and put on boots, and hurry at top speed through a small, narrow door into the eating room next to their sleeping quarters. One prisoner, a 70-year-old man, had to remain lying across the doorway. All the other 150 men had to run over him. The *Blockführer* stood at the door and distributed kicks and punches to the knots of prisoners trying to get through the door. But beneath their boots lay the 70-year-old man...

Alongside each *Blockführer* is a *Block-Ältester* [block elder], himself a prisoner and chosen from them by the *Blockführer*. He also has the power to give orders. He is also able to hit and often does so. These *Block-Ältester*, who for the most part have been in the camp for a long time, have the urge to be liked by those above them, in the hope that this may improve their own situation and might even speed up their release. The majority of these men are political prisoners. A former Communist named Hauer in Sachsenhausen distinguished himself through his foul beastliness. *Vorarbeiter* [foremen] who kept watch on outside work were also selected from the ranks of prisoners. They also had the right to mistreat prisoners. Yet few characters resist the temptation of improving their own situation through denunciation and brutality. It is worth mentioning one punishment here that was thought up by one of the *Block-Ältester* in Sachsenhausen during the isolation of one prisoner, a singer from Berlin: during the hot summer he had to sleep for six nights on the latrine with the windows closed! Another time, the 150 inmates of the barrack had to spend several hours in rank and file in the dining hall with closed windows in great heat, performing endless strenuous callisthenics until they were soaked through and mortally exhausted. This after a heavy day's work!

Jewish prisoners were also used as *Vorarbeiter*, singled out to be the superiors of their fellow believers. They are mostly subjects suited to this through inferior disposition. One name from Sachsenhausen should be denounced here: that of a certain Julius Woyda. Incidentally, corruption of the daily business occurred through these *Block-Ältester* and *Vorarbeiter*. Money donations were extorted from the prisoners.

It is worth mentioning the partial use of Austrian groups for the *Wachmannschaften* [guard teams] in Buchenwald and Sachsenhausen. Some of those sent to Buchenwald were Austrian SA, whilst an Austrian *SS-Sturm* [SS-troop]was sent to Sachsenhausen. They were here to be punished following inadequate discipline in Vienna. In Sachsenhausen the Austrians had to do *Strafdienst* [punishment duty], i.e. they were occupied the whole day and had no exit whatsoever in the evenings, always only staying in the camp. One can imagine the rage of these men. One can also easily imagine the inhumane ways in which this rage was taken out on the defenceless prisoners.

Camp punishments

All these – the humiliation, the abasement, the trials and tortures, the kicks and mistreatment – all these are by no means punishments in the true sense, but are what one might call the daily bread of prisoner existence. Nor is the "sport", as it is known in camp language, true punishment. The heavy work outside, which consisted mostly of moving earth with spades amongst other things, took place under the sharp gaze of the *Vorarbeiter* and observed by armed *SS-Posten* [SS guards]. In addition there were frequent visits by the more senior *SS-Führer*. The prisoners had to work constantly without respite. Work hard! At work the midday meal was often eaten hurriedly whilst standing. The prisoner was allowed to be as exhausted and distressed as he wished – but woe betide him if he showed traces of exhaustion! These would be punished harshly. He must not show the least sign of his exhaustion because a terrible hand was always ready to strike him from behind. Exhaustion was regarded as a refusing to be obedient. To revive the exhausted man's willingness to work – sport. "Sport" is e.g. the following: the prisoner must bury a small short stick in the earth and grasp the top in the right hand. Without letting go, in a sideways bent-over posture he must move round the stick in circles like a spinning top. Blows encourage him in this. He rotates in circles around the stick until his senses leave him. Or another sport: the prisoner has to lie on the ground at the top of a slope and roll to the bottom, through sand or mud, and over roots and rocks. At the bottom he must roll to the top of the hill in the same position, and this "sport" continues until he is "prepared". From these two examples one can recognise how creative the fantasies in the sporting area can be in the concentration camp.

Bunker, Galgen [gallows] and *Fünfundzwanzig vorm Arsch* [25 on the arse]

As has been said, none of all this is true punishment in the camp. They initiate the progression. For the prisoner, fear, horror stands behind everything that he undergoes and suffers. The "bunker" means confinement. Solitary confinement. But the bunker is not the shape of solitary confinement as we know it: the bare cell with *Pritsche* [plank bed] for sleeping and stool for sitting. In the bunker, the confined had to spend the time from half past 4 until 9 o'clock in the evening, that is, from waking up until *Zapfenstreich* [curfew], standing upright! Can one imagine what it means to stand up for 16½ hours in a cell? And thereafter with painful limbs to seek an exhausted sleep on the ground whilst shivering? And yet the bunker is perceived as the mildest punishment. More terrible is the "*Galgen*", a punishment applied particularly to Jewish prisoners. One who has heard the slowly extinguishing moans of the man hanging from the gallows will never forget it. The punishment is carried out in such a way that the arms of the prisoner are tied behind him at the wrists, just above the lower back; and in this way he is hanged from a thick post. The pain is inconceivable and only extinguished by loss of consciousness.

"*25 vorm Arsch*", as it is known in camp language, in the parlance of the *Lagerkommandanten* and *SS-Standartenführer* [SS Colonels], is the most terrible and terrifying of all punishments. It means that the victim is strapped to a *Bock* [whipping block] with his face to the ground and is struck on the buttocks with a baton 25 times. The entire personnel of the camp attends in rank and file when this punishment is being carried out. The prisoners only see the heavy thick baton – in Buchenwald they use a so-called *Ochsenziemer* [bullwhip] – rise overhead in a circular movement and then crash onto the victim below. The baton circles once in the air to achieve the strongest momentum. The strongest, most muscular of the SS men are selected for this duty and they replace one another as it is being carried out so that the force of the strikes does not decline. Thus one sees the movement of the instrument of torture but there is no sound to hear. The slightest sound the tortured man gives out results in an extra blow.

This punishment is imposed for apparent infringements of camp discipline, for disobedience, dissent, refusal to obey orders. Obviously no single prisoner makes the slightest effort to resist, or to refuse to carry out the most inhumane orders. Certainly not intentionally and willingly. The prisoner is defenceless, surrendering to every whim. Each will, each human emotion in him is broken and suppressed. He will do everything in his power not to worsen his unfortunate lot and call down upon himself the most horrible punishment. Despite this, corporal punishment is still imposed.

In the terrible June days of 1938 a certain Bartsch from Breslau [now Pol. Wroctaw] was brought to Sachsenhausen on one of the first transports. During "reception" – as yet in complete ignorance of the actual laws of camp life – he gave certain answers to certain questions that immediately marked him out as insubordinate. Even on the first day of his stay in the camp the punishment of 25 strikes was carried out on him. As he was unstrapped unconscious from the block the unfortunate man lost speech. But when a question was directed towards him and he did not reply he was prescribed 25 more strikes the following day for further insubordination. Once again 25 blows fell against his martyred, bloody body with merciless violence. Death was his salvation.

B. 329 General situation

One cannot really talk about a sharply oppositional mood making itself noticeable in Breslau [now Pol. Wrocław] and Niederschlesien [Lower Silesia]. The so-called educated classes, who have still retained a feeling for humanity and decency, are naturally repulsed by the entire behaviour of the leading circles of the Third Reich, but especially by the burning of the synagogues, and are holding themselves aloof as they have on other occasions. The vast majority in contrast regards the events with indifference or even with a certain sympathy for the government. By and large the people lack little. They are strongly influenced by clever propaganda and believe what they are given to read in black and white. The supply of foodstuffs is erratic, i.e. there is one kind of goods available, and then another, e.g. that happens with tropical fruit. Through this skilful policy of substitution they make sure that deeper dissatisfaction does not materialise. At the same time the intimidation is so great, even amongst people who were formerly in the opposition, that they dare not make their dissatisfaction known.

It must be stressed clearly that whilst these observations apply to Breslau, Lower Silesia, and partly also to Berlin, there might be a different picture in other parts of the Reich, especially in the west.

If there is a war the population, though not enthusiastic, would therefore go along with the war cry without resistance. How long this acceptance would last is absolutely impossible to say in advance.

The situation of the Jews

The professions that are still functioning can be counted on one hand. These are some few doctors, few lawyers (*Rechtkonsulenten* [legal advisers]), and municipal employees, namely teachers, hospital and welfare workers. All the others are living off their own money or from assistance.

So few doctors are authorised that medical care is barely sufficient. There is a completely inadequate number of lawyers. In fact only 15 lawyers are authorised in the whole district, but these have been picked arbitrarily. The nasty rumour is that it had to do with whether they are married to an Aryan woman. The lawyers who have been chosen were not asked in advance whether they were willing and nobody has checked whether they are suitable. As a result two thirds of them are tired of work because they are busy with their own emigration plans, and the others are so overloaded that they cannot take on any more. Some are also too old. An absolute legal famine prevails. Lawsuits play a minor role. At present it is mainly a matter of advice about winding up businesses and emigrating. There are only a few asset administrators and despite great demand there are only two or three foreign currency advisers.

Jewish population statistics

Since last year the population in the province has declined by 50%, that is from 5,000 to 2,500 souls. The Jewish population of Breslau has declined from 17,000 to 12–13,000 in the year 1938. This smaller decline in comparison with the province arises from the fact that some 2–3,000 of the people in Breslau have moved in from the province.

Only indirect difficulties have been put in the way of the people who have recently moved into the city, like *Vorladungen* [summonses] to the police, etc. But there are no prohibitions on moving in.

Yet the *Vorladungen* to the police and the Gestapo are nothing unusual. At present in Breslau they are busy calling in the entire Jewish population in alphabetical order of streets, leaving out neither old people nor young children. Those summoned are asked when they think they will emigrate.

The administration of the Jewish Gemeinde [community]

The *Gemeindevorsteher* [community board members] take the view: save yourself if you can! As a result the intelligentsia of the *Gemeinde* are leaving. There is no security for officials of the *Gemeinde* who remain behind. A permit would have to be available for such people to travel to England just in case. It is hard to find replacements for the people who move away. The reporter had a choice of three people to succeed her, of whom one was over 60 years old and frail, the other 50 years old and unsuitable, and the third younger and very suitable, but ill.

The *Hilfsverein* [*der deutschen Juden*; Aid Association of German Jews] has comparatively good people because the unemployed lawyers put themselves at its disposal.

The *Hilfsverein* is organised badly from Berlin downwards, even worse in the province. The main problem is that a shop that has no goods to sell does not need qualified salesmen. The abilities of these people and of the people who are seeking advice are being frittered away. There are hundreds of people standing in front of the doors of the *Hilfsverein* every day, waiting there for hours. In Breslau alone five advisers besides five stenotypists and around five registration staff are employed.

The arrests

In Lower Silesia around 100% of all Jewish men were arrested. Today five to ten people are still in the concentration camp. In Bunzlau [now Pol. Bolesławiec], the *Bürgermeister* [mayor] explained that he was not in a position to carry out the arrest order, which related to "all Jews", because there was not enough room in the jail for this. As a result nobody in B. was arrested.

It has become known just today that four people have been arrested because they were not arranging their emigration energetically enough. They have been held in detention for a week. Often, a rapid deadline for emigration is set.

Because the *Hilfsverein* cannot assist with legal immigration, people are now often going to Palestine and Belgium illegally.

The Wohlfahrtsgesetzgebung [welfare legislation] and the duties of the Jewish Gemeinde

The welfare decree has been changed. On the 19th November an addendum to it came out with the limitation: "Jews will basically receive no further public support, but are entrusted to Jewish agencies. In cases where public support is involved the circumstances are to be looked at exceptionally strictly." In practice i.e. private income of whatever sort without exception has to be set against the support. E.g. if the *Gemeinde* has previously been giving RM. 10.- and the city RM. 30.-, the contribution of the *Gemeinde* will be discounted from the RM. 30.- , so that the city will only provide RM. 20.-. The entitlements of small pensioners do not apply to Jews. The *Gemeinden* [communities] therefore, basically, have to take over all support. As a result, they will inevitably have to use up their capital, because the demand cannot be covered out of tax revenue. For fuller uptake of all demands Breslau would need RM. 30,000.- a month for public welfare alone, plus demands for hospitals, old people's homes, and so on, so that RM. 80,000.- would be needed every month, i.e. c. RM. one million a year!

Incidentally, pensions for the seriously war wounded will continue to be paid out, at any rate the pension payouts are continuing.

Effects of the Wohfahrtsgesetzgebung

In all cases where the word "basically" in the new decree is taken into account, the city and the province are paying out public support as before, because the Jewish *Gemeinden* have demonstrated that they would otherwise have gone through all their capital in half a year. Almost all the *Gemeinden* in the province have made these arrangements. The *Bürgermeister* have to some extent asked the *Gemeinden* what they ought to pay in particular cases. Unfortunately *Stadtrat* [city councillor] Less in Breslau has not pursued the issue energetically enough because he was proud that the *Gemeinde* was solvent and in a position to afford to make large payments. The cashier's offices have generally continued to be run by the city but in Breslau the payments were made from the Jewish *Wohlfahrtsamt* [welfare office], which is not designed to accommodate such an onrush of people.

On top of that, the costs of Jewish inmates of state or city asylums and hospitals still have to be borne by the Jewish *Gemeinden*. The *Landeshauptmann* [state governor] sent a whole bundle of documentation about these people. The offer has been made from the Jewish side to pay a contribution of 50 *Pfg.* [*Pfennig*; pennies] a day. The negotiations about this are still going on. But the *Landeshauptmann* is basically ready to accept such a deal. Yet in Breslau it will probably be a matter of fuller payment, because the *Bürgermeister* there has pushed the full costs of support onto the Jewish *Gemeinde*.

Jewish homes and institutions

The children's home in Flinsberg [now Pol. Świeradów Zdrój], which belonged to the *Jüdische Frauenbund* [Jewish Women's League] has been sold. The convalescent hospital in Warmbrunn [now Pol. Cieplice Śląskie-Zdrój] will probably be reopened as an old people's home or as a convalescent hospital. The Liegnitz [now Pol. Legnica] old people's home is still in Jewish ownership. The Jewish *Haushaltungsschule* [house-keeping school] in Breslau has been dissolved. It was no longer authorised as a school. The Breslau *Rabbinerseminar* [rabbinical seminary] is closed and its library and archive sealed up, as well as the library of the Jewish *Gemeinde* in Breslau. Some of the agricultural colleges have been left as *Hachshara* [agricultural training for Jews preparing to emigrate to Palestine], e.g. Groß-Bresen, after everything had been destroyed there. The reporter can say that she has seen a completely wrecked piano that had been "gutted", making a particularly bleak impression amongst all the other devastation.

The expropriation of the Jews

From the *Vermögensangabe* [statement of assets] one can observe in many cases that people overvalue them out of fear of being penalised by low statements. That is now coming back to haunt them in the *Besteuerung* [tax assessment]. Silver and gold had also been stated more or less exactly. These careful people are now the most wronged. Everything that has any value is taken, even the silver is removed at the last moment from possessions that have already been packed up.

Personal Experiences

The reporter underwent three house searches in the November days. She herself was on a business trip but her old mother of 80 was at home. Jewish men were being sought who were supposed to have hidden for fear of arrest. The people who pushed their way into the house ripped the phone line out of the wall in passing. When the reporter later enquired with the telephone company about repairing it an official was sent but who told her that because she was a Jew he was not allowed to repair it. After repeated enquiries with the office someone appeared who repaired the damage without asking anything for it.

Aryan friends have been very helpful. They looked after Frau X.'s silver and all valuables.

On 10th November the reporter was in a small town in Lower Silesia, Mielitsch [now Pol. Milicz].

There she and other people she was with in the *Gemeindehaus* [community house] were forced, under coarse insults from SA men, to search on the street for bits of broken glass from the smashed windows. The public looked on curiously without saying anything. She soon had the chance to escape and travelled to Breslau.

In general one could say that 10th November was worse the further one was to the East. In Liegnitz it happened most decently. But in Neusalz [now Pol. Nowa Sól] there was no Jewish shop, only four Jewish families. All four houses had been completely destroyed because it was believed that was the best way to obey orders.

Deaths

Dr. Emanuel Joel, Breslau, teacher, 40/45 y., died in Buchenwald

Erich Weyl, Breslau, businessman, 37 y., died in Buchenwald from pneumonia

Wormann, Breslau, shoe dealer, 60 y., died in Buchenwald

Karl Steinfeld, businessman, 60 y., died in Buchenwald

Cohn, Görlitz, manufacturer, dead in Sachsenhausen

Guttstadt, *Reichswirtschaftsgerichtsrat* [commercial lawyer], Berlin, 58 y., died after release from Sachsenhausen

Plachte, Glogau, around 60, businessman, died in Buchenwald

Jules Beer, Reichenbach, of firm Weil & Nassau, hanged himself after release from detention

Arthur Dresel, Görlitz, businessman, died (?) during the 1934 operation

Amputation as a result of frostbite in the concentration camp

Fritz Neumann, Brieg, 30 y., all toes amputated due to frostbite.

Numerous deaths as a result of illnesses or after-effects amongst people released from the concentration camps.

B. 330 The surrender of jewellery and precious metals in practice

Since December 1938 the various *Devisenstellen* [foreign currency offices] of the Reich have constantly changed their practice over retention of jewellery and objects made of precious metals. At one time it was completely forbidden for people to keep these with their effects when they moved, then their removal was allowed against a considerable deposit into the *Golddiskontbank* [Gold Discount Bank], then only partial export was allowed, and so on.

The issue now has a radical solution. All objects made of jewellery or precious metals had to be surrendered by 31st March, against compensation. The surrender had to be to pawnbrokers nominated for the purpose in the towns. However because a number of larger towns do not have institutions of this kind,

Jews in parts of Silesia were forced to pay travel costs to Breslau [now Pol. Wrocław] where they were to surrender their silver and so on. The compensation was paid out according to rules that even the neutral observer would have to describe as robbery.

What is paid does not approximate to the market value of the particular piece of jewellery. Instead, each piece of precious metal is paid for on the basis of its weight, at a laughable rate. It does not matter whether you are handing in an 800-year-old church chalice with delicate filigree chasings or a silver pocket-watch – for each gramme of silver you are paid between one and a half and two and a half *Pfennigs* [pennies]. In Breslau broken silver was and is paid for at one and a half *Pfennigs*, and silver in intact condition at two and a half *Pfennigs* per gramme. The bullying of the officials you surrender to is that they count completely intact pieces of silver as broken and so save themselves a *Pfennig* for every gramme. One Jew who had to give up some intact silver which had been declared to be "broken" defended himself against this by taking a hammer out of his briefcase and telling the thieving official that he would smash it up so that it really was broken. At which, following the intervention of the director of the pawnbrokers', the price of two and a half was paid to him.

A person who valued his historically or artistically valuable gold or silver items only by their weight value when he surrendered them would expose himself to the danger of having assessed his property at too low a value. So the more business-like Jews have their property assessed by an expert. In one well-known case an estimate of RM. 10,000.- was given for silver pieces from the Middle Ages. The owner today received RM. 700.- in weight value from the relevant pawnbroker.

A person who is required to give up his silver cutlery or old watches as an emigrant has *de facto* permission to obtain substitute items made of non-precious metal. However, this is only allowed if a deposit of a hundred per cent of the value of the new items is made into to *Golddiskontbank*, because these items were obtained after 1933. The author of these lines is in the following situation. In February 1939 he was permitted to take with him his father's old gold watch and a box of silver cutlery for 12 people. At the start of March this permission was invalidated by the overall requirement to hand these things in, and he is now only allowed to take with him four spoons, four teaspoons, four knives and four forks for himself and his wife.

He is allowed to buy a substitute steel watch if he pays double the purchase price into the *Golddiskontbank* and goes through a long-winded application process lasting four to six weeks. He can also buy knives, forks and the other bits of cutlery if he pays the hundred per cent deposit and receives permission. But because he is only getting about RM. 8.- in weight value for his gold watch and RM. 30.- to 40.- for the entire silver canteen, it is not possible for him to buy even the cheapest metal knives out of the proceeds, let alone pay the hundred per cent deposit. Invitations to friends will soon be going out asking them to bring their own cutlery because the host has had to give his up.

Many deeply religious people are in a tragic position, having had to hand over religious items such as *Sabbathleuchter* [sabbath lamps], *Kidduschbecher* [kiddush cups], etc. to the pawnbroker. The compensation does not stretch to the cost of obtaining substitute items of non-precious metal. Their owners are especially affected by their loss because they are mainly items that have been in the family for generations and have great emotional value.

The *Auslösebefugnis* [redemption authority] is developing into shameless robbery. It means that with a two-day deadline Jews would lose the right to retain their own jewellery and precious metal objects if they have paid equivalent value in foreign exchange, as laid down by an expert of the *Reichswirtschafts-ministerium* [Reich Ministry of Economic Affairs], which is not specified for the purpose. An example: the Jew X. has a *Kidduschbecher* that has been in the family's possession for 100 years. Artistic value RM. 60.-, sentimental value inestimable, proceeds from surrender to the pawnbroker according to weight on the standard basis RM. 1.80.

This Jew wants to keep the cup for sentimental reasons. Since the appearance of this decree he has had to complete the following, for which he is given two days:

1. A request to the *Reichswirtschaftsministerium* to retain the cup and nominate a valuer.

2. Surrender of the cup to a foreign currency bank. This leads to deposit charges for the next six months, within which the foreign currency must be provided. The deposit charge for one month might well be higher than the complete sum that the Jew would receive by weight on surrender to the pawnbroker.

3. Appearance of the expert valuer at the foreign currency bank to give the estimate. This involves considerable professional fees.

4. Communication of the valuation to the *Reichswirtschaftsministerium*.

5. Statement of the amount of foreign currency that the Jew must bring to Germany with the assistance of foreign relatives in order to be allowed to keep the cup.

6. After the deposit of the foreign currency a *Freigabeerklärung* [clearance certificate] is supposed to be issued by the *Reichswirtschaftsministerium*.

It is apparent that the Jew would get for his *Kidduschbecher*, with its market value of RM. 60.- proceeds of RM. 1.80 at the pawnbroker on the basis of its weight, or would have to bring foreign currency worth around 75 gold Marks into Germany to be able to retain his property rights in the cup.

The person primarily responsible for this pillage, as for the economic regulations on Jews in general, is most probably *Oberregierungsrat* [senior government lawyer] Dr. Gotthard of the *Reichswirtschaftsministerium*. He was *Gerichtsassessor* [court assessor] and active as an economics expert with the *Geheime Staatspolizei* [Gestapo]. They placed him in the *Reichswirtschaftsministerium* at the start of 1936, where he worked in the so-called "*Störungsstelle*" [faults department]. In reality he was there to keep an eye on the department, which had been set up by [Hjalmar] Schacht, and on its head *Ministerialdirektor* Pohl and *Ministerialrat* [ministerial adviser] Dr. Hoppe. The *Störungsstelle* had been set up by Dr. Schacht in order to deal with problems in the economy caused by the Party authorities.

B. 331 One observes preparations for the war cry: the Jews are guilty.

Great article by Alfred Rosenberg end of August or beginning of September in the general press. Quote in it from an American-Jewish journal with an essay presenting an ironical vision of the war.

The article by Rosenberg was put up on posters, the Jewish journal reproduced on the posters with a picture of Judith.

During the September crisis a special number of Der *Stürmer* [The Striker; Nazi tabloid newspaper] appeared: "The Jews and the War".

Prophecy by Hitler on 30th January 1939: the next European war will mean the end of the Jews in Europe.

Very dangerous article by Dr. Goebbels in a Saturday edition of the "V. B." [*Völkischer Beobachter*; National Observer] middle of March 1939, where the slogan "The Jews are guilty" is presented verbatim. One recalls the article by the same author in Der *Angriff* [The Attack; Berlin Nazi Party newspaper] of August 1932, where exclusion from the formation of government despite the election result provoked strong discontent in the party, which was set off through the same slogan "The Jew is guilty".

B. 332 On the alleged spontaneity of the pogroms of 10th November 1938

The measures of 10th November and the following weeks ultimately lead back to internal Party decisions taken in September 1937. It was decided at that time to solve the Jewish question radically. Any real influence of [Hjalmar] Schacht, who had always opposed the destruction of Jewish commerce, had been eliminated in August 1937. Schacht had not been at the *Reichswirtschaftsministerium* [Reich Ministry of Economic Affairs] since August 1937. A programmatic article in *Das Schwarze Korps* [The Black Corps; SS newspaper], which appeared around October 1937, after the 1937 Nuremberg Party Rally, laying down a systematic disadvantaging of Jews in the economy, can be viewed as evidence of the change of course in this respect. According to the article a rule had been in force until that point, at least officially, that the *Arierprinzip* [Aryan principle] should not be applied to the economy. There then followed official orders to cut back on business dealings with Jews and above all quota arrangements under which Jewish businesses were not to be treated in the same way as Aryan ones. This introduced the compulsory selling of Jewish businesses.

In February 1938 Hitler made a speech to old *Parteigenossen* [Party members] in the Munich *Bürgerbräukeller* [Bürgerbräu beer hall], which can be looked up in the *Völkischer Beobachter* [National Observer; Nazi Party newspaper] for the end of February (around 21. 2. 1938). For no obvious reason he set out the *Geiseltheorie* [hostage theory] and explained that the Jews of the world were enemies of National Socialism, that the Jews in Germany were part of World Jewry and would be dealt with accordingly. This was the first time that the *Geiseltheorie* was made official. In the first days of March 1938 news began to leak out that the idea of a mass arrest of Jews was being played with. [Rudolf] Hess apparently opposed this plan. At about the same time *Gauleiter* [Nazi Party regional leader] [Julius] Streicher gave a talk about the Jewish question to the foreign press in Berlin. He had no inhibitions about declaring that there would be no peace in the world "*bis die Juden mit ihrer ganzen Brut vernichtet seien*" [until the Jews are exterminated with their whole brood]. (The expression is word-for-word!) The open admission regarding the elimination of women and children (a foreign journalist asked specifically whether extermination should be understood as physical extermination, which was not answered) caused astonishment at that time. The first measures pointing towards expropriation of property (*Vermögensanmeldung* [asset registration]) followed in April. They were followed in June by the frightful *Verhaftungsaktion* [arrests operation] of Jews with so-called previous convictions, of whom at least 10% have died. The Jews arrested in June and other "*Asozialen*" [anti-socials] had the job of expanding the camps, at Sachsenhausen and Buchenwald. In Sachsenhausen the so-called "new" camp was constructed, that is barracks were put up for several thousand people. Even at that time the rumour was going round the camp that these barracks would be filled with Jews from a forthcoming mass action. The prisoners of 10th November were invariably greeted by their comrades from June 1938 and their Aryan fellow sufferers with the words "We've been waiting for you since August."

In October 1938, that is four weeks before the assassination of Legation Secretary vom Rath, *Das Schwarze Korps* published two leading articles which set out the prospect of a radical solution to the Jewish question in an absolutely programmatic way. In one of them there is brutally cynical discussion of how Jews who have been excluded from the economy are to be "interned", because there must be protection against the criminality that will necessarily ensue from their financial impoverishment.

Note the attempts to attack the synagogues in Kassel which were described in a special article. In fact, all the synagogues in Germany were destroyed in the same way five days later. The two attempts at wrecking in Kassel meant the campaign was being pressed ahead with at a time when the assassination in Paris had not yet happened. As a matter of fact in the week ending 5th November numerous acts of violence against Jewish shops, offices, and so on took place in the Kassel area, and also elsewhere, without any reason, in particular in Franconia, where the population in small places like Burgsinn and elsewhere were driven out of their homes. The daily increasing press hysteria at that time was the accompanying music for an internal undertaking to engage in a radical operation that was then motivated by the death of Herr vom Rath. "This same Mortimer died most conveniently for you, my lord" [from Friedrich Schiller's *Maria Stuart*].

B. 333 Concerning the spontaneity of the operation of 10th November

On Saturday 5th November the wrecking of the synagogue in Kassel was attempted. *Hitler-jugendtruppen* [Hitler Youth troops] moved in front of the synagogue, tried to force their way over the railings into the house of prayer, threw stones at the window panes, then however withdrew on the arrival of the police. On Sunday 6th November this attempt was repeated. During this they managed to force their way into the *Gemeindehaus* [community house], throw documents onto the street and cause substantial damage, especially by throwing stones at the synagogue windows. These serious riots were reported in the *Kurhessische Landeszeitung* (the title of the newspaper is not absolutely correct, possibly *Kurhessische Zeitung*) of Monday 7th or 8th November. At the same time comments appeared in the newspaper about antisemitic riots in the Hesse-Kassel region. In Kassel itself the area around the synagogue was cordoned off in a wide circle and access to the heavily damaged building was not permitted to the governing body.

This is one of the precursors of the *Aktion* [operation] of 9th and 10th November, as stated by a newspaper report in a National Socialist paper. Incidentally there was also an attempt to set it on fire. The onset in Kassel several days before the death of the legation secretary vom Rath proves that there can be no question of spontaneity concerning the events of the pogrom. Besides, after the death of Herr vom Rath on 9th November foreign journalists at the press conference asked the representative of the Propaganda Minister, Prof. von Böhmer, about the implications of the Grynszpan assassination for the position of the Jews. Prof. Böhmer replied literally that the question required a *Radikallösung* [radical solution] from now on. The *Völkischer Beobachter* [National Observer; Nazi Party newspaper] of 9th November then quotes a number of economic measures, which are now becoming reality in the "*Radikallösung*". (Disappearance of Jewish shops from the shopping streets etc.)

All these specified measures were harmless in comparison to what then took place: proof that at first strict measures indeed were planned in contrast to the Jewish economic policies pursued thus far, that however the radicals did not consider these measures to be sufficiently far-reaching and rapidly established an *Aktion* with vehemence unknown thus far. The order to carry out the pogrom was probably only given on the evening of 9th November. A credible source reports having heard from a Polish postal official that he was working in the *Rundfunkabhördienst* [broadcasting monitoring service] on the night of 9th to 10th November and, without intending to, by chance picked up an instruction that was directed at the Party or SA posts in German Upper Silesia. The clerk was on duty in Katowice. The contents of the instruction corresponded with what later happened.

The theory that the instruction was only given during the night of 9th to 10th November is inconsistent with a message from Krefeld, after the *Gemeindehaus* had already been visited on the morning of 9th. In the *Gemeindehaus* was the *Gemeinde* restaurant, which has carbon dioxide cylinders for the beer pumps. These cylinders were then removed under the expert guidance of an innkeeper during the night of 9th to 10th so that there would be no explosions during the fire.

Rioting in detail

In Beuthen [now Pol. Bytom] in Upper Silesia during the night of 9th to 10th November the Jews were taken from their beds, women and men brought in front of the burning synagogue, where they were shown the prestigious building burning amidst scornful laughter. They were forced to stand in front of the synagogue for many hours, in order to also watch the burning down of the dome. A Polish Jew was forced to kneel in front of the burning synagogue. He was photographed in this position by SS men. *Kreisleiter* [district leader] Röhl was in charge of the *Aktion* in Beuthen, who also excelled in forcing his way into homes, brutalities, destroying furniture etc. Besides, forcing people to visit the burning synagogue does not seem to have been an isolated occurrence.

In Landeck [now Pol. Lędyczek] in West Prussia the synagogue was burned down. On the day after the fire National Socialists turned up at the *Vorstand* [board] of the Jewish *Gemeinde* and presented an invoice for fuel.

In (Pomerania or West Prussia) the synagogue was sold. The district egg store was supposed to be kept here. The continuing presence of the building however caused serious offence in local Party circles, because everywhere in the neighbouring towns the synagogues had been burned down. The chairman of the Jewish *Gemeinde* was forced to revoke the contract of sale, repay the sale's proceeds, and then the synagogue was set alight after they had cleared out the egg store.

In individual places, such as Oppeln [now Pol. Opole] and Beuthen for example, the fires were set so expertly, that for insiders there is no doubt about the involvement of the *Feuerwehr* [fire brigade] in the arson.

Fire-fighting operations were so delayed everywhere that only the neighbouring buildings were safe. In response to direct questions to the heads of individual *Feuerwehr* it was explained that the *Feuerwehr* was only in a position to prevent the spread of the fires to neighbouring buildings.

In Chemnitz Grünberg, the *Gemeindesekretär* [community secretary] was shot when the *Gemeindehaus* was set alight. He lay in the garden. The arsonists came to his wife and announced to her, "Your husband is dead, he is lying in the garden." For about a day the wife was made to believe that her husband was dead, while in reality he was very seriously wounded and had escaped with his life.

In Berlin the synagogues were set on fire during the night of 9th to 10th November between 3 and 4 o'clock in the morning. At the same time the window panes of all the shops which the owners of the firms had marked with white letters were smashed in. Even in the summer, when the police president had ordered that Jewish shops were identified by white lettering, this order appeared to many to be a "*Pogromwegweiser*" [pogrom signpost]. On the morning of 10th November throughout the whole of Berlin the shards of the shop window panes lay on the street, however there was no looting.

While during the first hours of the morning the shop owners set about clearing out the debris and informing the insurance companies, some also arranging to have new window panes put in, at about 4 o'clock in the afternoon a new storm broke over the ruined shops. During this the shop shelves were overturned, the goods, books hurled onto the street. In one Jewish department store where the large and numerous display window panes were all smashed, there were attempts in several places to set it on fire, which failed.

The offices of the *Zionistische Vereinigung* [Zionist Association] in Meinekestraße were wrecked, typewriters thrown out of the window, while the attempt to destroy offices of other Jewish organisations failed because the office areas already had been closed and sealed previously by the *Geheime Staatspolizei* [Gestapo; Secret State Police]. The would-be assassins withdrew when they saw the seal of the *Geheime Staatspolizei.*

In general in Berlin homes have not been wrecked. The absence of such an *Aktion* to destroy homes is attributed to the fact that numerous Jewish foreigners live in Berlin; it is understood that there would also have been diplomatic intervention. Even in certain exclusive suburbs of Berlin not a single arrest has been made, reportedly because numerous villas are occupied by diplomats. (Wannsee). In Dahlem a large number of Jews was detained, taken to the appropriate *Polizeirevier* [police station] and held there until evening. The station superintendant had received no instruction to transport the arrested people further, and for that reason he released them late in the evening, whereupon the majority absented themselves from their homes and thus evaded arrest the next day. The number of Jews arrested in Berlin cannot have been greater than 3,000. Considerably more were sought, but in Berlin it was possible to go into hiding, and in the days between 10th and 20th November thousands of Jewish men led the existence of a hounded wild animal.

Individuals have been on the move day and night, were travelling back and forth in vehicles, spending each night somewhere different, often in the homes of Jews who had already been arrested, often with Aryans, some of whom behaved very helpfully. Eleven Jewish men were living in the villa of one Aryan businessman, some of whom were not known to the villa owner at all and were recommended by friends. In the small cigar shop of one Aryan owner, which is about 9 sq. m. in size, two Jews spent the night on chairs for 14 consecutive days. A female Aryan guesthouse proprietor – to report a particularly grotesque case – induced two of the SA men living with her to spend the night in a Jewish club which was located in the same building. The rooms of the SA men were given to "*Juden auf der Flucht*" [Jews on the run].

The selection of the Jews arrested in Berlin must have taken place according to the following criteria:

The basis was the police Register of Jews who possessed assets of more than RM. 5,000.-, and therefore were obliged to declare their assets.

Geheime Staatspolizei headquarters in Berlin ordered the arrest of all leading personalities from Jewish organisational life, with the exception of the *Gemeinde* chairman and Rabbi Dr. Baeck.

It is claimed, cannot however be verified, that the medical and legal professional associations have been used for the selection of the Jews to be arrested. Scarcely any Jews without means have been held in Berlin. Almost all of the prisoners accommodated in Sachsenhausen concentration camp possessed means of more than RM. 5,000.-. A few have been "taken away" accidentally.

In contrast – as is known – in the province all the Jews have been held with the exception of the very old; some Jews have been arrested in Hamburg, Breslau [now Pol. Wrocław] and Baden-Baden from the hotels, off the street, in the trains. In Hamburg e.g. a Jewish doctor who was seriously ill in bed and could not be moved was left in his home; the officials asked the servant who led them into the room of the sick landlord whether he was Jewish. He said that he was and was taken away. So e.g. even relatives who were staying in Jewish households, without coming from the town in which the arrest was made, were "taken away".

Occasionally sympathetic police doctors saved Jews under arrest from being transported off into the camp. In one large Westphalian city the police doctor sought out his medical colleagues and suggested illnesses to them on the basis of which he could certify them as "*nicht lagerfähig*" [not fit to go to the camp].

In Berlin on 11th and 12th November detainees with an E. K. 1 [*Eisernes Kreuz 1*; Iron Cross First Class], the seriously war wounded and those obviously seriously ill were not sent on to Sachsenhausen concentration camp, whereas on the first day of the mass arrests nobody escaped being transported off. In the camp itself no consideration was taken of even obvious illnesses and release from the camp did not follow, so that cripples with all kinds of the most serious disabilities had to submit to staying in the camp for weeks. Amongst others a *Studienrat* [graduate secondary school teacher] was also dragged off, who could not move along by himself as a result of polio in both legs and had to be carried to *Appell* [roll call] by two prisoners, hanging onto their shoulders.

B. 333 a It is reported that during the operation of 10th November the Jews in one Silesian town were driven through the town bound together with ropes in front of the burning synagogue. It is said to be Trebnitz [now Trzebnica]. The incident is undisputed, the place however uncertain.

B. 334 Current criminal proceedings

As a general rule for all criminal proceedings against Jews, a report filed against a Jew usually results in the person's immediate arrest. Jews are generally arrested immediately, even if the potential punishment is very small or the notice of an arrest warrant highly unusual in terms of the as yet unchanged *Strafprozessordnung* [criminal procedure code].

In addition to the old Jewish offences, there are the following new ones:

1.) Anybody who omits to use the first name Israel or Sara in legal or business dealings [*Zwangsnamen*] is to be punished with imprisonment. A fine is not admissible, arrest is to be effected immediately. A doctor in Pomerania, baptised, has been imprisoned for three weeks, because he did not sign some pointless declaration with the additional first name Israel.

Another graduate, who had been in prison for a trivial reason, reported the birth of his child to the registry office without giving the additional first name Israel for himself. Consequently, proceedings were instigated against him as a result of this omission.

A 73-year-old lady in Berlin, who had lodged a report with the police in January without giving the additional name Sara, received a penalty order of a week's imprisonment.

2.) Anybody who listed his jewellery in the *Judenvermögens-*

anmeldung [Jewish assets registration] of June 1938, and now does not hand in the full number of specified pieces, has to expect to have proceedings instigated and be arrested. It is not necessarily the case in this instance that part of the jewellery has been withheld from submission. In the time from June until December 1938 individual pieces of jewellery may have been sold or given away as a gift.

3.) Emigrants have to submit details of the goods they are transporting on long lists to the *Devisenstelle* [foreign currency office], which then levies surcharges for the *Golddiskontbank* [Gold Discount Bank] for all things purchased after 1933, including additional clothing. *Zollbeamten* [customs officials] are present when the goods for transportation are packed, comparing the packed items with the submitted list. If anybody packs anything that is not on the list, criminal proceedings are instigated and in the majority of cases the "criminals" are arrested. In one case where children's clothes, a few items of lingerie and a few ladies' blouses were packed, rather than jewellery or goods banned from export, a fine of RM. 1000.– was imposed. An emigrant whose wife had packed a curtain that was not listed was kept in *Schutzhaft* [protective custody] for seven weeks.

4.) On 6th April the shipment of suitcases by Jewish haulage companies was presented as a capital offence of the highest order in German newspapers, on the front page and with leading headlines. In fact it had been a shipment of suitcases without a permit from the *Devisenstelle*; the contents of the suitcase is generally irrelevant: extra items of clothing, sometimes also an individual's own jewellery and a bit of silver cutlery which evaded the process.

B. 335 Alteration of German-sounding surnames of Jewish people

Sometime in February 1939 the *"Völkischer Beobachter"* [National Observer] described it as intolerable that Jews bear surnames which indicate a connection with Germany or German towns. It is intolerable that Jews bear the names of German towns as surnames, Berliner, Deutsch etc. The Jews ought to change such surnames of their own accord otherwise decrees would be passed that would not be pleasant for them.

Jews have now been summoned to Berlin police stations as part of this trend. This concerns Jews with such names as Deutsch, Deutschmann, Deutschland, Deutschkron etc. They were told without any further explanation that they had to renounce their names immediately; they were asked for their mother's or paternal grandmother's maiden name and then left to use one of these names provided that it did not have any connection with Germany. A document was then signed within five minutes declaring the renunciation of the name Deutschmann and the taking of the mother's name.

The operation has only started; it is being continued systematically.

B. 336 REPORT ABOUT THE EVENTS IN PRAGUE ON 15TH MARCH 1939

The Gestapo reached Prague at 9 o'clock; by 10 o'clock the arrests had already started. Everyone who was in some way involved in the top jobs was arrested. Nobody was permitted to leave Czechoslovakia or return again across the border who was not in possession of the blue permit.

The *Durchlaßschein* [travel permit] was obtainable only with difficulty. Anyone who wants it has to queue up at the Gestapo, Perstyn [Cz. Na Perštýně] 9, and wait. If they have waited for a long time, it can happen that the officials suddenly stop whenever it crosses their mind. Hundreds who are waiting there outside must then go home empty-handed. However most do not do that, but they stay where they are and continue to wait until it is opened again; many stand there all through the night in snow, rain and wind until the next morning and even longer, for hours, until finally it is their turn. On 30th March a sign was put up with the announcement that Jews could no longer receive a blue permit. A flourishing business has developed in such *Durchlaßscheine*. Cases are known in which thousands of koruna have been paid for it. Initially about K. 2,000.- were paid; on 31st March it is said that up to K. 50,000.- have been paid. The reporter points out that the actual wording of the permit also allows re-entry to Czechoslovakia, however that this passage was frequently deleted for Jews, or the permits which still bore the endorsement allowing re-entry were taken from Jews at the border, e.g. in Bentheim. The reporter received his *Durchlaßschein* through the Dutch consul in Prague.

The Gestapo differentiates between *"echt"* [genuine] and *"unecht"* [fake] foreigners. *Echt* foreigners are e.g. Americans, British, French, Dutch, *unecht* are all Jews, Hungarians, Poles, Yugoslavs. Everyone however needed this *Durchlaßschein* and initially on arrival an *Einreisegenehmigung* [entry permit] from the German authorities. Even German nationals have to obtain an *Einreisegenehmigung*. If it is a case of business travel, they must request the permit at the *Reichswirtschaftsministerium* [Reich Ministry of Economic Affairs] and submit a *Befürwortung* [endorsement] from the *Handelskammer* [Chamber of Commerce].

The Czech Jews have provisionally received their passports. Incidentally the "J" has already been introduced from January for these passports. [František] Chvalkovsky had to go to Berlin at that time, because Hitler's wishes in connection with "Aryanisation" were not being implemented quickly and not precisely enough. At that time, suddenly, without further legal provision, *Schächten* [Jewish kosher slaughter] was forbidden, i.e., it was simply made impossible by means of locking the area set aside for this at the Prague abattoir.

The arrests were made by a Gestapo man and a Czech official, but these Czech officials were almost always Sudeten Germans. They all had command of the Czech language however. In Dresden it is said that Czech courses for officers have been taking place for a long time.

On 14th March there began to be unrest on the streets of Prague. Groups of young people roamed the streets with a clearly aggressive intent. Already by evening it was no longer possible to speak Czech on the streets without being jostled. Mostly they spat in the face of people speaking Czech. It was said that the groups roaming around were German students. They were however *Henleinleute* [[Konrad] Henlein men], who had come especially from the Sudetenland to Prague. Not only boys but men of 40 to 45 years of age could be seen among them. The reporter describes how groups of 20, 30 or more people were causing unrest in an unheard of insolent manner. They went up and down Wenceslas Square endlessly and accosted Jews and Czechs. In Heinrichsgasse a dreadful brawl developed in which the *Henleinleute* came off worse. These men already knew on 14th March exactly what was happening. The greeting was said to have sounded, "Hail 15th March!" The demonstrations lasted right into the night. Many hundreds of police officers were on Wenceslas Square and Graben.

Late in the evening came the news that Ostrava (Moravian Ostrava) [now Moravská Ostrava] was occupied by German troops. Pilsen [now Cz. Plzeň] was said to be occupied the following morning. By the following morning between 10 and 12 o'clock Prague was already occupied. The first thing that happened was that Gestapo vehicles drove up to the *Staatsbank* [State Bank] and took the gold. Motorised troops arrived in Prague. The officers sat in open cars without sides, as they usually are in the military. The populace spat at the men and waved their fists at the vehicles. The German military however did not let this ruffle them.

When the reporter returned to his hotel, two Gestapo officers came there and wanted 20 of the hotel rooms to be placed at their disposal. "The rooms must be free in two hours!" At 11 o'clock the hotel manager told him he had to clear out his room, the whole floor was reserved for the Gestapo. At half past 11 two Gestapo officers (in SS uniform) came back with the demand that the entire hotel be vacated by guests and placed at the disposal of the Gestapo. On the manager's objection that his guests were almost all out, a deadline of 5 o'clock was given. Other hotels (this was the Palast-Hotel) were also requisitioned. *Bankhaus Petschek & Co.* [Petschek bank building; now *Petschkův palac;* Petschek Palace] was the headquarters of the general staff.

The military behaved properly towards the rest of the public and did not bother with anyone in particular. It was noticeable that soon after the occupation by German troops all the literature which was forbidden in Germany was sold out. Books by Emil von Ludwig for example were immediately bought up. It is said that the officers were supposed to have even bought Konrad Heiden's *Hitler.*

The Gestapo appeared with complete arrest lists in their briefcases, so that already one hour after their arrival the arrests could be started. *Henleinleute* [Henlein men] who knew Prague well accompanied the Gestapo vehicles on these trips. In total in Czechoslovakia 13,000 people are said to have been arrested. In Prague about 6,000 arrests were made during the first two days. To begin with the former *Bürgermeister* [mayor] of Prague and some department heads of the city administration were arrested. In addition various politicians. [Wenzel] Jaksch fled to the British Embassy. The *Prager Tagblatt* [German language daily newspaper published in Prague] was occupied. Eight German *Landgerichtsräte* [district court counsels] arrived for the investigation. There is said to have been no mistreatment during the arrests. There was merely more than enough rudeness and insolence. The arrested men came first of all to the prison at Pankrasz [now Pankrác], then to the Sokol stadium, where they were accommodated in the cubicles set up for contestants in competitions. There is room for 3,000 people. Some have also had to spend the night standing up there, because they had no room to lie down.

Gradually life in Prague started to "normalise". The shop signs were changed. The people Aryanised themselves. In the windows there are signs with the inscription "pure Aryan shop" in Czech. Delivery vans were secured by simply painting over the firm's signs. On Wednesday Hitler seized Prague. On Thursday there appeared in all the newspapers a report that the *Anwaltskammer* [barristers' association] had requested all Jewish lawyers to stop practising. When walking through the streets all the shops, particularly the clothing shops, even Christian ones, looked as if they were closed. So much was being bought that the shops started to admit only a small number of buyers, to close the doors and some time later to admit the next ones. There was also hoarding. Food was bought up by people from Germany. Entire convoys of vehicles loaded with food drove off to Germany.

On the third day after the occupation of Prague came dreadful news of suicides among the Jewish population. Every day there numbered about 30 to 40 suicides. To date about 400 people who attempted to commit suicide in the days from 15th to 18th March have been taken to the hospitals. Entirely non-political people had been arrested. Among others e.g. Freisinger, the engineer who, with the approval of the *Fürsorgeministerium* [Ministry of Welfare] in Prague, organised a group emigration of 300 Jews and who had legally arranged this emigration to the Dominican Republic. The only difficulty still lay in the fact that there were people among them who were afraid of the journey across Germany. For that reason Freisinger negotiated with KLM in Holland, in order for the transport to be carried out by aeroplane to Rotterdam. He was arrested because he was "leader of a group of emigrants".

Frau [Maria] Schmolka and Frau Stein were arrested. All the money collected for the Sudeten German Jews was confiscated so that the Sudeten German Jewish refugees, who had been staying in Prague since the previous autumn, had to starve. Furthermore all the rich people were arrested. Even Dr. Stein, the *Rechtsanwalt* [lawyer] who had worked a lot for Petschek was arrested. He was only able to escape as he had been warned; on the sixth day he handed himself in to the police.

Many Jews fled to Poland. Ostrava, the only way out, was however first occupied by the Germans, so that the Jews were as if in a trap. Under these circumstances a human smuggling operation developed in Ostrava, starting from Restaurant Grün and Café Union. For about ten days it took place in the following way: those escaping were smuggled into the coal tunnels and led underground across to Polish territory. But the German authorities discovered this route and put a stop to it. Now it is necessary to pay a high price in order to be taken across. For K. 5,000 koruna people ought to get safely across to Poland. However the Sudeten German Jews have no longer got that much. People lend each another K. 300.- or K. 400.- koruna to escape.

Many Jews, as they cannot successfully get across the border, flee into hospitals and sanatoria, where they believe they are safe from the clutches of the Gestapo.

Many hundreds of those who have escaped stay in Czenstochau [Tschenstochau; now Pol. Częstochowa], many have also gone on to Gdingen [Pol. Gdynia] and hope to get a ship to England from there. Many also fled to Yugoslavia, for which it was easy to get a visa.

In Czechoslovakia in recent months many Jews have been baptised, and admittedly only for the purpose of emigrating to South America. Yet more are armed with baptism certificates which were obtained by corruption. Prices between K. 800.- and K. 1,500.- have been paid for baptism certificates, depending on whether only the parents or also the grandparents were recorded on them as Christian.

Soon after the occupation by the Germans regulations were already enacted which affected Jews. By 15th April all the Jews living in Bohemia and Moravia have to declare their wealth. Jews are allowed neither to sell nor assign nor gift pieces of land. The owners of shops may not sell nor Aryanise their shops. Jews may not go in cafés, cinemas or theatres.

Czech reaction: after Hitler had arrived, [Radola] Gajda believed that his hour had come. He issued an appeal on 15th March for the people to place itself under his leadership. Originally a National Guard was to be formed, of which Gajda was to be head. As early as the following day that was prevented by the Germans. Gajda is of no consequence, and [Emil] Hácha has taken over as head. The people learned from the fate of the Jews, but no conclusive judgement can be given about the mood of the Czech people. In any case the disappointment and bitterness are very great. It is said that acts of sabotage took place in the Škoda factories.

As a personal experience the reporter adds the following:

After the Gestapo had already moved into the Palast-Hotel and he along with other guests had had great difficulty finding private lodgings, he was compelled to go back to the hotel in order to fetch his post there. While the concierge was looking for and handing out his letters, the SS men who were present in the entrance hall, apparently as guards, stepped right up to him and asked him harshly whether he was Jewish, why he was in Prague, whether he travelled much, etc. He was required to show his passport. Thereupon it was said in a rude tone, "So, you're Dutch! And so you probably think that we can't touch you?" He said that he was due to go to Holland, but just like everyone else had to get hold of a *Durchlaßschein* [travel permit]. He answered calmly but firmly, whereupon the SS men relented and even informed him in a relatively polite way where he should collect the "blue permit".

B. 337 Addendum to the report from Prague

The following committed suicide between 15th and 18th March:

Paul Rittenberg in Prague shot himself in the Haus Schwarze Rose.

Dr. Beermann and his wife from Karlsbad [Carlsbad; now Cz. Karlovy Vary] poisoned themselves.

B. 338 Although omens pointing to an operation against Czechoslovakia planned for the middle of March had been evident for months, it was nevertheless more like a surprise for the great majority of the population of the *historische Länder* [historic states] (Bohemia, Moravia and Silesia) when, in the late evening of 14th March of this year the occupation of Mährisch Ostrau [now Ostrava, Czech Republic], the industrial and coal and steel centre and the surrounding areas, was announced. Shortly before this, it had become known that the President Dr. [Emil] Hácha escorted by the foreign minister Dr. [František] Chvalkovsky had travelled to Berlin on the afternoon of the same day to negotiate with the *Reichskanzler* [Reich Chancellor] Hitler.

If one had initially been inclined to think that this was a temporary or partial occupation, then one was disabused on the morning 15th March. From early on and in fiercely driving snow, lorries and other motorised divisions of all branches of the Reich army entered Prague, and few hours later offices of the army, the Gestapo and other organisations (SS, SA etc.) were already active.

The population was indescribably dejected, yet they accepted the knowledge of the troop invasion silently and without incident.

The commanding general, who was the highest authority, immediately issued bilingual decrees and which ordered the first curfew for between the hours of 8 o'clock in the evening and 6 o'clock in the morning. The Führer arrived at Prague Castle in the evening, where he was "enthusiastically" received the following morning by the Germans in Prague and by the Sudeten German high school students who had been sent to Prague with the troop invasion. He left Prague at around midday and betook himself to Brünn [now Brno], where he was acclaimed by the sizeable German population of the town and everyone in the surrounding area. After his departure the curfew was extended to midnight.

Understandably, the Jewish population was seized by a tremendous mood of panic, all the more so as it became known that Jewish institutions (HICEM [emigrants' assistance organisation], *Sozialamt* [*Jüdisches Sozialamt*; Jewish social services office], *Palästinaamt* [Palestine Office] etc.) had been closed and partly sealed administratively by the German authorities. The leaders of these organisations had to undergo police interrogation, some were imprisoned, e.g. Frau Dr. Schmolka, the commendable leader of HICEM, of whom it is said that she was taken to the newly established concentration camp near Michalovce, the existence of which is denied by the German and Czech press, etc. Owners of the numerous retail and wholesale firms in Jewish possession in most cases were immediately subjected to "*Arisierung*" [Ayanisation] of their businesses through handover to reliably Aryan employees etc.

However, the intention of most Jews to depart for abroad, apart from the difficulty of entering other countries, was made impossible from the moment of the occupation onwards by tying it to the approval of the German authorities. Whilst the procurement of an *Ausreisegenehmigung* [exit permit] had been relatively easy in the very first days as the German military command was responsible for this, in the course of the first weeks the Gestapo took control of the agenda and thereby of a life of suffering for many. There are many cases where Jews queued many long nights to obtain the *Ausreisegenehmigung* and just before they reached their turn they were dispersed by the police. Many did not spend the nights in their homes from fear of the Gestapo, and very many who were afraid to show their passport to the Gestapo because of political or other reasons crossed the Polish border illegally, an attempt that often cost many 1,000 *Kronen* [Cz. *Koruna*]. In many cases, however, crossing the border in this manner was not successful, and the Polish guards chased the refugees back over the Czech border, where their belongings up to RM. 3.- were confiscated by the German Gestapo men. They were then taken across the border by the Gestapo by a different route.

The situation in Prague intensified in the final days of March, the official decree appeared stating that *Ausreiseansuchen* [exit applications] from Jews would no longer be accepted, a measure that is hopefully only temporary.

The circumstances must be regarded as better than might otherwise have been, as the Czech fascist movement of [former] Legion General Radola Gajda, who began to develop a very active function through the German troops immediately after the occupation of the country, was stopped by the German authorities at the beginning, for it cannot be foreseen what harm the goings on of the Czech fascists meant for the Jewish population. The Czech population as a whole rejected the nasty antisemitic deeds of this vanishingly small group, much as its attempts to incite hatred in these people in previous months remained almost without resonance. Nevertheless one should not overlook the fact that another tactic for excluding Jews from all occupations and trades etc. was in progress with hundred per cent success. The exclusion of Jewish and non-Aryan members in which they often played significant roles was carried out by professional etc. organisations in the minimum time, not officially.

The situation was also very threatening for the thousands who had attempted to flee to the *historische Länder* after the occupation of the Sudetenland, as well as the *Reichsdeutsche* [ethnic German] and Austrian emigrants living there.

The Gestapo has been carrying out continual arrests amongst these people, and in that context are the suicides of many exceptionally well-known personalities.

Gestapo headquarters in Prague has been established in the building of the well-known Jewish banking house Petschek.

The hope of many of those remaining in the *historische Länder* is that those nations willing to help will undertake a mass evacuation operation of those who still find themselves there, to find asylum anywhere else through their own efforts, because many of them lack even the smallest connection to abroad.

B. 339 Amsterdam, 1st February 1939

The contemporary situation of the Jews in Austria

The following facts illuminate the current situation of the Jews in Austria. It is more than catastrophic.

The total population today consists of roughly 110,000 souls, but consisted of over 180,000 Jews at the *Machtergreifung* [seizure of power]. At least 35,000 Jewish people are homeless. Of the c. 40,000 Jewish people who were in Vienna's prisons, in the various concentration camps, Dachau, Buchenwald etc. c. 11,000 are still there today. The number of dead would not be given as too high at 1,000. Many were culled by the inhumane exertions, many were "auf der Flucht erschossen" [shot whilst escaping]. The Jews live in constant fear of arrest, and psychological breakdown is unavoidable as a result of the crippling situation. Of the 180,000 Jews living in Austria at the accession of the Hitler government, every second Jew over the age of 16 has been in prison.

Only in the rarest cases are children aged up to 14 years of age "taken along"; if one therefore deducts the number of children from these 180,000 souls, and the women, who were only arrested in small numbers, one comes to the shocking result that every second Jew filled the National Socialist prisons. This naked fact entails awful consequences. An indescribable feeling of panic seizes each Jew, which increases, because he must have the conviction that it will be his turn too. These purposeful and systematically carried-out arrests on the streets, at night in homes and suchlike also have one more very sad effect. As a result of cramming ten to twelve or more people in one room, which is hygienically bad, these people live in stuffy air, malnourished. In the shortest time possible they inevitably become unable to work, and therefore also unable to emigrate. Evacuation of these people at the earliest must happen if one still wants to prevent their doom in time.

Over 2,500 people are waiting to be moved to the expanded old people's homes, and cannot find a place in this country because neither homes nor beds are available.

Of about 60,000 Jewish companies and businesses that were in Austria, barely 2,000 have been *arisiert* [Aryanised], the other 58,000 have utterly perished. The process of complete economic expulsion set in immediately after the *Machtergreifung*, there have been no more Jewish businesses at all since the *Pogromtagen* [pogrom days] (10th November).

20 *Tempel* [synagogues] and 70 houses of prayer have been burned and destroyed, there are no longer any religious services in the places of worship, one cannot say Kaddish [Prayer for the Dead].

Restaurants, cafés, cinemas, theatres, concerts, public baths, gardens are closed to Jews. Jews are not allowed to sit on any of the benches within the city's limits.

The perpetual house searches are carried out sadistically. Everything is smashed to pieces, torn apart, taken away.

Vorladungen [summonses] or being taken to the Gestapo, and the perpetual agonising interrogations invariably provoke an indescribable feeling of panic.

Community life has ceased; of the 33 *Gemeinden* [communities] only seven remain in all, of Austria today.

All, absolutely all, Jews are informed by one goal today: emigration. A methodical emigration carried out from abroad is not only in the interests of the Austrian Jews but also of Jews of the world. The "*Sesshaftmachung*" [settlement arrangement], which has been implemented for several years, is now being completed, because of the 110,000 Jews still living in Austria, roughly 35,000 have *Einreisemöglichkeiten* [entry opportunities] in various countries whilst the 60 to 65,000 Jews are in camps, camps to be annihilated at the earliest.

This solution is possible and is the prayer of the hour!

B. 340 SACHENSENHAUSEN CONCENTRATION CAMP

A factual report

On the afternoon of the fateful 10th November I was sitting at my desk at around 5, full of disquiet not only on account of the reports of looting of Jewish businesses and burning of the synagogues, reports that had spread at great speed, but also by what I myself had observed of these events in a number of streets, when the doorbell rang furiously. Two gentlemen were standing at the door, one of whom identified himself as a *Kriminalbeamter* [detective] by pointing to his badge and told me that they were under orders to take me to the *Polizeipräsidium* [police headquarters]. They were either unable or unwilling to respond to my question as to what the reason might be. My wife and daughter happened to be ill in bed in their bedroom. I was permitted to let them know what was happening and take some things for the night, because knowledge of earlier incidents involving arrest suggested that I could expect to have to stay for at least the coming night. The officials stood by the door in order to check what I was saying. My wife, who was understandably very shocked by the news, packed some nightwear, underwear, socks, and a pullover for me, I took RM. 20.- with me and the three of us left.

I tried to elicit some information as to the reason and purpose of my arrest, but to no avail. The officials were civil but guarded and perhaps themselves not fully informed as to the details of their brief. We spoke about the murder in Paris and they took an interest in my financial affairs. We then travelled by ordinary bus amongst the public, quite inconspicuously, to the *Polizeipräsidium*, each paying his own fare. There were large gatherings of people on the streets staring inquisitively at the looted businesses. We passed through the grand entrance of the *Polizeipräsidium* into the courtyard where a fairly large group of people was already gathered: those who had been arrested, detectives, SS men. As we passed the checkpoint my escorts made an announcement that I was later to observe repeatedly: two detectives with one Jew (or with two Jews, etc.). Ordinarily only one or two people under arrest came with their officials, which means that a very large number of officials must have been called in for the operation. Whilst the tone of the officials had been quite correct and their behaviour towards me on the street entirely inconspicuous, the tone in the courtyard of the *Polizei-präsidium* was entirely different: military, full of cruel ferocity and scorn for the defenceless Jews under arrest. The tone was that of a military camp with phrases such as "*Drecksau*" [filthy swine], "*Judenschwein*" [Jewish pig] etc. repeated endlessly, such that they have doubtless remained indelibly imprinted on the minds of everyone who was there. It was about half past 7 in the evening. Already circa 50–70 prisoners were standing in the courtyard, more arrived every minute.

Without being given an inkling of what was planned for us, we were lined up in rows of five or ten. Some tried to be released by presenting completed emigration papers. With the exception of one individual who proved that he had foreign nationality nobody, to my knowledge, was released, be it on the grounds of illness, war wounds or anything else for that matter. One already discovered friends and felt oneself to be the victim of a comprehensive operation. In the darkness I noticed a disproportionately large number of academics amongst the crowd.

After about another half an hour large police vehicles drew up and we were ordered to board them, which was no easy matter given that the vehicles were tall and only open at the back, without any steps, making it difficult for the less nimble and for the old people. Insufficient speed in climbing aboard immediately resulted in energetic vocal and physical assistance from the SS. One had to stand in the vans (although there may have been a few benches to the side), holding on to one another or the walls. There were probably 40–60 people squeezed together in each van. The vehicles drove through the centre of Berlin and out to the north. The streets were full of people who watched the procession of vehicles and in some cases greeted it with jeering. The further we came from Berlin the clearer it became to us what was facing us: that we were not heading for an interrogation in a prison but for a concentration camp. In the van I discovered an old friend standing right next to me, we shook hands and promised to hold together. I was determined to summon all my strength in order to get through the ordeal and not offer the enemy the pleasure of seeing me "*Verrecken*" [perish].

We arrived at the iron gate of Sachsenhausen camp at circa nine and were greeted with what would become the standard form of address, the "*Drecksau*" that was later to become monotonous, the presumption of the informal "*Du*" [you], the threat of punches, blows and slaps in the face, the administering of these kindnesses, the compulsion to run everywhere ("*Bewegung*", "*Bewegung*" [move, move] still rings in my ears). Anyone who did not climb down quickly from the van was punished with a punch. No one could see anyone else properly in the darkness; in accord with the principle of "*sauve qui peut*" [every man for himself], which generally dominated camp life, everyone was determined to protect themselves as best they could from an encounter with the *Sklavenaufsehern* [slave drivers] by running as fast as possible. I do not know how many were beaten in the process. Thanks to being driven to the entrance of the camp we were much better off than other camp inmates who arrived by train who later told us they had been chased like cattle at the double under blows, or rather much worse than cattle, from the outlying railway station to the camp.

From the vans we were herded through the iron gate with the beautiful wrought iron inscription, the one we subsequently read on a daily basis, "*Arbeit macht frei*" (work frees you), to the *Appellplatz* [parade ground] where we were lined up in rows of five. At that moment the last bit of freedom that we had experienced in that great concentration camp known as Germany evaporated. The camp is surrounded by high stone walls topped with a barbed wire fence and in front of it a further barrier also of barbed wire. The fence and barrier are electrified, at least at night (I do not know if that is also the case during the day), and the slightest contact with it is fatal – many a suicide candidate made successful use of this method, if he was not caught first and severely punished. Huge watch towers punctuate the wall; these have machine guns installed in them and from there the guards ceaselessly check the camp, illuminating it at night with enormous searchlights that also light up the barracks with a ghostly semblance of daylight. If and when work is carried out outside of the camp – beyond the walls – there is not only supervision by patrolling guards but also endless counting off, repeated at every opportunity, of prisoners leaving and entering the camp in order to identify any absentees as soon as possible. For this reason successful escapes are very rare and regularly end in those concerned being rediscovered sooner or later.

The sense of being cut off from the rest of the world for no obvious reason, indefinitely, with no legal justification, and entirely arbitrarily is almost impossible to convey to someone who has not experienced it. It weighs down on one all the time like a terrible burden – one hopes, hopes, and hopes again that the hour of freedom will come, but one never knows if and when it will. A criminal who is locked up for a given act for a given amount of time knows why he is incarcerated and for how long, and can calculate the length of time that he will be denied his freedom; the "*Schutzhaftling*" [prisoner in protective custody], who is in *Schutzhaft* [protective custody] despite the fact that he has done nothing which would amount to a criminal act, faces total nothingness, as a political convict having already served his sentence, for being politically unreliable and, as such, someone for whom even today's "*Strafrecht*" [criminal law] cannot envisage any form of conviction, for being a so-called *Asozialer* [asocial] who happens presently not to have a job and is denounced by his caring neighbour or the Party, for being a *Bibelforscher* [Jehovah's Witness], or for being a Jew who has nothing against his name beyond his indelible birth mark and who can therefore never eliminate the root cause of his incarceration. Outside one could hear the trains whistle on their way to Berlin. In the camp there were thousands upon thousands of inmates, Jews and non-Jews, all in all around 14,000 people (around half of them Jews rounded up in the *Novemberaktion* [November operation]) at the mercy of a senseless and despotic rule, the entire thing almost inconceivable in a world which but a few years previously had held itself to be so progressive, and which now afforded those responsible international respect for this system where once a single example of such a tragic miscarriage of justice, such as in the Dreyfus case, could have shocked the whole world. But I have allowed myself to be deflected from describing the events as they unfolded.

We stood, as already mentioned, on the large *Appellplatz*, large enough to accommodate all 14,000 occupants that the camp held at the height of the *Judenaktion* [Jews operation]. We stood and stood. After a certain period of time our briefcases, bags etc. were taken away; we were only to see them again on our release, untouched I should add (albeit without any food that they may have contained). Some time later we were called into the office to have our personal details recorded on index cards. The evening came and went, night came and we were still standing, night passed and morning came and we were still standing there. We looked over to the large clock on the tower above the camp entrance and the hands moved onwards inexorably. The winter sun rose, it was early and we had been up all night, something that would have seemed impossible if someone had announced it the previous day. The monotony of waiting was only interrupted on one occasion by a terrible incident: one of the new arrivals, a professor of mathematics it was said, whose nerves were not up to it immediately became involved in an altercation with one of the *Aufseher* [overseers] and was punished for his insubordination with immediate blows. The punches and the moaning of the unfortunate man strapped to the *Bock* [whipping block] were gruesome in the night; apparently he continued to be in all kinds of trouble thereafter.

We had not been given anything to eat and most of us had not eaten since lunchtime. One or two had managed to sleep a little whilst standing up, others had fainted and were propped up by their comrades. Our *Aufseher*, who stood in front of us and kept coming and going, were already clearly divided into two different groups: the brutal SS men, our "lords", with corresponding manners, and political prisoners, our fellow sufferers, who dealt with us in a friendly way from the outset and who passed on rules of conduct that would enable us to master as well as possible the difficult situation facing us. They also allowed us, when the others were out of sight, to step out of line a little and answer the call of nature; more was not possible despite the length of time. We continued to stand there through the morning. In the course of the morning military clothing was distributed. To this end we were herded, about ten at a time I think, into the camp's washing block, always at the double every step of the way to avoid the punches and blows. There we first had to hand over any jewellery or other valuables (watches, rings, also earrings, tie pins, cuff links etc.) as well as money, which, incidentally, we received back again on our release. Then we had to undress and hand over our civilian clothes, we were only allowed to keep shoes, handkerchiefs, and glasses. A quick physical check by a *Sanitäter* [medical orderly] followed to identify any skin complaints and, above all, sexually transmitted diseases; it was carried out in a rough manner, followed by a head shave, perhaps a hygienic measure but one considered by many to be belittling, then a cold shower augmented by a powerful hosing down to the face from a thick hose pipe, conceived as an amusement for the SS and as torture for the victims, and administered with even greater force if the victim did not control himself and seemed unable to cope with the situation, all followed by finally getting dressed.

The clothing consisted of a mixture of old and new military and camp uniforms, ranging from good old military materials to the latest substitute materials. We obtained whatever was available at the moment haphazardly, not individually fitted of course, a cap, pair of socks, underpants, a jacket, trousers and a towel. Those who came later for the most part did not get a cap at all because there were none left and for weeks until their release they had to run around without any head covering, at this time of year! Some people, those who were sent to work outside the camp, later also received work shoes. The underwear was part cotton, part linen, socks were woollen, the clothing more or less weatherproof depending on its age. The caps were grey, blue, red, black, from all arms of the service, as were the jackets and trousers, all from different ranks, including some officers' dress which seemed strangely elegant in this place. The new uniforms from substitute materials were striped blue and grey and looked like pyjamas. It all gave the impression of being thoroughly motley, carnivalesque even, and one could have burst out laughing if the situation had not been so serious, and we did indeed laugh sometimes because humour is a real consolation, even in a situation like this. We did not receive any more clothing throughout our entire stay, a few fortunate souls apparently obtained gloves during the really cold spell that began on 15th December, but most did not, which explains why much evidence of frostbite was associated with those days.

The underwear and clothes were missing a lot of buttons. That might appear insignificant to someone who dons proper underwear on a daily basis, but it certainly is not for two reasons: first, because underwear and clothes that cannot be closed are much more open to the wind, second because the missing buttons offered one of the best opportunities for bullying. The "*Sklavenhalter*" [slave owners] demanded that all buttons be present, e.g. opening up jackets at random during *Appell* [roll call] to check that they were all present and correct, but never provided buttons or sewing materials to make good the missing ones. The longest standing detainees did indeed have their own sewing kits, which they sacrificed (they were the "*Politischen*" [politicals]!) and also managed to conjure up some buttons, but there were not anything like enough to go round, so the whole time everyone was scrambling to find needles, thread and buttons to repair their clothes and underwear, and it was a strange sight to behold when of an evening everyone would crowd around the proud owner of sewing materials and buttons waiting their turn. Gradually one learnt the camp custom of tearing off the button from dirty shirts and underwear before handing it over in order to be well equipped for the new, probably buttonless ones, a completely senseless activity which meant that everyone had to sew on all their buttons again every time they had a change of clothes. Shirts, socks and towels were changed weekly, underwear every two weeks; the state everything was in by that time is best left to the imagination when one consider that everyone spent the night in their shirts and underwear on the straw mattresses, which will be described below.

On being fitted out everyone received a number to sew onto their jacket. We were now merely numbers, which, however, also had a positive dimension to it: our name, job and so on, in short every aspect of individuality, which could all too easily have provided our "lords" with another target, was extinguished for them. They were inquisitive enough as it was, often enquiring about our job, intended country of emigration and the like. A few days later a coloured mark that designated us as Jews of the *Novemberaktion* was added to the number. All camp inmates were labelled with a number and a mark, a triangular symbol of a particular colour which was supposed to make it easier for those in charge to identify the group to which a particular prisoner belonged and deal with him. The colours were as follows:

a) Red for political prisoners; mostly Communists (and amongst them many former members of parliament), a small number of social democrats, oppositional Protestant ministers, Nazis who had made themselves unpopular or other grumblers, all in "*Schutzhaft*" following a judicial conviction which seemed too lenient to the Gestapo, or because some action or thought was not sufficient for a conviction; many of them had been in custody for years, often since 1933, indeed some who had been punished for being Communists before 1933 had been there even longer.

b) Green for *Berufsverbrecher* [professional criminals]; doubtless real criminals who are sent to the camp nowadays once they have served their sentence, undoubtedly a serious issue in relation to maintaining a safe society, but just not one that should be solved by means of a German concentration camp. Before the green marking was introduced they had the designation "B.V." (*Berufsverbrecher*) painted onto the back of their jackets in large black letters; some of us had received jackets of this kind when we were fitted out and now walked around with this horrible B.V. on our backs.

c) Brown for the *Asozialen* [asocials]: as well as truly asocial elements (tramps, beggars), people who were temporarily unemployed or who as covert opponents of the system had avoided participating in Party activities or who had a more or less minimal criminal record. The presence of a criminal record was known to have been the excuse for the imprisonment of Jews in June 1938 (the so-called *Juni-Aktion* [June operation]). At that time people were imprisoned with harmless previous convictions (commercial, tax, or driving offences sometimes dating back many years). I know of the case of a 67-year-old man who faced criminal prosecution for a political utterance, who was not required to serve his sentence as a result of an amnesty, but who was arrested for the same incident once again. He died in the camp two months later from blood poisoning shortly before he was due to be released. The true cause of death was suppressed, it was, of course, the result of the entirely inadequate, unhygienic conditions in the camps, clearly intended to destroy rather than preserve life. These prisoners, designated "*alte Juden*" [old Jews] and of whom there were still several hundred despite the fact that many had been released in order to emigrate, bore a yellow symbol on top of the brown one so that the two triangles together constituted a *Mogen Dovid* [Star of David].

d) The colours pink, blue and purple were handed out to Bibelforscher, and returning emigrants (Germans and Aryans who seemed untrustworthy); of these the were particularly harshly treated in that they were only allowed very restricted contact with other inmates of the camp, limited access to post and use of the canteen. Their beliefs were unshakeable and they stubbornly rejected any approaches demanding that they acknowledge the superiority of National Socialism over and above their own faith. The German concentration camps hold many true martyrs of all imaginable political, religious, and other groups.

We, Jews from the *Novemberaktion,* received, along with the number, a red and yellow symbol, two triangles to be sewn crosswise, evidently as a symbol of our political and also "racial" inferiority and untrustworthiness. During the first few weeks the markings, which combined to form the *Mogen Dovid*, were mechanically sewn onto our jackets, and later our trousers, by camp tailors (who were prisoners too). This red-yellow colouring thus dominated the camp thanks to its ubiquity (6–7,000), not least because the colours were still strong and fresh and brightly visible everywhere.

Fitting out constituted the last interruption to the protracted period of standing which had begun with our arrival on the previous evening. Finally, it must have been around 4–5 o'clock in the afternoon, we were led to our allocated barracks where, circa 24 hours after our arrest, we received our first meal, the usual stew from a pot which many of us still remembered from our time in the army. The whole period of waiting had, of course, been a deliberate form of torture, since it would have been quite possible to allow new arrivals to wait in the empty barracks and lie down, despite the undoubted technical difficulties presented by such a massive influx of people.

We Jews were housed in a number of spacious barracks connected to one another, called "blocks", and we were separated from the other camp inmates. Prisoners lived in about 50–60 barracks surrounding the camp's *Appellplatz* in a series of rows. In this huge camp there were also barracks for the kitchen, for stores (clothing etc.), for the offices, the medical barracks, the washing block, as well as rooms to accommodate more than 1,000 guards, well equipped of course, and comfortable little houses for the SS leader gentlemen of various ranks right up to the *Lagerkommandant* [camp commandant]. Each block had two wings A and B, each wing consisting of large sleeping quarters and a day room, in the middle were the washroom and toilets for both parts. In the sleeping room there were c. 140 men, literally squeezed together like sardines. We lay on straw, over which thin cotton blankets were spread each evening, and which were piled up in a corner during the day. As a covering we each obtained a single blanket, on occasion some people obtained two if there were extras when people left and their space had not been taken again. The blankets varied in quality, some better some worse, some thinner some thicker. They were distributed in the evening and piled up again in the morning; as they were not distributed and retained individually a certain communism of blanket use prevailed, hard to comprehend for the outsider in terms of hygiene, yet which had to be endured "*nolens volens*" [whether one liked it or not].

We lay in five rows of 28 men on average, mostly back to back, not back beside back, so that a change of sleeping position was only possible if one's neighbour also moved or if one got up with considerable effort and lay down the other way round. It was less tightly packed for a while after a certain period of time when people began to be released, but then after a few days the barracks were filled up again and a number of blocks combined, so that the sardine state of affairs returned. When occupation was at its greatest one could not walk through the sleeping quarters, therefore the large number of people who had to make their way to the toilet had to balance their way over the heads and legs of the sleepers, which was of course not conducive to rest and sleep. We generally had to go to bed at 7 o'clock, although most people were happy to lie down earlier: the need for sleep and the impossibility of engaging in other activities was so acute that all these people normally used to going to bed late quickly adapted to the change in lifestyle. The lights were put out usually at around 8 o'clock, following the inevitable counts and checks to make sure everyone was present. Everyone had their own particular sleeping place which had happened by chance. Those who had to go out most often during the night were placed as close to the exit as possible.

We were woken at 5 o'clock in the morning, later on at half past 5. Thus the night was much longer than in civilian life; given the absence of watches and the impossibility of knowing how late it was, this merely increased the agonising uncertainty, something that is hard to imagine if one normally takes it for granted that one can check the time, even at night. To sleep one had to remove jacket, trousers and socks but keep shirt and underpants on. The clothes removed served as a pillow, the boots at the very bottom, the rest on top. A further 15–25 people were put up in the day room, initially on the bare ground, later on straw sacks. Despite all this, accommodation on the straw was more pleasant than being billeted to the military beds stacked one above the other, as was commonly the case with a number of the long term prisoners. With these there was always the "*Bettenbauens*" [bed making], so beloved of the German military, in which everything, i.e. straw sacks, sheets, blankets, pillows had to be dead straight and plumped up into perfect right angles, which offered the perfect opportunity for endless bullying as those in charge repeatedly destroyed the beds and had them made all over again. In this way the victims of this mistreatment were deprived of the last remnants of their free time and tortured to within an inch of their lives.

The washroom and the toilet, situated between the two wings of the block, were actually quite hygienic. The washroom contained eight to ten footbaths and two large round washbasins, each with eight taps in a circle; the toilets had eight to ten bowls and six small sinks, all with running water. The problem was that both sets of facilities were far too small for 340–350 people, and using them involved massive problems. Initially there were c. 1½ hours for getting up, washing and having breakfast, later for some obscure reason we were only allowed to get up half an hour later which meant that all these activities had to be squeezed into a shorter period.

Getting up too early was strictly forbidden, but woe betide anyone who did not rise as soon as the electric light came on, the signal to wake up! If one of the torturers felt in the mood to inspect the getting-up procedure, then the unfortunate man would be dealt a slap in the face. One day a man in his late 60s was punched in the face for this very reason despite the fact that he pointed to a disability he had sustained in the war. The slaps rained down on him. One put on socks, shoes, trousers, took one's jacket under one's arm, put one's cap in one's trousers or jacket and rushed down the narrow corridor leading from one wing to the other and off which the toilets and washroom led. One group used the toilet first, the other the washroom. In the toilet people "queued" in four or five rows, with the room full to bursting with people. As it is not everyone's thing to follow the call of nature in front of such a large, impatient crowd of onlookers, all kinds of physiological problems ensued, a slowing down rather than speeding up, which in turn led to even greater pressure from the others, in short increasing nervousness. People with irregular digestion suffered enormously. There was the same jostling in the washroom and washing had to be done with a bare torso, which was justifiable in itself. Woe betide anyone who contravened this rule and was caught by one of the *Aufseher*.

A serious problem, at least in the early days, was keeping hold of one's own towel. Initially the towels were hung up on nails in the sleeping quarters without any label and of course all got mixed up. Then small pieces of card to write one's number on were distributed along with string to tie them on. Despite this, individual ownership of these towels was not recognised for some time. Who could make sure that someone did not take someone else's clean towel if theirs had, for example, already got dirty from washing feet or whatever. It took some time before the necessary mutual consideration won through here. One could often observe the lack of consideration amongst the Jews despite the fact that they were so dependent on one another. It is in general an interesting question as to whether crises of this kind encourage egotism or altruism.

Once a week we availed ourselves of the one and only welcome camp institution, the chance to take a shower. In the washing block there were 100 showers next to each other in rows, which were a substitute for a really nice hot bath. We had to get undressed in the next door changing room in double quick time, which was followed by the shower lasting seven minutes and for which we received a small piece of soap; it was overseen by friendly political prisoners in charge of the washing facilities; getting dressed had to happen just as fast to make room for the next group. In the circumstances one had to appreciate that this rigid organisation was necessary for the weekly clean of all of the prisoners.

Haircutting and shaving also belong in the territory of physical cleanliness. It was compulsory to have one's hair shaved off completely at regular intervals and it was ensured in accordance with Prussian militarism that everyone shaved regularly. Both activities were carried out free of charge by prisoners under orders, in their own time, of course. Anyone whose hair was too long or who had too full a beard could expect to be yelled at or punched in the face during *Appell*.

We had been admitted on Thursday evening, had stood until Friday afternoon, and now had the chance to sleep for the first time that night as part of this modern slavery. Saturday and Sunday were still work-free; usually the concentration camp does not recognise Sundays, there is work every day. On both days there was *exerzieren* [punitive drill] on the camp paths between the barracks, partly on the orders of the *Blockälteste*. Within the *"Judenblocks"* [Jewish blocks] one was allowed to move freely on the paths, as long as work allowed it. Entering other blocks was forbidden, although the ban was not observed strictly. During these days new groups of Jews kept arriving at the camp from the provinces. We kept seeing new people standing on the *Appellplatz*, some of whom had to wait for a shorter time than us, some for longer. The camp quickly filled up with the objects of the operation.

As they told us later, many of the fellow sufferers admitted from the provinces had experienced days that were much more unpleasant than we had. In small- and medium-sized towns they were not arrested with the semblance of correct procedure that had been adhered to in Berlin; instead they had been dragged out of their homes by looting gangs of SA at night, straight out of bed, from their offices, from building sites or wherever they happened to be, in their work clothes, often without a jacket or hat. They had been sent to regional police headquarters, had often spent days there and then been transported here by train on journeys lasting several days, already exhausted, having received little or nothing to eat, often without any money because it had already been taken from them *en route*. So there they stood on the *Appellplatz*, young and old, men from all parts of the country waiting to be processed just as we had been. We learned about the true scale of the catastrophe across Germany from them, heard how synagogues had been burned down all over the place, possessions wrecked, even the women and children chased out of their homes. Some groups were forced to carry signs, these were thrust into rabbis' hands particularly, bearing such inscriptions as "*Die Juden sind unser Unglück*" [The Jews are our undoing] or "*Wir sind das auserwählte Volk*" [We are the chosen people]. I do not know whether the signs came from their local areas or were forced on them in the camp, I suspect the former was the case.

One incident during what was otherwise a reasonable Saturday demonstrated to us where we were. We were doing marching practice in small groups when one of the *SS-Führer* [SS leaders] who happened to be passing had the idea of getting my section to "hop" around in a circle with our knees bent as low as possible, one of the favourite methods of torture as we were later to discover in countless individual incidents. He positioned himself in the middle, gave orders and counted, and we had to "hop" in rows of five, round and round, on and on, faster and faster, keeping in step, regardless of how much our unpractised limbs hurt and threatened to give in. In fear we pressed up against one another and side by side, supporting each other, tried to evade the gaze of our tormentor, straightened up a little when one or other of us caught his attention and he hit out at them, thereby momentarily distracted from the crowd as a whole.

Here as always in the camp it was fat, clumsy, or especially "Jewish"-looking types who had to suffer most. Our tormentors apparently only knew Jews from *Der Stürmer* [The Striker; Nazi tabloid newspaper] and *Das Schwarze Korps* [The Black Corps; SS newspaper]; they invariably spoke using the jargon of these papers and made a special effort to translate their words into deeds, so they attacked anyone who reminded them of the images in these papers. There was just such a fat, middle-aged man amongst us and, not surprisingly, he had a much more difficult time than average with the hopping, with the result that our executioner dragged him out of our midst and had him "hop" on his own for him. When he failed he got repeated kicks in the backside and whimpered for mercy like a dog, without success of course, collapsed, was forced up again with kicks and so it went on. We thought something would happen to him, but his heart was obviously in order and as a result he apparently survived the torture with no further injuries. I do not know how long the "hopping" lasted, to us it seemed endless, until our tormentor had had enough and released us. We were lucky, thank God, and did not have to go through this again.

That was on Saturday afternoon. The following day, on Sunday afternoon, we were allowed, as mentioned, to move up and down the camp streets between the *Judenblocks* and so – the weather was beautifully mild – went in search of friends.

It was then that we discovered, from mouth to mouth, face to face, the true extent of the operation of which we were the objects. One quickly encountered friends, one discovered from which parts of Germany people had been sent to Sachsenhausen (North and East Germany, but also some of West Germany). We took heart from each other. One realised that in the big cities of Berlin and Hamburg it was evidently academic and senior business people who were the main focus, whilst in smaller and medium-sized places almost everyone was deported, and in many cases it really was everyone. Numerous former *Richter* [judges], from *Amtsgericht* [county court] to *Reichsgericht* [supreme court], teachers of all kinds, lawyers, many doctors, both licensed and unlicensed, numerous rabbis and other cultural leaders, important businessmen and bankers, office holders from Jewish communities and organisations up to the *Reichsvertretung [der Juden in Deutschland*; Reich Deputation of Jews in Germany], editors of the Jewish press, independent writers, artists, actors all wore the same motley slave costume. Brothers, fathers and sons who had not known anything of each other's fate since the dreadful 10th November, even when they had been in the same place at the time, now found one another again in the camp, often with the help of third parties. One heard directly from leading figures in Jewish life that the communities and organisations had already been brought to a standstill on the morning of 10th November through bans and closure. One heard about the violent closure of the Hachshara centres [agricultural training for Jews preparing to emigrate to Palestine] and imprisonment of the youths who had been there. This verbal newspaper immediately provided an image of the overall situation of Jews in Germany; it developed into what someone labelled a "news exchange" with all kinds of speculation about the fate awaiting us, the response abroad etc. The mood oscillated between blackest pessimism and moderate optimism when it came to the single question that preoccupied all of us: "How long?"

Yet even on that day by no means all of the Jews who were supposed to be admitted to the camp had actually arrived; for days to come groups continued to arrive, the last being 300 Jews immediately labelled "*Sudetendeutsche*" [Sudeten Germans] within the camp, all from the German areas of Czechoslovakia recently ceded to the Reich, perhaps the most unfortunate and certainly most unexpected victims of the operation, a number of whom had been serving in the Czech military forces only a few weeks previously. They had had an *Optionsrecht* [option to move to Germany] until March of this year and now within a mere four weeks had experienced a material and spiritual collapse more drastic even than the fate which had befallen the Austrians in the previous year. In terms of age almost all groups of *Sudetendeutschen* were represented from 14 years to 82 (according to the most reliable sources). The 14-year-old was admitted with his father. The camp's card index, were it ever to become accessible, would show how high the percentage of over-60s actually was.

Given that the arrests were not carried out under the customary legal stipulation that physical suitability should be a condition of imprisonment, but rather at random, people suffering from all kinds of illnesses were also admitted, people with serious internal disorders, with paralysed limbs (arms and legs), people with mental retardation, there was even a dwarf amongst them with whom, according to the evidence of a reliable witness, the brutal SS men played a ball game by throwing him back and forth. The *Appellplatz* often presented a picture of misery when one saw – on top of everything else – sick and disabled people of this kind dragging themselves or being dragged there. The revocation of Germany's customary principles in matters of race naturally resulted in the imprisonment of many Jews who belonged to other religious communities for the purposes of the Nuremberg Laws. Thus there were also a number of famous Protestant clergymen of Jewish descent in the camp.

One of our greatest worries from the outset was "Do our relatives know where we are? When will we be able to inform them? How are they? What will we be able to write to them for them to assist our release?" Many of us knew from earlier operations that the strongest reason for release of Jews always was proof of emigration. Others hoped for deliverance in the form of the business *Arisierung* [Aryanisation], winding up of legal practices (the end of the Jewish legal profession, scheduled for 1st December, was imminent), disposal of funds for the *Judenkontribution* [tax on Jews for the cost of *Novemberaktion* damage], which was also announced in the camp after only a few days.

One of the most spiritually gruelling institutions in the camp was the almost diabolical control of post in both directions, from and to the camp, gruelling for the prisoners and the relatives, perhaps most of all for the latter because the prisoner after all knows minute by minute how feels, that he is "alive", whilst the relatives only discover after a long period of time that the prisoner "was still alive" at that past moment. We were given permission to send a postcard home for the first time on the second Sunday (20th November), ten days after being arrested. According to the stories told by older prisoners this was unusually early, normally following imprisonment there was a total ban on post for four weeks. Comrades who had been admitted with larger sums of money had enough for cards, stamps and to obtain pens, ink and nibs so that no one was excluded from writing on financial grounds. The postcards were lined and the lines had to be observed precisely. Communicating information about the camp was forbidden, as was reference to acquaintances one had met there; content was allowed to relate to familial, business and emigration matters. In any case no one would have dared to reveal their innermost feelings to the camp censor.

People wrote in groups of 15 or 20 (as many as there were pens), the time was precisely calculated so everyone had their turn. The card contained the pre-printed notice that a card or a letter could be written or received every two weeks. One can imagine the emotions in those who wrote the cards and the calculations as to the date on which they would be received and replied to. As we later discovered from the replies, the cards were in the hands of the addressees on or around the following Friday, i.e. c. 15 days after arrest. The camp censor had taken that long for approval.

Astonishingly, some post sent on the off chance by relatives was handed out to prisoners as early as the second or third week, although by no means to everyone. (The location of the camp had meanwhile leaked out in Berlin.) Some resourceful wives had also sent notaries to the camp to draw up banking mandates and similar documents in order to give and receive initial signs of life. The prisoners concerned had indeed been allowed to see these notaries. As far as I know this situation was changed some time later so that only a single local notary was responsible for files of this kind. In the eyes of the other camp inmates, even these small gestures, such as the exceptional handing out of post, which still did not represent an answer to our first post, were special favours for us Jews; in discussions during work they let us know again and again that our treatment, which to us already appeared pretty barbaric, was "worthy of a sanatorium" in comparison with the treatment of the victims of other operations, in particular the so-called "*alten Juden*" of June 1938!

Replies to our postcards of 20th November, which had reached the addressees on or around 25 November, gradually started to arrive at the end of the following week (that was the 3rd December), although the relatives must certainly have replied immediately. The camp censor gave himself time to look through the 6–7,000 replies. The main day for distributing post was Saturday even if this, at least in our case, was not adhered to strictly. Thus the distribution of replies to our first communication was drawn out over a number of weeks. Some people who were released after three to five weeks had not received an answer at all, and were consumed with worry about what had become of their relatives, their homes, their businesses etc., and they were only able to console themselves with the thought that others were in the same situation, which meant that silence was not necessarily a bad omen. Moreover, the delivery of post was not always complete, e.g. I was handed only part of a letter, the other part having been torn off.

The second writing day was 4th December, at which point most people had not received a reply to their first missive. On this particular day we were allowed to write either a letter or a card, but suddenly, apparently because of a lack of time, only one wing in some of the blocks was allowed to sit down to write, with the other wing postponed until the following Sunday, which meant a three-week gap. What did it matter to the "lords" whether an order of this kind resulted in renewed unease and spiritual suffering for those affected! Was not that, after all, the intention of the camp and all its individual measures? Jews in the camp and outside were to be worn down, made ready for emigration, a goal that was achieved more effectively this way than through any previous measures. Many who were allowed to write just chose a card based on the entirely reasonable assumption that a card would pass the censor more quickly. A few days later a number of the letters were returned as not permissible. There was no explanation why. As a result the letter writers were denied the possibility of sending out a sign of life for an entire writing period.

The standard restriction of postal communication in the camp to once every two weeks meant that if post arrived for one recipient from a number of different sources it was pure chance which piece he would receive. A well-meaning letter from a friend or relative could be at the expense of letter from a wife or the children, a truly inhuman system. Occasionally wives who were in the know regarding this very slow and unreliable postal system send telegrams with important news, perhaps also in order to send some sign of life. Initially the telegrams were handed out quickly, then they too slowed down as those "above" presumably noticed that they were increasing in number, until finally they were apparently not handed out at all, or at least no more quickly than other post. I trust the reader will forgive this very precise description when he realises how enormously significant any sign of life becomes in a situation like this. No one in everyday life can imagine what it means when the exchange of letters and replies within Germany's own postal system is only possible over a period of weeks. The families who have gone through it, however, will certainly never forget.

The internal organisation of the barracks was such that every block was under the overall control of an *SS-Blockführer* [SS block leader], a kind of officer, and the day-to-day supervision was delegated to the *Blockältester* [block elder] who lived in the day room of one wing, had a small cupboard and was supported in his duties by a *Stubenältester* [room elder] who lived in the day room of the other wing; in the case of the Jews both elders were generally "Reds" (i.e. see above, political prisoners); apart from them there was also – likewise "Red" – a *Blockschreiber* [block clerk] and one or more prisoners responsible for *Stubendienst* [room duty]; they were what one might term the *Feldwebel* [sergeants] and *Unteroffiziere* [non-commissioned officers] of the barracks. They generally tried to make the difficult situation bearable by means of friendly encouragement, at least in the barracks, and avoid intervention by the *Blockführer*, which was not always easy when they were faced with unreasonable elements, in which case they had to be energetically supported.

For camp life in general and life in the barracks in particular, the old military rule of thumb applied: do not be noticed, never generate conflict, which could always be triggered off by something insignificant and would always have to be paid for in extra drill and other individual or collective punishments. On one occasion one of the barracks would be too loud – with 170 men there was bound to be a certain amount of noise even if conversations were hushed; moreover stress and irritability, with the agonisingly terrible lack of space and absence of places to sit, led to many tense situations amongst one another and nervous outbursts. On one occasion the food bowls and drinking mugs had not been washed up properly – the system of cleaning was constantly changing and differed from block to block, at one point everyone had to wash their own things, subsequently a number of us were enlisted to take over the *Stubendienst*, and finally this enlisting of help was prohibited. Of course the Jews are not all angels either, and there were some who were less clean than others, some who were more stubborn, others who were less educated, and these "lesser" ones could in an instant be the cause of night-time drills or "*stehen am Tor*" [standing to attention by the gate], a popular punishment for individuals and larger groups, sometimes – this also happened – without shoes, just in socks and without jacket, or in shirtsleeves and underpants. Again and again the *Blockältesten* would plead with people to be reasonable in order to spare us being woken up at night, as was so often the case. They were like buffers between *Blockführer* and us and of course also had no desire to be punished themselves on account of the unreasonable occupants of the barracks, and when there was night-time drill they too had to participate.

With the new week on Monday the 14th November normal camp began life for the Jews, as it did for all the other camp inmates: *Appell* – work – *Appell*. In the morning at half past 6, a little later in the darkening season, a *Gesamtappell* [full roll call] of the entire camp on the large *Appellplatz*: initially the same *Gesamtappell* was repeated at midday for everyone except those working a long way away outside the camp, who worked through; later, when continuous working was introduced because of the season, the *Mittagsappell* [midday roll call] and lunch were scrapped and replaced by so-called *Zählappelle* [roll call head counts] at the various workplaces. In the afternoon at 4 there was a further *Gesamtappell* as in the morning, followed by a hot meal. Every time endless standing around accompanied by much counting, announcing of numbers to the *SS-Blockführer* by the *Blockältesten*, further conveying of the information by the *Blockführer* to the camp leadership. Except for those in the *Revier* [sick bay] everyone had to attend the *Appell*: the lame, people with a fever though not yet ready for the *Revier* or had not got there, those with foot injuries, all had to attend the *Appell* come what may. They were dragged or carried there by others, a woeful sight. Perish the thought that the total did not add up! Old inmates told stories of

times when a mistake in the counting or a real escape had immediately led to everyone having to stand there until late at night
when either the mistake was rectified or an escape proven.

It is worth interposing that we were incredibly lucky with the
weather until 15th December, as though the dear Lord wanted to
prove himself merciful at least in this respect. Throughout this
period the temperature remained very bearable for the time of
year and above all it remained dry, only raining during the day
briefly one afternoon and on a Sunday, otherwise only a few times
at night. We looked skywards every day, afraid on account of our
inadequate clothing, something that would not have had much
meaning for us in the city, and thanked God for this mercy. Even
so standing around, particularly on a cold morning before sunrise
and in the afternoon after work, was exhausting enough, we froze
and naturally were not allowed to put our hands in our pockets
(the guards and *Blockführer* had good coats and thick gloves)
without risking slaps in the face or other punishment, and waited
longingly, in the morning, for the warmth from marching and
work, for the moment of arrival in the barracks in the afternoon.

Initially the barracks were not heated. When it got colder they
were heated in the afternoon, the fire went out at night and was
lit again for the time spent getting up. When, on one occasion,
one of the barracks was improperly heated during the day the
result was a week-long general ban on heating, although this was
later shortened by a day. The heating was also important because
those who set store by the use of a towel – others quickly got
used to doing without – needed to wash it out with cold water
and soap in the evening and dry it by the stove, with the result
that a major battle raged by the stovepipe. But I have strayed
from my description of the *Appell*.

The afternoon *Appell* was frequently extended artificially by a
particularly insulting institution common to such camps, namely
singing. At the end of the *Appell* one afternoon we novices were
surprised when the order was given to sing various songs, a
"Sauerland march", which described the beautiful Sauerland that
apparently everyone wants to visit (and from which the Jews are
doubtless excluded), as well as two sentimental songs, "*Das alte*

Mütterchen" [The Aged Mother] and "Postillion". Then the order was immediately given that we Jews also had to learn the songs. So a singing lesson was instituted after supper for the *Stubenält-ester* to teach us these three songs, the words and the music. One can imagine the feelings that accompanied our learning of these songs! But our singing teachers told us that this was a duty like any other and that anyone who did not sing or had not learnt the text by heart could expect to be punished just as he would be for any other infringement of camp discipline. This singing lesson was repeated a number of times, and after a few days we Jews had to sing along at the *Appell* despite the fact that we privately felt this singing amounted to a ridiculous mockery of our situation, one in which we were certainly not disposed to singing. When the Jews' singing did not go smoothly on one occasion the Jewish blocks were ordered after a hastily downed supper to participate in a special singing lesson in the open on the *Appellplatz*, a bullying torture for us and the chorus master (a prisoner). But what could we do? We had to make an effort and, despite inwardly rebelling very much, sing with greatest "love" and "enthusiasm" just in order to avoid prolonging the singing lesson. The other prisoners doubtless felt very much the same way about the singing. It was just another link in the endless chain of human degradation, singing in this environment of the most terrible incarceration and brutal uncertainty.

More generally the *Appell* invariably provided the opportunity for all kinds of acts of bullying. Counting went wrong in the front row of the block on one occasion – most people's thoughts were probably somewhere very different –, on another the eye of the *Blockführer* spotted a missing button on one of the beautiful uniforms, on another someone's hair was too long, a beard too bushy, on yet another caps were not removed quickly enough when the salute "*Mützen ab*" [caps off] was called, which here replaced presenting arms and was practised *ad nauseam*. Every fault of this kind could result in individual or collective punishment as already mentioned: night-time drill, "*stehen am Tor*", *Blocksperre* [block ban] (i.e. not being allowed to go out for a long period) or a resounding slap on the face for the comrade who had not shaved properly. I often had a strange feeling standing amongst this large Jewish crowd of 6–7,000 militarily attired people, I wondered whether this was perhaps the largest paramilitary Jewish formation in one spot in the whole world. All we lacked were the weapons which, concentrated in their most modern manifestations in the hands of a small minority, turned us into defenceless victims of the capriciousness of our tormentors. This is how the Potemkin sailors must have felt, except that they had weapons with which they could rid themselves of their tormentors. And yet this mass did give everyone a certain feeling of security, a feeling of belonging very different from individual Jews finding themselves in such hostile surroundings.

On the first regular working day, the first Monday, we were made to listen to a speech by the *Lagerkommandant*, strangely employing the formal "*Sie*" [you] form of address, otherwise entirely untypical there. In it he revealed to us that the camp was neither a sanatorium, nor a prison, nor a penitentiary, but a special kind of educational institution, that we had to abide by all the rules of the camp, a listing of which he deemed superfluous, and that any contravention of camp rules would result in severe punishment. We had already heard enough about the *Prügelstrafe auf dem Bock* [flogging on the whipping block] to be at a loss about what it meant. On this and other occasions it was impressed upon us that every guard was our absolute superior regardless of age just like any other SS officer: this was important because some of the guards were certainly no more than 17–18 years old.

Work, which began at this point, took many different forms. One could distinguish between about three kinds: *Exerzieren* in the camp, work in and around the camp in the workshops and in construction and road building, and finally industrial work further away. In addition one could be commandeered to peel potatoes, darn socks, *Stubendienst* etc. Allocation to the various kinds of work was based on age, certainly not on humanity, but to maximise productivity, which could clearly not be squeezed out of the old to the extent that it could from the young. The age brackets kept changing however. As departures became increasingly noticeable the age limits were lowered and the elderly were also called on to engage in heavy work. Every day each block had to provide its specific number of people to undertake the heavier work outside the camp, which directly determined how many of the older men had to be called upon for this purpose, irrespective of whether they were physically suitable or not. In the case of *Exerzieren* generally viewed as lighter work because it was carried out on the *Appellplatz*, the over sixties were called upon, for work in the factories those under forty five; the other kinds of work were in between but as time went by the age limits increasingly only existed on paper and one found comrades in their late fifties doing industrial work.

Exerzieren consisted of marching in step and at the double up and down the *Appellplatz* from c. half past 7 to c. half past 3 with a half-hour standing break at lunch. It was so exhausting, even if there was no additional bullying, that the old people were very keen to avoid it and frequently tried to be transferred to less strenuous work in the camp.

Work in and around the camp took different forms. For instance sand was shovelled around in circles for no reason. Elsewhere, in order to level the ground sand was shovelled away again by a long line of people and conveyed into trucks. Other gangs had to sort felled tree trunks, cut them up and then carry or drive them to a large warehouse where the trunks were prepared by electrically powered saws for use as timber to build houses. In fact the camp was situated on former woodland and the previous year had been expanded into the camp as we encountered it using the heavy forced labour of prisoners; the timbers were from this period of construction. Other gangs were simply deployed to transport materials. The timber was taken from the saw mill to building sites where nice little houses were built for the SS (for married couples apparently). Much slave labour here achieved what transport vehicles and a couple of people could accomplish in the shortest time; whether it was cheaper must be very doubtful. We carried large and small planks, iron rails, bedsteads and various implements made of iron. The *Vorarbeiter* [foremen], "Reds" and "Browns", who demonstrated as little interest in the work as we did, simply had to make sure that there were not too many people carrying one track or plank and that no single individual was carrying too light a load of planks in case a passing SS man or guard became suspicious and unleashed some arbitrary act of cruelty on us, or even punished the *Vorarbeiter* himself.

In the transport gangs, to one of which I belonged for several days, one tried to drag out the work and make the journeys last as long as possible. Transport work was very popular even if it was sometimes quite demanding – the unaccustomed weight on the shoulders was initially extremely wearisome. One went on one's way without being accompanied by the much-hated guards, was permitted to move when it was cold, and the time passed much more quickly when one undertook a number of long marches from one end of the sprawling camp to the other than when one was shovelling all day in the same spot, probably in the clutches of a sentry overseeing and pressurising one. The transport gangs often had to carry cement sacks, each weighing a hundredweight, from the materials store to the building sites (15–25 minutes). Initially each man had to carry a sack on his own, but they were too heavy and almost impossible to lift for older or weaker people, then it was tacitly allowed for two people to do the work by using a carrier, a board resting on the shoulders and onto which the sack was loaded – with a bit of practice it worked quite well. In this context the older camp inmates told us that reprieves of this kind would previously have been unthinkable, everyone had had to carry a sack on their own even if they had collapsed in the process, [deleted: and indeed for many hours at a time, during the previous summer from early in the morning until late in the evening] and indeed a number had died during the previous summer, particularly amongst the Jews from the *Juni-Aktion*. We shuddered on hearing these earnest reports of tragedies that had occurred in the camp. In itself the workload was really less of a problem than the treatment we received when carrying it out, or what might happen at any moment if an SS man or guard appeared.

Then there were other gangs busy with nails, i.e. they had to remove the nails from pieces of wood, planks, boxes and the like, sort them, clean them and make them fit for use again, although no one checked the results. They stood (in the open air) at long tables on which there were boxes containing a huge number of nails of different lengths and grades. But hardly any work was done; everything that had been sorted was tipped out again in the afternoon and on the following day the work began again. As they worked they clutched a few good-quality nails in their hands to show how much they were achieving if a guard came by, but otherwise they just talked non-stop, always discussing the same things: How long now? On what grounds can one be released? What are things going to be like in the family, in the local community? What are those at home doing to ensure our release? The desire for freedom dominated every discussion as well as important questions about eating and sleeping.

Other gangs worked on the so-called wood yard. There tree stumps were chopped into firewood for the stoves, a task that was unfamiliar and back-breaking for many. The firewood was piled up into enormous stacks at the same time. These stacks were repeatedly taken down and rebuilt in a different spot just a few paces away. Those working here were constantly marching back and forth in single file over a distance of 100–200 metres with a couple of pieces of wood under their arms. They then hid behind the stacks of wood for a while before making their way monotonously back again. Now and then the guards would appear, chasing their victims and making them move at the double. When they left the whole rigmarole started all over again. Many of us, especially amongst the nail people and those in the wood yard, had the feeling that the whole thing was worthy of being captured on film, especially if one imagined for a moment all these workers in their former civilian activities at hospital beds, in court, in shops, in banks and so on.

Elsewhere people were occupied building a road for a new SS settlement. They dragged road building materials or broke stones sitting by the roadside (those with foot or leg ailments were selected for this activity), which was very unhealthy in the cold autumn weather, or pounded the sand which was delivered by others in wheelbarrows. Strange sensations crept over one on seeing Berlin cars and harmless civilians whilst engaged in these activities which for the most part took place outside the walls of the camp: namely that one had so recently walked through the streets just like these passers by and yet had done absolutely nothing that anywhere else or at any other time could possibly have given any authority the right to lock one up and place one at the mercy of the whims of feral young people.

We heard radio music from the windows of the pleasantly furnished rooms of the SS block houses as if coming from somewhere far off, from another world, as we went past laden with cement sacks. A bird-house in the middle of the one completed SS settlement bore a label requesting that the birds be protected. What were we in comparison to the birds? In the eyes of our tormentors vermin to be eradicated just as they had learnt from the new German Bible "*Mein Kampf*" [My struggle; book by Hitler] and could read weekly in *Der* "*Stürmer*". If they had asked about our profession and received the reply "businessman" or "*Rechtsanwalt*" [lawyer] they would doubtless have retorted: "Well at least you can't f*** about with anyone here any more" or something similar.

Industrial work about half an hour away (shovelling sand, unloading cement sacks, pulling wagons, laying tracks) was rightly viewed as the toughest, but was also increasingly allocated not just to the young but to more and more old people. The young men, some of whom came from the *Hachshara* or were used to physical labour for other reasons, could cope with it much more easily than the older academics and businessmen who had never done anything like it. Moreover, the ability of people to adapt to new situations varies hugely. I myself worked there for c. ten days and was lucky. I was a member of a gang who shovelled sand for levelling off the ground and was able to keep up quite easily – indeed as a result of a good constitution I generally suffered no lasting physical damage from my time in the camp – but that does not affect my assessment of the set up as a whole. Most of the young comrades with whom I worked were friendly and also helped a bit. The *Vorarbeiter*, a politically well versed Communist who had become a despiser of mankind and was now simply waiting for the day of retribution, was content with anything that did not make him an object of attention for the *Aufseher* who would pass by now and then. One could have a good conversation with him about all the political problems of the last 20 years and it cheered him up now and then to declaim revolutionary songs and poems with real pathos.

The piled up sand was then transported onwards in wagons. We had to pull these wagons ourselves, I believe because the existing mechanical haulage machine was always broken. So around 15–20 men were deployed for each wagon, which was moved forward perhaps 1 km by the most primitive method of pushing and pulling, and then emptied. If one saw the six or seven wagons being moved in this way one was unavoidably reminded of those pictorial representations of galley convicts from earlier times who seemed to be celebrating their resurrection here. How often on this and many other occasions we were reminded of the Jewish servitude in Egypt, and how often the words of the Haggadah were quoted: "We were slaves in the land of Egypt", something we had never experienced so literally before. Those comrades engaged in unloading the cement each had to carry a sack quite a distance on their own and complained bitterly about brutal treatment by the *Aufseher* if they did not move as fast as they were told or even dropped one of the sacks.

Yet by common consent the worst thing about this work outside the camp was the journey to and from work. Every day 3,000 men went to this work in three convoys of 1,000 men. The convoys marched in rows of five but were otherwise not subdivided. To the side, a few metres apart, and at the front and rear were guards with weapons under their arms. They amused themselves by walking with rapid steps until they had the whole convoy of people running. Whilst it was possible to keep up by walking fast in the front rows, those behind alternately had to run to catch up with those in front and wait until the crush of people thinned out a bit, and then, after walking normally for a short while, start running fast again. The whole thing was like an accordion squeezed together and then drawn apart. However, the guards running at the side chased and drove the rows forwards, pushed and shoved, sometimes with their rifle butts if one of the rows lagged behind even for a moment. This whole thing began on leaving the camp and lasted for the full 20–25 minutes of the journey, the way back was just the same and both marches were often embellished by the order to sing.

These journeys thus became a wild chase through the forest of the Mark Brandenburg, a real torture for all those who had breathing problems, with the consequence that some comrades simply collapsed and had to be carried. A number of deaths resulted from this madness. We felt like a herd of sheep when we left the camp in this manner and returned in the afternoon, parading past the *Lagerkommandant* at the entrance gate, cap in hand, thumbs on trouser seams. There was no chance of marching in step during the chase as we passed astonished pedestrians walking on the country roads and civilian cars. Running simply aggravated the situation, those behind cursed those in front, everyone was terrified of the guards chasing us, no one wanted to be on the end of the rows of five, there was no chance of taking care of one another, the most naked survival instinct was the order of the day. Worst off were the final few rows of the convoy, so that when it came to lining up at the end of work there was immediately a fierce battle to occupy one of the places at the front. This journey to and from work will remain an indelible memory for everyone.

One of the most primitive and excruciating working methods that typified the camp was the so-called *Sandlaufen* [sand running]. As there were not enough shovels, jackets were sometimes taken off and put on back to front, two men with shovels were stationed at a pile of sand as the starting point and the others had to run past them and lift up their jackets at the front to form a bag so they could be filled with a large load of sand, which they then deposited a few hundred metres away. That not only meant using fewer shovels but also that everyone was working in a chain, but it was very exhausting when it lasted any length of time and at a running pace and provided a good opportunity for persecution.

In contrast to the strict separation of Jews and non-Jews in the barracks, work was often mixed. The *Arbeitskommandos* [work squads] were often, but not always, made up of all different kinds of camp inmates, and so it was possible in these circumstances to make interesting new friends and discoveries. The allocation of blocks to different work places took place each morning on the *Appellplatz* and changed constantly so that one never knew if one would be returning to the workplace from the previous day. It apparently depended on the demands of the technical managers of the different sections of the organisation (also SS men). From an economic point of view there was certainly no need for such a huge camp workforce, but that was not the decisive factor in running this special kind of educational institution, to adopt the terminology of the aforementioned *Lagerkommandant*.

I have mentioned the guards on a number of occasions in this report because they repeatedly came into contact with us when we were working. They were very young lads, perhaps 17 and upwards, who seemed to have been trained specifically to torment us prisoners, who in many cases could have been their fathers and grandfathers. They patrolled up and down in the camp and accompanied us on the journey to and from the industrial work as described above. We had to stand to attention in front of them, take off our caps if they spoke to us and reply in military fashion. They invariably wanted to know what these Jews had been in civilian life and interrogated us. As a camp joke would have it, someone claimed that their profession was a *Syndikus* [legal adviser] and on being asked what that was supposed to be, replied that he worked at the bar, to which the guard replied "Well you should've just said you worked in a pub." Whenever one set eyes on them one asked oneself what sort of young people they were, growing up without any respect for their elders, without a glimmer of humanity, sadists who belong in *Sicherungsverwahrung* [preventive detention] rather than tormenting the innocent whenever they feel like it.

The food in the camp usually consisted of semolina, skimmed milk or some other kind of soup in the morning, a warm stew after work at around 5 o'clock (cabbage or other vegetables, frequently whale meat), half a *Kommissbrot* [army loaf] daily, later a third, a piece of liver sausage, brawn or margarine in the morning to be shared out and intended as a spread for the bread at breakfast, eaten during the working day at the *Zählappell* (at about half past 11). The food itself was not that bad, but for people undertaking physical labour in the outdoors it was insufficient in quantity and quality. The reduction of the bread ration was doubtless a result of the fact that we Jews initially left a lot of the bread because we were not sufficiently hungry. Then when our appetites understandably increased as a result of working outdoors, the reduction had already been implemented and now there was not a crumb left over. The inadequacy of the food was clear to see in the hunger experienced by the older inmates who threw themselves like wild animals on every last bit of bread they spotted on the floor. At work they repeatedly came over to us, particularly in the early days when we were better provided, and begged us for some bread, although this was strictly forbidden (as was handing over bread). Worse was the lack of fat. The spreads mentioned above were completely insufficient and did not contain enough fat. The power of resistance of those who had been in the camp for longest had declined inordinately.

As a result of this lack of nutrition the opportunity and entitlement to buy extra food from the canteen became very important. In principle the idea was that everyone would be sent RM. 15.- per week and would be able to use it to buy things in the canteen. However, at least during the period I spent there, this entitlement was partly on paper only and according to the stories told by older inmates there were frequent interruptions in the shape of canteen bans as a form of punishment. The payment system was clearly incapable of dealing with such an enormous influx of relatively moneyed prisoners with the result that it was about 14 days before we were handed RM. 15.- from the money that we had arrived with and which had been confiscated. Every day several hundred of us turned up to be paid and then for some unknown reason there would always be a delay in making the payment and a number of the comrades did not get anything at all. The possibility of buying things represented a substantial relief amidst all the deprivation. It is hard to imagine how significant eating can suddenly become for people who were normally not very bothered about it. The atmosphere improved at the mere thought of being able to bring some variety into the nutrition, e.g. being able to get chocolate, margarine, butter, sausage, ham, cheese, milk, sweets, cakes, white bread etc. Initially smoking was forbidden in the Jewish blocks; the ban was lifted, I believe, with the payment of the canteen money and was a great relief for the smokers.

The canteen was well stocked with variety and the prices were normal. It was interesting to observe the order in which individuals satisfied their needs after food and cigarettes. One person would first buy toilet paper, the next a shaving brush which the hairdresser was only to use for him, the next tissues, the fourth a toothbrush. Organising the purchasing represented a technical problem which was the object of numerous experiments. Individual purchasing in the canteen, which was located in a basement, was impossible with so many people, not least as there was at most an hour available for shopping between the evening meal and going to sleep, and it was often curtailed, e.g. by the shower, distribution of new underwear, *Strafexerzieren* [punitive drill], sewing on buttons. So for a time there were buyers for each block who did all the shopping for the entire block, or the orders were handled by the *Tischältester* [most senior people at table] who were later deployed to organise the distribution of food more effectively. In addition people also made individual purchases in the canteen, which involved long queues there.

When the money was paid out for the first time the *Stuben-ältester* "suggested" to us under instructions from above that we "voluntarily" subscribe to the permitted Nazi newspapers, and that there should be as many copies as possible of them in each block (*Der Angriff* [The Attack], *Völkischer Beobachter* [National Observer], *Das Schwarze Korps* and presumably *Der Stürmer*). *Die Illustrierte* [The Illustrated] and, as far as I know, a scientific journal were also allowed. We ordered the newspapers under duress, not least because they might help to alleviate the lack of toilet paper. The payment of subsequent canteen money did not work at all despite the fact that relatives had generally paid in the money punctually. The next payment happened not after two weeks but four; the money that had arrived from home had generally not yet been credited, so only the remainder of the money brought with us was handed out. Most people had spent their RM. 15.- by this time and in some cases borrowed extra (which incidentally was forbidden) and were therefore very disappointed at the delays in the system. Incidentally, he money that was not paid out was handed over on our release or returned later in accordance with the rules. In this respect there was nothing to complain about, sometimes bureaucratic orderliness is stronger even than the desire to loot.

Paying out canteen money led to the emergence of all kinds of interesting community problems. There were comrades who were immediately happy to give or lend money or things they had purchased, although there were also egoists who spent everything on themselves or who even preferred to consume their treats in front of everyone else. Anyone who is regularly sent and receives their RM. 15.- and is able to shop with it can compensate for the inadequacy of the provision in the camp of course. But how few of the regular inmates could expect help of this kind from their relatives! Most people were happy if they occasionally got part of this sum. There were many who were never sent anything and who, like wild animals with greedy eyes, were always on the lookout when one of their better-off comrades took a piece of sausage or a bit of chocolate out of their pocket, in the hope that there might be some leftovers for them. They begged to be allowed to take a puff from someone's cigarette. In the camp jargon cigarette ends were known as "*Kippen*" [fags]. And how many there were who were willing to throw themselves at any *Kippe* on the path and grab it just to experience the precious pleasure of tobacco that they had been deprived of. Here one could see how scarcity and deprivation turn people into animals, how hygiene is forgotten and nobody cares if a single cigarette is passed from mouth to mouth.

I cannot easily pass judgement on the health situation in the camp. Amongst the older inmates in particular there were many, many who had skin diseases, sores of all kinds, boils and the like, obviously the consequence of the lack of hygiene and diminished power of resistance (shortage of fat!). Open wounds, which often come about through cuts, small injuries and grazes when undertaking the kind of work we were doing, only healed very slowly. The period of sharp frost after the 15th December multiplied the signs of frostbite that had already started to appear on the limbs of many people. All these illnesses were treated in the *Revier* staffed by prisoners. I was told again and again that they were very friendly and really wanted to help their comrades. The only problem was that there was such a huge demand that it was very difficult to gain access to the *Revier*, one sometimes had to wait for many hours, even days, outside the *Revier* barrack before one could be admitted. The *Revier* was the first port of call for all illnesses, including fever, flu, stomach conditions, asthma, kidney and lung problems. The only way to see a doctor was through the *Revier*, and the doctor had a reputation for not wanting to treat Jews. Anyone presented to him who he felt should not be there was in danger of being punished. Fortunately I never got to know either the *Revier* or the doctor so cannot report anything based on personal experience.

These official channels were disastrous for any illnesses which could not cope with such procedures. As a result some died before their time who could have been saved. Being ill in the camp was easily the worst. Even someone with a fever had to attend *Appell* early in the morning, had to wait for hours outside the *Revier* barrack to be treated and still risked not having their turn. Unfortunately the number of fatalities as a consequence of inadequate medical treatment of prisoners who had been arrested without any attention to whether they were fit to be arrested is not known. In Sachsenhausen, according to reliable sources, c. 60 people died in the first four to five weeks, later this number apparently rose substantially as a result of the cold.

In this context another camp institution should be mentioned. There were (see above) hundreds of sick people who, as a result of skin diseases or injuries to their limbs, had to walk around with thick bandages and were literally unable to undertake any work duties because they could not grasp anything. However they were not relieved of their duties, but instead formed the so-called "*Schleichkommando*" [creeping squad], i.e. for the working hours they had to march ("creep") continuously in rows of five, one behind the other, through a large sandpit next to the camp wall (the so-called "hole"). This was clearly meant to discourage anyone from trying to shirk their duties. Thus this gang, consisting of people with bandaged heads, arms and hands, legs and feet, and reminiscent of pictures of the Napoleonic retreat from Russia, trudged on indefatigably. A lamentable sight!

There is a lot more that could be said about Sachsenhausen concentration camp, about its people, its institutions, its methods for humiliating, brutalising and demeaning people. We Jews of the *Novemberaktion* were there only for a relatively short time, we were to be made ready for emigration and set an example to all the others who had not been arrested. They achieved this goal. Nonetheless it seemed to us like an eternity. As the releases began to occur in large numbers on a daily basis they were announced to us every evening in the sleeping quarters. Those whose names were called out had to line up for the complicated release procedure (to be dressed in civilian clothes, receive valuables) the following morning, freshly shaven (this was emphasised to the end). In the evening everyone waited excitedly to see if they had perhaps won the jackpot this time; the faces of those whose names were read out shone, some wept for joy when their name came up and they now knew that their enslavement would only last one more day! And then came the requests from those left behind to those leaving: greetings to the family, the plea to do anything possible to help (one was not allowed to note anything down, so addresses and telephone numbers had to be learnt by heart).

One could still feel the iron fist pressing down on one until leaving the camp. Already in civilian clothes (one's own things, what a precious feeling!) one had to stand for hours, hat in hand, until everything had been painstakingly completed. Even here the *SS-Führer* enjoyed wreaking their capriciousness on the prisoners, on occasion making them run around at the double, execute knee-bends and slapping them round the face. Finally a written oath that one would not do anything against the National Socialist state. Then we were led to the exit of the camp by a guard, a barrier opened up to the ordinary street and we could move about freely. What a feeling! It did not matter to us in the least that our things had been de-loused and looked terrible and people could mistake us for vagabonds. We were free like all the others on the street and no one would now freely insult us, slap us round the face and order us around. We were free, even in this Germany where the position of the Jews had worsened catastrophically during the weeks we had been away. The people on the street and in the train to Berlin, who daily saw such camp inmates travelling home, looked at us and were presumably a bit ashamed about what was going on here. And during these weeks one heard many stories of Aryans at Berlin stations who helped the Jews, easily recognisable by their outfits and shaven heads, and who wanted to atone a little for what a state government did not merely tolerate but established, supported, and remunerated.

It is a terrible notion that thousands upon thousands of people of all kinds and for different reasons have been languishing in camps like this for years without due legal process, solely through the shadowy intrigues of an unchecked *Geheimpolizei* [secret police]. It is not National Socialists that are being bred here but despisers of mankind, desperate people seeking revenge, broken characters; and so-called civilised humanity accepts it passively, like so much injustice.

B. 341 THE DESTRUCTION OF THE SYNAGOGUE IN POTSDAM – AN EYEWITNESS REPORT

The beautiful synagogue in Potsdam, which had been festively inaugurated in June 1903, on the same site on Wilhelmsplatz as the Jewish *Bethaus* [house of prayer] founded by Frederick the Great long ago, was destroyed during the *Pogromtagen* [pogrom days], much as almost all the synagogues in Germany were. An eyewitness report follows:

The doorbell of our home rang at half past 5 in the morning on 10th November, a ringing that was gruesome and that I will not forget to the end of my life. I knew the meaning of this ringing immediately, and when I opened the door having dressed myself provisionally, I found my fears were confirmed: five men in plain clothes stood before me. Their leader identified himself as a Gestapo officer and explained to me immediately that I was being arrested, with the comment that any attempt to escape would lead to the use of their weapons. As my son came out of his room at that moment, he was also arrested. We had to dress in the presence of the officer, then I was ordered to hand over the keys to the synagogue and the *Gemeindebücher* [community ledgers]. When I remarked that I did not have them, but the keys were with the Aryan *Kastellanin* [female warden], and the ledgers with the *Rendant* [treasurer], we were both loaded into a car that drove us to the *Polizeipräsidium* [police headquarters], where my son was deposited.

I myself had to go back to the synagogue with the men. A dark bunch of Catiline [reckless, conspiratorial] shapes in plain clothes was already waiting there, dangerous looking young lads holding sinister-seeming tools. Because the main door to the synagogue would not yield to the storming by this strong gang of approximately 20 to 25 men, I had to take the leader to the side door, where the *Kastellanin* was rung for. As it was taking too long for the men until the old woman appeared, the door was pushed in, and I now took the leader through this side entrance into the synagogue. It did not appear solemn enough for the head of the gang, and so he screamed at me "We still want to be led to the holiest of places!" I retorted to him that we were just on the way there. We were soon standing between the *Kanzel des Rabbiners* [Rabbi's pulpit] and the *Vorbeterpult* [prayer leader's lectern].

At the same moment the gang that had assembled in front of the main door to the synagogue pushed forwards again, and now an atrocious picture was acted out at lightning speed before my eyes. In a few minutes – as I myself probably lost consciousness temporarily I do not know precisely how many minutes it was, even though I remember the entire process in all its detail, but it cannot have been more than four or at most five minutes – the entire house of prayer was turned into a barren heap of rubble. All the windows were smashed with thoughtfully brought along wooden hand grenades of the type used for practice by the army, all the lights were pulled down, the benches were wrecked, the *Frauenempore* [women's gallery] was demolished,

the *Sitz des Rabbiners* [Rabbi's seat], the *Vorsteherbank* [chair-
man's bench] chopped up, the *Vorhänge* [curtains] torn to shreds,
the *Thorarollen* [Torah scrolls] ripped to pieces, the large *Chanuk-
kahleuchter* [menorah] used as a crowbar, in short: nothing, but
absolutely nothing remained whole. It was so horrible and brutish
that the leader of the gang – certainly not a weak person – said to
me: "It's probably better if we go now."

On leaving I saw small flames leaping up in the *Vorraum* [ante
room]. But as I later heard, the *Oberpostdirektion* [district postal
authority] had pronounced an energetic veto against setting the
synagogue on fire, not because of any humane considerations,
but rather, as was apologetically added, because the large post
office building situated right next to the synagogue would have
been too endangered.

I was then taken to the police prison (Priesterstraße), where I
remained alone in my cell for c. three hours. Then at about half
past 9 the door opened, and the 70-year-old Herr H. appeared,
an hour later the 73-year-old Herr S. and a further hour thereafter the dentist Dr. P.

I mention further that at the same time as the destruction of
the synagogue was playing out, a second gang had broken into
the Potsdam Jewish cemetery, admittedly so quietly that neither
the cemetery attendants, a married couple, nor their dog noticed
anything about it. The mortuary was gutted; apart from that the
cemetery was not damaged.

B. 344 Report from Nordhausen

In November 1938 the Jewish population of Nordhausen still
consisted of c. 400 souls.

"On various occasions on 9th November we were already
warned that something was going to happen to us that night.
Thus a Nordhauser *Sipo* [*Sicherheitspolizist*; security policeman]
who knew me came to me and counselled, "If I were in your
position I would get out." During the day refugees had been
arriving from Witzenhausen, where the synagogue had been
burned down and the Jews had been mistreated.

It started during the night punctually at half past 1. SA and SS from Nordhausen and further afield came in cars from an assembly. They were all drunk. One could hear hooting in the streets, the smashing of window panes and shouts: "To the synagogue!" Everything was dragged out of the synagogue and burned. A *tallit* [Jewish prayer shawl] was burned in front of my door, and then the synagogue itself was set on fire. The *Feuerwehr* [fire brigade] was on the scene promptly and made sure that the fire remained localised. Meanwhile the drunken SA and SS men fetched all Jews, men, women and children, even seriously ill and elderly out of their homes. Some still in nightclothes, we were then taken in cars to "Siechenhof" (a homeless shelter). Of course the homes were wrecked whilst we were being fetched, beds were ripped apart, chair legs were broken off, all window panes of Jewish shops smashed... Apart from very few people who had evidently been forgotten (these were fetched out the following morning in a relatively friendly manner), everyone arrived at Siechenhof beaten and battered. Even two- and three-year-old children were in the group. At Siechenhof there was further battering. I recognised an *Oberscharführer* [SS staff sergeant] amongst the thrashers. *Sturmbannführer* [Major] Sander had excelled himself hitting and kicking as though insane. The police partly tried to prevent the worst but could not do much. We were kicked and chased around in the yard at Siechenhof. It was cold and some were almost naked... Even the women were ordered to run back and forth. They were only released at 8 o'clock the next morning. Men aged 15–85 were separated from the women. Nobody was allowed to leave, and the SS men yelled: "Shit in your trousers!"

Particularly mistreated were:

Walter Eisner, a small industrialist, who had incurred the particular displeasure of the Nazis for an unknown reason. He was battered dreadfully and chased through the town.

Herrmann Stern (still in Germany!) a former *Reichsbannerführer* [leader of the Social Democratic Party Reichsbanner Schwarz-Rot-Gold], was badly mistreated.

On the next day (10th November) in the morning we were all taken to Buchenwald (90 km) by *Überlandautobussen* [country buses], even those who had been forgotten in the night. We were 78 men from Nordhausen. In Buchenwald things really got going even more... the SS literally whipped us into the camp with cat-o'nine-tails. Fared particularly badly from that:

Gerson, an *Amtsgerichtstrat* [local court judge], who had been baptised aged 6, with Aryan wife and one son. He was dreadfully battered.

Plaut, a semi-idiot, who was struck on the head not only with whips but with a bunch of keys and was completely bleeding.

After us 600 men from Erfurt arrived. They had all been beaten bloody, one had lost an eye, they were battered like that with sticks and iron rods. Two of the men from Erfurt were in nightclothes and slippers. All had bandages. The men from Erfurt were not struck more in Buchenwald, because even the SS were of the opinion that they had already received enough.

We then had our hair shorn and our personal details taken etc. Then one was informed that until further notice all Jews were banned from post or canteen. We received nothing to eat until Friday evening (we were admitted on Thursday).

At the time there were two barracks in Buchenwald, which could normally accommodate 500 people. We were 2,500 in a single barrack! There was even whipping during the night. Many, many were driven crazy. On the first night in our barrack alone 260 men went mad. The crazy ones were bound and whipped and then dragged to the wash house where they were beaten to death.

Of those from Nordhausen, the following died in the concentration camp:

Singer, father of Nordhausen teacher, aged 60. He was driven mad in the night of Sunday to Monday and was beaten to death in the wash house.

Son of Singer, a teacher, went into the barbed wire because he could not bear to watch as his father had his hands bound, was dragged around the whole yard.

Amtsgerichtsrat Gerson, wanted to go into the barbed wire, was then bound and beaten to death.

Ernst Plaut, dispatched in the wash house.

Bacharach, 81 years old, beaten to death.

Lewin, 70 years old, beaten to death.

Wolf, did not die in the concentration camp but as a result of his mistreatment there upon his return to Nordhausen."

Of the 78 people from Nordhausen, seven are dead.

B. 345 ... The judgements against Jewish *Rassenschänder* [racial defilers] are harrowing, not only through the severity of the sentences passed but because the young people concerned plunge themselves and their families into indescribable misery through their incredible recklessness. The second man sentenced, Georg Rau, was found dead in his cell on the morning after the sentence was passed. "Heart attack" is what the poor parents were told – very unlikely for a young man.

B. 346 *Pester Lloyd* [German language newspaper], Budapest, 15th June 1939

Last night in Mährisch Ostrau [Moravian Ostrava] the largest synagogue and the building of the Jewish *Kultusgemeinde* [community] burned down.

Neue Zürcher Zeitung, Zürich, International edition, no. 163, 14th June 1939

Berlin, 14th June. (Tel. from United Press). The synagogue in Mährisch Ostrauhas has been burned to the ground.

B. 347 Today I want to describe my Wild West story quickly to you. So, the Gestapo checked our passports the first time in the local train to the border – all of us – and, guessing our intentions, sent us back. The second time, the company that arranges these things suggested the same route at a different time. Everything went to plan at first, we went through the German customs which had been bought off – were checked with our things, and then quickly off to an inn three minutes away. In the evening we crept into the station restaurant, whose owner is also the proprietor, planning to disappear from there one by one. But two minutes later a few Belgian gendarmes arrived and because a train had just left for A. and we were still sitting in the waiting room they suspected our purpose and did not move from the place. We did manage to hide, but did not come to the inn, were detected with torches and arrested with five other people, handed over to the German Gestapo, who put us in prison for that night and the following day. I.e. it was a room, ice cold, with three double-tier bunk beds, rather than *Pritschen* [planks]. It was locked tight from the outside so we could not disappear. We were four men and three women. You can imagine how wretched it was, as one knew not whether one would have to spend one or more days there. I was actually in rather good heart to have so many interesting new experiences. The next day we were fetched by the Gestapo, who spoke to us in a tone as though to criminals, everything "*Du*" [familiar "you"], and taken for interrogation. Two and a half hours of cross-questioning, but I was so peaceful as never before in my life. The only thing that annoyed me was the *Passus* [release form] I had to sign at the end, in which I had to agree never to let myself be seen in that area again and to undertake to travel to Berlin or be put in a concentration camp or prison.

Arrived back in Aachen, now without M., I rested for a couple of days, took my pack and set off with two old ladies of 65 years of age and a Viennese boy of 18. The journey was arranged by a reputable first-class firm, known as top notch in A. and K., and the old ladies went along with it too, in fact the guide was sent by the son of one of the ladies, who has lived in Belgium for many years, and I joined the group. When I asked the guide whether the journey would be safe, he answered that it was more of a gamble for him than for us, he worked at the Western Front – espionage zone. So as we drove in the car through the darkness I knew what danger we were putting ourselves into. After a half-hour journey we were set down and went across country in the pitch dark over ground so completely soaked that we got stuck in the mud, through barbed wire. Suddenly we had to remain stock still, hide, not speak, hardly breathe, so as not to give ourselves away; then onwards as before, again through barbed wire which tore our clothes to pieces. Now he left us hidden behind the fence of a cottage and went forward to see whether everything [was] safe. He did not come back because the police already knew about our presence in the area and that he was helping us.

We now sat on the ground all hidden by the small house so as not to be seen in the dark. Suddenly a light came on in the house and a frightened lady saw us lying on the ground. We asked if she could put out the light, we were Jews, we just wanted to cross over here – we were still on German soil – and she did that right away, after she had also told us that the little house belonged to the *Kriminalpolizei* [criminal police]. After half an hour a large dog suddenly arrived and leapt up at us at the fence, a light flashed on and a *Zollpolizist* [customs policeman] was standing in front of us with a revolver, hands up or I shoot. Then hands behind our backs and march, march. Actually the car in which we had travelled had been picked up – as the officers themselves said to us – and the driver questioned, because of the espionage zone, everything was checked there, thus our presence there was already known for a long time.

If we had not been Jews, who everybody knows want to do nothing more than get over the border illegally, things would have gone very badly for us, I thought that straight away. The guide had also been discovered by patrols and so after questioning and a body search we were brought by car to the police prison in Aachen still in the night. Yet more hours-long interrogations there – sign the *Passus* again, saying that I had to go back to Berlin and not be seen at this border again, and we were lucky, we were let out and were back at the hotel at half past 3. I had always told the gentlemen of the Gestapo that my whole crime consisted only of wanting to go to my husband and children, that I am ordered to leave Germany anyway and how I should go now, as I cannot obtain a visa anywhere it was in their own interest to be rid of me. The answer was, we are not allowed to permit it any more on foreign policy grounds, and I must try to obtain visas. I had had enough of it now, and fearing never to be with H. and the children again I was gripped by despair – so much misfortune at once was too much. I decided quickly to put myself on the train, travelled to Cologne.

I then travelled here with my husband to my child, we had Swiss passports, through Basel, France and Luxembourg. We arrived successfully after a 20-hour journey. I cannot describe in detail all the interesting things that happened on the way, or I would have to write books. In any case, when one returns from such a journey one always has no money because one can only take RM. 10.- across and one does not reckon one will need more money in case one is sent back. So there are dreadful conditions. People hang around desperately for days or sometimes weeks waiting for a suitable journey. The two old ladies on the same journey that I was on it made it again three days later after a lot of encouragement from their sons and me, with another guide – sent by the same firm, however – and this time it worked out, and they were on Belgian soil in two and half hours. They had suggested that I go with them again, and I had refused because it was the border where I had agreed in writing never to let myself be seen again . . .

B. 348 From the *"Jüdische Telegraphen-Agentur"* [Jewish Telegraphic Agency] (J.T.A.) no. 133, 14th June 1939

Two more synagogues in the *"Protektorat"* [Protectorate of Bohemia and Moravia] were set on fire

London, 13th June (J. T. A.)

It has been reported from Prague: in Zabreh on the Oder (in Mähren [Moravia]) during the late evening SS men equipped with petrol cans broke into the synagogue, poured petrol over the benches and the Ark of the Covenant, besmirched and ripped up the *Thorarollen* [Torah scrolls], and finally threw a burning torch into the interior after they had left the synagogue. The building immediately went up in bright flames. SS men also set the synagogue on fire in Oderfurt [now Cz. Přívoz], not far from Mährisch Ostrau [Moravian Ostrava].

B. 349 From *Der Neue Tag* [The New Day], Prague, no. 72, 19th June 1939

BUDWEIS SYNAGOGUE BECOMES CIVIC PROPERTY:

The *Israelitische Kultusgemeinde* [Jewish community] in Budweis [now Cz. České Budějovice] has informed the *Polizeidirektion* [police authority] in writing that it is prepared to transfer its synagogue in the Gerstgasse to the administration of the municipality. This proposal was accepted in principle by *Bürgermeister* [mayor] David. The way the building will be used will be decided in the very near future.

B. 350 *Die Zeit* [The Times], Reichenberg [now Cz. Liberec], 16th June 1939

Jewish *Tempel* [synagogue] incinerated. Friedeck [now Cz. Frýdek-Místek]: Last night, a fire broke out in the *Tempel* at Friedeck the causes of which are still unknown, which soon spread to the entire building. The interior and a part of the building itself fell victim to the flames.

Neue Zürcher Zeitung [New Zürich Newspaper], no. 166 (International edition), 18th June 1939

Prague. 17th June. (Havas) The synagogue in Frydeck in Mähren [Moravia] has been destroyed by a fire.

B. 351 From *Der Neue Tag* [The New Day], Prague, No. 64, 11 June 1939 (National Socialist)

Synagogue fire in Oerfurt [Oderfurt; now Cz. Přívoz; Prziwos; within city of Ostrava, Moravia-Silesia region] (Own report)

On Saturday night the Oderfurt Synagoge was beset by fire. Before the *Feuerwehr* [fire brigade] rapidly appeared at the fire scene, the fire had already spread to such an extent that the whole building was alight. The firemen sought to master the fire with all the skill at their disposal. Suddenly a westerly wind set in, so that the neighbouring buildings were much endangered by the blazing flames and fierce sparks. As the wind powerfully fanned the fire, it was fuelled by highly dangerous constant explosions which came from the large quantity of revolver ammuntion and explosives as well as numerous hand grenades hidden in the synagogue by criminal elements. Only thanks to a particular stroke of luck was no one harmed from the team of firefighters and security services. In these circumstances, after all their efforts to extinguish the fire were unsuccessful, the *Feuerwehr* eventually had to restrict the neighbouring buildings and their inhabitants in the interests of safety and protection. If the rising wind had had greater strength, then the buildings fringing the Ringplatz fire would also have been encroached inexorably by the fire.

B. 352 *Völkischer Beobachter* [National Observer], Vienna, 19 June 1939

Znaim [now Cz. Znojmo] blemish removed

18 June [1939]

Prof. Erwin Ilz has just elaborated a new regulatory plan that provides for the removal of the Jewish *Tempel* [synagogue] and the construction of a pleasure ground in its place.

B. 353 *Neue Zürcher Zeitung* [New Zurich Newspaper], foreign edition, Zürich, No. 167, 19 June 1939

PALESTINE

Haifa, 18 June (Havas)

Last night the synagogue in was burnt down. The fire is probably attributable to malevolence. The damage is estimated at many thousands of pounds. More fires have occurred in the region in recent days.

B. 1001 London

When I heard on the radio on 9th November that Legation Secretary vom Rath had died in Paris, I immediately said to my wife, "If only nothing happens!"

At a quarter to 5 in the morning on the night of 10th November I heard a lot of noise. A policeman whom I knew appeared, in a very angry state, and told me I was under arrest. He released the safety catch on his weapon and said that he would shoot any attempt to escape. I replied extremely calmly, "You needn't worry about that with me."

As the officer and I went through the front garden I saw two typical SS men whom I did not know, standing there wearing leather jackets. The policeman accompanying me whispered with them both. He said to me "Go on!" and let me go forward alone in the dark.

After I had gone on for a little while three shots suddenly sounded. The first shot missed. The second hit me in the back, the third was a shot in the stomach which caused me serious injury. The shots were fired from a Luger pistol. Before the shooting I had noticed that the two SS men I did not know were the culprits, because they were circling round towards me. I had the presence of mind not to cry out. The SS men ran off. I crawled into a front garden. The policeman suddenly appeared on the other side and satisfied himself that I was lying there. Then he got into a car that stopped nearby and drove away. I was gurgling loudly, especially after I noticed one of the murderers coming back after about ten minutes. "*Solche Schweinerei!*" [such filth] he shouted.

I knew better than to call for help straight away. When I noticed that the murderers and their helper's helper had apparently disappeared I dared to do so. Ten to twelve people turned up despite the early hour. I asked them first to tell my wife that I was not well. The emergency ambulance did not come. After I learned of reports about how difficult it was to call it out, I take it to be certain that the departure of the emergency ambulance was deliberately held up by the Gestapo.

I was then taken to hospital by the ambulance and had to undergo an operation lasting one or two hours. It was a shot through the bowels. The fact that I had gone to the toilet before the policeman led me out of my house significantly contributed to my surviving the serious gunshot wound and the operation that that which resulted from it. I was released from hospital after seven weeks on my sickbed. My release only took place with the approval of the Gestapo. Because I had been living in my home town for years, many Christian friends and acquaintances sent me their best wishes for my recovery when I began to walk again. Strangers sent flowers to my house, and I received anonymous letters that brought me evidence of sympathy. A lady I knew who belonged to the NSDAP [Nazi Party] wanted to protest against the outrage by sending a reader's letter to the appropriate National Socialist newspaper. Only the fact that she had been a National Socialist for a long time protected her from serious consequences. An engineer (a naval officer) whom I know and his secretary were arrested because they had supposedly spoken up for me.

As the Gestapo observed that my presence produced an atmosphere and reports that were detrimental to the Party, I received the order to leave my home town on 16th January. I was also told to report to the responsible police station in Berlin. I was not allowed to leave the territory of the Reich, although a permit to travel to England was already available for me and my wife too.

I was repeatedly told during my seven-month -ong stay in Berlin that I would receive my passport for the journey out. I received it eventually, after, as I was told, Herr Himmler himself had taken a decision on the matter. I then went to London with my wife.

B. 1002 London

Report on the events on 9th and 10th November 1938 in Kiel

1) Attempted murders. The Chairman of the Jewish *Gemeinde* [community], Gustav Lask, who had lived as an independent gentleman in the Villenviertel area of Kiel since the sale of his business, was shot and seriously wounded by two SS men after his arrest on the night of 10th November. He was shot in the stomach and lay between life and death in hospital for seven weeks. Herr L. now lives in London. Furthermore, the owner of S. Mastbaum silk dealers, who also lived in the Villenviertel area of Kiel, was shot down by five shots. He received a graze to the lung, a graze to the head and an especially dangerous shot to the

jaw. Herr L., who is 59 years old, now lives in London (15 Wood-church Rd., NW6, at Mrs Joseph's).

2) Arrests. About 55 people, Jews and non-Aryans, were arrested in Kiel and taken to Sachsenhausen. Amongst those arrested was the former second *Bürgermeister* [mayor] of Kiel, Gradenwitz, who is non-Aryan. Some 15 Jewish shops were destroyed, as well as a few houses, amongst them those of Gradenwitz and Rosenstein.

3) The synagogue was burned and completely destroyed inside. The *Thorarollen* [Torah scrolls] were ruined. A brass candlestick donated in memory of the Jewish fallen has not been found and was probably stolen. The memorial tablet in honour of the Jewish fallen was discovered in the ruins of the synagogue and later rehung in the cemetery mortuary.

Addendum

As the synagogue was being set on fire, the Christian *Kastellanin* [warden], a widow, was driven into the street in her nightshirt. Her home was destroyed. The woman fainted as a result.

GLOSSARY

All non-English glossary terms are in German unless otherwise specified

Abbreviations
abbr. = abbreviation
lit. = literal meaning
USHMM = US Holocaust Memorial Museum

24 auf den Nackten	abbr. for *24 auf den nackten Hintern* [24 on the naked backside]; see *25 vorm Arsch*
25 auf das Gesäß	(lit. 25 on the backside); see *25 vorm Arsch*
25 vorm Arsch	(lit. 25 on the arse); punishment by whipping
175-er	homosexual prisoner; paragraph 175 of Germany's criminal code outlawed homosexual behaviour; *175-er* prisoners were denoted by a pink triangle on their clothing
Abschiebungshaft	custody pending deportation
Abtreibungsparagraph	(lit. abortion paragraph); although paragraph 218 of the Penal Code for the German Reich 1872 outlawed abortion, during the Nazi period and under the Nuremberg laws the courts acquitted cases of Jewish women having abortions
	Source: Henry P. David et.al., 'Abortion and eugenics in Nazi Germany', Population and Development Review, 14/1, March 1988, pp 81–112
Aguda	Hebrew: *Agudath Israel; Agudas Yisroel;* Union of Israel; political movement associated with orthodox, non-Zionist Jewry in Eastern Europe founded in 1912
Aktion	(lit. operation); Nazi term for a campaign against Jews involving mass arrests, assembly, deportation, and sometimes also dispossession, torture and murder; see also *Aktion-Gildemeester, Aktionsjuden, Juni-Aktion, Novemberpogrom, Polenaktion, Sonderaktionsjuden*

Aktion-Gildemeester   abbr. for *Auswanderungshilfsaktion Gildemeester*; Nazi operation to accelerate the evacuation of Jews from Vienna, run by Frank van Gheel Gildemeester (b 1881) who had previously helped the Nazis in various ways, thus gaining their confidence; the *Aktion* used 10% of the assets seized from wealthier Jews to finance an emigration fund for impoverished Jews, and it also assisted the wealthier Jews to expedite their own emigration; before its activities were integrated into the *Israelitische Kultusgemeinde Wien*, Gildemeester helped some 30,000 non-Aryans to emigrate

Source: Republik Österreich Historikerkommission, Final Report, 2003; Peter Berger, 'The Gildemeester organisation for assistance to emigrants and the expulsion of Jews from Vienna, 1938–1942', in Terry Gourvish, ed., Business and Politics in Europe, 1900–1970: Essays in Honour of Alice Teichova, Cambridge University Press, 2003, pp 215–245

Aktionsjuden   (lit. operation Jews); sometimes *Sonderaktionsjuden*; Jews arrested in the *Juni-Aktion* and/or the *Novemberpogrom*

Alex   see Alexanderplatz

Alexanderplatz   public square in central Berlin; location of the *Polizeipräsidium* Berlin [Berlin police headquarters]; sometimes abbreviated to Alex

Alt-Bentschen   town in Upper Silesia; now Zbąszyńek, Poland; see *Polenaktion*

Altreich   Old Reich; designation of the German state prior to the *Anschluß* [annexation] of Austria in March 1938

am Tor stehen   see *stehen am Tor*

Amtsgerichtsrat   local court judge

Angriff, Der   The Attack; Berlin Nazi Party newspaper (1927–1945) founded by Joseph Goebbels as a mass circulation paper for communicating propaganda and antisemitism

Anschluß   also written *Anschluss* (post 1966); Nazi German occupation and annexation of Austria on 12 March 1938, which was widely welcomed and endorsed by the non-Jewish population; there were about 192,000 Jews in Austria at the time, 4% of the total population, the great majority in Vienna, where they comprised 9% of the city's inhabitants

Source: USHMM

antisemitic insults	antisemitic insults cited in the *Novemberpogrom* testimonies:

Saujud [Jewish pig/swine] see *Saujud*
Saukerl [pig fellow/chap; bastard]
Drecksau [filthy swine]
Derstickts, Saujuden [Choke, Jewish pigs!]
Schwein [pig, swine*]*
Judensau [Jewish pig/swine] see *Judensau*
Judenschwein [Jewish pigs/swine]
Schweinejuden [Jewish pigs/swine]
Schweinehund [pig dog; bastard]
polnisches Schwein [Polish pig]
intellektuelles Schwein [intellectual pig/swine]

alter Dreckjude [old filthy Jew]
Juda verrecke [Perish Judah!]
Talmudgauner [Talmud crook]

Betrüger [fraudster]
Volksverräter [traitor against the people]
Zuhälter [pimp]

Antwerp incident	incident involving an alleged attack on two German journalists from the newspaper *Der Angriff* who were passengers on the steamer Cordilleras on 26 October 1938, and who took photographs in the Jewish district of Antwerp; for more information, see press reports on the alleged attack Source: The Times, London, 27 October 1938, p 1
Appell	roll call of prisoners in concentration camps, who had to line up on the *Appellplatz* [parade ground] and stand to attention, two or more times per day, each *Appell* could last several hours and was held in all weathers; see also *Zählappell*
Appellplatz	parade ground where *Appell* [roll call] was held
Arbeitseinsatzgesetz	work deployment law; under which male German nationals between the ages of 18 and 60 could be ordered to perform certain types of work as required by the authorities; used for transfer to concentration camps for forced labour
Arbeitsfront	abbr. for *Deutsche Arbeitsfront* (DAF); German Labour Front; it replaced trade unions and obtained their assets after their forced dissolution by the Nazis and was supposed to represent employers and employees alike, with 25 million members
Arbeitskommando	work group for forced labour

Arbeitsscheu	work shy; label for a category of concentration camp prisoners, many arrested in the *Juni-Aktion* called *Aktion Arbeitsscheu Reich*; designated by a black or brown triangle on the prisoners' uniforms; see also *Asoziale* Source: Deutsches Historisches Museum
Arier	Aryan; Nazi term for non-Jewish, non-Gypsy Caucasians; the Nuremberg Laws of 1935 defined an Aryan as a person with four Aryan grandparents; only Aryans could be Reich citizens; so-called *Halb-Arier* [half Aryans] had only one Aryan parent; so-called *Rein-Arier* [pure Aryans] were Aryans who could prove that their ancestors were pure Aryans in the period before 1800 Source: USHMM; Yad Vashem
Arierbeweis	Aryan permit
Arieresung	see *Arisierung*
Ariernachweis	Aryan certificate
Arierprinzip	Aryan principle
arisiert	see *Arisierung*
Arisierung	Aryanisation; the forced transfer of Jewish-owned businesses to non-Jewish *"Arier"* [Aryan] German ownership throughout Germany and German-occupied countries; the process included two stages: from 1933 to 1938 the Jews were gradually removed from German economic life, termed "voluntary" exclusion by the Nazis; after 1938 forced confiscation of Jewish businesses and property was legalised; eventually all Jewish money and property was confiscated by the Nazis and used to finance the deportation of the Jews Source: Yad Vashem
Arisierungsabgabe	Aryanisation duty
Arisierungsbefehl	Aryanisation order
Arrest	detention
Arreste	see *Arrestlokal*
Arrestlokal	detention centre
Aryan	see *Arier*
Asoziale	asocials; label for a category of concentration camp prisoners, many arrested in the *Juni-Aktion* called *Aktion Arbeitsscheu Reich*, who were regarded as inferior by the Nazi regime; they included vagrants, beggars, alcoholics, drug addicts, prostitutes, nonconformists, pacifists and Gypsies (Sinti and Roma); designated by a black or brown triangle on the uniform; see also *Arbeitsscheu* Source: Deutsches Historisches Museum; Holocaust Memorial Day Trust

Auernheimer, Raoul	(1876–1948); lawyer, journalist and writer in Vienna; President and Vice-President of PEN (an international association of writers) in Vienna; arrested in March 1938 and imprisoned in Dachau concentration camp until late 1938; emigrated to New York with his family; see also B. 142
auf der Flucht erschossen	shot whilst escaping; Nazi term for concentration camp prisoners shot dead by the SS guards
Aufenthaltsbewilligung	see *Aufenthaltserlaubnis*
Aufenthaltserlaubnis	residence permit
Aufenthaltsgenehmigung	see *Aufenthaltserlaubnis*
Aufenthaltsverbot	exclusion order
Aufseher	overseer or supervisor of prisoners
Ausfuhrsteuergenehmigung	export tax permit
Auskunftserteilung	disclosure of information
Auslandsdeutsche	Germans living abroad
Auslösebefugnis	redemption authority; decree controlling the financial arrangements imposed on Jews who wanted to retain precious metal or jewellery items Source: Wiener Library, *Novemberpogrom* eyewitness account B. 330
Ausreiseansuchen	exit application
Ausreisegenehmigung	exit permit
Ausreisepapiere	exit papers
Auswanderungsberatungsstelle	emigration advice centre
Auswanderungspass	emigration passport
Auswanderungsvisum	emigration visa
Ausweisungsbefehl	deportation order
Ausweisungshaft	see *Abschiebungshaft*
Bänke, gelbe	yellow benches; public benches marked with yellow paint; Jews were not allowed to use other benches
Barackenältester	barrack elder
Baranowski, Hermann	(1884–1940); *Lagerkommandant* of Sachsenhausen concentration camp (1938–9)
Baumhängen	tree-hanging punishment, in which the prisoner's hands were chained to a tree behind him and supported his whole weight
B.D.M.	see *Hitler-Jugend*
Beer Hall Putsch	see *Bürgerbräukeller*
Bentschen	town in Upper Silesia; now Zbąszyń, Poland; see *Polenaktion*

Berufsverbrecher   abbr. BV; career or professional criminal who made crime their business and who lived in part or whole from the gains of their crimes; sentenced at least three times for a minimum of three months; category of concentration camp prisoner, designated by a green triangle on their clothing; officially known in full as *Befristete Vorbeugungshaft* [limited term preventive custody] or *Beschränkte Verhaftung* [limited or short term imprisonment]; see also *Gewohnheitsverbrecher*

Source: USHMM; Robert Gellately, Backing Hitler: Consent and Coercion in Nazi Germany, Oxford University Press, 2001, p 296

Beschlagnahme   confiscation

Besteuerung   tax assessment

Beth Neorim   Hebrew: *Beit Hanarim*; youth hostel

Bethaus   house of prayer; often interchangeable with "synagogue"; premises of a private person left to a Jewish community in order to perform the community service; only furnished in a makeshift manner for worship; a Jewish school can also be used

Bethaus (cont.)   Source: Manfred Jehle ed., Die Juden und die jüdischen Gemeinden Preussens in amtlichen Enquêten des Vormärz Einzelveröffentlichungen der Historischen Kommission zu Berlin, Band 82/1–4, Munich, K.G. Saur Verlag GmbH & Co., 1998

Bewilligung   authorisation

Bezirk   district; term used particularly in Vienna

Bezirkskommissariat   district police station

Bibelforscher   bible students or Jehovah's Witnesses; also *Ernste Bibelforscher* [earnest bible students]; abbr. of *Internationale Bibelforscher-Vereinigung* (IBV) [International Bible Students Association (IBSA)]; comparatively small Christian denomination; first religious denomination in the Third Reich to be banned; Nazi legal authorities persecuted them as conscientious objectors on the charge of demoralisation of the armed forces; no other religious denomination opposed the coercion of the National Socialists with comparable determination; as prisoners denoted by purple triangle on their clothing

Source: Detlef Garbe, Between Resistance and Martyrdom: Jehovah's Witnesses in the Third Reich trans. Dagmar G. Grimm, University of Wisconsin Press, 2008, pp 3, 4

Block   group of barracks in a concentration camp

Blockältester	block elder in a concentration camp; senior prisoner with disciplinary powers, appointed by the SS
Blockführer-SS	see *SS-Blockführer*
Blockschreiber	block registrar in a concentration camp
Blockwart	block warden
Blut und Ehre	(lit. blood and honour); motto etched on the blade of Hitler Youth daggers
Blutorden	(lit. blood order); prestigious medal awarded by the Nazis
Bock	whipping block
Braune Schwestern	brown sisters; nurses, members of the *NSV-Schwesternschaft (Nationalsozialistische Volkswohlfahrt)* [National Socialist People's Welfare Nurses]
Buchenwald	Nazi concentration camp on the Ettersberg, ten kilometres north west of Weimar, Germany, opened in July 1937; most of the early inmates were political prisoners; however, in the aftermath of the *Novemberpogrom* in November 1938, German SS and police sent almost 10,000 Jews to Buchenwald; 600 prisoners died there between November 1938 and February 1939 Source: Jewish Virtual Library
Bund Deutscher Mädel	see *Hitler-Jugend*
Bürckel, Josef	*Reichskommissar* for the unification and integration of Austria with the German Reich, 1938–40
Bürgerbräukeller	Bürgerbräu beer hall in Munich, from where Hitler led a failed attempt to seize power in Munich on 8 November 1923; also called the Beer Hall Putsch and *Ereignis am Biertisch* [event at the beer table]; subsequently the location of annual Nazi Party commemoration of that event
Buß- und Bettag	Day of Prayer and Repentance; regional Protestant Christian holiday on the Wednesday eleven days before the First Sunday of Advent
B. V.	see *Berufsverbrecher*
Capo	see *Kapo*
Centralverein deutscher Staatsbürger jüdischen Glaubens	abbr. *CV*; Central Association of German Citizens of Jewish Faith; founded in 1893 as a reaction to growing antisemitism, it monitored and documented the prevalence of anti-Jewish actions throughout Germany, as well as the Jewish communities' responses to them
Chaluz	Hebrew: pioneer; Zionist youth organisation with offices in Europe, providing preparation for settlement in Palestine
Chevra kadisha	Hebrew: preparations for Jewish burial

Comité	Dutch: committee; refers to several relief organisations active in the Netherlands: *Comité voor Bijzondere Joodsche Belangen* [Committee for Special Jewish Affairs]; *Comité voor Joodse Vluchtelingen* [Committee for Jewish Refugees]; *Nederlands Kinder Comité* [Dutch Children's Committee]
C.V.	see *Centralverein deutscher Staatsbürger jüdischen Glaubens*
C.V. Zeitung	weekly newspaper of *Centralverein deutscher Staatsbürger jüdischen Glaubens* from 1922 to 1938
Dachau	concentration camp near the town of Dachau, 30 kilometres north west of Munich; the first Nazi concentration camp to be opened in Germany, in March 1933, in the grounds of an abandoned munitions factory; its layout and building plans were the model for all other Nazi concentration camps; it was a training centre for SS concentration camp guards, and the camp's organisation and routine became the model for all Nazi concentration camps; about 10,000 Jewish men arrested in the *Novemberpogrom* were held at Dachau Source: Jewish Virtual Library
Daluege, Kurt	(1897–1946); Nazi official; after serving as a German army officer in WWI and the Rossbach Freikorps, in 1926 he joined the SA then transferred to the SS in 1928; he became a member of the *Reichstag* [German parliament] in January 1933 and chief of the Prussian police department; in 1934 he ran the regular uniformed police and in 1942 became acting governor of the Protectorate of Bohemia and Moravia; he was executed in 1946 for crimes such as the Lidice massacre Source: Yad Vashem
Deutsche Arbeitsfront	see *Arbeitsfront*
Devisenabfertigung	foreign currency clearance
Devisenbeamte	foreign currency official
Devisenstelle	foreign currency office
Drillichanzüge	concentration camp prisoners' uniforms made from *Drillich* [cotton drill]; see also *Zwilchanzug*
Dolfuss, Engelbert	(1892–1934); Chancellor of Austria (1932–34); Catholic, Austrian nationalist dictator who sought to maintain independence from Germany and the rising Nazi Party; assassinated in an attempted putsch by Austrian Nazis Source: A. D. Harvey, 'Austria's diminutive dictator', History Today, 7/2009, pp 41–47

Durchgangslager	transit camp
Durchlaßschein	travel permit
Ehrenhaft	honourable custody
Eidesstattliche Vermögenserklärung	declaration of wealth issued in lieu of an oath
Einreise	entry
Einreise-Zertifikat	entry certificate
Einreiseerlaubnis	entry permit
Einreisegenehmigung	entry permit
Einreisemöglichkeit	entry opportunity
Eintopfsonntag	stew Sunday; a day when all citizens eat only simple, cheap foodstuffs
Elisabethpromenade	street in Vienna IX., renamed Rossauer Lände in 1919; location of police prison within the Imperial Royal police headquarters, built in 1905 to replace police prisons at the Theobaldkloster and on Sterngasse; despite the street name change it continued to be referred to as Elisabethpromenade or Liesl; the prison contained c. 148 cells for 300 prisoners and had plumbed toilets in every cell Source: Wikipedia; dasrotewien.at
Enteignungsverfahren	expropriation procedure
Entlassungsgesuch	petition for release
Entlassungsschein	release certificate
Ereignis am Biertisch	(lit. event at the beer table); see *Bürgerbräukeller*
Ernste Bibelforscher	(lit. earnest bible students); see *Bibelforscher*
Evian Conference	32 countries were invited by US President FD Roosevelt to attend a conference at the Hotel Royal in Evian, France, on 23 March 1938 to tackle the problem of accommodating refugees from the German Reich; Germany and Portugal were not invited, the USSR and Czechoslovakia did not send representatives, Italy refused the invitation and Hungary, Romania, Poland and South Africa sent observers; all except the Dominican Republic refused to increase their respective immigration quotas Source: Mémorial de la Shoah
Exerzieren	punitive drill; military-style physical exercises in concentration camps
Festhalle	(lit. festival hall); large hall used for trade fairs, amongst other things, e.g. in Frankfurt am Main
Finanzamt	tax office
Fluchtsteuer	flight or escape tax; tax on departure; see also *Golddiskontbank* and *Sperrmark*
Frauenschaft	see *Nationalsozialistische Frauenschaft*

Freigabeerklärung	clearance certificate
Fremdenamt	foreigners' registration office
Fremdenpolizei	aliens' branch of the police
Frondienst	socage; forced labour, slave labour; see also *Zwangsarbeit*
Fuhlsbüttel	concentration camp in Hamburg
Führer	leader; designation for Adolf Hitler
Führer-SS	see *SS-Führer*
Fünfundzwanzig vorm Arsch	see *25 vorm Arsch*
Fürsorgeministerium	Ministry of Welfare
Gauleiter	Nazi party regional leader
Gefängnis	prison
Geheime Staatspolizei	see *Gestapo*
Geiseltheorie	hostage theory; Hitler was convinced of a Jewish world conspiracy and regarded the Jews of Europe as political hostages against the United States; an earlier version referring to WWI foresaw an attack against France as a means of influencing British policy and of compensating for the confiscation of German colonies and shipping by Britain in the event of an Anglo-German war
Geiseltheorie (cont.)	Source: Boris Barth, Genozid: Völkermord im 20. Jahrhundert: Geschichte, Theorien, Kontroversen, CH Beck, 2006, p 99; Mark Hewitson, Germany and the Causes of the First World War, 2004, Bloomsbury, p 176
Gemeindebezirk	see *Bezirk*
Gemeindehaus	(Jewish) community house
Gemeindevorsteher	(Jewish) community chairman and/or council member(s)
Genehmigung	permit
Gestapo	abbr. for *Geheime Staatspolizei* [Secret State Police]; formed in 1933 by Hermann Göring; see also *Sicherheitspolizei; Kriminalpolizei*
Gesuch	petition; in the *Novemberpogrom* context for release from arrest or imprisonment
Gewohnheitsverbrecher	habitual criminal or repeat offender; in Nazi terms not a professional criminal but regarded as being driven by a similar predisposition; sentenced at least three times for a minimum of three months; see also *Berufsverbrecher*
	Source: Robert Gellately, Backing Hitler: Consent and Coercion in Nazi Germany, Oxford University Press, 2001, p 296

gez.	abbr. *for gezeichnet*; signed
Gildemeester, Frank van Gheel	see Aktion-Gildemeester
Goebbels, Josef	(1897–1945); Nazi Minister of Public Enlightenment and Propaganda
Golddiskontbank	Gold Discount Bank, established in 1924, became a subsidiary of the Deutsche *Reichsbank* [German central bank]; the transfer of Jewish emigrants' assets abroad was made more difficult by the large deduction that had to be paid in foreign currency to the Golddiskontbank, which could amount to 90% of the capital; see also *Fluchtsteuer* and *Sperrmark*
	Source: Philipp Gassert and Alan E. Steinweis, eds, Coping with the Nazi Past: West German Debates on Nazism and Generational Conflict, 1955–1975, Berghahn, 2006, p 92 n29
Göring, Hermann	(1893–1946); Nazi politician and military leader; founded the Gestapo in 1933; commander-in-chief of the Luftwaffe (1935–1945)
Grensbewaking en Rijksvreemdelingendienst	Dutch: Border Control and State Aliens Office
Grenzschein	border permit
Grenzstation	(lit. border station); border railway station
Grüne Heinrich, Der	Green Henry; popular name for a type of low, narrow police vehicle used in Vienna
Grynszpan, Herschel	(1921–?1960); Polish Jew living in Paris, on 7 November 1938 protested against the recent banishment of Polish Jews living in Germany (including his parents) to beyond the Polish border by mortally injuring Ernst vom Rath, a third secretary at the German legation; the Nazis took this as a pretext for the *Novemberpogrom*; see also *Polenaktion*
	Source: Mémorial de la Shoah
Haavaramark	Haavara [transfer] marks: payments under the Haavara Agreement, negotiated by the Jewish Agency in 1933 with the Haavara Co. in Palestine and the Nazi authorities to allow Jewish emigrants to deposit money with the company; it enabled 50,000 German Jews to emigrate to Palestine and export some of their assets there; see also *Reichsmark; Sperrmark; Papiermark*
	Source: Encyclopedia Judaica
Hachshara	Hebrew: training, preparation; German: *Hachschara*; agricultural training facilities for young Jews preparing to emigrate to Palestine (1933–39)
	Source: Jewish Virtual Library

Halb-Arier	half-Aryan; see also *Arier*
Handelsgerichtsrat	commercial court lawyer
Hehalutz	see *Chaluz*
HICEM	Jewish emigrants' assistance organisation, with head-quarters in Paris and offices all over Europe, Central and South America and South East Asia; HICEM is an acronym of HIAS (Hebrew Immigrant Aid Society), ICA (Jewish Colonisation Association) and Emig-direct, three Jewish migration associations which merged in 1927 Source: Yad Vashem
Hilfsverein der deutschen Juden	Aid Association of German Jews, 1901–1939; provided financial and practical assistance to Jews seeking to emigrate; see also *Palästina-Amt* of the Jewish Agency, which assisted emigrants to Palestine Source: Yad Vashem
Himmler, Heinrich	(1900–1945); *Reichsführer-SS*, head of the Gestapo and the Waffen-SS, Nazi Minister of the Interior (1943–45), responsible for overseeing the Nazis' "Final Solution to the Jewish Question"
Hirschfeld, Oskar	(b ?1900); former secretary-general of the Union of Austrian Jews and final editor-in-chief of the Vienna Jewish weekly *Die Wahrheit* until it was closed down and he was arrested and imprisoned in Vienna in March 1938; released on condition that he emigrated; went to the USA via England; contributed nine reports to the JCIO (102 136 142 149 153 173 179 190 197); see also B. 142 Source: Jewish Telegraphic Agency (4 Jan 1940)
historische Länder	historic states: Bohemia, Moravia and Silesia
Hitler-Jugend	abbr. *HJ*; Hitler Youth; paramilitary youth organisa-tion of the Nazi Party founded in 1926 for boys, to indoctrinate young people in Nazi ideology; a parallel organisation for girls was set up in 1928, later called *Bund Deutscher Mädel (BDM)*; 90% of German youths were members of *HJ* and *BDM* by 1939 Source: Jewish Virtual Library
Hochverräter	person guilty of high treason
Horst Wessel song	marching song of the SA and later the official song of the Nazi Party and unofficial national anthem of Germany, with words by Horst Wessel (1907–1930), an SA Storm trooper whose death Goebbels claimed was a Communist plot; also known as *Die Fahne hoch* [the flag held high] from its first line Source: Jewish Virtual Library

Illegale	illegals; category of prisoners
Innenministerium	Ministry of the Interior
Inschutzhaftnahme	so-called protective detention
insurance	Jewish policy holders were unable to obtain compensation from insurance companies for destroyed shop window displays, windows and the contents of destroyed synagogues and houses of prayer; the insurance companies had to pay the German Reich, not the policy holders, who were obliged to continue to pay premiums to the insurance companies
	Source: Republik Österreich Historikerkommission, Final Report, 2003
Israelitisch	Israelite; of Israel; Jewish; in the biblical sense a descendant of the Jewish patriarch Jacob, whose name was changed to Israel after an all-night fight at Penuel near the stream of Jabbok (Genesis 32:28); a native or inhabitant of the ancient, biblical Northern Kingdom of Israel; see also *Israelitische Gemeinde* and *Zwangsnamen*
	Source: Encyclopædia Britannica Online, 'Israelite'
Israelitische Gemeinde	Jewish community; used mainly in Austria, also in Germany and Switzerland; the official name for Jewish communities in Austria is *Israelitische Kultusgemeinde (IKG)*; originates in a speech by Emperor Franz Joseph I on 3 April 1849 referring to the "*Israelitische Gemeinde von Wien*" [Jewish community of Vienna]
	Source: Schencker Documents Online; accessed 16 June 2014
Jahrzeit	Yiddish: anniversary of a death; mainly observed for deceased parents or outstanding individuals
JCIO	see Jewish Central Information Office
Jehovah's Witnesses	see *Bibelforscher*
Jewish Central Information Office	abbr. JCIO; Jewish Central Information Office; organisation set up to gather intelligence about the Nazi regime and antisemitism and disseminate it internationally; led by Dr Alfred Wiener in Amsterdam (1933–39), following his similar work at *Büro Wilhelmstrasse* for the *Central-Verein deutscher Staatsbürger jüdischen Glaubens* in Berlin (1929–1933); it had 17 staff , 8,000 books and pamphlets and many thousands of press cuttings by the time it was moved to London in 1939; it is now known as the Wiener Library for the Study of the Holocaust & Genocide; for biographies see document: "Jewish Central Information Office: people"

Juda verrecke!   see antisemitic insults

Juden unerwünscht   Jews not wanted; sign displayed in restaurants, etc.

Judengesetze   laws relating to the Jews

Judenknecht   servant of the Jews; Gentile person assisting Jews with domestic work etc.; also Jewish lackey, used in antisemitic parlance to label non-Jews servile to the Jews, for example term used to insult people who approached Jewish shops and offices of Jewish lawyers and doctors as well as workshops of Jewish artisans, shoemakers and tailors, despite the boycott of April 1, 1933

Source: Theodore Herzl, The Jews' State, transl. Henk Overberg, Rowman & Littlefield, 1997, p 225; Thomas Dunlap, ed. and transl., Before the Holocaust: Three German-Jewish Lives, 1870–1939, Xlibris, 2011, p 389

Judenkontribution   tax of RM 1.2 billion imposed on the Jews in 1938–9 for the cost of the *Novemberpogrom* damage; see also *Judenvermögensabgabe*

Judensau   also *Saujud*; Jew pig/swine; a popular image in German religious texts and sculptures since the middle ages, seen in prints and sculptures and carvings on cathedrals, churches and public buildings (e.g. Cologne, Leipzig, Regensburg, Wittenberg); a few examples also in Austria, France, Belgium and Switzerland; it depicts Jews, sometimes rabbis, in obscene activities with a pig, sometimes in consort with the Devil, sometimes copulating with the pig or with pig faces, or eating pig excrement or suckling from the sow; it is often combined with depictions of the blood libel and is based on the Jewish ritual prohibition against eating or touching pigs; the image was revived in the Nazi period, and the word was turned into an insult; see also antisemitic insults

Source: Zionism & Israel Center

Judenvermögensabgabe   Jewish assets/property tax; *Sühneleistung* [punitive tax] introduced by Hermann Göring on registered Jewish assets for "the hostile attitude of the Jews towards the German people" following the assassination of Ernst vom Rath and the *Novemberpogrom*; it imposed a *Strafmilliarde* [punishment billion] compensation payment of one billion RM; all German Jews with property in excess of RM. 5,000 including those living abroad had to pay 25% of their remaining wealth in five instalments up to the end of 1939; see also *Judenkontribution* and *Sühneleistung*

Source: USHMM

Judenvermögens-anmeldung registration of Jews' assets; Jews seeking to emigrate had to submit a statement of their assets, which were then confiscated or heavily taxed

Jüdischer Kulturbund Jewish Cultural Federation; supported and promoted segregated Jewish art, music, writing and publishing in Germany for Jewish-only audiences between 1935 and 1941 as prescribed by the Nazi regime; it replaced the *Kulturbund Deutscher Juden* [Cultural Federation of German Jews] (1933–1935); see also *Kulturbund*

Jüdische Rundschau Jewish Review; twice weekly paper published by the Zionistische Vereinigung für Deutschland [Zionist Federation for Germany] between 1896 and 1938

Jüdischer Frauenbund Jewish Women's League; founded in 1904 by Bertha Pappenheim (see Pappenheim, Bertha); closed down in 1938; revived in the 1950s

Jüdischer Krankenpfleger see *Krankenbehandler*

Jüdisches Nachrichtenblatt (1938–1943); The Jewish News Bulletin; after the *Novemberpogrom* the many Jewish newspapers were shut down and the Nazis ordered the creation of this one new Jewish newspaper; it was kept under close watch by the Nazi authorities; it published discussions and news items about the Jewish community that were found "acceptable" by the Nazi authorities; many of the articles and advertisements concerned Jewish emigration from Germany
Source: Leo Baeck Institute

Jüdisches Sozialamt Jewish social services office; a Jewish emigrant aid society in Prague in 1939
Source: Jean-Michel Palmier, Weimar in Exile: the Anti-Fascist Emigration in Europe and America, transl. David Fernbach, London, Verso, 2006, p 275

Juni-Aktion June operation; mass arrests in Germany between 13 and 18 June 1938 of more than 10,000 men categorised by the Nazi regime as so-called *Asoziale* [asocial] and *Arbeitsscheue* [work shy], mostly unemployed or with a criminal record; over half were sent to Sachsenhausen; the operation was called *Arbeitsscheu Reich*; about 20% of the men were Jews
Source: Deutsches Historisches Museum; Dieter Pohl, 'The Holocaust and the concentration camps', Concentration Camps in Nazi Germany: The New Histories, Jane Caplan and Nikolaus Wachsmann, eds, Routledge, 2009, p 150

Justizrat	state prosecutor
Kapo	also *Capo*; concentration camp prisoners given a supervisory role over other prisoners by the SS; carried out the orders of the SS; after the war some *Kapos* were prosecuted as war criminals
	Source: Jewish Virtual Library
Karajangasse	Karajangasse 14, Vienna XX.; police station in the former Brigittenauer Gymnasium and Volkschule, used to detain Jews arrested in November 1938; it was also used as a *Durchgangslager* [transit camp] in 1939
	Source: http://www.carto.net/judenplatz/wien/jp_wi_center.html; 'Ein fremdes, fernes, unbekanntes Land', testimony of Ernst Otto Allerhand (born 1923, Vienna), in Erinnerungen: Lebensgeschichten von Opfern des Nationalsozialismus, Vienna, National Fund of the Republic of Austria for the Victims of National Socialism, 2012, p 75
Kennkarte	identity card
Kenyongasse	Kenyongasse 4–8, Vienna VII.; *Notgefängnis* [temporary prison] in a former convent school; the school was dissolved in 1938 and the building used as a *Fachschule* [technical college], possibly for teacher training, and for c. 300 refugees from the Sudetenland and 2,062 Jewish prisoners interned there on 12 November 1938; the custody regime was particularly brutal; prisoners were killed and committed suicide there
	Source:http://www.gedenkdienst.at/fileadmin/zeitung/gd2011-1a.pdf
Kinderausweis	identity papers for children
Kindercomité	see *Nederlands Kinder Comité* and *Comité*
Kippen	cigarette ends
Kniebeugen	knee-bends or squats; a punishment exercise
kochende Volksseele	seething populace; see *Volkswut*
Kom. Rat.	see *Kommerzialrat*
Kommandantur	headquarters
Kommerzialrat	abbr. *Kom. Rat*; commercial councillor; honorific title given to distinguished businessmen in Austria
Kommissar vom Dienst	duty police inspector
Kommissariat	police station
Kommissbrot	army bread; a coarse rye bread
Kontribution	see *Judenkontribution*

Konzentrationslager	abbr. *KZ*; concentration camp; type of prison used to detain and confine large numbers of people without judicial process, usually under harsh conditions, especially political prisoners or members of persecuted minorities, in a relatively small area with inadequate facilities, sometimes to provide forced labour or to await mass execution; the Nazi regime established about 15,000 concentration, labour and death camps between 1933 and 1945 in Germany and elsewhere; men arrested in the *Novemberpogrom* were held in three concentration camps: Buchenwald, Dachau and Sachsenhausen Source: Oxford English Dictionary; USHMM; Jewish Virtual Library
Krankenbehandler	Jewish doctors licensed by the Nazi authorities to treat Jewish patients
Krankenrevier	see *Revier*
Krankenstube	see *Revier*
Krankenwärter	see *Sanitäter*
Kreisleiter	Nazi municipal leader
Kreisleitung	Nazi municipal authorities
Kriminalbeamte	police detective
Kriminalpolizei	criminal police; plain-clothes police detectives; in 1936 became part of the Sicherheitspolizei together with the Gestapo; see also *Sicherheitspolizei; Reichskriminalamt* Source: Encyclopædia Britannica Online, 'Gestapo'
Kriminalrat	detective superintendant or captain
Kristallnacht	also *Reichskristallnacht*; night of broken glass; see *Novemberpogrom*
Kulturbund	*Kulturbund Deutscher Juden*; Cultural Federation of German Jews (1933–1935); replaced by the *Jüdischer Kulturbund in Deutschland* [Jewish Cultural Federation in Germany]; see also *Jüdische Kulturbund*
Kultusgemeinde	see *Israelitische Kultusgemeinde*
Kultusverband	Jewish Association of Cultural Affairs
Kultusvorsteher	Jewish community council chairman and/or member(s)
Kündigung	notice to quit
Küster	see *Synagogendiener*
KZ	see *Konzentrationslager*
L'Univers Israélite	Jewish Universe; weekly journal published in Paris 1844–?1939
Lagerältester	camp elder
Lagerführer	camp leader
Lagerkommandant	camp commandant
Landesgericht	regional court
Landeshauptmann	state governor

Landesverwaltungsver- abbr. *LVO*; regional authority regulation
ordnung

Landungsgeld   landing money; charge paid by relatives of Jewish refugees living outside of Germany, upon the refugee's arrival in the country to which they have emigrated

Lazarett   usually: military hospital

Legationssekretär   legation secretary

Legitimationskarte   identity card

Lehrhaus   Jewish house of study

Leopoldstadt   name of the *II. Bezirk* [second district] in central Vienna, on the west bank of the River Danube, first granted to the Jews in 1624; by 1923 Jews comprised almost 40% of its inhabitants
                        Source: Wikipedia

LVO   see *Landesverwaltungsverordnung*

Machtergreifung   Hitler's seizure of full power following his appointment by the President, Paul von Hindenburg, as *Reichskanzler* [Reich Chancellor] on 30 January 1933

Mannschaft   team; see also *Wachmannschaft*

Marechaussee   Dutch and Belgian police performing military and civilian duties

Mein Kampf   My Struggle; autobiographical book by Adolf Hitler, published in 1925, containing his ideas, beliefs and plans for the future of Germany
                        Source: Jewish Virtual Library

Ministerialdirektor   senior government official

minyan   Hebrew: quorum; ten adult Jewish males must be present for public worship

mitzvah   Hebrew: commandment; good deed

Mogen Dovid   also *Magen David*; Yiddish: *Mogein Dovids*; (lit. Shield of David); Star of David; two overlaid equilateral triangles form a six-pointed star; historically a common symbol in the Middle East and North Africa, which was never an exclusively Jewish symbol; it was adopted as the emblem of the Zionist movement in 1897 and continued to be controversial for many years afterward; the yellow badge that Jews were forced to wear in Nazi-occupied Europe invested the Star of David with a symbolism indicating martyrdom and heroism; it was used in badges on prisoners' uniforms in Nazi concentration camps; see also prisoner badges
                        Source: Encyclopædia Britannica Online, 'Star of David'; Jewish Virtual Library

Morgan, Paul	(1886–1938); prominent and successful Austrian cabaret director and film actor; arrested in March 1938 for his anti-Nazi cabarets; sent to Dachau then Buchenwald, where he died in December 1938 Source: ORT, Music and the Holocaust (online)
Munich Agreement [Pact]	agreement signed by Hitler, Chamberlain, Mussolini and Daladier on 30 September 1938 in Munich for Czechoslovakia to cede the Sudetenland to Germany in return for Hitler pledging peace; see also Sudetenland
Nathan Israel	Kaufhaus Nathan Israel; Nathan Israel department store; founded in 1813, became one of the largest retail establishments in Europe by 1930
N. N.	abbr. for Latin: *nomen nominandum* [name to be confirmed]
Nazionalsozialistische Deutsche Arbeiterpartei	abbr. *NSDAP* [National Socialist German Workers' Party; Nazi Party]; state party of the German National Socialist dictatorship; founded in 1919 as the *Deutsche Arbeiterpartei (DAP)* [German Workers Party]; Hitler joined the DAP in 1919, became its head of propaganda in 1920 and helped to draw up its anti-semitic, anti-Versailles Treaty manifesto; the Party was renamed *NSDAP* in 1920 and Hitler became its chairman and Führer in 1921
Nationalsozialistische Frauenschaft	National Socialist Women's League; founded in October 1931 as an umbrella body for several national and National Socialist women associations; it was declared the only official Nazi Party organisation for women and had a membership of 2.3 million, led by Gertrud Scholtz-Klink; members had to attend at least one evening meeting per month; the focus was the preparation of women for their duties as house keepers and mothers Source: Deutsches Historisches Museum
Nationalsozialistisches Kraftfahrkorps	abbr. *NSKK*; National Socialist Motor Corps; paramilitary organisation within the Nazi Party (1931–1945)
Nazi Party	see *Nazionalsozialistische Deutsche Arbeiterpartei*
Nederlands Kinder Comité	Dutch Children's Committee; see also *Comité*
Nederlandsche Nationaal Socialist, De	The Dutch National Socialist; official newspaper of the *Nationaal-Socialistische Arbeiderspartij* [Dutch Nazi party]
Neu-Bentschen	town in Upper Silesia; now Zbąszynek, Poland; see *Polenaktion*
Neue Freie Presse	New Free Press; daily newspaper published in Vienna from 1844 until the *Anschluß* [annexation of Austria] in March 1938

Neue Zürcher Zeitung	abbr. *NZZ*; New Zurich Newspaper; internationally well-regarded daily German-language paper published since 1780; daily since 1869; banned in Nazi Germany from 1934
Neues Wiener Tagblatt	New Vienna Daily Paper; published 1867–1945; from 1938 a vehicle for Nazi propaganda
Notarrest	emergency detention (unit); in Vienna Karajangasse and Kenyongasse were two of the *Notarreste*; two others were Sofiensäle, on Marxergasse, Vienna III., a concert hall that continued in use after November 1938 as a *Sammelstelle* [collecting point] for people being deported; at Pramergasse, Vienna IX. the police *Reitschule* [rider training school] was used to detain Jews; see also Karajangasse; Kenyongasse
	Source: http://www.planet-vienna.com/spots/ sofiensaele/sofiensaele.htm; Christa Mehany-Mitterrutzner, 'Vor 75 Jahren: Novemberpogrom 1938', Österreich Journal, 125 (12.11.2013), pp. 32, 34
Notgefängnis	emergency prison
Notgemeinschaft deutscher Wissenschaftler im Ausland	Emergency Association of German Scientists Abroad; self-help organisation founded in 1933 by Philipp Schwartz (who had himself fled to Switzerland) for German scholars abroad, which acted as an intermediary for jobseekers without regard to race or creed
	Source: Christian-Albrechts-Universität zu Kiel
Novemberaktion	November operation; see *Novemberpogrom*
Novemberjuden	November Jews; Jews arrested during the *Novemberpogrom*
Novemberpogrom	November pogrom; also *Novemberaktion* [November operation], *Kristallnacht* [Night of Broken Glass]; *Reichskristallnacht* [Reich Night of Broken Glass];
	Terminology: each of these terms is problematic because (a) some dispute that this was a 'pogrom' which they regard as 'exterminatory violence against a social group',rather than 'state-directed terror against the Jews'; (b) some wish to avoid Nazi vocabulary, for example the word '*Aktion*'; (c) some wish to avoid the term 'Kristallnacht' because they regard it as misrepresenting what happened by implying only windows were broken, thus diminishing the extent and severity of the murders and other harms caused to the Jews; see also *Volkswut*; the OED offers two definitions for 'pogrom': (i) In Russia, Poland, and some other East European countries in the late 19th and early 20th centuries: an organized massacre aimed at the destruction or annihilation of a body or class of people, esp. one conducted against Jewish people; (ii) an organized, officially tolerated, attack on any community or group.

The events: on the night of 9–10 November 1938 in hundreds of towns and villages in Germany and Austria, thousands of Jews were simultaneously terrorised, persecuted and victimised; antisemitic persecution and mistreatment had already occurred before those dates through the increasing restrictions and disenfranchisement of Jews in Germany and Austria, a wave of arrests in June 1938, the expulsion of Polish-born Jews from Germany to the border with Poland in October 1938; that last event prompted Herschel Grynszpan's mortal attack on German diplomat Ernst vom Rath in Paris on 7 November 1938, which was the pretext for the November incidents, in which a centrally orchestrated attack was unleashed upon the Jews: over 1,200 synagogues were desecrated, looted and burned, thousands of Jewish shops, businesses and homes were damaged and looted,countless individuals were attacked, abused and beaten; over 90 people were killed; over 25,000 men were arrested, deported and detained in the concentration camps at Buchenwald, Dachau and Sachsenhausen for months, where they were brutally tortured and mistreated; many more died there

NSDAP	see *Nazionalsozialistische Deutsche Arbeiterpartei*
NSKK	see *Nationalsozialistisches Kraftfahrkorps*
Nuremberg Laws	the Reich Citizenship Law and the Law for the Protection of German Blood and German Honour were adopted on 15 September 1935, depriving Jews of citizenship and barring them from flying the German flag; Jewish families employing a Christian household servant under the age of 45 could be convicted of racial contamination, as could any couple circumventing the law by marrying abroad; mixed marriages and all sexual relations between Jews and non-Jews, which were said to contaminate the race, were forbidden; related regulations defined a Jew as someone with three or four Jewish grandparents, and removed Jews from all spheres of German political, social, and economic life

> Source: Mémorial de la Shoah; Jewish Virtual Library

Oberbaurat Ing.	senior architect and engineer
Oberführer-SS	see *SS-Oberführer*
Obergruppenführer-SS	see *SS-Obergruppenführer*
Oberlandesgerichtsrat	senior lawyer at the regional high court and court of appeal

Oberschammes   Hebrew: *Shammash;* servant; German/Yiddish: senior
                          synagogue attendant
Oberscharführer-SS   see *SS-Oberscharführer*
Obersturmbannführer-   see *SS-Obersturmbannführer*
SS
Optionsrecht   option to move from Czechoslovakia to Germany
                          before the end of March 1939; see Article 7 of Munich
                          Agreement, 29 September 1938
Oranienburg   now Oranienburg bei Berlin, about 40 kilometres north
                          of Berlin; German concentration camp set up in an
                          abandoned brewery in central Oranienburg during
                          1933 and closed in 1934; later there was a satellite camp
                          of the main concentration camp at Sachsenhausen at
                          the Heinkel-Werke in Oranienburg from 1943 to 1945
                          (prisoners had been working there since 1939), also
                          referred to as Oranienburg; see also Sachsenhausen
Ordensburg   (lit. castle of the [medieval, knightly] order); elite Nazi
                          training establishment for military leaders, open only
                          to the landed nobility
Ortsgruppenleiter-SS   see *SS-Ortsgruppenleiter*
Ostmark   Eastern Marches; originally eastern territories of the
                          German Empire ceded to Poland in 1919; applied to
                          Austria between 1938 and 1942, after which the desig-
                          nation was forbidden
Packgenehmigung   packing permit
Palästina-Amt   Palestine office; offices set up in most European capi-
                          tals and exit ports by the World Zionist Organisation
                          from 1918, later under the aegis of the Jewish Agency,
                          to handle the organisation, regulation, and imple-
                          mentation of Jewish immigration to Palestine; see
                          also *Hilfsverein der deutschen Juden*
Palästina-Behörde   Palestine Authority
Palästina-Pionier   organisation active across Europe training young
                          people for relocation to Palestine
Papiermark   (lit. paper mark); German currency (1914–1923) as
                          coins and banknotes; see also *Reichsmark; Sperrmark;
                          Haavarmark*
Pappenheim, Bertha   (1859–1936); founder of Jewish girls' home in Isen-
                          burg [now Neu-Isenburg] near Frankfurt am Main;
                          founder of the *Jüdischer Frauenbund* [League of
                          Jewish Women]; received psychological treatment
                          from Josef Breuer written up as Anna O. in Breuer
                          and Sigmund Freud's Studies in Hysteria (1895)
Parteigenosse   abbr. *PG*; party member
Passus   passage; release form
Pfg.   abbr. for *Pfennig*; penny; 1/100 of the RM

PG	abbr. for *Parteigenosse*
Polenaktion	operation in Poland; in mid-October 1938 a Polish decree was issued cancelling passports of Poles living abroad who did not obtain a special authorisation to re-enter Poland by the end of the month; over 30,000 Jews living in Germany and 20,000 in Austria were born in Poland and this decree seized their Polish nationality and made them stateless on 1 November 1938; the Nazi government in Germany did not wish to absorb this population, and on 27–28 October 1938 the police and the SS arrested and transported about 17,000 to Neu-Bentschen, near the Polish border town of Zbąszyń, 90 kilometres west of Poznan and 110 kilometres east of Frankfurt an der Oder; the Polish border police sent them back; they were stuck in no man's land close to Zbąszyń; a few with relatives in Poland were admitted; in January 1939 following negotiations between Germany and Poland, Jews with family members living in Poland were allowed to join them; the others were allowed to return to Germany in small groups to sell their businesses and emigrate; approximately 16,000 Polish Jews were expelled from Germany in this way; see also Grynszpan, Herschel
	Source: Mémorial de la Shoah; Bundesarchiv: Memorial Book (with further details at http://www.bundesarchiv.de/gedenkbuch/zwangsausweisung.html.en?page=1)
Politischer Häftling	political prisoner; mainly communists, also social democrats, liberals, conservatives and some former NSDAP; denoted by a red triangle on their clothing, which until 1939 was seen as a badge of honour for enemies of the fascist regime
	Source: Gertrude Schneider, Exile and Destruction: The Fate of Austrian Jews, 1938–1945, Greenwood Publishing Group, 1995, p 19
Polizeiarrest	police detention
Polizeigefängnis	police prison; police cells
Polizeihauptmann	police captain
Polizeipräsident	Chief of Police
Polizeipräsidium	police headquarters
Polizeirevier	police station
Polizeiverfügung	police order
Polizeiwagen	police car/vehicle
Pritsche	plank bed; sometimes bunk bed
Privataktion des Führers	personal operation by the Führer [leader]
Prokurist	authorised signatory, proxy; company secretary

Prügelstrafe auf dem Bock	flogging on the whipping block
Quinta	Latin: fifth; second year of schooling in German grammar school
Rassenschande	racial disgrace, defilement; Nazi term for sexual relations between Aryans and non-Aryans, punishable by law; initially it referred to relations between Germans and Jews, later to relations between Germans and all foreigners brought into the Third Reich as slave workers
	Source: Gregory Wegner, Anti-Semitism and Schooling under the Third Reich, Routledge, 2002, p 64
Rathaus	town hall
Referent Reg. Rat	*Referent Regierungsrat*; consultant (senior) civil servant
Reg. Rat.	see *Regierungsrat*
Regierungsbaurat	building officer employed by the government
Regierungsrat	civil servant
Reibekolonne	scrubbing or cleaning gang; arrestees or prisoners forced to wash pavements and walls
Reichsbank	German central bank 1876–1945
Reichsbannerführer	leader of the *Reichsbanner Schwarz-Rot-Gold* [Reich banner black-red-gold], a political organisation and paramilitary force associated with the German Social Democratic Party
Reichsbund jüdischer Frontsoldaten	Reich Association of Jewish Front-line Soldiers
Reichsdeutsche	Germans of the Reich; Nazi term for ethnic German citizens living in the German state following unification in 1871, as contrasted with *Volksdeutsche*, ethnic Germans born outside of Germany
Reichsfluchtsteuer	see *Fluchtsteuer*
Reichsführer-SS	highest rank within the SS; see also Himmler, Heinrich
Reichsführung-SS	SS High Command
Reichskriminalamt	Reich Criminal Investigation Office; central office of the *Kriminalpolizei*; a department within the *Reichssicherheitshauptamt* (RHSA) [Reich Security Main Office]
Reichskristallnacht	see *Novemberpogrom*
Reichsmark	abbr. RM; German currency (1924–1948); see also *Papiermark; Sperrmark; Haavarmark*
Reichsnährstand	Reich Food Corporation; statutory corporation of farmers and other food producers in Nazi Germany; set up in 1933 to control production, distribution and prices of agricultural products
	Source: Deutsches Historisches Museum

Reichspost	Reich postal service
Reichsstelle für Wanderungswesen	Reich Office for Emigration Affairs
Reichsvertretung	*Reichsvertretung der Juden in Deutschland* [Reich Deputation of Jews in Germany] (1933–35); chairman Leo Baeck, director Otto Hirsch; renamed *Reichsverband der Juden in Deutschland* [Reich Federation of Jews in Germany] (1935–39) and *Reichsvereinigung der Juden in Deutschland* [Reich Association of Jews in Germany] (1939–43); before the *Novemberpogrom* it was a federation of Jewish organisations and regional and local Jewish communities that aimed to provide a unified voice for German Jewry in dealing with the Nazi authorities; it was then taken into the *Reichssicherheitshauptamt* (RHSA) [Reich Security Main Office] and supervised the communication to and implementation by the Jewish community of Nazi laws and regulations
	Source: Wikipedia; Archiveshub
Reichswirtschaftsgerichtsrat	state counsel for commerce; the Reichswirtschaftsgericht [Imperial Commercial Court] was established in 1915 to deal with disputes related to the expropriation of civilian property to finance the war effort; it became part of the *Reichsverwaltungsgericht* [Reich Administrative Court] in 1941 Source: Wikipedia
Reichswirtschaftsministerium	Reich Ministry of Economic Affairs
Rein-Arier	see *Arier*
Reiselegitimationskarte	travel permit
Remigrant	re-emigrant; category of prisoner in concentration camp who had returned to Germany after emigrating abroad
Revier	sick bay in concentration camp
RM	see *Reichsmark*
Rollen	(lit. rolls); punishment in concentration camp; in Sachsenhausen the prisoner had to roll over and over on the ground down a hill: see also *zur roten Fahne*
Rollkommando	raiding party
Rosenberg, Alfred	(1893–1946); leading Nazi propagandist, editor of the daily paper *Völkischer Beobachter* [National Observer]; in charge of Nazi looting of works of art; *Reichsminister für die besetzten Ostgebiete* [Reich Minister for the Occupied Eastern Territories] from 1941; tried for war crimes in Nuremberg and executed in 1946

roten Fahne, zur	see *zur roten Fahne*
Rückwanderer	see *Remigrant*
S-Bahn	*Stadtschnellbahn* [city rapid railway]; urban transportation network
SA	*Sturmabteilung*; Storm Detachment or Assault Division; storm troopers or brown shirts; original paramilitary wing of the Nazi Party
Sachsenhausen	sometimes Sachsenhausen-Oranienburg, i.e. Sachsenhausen bei Oranienburg, later a suburb of Oranienburg; German concentration camp founded in 1936, 40 kilometres north of Berlin near the town of Oranienburg; prisoners were brought to Sachsenhausen via both Oranienburg and Sachsenhausen railway stations; there was a separate concentration camp at Oranienburg; see also Oranienburg
Salzgasse	(lit. salt alley); a torture method used in concentration camps, making a person go along a double row of fellow inmates who have to beat him with clubs

    Source: Felix Mitterer, 'Drei Geschichten über Kinder, und wie es weiter ging', ESRA-Lesung, 16.11.04, Context XXI, 3–4/2005, 4: "Danach muss er durch die "Salzgasse" gehen. Dabei stehen links und rechts aufgereiht die anderen Kinder, mit Stöcken in den Händen, und schlagen auf den durchmarschierenden Delinquenten ein."

    "The name might just be a case of random euphemisms; many Jewish quarters had a Salzgasse, as in the middle ages, trading (salt) was one of the professions that they were allowed, and the roads with Salz in their name in Vienna are close to the Judengasse."

    Source: Wiener Library

Sammellager	assembly camp
Sammelstation	assembly point
Sammeltransport	group transport; see also *Sonderzug*
Sanitäter	medical orderly
Sanitätspersonal	medical orderlies
Sanitätsrat	medical consultant
Saujud	Jewish pig/swine; see *Judensau* and antisemitic insults
Scharführer-SS	see *SS-Scharführer*
Schiva	*Shiva*; also: *Schiwo*; from Hebrew: seven; Jewish customary period of seven days' mourning
Schlafpritsche	see *Pritsche*
Schupo	abbr. for *Schutzpolizei*
Schuschnigg, Kurt	Chancellor of Austria from 29 July 1934 to 11 March 1938

Schutzhaft	so-called protective custody; the arrest without judicial review of real and potential opponents of the Nazi regime; such prisoners were not confined within the normal prison system but in concentration camps under the exclusive authority of the SS; see also *Vorbeugungshaft* Source: USHMM
Schutzhaftbefehl	so-called protective custody order
Schutzhaftjuden	Jews in so-called protective custody
Schutzpolizei	lit. protection police; abbr. *Schupo*; uniformed police
Schutzstaffel	see SS
Schutztruppe	so-called protection force
Schwarze Korps, Das	The Black Corps; official SS weekly newspaper (1935–1945)
Schweigepflicht	duty of confidentiality
Schwein	see antisemitic insults
Schweizer Israelitischer Gemeindebund	abbr. *S. I. G.*; Swiss Jewish Community Federation
Sesshaftmachung	creation of residence
Shabbos	Yiddish: sabbath
Sicherheitspolizei	abbr. *Sipo*; security police; see also *Gestapo; Kriminalpolizei*
Sicherungsverwahrung	so-called preventive detention
S. I. G.	see *Schweizer Israelitischer Gemeindebund*
Sipo	see *Sicherheitspolizei*
Sonderaktionsjuden	special operation Jews; sometimes *Aktionsjuden* [Jews arrested in the *Juni-Aktion* and/or the *Novemberpogrom*]
Sonderzug	special train; see also *Sammeltransport*
Sozialamt	see *Jüdisches Sozialamt*
Spartacist uprising	general strike in Germany in January 1919, in which left wing groups mounted an armed protest against the government led by Friedrich Ebert and were violently suppressed
Sperrmark	blocked Marks; the removal of Reichsmarks from Germany was prohibited; the government placed the liquid assets of German Jews who had emigrated in special *Sperrkonten* [blocked accounts] which contained *Sperrmarks*, of little value outside Germany; the rate of exchange for converting *Reichsmarks* to *Sperrmarks* was cut from about 37% in 1935 to about 10% in 1938, by which time the transfer of any funds of Jewish and most foreign emigrants was prohibited; see also *Reichsmark; Papiermark; Haavarmark; Fluchtsteuer; Golddiskontbank*

Source: Brian Amkraut, Between home and Homeland: Youth Aliyah from Nazi Germany, University of Alabama Press, 2006, pp 89, 191 n133; Jewish Telegraphic Agency, 28 September 1936 and 9 June 1938

SS	*Schutzstaffel*; Defence or Protection Squad; established 1923 as Hitler's personal guard, later transformed by Heinrich Himmler into major paramilitary organisation of the Nazi Party
SS-Blockführer	SS concentration camp block leader
SS-Führer	SS leader
SS-Oberführer	SS senior leader, equivalent rank to brigadier general
SS-Obergruppenführer	SS senior group leader; senior SS rank
SS-Oberscharführer	SS sergeant
SS-Obersturmbann-führer	SS rank equivalent to a lieutenant colonel in the German army; also used by SA
SS-Ortsgruppenleiter	SS local area leader; local representative of the Gauleiter
SS-Reichsführer	see *Reichsführer-SS*
SS-Reichsführung	see *Reichsführung-SS*
SS-Scharführer	SS company leader; staff sergeant
SS-Standartenfüher	SS standard leader; SS colonel
SS-Sturm	SS troop
SS-Sturmbannführer	SS rank equivalent to major in the German army; also used by SA
SS-Sturmführer	SS rank equivalent to lieutenant in the German army; also used by SA
SS-Sturmhauptführer	SS rank equivalent to captain in the German army; also used by SA
SS-Verfügungstruppe	SS combat support troop; auxiliary troops formed in 1934, renamed *Waffen-SS* [Armed SS] in 1940
Staatsanwaltschaft	public prosecutor's office
Staatspolizei	abbr. *Stapo*; state police
Stabsarzt	(army) medical officer
Stadthausierschein	city hawker's licence
Stadtpräsident	mayor
Stahlhelm, Der	steel helmet; *Bund der Frontsoldaten*: League of Front Line Soldiers; German paramilitary nationalist organisation (1918–1935)
Standartenfüher-SS	see *SS-Standartenfüher*
Stapo	see *Staatspolizei*
Stehappell	standing roll call
stehen am Tor	standing to attention by the gate; punishment in Sachsenhausen concentration camp
Stehrapport	reporting to inspection patrols in concentration camp
Steuerbestätigung	tax confirmation certificate

Steuerunbedenklichkeit	see *Unbedenklichkeitsbescheinigung*
Steuerverwaltung	tax administration; see *Finanzamt*
Strafdienst	punishment duty
Strafe des Baumhängens	see *Baumhängen*
Strafexerzieren	see *Exerzieren*
Strafkompanie	punishment company
Strafmilliarde	see *Judenvermögensabgabe*
Strafprozessordnung	criminal procedure code
Streicher, Julius	founder and publisher of antisemitic tabloid weekly newspaper *Der Stürmer* [The Striker]; Nazi Gauleiter of Franconia; see also *Stürmer, Der*
Stubenältester	room elder in concentration camp
Stunde, Die	The Hour; daily newspaper published in Vienna from 2 February 1923 to the *Anschluß* [annexation of Austria] in March 1938
Sturm-SS	see *SS-Sturm*
Sturmabteilung	see *SA*
Sturmbannführer-SS	see *SS-Sturmbannführer*
Sturmführer-SS	see *SS-Sturmführer*
Sturmhauptführer-SS	see *SS-Sturmhauptführer*
Stürmer, Der	The Fighter; weekly antisemitic tabloid newspaper (1923–1945) founded and published by Julius Streicher; it was an influential element in Nazi propaganda
Sudetenland	Germany demanded the return of the Sudetenland, a border area of Czechoslovakia containing a majority ethnic German population; in late Summer 1938 Hitler threatened Europe with war unless the Sudetenland with its German population was ceded to Germany; leaders of Britain, France, Italy and Germany held a conference in Munich on 29–30 September 1938 and signed the Munich Pact allowing Germany to annex the Sudetenland in exchange for Hitler's pledge of peace; nevertheless on 15 March 1939 Nazi Germany invaded and occupied the Czech provinces of Bohemia and Moravia and turned them into a German Protectorate; see also Munich Pact Source: Yad Vashem
Sühneleistung	reparations; an extra tax paid by Jews to the German state after the *Novemberpogrom*; see also *Judenkontribution* and *Judenvermögensabgabe*
Synagogendiener	synagogue sexton
Syndikus	legal adviser
tallit	Jewish prayer shawl
Tempel	temple; synagogue of Reform Judaism

Tempelverein	Temple Society; community of Reform Judaism
Thorarollen	Torah scrolls; the most sacred Jewish ritual object; the Five Books of Moses inscribed by hand on the specially prepared skin of a kosher animal; in the Ashkenazi tradition the scribe writes with a quill on parchment; the Sefardi scribe uses a reed to write on parchment or leather
	Source: Jewish Virtual Library
Tischältester	table elder; most senior person at meal table in concentration camp
Tor stehen, am	see *stehen am Tor*
Totenkopfverbände	Death's-Head units of the SS, founded in 1936 to administer the concentration camps, led by Theodor Eicke, first *Kommandant* of Dachau who directed the design, operation and training for all concentration camps until 1940; *Totenkopfverbände* troops were trained to be extremely harsh towards prisoners
Transitaufenthalt	transit residence
Überwachungsbeamter der Zollstellen	customs officer supervisor
Umsatzsteuer	turnover tax levied on businesses
Unbedenklichkeitsbescheinigung	(lit. certificate of non-objection); tax clearance certificate; needed by Jews seeking to emigrate
Unbedenklichkeitsschein	see *Unbedenklichkeitsbescheinigung*
Unterwerfungsverfahren	submission process in connection with the financial arrangements imposed on Jews who wanted to retain precious metal or jewellery items
Verfügungsberechtiger	person with power of disposal
Verfügungstruppe-SS	see *SS-Verfügungstruppe*
Vergeltungsmaßregel	retribution measure
Verhaftungsaktion	arrests operation
Verhaftungswelle	see *Verhaftungsaktion*
Verkehrsfalle	traffic trap; ".... it was for some time the practice in this police district that Jewish looking persons, who had allegedly disregarded the traffic regulations when crossing the Kurfürstendamm, were taken to the police station..."
	Source: AJR Information, VI/2, February 1951, p 7
Vermögensabgabe	see *Judenvermögensabgabe*
Vermögensanmeldung	see *Judenvermögensanmeldung*

Verwundetenabzeichen	wound badge; military decoration initially awarded to German Army soldiers wounded in World War I, reinstituted by Hitler in May 1939 for German volunteers wounded in the Spanish Civil War (1936–1939), and awarded during World War II; the badge was similar to that of World War I with a swastika added to the steel helmet Source: Jean-Denis G.G. Lepage, An Illustrated Dictionary of the Third Reich, McFarland, 2013, p 193
Vienna	Wien; capital city of Austria; see *Anschluß*; Auernheimer; Dolfuss; Elisabethpromenade; *Gildemeester-Aktion; Grüne Heinrich, Der;* Karajangasse; Kenyongasse; Leopoldstadt; *Neue Freie Presse; Neues Wiener Tagblatt; Notarrest; Schuschnigg; Wahrheit, Die; Stunde, Die; Wiener Tag*
Vierjahresplan	four year plan; economic reforms (1936–1940) to make Germany self-sufficient
Vizebürgermeister	deputy mayor
Vizekommandant	Vice Commandant; also *Vizelagerkommandant*
Vizelagerkommandant	Camp Vice Commandant; also *Vizekommandant*
Völkischer Beobachter	National Observer; daily newspaper (1923–1945) published by the Nazi Party and owned by Hitler; edited by Alfred Rosenberg, a leading Nazi and antisemite
Volksseele	see *Volkswut*
Volksverräter	traitor against the people
Volkswut	people's rage; in the *Novemberpogrom* context the term was used sceptically by Jews who regarded that outbreak of violence and persecution against them and their communities as being officially directed and coordinated rather than having arisen spontaneously and locally in the mass population; the term *kochende Volksseele* [seething populace] is also cited sceptically in some of the testimonies
Volkszorn	see *Volkswut*
vom Rath, Ernst	(1909–1938); a third secretary at the German legation in Paris, shot on 7 November 1938 by Herschel Grynszpan, a Polish Jew living in Paris, in protest against the recent banishment of Polish Jews living in Germany (including his parents) to beyond the Polish border; vom Rath died on 9 November and the Nazis took this as a pretext for the *Novemberpogrom*; he was buried in Düsseldorf on 15 November; in the week of the funeral special restrictions and punishments were imposed for Jewish prisoners in concentration camps Source: Mémorial de la Shoah

Vorarbeiter	foreman in charge of a work group of concentration camp prisoners
Vorbeter	prayer leader
Vorbeugungshaft	preventive custody of those with previous convictions; see also *Schutzhaft*
Vorgesetzter	supervisor
Vorladung	summons
Vorsteher	chairman(men) and/or council member(s)
Vorvisum	preliminary visa
Wach- und Schließgesellschaft	security company
Wachbeamter	*Waffen-SS*
Wachmannschaft	guard team; see also *Mannschaft*
Waffen-SS	Armed SS; see also *SS-Verfügungstruppe*
Wahrheit, Die	The Truth; weekly Austrian Jewish newspaper published in Vienna 1885 until the *Anschluß* [annexation of Austria] in March 1938; Oskar Hirschfeld (see Glossary) was its last editor
Weimar	town in Thuringia; Buchenwald concentration camp was 10 kilometres north west of Weimar
Wiener Library	see Jewish Central Information Office
Wiener Tag	Vienna Day; daily newspaper published in Vienna until the *Anschluß* [annexation of Austria] in March 1938
Winterhilfswerk des deutschen Volkes	abbr. *WHW* and *Winterhilfe*; Winter Relief for the German People; Nazi-controlled relief agency for non-Jewish German people in need of material support
Wippen	squats or *Kniebeugen* [knee-bends]; a punishment exercise
Wunderrabbi	erudite rabbi who could work miracles
Zählappell	roll call count of prisoners in concentration camps; see also *Appell*
Zeitschrift für die Geschichte der Juden in Deutschland	Journal of the History of the Jews in Germany, published in Berlin from 1887 until it was banned in November 1938
	Source: CompactMemory.de
Zentner	hundredweight; c. 50 kilograms
Zerstörungsaktion	destruction operation
Zerstörungskolonne	see *Zerstörungstrupp*
Zerstörungstrupp	destruction squad
Zertifikat	certificate
Zertrümmerungsaktion	see *Zerstörungsaktion*
Zionistische Rundschau	Zionist Review; weekly journal of the *Zionistischer Landesverband für Deutschösterreich* published between 20 May 1938 and 4 November 1938

Zionistische Vereinigung für Deutschland	Zionist Union for Germany; founded in 1894 by Max Bodenheimer; it promoted emigration to Palestine rather than further assimilation in Germany; it was banned after November 1938 Source: Arbeitskreis Shoa.de e.V.
Zollfahndung	customs investigation department
Zollfahndungsstelle	customs investigation office
Zuchthaus	prison normally administered by the regular legal apparatus rather than the SS; some were used as temporary detention centres for people arrested in the *Novemberpogrom*; usual *Zuchthaus* sentences were harsher and much longer than *Gefängnis* sentences; by June 1935 almost 28,000 (about 25% of all prisoners in Germany) were serving *Zuchthaus* sentences Source: Nikolaus Wachsmann: Hitler's Prisons: Legal Terror in Nazi Germany, Yale UP, 2004
zur roten Fahnen	to the red flags; punishment in Sachsenhausen concentration camp: In Sachsenhausen *"Rollen"* [rolling] was practised; during their work, prisoners were not allowed to cross a line marked by small flags; prospective victims were made to walk to the top of a hill and were commanded to "lie down and roll"; those made to roll had to brake their bodies before the flag boundary; vigorous individuals succeeded as long as they had not become dizzy; to induce dizziness, the procedure of walking up and rolling down the hill was repeated many times, until the rolling body rolled over the flag boundary; then they were shot Source: Wiener Library, *Novemberpogrom* eyewitness account B. 330
Zwangsarbeit	forced labour; the imposition of work duties on prisoners; over 20 million foreign civilian workers, concentration camp prisoners and prisoners of war from all the occupied countries had to perform forced labour in Germany between 1940 and 1945; Germany's agriculture and armaments industries relied on them and most other sectors also used them Source: USHMM; Freie Universität Berlin; Stiftung Topographie des Terrors
Zwangsnamen	compulsory first names; from 1 January 1939 Jewish women and men were compelled by Nazi decree to take the additional first name of Sara and Israel respectively; see also *Israelitisch*
Zwilchanzug	cotton drill uniform; drill, a strong woven cotton fabric, has long been used for military and other uniforms; see also *Drillichanzüge*

LIST OF SELECTED NAMED INDIVIDUALS

1.1. Reporters (alphabetical)

1.1.2. Reporters (numerical)

INDEX

PART II

PRESS REPORTS 1938–39

Neue Zürcher Zeitung, 10 November 1938
Assassination in the German Embassy
in Paris

Retaliatory action against the German Jews – Arson in the synagogues – Looting

Legation Secretary vom Rath dead

Paris, 9th Nov. (*United Press* telegram) The German Legation Secretary vom Rath died today at 5.25 am.

Berlin, 9th Nov. agency (*DRB [Deutsche Presse Bureau*; Reich Press Bureau]) The French Chargé d'affaires has expressed his sympathy on behalf of the French Government, the French President and the Foreign Minister on the death of Legation Secretary vom Rath.

Paris, 10th Nov. agency (*Havas*) Following the news of the death of Legation Secretary vom Rath, the President of the Republic, the Prime Minister and the Foreign Minister have expressed their sympathy to the German Ambassador. A commemorative service took place in the Protestant Church, at which the German Ambassador spoke. The body was taken from the clinic to the Embassy and laid out there.

Paris 10th Nov. (*United Press* telegram) The death of the German Legation Secretary has made a considerable impression upon the French population. In right-wing circles, there are signs of a growing antisemitic and concurrently xenophobic movement, which is finding expression in pamphleting and placards and is directed with particular vehemence at immigrants living in France. That is, the French Government has prepared new regulations concerning the residence permit [*Aufenthaltserlaubnis*] for aliens in France, and has tightened police checks concerning aliens.

The charge against Grynszpan, following the death of his victim, will probably be changed to murder; hitherto it was attempted manslaughter.

Tightening of Jewish Policy in Germany

Berlin, 9th Nov. (Telegram from our Senior Correspondent) The Jewish question is assuming-ever greater significance in Germany. Negotiations between Germany and Poland concerning the settlement of the fate of 8,000 Jews deported from the Reich had almost been decided when the assassination in the Embassy in Paris became known; they then suffered from the news of retaliation and have never since got back on track. Both Governments had agreed in principle that those Jews deported could temporarily return to Germany, in order to settle their affairs and take moveable possessions with them. Their money is to be paid into a joint account and, after a clearing period, converted into Polish currency at an as yet undetermined rate of exchange on their return to Poland under the auspices of the Polish Government. The deported Polish people might be able to save half their assets. It was generally accepted that they were happy with this, as, otherwise, Jews emigrating would only keep five to six percent of their assets. Germany has excluded all possibility that those deported Jews could ever return. Since Grynszpan, the 17-year-old Paris assassin, comes from the circle of Polish Jews in Germany, of which there are 50,000 in total, and has sounded the death knell of the reputation of all foreign Jews after general deportation, it now seems questionable whether a Germano-Polish agreement could be reached under the terms mentioned. The *Völkischer Beobachter* has stated today that all Jews in Germany, regardless of whether they possess a German or foreign passport, must be included in atoning for the Paris crime.

The German press reports "substantial spontaneous demonstrations by the population against the Jews" in Kurhessen. Those who are acquainted with the jargon and how it is used in such operations can easily imagine what the events in Kurhessen signify. After riots emerged in Kassel, in which the synagogues were also damaged, a department of the German News Bureau, that has since been dedicated solely to reports from abroad that have not been published in Germany, released a statement that the German authorities would not tolerate any lack of restraint. In the Berlin papers, there are detailed reports concerning the "disarming" of the local Jewish population undertaken by the police, where "a large quantity of weapons" came to light. Those looking around in the capital city of the Reich will more likely receive the impression that local Jews are far from having anything to do with aggressive plans, for the most part no longer venture onto the streets.

*

Berlin, 9th Nov. (agency) The German News Bureau reports that as a result of indignation concerning the assassination in Paris of Legation Secretary vom Rath, statements against the Jews are being made in Hersfeld. Many synagogues went up in flames during raids and were completely burnt down.

Berlin 9th Nov. (pt) *Der Reichsanzeiger* [Reich Advertiser] has published the names of 114 Jews who have forfeited their German nationality.

A Night of Terror in Berlin

Berlin, 10th Nov. (Telegram from our Senior Correspondent). The most terrible wave of antisemitism since the regime change of 1933 swept over Germany last night and early on Thursday morning. In Berlin the synagogues were set alight. The largest Jewish temple in the capital of the Reich, which is situated in Fasanenstraße near to the Kurfürstendamm, was entirely destroyed inside. The three cupolas and the soot-black surrounding walls are still standing, whilst the ceiling joists have collapsed and all windows are shattered. Clouds of smoke were still rising out of the synagogue around midday. A penetrating smell of burning is spreading throughout the whole quarter. The fire brigade had to intervene to prevent the fire spreading further. Early in the afternoon, jets of water from hydrants were still directed at the source of the fire. The fire has been extinguished at the synagogue on Adlerstraße in Charlottenburg, whilst it is reported that other synagogues are still burning.

A systematic, destructive operation with merciless consequences has been directed at Jewish shops and businesses, which have been made identifiable over the last few months by white, 25 centimetre-high inscriptions. The storm began at half past two in the morning. Dark figures infiltrated the streets and started using paving stones to bombard shop windows, from which all the objects suitable as missiles were taken and used to smash the mirrors, glass containers and light fittings. The police remained invisible and also did not answer telephone calls from the angst-ridden business owners, who were sleeping nearby, as is usual with small businesses in Berlin. At half past six in the morning large groups of men mobilised, 8–12 in each, dressed in civilian clothes as a precaution.

All remains of the windows, containers and business desks were smashed to pieces with sticks and iron bars, until the pavement was covered with shards of glass and splinters. Some of the clothes shops were emptied and the stock burnt on the street.

Parts of the Kurfürstendamm, Laurentzienstraße and particularly the Wilmersdorfstraße, where there are still a great many Jewish shops, presented a miserable sight in the morning. Many Jews have fled and have abandoned their shops; others are clearing the debris with a resigned air. Paving stones are still lying about in the shops and on the streets. The contents of a chocolate shop are in a desolate state, scattered on the street; passers-by wade through sweets and confectionery. As far as one knows, insurance companies are not denying their liability for the damage, but are rather advising the aggrieved Jews to board up their shops, as not enough glass is available for the repairs so soon. Those shops unable to board up their windows by this evening have no means with which to protect themselves from looters. Many tenants in private houses that have Jewish shops on the ground floor are worried as they fear arson. The population, to the honour of the German people, it has been said, are, for the most part, disgusted with the excesses and many people on the streets do not hold back their criticism.

*

According to a report from the Havas agency five further synagogues are burning in the West of Berlin.

The German News Bureau reports that throughout Germany in countless places, spontaneous anti-Jewish demonstrations have taken place and in most cities the synagogues have been set on fire by the population. The Havas agency reports the looting of two synagogues in Vienna and the fire at the synagogue in Bayreuth.

Anti-Jewish Riots

Berlin, 10th Nov. (United Press Telegram) Throughout Berlin last night the windows of most of the shops that have not yet been Aryanised were smashed. In many places the street is covered with shards of glass and, in part, also with the letters torn off the business hoardings. However, in numerous cases the flying squad usually arrived too late after the culprits had already disappeared. Nobody has been arrested. Particularly in the West, at Kurfürstendamm and in the centre in Friedrichstraße, many shop windows and, in part, the furniture was wrecked.

Neueste Zeitung, Innsbruck, 10 November 1938

Out with the Jews!

Kth. *Innsbruck*, 10th November.

The Jewish murderer Herschel Feibel Grünspan has now achieved his objective. Legation Secretary vom Rath is lying on the bier. A young German who was doing nothing but his duty abroad was cowardly and maliciously attacked and shot down by a Jewish criminal. Now where is the indignation of the democratic world? The whole mob from all continents *cried out loud* when Germany took justifiable measures to remove Jews from our economy. They cried out about brutal oppression, appealed to humanity and thereby meant money bags. Anywhere in Germany if a stop is put to an immigrant Jew's fraudulent trade, then in an instant there is unanimous wailing from the whole mob of world Jewry. What happened to Isidor in Germany was sympathised with by world Jewry exactly thus in beautiful solidarity, and this sympathy was so stark that in all capital cities and centres of Jewry a large-scale hate campaign against the Third Reich was staged. For years the Jewish Press has pursued an excessive campaign against the person of the Führer, nothing was too vulgar to fan the flames.

This agitation has once more borne sad fruit. Now it is truly high time that the German people finally turn the tables and the whole Jewish population is blamed for the crime of the individual, of the bought subject Grünspan. We have often and for a long time now noted the ever-effective solidarity of world Jewry, Jewry in Germany will now have to atone for this same solidarity. The message is as clear as day: never would the degenerate Jewboy Grünspan have struck with the revolver if his racial comrades in the whole world had not openly and explicitly rushed to murder. We remember the fact all too well, how, after the cowardly murder of Wilhelm Gustloff the Jewish emigrant press glorified the crime of David Frankfurter, the murderer, in glowing editorials. A few hours after the wretched murder, a Jewish newspaper then wrote: "Dear Frankfurter, we love you for your great deed!"

This love will now come to be costly for our Jews. We truly treated the Hebrews in Ostmark with kid gloves after the *Anschluß*, no hair on their heads was harmed, and that we proceeded thus with thoroughly legal means to cleanse our business world of this parasitism is now really our right of self-preservation. We have, of course, on the contrary, been very badly paid for our decency. Now, however we are no longer thinking of looking on watching passively, as cowardly murderers shoot down our Germans abroad like dogs in a row. Justified self-defence compels us today to resort to the only possible means of protection from future bloody deeds available to us: for every crime committed against a German anywhere abroad, the Hebrews, who still enjoy our hospitality, will have to atone for it! We have no more sympathy for Palestine-manners in our country.

Today we hear with disgust that the Jewish rabble is already busy at work cleansing itself free of all guilt. At the Frankfurter murder, it was written that it doubtless concerned a "pitiful" person, who was "abnormal". With Grünspan today they come to the astonishing recognition that the culprit could not be held guilty for his deed, as he is still of "youthful age".

Such Jewish tricks do not bring the Legation Secretary back to life and, as far as the first argument is concerned, we Germans have for a long time been of the view that at least in our eyes and from our point of view all Jews are abnormal. To us, they are unnatural and, admittedly, so unnatural that for the last time we advise them in a peaceful way as quickly as possible and we mean as quickly as possible to pack their things and get out of Germany once and for all. The Jews of the world should not forget one thing: in our veins runs not jam, but blood! The hour can and will come when we will lose our temper once and for all with such cowardly murderers. Then, it will be too late for the Jews!

We too in the Tyrol have all sorts of Jews still and we Tyroleans knowingly allow all kinds of things to happen to us before we really hit back. But, when we do, we really do! Tylorean fists have lost nothing of their power and anyone who has a fair idea of history will understand this threat.

With this "mindless flexing of muscle", it naturally depends upon whether, according to Emil Ludwig Cohn, every German is belligerent and subservient. In the paragraph entitled "French and German Ways" it states:

"When the Frenchman sees something funny, he says "How funny!". The German calls: "That's a riot [*das ist zum Schießen*]!", because he finds the greatest increase in delight in life in shooting [*Schießen*] ..."

The Frenchman loves the cat, which lives its interesting life alone and does not allow itself to be ordered around, just like its master; the German tells his police dog, which obediently asks with its eyes which foe to attack, just like his master ...

How should an understanding be reached if, on the one hand, the national sport is angling, a lonely and quiet game, and on the other the rules are a mutual and loud trade? ...

In Germany, one only has to shout, to gain obedience and respect. Fear and not inclination win a following there, which make the red stripes of the dumbest general blanch.

According to Emil Ludwig Cohn, therefore, the entire German nation longs incessantly for revenge and to exert it around the world! German racial legislation has the strangest principles, according to Emil Ludwig Cohn. In the section entitled "Bombing as a hygienic measure", he states impudently that the German officer regards dropping bombs on the German people as a means of racial improvement. According to the rule that the person in a panic is hit first and the superior person last, the following view was presented by the Air Ministry:

"Losses through bombing will increase as talent decreases. As pitiful as each loss is from a human perspective, this distribution can be understood as an act of racial hygiene."

Against this "State of stupidity, vengeance mania and slavery", Emil Ludwig Cohn calls for war.

The Call to Arms

Then the call to arms resounds: "We are no longer obliged to let ourselves be bullied by the arrogance of chosen people or races. We are coming together and are ready to defend with weapons the rational dealings between competing nations and their new holy alliance. Presidents of all countries, unite!"

The Jew places his greatest hope in Roosevelt: "Roosevelt guards! Since he has been in power he has led the United States in five great demonstrative speeches on the side of the Democrats with an open front against the dictators. As long as he lasts, America will, with all that a great nation and rich country has to offer, wage war against the dictators with everything except with puppets.

"The new holy alliance is possible as each of the three founding States has one, two or three dictator States as its enemy.

"Void of spirit and love, the once so graceful German people today stares full of hate into a world that has become alien. The world waits prepared for the outbreak."

We have intentionally allowed this authoritative Jew to say his piece, in order to picture the frame of mind, just as millions of his racial comrades do who do not grant peace for the world and dream of revenge.

But this dirty business is ever-faster becoming too much, even for those people who conduct their belligerent activities with us with almost incomprehensible patience and false generosity. We have already pointed out that the impregnable bastions of world Jewry have collapsed and disappeared in Prague and Vienna; in Italy the enemy has been identified and in Paris they are at the point of opening their eyes.

Of all papers, the Jewish newspaper *Le Droit de Vivre* has reported on this awakening; the official organ of the Jewish World League and the favourite journal of the murderer David Frankfurter. In a broadsheet edition of this paper it states "Arrest the enemies of Jews!" And then a lament was published, which could not sound more sweetly in our ears. According to information by senior Jews in the World League, mobilisation in the whole of France has led to large scale anti-Jewish demonstrations. "It seems almost to us as though we are breathing German air," the reporter laments.

Westfälische Landeszeitung, Dortmund, 11 November 1938

Demonstrations against Jews
Indignation of the population of West Germany

Cologne. The news of the cowardly treacherous murder in the German Embassy has also evoked clear indignation among the population of Cologne. Everywhere in the old city and the suburbs of Cologne it came to passionate demonstrations against the Jews on Wednesday and Thursday. The anger amongst the population about the Jewish crime was so great that the windows of Jewish businesses everywhere and particularly the synagogues were smashed.

Düsseldorf. Out of sheer disgust at the crime of the murderous clique in Paris, there were already spontaneous rallies against the Jews in the evening hours of Wednesday. The population of Düsseldorf proceeded in large groups through the streets and it is only thanks to their extraordinary discipline that fellow members of the race of the cowardly murderer Grünspan were spared from harm or loss of life. However, the crime in Paris was too inhuman to remain with public chanting. Jewish businesses, which themselves – a sign of the impudence of the chosen people – even in the sixth year of the new Germany make themselves at home in the main shopping streets of Düsseldorf, fell prey to the justified rage of the people.

During the course of Wednesday night the Düsseldorf synagogue was stormed by ever greater crowds of people. The internal fixtures were completely destroyed as a result; later there was a fire. The fire quickly took hold of the entire building, so that the endeavours of the fire brigade could not achieve anything more. Cleansing the inner city of Jewish businesses also continued on Thursday morning.

Essen. Here the synagogue in Steeler Straße was set on fire. The internal fixtures of the building were burned. Likewise the synagogue in the district of Essen-Steele and the youth centre in Moltkeplatz were also set on fire. In the course of the anti-Jewish demonstrations in the centre of Essen on Thursday morning, shop windows of Jewish retail premises were destroyed.

Volksstimme Steyrer, 11 November 1938

Retaliation for the Jewish Murder
All Jews in Protective Custody

The greatest embitterment prevails in German districts concerning the malicious murder in Paris. Once again, it has been played out before our eyes how the Jews not only feel themselves bound through their religion, but that the drive towards world power is at the innermost core of the Jewish people. The cowardly act of the Jewish boy-murderer, Grünspan, give us just cause to say "This far and no further!" We must confront the temerity of world Judaism and give the gang of Jewish criminals their final warning: Our patience is at an end! If the international Jewish string-pullers do not to want to hear, then we will call in the Jews, who still enjoy the protection of the German Reich, to atonement according to the principle of retaliation and then, perhaps, on a value scale a hundred Jews will have to atone for one murdered German.

In order to make this unflinching resolution clear, the SS Reichsführer ordered the arrest of all Jews last night.

Even in Steyr the SS was alerted and all the Jews were hauled from their beds by the men in black. Once again the intricacies of Jewish organisation are displayed, for strangely almost all the male Jews were away on "business". Those Jews found in their homes were taken to the police barracks and held there in order to prevent the justified indignation of the embittered population. This time they were still dealt with politely. But with a repetition we could not undertake to guarantee it further. May this all be a warning: whosoever wilfully resists us will be destroyed.

Westdeutscher Beobachter, Cologne, 11 November 1938

Public anger

Demonstrations against Jews took place in Cologne during yesterday, as in the other German cities. This fact can be regarded as a healthy reaction of the German people to the recent despicable treacherous act of a Jewish murderer towards a German compatriot. In a spontaneous operation, the population of Cologne forced a cessation of business in all Jewish shops in our city, as well as making the Jewish houses of prayer, the synagogues, which still stand as monuments to bygone Jewish power in our city, unfit for further use.

The broadcaster in Lemburg found it necessary to speak about the looting of Jewish shops. On walking through the city we were able to ascertain that the windows and placards on Jewish businesses had indeed been smashed and destroyed. However, nobody has enriched themselves from Jewish property. Moreover, no looters or uncontrollable elements were located there, here German compatriots merely gave expression to their disgust about the murder born from the atmosphere of incitement prompted by international Judaism.

Incidentally, this operation borne of public anger, has supported the extraordinary fact that a huge number of Jewish businesses can still be found in Cologne. Jews in Germany and in Cologne are in no way subject to as much gagging and subservience as those abroad would have one believe. These ladies and gentlemen are above all still doing extraordinarily well economically, an assumption that can be explained in that they are visible in public life time and again.

After the spontaneous demonstration against Jewry by German compatriots is over, we can say this: the National Socialist German government will find further ways and means of applying the various measures of atonement with regard to the representatives of every race who has again outrageously sullied themselves with blood.

Westdeutscher Beobachter, Cologne, 11 November 1938

The People's Answer

Cologne, 11th November

The huge disgust that has seized the German people on the news of the death of the young German diplomat assassinated by the cowardly Jewish murderous hand has prompted spontaneous rallies and demonstrations against Jewry in all German districts. As reports from the Reich say, the windows of many Jewish junk shops were smashed by the disgusted masses in many cities as well as the capital of the Reich, and some Jewish temples too, in which the teachings of the Talmud, songs of hate against everything non-Jewish, were disseminated, have gone up in flames. Judaism has thus for the first time received a clear answer to its hate and slander campaign of many years against Germanness throughout the world, whose victims were Wilhelm Gustloff and now also Party member vom Rath. For years the German people have dispassionately allowed the daily insults of Jews throughout the world to pass over their heads. All of the dirt and filth fabricated in the known centres of immigration of Paris, London and New York, and guided by the Jewish-influenced world press, could not even reach the soles of our feet. We know that the Jewish machinations throughout the world have recently brought the German people to the brink of a war. Even this possibility was anticipated cold-bloodedly and resolutely by the German people. Once the moment occurs, however, patience ends. The murderous boy Grünspan scornfully announced that he was shooting in the name of all Jewry and that he wanted to hurt the German people in the innocent victim of his vindictiveness. No Jews can cleanse themselves of this blood guilt, twist and turn though they may.

What has played out over the last 24 hours in Germany is the expression of a righteous disgust amongst the broadest strata of the German people. It cannot be regarded as retaliation. One murder by provocative Jewish louts is not atoned for through splintered window panes or perhaps a few well-deserved slaps round the face, the German people are also much too disciplined to allow themselves to be carried away by such "acts of revenge". Whoever was witness to the demonstrations must much more wonder at the admirable discipline that was observed by the masses despite the unheard of disgust at the shameless cowardly murderous deed.

It has not come to "pogroms", as the Jewish-Marxist foreign press already thought could be announced yesterday.

It is self-evident that the German people will continue to preserve discipline. The events may, however, show world Jewry that the German people will no longer allow themselves to be toyed with. Were the murder weapon to be raised against German compatriots, yes, even against the official representative of the Reich, then one cannot expect that the racial comrades in Germany will be dealt with kid gloves.

For this cowardly act of murder in Paris, as Dr. Goebbels stated, Jewry will receive a final answer through legislative channels.

Berliner Börsenzeitung, 12 November 1938

"Civil War"
World Jewry's relief offensive

The dark figures who set world public opinion in motion in the democracies have found a way to cover up the devastating impression of international Jewry that the murder of Legation Secretary Herr vom Rath has evoked throughout the entire civilised world. They use common tricks to construct a "scandal" and give suitable documents with false horrific reports according to the usual methods. The justifiably deep disgust which prevails in every German as a result of this despicable murder of a German diplomat has led to spontaneous retaliatory measures against the Jews. It was the natural reaction of a people to unbearable provocation by the Jewish world press concerning unconscionable pressures by international warmongers and catastrophe politicians. For a people of honour it is no longer tolerable to be the object of acts that are dangerous to the public committed by an international clique, whose Jewish inspirers, to use a word of its craftsman, the murderer Grünspan, want to take "revenge" in National Socialist Germany. The German people are intelligent enough to see through what these dark figures are seeking, whose most fervent wish is to rush the peoples of Europe into war, from which these illusionists promise the fall of Germany.

We accepted the cowardly murder of Gustloff without appropriate action, but – this should be kept in mind abroad – after this second murder we are no longer willing to keep silent. The international Jewish political criminality should know once and for all that the patience of the German people is herewith exhausted. They are no longer in the mood to allow themselves to be provoked and to accept with humility that German diplomatic representatives lose their lives for this society.

It is typical that even foreign papers, which want to be taken seriously, do not shy from presenting their "information" to the reader on the side of the relief offensive of the Jewish world press. They are suddenly no longer interested in the dark background of the murderous deed and the person of the murderer, they direct their friendly attention to full extent at the spontaneous consequences the murder in Germany. What horror stories can be thought up in terms must serve. From the smashed-in shop windows they make a sort of civil war. In one it was 100-200 people, in another 20,000-30,000 who dashed through the streets in violent turmoil. Apathy and cries of joy from every citizen are evoked by the talent for fantasy. In short, it is a wild tumult of contradictory comments, which are concocted to cater for every taste of sensation-hungry reader. If one is told, among other things, that the demonstrations by the people were carried out by "organised groups", we can only say that they would have been a great deal more drastic if they had been "organised".

The spontaneous operation against Jewry was denounced in the shortest period by the Government. But World Jewry should base no new "hopes" on that. It could be said to them that the position of the Jews in Germany in private, public and commercial life depends on the restraint of World Jewry. They do not strike the German people, only their racial comrades with their provocation. Insofar as foreign countries are interested in them, they are free to take in as many of them as their needs require. The German Government will now settle the Jewish question in Germany in the shortest period via laws and regulations. Germany has been provoked most gravely by this second murder; it will issue an appropriate response.

News Chronicle, 12 November 1938

[...]

During the night, private houses and villas owned by Jews in Berlin suburbs were raided by young Nazis who drove up in cars. They hurled paving stones through the windows and destroyed all they could lay their hands on, shouting obscene insults at their victims.

Heavy stones crashed onto the beds of sleepers. One Jewish couple, both deaf and dumb, were not spared. Some dwellings were smashed up inside, too.

MANY JEWS VANISH

Today hundreds of arrested Jews were sent to Sachsenhausen concentration camp, where Pastor Niemeller is interned. Apart from the thousands arrested, there are numbers of Jews who have just "disappeared". Their families do not know where they are.

The caretaker of the Prince Regent Street Synagogue and his wife and child, who had not been seen since the synagogue was destroyed by fire two nights ago, have, I learn tonight, been taken to hospital. The custodian and the child are badly burned and his wife is suffering from a nervous breakdown.

When the incendiaries appeared, neighbours warned them that the caretaker and his family lived on the premises.

The new Aryan owners of smashed Jewish shops, mostly put up for ownership by the Party, today surveyed the ruins which they were to buy for a song and secretly wished that their fellow-Aryans had not been quite so thorough in giving vent to their ideals.

Some shops are worth nothing more than the site on which they were built.

Near Breslau, the Gross Bresen Apprenticeship School for Jews who want to take up agriculture in foreign countries, was raided by the secret police. Professor Bondy, the Principal, and 20 pupils were arrested. One Jew of 17 was told: "Grynszpan, the murderer, was only 17. That is why we are arresting you."

The Scotsman, 14 November 1938

SENT TO CONCENTRATION CAMPS
Another Train Load of Jews Leaves Vienna
[FROM OUR OWN CORRESPONDENT]

VIENNA, Sunday. – Another train load of a thousand young Jews has left Vienna for concentration camps – it is believed at Mauthausen and Buchenwald. There is utter consternation among the Jews in Vienna in consequence of the announcement made by Field-Marshal Göring. There is the greatest anxiety as to how they shall obtain essential food supplies, as Jews cannot open their shops, and may not buy in "Aryan" shops. The High Commissioner will announce tomorrow what provision is to be made to meet this situation.

It appears that a number of old men and women, some of them invalids, were locked in their homes on Thursday by rioters, who took away their keys and also those of the house master, and sealed the entrance doors of the flats so that these old people could not get out, and no one could get into them until the doors were broken in on Saturday by police orders.

National Zeitung, Basel, 16 November 1938

Help for the persecuted Jews
America in the lead for a campaign

Roosevelt's declarations
Washington, 16th November. (agency) (Havas) President Roosevelt's declarations concerning the events in Germany read as follows:

"The news coming from Germany over the last few days has profoundly affected the American people. If we received such news from other parts of the world it would have evoked the same reaction in all classes of the American people.

"I had difficulty believing that such things could occur in the 20th century.

"In order to be informed first hand about the situation in Germany, I have issued instructions to the Secretary of State to recall the American Ambassador in Berlin back to Washington immediately."

The President emphasised that the recall of Ambassador Wilson does not diplomatically signify a denunciation, rather an invitation for purposes of consultation. He added that he could not state how long the Berlin Ambassador would remain in the United States and emphasised that at present the official protest to the German Government for the damage suffered by American Israelites in Germany has not yet struck. The President closed with the remark that the Intergovernmental Committee in London will do its best to render practical assistance and that he will examine all possible options for Jewish immigration personally. He said, however, that he could not yet give any details concerning this matter.

The *New York Post* described President Roosevelt's gesture to recall the American Ambassador in Berlin to Washington as: a slap round the face for the National Socialist Government.

The leaders of American politics are busy with the assessment of practical measures that would be suitable to strike harder at National Socialist Germany. The *Washington Post* is of the opinion that Roosevelt wanted to make clear to Germany with his gesture that the United States could step into the lead of a protest. In political circles it is understood that at the moment no other opportunities exist to express disapproval of the persecution of the Jews.

The American newspapers defended themselves from threats expressed in National Socialist newspapers.

In the United States, the general impression is that Ambassador Wilson will not return to Berlin as long as Germany does not entirely change its position.

Exchange of opinions between London and Washington

London, 16th November. (agency) (Havas) English diplomatic circles consider an exchange of opinion between London and Washington about the Jewish problem a distinct possibility.

The *Evening News* writes: "Great Britain, France and the United States could together create a new home for the Jews from Germany and Central Europe. It is to be assumed that Chamberlain will present the proposal to the American President Roosevelt, to lodge a complaint directly to the German Government together.

"This proposal is currently being discussed between Washington and London, and the intention is to invite France to participate in this campaign. The United States Ambassador in London discussed this question on Sunday with the British Minister of Colonies and Dominions, MacDonald, and therein expressed the wish of his government that a decision is made immediately on this question. England together with its dominions intends to allow Jews to settle in the less populated regions, whilst the United States will itself turn to the South American republics, so that these countries can accept Jewish immigration on a larger scale than hitherto promised. The United States itself is ready to accept 30,000-40,000 refugees."

Holland is prepared to accept a few thousand refugees
The Hague, 16th November. (agency) (Reuter) Prime Minister Colijn stated in the Lower House that the Dutch Government with the Governments of Great Britain, France, Denmark, Belgium and Switzerland has entered into negotiations with regard to easing the immigration of German Jews.

Holland will build refugee camps, which could take in a few thousand Jews. The city council of Amsterdam unanimously agreed to a Socialist application, whereby the Mayor will be asked to take the necessary measures to accommodate German refugees in municipal inns.

Leading Jews in England with Chamberlain
London, 16th November. Prime Minister Chamberlain received a delegation of the leading Jews in England on Thursday amongst whom were Lord Samuel, Lord Bearsted, Senior Rabbi Dr. Herz, Rabbi Dr. Weizmann. The delegation raised the idea of easing restrictions on the ability of Jews to migrate from Germany to English territories.

The Spectator, 18 November 1938

THE NEW BARBARISM

This week's outbreak of barbarism in Germany is on so vast a scale, is marked by an inhumanity so diabolical and bears marks of official inspiration so unmistakable that its consequences internal or external are, as yet, beyond prediction. Internally, there is sufficient evidence of the pity and disgust inspired in the ordinary, decent German citizen to make it both unreasonable and unjust to draw an indictment against a nation for crimes that are to be laid at the door of a party. That is the more to the credit of the German people, in that Dr Goebbels, whose apologia for what is happening is repulsive in its cynicism, is able through his control of the Press to disseminate utterly distorted accounts of events which have aroused the horror and approbation of the civilised world. Mr Hoover may have exaggerated when he said there had been nothing like it since the tortures of Torquemada – Russia might provide some parallels – but there will be few purists disposed to insist on a meticulous precision of comparison in such a case. President Roosevelt's condemnation is, in view of the restraint his position imposes, even more impressive than his predecessor's.

It is true that Jews in Germany have not been formally condemned to death; it has only been made impossible for them to live. Their crime is that they are of the same race as a frenzied boy of seventeen, who, distraught by the sufferings inflicted on his parents by the Nazi rulers of Germany, shot a member of the German Embassy in Paris. Nothing but unequivocal condemnation can be pronounced on political assassination by civilised men. It is only people of the type of the Nazi leaders who condone and even glorify it. They have exalted to heaven the murderers of Rathenau and Erzberger and Dollfuss, and their own record in the matter of assassination is too pertinent to be ignored at a moment when a political murder is being taken as a pretext for a mass-persecution that throws Germany back to the level of the Middle Ages. The so-called "blood bath" of 30th June, 1934, was simply a massacre – of women as well as men; General von Schleicher's wife was shot with him – without semblance of trial. An assassination only becomes an outrage when its author is a Jew, and if he is a Polish Jew it is on Jews, not Poles, that a vengeance which strikes the innocent alone is visited.

What form that vengeance has taken has been recorded in the British, French and American papers, if not in the German. On Thursday morning of last week, twenty-four hours after the death of Herr von [sic] Rath from the Polish Jew's bullet, by an obviously concerted plan – whether attributable to the Government or to the Party is immaterial –Jews were beaten up, Jewish shops were wrecked and looted, Jewish synagogues were set on fire throughout what is now known as the Greater Reich – for one result of the annexation of Austria and Sudetendeutschland is that Jews in those areas can now be subjected to the treatment to which their co-religionists in Germany proper were always exposed. Dr Goebbels imposed a veto, and the Government itself took the situation in hand. It began with arrests and consignments to concentration camps on an extensive scale. A reign of terror set in. Jews everywhere fled from their homes and hid shelterless and foodless in woods. By Monday the first set of anti-Jewish decrees had been promulgated. A collective fine equal to about £84,000,000 is imposed on the Jews of Germany – much to the benefit of the Government's precarious financial system. All the damage done to Jewish premises by Nazi mobs is to be repaired at the expense of Jews; but Jews will not be able to use the premises so repaired, for they are to be excluded from all economic activity in Germany from the end of the year onwards. No Jew may attend any public entertainment, no Jew may attend any German university, no Jewish child may attend any German school – but no Jew apparently may emigrate, or if he does he will go without a penny to support him or start him in a new life elsewhere. It is recorded that Jews who tried to escape from Sudetendeutschland were compelled to crawl on all fours over the frontier and were then sent back by the Czechoslovakian authorities at the behest of the Germans. Not one of the half-million victims is guilty of anything but the crime of being a Jew.

For the world outside Germany two problems, baffling in their magnitude and complexity are presented. One is the age-long problem of evil. Never before in living memory, or for generations before that, has brute force divorced from every canon of morality been erected into a national policy on a scale comparable with this, and there are no precedents to determine the attitude to be adopted towards it. No foreign Power can do anything for the Jews still in Germany. Any attempt to do that, even any expression of opinion on what has happened, may well make their lot worse, though silence would inevitably be interpreted as indifference or condonation. Even the protest our own Government has made is prompted, not by the pogrom itself, but by the outrageous charges brought by the controlled German Press against certain British public men, and the American Government, while indicating its judgment plainly by calling its Ambassador home, has refrained from official protest. In view of this impossibility of helping the victims of the Nazi terror so long as they remain in Germany, the impulse of most normally-minded people would be to reduce to the minimum of strictly official relations all contact with a country whose rulers apply the methods of barbarism in the midst of a civilised continent. To a large extent that must happen, for the events of the past week have obliterated the word appeasement, for the present at any rate, from the political vocabulary – a bitter and wholly undeserved reward of Mr Chamberlain's endeavours.

But that is only one problem. The other is how the Jews who have escaped from Germany, and those who may yet be expelled, may be helped. Execration of Nazi methods is dishonest and hypocritical unless every possible step is taken to give succour to the victims of those methods. As a whole the problem may be insoluble, but something at least can be done to alleviate suffering, and the duty to do that is a solemn charge on civilisation. A totally new effort on a totally new scale is called for. The Evian Conference of last July has led to nothing. Palestine could only accommodate a few thousand Jews at the outside. The United States is receiving some and could take more. Australia is receiving some and could take more. The Indian States are receiving some. It is incredible that in the vast spaces of the British and French Empires and on the North and South American continent there should be no room for a singularly industrious and resourceful people. The four African territories of Uganda, Kenya, Tanganyika and Northern Rhodesia have between them a white population of less than 40,000. Is there no room for any Jewish settlement there? The question must be faced at once and resolutely, and, if necessary, at some cost, by countries like Great Britain and the United States and France in the name of humanity. Ultimately, they will be enriched, not impoverished, by the harbourage they offer, though that should not be the operative motive. And there can be little doubt that hundreds of thousands of Germans, who have watched the pogroms with a shame and disgust as profound as our own would view any move to help the victims of their rulers with thankfulness.

*

The Week in Parliament
Our Parliamentary Correspondent writes: At no time since the summer of 1931 has the immediate political outlook been so uncertain. [...] On the wider issue of foreign affairs, no one doubts that Mr. Chamberlain's policy of appeasement has been gravely jeopardised by the news from Germany. As regards the Nazi persecution of the Jews there is, of course, only one opinion, and the stoutest die-hards are as indignant as the most rabid Socialists. Nor have the latter attempted to make any party capital out of the sufferings of German Jewry. But the present Ministers are necessarily regarded by the public as men who are trying to make friends with the dictators and who are prepared to trust their assurances. Since the Munich Agreement was signed Herr Hitler has done everything in his power to strengthen the hands of the Government's critics.

Le Droit de Vivre, 19 November 1938

10th November in Germany

BALANCE SHEET
of a day under Hitler

Murders

- At Buchenwald concentration camp, 146 Jews have been murdered.
- In Munich and Vienna, news of more than 80 "suicides" was known.
- In Polzin, in Pomerania, an industrialist, father of three children, was murdered.
- In Frankfurt am Main, amongst the Jews arrested, 60 have "disappeared".
- Entire families kill themselves.

Pending death ...

- 8,000 Jews, suffering at a camp in Zbonszyn, on the Germano-Polish border, following the breakdown in negotiations between Poland and the Reich.
- Jewish women and children of Frankfurt am Main are threatened with starvation. Refusal to deliver milk for Jewish babies.

Blows and injuries

Jews grievously injured:
- At Osnabrück.
- At Düsseldorf.
- At Nuremberg.
- At Danzig.
- In Munich and Vienna, manhunt in the streets.

Arrests

- 4,000 in Berlin.
- 1,000 in Hamburg.
- Thousands in Munich and in Vienna.
- All the Jews of Nalbach (Saarland).
- All the Jews of Diefflen (Saarland).
- All the Jews over 18 years and less than 60 years of age of Frankfurt am Main, and locked in a concentration camp.
- Jewish lawyers, judges, assessors and doctors regardless of age.

– All Semitic travellers are apprehended at railway stations.
– In total, all over Germany: 35,000.

Sabotage, pillage, etc ...

News of the death of Embassy Secretary von [sic] Rath was broadcast by radio to Berlin at 7.00 pm. "Spontaneous" reactions did not begin until six hours later, at 1 o'clock in the morning.

20 HOURS OF VANDALISM
THROUGHOUT GERMANY
from 1.00 am to 7.00 pm on 10th November 1938.

Fires
– In Berlin: nine out of twelve synagogues.
– In Danzig: two synagogues.
– In Hersfeld: one synagogue.
– In Cottbus: one synagogue.
– In Potsdam: one synagogue.
– In Vienna: two synagogues.
– In Constance: one synagogue.
– In Bamberg: one synagogue.
– In Bayreuth: one synagogue.
– In Leipzig: one large shop (Bamberger and Hertz).
– In Reichenberg (in Sudetenland): one synagogue and numerous Jewish shops.
– In Old Brisach (Baden) [sic]: one synagogue.
– At Ihringen (Baden): one synagogue.

Expulsions
– At Munich, all the Israelites, the majority of whom were dragged from their beds in the middle of the night, had to hand over to the police the keys to their homes and garages.
After which, they were given 48 hours to leave the town.

Thefts, ransoms, confiscation
– One billion marks fine has been imposed upon German Jews as a whole.
– Reparations by the Jews themselves for the damage that they suffered on the day of 10th November.
– Confiscation in favour of the State of the sums due to Jews from insurance companies.

- The Israelite community of Frankfurt am Main is obliged to meet the costs of the Jews (all the men over 18 years and under 60 years of age) sent to concentration camps.
- Of three thousand establishments in Berlin that have Israelites, almost 1,500 have been "surrendered" to "Aryans" in less than 48 hours.
- All Jewish fortunes exceeding 3,000 marks will be confiscated in favour of the State.

Prohibitions

- Prohibition of Jews from owning retail and wholesale businesses, partaking in intermediate trade or practising a handicraft, even at home, from 1st January 1939.
- Prohibition of business owners from retaining a Jew in any managerial post. Work contracts of Jewish employees will be cancelled.
- Prohibition of Jews from frequenting theatres, cinemas, concert halls and all other entertainments.
- Prohibition of Jewish newspapers.
- Prohibition of cultural institutions and Jewish culture.
- Prohibition of Jews from advertising in the press.
- Closure of Jewish schools.
- Prohibition of the minority of Jewish children entitled to attend Aryan schools from further attendance.
- Prohibition of Jews from owning any weapon, not even a knife.
- Prohibition of Jews from attending universities where they were only admitted in very small numbers.
- Prohibition of Jews from selling their shares on the stock exchange.
- Prohibition of the Catholic Church from baptising Israelites.

Restrictions

- Obligation will be placed on Jews to wear a distinctive sign.
- Preparation of the medieval ghetto.
- Review of mixed marriages and divorce imposed on couples of Jews and Aryans.

After the Jews …

- A short time after the attack carried out on Cardinal Innitzer's Palace in Vienna, the Nazis protested and smashed the windows of Cardinal Faulhaber's Palace in Munich.
- The Cardinal was prevented from delivering his sermon.

It is right to add to this tragic list the doubtless extremely numerous and serious facts, news of which has not crossed the frontiers.

Manchester Guardian, 21 November 1938

THE GERMAN POGROM
Not Sudden Outbreak, but Carefully Planned
Mr Neville Laski's Charge

The Board of Deputies of British Jews at its meeting in London yesterday adopted on behalf of the Anglo-Jewish community a resolution in which "it records its sense of the tragedy which led to the death of a member of the German Embassy in Paris at the hands of a Jewish youth made insensate by the suffering of his parents following their expulsion from Germany, joins with the rest of the civilised world in the expressions of horror at the organised terrorism directed against the defenceless Jewish population of Germany, already brought to distress and misery by five years of unremitting persecution," and expresses its gratitude "for the sympathy with victims of Nazi persecution shown by our fellow-citizens of all denominations and all political parties and for the general support given to proposals that larger opportunities shall be given in the Empire and Palestine for the permanent settlement of refugees."

The resolution also appeals to the Government "to use its good offices in any way appropriate for the amelioration of the position of the Jews in Germany, trusts that in the forefront of any approaches made by the British Government to the German Government may be placed the necessity for permitting intending emigrants to remove their property with them, offers its wholehearted co-operation in any immediate and effective steps which have the purpose of affording relief and refuge to the victims of persecution, affirms the determination of the community to continue by unified efforts to overcome the terrible problem of human suffering created by recent events in Germany, and appeals to the community to give its generous and prompt support to the appeal for funds for the rescue of those in Germany whom it is still possible to save."

Mr. Laski's Statement
Before passing the resolution the Board heard a statement by Mr. Neville

Laski in which he declared that there was ample proof that the whole action against the German Jews had been carefully and systematically prepared by the Nazi party. In this country and other civilised countries the view was widely held that the recent outbreaks in Germany were rather sudden developments, the result of a foolish act committed by a maddened Jewish youth in Paris. This view was false. The Paris crime was used as a pretext by the Nazi rulers.

"I use the word 'pretext' advisedly," said Mr Laski, "for I am firmly convinced that the Nazis were bent upon the entire destruction of the Jews in Germany and would have found an occasion sooner or later even if what happened in Paris had not occurred."

"Dr. Goebbels said that the Government knew nothing of the happenings until they had started. It is possible that the Minister of Propaganda knew nothing about the plans, but it is certain that the district leader of the Nazi party of Berlin, the same Dr. Goebbels, knew perfectly well what was going to happen. It is possible that the head of the Secret Police, Herr Himmler, knew nothing about it until he ordered the arrest of the Jews, but it also certain that the head of the Black Guards, the SS, the same Herr Himmler, knew perfectly well what was going to happen."

Jewry's Thanks

"No words can adequately express the gratitude of us Jews for the sympathy shown us during the present German persecution," said the Rev. Leslie Edgar, Associate Minister of the Liberal Jewish Synagogue, London, at a service held there yesterday, adding that Jewry was most thankful, too, for the prayer for the persecuted Jews offered at the Armistice service at Westminster Abbey, to the Archbishop of Canterbury and British statesmen for their protests, and "for many acts of helpfulness of our Christian neighbours".

"In all this" Mr. Edgar continued, "we have seen once again the power of the Christian spirit in England, that love of humanity, of justice and tolerance so characteristic of our country."

There was a widespread realisation that not only the fate of half a million German Jews was at stake but the whole future of civilised standards in the western world. England had already shown to the Jews her traditional and generous hospitality. But if the onslaught against human rights was to be effectively answered, some even greater gesture to the world was needed.

"Our hopes are pinned to England," Mr. Edgar concluded, "and our fervent appeal is addressed to her as a nation of vast resources and great influence who could give the lead to others and find in one of the wide spaces of the British Empire a home for our persecuted brothers."

Scientists' Sympathy

The Council of the Association of Scientific Workers at a meeting in London on Saturday passed a resolution "strongly condemning the policy of deliberate oppression and brutal persecution of the Jewish minority in Germany on unscientific racial grounds as fundamentally opposed to the cultural views of an age of scientific enlightenment." The Council also decided to try "to ensure that no obstacle be placed in the way of immigration of refugee scientists."

Völkisher Beobachter, South German edition,
Munich, 22 November 1938

No Jews in German homes

Notice to quit permissible for Jewish tenants – actions to terminate tenancies well-founded

Even before the shots in Paris steered attention towards the Jewish problem once more, the question whether landlords may serve notice to quit on their Jewish tenants or whether they are prevented from doing so by the Rent Act [*Mieterschutzgesetz*] had become pressing, particularly in Berlin.

It is known that there is an urgent need for accommodation almost everywhere in the Reich, but particularly in the large cities. This applies most especially to medium-sized and small homes. Also the numerous new and estate buildings that have already been built since the seizure of power and are still constantly being built could not meet demand up to now, as demand always continues to increase chiefly due to the numerous marriages. Amongst the people it has for a long time been felt to be an unstoppable situation that members of the Jewish people possessed huge homes, whilst working Germans were left without accommodation or had to help themselves in the most primitive ways.

Through an amendment made to the Rent Act in 1933, a certain compensation was introduced in that the Rent Act does not apply if the tenant did not have his home in Germany on 1st January 1914. However, this amendment does not suffice in order to do justice to the demands of everyday life. The question was therefore whether or not the Rent Act permits revocation of Jewish tenancies on other grounds. This question must be affirmed. The New Order in German society and in German landlord and tenant law has led to households becoming a significant constituent element of the landlord/tenant relationship and in landlord and tenant law. This means that house tenants should not only live alongside each other but care for the spirit of National Socialist society. The term household as it exists between landlord and tenant and between the tenants amongst themselves requires that all are bound by the same spirit and objectives; the National Socialist ideology.

From this reasoning, various German courts have seen fit to grant landlords' applications for terminations of leases of Jewish tenants. This is stated in the German legal journal *Juristische Wochenschrift* of 1938 page 2975, published judgment of the *Amtsgericht* [local court] in Halle on 18th August 1938:

"Even in the household individual selfish interests can endure. A true household in the sense of this thought can only be formed and nurtured by right-thinking, German-thinking people and house occupants of Aryan descent; it is, of course, absolutely impossible with persons of Jewish origin, due to the existing racial differences. As the National Socialist state places particular value on forming and nurturing a true household and requires this attitude towards the sense of household from every member of the population, in the interests of the preservation of this household landlords and tenants of Aryan descent are not permitted to form and nurture such with tenants of Jewish origin and to live with them in the same household. The landlord must, therefore, be promised the right to exclude tenants of Jewish descent from this household and to demand they vacate this accommodation of their home. If such a tenant of Jewish descent does not comply with the landlord's eviction demand and the landlord of Aryan descent rejects the household with him, he interferes with the household between the landlord and other tenants of Aryan descent and by his further remaining in residence is guilty of a relevant harassment in the meaning of § 2 of the Rent Act."

This view, which had already been expressed before the assassination of Legation Secretary vom Rath, has found particular emphasis and support as a result of the events in Paris. After what has happened in

Paris, no German tenant can be expected to live in a house with Jewish tenants. Applications by German landlords against their Jewish tenants must therefore be affirmed for the reasons stated.

Völkisher Beobachter, South German edition,
Munich, 22 November 1938

Jews unwanted in the whole world

England

The support of Jewish emigrants and, in particular, the question of where the "poor German Jews" should be brought occupied the British lower house [House of Commons] on Monday. As far as the Government's intention is known, joint action is planned to bring together as many States as possible to make progress on this issue.

At the moment when English helpfulness should be turned into actions, it seems not to be quite so glowing as newspaper reports had us believe last week. The various plans to allow a greater number of Jews into England have already encountered manifold resistance. It would seem they are only prepared to allow these Jews merely to use England as a transit stop for the overseas colonial empire.

The mendacity of the parliamentary debate was recognised by the *Daily Express*. The newspaper asks what good the debate can actually bring about and whether there was any intention to allow more emigrants into England. It would, of course, be a dangerous intention.

"We have already taken up our full quota of foreign Jews. We cannot assimilate them. Should we open the Crown Colonies to the Jews? Of course. There is sufficient space there and many undeveloped areas from which a man, through the sweat of his endeavours, and through unrelenting work could draw a wage of a thousandfold. But will the Jews go to these distant countries? Of course not. At most to Palestine, which cannot accept any more. The emigrant problem is an administrative issue that must be dealt with by Mr. Chamberlain and his colleagues.

"Only one thing will be achieved as a result of this parliamentary debate, some elected representatives will succeed in directing general attention to their extreme views, which they would be able to give free rein to in the lower house. We do not see how far we or the Jews are served by constant accusations against Germany."

Switzerland

The clear response from the Swiss *Bundesrat* [upper house of parliament] to the Dutch request regarding accommodating new multitudes of Jewish emigrants was met with tacit approval by the Swiss public. The *Bundesrat* statement should chime with the position of the governments of other European countries who have likewise repeatedly pointed out that they are already overrun with Jewish emigrants. In this context it is pointed out that these highly unpleasant "guests" are anyway only granted temporary residence in the expectation that those powers with large overseas territories would create the possibility of lasting accommodation.

Nothing tangible on this matter has occurred in recent months though, so that the small countries ask with a certain amazement why London and Washington constantly direct new unreasonable demands on the hospitality of these small lands. Switzerland regards itself per se already swamped as about 10% of its inhabitants are foreigners, of whom the majority have permanent residence, i.e. possess opportunities for unrestricted activity in working life.

Already in July of this year, as a new wave of Jews from abroad, namely Austria, came forth, Switzerland saw itself as obliged to close its borders and to even to install military supervision. Nevertheless a few thousand Jews came in and the population harbours the fear, mostly justifiably, that their accommodation in their own camps in the long run cannot be carried out and that over the course of time these Jews will then suddenly surface in more or less productive positions.

Switzerland is one of the most interesting examples where there too, where it is believed that anti-Jewish attitudes have been fundamentally rejected, anti-Jewish measures are perceived as unavoidable as soon as certain facts speak for themselves.

Poland

The Jewish question has once more been dealt with by *Dziennik Narodowy* [National Journal]. The paper writes that the nation in Europe that is free from the influence of Judaism will have a great and indisputable predominance over the other nations. Therefore Poland also gradually has to remove all Jews from its territory. This also holds true for all other countries in Europe. Such settlement of the Jewish question is a necessary precondition for a renewal of Europe.

Efforts in Poland hitherto undertaken towards the elimination of

Jews from political, cultural and economic life must be doubled, tripled and increased tenfold. In order to maintain a happy, independent Poland, all political rights of the Jews in the State must be taken; they must be eliminated from cultural and economic life and then, finally, absolutely removed from Poland.

America
In answer to the hysterical cry of Jewish organisations in recent days, Senator Borah expressed his conviction that every attempt to amend the American immigration laws in favour of the Jews would falter from the strongest opposition in Congress.

Borah stated further: "I do not consider it desirable to amend the immigration law now. We could, at most, implement completely insufficient measures."

Roosevelt's instruction to the Labour Ministry too, to extend the visas of 15,000 refugees who are currently visiting America, was strongly criticised. The Chairman of the well-known House Committee on Un-American Activities, [Martin] Dies, stated in this regard that Roosevelt was not allowed to implement such an order. His actions contravene the sense of the law.

Finally a member of the Senate Immigration Committee also determined that even the Trades Unions would protest most keenly against a further increase in Jewish immigration. Even the Union men Lewis and Green, who are known as passionate supporters of a boycott against Germany, are of the opinion that Jewish immigration will not only increase current unemployment but would in particular increase significantly pre-existing antisemitic tensions.

Australia
Almost daily, reports are appearing in the London Press from which it can clearly be seen that in many parts of the Empire do not at all want to allow their countries to be deluged with Jews.

Thus stated the Australian Prime Minister Lyons, that the Australian Government is resolute in its stance to prevent the mass immigration of foreigners and that the associated settlements also will in no way be tolerated. A proposal apparently made in London, to settle Jewish emigrants *en masse* in Australia, was entirely out of the question. The Australian High Commissioner in London, Bruce, was very well aware of the stance of the Australian Government and will maintain it strongly.

Ceylon

"Only important Jews" (!), the Governor of Ceylon Sir Andrew Caldecott spoke thus in response to the Colonial Minister MacDonald. The current trade situation and unemployment in Ceylon allow no unrestricted admission of Jews. The Health Minister of Ceylon cautiously brought in a bill in the State Council, in which holding a medical surgery for foreigners would be prohibited.

Daily Telegraph, 22 November 1938

32 Powers to Concert Refugees Plans

Hope of swift decisions at London conference

*

Premier on available areas in colonies

*

All parties united in deploring persecution in Europe

The Home Secretary, Sir Samuel Hoare, stated in the House of Commons last night that joint action by 32 States in solving the problem of refugees from Germany was hoped for in the immediate future.

Announcing that the Evian Committee, on which these Powers were represented, would meet in London in 10 days' time, he declared that inquiries as to how many refugees each country could take had already been made and had proved useful.

On behalf of the Government, he accepted an Opposition motion deploring the treatment of minorities in Europe and welcoming an immediate concerted effort by the nations to afford relief.

In a statement made earlier in the House, the Prime Minister disclosed that surveys were being made in the Colonial Empire to ascertain the possibilities of settlement. Tanganyika might provide 50,000 acres; British Guiana 10,000 square miles, Kenya, Nyasaland and Northern Rhodesia smaller areas.

Mr. Chamberlain, appealing to all nations to co-operate in solving the refugee problem, declared that the country of origin should permit emigrants to take their property with them.

In a statement on Anglo-German relations, he said that no early meeting between the British and German Governments was contemplated.

*

10,000 Square Miles in Guiana

BY OUR SPECIAL REPRESENTATIVE

WESTMINSTER, Monday. "Greatly impressed by the urgency of the problem." That phrase was the keynote of the brief statement on Jewish refugees from Germany in which the Prime Minister indicated to-day some of the lines of action of our Government.

The number of refugees whom we can receive in the United Kingdom, said Mr. Chamberlain, is limited. Eleven thousand have come here since 1933.

In the Colonial Empire he suggested important possibilities:

Tanganyika might provide about 50,000 acres of land for large-scale settlement.

Kenya, Northern Rhodesia, and Nyasaland might receive small numbers of settlers.

British Guiana could offer not less than 10,000 square miles.

Mr. Chamberlain made it clear that much consideration had already been given to the resources thus available. He pointed out the necessity of action through voluntary organisations, which must conduct surveys and undertake the responsibility of preparing the land and settling upon it refugees of suitable types.

Palestine could not provide a solution.

PROPERTY QUESTION

Helping Emigrants

Then, in significant sentences, Mr. Chamberlain hoped that other countries would join with us in developing the work of the International Committee established at Evian-les-Bains, France, in July, and would make what contribution they could to the urgent need of facilitating emigration from Germany.

He had always declared that the Government had in mind the view expressed at Evian that the country of origin should enable emigrants to take with them their property.

This statement was the preface to a debate later in the evening when Mr. NOEL BAKER, from the Socialist Front Bench, brought forward a motion deploring the treatment of minorities in Europe and welcoming an immediate concerted effort among the nations, including the United States, to secure a common policy.

The motion made no mention of Germany, but Mr. Noel Baker, in a speech of emotion and fire, supplied that omission.

MURDER CONDEMNED

Always detestable
He began with the murder of the German Diplomat, Herr vom Rath, in Paris, declaring that political assassination was always detestable but not less detestable when it was the method by which a party climbed to power.

Then – he quoted THE DAILY TELEGRAPH AND MORNING POST's first summary of what occurred in Germany after the assassination. That upheaval, he maintained, was not spontaneous, but organised in advance.

The campaign was not supported by the German people. Germans were now helping the Jews whenever they dared.

Dr. Goebbels meant to rob the Jews of all their possessions for his party fund and to meet the bankruptcy of State finance. If he succeeded, antisemitism might blaze up in Eastern Europe; and Poland and Rumania might expel 4,500,000 Jews.

Mr. Noel Baker offered a programme of remedies. We should protest, we should make it clear that no cordial relations could exist between the German Government and the British people while persecution went on.

We might have to consider active self-protection. The number of Germans receiving our hospitality could be reduced.

LOANS PROPOSED

Charity Not Enough
To meet the grave financial problem, we could take economic measures in the taxation of German goods and the control of German assets here.

Settlement of emigrants must be the work of a strong international machine. The League of Nations High Commissioner for Refugees was Mr. Noel Baker's choice for its chief.

We should, with other countries, guarantee a long-term loan. Private charity could not suffice. The nations which guaranteed loans would not lose their money.

Mr. HAMMERSLEY, from the Conservative benches, pronounced the problem of settlement well within the capacity of the world and the British Empire able to give great help.

Mr. MANDER suggested that financial pressure might be exerted, that Nazi Germans carrying on propaganda might be sent back to their country, or that the question of appropriating German property in this country might be considered.

Mr. LOGAN expressed the view of the "orthodox" Roman Catholic, declaiming strongly against the persecution to which the Jews had been subjected and demanding that the inevitable exodus should be treated as an international problem.

Sir ARCHIBALD SOUTHBY suggested that Jewry at large should help and asked for the strongest possible representations that refugees should be allowed to bring with them out of Germany sufficient to enable them to establish themselves elsewhere.

ISSUE NOT DOMESTIC

International Question

Sir SAMUEL HOARE, the Home Secretary, who spoke for the Government, showed a practical and constructive sympathy with the plight of the Jews in Germany, which was approved by both sides of the House.

Having accepted Mr. Noel Baker's motion, he proceeded to avow that, although a believer in Anglo-German friendship and a staunch supporter of the Munich policy, he could not conceal deep feeling on the suffering of thousands for a crime with which they had no connection.

Measures taken against the Jews in Germany could not be an exclusively domestic question. Scores of thousands were made destitute and driven to seek admission to other countries.

The problem must remain international. No single country could hope to solve it.

BRITAIN'S SHARE

Responsibility Accepted

Amid general applause, he announced that the Evian Committee representing 32 States would meet in 10 days. Mr. Myron Taylor, the United States Representative, was now on his way here.

Inquiries already made among the 32 Governments, as to how many refugees they could receive, had proved useful and they hoped that action would be taken in the immediate future.

Although the problem was not insoluble, international effort, with the active co-operation in effective organisation of all nations, was needed. We accepted the responsibility which fell upon us, as possessors of a great part of the world and large resources, to do our share.

The Dominions would speak for themselves. Their Governments had given the matter urgent attention and already admitted a substantial number of refugees.

To the Prime Minister's statement on the possibility of our colonies, Sir Samuel added that the survey would be expedited to find where immigration was likely to succeed. To a criticism put in an interjection by Mr. Noel Baker to Mr. Chamberlain that a tract in British Guiana had been refused for settlement of the Assyrians, he replied that the area now under consideration was of much greater extent and, if it proved suitable, large sums of capital would be found by co-religionists of the refugees.

Antisemitism Danger

Then he dealt at length with his own task as Home Secretary in controlling immigration to this country. He warned the House that his department had evidence of an underlying current of suspicion and anxiety about an alien influx.

If it rose to a big scale there was the making of a definite anti-Jewish movement. He did his best to stamp on animosity, but he had to be careful to avoid mass immigration.

Checks involved delay, but whenever a Jew could help himself or had friends who would look after him, he was admitted; 11,000 refugees from Germany and Austria had settled here and been instrumental in giving employment to 15,000 British workmen.

Extensions of the machinery for giving visas in Germany had failed to cope with the demand in the last 10 days, and much greater expansion would be necessary.

Then came a statement which made the House audibly uneasy. Though large numbers of visas had been given only a small number of immigrants had yet reached our shores. Many must have stopped en route.

"Concentration camps", Members commented.

Two classes, Sir Samuel went on, he was ready to admit en masse, transmigrants and children.

Successful Experiment

Numbers of transmigrants could come for intensive training. An experiment of that kind had already been successful with hundreds.

He announced a promise this morning to Viscount Samuel that the Home Office would provide facilities for a large number of "non-Aryan" children, Jewish or half-Jewish. Lord Samuel and others had arranged to bring all such children from Germany whose maintenance is guaranteed by anybody.

Sir SAMUEL HOARE "commended to his fellow countrymen in general" this opportunity of saving the younger generation of a great people and mitigating the suffering of their parents and friends.

He admitted a "terrible dilemma" for the Jewish fathers and mothers in Germany, but he had been told by someone who had just returned from work among them that they were almost unanimous that their children should go.

Dr. Colijn, the Prime Minister of Holland, had offered a temporary refuge in his country if there was hope of the children coming here. We should offer no obstacle.

International Loan

For the larger effort, an international loan must be considered by the Evian Committee. We were ready to take our full part.

No Government was more sympathetic than our own, none more anxious to solve the problem or mitigate to the utmost the present suffering.

Mr. GRENFELL closed the debate with feeling untinged with vehemence. The quiet sincerity of his tones preceded immediately the passage, *nemine contradicente*, of the motion.

He spoke of the persons who came to the passport control office as if they were facing a tribunal which was to decide their life or death – and the help which was offered to them. The Jews had never failed to make their contribution to the destinies of the nations which had befriended them.

The Scotsman, Edinburgh, 22 November 1938

The Refugee Problem

Germany's latest drive against her Jewish citizens has given increased urgency to the refugee problem, which was the subject of an international conference at Evian last July. It was recognised that, while there was no lack of goodwill on the part of the nations taking part in the Conference, the practical problem of finding a permanent home for these unfortunates was beset by the greatest difficulties. Last night, the subject was discussed in the House of Commons, and again sympathy was freely expressed, but sympathy which cannot be translated into concrete schemes of settlement is of little avail. The most important contribution to yesterday's discussion in the House was made not during the debate but at question time by the Prime Minister. Mr. Chamberlain stated that, following the Evian Conference, the subject had been closely and constantly under examination by the Government. The practical outcome so far is not, however, very substantial. The United Kingdom itself cannot take any large number of immigrants. We have our own unemployment problem, and the admission of destitute refugees throws a heavy financial burden on the voluntary organisations who are undertaking responsibility for selecting, receiving, and maintaining these fugitives. Since 1923, about 11,000 men, women, and children have been settled in this country, in addition to some 4,000 or 5,000 who received temporary refuge pending settlement overseas. The Prime Minister did not hold out much hope of an increase in that rate of succour. Clearly, settlement in the United Kingdom offers no solution of a very large problem. What of the Colonial Empire? A large part, as Mr. Chamberlain pointed out, is not suitable for European colonisation, and, in addition, the interests of the native populations must not be prejudiced. But inquiries – which are being continued – show that provided suitable schemes are formulated and carried out by responsible organisations with a certain amount of financial backing, it may be possible to arrange for the settlement of parties of refugees in Tanganyika, Kenya, Northern Rhodesia, Nyasaland and, perhaps, British Guiana. About 50,000 acres might be available in Tanganyika – formerly German East Africa – in addition to a small scale settlement for 200 persons. The biggest, but also the most doubtful area lies in the interior of British Guiana. There, 10,000 square miles or more are available of land and climate deemed suitable.

The Socialists who raised the subject in the House of Commons last night appeared to be more concerned with an indictment of Germany than with the practical problems of finding new homes for these political and racial refugees. There is no excuse for Germany, just as there is and was no excuse for the horrible misdeeds of the Communists in Russia, about which Socialists and anti-Fascists are usually dumb. Germany has shown herself to be the brutal, domineering Power that many in this country and still more in France knew her to be at the time when those who are foremost in denouncing her were her sentimental champions. That she has been allowed to acquire the power to tyrannise over her own people and threaten Europe is due to the softness of those who wished to release her from the shackles of Versailles. Now they would willingly put her back in fetters, but it is too late. We have to accept things as they are and one of the problems that a resurgent Germany has presented to the world – unfortunately it is not the only problem – is this matter of the refugees. Something must be done, and it must be something on a big scale. But for the hostility of the Arabs Palestine would have provided an ideal outlet. It is obvious, however, that at the present time we must proceed cautiously in that country. The need of caution was ignored by several speakers in the House last night, but theirs is not the responsibility. The problem would be eased if Germany could be persuaded to allow her expelled subjects to take out with them at least a proportion of their capital; and a strong demand in that sense should be lodged in Berlin by the Powers jointly. It is improbable, however, that it would have any effect, for Germany's financial plight is so desperate that she positively craves the confiscation of Jewish capital. The problem is so big that no one country alone can solve it. The Socialist resolution – which the Government accepted and which was adopted unanimously – called for concerted efforts. The Standing Committee of the Evian Conference, on which 32 Powers are represented, supplies an international basis for joint action; and surely, with all the goodwill so lavishly expressed in the United States of America as well as here, means can be found for rescuing a large number, if not all, of these helpless sufferers, especially the children.

L'Ordre, Paris, 1 December 1938

UNDER THE SWASTIKA

No, the antisemitic violence was not spontaneous

On the contrary, it was wanted, organised by the Government and thoroughly prepared.

Information coming to us from Germany brings out with painful precision the character of the preparations and the desired cruelty that provoked the antisemitic excesses, or rather pretexts through the assassination of Herr vom Rath, and which at times assumed the veritable aspect of a pogrom.

In Stuttgart, everything was methodically organised. SS squads in civilian clothing, under the protection of the Gestapo, set fire to all the synagogues in the city according to a predetermined plan. Systematic acts of vandalism committed against Jewish shops made the population indignant. Moreover, numerous passers-by were arrested in the street for expressing critical remarks addressed to the Nazis.

In Aix-la-Chapelle, the excesses were such that equivalents were sought in vain in the chronicles of the Middle Ages. It seems to have been demonstrated today that the leaders of the Nazi Party and the Hitler Youth organised the operation well before the assassination in Paris. Several weeks, indeed, before the murder of Herr vom Rath, there was talk in National Socialist circles of a "radical clean-up" before freeing Aix-la-Chapelle of all of its Jews. Just as the burning of the Reichstag had been the signal to Hitler's hordes for the hunt for Socialists and Communists, similarly in Aix-la-Chapelle, the murder in Paris would have been the signal for antisemitic persecution.

At 2 o'clock in the morning, when the death of Herr vom Rath was made known, all the heads of Hitlerian organisations were pulled from their beds by specially sent emissaries, and received the order to assemble with their men at specific locations in the city. Shortly beforehand, the usually very calm streets in Aix-la-Chapelle rang with the cries of hounded people and the crashing of broken window panes. In troops of several dozen men, Hitlerians in uniform covered the city. The head of each troop was in possession of a list of Jewish shops and homes. Lorries loaded with stones went from one troop to another to resupply them with projectiles. The police forces were sufficient, but it seemed that their function consisted of showing the gangs the shortest route to the place of looting and devastation.

The troop that gathered at the synagogue was accompanied by policemen who asked the Nazis to dispose of their cigarettes as they carried gasoline and petrol in uncovered containers. The doors of the synagogue were forced and flammable liquid spread artfully and then lit. The fire brigade was on scene before the fire, and they had been ordered not to intervene until the flames threatened the façade of the synagogue.

Meanwhile, on the streets, terrifying scenes were unfolding. It started with the looting of the shops. The author of these notes heard three men from Hitlerian groups complaining irritably about finding shoes that were too small. After which, when all the Jewish shops had been ruined, Jewish residences were stormed, unfortunate occupants were hurled onto the streets, surprised out of their sleep, without being given time to dress; they were beaten with clubs and cudgels and were forced to move as a group.

The crowd, which until then had passively watched the spectacle, found that the limit had been exceeded. When an old Jewish lady collapsed to the ground, beaten by a Hitlerian, and other uniformed criminals continued their blows, shouting "Kill this Jewish sow!", a brawl ensued between the perpetrators and the crowd, who wanted to make them the wrongful party, and was stopped by the police. In spite of the immense danger of such a gesture, many people took the black and blue persecuted Jews who were on the brink of being unrecognisable into their homes and gave them shelter as well as provisions to enable them to flee.

Especially in Catholic circles disapproval was shown. "Today, they are burning the synagogues", one often heard, "tomorrow they will burn our churches."

In the Saarland, the pogroms have surpassed in terror and ignominy everything that has been seen from the Nazis up to now. But, even there, the people demonstrated their disgust and disapproval courageously. Indicating the true culprits were not feared, who were, as was underlined. This indicated the Nazi government and in particular Messrs Streicher, Goebbels and Himmler, and not the Jewish youth who assassinated M. vom Rath. Furthermore, one does not cease from pointing out that the perpetrators are solely recruited from amongst venal elements, and notably amongst those with debts at Jewish shops.

In Saarbrücken, those Jews torn from their beds with their families were taken to the synagogue and had to set fire to it themselves with straw prepared by the Nazis. Some of the young hooligans wanted to lock the rabbi in the burning temple, but the police opposed it. After which, the Jews were led through the town in procession. But the population displayed its great disapproval. A worker's wife burst into tears and asked the Nazis to let the unfortunates go without torturing them so. She was, naturally, arrested immediately.

In all places in the Saarland, incidents of the same magnitude can be reported, as well as a comparable disapproval on the part of the inhabitants. Certain details suffice to show the base degree of the Nazis' actions. In Ludweiler, for example, Hitlerians throw themselves like wild beasts on a Jew, a tailor by profession, and shout: "We want to pay you for the uniforms you made us." In another place, in Losheim, the Nazis throw all the furniture and crockery of a Jew called Silve onto the street. After which they required the family to clear everything off the street in the next hour. When they returned, everything was, naturally, in the same state as before and the Nazis reiterated their demand, giving another quarter of an hour to the unfortunates to remove the traces of this devastation. When they returned, after this brief delay, Silve had hanged himself from a tree and his wife had cut her wrists. Note that Silve is a severely war disabled person. For him, as with all the other Jews, the Nazis stole all the money they found in the house and drank it away.

Such instances could be multiplied ad infinitum. Everywhere is the same ferocity, the same spirit of plunder, everywhere these crimes are only committed by teams specially organised by the Gestapo and its head, M. Himmler, and finally everywhere the German population in its great majority either has watched this repugnant spectacle with an expression of silent disgust or has expressed its sympathy for the benefit of the victims.

Robert Dreux.

La Lumière, Paris, 2 December 1938

The assassin's racism

On the day after the German pogroms, which have aroused the indignation of all the people and all the governments, except that of M. Daladier, *L'Action Française*, organ of total nationalism, flew to the rescue of Hitler's Reich. On 20th November, M. Charles Maurras pressed the impudence as far as writing that the German Jews have been scolded at the most; the man with the kitchen knife, brimming over with hatred against a republican and disarmed Germany, tuned himself into a benevolent helper of the conquering and racist Germany. Charles Maurras' insolent lies have been taken up in diverse organs of international fascism published in French, notably by *Le Petit Marseillais*.

They are answered not with arguments, but with figures. Thus, here are incomplete and provisional statistics of the murders committed by the National Socialist gangs. We have drawn them up by referring solely to testimonies in the major conservative or liberal papers of Great Britain, the information of which has never been denied and whose professional scruples are universally recognised.

BUCHENWALD CAMP	146 deaths
DACHAU CAMP	70 deaths
JEWS BURNED ALIVE IN VIENNA DURING THE NIGHT OF 10th to 11th NOVEMBER	3 deaths
NUREMBERG POGROMS	15 deaths and 72 seriously injured
DÜSSELDORF POGROMS	6 deaths
"SUICIDES" IN MUNICH AND VIENNA	60 deaths
PRINCIPAL INDIVIDUAL MURDERS	Karl Herz, killed at Hilden, near Düsseldorf Karl Markus, owner of the café "Karema", in Düsseldorf, shot dead before the eyes of his seriously injured wife Leo Levy, miller, shot dead in Polzin, Pomerania Pintus, killed at Ludwigsburg, near to Stuttgart
"SUICIDES"	Dr. Bernhardt Rosenthal, gynaecologist in Berlin Dr. Loewe, radiologist in Frankfurt am Main Emil Kramer, from Munich Paul Wallisch, from Berlin

The Sachsenhausen concentration camp affair merits special mention. On 11th November, 62 hostages arrived there under escort; the majority of them were lawyers, doctors and professors. Under blows from whips, cudgels and bludgeons, the prisoners were immediately set upon. Twelve of them were killed. Amongst the injured, several of them had their eyes gouged out and the majority were taken away unconscious.

We have only reported limited information. The majority of the victims of the brown shirts could not be counted, let alone identified. On the other hand, it goes without saying that hundreds of Jews have died or are dying from their injuries. As M. Max Ferville wrote in *l'Intransigeant*, "the arrest of all Jewish doctors so that the wounded cannot receive treatment, leads to many of them dying."

Moreover, this violence and these murders have provoked indignant reactions on the part of the German people. Messrs Goebbels and Streicher have publicly taken sides and insulted "those who sympathise with the Jews". We have counted at least 500 arrests of "Aryans" who demonstrated their disapproval of the pogromists.

Manchester Guardian, 6 December 1938 –
LETTERS TO THE EDITOR

THE NAZI PERSECUTION OF JEWS
What is Happening in Vienna

To the Editor of the Manchester Guardian

Sir, – Like most other Left organisations, we are overwhelmed at the present time with the problem of dealing with refugees from the Fascist countries. Most urgent are the cases of anti-Fascists who were living in the Sudeten area and who are now given the alternative by the Czecho-Slovakian Government to leave the country or to return to the Sudeten area within a limited period.

Typical of one of these is a German who was sentenced to fifteen years for anti-Fascist activities in the Reich, who escaped across the Czecho-Slovakian frontier, and whose time limit to leave the country or to be deported to Germany expired last Saturday. We believe he is still in hiding in Czecho-Slovakia and hope to be able to get him away, but one of the difficulties is the limitation placed upon the visas by the British authorities. Only 100 visas have been allotted to all German anti-Fascists.

But my object in writing is not to draw attention only to the desperate plight of the refugees in Czecho-Slovakia. We tend to forget the tragic position of opponents of the Nazi regime, particularly if they belong to the Jewish race, who are left in Vienna. I attach a copy of a letter received from a Jewish Socialist in Vienna. It speaks for itself:

I want to tell you as shortly as possible how everything is. I think it is important that you should know what is going on and how urgent it is that help should still be given to enable the sufferers here to get out of the country. I do not think people in England can imagine what happens here to human beings. Hand-grenades have been thrown into the synagogues, and the crematorium looked like a battlefield. Flats have been totally robbed. If the Nazis could not find what they needed they smashed everything into pieces and the people were chased through the streets. They had to leave their flats with hardly anything on, sometimes in nightshirts and pyjamas. In some flats there now live from seventeen to thirty people because they are not allowed to live anywhere else. Other flats are empty because they have been closed officially.

Often when a Jew was caught in the street all his money, to the last penny, was taken away. All Jewish men who could be traced were arrested. They were fetched from their flats, from the headquarters of the Jewish Emigration Organisation, from public offices, passport offices, consulates, and even from hospitals. Poor Jews were arrested at the canteens where they got food; the food was either spilled on the streets or divided among other people. People were beaten in the streets, some of them so severely that they could not walk and fainted. Most of the people who were arrested have been freed, and they look as if they had undergone a serious illness. Some men were not ill-treated bodily; only their hair was shaved off. The men are not allowed, of course, to tell what happened to them while they were in prison, and they are threatened with the most terrible punishment if they do. But one hears one thing and another. It was, for instance, one of the great jokes among the Nazi guards to make one Jew beat another. God help them if they did not do it thoroughly! Once a boy declared that he would not beat his father, so the father was first beaten before the eyes of the son, and then the son before the father.

I have been told by a doctor who works in a Jewish hospital that many of the men have wounds of a most terrible and serious kind. There are many cases every day. People are brought with broken skulls. Some of them must lie on the floor, as there is not enough room for the many patients. Many die. Still more commit suicide. I have heard of seven acquaintances of mine who have killed themselves in these last few days. Most of them are women. The other day I saw four ambulances in fifteen minutes and that is no exception.

Friends of mine who lived in a small village were fetched the other day from their house. It was seven o'clock in the morning. There was an old man among them of seventy, a woman who was not much younger, their two daughters with their husbands, and two little children of seven and three years. They were driven like a herd of cattle through the village and brought to the police station at —. There the women and children were released after a short examination; the old grandfather was imprisoned for 24 hours without food (though he begged on his knees to get a tiny piece of bread) and then he was dismissed. Nobody knows where the two young men are, whether they are dead or alive. Their house and the money they had was confiscated. All that was left to them was 150 marks.

I know of another case where a man was missing for a week and then his wife found out that he was in a police prison. She was told that he would be taken to the concentration camp at Buchenwald. I think they tell this always to torture people, because I know of many cases where women were told by the Gestapo that their husbands or sons would be sent to a concentration camp and the men came home the following day. In this particular case, however, the man has not returned. Believe me, there is not one word in this letter which is not wholly true.

–Yours, &c.,

FENNER BROCKWAY General Secretary I.L.P.

35, St. Bride Street, London, E.C. 4, December 5

L'Ordre, Paris, 6 December 1938

At the Sachsenhausen concentration camp, 12 Jews have been beaten to death

We have just learned the dreadful fate that was reserved for 62 Berlin Jews, arrested as hostages during the pogroms. They were, for the most part, lawyers, doctors, engineers, traders and two rabbis. They were transferred to Sachsenhausen concentration camp in a single transport, led by a Berlin police officer and supervised by 12 policemen.

At the entrance to the concentration camp, the transport was awaited by two sections of SS in black uniforms. The police officer offloaded the Jews from the lorry which brought them and, at the entrance, ordered them to proceed to the camp commandant's office and present themselves there. Only, the unfortunates had to begin by parading past two rows of thugs in black uniform, holding whips, cudgels and clubs.

The police officer, fearing the worst, asked the SS chief to let the Jews pass freely. The SS chief responded dryly that his duty consisted solely of taking the hostages to the required place. The Jews therefore had to pass through the two rows of SS whilst the most savage blows rained down on them. The policemen, unable to bear the cries of the martyred men, turned away. Those Jews who fell to the ground were beaten black and blue. This orgy of brutality lasted for half an hour. Then, other detainees were called on, and ordered to carry the unfortunates lying on the ground. Of the 62 Jews, 12 were dead, having had their skulls fractured.

The majority of the others lost consciousness, their faces were unrecognisable and all were covered in wounds and injuries. The chief of the SS section handed the police officer an "acknowledgment of receipt" confirming that he had brought the exact number of hostages.

This all took place on the 11th November 1938, in the afternoon, within Sachsenhausen concentration camp. As awful as these scenes of horror are, they only constitute one example among hundreds of similar occurrences which have taken place throughout the Third Reich during the month of November 1938.

L'Ordre, Paris, 15 December 1938

What I saw at Dachau camp

Eighteen thousand opponents of Hitler's regime, of whom twelve thousand Jewish, are subject to the cruellest treatment

The *National Zeitung* of Basel publishes an interview about an escape from the Dachau concentration camp where 18,000 people are interned, many of whom are Jews and a group of Austrian opponents of Hitler's regime. For reasons one can easily understand, the Swiss newspaper does not communicate the name of its informant. The article is signed Meyer, a name as common in Switzerland as Durand is amongst us.

The number of Jews interned in Dachau following the night of the pogroms on 10th November is in the region of 12,000. It is easy to make the calculation as there are 14 barracks, called blocks, each of which is fitted out to accommodate 800 men.

M. Meyer evidently had trouble remaining as objective as possible and avoiding giving the impression that he was seeking to arouse indignation through exaggerated stories. Thus when I asked him if it was true that they intentionally or out of negligence allowed prisoners to die from cold, he answered animatedly . . . ,

I must clear things up. War was expected last May. In that case it was the intention to intern all Jews, for whom they had 10,000 suits made of blue and white striped canvas. Meanwhile, winter came and the clothes of very thin material provided only a very relative protection against the cold and humid climate in this marshy region where Dachau camp is located. The last arrivals could be counted amongst the most fortunate, as they were permitted to keep their own clothes. But the first 10,000 had to swap their warm and comfortable suits and underclothes for the canvas uniforms; their belongings were kept in numbered sacks. Those who have the chance to leave the camp alive see all their belongings back on leaving.

M. Meyer also consoles himself for having to sleep on hard planks. He explains this by the fact that every day, on cleaning the dormitories, some of the straw supplied at the beginning was lost. As it was never renewed, it ended up disappearing entirely. But, he adds, it would be wrong to attribute this to deliberate intention. In order to protect themselves from the cold at night, each prisoner had a blanket. For those who had the good fortune to be able to sleep, not in one of the dormitories but in a heated room, this sufficed. Nevertheless one was required to remove clothes and shoes on pain of receiving 25 strokes of a cane.

M. Meyer states that, as in Württemberg, the arrests were normally operated by law and order organisations, it was quite different in particular towns in Baden, where scenes of unspeakable barbarity could be seen to occur. In Kiel for example, just as in Offenburg, where the poor people were forced to march in step whilst singing Nazi songs. The only consolation which befell them was to note that the population did not hide its disgust and indignation at the sight of these proceedings.

After an interminable journey by rail and by bus, at last we arrived at Dachau, M. Meyer recounted. There was a roll call of all those who had brought a parcel with them which they had had to hand over to the guards before the journey. These were returned to them, but accompanied by a volley of blows with sticks administered by the SS guards. As for me, I congratulated myself for not having had a parcel; all the more so because their contents had to be given up to the authorities later with the clothes. Thus the unfortunates drew no advantage from their foresight.

I will never forget my first night; night of terror in a waiting room full of poor people sobbing with despair and terror, fearing death, completely demoralised by the brutal treatment administered by young delinquents of 18 years of age. The following morning, there was registration of new arrivals, medical inspection, shower, clothing and allocation to different blocks. For the majority of us, these formalities saw the end of the beatings, except as punishment for some so-called offence. One was beaten more for simple pleasure of beating us. Indeed, respect for the uniform amongst these people is held to such a degree that in their eyes a prisoner wearing convict's clothing has a right to more consideration than one dressed in civilian clothes.

The daily schedule begins at 5 o'clock in the morning on weekdays and 6 o'clock on Sundays. Ablutions are supervised by the room elder, who has 200 people under orders. Basins of water are placed in the middle of the room. Those who have the means can buy a toothbrush, soap and a mechanical razor at the canteen. One is allowed to have up to 15 marks sent from outside each week, but this money disappears in no time at all, as the price of food and clothing are exorbitant. I will have the opportunity to say more about breakfast, which followed morning ablutions.

At half-past five, everyone had to gather on the main road alongside the blocks. Those with cleaning duties in the rooms can count themselves lucky, as they have half-an-hour less to stand still in the cold. As soon as the barrack has been made orderly, detachments march block by block to gather for general assembly on the main square where every morning there is roll call of the 18,000 internees. Not only in the morning, however, but three times daily: at half past two, and again at half past six. The eldest in each block is charged with checking with the aid of their lists. Of a morning, this usually lasts until half past seven, but when there is any complication, departures, lost glasses or I don't know what, this can only finish towards 10 o'clock. You can imagine what this means for the elderly of 60 or 80 years dressed in thin clothes, remaining at attention in the rain, the cold, shoulder to shoulder, former professors, bank directors.

Aryan internees, "political prisoners", the "dodgers of the labour law" [work shy], "Bible Students" [Jehovah's Witnesses] (American religious sect heavily persecuted by the Third Reich), are recognisable by their respective badges; after the roll call they have to work, mostly in the construction of new barracks.

A group was pointed out dragging an enormous roller; they were the former governors of Austria. One recognised the former minister Kienboeck, and the mayor of Vienna, Schmitz.

As for the 12,000 Jews, they are not even judged worthy of working. They have to march, exercise and do gymnastics; at first they were allowed to sing, but not any more. You could cite many an example of the goodwill of junior officials, who are themselves former internees; but all indulgence on their part represents a danger to themselves. When there are SS guards close at hand, one walks faster, carries out exercises on tiptoe or they make you run kilometres. The more the underlings are hard on the internees, the greater their chance of being freed.

There are individual or collective punishments. The latter are generally a prolongation of the painful physical exercises. The less severe individual punishment is to find oneself going without supper. On the slightest infraction, a cross is placed by you on the register: it is a warning there. On the third cross, they give you 25 blows with a stick. There are more severe punishments which I only know about through hearsay: such as being tied to a tree with your head hanging [Baumhängen], or you are thrown into a dark dungeon. As for insults such as "load of filth", "shit", "pigs", one does not pay much attention as they are frequent.

There are many deaths at Dachau. I know of cases where in 20 days there were 5 to 7 deaths in a block of 800 men; after all it is only 1 per cent in 20 days! Cases of pneumonia are frequent. One man was shot by a patrol for having probably inadvertently opened the door to the room at night. Another received the same fate for calling the camp authorities assassins aloud. A third died from an embolism.

Moving on to the everyday, breakfast consists of coffee and dry bread. In the beginning there was butter; but this was withdrawn from Jews, supposedly because they could use it to protect themselves from the cold! At midday there is soup during the week and stew on Sunday; fish on Friday. There is, of course, no notice taken of the prejudice of the Jews against pork. No "kosher" food. But although the usual is not copious, the cooking is not bad and one can say that the electric fittings are models of their type. In the evening there is tea with a piece of sausage or cheese. Those who have pocket money can supplement their rations in the canteen.

M. Meyer assured me that the most terrible thing about Dachau was neither the cold, nor the hunger, nor even the fear, but the uncertainty. The common law prisoner in prison knows the length of the sentence that he has to undergo, but in Dachau one is dependent on the whim of the authorities or dark and unknown forces.

Do not forget that this does not only relate to Dachau. Besides the 12,000 Jews who are interned there, there are many more of them in other concentration camps such as Buchenwald, Oranienburg [Sachsenhausen] and Chemnitz. It is estimated that around 80,000 is the number of those who have been torn from their occupations like this, from their families, without knowing anything to be blamed for.

One asks oneself what all this may well mean. M. Meyer gives an explanation: according to him it concerns an intention of the Nazi leaders to rid Germany of all the Jews without exception at any cost. There is no longer a single Jew within Germany who does not wish fervently to leave the country, whatever it may cost them. "These persecutions have another consequence, certain countries, and notably the United States of America and the British Empire show greater disposition to open their borders to unfortunate German Jews."

Very recently I heard a senior German official complaining about the bad attitude of many Swiss towards Germans make the following remark: *"Our measures are without doubt special, but what does that signify abroad?"*

"Special measures"? Without doubt! But when, as in the case that concerns us now, that of the Jews, these methods are applied precisely in view of the impression they create abroad, the foreigner has the right to express his opinion. The authors of these pogroms, which have reached the depths of baseness and barbarity without equal, even in the Middle Ages, do not have the right to be surprised if the reaction abroad is not confined to a simple expression of pity for the Jewish victims.

Evening Standard, 22 December 1938

20,000 Jews Freed from Camps Tell of Hardships

BERLIN, Thursday.

Twenty thousand Jews, put in concentration camps during the recent antisemitic campaign in Germany, have been released within the past month. All of them had to sign forms when they left stating that they would not give any information about the camps.

Nevertheless, certain statements have been made. Here are some of them:

In some camps one form of punishment was to have to stand to attention for 30 minutes in the glare of searchlights.

At one time in one camp 16,000 men were in quarters designed for 7,000.

Camp inmates have to sing joyous songs to visitors to show how happy they are.

Conditions Improved

During a cold spell, a rumour was spread in Buchenwald that caps would be distributed, as the inmates up till then had been bare-headed. Those who inquired about the rumour were made to do physical jerks. But conditions have improved there in recent weeks. Men are not forced to work, and they are allowed to receive warm clothes from friends and relatives.

At Sachsenhausen, it is said that in some cases men were required to sign a form handing over such gifts to the winter help campaign. One man had to have his leg amputated. Gangrene had set in after the leg had suffered from a contusion.

Almost all those released have badly inflamed hands, because they were made to do heavy work and were not allowed gloves. They worked in the rain, snow, or frost without any change of clothes. Their clothing became frozen into a solid mass and then they had to sleep at night in the same attire while it partially thawed out.

146 Deaths in Seven Months

During the last seven months, it is calculated there have been 146 deaths in all the camps.

At present Sachsenhausen is rated as the worst camp. Until recently, it had 2,000 inmates. Two groups of business men from Hamburg, after they had been admitted to the camp, had to stand continuously in the courtyard – one for 16 hours and the other for 26 hours.

In all camps Jews wear on their shirts a Star of David on a coloured background. The colour indicates their offence – green for those who had previously been sentenced to concentration camps, red for race pollution, blue for political offences.

Precedence is being given to ex-servicemen in releases and they are not forced to sign the customary promise to emigrate. Others are ordered to leave the country, often in as short a period as 10 days. Naturally they cannot obtain a visa, and they have either to go into hiding or try to leave the country illegally.

If caught again they are taken back to the camps, but most of them seem to vanish. – British United Press.

JEWISH CENTRAL
INFORMATION OFFICE

People

C.C. Aronsfeld (1910–2002)
Alfred Wiener's assistant in London, where Wiener recruited him in 1938. He obtained accreditation as a journalist for a succession of short visas for the Netherlands which enabled him to work intermittently in Amsterdam and in London for the JCIO; after WWII he edited the *Wiener Library Bulletin* and in 1961 became acting director of the Wiener Library until he left in 1966 to become Senior Research Officer at the Institute of Jewish Affairs.

Louis Bondy (1910–1993)
Born into a cultured Jewish family in Berlin, his father was a well-known journalist. Bondy studied architecture in Berlin and Geneva; between 1932 and 1936 he found work as a journalist, translator, barman and photographer in Paris, Spain and London. He applied for a job at the JCIO in Amsterdam and Alfred Wiener recruited him in 1937; in Amsterdam he met Elisabeth Leda, a secretary at the JCIO from 1934 onwards, and married her in 1939; Bondy was the first of the JCIO staff to go to London to find premises. From August 1940, when Wiener left London for New York, Bondy became de facto head of the Wiener Library; after the war he became a bookseller in Bloomsbury and specialised in miniature books.

Prof. Dr. David Cohen (1882–1967)
Born in Deventer, he studied classics at Leyden, Leipzig and Göttingen. He set up the Zionist students' organisation as well as

the first Dutch Zionist youth groups; he taught classics in Leyden and became professor of ancient history at Amsterdam in 1926. Together with Abraham Asscher and three others he founded the *Comité voor Bijzondere Joodse Belangen* [Committee for Special Jewish Affairs] and *Comité voor Joodsche Vluchtelingen* [Committee for Jewish Refugees] in the early 1930s to assist the increasing numbers of refugees arriving in the Netherlands. Alfred Wiener approached Cohen in 1933 for assistance to establish the JCIO in Amsterdam, and Cohen became its president and lent his prestige and influence to its work. From February 1941 Cohen and Asscher led the *Joodsche Raad* [Jewish Council], which cooperated with the German authorities in the Netherlands and implemented its antisemitic policies, attracting much criticism at the time and later. Cohen was amongst the last Jews to be deported to the Theresienstadt Ghetto; after his release in May 1945 he was convicted of collaboration (which was annulled in 1950); he resumed his university work in Amsterdam.

Dr. Eva Reichmann (1897–1998; née Jungmann)
Historian and sociologist, she worked for the *Central-Verein deutscher Staatsbürger jüdischen Glaubens (CV)* [Central Association of German Citizens of Jewish Faith] (1924–1938). She married a prominent CV official, Hans Reichmann (1900–1964), and edited the monthly magazine *Der Morgen* [The Morning] (1933–1938). The couple emigrated via the Netherlands to Great Britain in 1939, where she worked for the BBC and for the Wiener Library (1945–1959), becoming the Library's research director; she was also on the boards of the Association of Jewish Refugees and the Leo Baeck Institute. *Novemberpogrom* report B. 87 has handwritten comments by her.
    [Source: Wikipedia; Jürgen Matthäu and Mark Roseman, Jewish Responses to Persecution, 1933–1938, Rowman & Littlefield, 2009.]

Dr. Alfred Wiener (1885–1964)
Born in Potsdam, Wiener studied history, philosophy, Jewish theology and Arabic in Berlin. He was in the Middle East from 1909 to 1911 and was a soldier in the German Army in WWI, awarded an Iron Cross. From 1919 he worked in the *Central-Verein deutscher*

Staatsbürger jüdischen Glaubens [Central Association of German Citizens of Jewish Faith], where he identified the NSDAP as a threat in 1925. He helped to found the *Büro Wilhelmstrasse* in 1928 to gather intelligence about the Nazi regime and antisemitism and disseminate it internationally; he continued similar work in Amsterdam between 1933 and 1939 by setting up the Jewish Central Information Office (JCIO) with Dr David Cohen. In the summer of 1939 Wiener obtained visas for all the JCIO staff (which Kurt Zielenziger apparently hid) and much of its books and documents were taken from Amsterdam to London. His wife and three daughters stayed behind and were later caught and deported to Bergen-Belsen and liberated in 1945 but his wife died shortly afterward. Wiener spent most of WWII in the USA, continuing intelligence gathering work for the British government and others, and returned to London in 1945. He reorganised the former JCIO into a library and research centre (subsequently named the Wiener Library for the Study of the Holocaust & Genocide); he retired in 1961.

Kurt Zielenziger (1890–1944)
Born in Potsdam, he studied social sciences and graduated in 1912, and worked for various chambers of commerce and as a journalist and scholar. In 1919 he became deputy chief and later chief of the Berlin Press Office. He met Alfred Wiener in Berlin and occasionally contributed to the *CV Zeitung*; from 1926 he was Political Editor of the *Vossiche Zeitung* [oldest Berlin daily paper, liberal]. His best known book on the Jewish contribution to the German economy (*Juden in der deutschen Wirtschaft*) was published in 1930 and he also wrote for the *Encyclopedia Judaica* and *Handwörterbuch der Staatswissenschaft* [Concise Dictionary of Political Science]. He and his family left Germany for Paris in 1933 but moved to Amsterdam at Wiener's invitation to Zielenziger to join the Jewish Central Information Office as office manager and deputy director. Wiener left for London in 1939 but Zielenziger apparently did not wish to close the JCIO or leave Amsterdam, and he hid the visas that Wiener had obtained for the staff; Zielenziger was caught by the Nazis and taken to Bergen Belsen concentration camp he is believed to have perished there in 1944.

Other staff

Miss C. Asser
– archives

Joseph Bettelheim
– office manager

Anneliese Bielschowski (b 8.7.1907 Berlin)
– Wiener's private secretary (1934–1939)
– continued to work at the JCIO until the German invasion

James Cohen
– Krieg's assistant

Miss S. Delde
– Krieg's assistant

Mrs Friedlaender
– typist

Philipp Hart
– office boy

Miss N. Kohn
– archives

Bernhard Krieg (b 8.10.1908 Berlin or 20.4.1905)
– JCIO book keeper and cashier
– first taken to the transit camp Westerbork with Wiener's wife
  and children
– deported to Bergen-Belsen; perished

Miss Leda
– assistant secretary

Miss E. Mendelson
– typist

Mrs Veltman
– archives

Reports 1938–39

When ordering please quote: R 38/973
Amsterdam Z., Jan van Eijckstr. 14, I.
December 12th, 1938

Dear Sir(s),
We beg to inform you confidentially that KONRAD HEIDEN will finish soon a book he is writing on the *German pogroms*, which will be of about 5–6 sheets (80 pages) and will contain valuable documentation.

The work shall probably appear in German, English, French, Dutch, Norwegian and Swedish. Its price is not yet definitely established, but shall not be high.

We are at your disposal for all informations and subscription orders.
Yours faithfully
JEWISH CENTRAL INFORMATION OFFICE
Public Service Institute

The German Pogrom: November 1938

Under the date of December 12th, the *Deutsche Nachrichten* – the official German Government News Agency, publishes a lengthy statement regarding the treatment, now and to come, of German Jewry, and also concerning the manner of carrying out their entire emigration.

This official statement calls for the following comment:

1. The German Government deny their intention of establishing for German Jewry special residential quarters and municipal ghettos. Whether or no they actually did establish such quarters, seems, however, entirely immaterial.

   Now that in towns without number, savage hordes have reduced Jewish dwellings to matchwood,

Now that in a large number of cities Jewish families have had compulsory notice served to quit on, or shortly after, January 1st,

Now that in various districts of Germany, such Jewish dwellings as have yet been left intact are crowded with families from destroyed houses, or refugees from the country,

Now surely it is bordering on hollow mockery for the German Government to declare that they were not indeed intent upon establishing any ghettos.

2. The German Government refer to a "strictly lawful elimination of the Jews from economic life". This "strictly lawful" elimination is attested by thousands of Jewish shops and businesses, also many solicitors offices and surgeries, being demolished, and even looted during the night of November 9 to 10.

Compulsory "Aryanisation", as had been practised for well over a year, by means of blackmailing Jewish shop owners into giving their signatures, and threatening imprisonment to anyone refusing to surrender of his own free will, the tactics of bringing false charges of all kinds for the sole purpose of dragooning the Jews into "Aryanisation" – all this had been the forerunner of the now proclaimed "strictly lawful regulation".

The German Government proclaim that the Jews would be forbidden to carry on retail trade, etc., as from January 1st; they would be allowed, however, to make their purchase in all German shops and take residence in all German hotels.

The facts are that thousands of German business establishments, especially in the provinces, will, in compliance with higher orders, sell nothing to Jews – that in thousands of hotels, even since 1935, no Jew is permitted to stay, those recognised as Jews are chased into the streets like dogs.

If it is lawful – as it is alleged – for a Jew to be in charge of purely Jewish establishments, this has been responsible for two owners of Jewish coffee houses, at Dusseldorf and Nuremberg, to lose their lives in the pogrom during the night of November 9–10.

3. What the German Government suppress, however, is the following: The synagogues, prayer-houses, and many mortuaries, in nearly every congregation of Germany, Austria, and Sudetenland, have been set on fire, or blown up. In many cases the scrolls of the law and the ritual objects were separately burnt, or soiled and defiled. Some 30,000 Jewish men were, by brutal force, dungeoned in

concentration camps, often compelled to do hard labour under degrading circumstances. The suffering entailed by that exertion and ill-treatment, has actually driven many into death. Owing to systematic false reports, it has not yet been possible to ascertain anything even near the actual number of deaths caused by "pneumonia", or "heart failure". That in the course of the pogrom, a number of people died or were killed, is established through the evidence of absolutely reliable sources.

Driven to despair, with no prospect of either work or food, tormented with the likelihood of renewed imprisonment, those released from the concentration camps, and those hitherto yet spared, seek hurriedly to leave the country, with wife and child. Then they are again seized by a merciless legislation that will rob them of nearly everything yet left, by means of taxes, money devaluation, indemnity, and the licence indulged in by some officials. So they are forced, in some other country – if any be still open to them – to begin anew the struggle for life, with 10 marks in their hands, and if they are lucky, with the remnants of a once well-furnished household. Suffering and tears are the marks of their progress.

The German Government, in their reference to "strictly lawful measures", feign that the Jews in Germany have not had a hair touched, and that they will be able to carry on, even without a trade and income. The noted *Neue Zürcher Zeitung* (Zurich), on November 24, writes:

"The SCHWARZE KORPS to-day in a leading article, foreshadows a new series of anti-Jewish measures, the final act being the assassination of all Jews in Germany, unless foreign countries provide for their removal and resettlement. It would be amiss to regard this threat as a mere dummy or a manoeuvre which was not meant seriously".

In the "Official Journal of German Jurisdiction", "*Deutsche Justiz*", published by the Reich Minister of Justice, Dr. F. Gürtner, the Supreme Party Judge of the Nazi Party, Herr Buch, writes: (p.1660, No. 42) "The Jew is not a man . . ." That in fact he is treated worse than the lowest beast in Germany, has been realised by the civilised world, since 1933 and more especially since the pogrom of November 9–10.

When ordering please quote: R 38/934
                          Amsterdam Z., Jan van Eijckstr. 14, I.
                                          December 12th, 1938

Dear Sir(s),

We enclose to-day the fifth instalment of the reports on the
German Pogrom.

Again the reports are published in English, French, German, and
Dutch, and any quantity of them may be obtained from this office,
free of charge.

Now that the general Press is ceasing more and more to report
on the fearful events in Germany, it would seem, even more than
before, advisable to secure for information such as that enclosed,
due distribution, especially among Christian acquaintances and
business friends.

You are at liberty to publish the reports, save where an express note
to the contrary has been affixed. As usual, no mention must be
made of our office being your source.

Yours faithfully
JEWISH CENTRAL INFORMATION OFFICE
Public Service Institute

The German Pogrom

November 1938

Devastations in Halberstadt, Central Germany

Although the ground work of the synagogue still stands, the ancient
interior, of considerable artistic value, has been smashed to bits. It
seems probable that the chandeliers too, a 17th century piece of
work, have been destroyed. The Holy Ark in the synagogue was
covered with a curtain, overlaid with precious embroideries, dated
about 1650: this too has probably gone.

As in the case of so many cities, even the mortuary, built in 1895,
was blown up.

Defiling prayer books and scrolls of the law

Reports from various parts of the Reich, more especially from Vienna, tend to confirm that more than usual savagery was applied to objects of ritual use. On the other hand, certain stray reports received also state that such objects had been put to safety, not indeed by the S.A. but by policemen who still had a spark of religious sentiment. But these are rare exceptions.

As a rule, the scrolls were torn up, or subjected to even worse blasphemy which, from consideration of readers' religious feelings, we do not propose to describe in detail. It is known, for example, that in front of the Pestalozzi Strasse Synagogue, Berlin, which together with the adjoining Middle Class Kitchen has been smashed to atoms, scrolls, altar cloth, and prayer book have been lying in the street for hours, befouled and defiled. Nor is this sort of thing known from Berlin only: it has happened in other cities in even grosser form.

The pogrom in the Rhineland

There is now an ever-growing number of eye-witness reports available on the occurrences in the big cities. The eye-witnesses include many non-Jews who, during the relevant time, had been engaged in Germany in business, or otherwise, and now, filled with indignation and shame, tell their tale of what human bestiality is capable. Out of the mass of reports of that kind – there are hundreds of them – the following is quoted, giving a description of the pogrom in a big city in the Rhineland.

"Not only men but also women and even children were manhandled by the pogromists, and hounded, in their shirts, into the streets during that terrible night. Anything at all subject to damage in the dwellings, was destroyed. Linen, suits, and dresses were torn up with daggers. Wall washing stands, even wall Majolika baths, were demolished with hammers. Even wall paper and linoleum floor cloth was destroyed.

"Nearly all men were arrested. No regard was had to age. First into prison, then the prisoners were taken away, apparently to Dachau, near Munich. It must be born in mind that this is a distance of some 600 kilometers, so probably a journey by rail of at least 12 hours. As late as mid-November, a fortnight after the arrests, the women were still without any news as to the where-abouts of the men. The mental condition of the unhappy women beggars description. The immediate consequence was nervous break-downs and fits of depression, which, for all we know, may last for the rest of their lives.

"Having gradually been deprived, during the last few years, of their income and business, the Jews have now had most of their very last possessions destroyed: house or room, clothes, linen. There are many in our city that will sink into hopeless debt as money must be found for the officially enforced repairs of the window panes, fire places, water pipes, etc. – under pain of new reprisals. Those engaged in professions, as far as that was still at all possible, their entire library destroyed, upon which in many cases they must depend for their work".

"May God have compassion on the poor refugees"

Throughout Holland, a street collection was held, on December 3rd, in aid of Refugees of all creeds, including the children of refugees.

Moving evidence of readiness to help and gladness of sacrifice has, on that occasion, been evinced, especially on the part of the poorer classes. A woman, herself unemployed, gave the money she had received that week from the local unemployment relief. A Christian policeman gave his week's salary.

A poor woman sent a gold ring and two ear-rings with precious stones; in a letter enclosed, she wrote to the Collection Committee: "This, my gift is the best I can do. May God bless it, and may He have compassion on the poor refugees".

The total yield of the nation-wide Dutch collection on behalf of the refugees is estimated at hfl. 500,000. –, i.e. about £55,000, or 10 million French Francs.

Robbing ritual silver implements

According to eye-witness reports, the synagogue fires at Frankfurt am Main were marked by a very special savagery. At the Friedberger Anlage Synagogue, the fire was rekindled, the first attempt at arson being thought inadequate. Large quantities of benzene were used for that purpose. On the day of the first act of arson, the safe containing the silver ritual implements was unwolded [sic], and its contents stolen. Afterwards the police proceeded to accuse the Jews of having laid the fire, and actually brought a formal charge against them.

They who are persecuted for the sake of their race and their faith.

Nation-wide collection in Holland in aid of the refugees

A nation-wide collection has been held in Holland in aid of those persecuted "for the sake of their race and their faith". This big collection is to benefit above all the refugees from Germany. The members of all Dutch Youth Associations and numerous other organisations had promised their support of this idealistic action. The Prime Minister, Dr. H. COLIJN, delivered a broadcast address on December 1st, in support of this collection.

"If there be any doubts, he said, as to whether it is at all necessary to stress our people's good will and readiness to succour those in deepest distress, these doubts are legitimate, for the good-will of our people is there. But what might not yet be known to all, is the extent of the distress owing to the large number of people who have been seeking a refuge in this country since the first days of November. On the eve of the collection day, the number of the persons who have been allowed to come to Holland during the last few days, will be nearly 4,000. Computing the cost per day and head, for housing, feeding, and clothing, at about hfl 1.50, this would – were these 4,000 to live on public expenses only – require an amount of some hfl 2,000,000 per year... What is needed here is not the alleviation of distress for a few days, or a single act of more or less generous relief: what is needed now is a continuous support for a large number of people during prolonged period... And in giving our help we are fulfilling God's Commandment respecting our neighbour, for though there is much distress in our own country requiring help, this is a case where suffering must be alleviated such as cuts far deeper into life than we have ever experienced yet."

The Lord Mayor of Amsterdam, (Dr. W. de Vlugt) has also issued a manifesto in support of the collection.

"Never have I appealed in vain to my fellow citizens when the call was for the alleviation of distress... How could it be otherwise now? I wish to tell my fellow citizens only this one thing: Let the size of your donation square the size of your horror at the fact that a treatment such as countless innocent men have had to endure, should be possible still in these days; let it be in accordance with your sympathy with so many utterly unhappy, and worthy of your pride of living in a country where man is man still."

Temples in flames
A propaganda cinema picture in favour of the nation-wide collection bearing the title of TEMPLES IN FLAMES has been produced in most of the Dutch cinemas during the last days of November.

Two folded hands appeared. The figure of a man, explaining the pictures was then to be seen. Airship, motorcars, express trains, all the marvels of modern technique were shown on the screen, but all the wonders which diminish space seem to increase the distance between human beings and do not prevent persecutions and medieval tortures used even in 1938, these facts having seemed to be impossible in view of civilization's progress.

House in flames, crumbling walls explosions further appear on the screen; desperate people amongs [sic] debris, horrible pictures of human misery are seen, whilst the human voice calls to support the victims of persecution.

The result of the nation-wide collection in Holland has surpassed, following latest information, 400.000 florins.

Note:
There are still available a number of profoundly distressing reports – supplied by trustworthy correspondents – on the occurrences in the Concentration Camps. No publication however can be contemplated in those cases as, on the one hand, some kind of reprisal must be feared for the thousands that are still in German concentration camps, and on the other hands, the informations are in themselves so appalling that German Jews, with their relatives still in the camps, would almost certainly be disastrously affected.

The extracts given below, not by any means the very worst yet of their kind, are reproduced here with the very earnest request not to forward them to German Jews.

The informations are confidential. No publication can be authorised.

From "Hell"

"On our arrival at the camp we were received by a large number of SS who at once began to kick us and manhandle us with bludgeons and rifle butts – so much so that the Police, up to now in charge of us, stood dumbfounded, and then speedily made off. We were then lined up, and made to march, or rather run. This physical exertion, lasting for 15 minutes, and the continuous kicking and beating by the SS resulted in two men fainting and dropping. I got the impression that they were dead, but as I could not verify it, I would not insist."

"The most terrible thing was – though negligible when compared with the severe physical ill-treatment – that we were forced to remain standing in the camp for more than 15 hours. When a man broke down, kicks and rifle butts were applied to him. Another had to carry about the camp a poster, bearing an offensive inscription, for 8½ hours, with his arms stretched out all the time. The SS men, the oldest of whom was hardly 25 yet, made a point of going for Jewish looking prisoners. But those belonging to a higher class, such as professionals, teachers, etc., were also put to severe suffering. Younger people, especially of a sporty type, met with some clemency."

"Everything in the camp had to be done running. Work and all. We had to carry sand and cement bags. For carrying the sand the prisoners had to take off their coats and put them on again the other way around. The coat was then filled with sand, so far down as room would permit. This heavy load would then have to be carried about for 5 minutes. Worse still were the cement bags. Heavy weights – I would put some of them at hundredweight – were indiscriminately thrust upon the necks of men aged 60 or even 65. Sometimes the sand was carried on a so-called stretcher. The wood then would cut deep into the hands, and caused injuries.

One morning we were forced to stand for 12 hours in the pouring rain, without any cover on our heads. The following day, for 4 hours, without food and without being allowed the natural convenience."

Certain sections in the Concentration Camps, now gorged with thousands, form an exception, however rare, in that the inmates there are accorded a reasonably tolerable treatment.

The German Pogrom

November 1938

Up to December 15th, 213 burnt houses of worship ascertained
According to a list which, in an alphabetical order, gives the localities of the burnt synagogues, and has been borne out, item by item, by trustworthy eye-witnesses or otherwise, so far 213 synagogues, prayer houses, and mortuaries have been set on fire. Most of them are completely burnt out. In some cases, the fire has not destroyed the whole synagogues but only part of it,

This number of synagogue fires is merely a first estimate. The final figure may be assumed to be much higher.

Two messages from France
Two French authors of world-wide fame have published recently messages concerning the German pogrom.

The first comes from M. François MAURIAC, one of the leading Catholic authors of France and member of the French Academy. It runs as follows:

"We might write that there is no comfort among men for the martyrs in Germany and Austria, that no words will avail save those that rise before God and earnestly plead justice.

"Yet there is one thought that might help them not to despair: this time they have not suffered in vain. The abundance of their suffering has awakened the world. The nations of the earth all abandon themselves to a feeling of shame and disgust.

"This time again the cross will prevail. The cry that rises from the hell of Dachau will prevent us from falling asleep again. And a day shall come, a day of joy and atonement, when we shall remember that we, even we Christians of all Churches, had prayed and suffered in communion with the sorrow-stricken of Israel, and that we are mindful of that fraternity which unites us in the God of Abraham, Isaac, and Jacob, in the "God of clemency and comfort", as Pascal calls Him.

"And we turn to one German who would assuredly also have been driven from Germany to-day we turn to Beethoven to join all in the Love Hymn of his ninth Symphony: ALL MEN SHALL BE BROTHERS...»

The second message, by M. ROMAIN ROLAND, reproduced in *L'Univers Israélite*, Paris, No. 13, p.203, contains the following passages:

"O ye great Germany, that I have loved and that I am loving still – I know that your best sons, that thousand unblemished men are under the sway of the terror, that they are crushed by the ignominy of the nefarious deeds of criminals and madmen.

"I doubt not that the proudest and most righteous amid your hosts are deeply humiliated, and stirred, by the indignity of the deeds which are the Government's doing, and which they are made to witness without being free to speak – deeds of a cowardly licence indulged in by ordered mobs, committed against thousands of peaceful and industrious, even defenceless, men, women, and children of Germany.

"They are profoundly stirred by the savage outbursts of brutality on the part of the authorities, against a race though it be struck down, be there never so many of its fighters that spilt their blood for Germany in the Great War, be there never so many its geniuses that have enhanced the glory of Germany.

"No enemy of Germany could have inflicted upon that country disgrace like this, nor such not to be guessed at harm, as did these wretched adherents of a race doctrine which is dishonoured before the eyes of the world..."

So far 34 deaths ascertained
The names and addresses of 34 Jews who either perished in the concentration camps, or were killed during the pogrom, or committed suicide in the wake of the pogrom, have now been ascertained.

The figure is undoubtedly higher by far. The exact and attested figure will only be known in a few weeks' time.

When ordering please quote: R 39 / 934 H
Amsterdam Z., Jan van Eijck Straat 14.
January 8, 1939

Dear Sirs –

We beg to enclose to-day two reports, one of them containing a provisional survey which is needs incomplete.

As usual, these reports have been published again in English, German, French, and Dutch, and any quantity may be obtained from this office free of charge. You are authorised to make such use of the reports as you deem fit without naming us as your source.

We herewith conclude the series of our reports on the German Pogrom. Any information supplementing our materials will be welcome, especially information concerning deaths, which must however bear precise details as to persons, locality, etc.

Yours faithfully
JEWISH CENTRAL INFORMATION OFFICE
Public Service Institute

The German Pogrom: November 1938

The Child's sobbing: "Bread! That Bread!"

The "*Ostschweizerisches Tagesblatt*", published at Rorschach, Switzerland, has in its Number 276, a report on experiences and impressions of a Swiss lady who had been to Frankfurt-am-Main immediately after the Pogrom.

As the accuracy of the story as well as the trustworthiness of the author had been called in question, the Editor of the "*Ostschweizerisches Tagblatt*" issued, on December 22, the following statement:

"The author is a Swiss lady, well known to us, who, in her outlook on life stands as remote from Judaism as the writer himself. That she has related only her own experiences, and not any one word exaggerated, we infer from the identical reports, both written and oral, which we have received from Swiss and German witnesses to this undying shame of civilisation".

The report runs as follows:

... Frankfurt am Main. I stop in front of a destroyed synagogue, the guard stalking up and down in the rain, dull and worn out. Somebody has stopped next to me, and says: 'Struck down and humiliated we are, deprived of all human dignity.' A burning shock flashed all over me: 'A Jew! He'll be arrested on the spot.' I am looking at him in horror: it isn't a Jew, it is a man wearing the Party and ex-Servicemen's badge.

Struck down and humiliated, deprived of all human dignity. Who amongst us Swiss, who are happy indeed to be Swiss, is going to suffer himself to be of his own free will humiliated like this – who is going knowingly to drive us towards that sort of redemption?"

Two children passing by, aged about 5 and 8. 'Oh!', says the little one, pointing to the burnt out synagogue , 'Look what been doing to it. Them poor Jews'; and ere she has finished, the older girl hast slapped her face, saying in terror: 'Shut up, yer must not say such things, don't yer know!' Girls of 5 and 8. The little scene is unforgettable, unforgettable the timid look (the German look, Oh poor, poor Germany!) of the children as they hurry along.

'God, my God, dry bread all my life rather than play the executioner another night', these are the words screamed by a high police official, in office, in front of people that might have at once brought him to Dachau.

"My brother-in-law has shot himself, you know that, don't you?", a friend says to me by the by, and a little subdued: 'Well, he was a policeman, and one day he could stick it no longer'.

'My friend is in the Gestapo', a young girl tells me: 'he would give everything to get out of it, but the only way out is to the concentration camp.'

'We have only this choice left: either no honour, or no bread' – so a high school official tells me.

These are but observations at random.

At the station another 'consignment'. Dozens of Jews, and others guilty of making invidious remarks. They jump off the dark luggage vans, run the few yards to the dark railway truck. SA and SS lining the path, behind them the crowd, many of them with tears in their eyes, and flashed over their faces: "Shame, shame on us!", again and again. No snarling by the police to-day; they say almost gently: 'Pass on please, don't stop.' I feel like screaming, screaming, screaming – all of us screaming till the world quake in its foundations! Instead we pass on in silence, as the police order us to do, and we suffer hundreds of men and women to be driven into distress, and torture, and ruin. Were it only 'into death', it would be mercy, but these are a hundred deaths of body and soul.

The housewife will be punished for throwing away a cabbage heart or a zinc tube, fight the waste, all over. But the destruction wrought here in a few hours according to plan, not merely to everything beautiful and useful, no, even to indispensable things, is beyond computation. Not only confectionery and sweetmeat, e.g. in the Rothschild Café, have been smashed to bits and trampled upon, together with broken window glass and the rest of the stock: heaps of flour and eggs are gone. Spades have I seen used in clearing the shops – spades full of food, broken glass, etc. I still hear it clash. I still smell the smoke from the open cellar peep-holes, where the havoc has raged.

Then all the destroyed shops were boarded up with white planks. That on these unique hoardings, everywhere and over night, *Der Sturmer* should have posted its pictures, is not really surprising. It is in keeping with the rest. The stage management works well even here. But that on these planks, the distressing background of which is evident to every single passer-by, bills should be posted such as these: 'Laughter, and Mirth', and 'Melodious Review – Why not come and enjoy it too? At the Winter Grand Ball. Tickets sold at the Popular Education Settlement.' What is this other than immeasured bestiality? It leaves one horror-struck.

Again someone approaches me, my little cross being like a light. 'What are they saying in Switzerland about all these things?' And yet, do you know that the Jews are not the poorest yet? The poorest are we, the executioners, the despised, they that have lost 'all honour'.

. . . I will say no word about hundreds of individual cases which I have seen and heard of: crying children – at night in the parks – seriously ill dragged out of their beds – hunting people like animals – arrested . . . it burns and burns within you, because you are unable to help.

In the evening a child draws me near his little bed, and whispers: 'Auntie, they've smashed a baker's shop, and the bread was in the streets, Auntie, and they've been trampling on it, on the bread, I've seen it', and the child, overwhelmed, keeps sobbing into his cushions: that bread! that bread!

A *total survey attempted*

Below a survey is ventured of the German pogroms as from November 9 and 10, 1938. It is however exceeding difficult to render the survey correct in every detail, as it has proved almost impossible so far to obtain sufficient evidence for certain important figures. Estimates being unavoidable in most cases, great care has been taken to ascertain the available data through conscientious and responsible enquiries. The results may be assumed to have been put too low rather than too high.

Killed: At least 30, though the figure may be higher.

Deaths: Either as a result of fatal deterioration of an illness contracted in a concentration camp, or as a result of confinement in a concentration camp altogether.

1. At Buchenwald Camp, near Weimar, about 180 deaths.
2. At Sachsenhausen Cmp, near Berlin, about 45 deaths.
3. At Dachau, figure below 45, though not yet ascertained.

   These deaths mark the stand of December 1st, before the severe cold spell, as a result of which the death roll has probably mounted considerably.

Suicides: Though the exact figure cannot be stated with certainty, it may be said to be running into a few hundreds.

Burnt synagogues: About 500, not including small prayer rooms and mortuaries. In many cased, the demolition is complete, in others only parts have suffered. Further use of the synagogues is nearly always impossible, and besides forbidden by the police.

According to the latest reports, not only the *Worms* synagogue has been destroyed but also the adjacent revered Rashi Chapel with which are bound up many religious and historical memories.

Destroyed dwellings: No estimate, even approximately correct, has as yet been possible. Nor were dwellings destroyed in all towns. In Nuremberg, at least 700 dwellings may be said to have been

demolished, also solicitors' offices and surgeries. The final figure
may be assumed to be running into the thousands.

Business establishments: No reliable estimate possible. The figure is
certain to be running into the thousands.

Material damage

The material damage is so tremendous that it must be described
as beyond computation. Estimates from reliable English quarters
(*The Times*, New Year's supplement, of 2nd January, 1939, p. VI)
put the damage in Berlin alone at 13 million marks. Appraising the
middle value of a fully furnished dwelling at about 5,000 marks,
this would yield for Nuremberg alone, with its 700 destroyed dwellings, a material damage of 3,500,000 marks.

The indemnity

According to the Official Reich Gazette, No. 189, of November 14,
1938, the indemnity for the whole of German Jewry is fixed at one
milliard marks. Subject to the contribution are also the German
Jews living abroad as far as they have registered their property
in accordance with the decree of April 26, 1938. There will be
no summons for payment. The first 20% of the sum was due on
December 15, it being insisted on payment in cash.

Emigration

1. *Figures:* As a result of the pogroms, the emigration has been accel-
erated, partly in the form of illegal frontier crossing. The number
of these emigrants is estimated at between 5,000 and 10,000. The
number of the Jews still in Germany is difficult to compute; there
may yet be about 400,000. The number of the Jewish children still
in Germany is put at 50,000. Up to the present about 2,000 children may be said to have emigrated.

2. *More Impediments:* As a result of new foreign exchange decrees
the emigrant will not even be free to take with him the luggage he
pleases. It will therefore hardly be possible to take with him in the
luggage the sufficient supply of clothes, underwear, etc, unless the
excessive dues are paid, for each separate item. These decrees go so

far as to forbid the disposal of any kind of jewellery, not excluding wedding rings. These must be officially sealed in a case, before departure, and in that state taken over the frontier, after payment of the dues. The selection of what jewellery may be taken, is left entirely to the discretion of the authorities.

3. *Losses:* No affluent person can emigrate to-day without losing all but an insignificant fraction of his fortune. All according to what his assets consist of (cash, business, real estate), the rest actually at his disposal abroad is not likely to amount to more than 4 or 4½% of the fortune originally in Germany. In a large number of cases, the rate may be lower still.

Buying and selling

The Jewish shops are closed without exception. In a number of towns, Jews may yet buy in non-Jewish shops, in others they may not. In Kassel, Central Germany, the authorities have already had a first floor shop established where Jews may buy from Jews. This shop must not be marked by any external sign. It would seem that a ruling on some such lines is being prepared for the whole Reich, but nothing definite has as yet been made public. In the meantime, Jewish booksellers and publishers have also been forbidden to carry on their trade. It is learnt that the *Kulturbund* [Jewish Cultural Association] is going to open a Jewish book-shop.

Administration

The Reich Representation [Deputation] of the Jews in Germany, with its seat in Berlin, has ceased to exist in its old form. In its stead, the Gestapo has appointed a Committee consisting of six Jews who have to stop in Germany and whose task is, on the one had, to ensure Jewish emigration, and on the other, provide relief for those left behind. Most offices of the *Hilfsverein* as well as the Winter Relief have resumed work.

Cultural Activities

Immediately after the pogroms, such practising *Kulturbund* members as had recently been released from the concentration camps, albeit for this special purpose, were forced to resume work. Thus, for example close upon the pogroms, a review had to be staged, entitled *Gemischtes Kompott* [Mixed Fruit], (see the newly licensed *Jüdisches Nachrichtenblatt*, No. 1, of November 23, 1938). While daily women were receiving for burial, the ash urns of their husbands that either died or perished otherwise in the concentration camps. The National Socialist press published jubilantly, as evidence of the well-being of German Jewry, the fact that the *Kulturbund* performances were being continued without interruption.

The Jewish Press

The entire Jewish Press in Germany has been banned for an indefinite period. Reich Commissioner (*Jüdisches Nachrichtenblatt*), of which so far 9 issues have appeared. It is published twice weekly. Editor is, by order, Herr Leo Kreindler, of Berlin.

Available in ebook and in a hardback edition

"It is to our part of World War II what *Uncle Tom's Cabin* was to the Civil War." Kurt Vonnegut

Address Unknown

Kressmann Taylor

Originally published in the United States in 1938 *Address Unknown* was an instant sensation and international bestseller. Now already reprinted 12 times in its Souvenir Press edition.

It was written before World War Two to alert the American public to the reality of Nazi power and its power remains undiminished after decades. The series of fictional letters between a Jewish art dealer in San Francisco and his German business partner in Munich traces their relationship as it changes after the coming to power of the Nazis.

"An overnight sensation at the time, it remains every bit as powerful and, sadly, as pertinent today." 'The Daily Mail'

Address Unknown is a perennially topical assertion of the power of the word against warped ideologies and intolerance.

"Only 70 pages long, Kressmann Taylor's *Address Unknown* will stay in the memory for ever." 'Guardian'

Available in ebook and in a paperback edition

"*Outwitting History* is the charming and compelling epic about how Lansky and a few volunteers saved Yiddish books from extinction." 'The Times'

Outwitting History:
How a Young Man rescued a Million Books and Saved a Vanishing Civilisation

Aaron Lansky

In 1980, an entire body of Jewish literature – the physical remnant of Yiddish culture – was on the verge of extinction. Precious volumes that had survived Hitler and Stalin were being passed down from older generations of Jewish immigrants to their non-Yiddish speaking children only to be discarded or destroyed. A twenty-three-year-old student named Aaron Lansky set out to rescue the world's abandoned Yiddish books before it was too late. As he takes us along on his groundbreaking journey, Lansky explores the roots of the Yiddish language and introduces us to the brilliant Yiddish writers – from Mendele to Sholem Aleichem to Issac Bashevis Singer – whose lasting cultural relevance is evident on every page.

"An adventure story to delight bibliophiles." 'Daily Mail'

Aaron Lansky enables us to see how an almost-lost culture is the bridge between the old world and the future.

"Lansky recounts the history of his decade-long pursuit of an impossible dream in a warm, witty narrative as instructive as it is entertaining." 'Times Literary Supplement'

Available in ebook and in a paperback edition

"Renders him heir to Lenny Bruce, Leo Rosten and your favourite Yiddish teacher, all rolled into one." 'Jewish Chronicle'

Born to Kvetch:
Yiddish Language and Culture in All of Its Moods

Michael Wex

Kvetching is to the Jewish soul what breathing is to the Jewish body. For Jews, kvetching is a way of understanding the world. It is rooted, like so much of Jewish culture, in the Bible where the Israelites grumble endlessly. They complain about their problems, and complain as much about the solutions. They kvetch in Egypt and they kvetch in the desert; no matter what God does, it's wrong.

"A rich book from which one derives much pleasure and more than a little knowledge." 'Jewish Renaissance'

In *Born to Kvetch* Michael Wex looks into the origins of this surplus of disenchantment, and examines how it helped to create the abundance of striking idioms and curses in Yiddish.

"Here we find an impressive taxonomy of slapping, a vivid way to encourage haste . . . and a splendidly verbose curse . . . Wex evinces a great sense of fun as well as a high linguistic seriousness." 'The Guardian'

Available in a paperback edition

A contemporary interpretation of the teachings
of one of the great figures of Judaism.

The Tales of Rabbi Nachman

Martin Buber

Nachman of Breslov was born in 1772 and combined his
knowledge of the esoteric secrets of Judaism (Kabbalah) with
a remarkable Torah scholarship. His religious philosophy was
based on speaking to God in normal conversation 'as you would
with a best friend'. He received much acclaim in his lifetime and
as a teacher is a seminal figure in the history of Hasidic Judaism.
After his death in 1810 his Torah lessons and stories were
published by a disciple and have been studied ever since. Martin
Buber, one of the great spiritual figures of the twentieth-century,
has recreated and introduced, together with an essay on Jewish
mysticism, the classic tales of Rabbi Nachman, whom Buber
describes as "perhaps the last Jewish mystic".

"I have not translated these stories of Rabbi Nachman, but retold
them in all freedom" Martin Buber

Rabbi Nachman's mystical tales are revered as much today as
during his lifetime because Hasidic tales have become a source
of cultural renewal for Judaism as they do not separate religious
experience from daily experience. In these stories we find the
universal truths of the Kabbalah.

Available in a paperback edition

"Kattan ... brings a first-hand immediacy to his Baghdad
memoir which marks it out as a minor masterpiece of the genre."
'Sunday Telegraph'

Farewell, Babylon:
Coming of Age in Jewish Baghdad

Naim Kattan

Farewell, Babylon is a memoir of a lost world, Baghdad, the
magical city in which Iraq's Kurds, Bedouins, Muslims, Jews
and Christians lived together in a rough sort of harmony. The
Iraqi Jewish community dates back 2500 years to Biblical
Babylon, but by Kattan's childhood in the 1940's anti-semitism
was on the rise and Nazi-sympathisers were threatening
Baghdad's Jewish community. Naim Kattan takes readers into
the heart of Baghdad's then-teeming Jewish community. His
Baghdad is a hot, quarrelsome city beset in equal parts by fear
and desire. Its politics are frantic, its street life a mystery.

"The plight of Jewry is recorded in *Farewell, Babylon* in spare,
elegiac tones ... A vital book." 'Sunday Times'

Kattan evokes the colonial, Muslim-dominated society of his
childhood and leaves an unforgettable portrait of Baghdad's
exoticism, and the political forces that shape it today.

"The question at the heart of Naim Kattan's book, whether it is
possible to be a Jew and an Arab, goes to the heart of unresolved
conflicts in the Middle East today." 'The Times'

Available in a paperback edition

"Classic history of Jews in the Netherlands during the Second
World War both chills and challenges a few assumptions."
'Jewish Chronicle'

Ashes in the Wind:
The Destruction of Dutch Jewry

Jacob Presser

Beginning in 1940, 110,000 Jews were deported from the
Netherlands to concentration camps. Of those, fewer than 6,000
returned. *Ashes in the Wind* is a story of murder, on a scale
never known before, with organised malice and forethought.
Jacob Presser documents the destruction of Dutch Jewry, from
isolation to deportation and, ultimately, to extermination. Using
15 years of research Jacob Presser graphically recounts stories
of persecution, life in the transit camps and the process of going
into hiding.

"Presser ranged widely over sources ... letters, interviews, even
his own memories and anecdotes ... It remains moving and
worth reading." 'Times Literary Supplement'

In this detailed narrative, the author conveys the utter despair
felt by people whose whole world had crumbled and would be
destroyed, with a historian's dispassion.

"A graphic and detailed account of the destruction of Dutch
Jewry ... Despite our familiarity with the events of the Shoah
this book retains an ability to shock." 'Tribune'